ISBN 978-0-265-14965-2
PIBN 10927218

1 MONTH OF
FREE
READING

at

www.ForgottenBooks.com

By purchasing this book you are eligible for one month membership to ForgottenBooks.com, giving you unlimited access to our entire collection of over 1,000,000 titles via our web site and mobile apps.

To claim your free month visit: www.forgottenbooks.com/free927218

REPORTS OF CASES

DECIDED IN THE

COURT OF APPEAL,

DURING PARTS OF THE YEARS 1884 AND 1885.

REPORTED UNDER THE AUTHORITY OF
THE LAW SOCIETY OF UPPER CANADA.

VOLUME XI.

TORONTO:
ROWSELL & HUTCHISON.
KING-STREET.

1885.

58,730

ROWSELL AND HUTCHISON, LAW PRINTERS, TORONTO.

JUDGES

COURT OF APPEAL

THE HON. JOHN HAWKINS HAGARTY, C. J. O.
"   "   GEORGE WILLIAM BURTON, J. A.
"   "   CHRISTOPHER SALMON PATTERSON, J. A.
"   "   JOSEPH CURRAN MORRISON, J. A.
"   "   FEATHERSTON OSLER, J. A.

Attorney-General :
THE HON. OLIVER MOWAT.

A TABLE

CASES REPORTED IN THIS VOLUME

A TABLE

NAMES OF CASES CITED IN THIS VOLUME.

A.

B.

C.

D.

D.

F.

G.

H.

H.

I.

J.

M.

Mc.

N.

O.

P.

W.

X.

ONTARIO
APPEAL REPORTS.

LETT v. ST. LAWRENCE AND OTTAWA RAILWAY COMPANY.

Railway accident—Death of married woman by accident—Rents or other income—Pecuniary loss.

Held, [reversing the judgment of the Q. B. D. (1 O. R. 545) BURTON, J.A. dissenting] that under the provisions of Lord Campbell's Act, Imp. Stat. 9-10 Vict. ch. 93, R. S. O. ch. 128, the husband of a woman killed by accident, suing as her administrator is entitled to recover damages for himself and her children, although there may be no evidence shewing that she was entitled for life to rents or other income.

Per BURTON, J.A.—The injury contemplated by the statute means injury resulting in the loss of money present or prospective, but proximate or direct.

THIS was an appeal from the judgment of the Queen's Bench Division, reported 1 O. R. 545, where the facts are clearly stated, and came on to be heard on the 9th of September, 1884.*

Osler, Q.C., for the appellant.
Bethune, Q.C., for the respondents.

The points and authorities cited are mentioned in the former report, and in the present judgments.

December 18, 1884. BURTON, J. A.—I have read with great care and much interest the very able opinion of the dissenting Judge in the Court below but am unable fully to agree with his conclusion.

My Brother Patterson has displayed his usual industry in collecting most of the English decisions to be found bearing on the construction of the statute of which ours is

---

* *Present:* BURTON, PATTERSON, JJ.A., GALT and ROSE, JJ.

a transcript, and has arranged them in their chronological order in the judgment he will deliver. I have also called to his notice one which he had overlooked, to which I shall have occasion presently to refer.

They seem to me to follow and confirm the construction placed upon Lord Campbell's Act very shortly after its passage in *Blake* v. *Midland*, 18 Q. B. 93, that the damages to be recovered do not extend to a solatium to sooth the feelings of the family for the loss of their relation, but are strickly confined to injuries of which a pecuniary estimate may be made. To what this may extend is a question upon the evidence in each particular case and it may sometimes be found difficult to draw the line. It was also held very shortly after the passage of the Act that the condition referred to in the Act restricting the action to cases in which the deceased might have maintained an action if death had not ensued, had reference not to the nature of the loss or injury sustained, but to the circumstances under which the bodily injury arose and the nature of the wrongful act, neglect, or default complained of. Thus if it were established that the injury was the result of the deceased's own negligence, or where he had received satisfaction during his life, no action was maintainable by the personal representative. The statute did not however transfer the rights which the deceased would have had, but created a new right of action on entirely different principles. The action being not for the loss or suffering of the deceased, nor the injury to the feelings of his surviving relatives, but a new remedy, creature of the statute given to the estate of the deceased in trust for the persons named according to the actual pecuniary loss sustained by each.

The word " pecuniary " is not to be found in the English, as it is in most, if not all, of the American Acts, but that was the interpretation placed upon it by the English Courts shortly after its passage and continuously followed. The injury forming the basis of calculation must be pecuniary, nothing else can enter into the estimate. There can be no recovery, it is admitted, for loss of society or wounded feelings, nor for anything else, in my opinion, which cannot be measured by money and satisfied by a pecuniary recompense.

What is included in that definition is the question, and is one which might in some cases be very difficult to decide. I shall confine myself to considering whether there was any evidence in the present case of such a pecuniary loss as comes within the meaning of the statute.

I agree that legal liability is not the test, but that a person named in the statute may recover if there was a reasonable expectation of pecuniary advantage by the relatives remaining alive. To prove, however, *that* reasonable expectation, there must be evidence from which a jury may be able to arrive, otherwise than by guess or conjecture, at the conclusion that there was in effect such reasonable expectation.

Thus upon proper evidence, a parent may recover for the loss of the probability that his son would have continued to contribute to his maintenance. The case of *Pym* v. *The Great Northern,* 2 B. & S. 750, 4 B. & S. 396, is a case which proceeds partly upon this principle.

There, the parent's means being proved, it was a reasonable inference that a part of that income would be applied to the education and comfort of the children, and it was in fact assumed in that case that at the time of the death the deceased was living with his family in the ordinary manner, bringing up his children in the position in society which that income would command.

It is true that it must always remain a matter of uncertainty, whether the deceased parent would have applied his income to the securing for his family the social and domestic advantages of which they were deprived by his death, or whether he would have laid by any portion of his income to make provision for them at his death ; but there being a reasonable expectation that the income would be so applied, the extinction of such expectation by negligence occasioning the death of the party from whom

it arose is sufficient to maintain the action, it being for the
jury to say under all the circumstances, taking into
account all the uncertainties and contingencies of the particular case, whether there is such a reasonable and well
founded expectation of pecuniary benefit as can be estimated in money, and so become the subject of damages in
such an action.

There is, therefore, always a preliminary question for the
Judge before the case can properly be submitted to the
jury, of whether there is any evidence that the person for
whose benefit the action is brought did sustain any pecuniary loss by the death of the deceased, or whether there
was any reasonable probability of a pecuniary benefit
accruing to him in consequence.

In an Irish case, *Condon* v. *Great Southern R. W. Co.,*.
Ir. R. 16 C. L. 415, very slight evidence was held
sufficient to go to the jury.

The action was by a widow for the death of her son
aged 14. Her husband had been killed by the same accident and she recovered for his loss £400. The boy was
being sent to school, but when at home used to work on
the farm in his father's absence. He never earned any
wages, but his capabilities were valued at 6d. per day. It
was held that the probability (increased by the past filial
conduct of the boy) that he would have enabled his
mother to earn more or would have devoted part of his
earnings to her support, was evidence to go to the jury.

I think that such a case could scarcely have been withdrawn from the jury, but in a case of *Holleran* v. *Bagnell,*
Ir. R. 6, C. L. 333, where an action was brought by a
father for the death of his daughter, who was about the
age of seven, where the only evidence given to shew that
the plaintiff had sustained a pecuniary loss was that she
had been in the habit of rendering trifling household services but which were incapable of being estimated at any
pecuniary value, the Court held that there was no evidence
fit to submit to a jury.

The only two cases in which I can find any distinct rulings in the case of a husband or child suing for the loss of a wife are : one in the English Courts decided in 1866, and of which a very meagre account is given in the Weekly Notes, and one in the State of New York—the case of *Mitchell* v. *The New York Central,* reported in 2 Hun 535.

In that case the plaintiff recovered a verdict of $4,000, which was moved against on the ground, among others, that in this class of actions the recovery must be confined to pecuniary loss sustained by the death of the deceased, and that these could only be awarded on proof of loss, the burden being upon the plaintiff to shew this.

In that case no pecuniary loss was shewn, except what might be inferred from the two facts that the deceased was a married woman; and aged 20 years. There was no evidence given of her capabilities, mental or physical, nor of her situation and circumstances in life, nor how she had or could be of benefit to her husband and next of kin.

There was no proof whatever shewing that her life was of any pecuniary advantage to anyone, and therefore there was no proof of any pecuniary loss to anyone by her death, and the Court set aside the verdict.

In the other, the case of *Chant* v. *The South Eastern R. W. Co.,* the only report of which I have been able to find is in the Weekly Notes of 1861. In that case no evidence was given of the pecuniary loss, but the jury returned a verdict for £200, which was moved against and a new trial asked for, simply on the ground of excessive damages, or to reduce the damages.

It was contended that there was no evidence of pecuniary assistance rendered to the plaintiff by his wife, and that she might have been an invalid, and so a burden to him. But the Court thought that in the absence of evidence to the contrary it must be assumed that she was a person of average health, industry and good character ; that to a poor man such a wife gave pecuniary assistance in keeping house, &c.; that they could not grant a new trial on account of the amount being excessive, and as no

change in this respect has been made by the Statute, but
that the damages to be recovered, and which may be
recovered not by the husband only but by any of the class
mentioned in the Statute, are of an entirely different
character, and must be such as would readily admit of a
pecuniary estimate.

If those attentions and services which a wife ordinarily
renders to her husband can be made the basis of a recovery,
the inconvenience would be as great as in cases in which
the allowance of compensation for mental anguish has
been disallowed, in fact juries would in effect give verdicts
upon that basis without any means of correcting their
errors.

The difficulty in giving direction to juries and in juries
acting upon the direction as to the proper estimate of
damages, is great enough where the evidence deals with
the profits of the deceased, or the amount of his income,
even with the assistance of experts and annuity tables,
but this will be light as compared with those with which
the inquiry will become entangled, if the jury are to be
called upon to fix a pecuniary estimate upon the loss which a
husband sustains by being deprived of the ordinary services, care and attention of a wife. Where she is herself
contributing to his income by moneys of her own earning,
there is something tangible to deal with, and the means
are thereby afforded of enabling a jury to come to a conclusion upon some well defined ground, and the Court to
deal with the amount of the verdict in case it should subsequently be moved against as excessive. If damages can
be given on the general grounds I have stated, it would
seem to follow that evidence would be receivable to shew
the character and capacity of the deceased, which in many
cases, might be of a very painful character.

The care, intellectual culture, and moral training which
the mother could supply are no doubt " pearls of great
price," but they are not to be measured by money, and it
was never the intention of the Legislature, in my opinion,
that they should be made the subject of estimate or

inquiry by a jury leading to the inquisitorial and painful investigation to which I have already referred.

The injury contemplated by the statute means, I think, an injury resulting in the loss of money present or prospective, but proximate and direct; and it is because I do not find any evidence proper to submit to a jury of any loss to the husband of this character that I come to the conclusion that the judgment in the Court below was correct.

I think also upon the finding of the jury as to the income from the real estate that the evidence fails as to the children who were deprived no doubt of the care and attention of a kind parent, but who are not shewn to have suffered any pecuniary loss within the meaning of the statute.

I am of opinion that the appeal should be dismissed.

PATTERSON, J.A.—The plaintiff sues as administrator of his wife, under the statute R. S. O. ch. 128, secs. 2 and 3.

The action was tried before my Brother Osler, with a jury.

There was a verdict for the plaintiff for $5,800, distributed $1,500 to the plaintiff himself, and the remainder in sums of different amounts to five of the children of the deceased and of the plaintiff.

The jury stated that no part of the damages was assessed in respect of income derived by the deceased from some property.

The case is one which has not an exact parallel in any case reported in the English reports or in those of our own Courts; because it raises the question of the right to recover damages for the death of a wife and mother, based altogether on the expectation of benefit from her personal services, and not at all upon any actual income, or earnings in money, of which she was in receipt.

There was an objection taken to the verdict for misdirection as to a matter which formed part of the evidence of negligence. I think it was properly disposed of in the Court below, and I do not propose now to discuss it.

The main question has been elaborately discussed, and most of the decisions bearing upon it have been commented on in the judgments delivered in the Court below, and I believe they have received equal attention from my learned brothers in this Court; but the novelty as well as importance of the matter for decision, and the fact that we necessarily rely very much upon the views held by the English Courts in dealing with Lord Campbell's Act (9 and 10 Vic. ch. 93) from which our statute is taken, and the existence of different opinions in the Court whose judgment we are now reviewing, must be my justification for again referring to them.

I propose to trace the history of the administration of Lord Campbell's Act in England by glancing, as briefly as may be consistent with perspicuity, at all the reported decisions I have been able to find which involve anything beyond matters of practice or pleading.

The enactments we are to keep in mind are that " wherever the death of a person has been caused by such wrongful act, neglect, or default as would (if death had not ensued) have entitled the party injured to maintain an action and recover damages in respect thereof, in such case the person who would have been liable if death had not ensued shall be liable to an action for damages, notwithstanding the death of the person injured, and although the death has been caused under such circumstances as amount in law to felony," and that " every such action shall be for the benefit of the wife, husband, parent, and child of the person whose death has been so caused, and shall be brought by and in the name of the executor or administrator of the person deceased," and " in every such action the Judge or jury may give such damages as they think proportioned to the injury resulting from such death to the parties respectively for whom and for whose benefit such action shall be brought."

The English Act passed in 1846. The earliest case under it, of which I have seen a note, is *Armsworth* v. *South Eastern Railway Company*, 11 Jur. 758, before

Parke, B., at *Nisi Prius*. He charged the jury that damages were not to be estimated according to the value of the deceased's life calculated by annuity tables; but that they should give what they considered a fair compensation to the widow and children.

Then there is the case of *Tucker* v. *Chaplain*, 2 C. & K. 730, in 1848, in which Lord Denman, at *Nisi Prius*, laid down the rule which has always been acted on, and which was affirmed in subsequent cases to which I shall refer, that the inquiries as to negligence of the defendant, and contributory negligence of the deceased, were as applicable in the action by the personal representative as if the action had been by the person injured. There was no question in this case as to the principle on which damages were to be assessed.

At the end of the same year, 1848, the case of *Gillard* v. *Lancashire and Yorkshire Railway Company*, 12 L. T. 356, was tried in the Exchequer before Pollock, C.B., and a jury. The plaintiff claimed as widow and admistratrix of the deceased, and did not claim on behalf of any of his children. Some remarks, reported as having fallen from the learned Chief Baron, have sometimes been quoted as if they indicated his opinion that a husband could not claim damages under the Statute in respect of the death of his wife except in the one case of the wife having had a pension or annuity which died with her.

I do not read the language as fairly open to that construction, and that it was not intended to be so understood is plainly indicated by the Chief Baron's placing the case of a wife claiming for the death of her husband on precisely the same footing. It is evident from the whole report that the Chief Baron was combating an attempt to recover damages for injury to the feelings, and that his object in what he said was to confine the right to damages such as have been described in other cases as damages capable of being estimated on a pecuniary basis.

If he had any idea of laying down a narrower rule, it will clearly appear from the judgments afterwards pronounced by the same learned Judge, to which I have to advert, that the idea was soon given up.

I shall make some quotations from the remarks attributed to the Chief Baron for the purpose of shewing that he really was not laying down any narrower rule than that followed in later cases ; and that at all events he made no distinction, unfavorable to a surviving husband, between the cases of husband claiming for the death of his wife, and wife claiming for the death of her husband. The report does not state the circumstances of the husband whose death was the foundation of the action, nor whether his income was earned by his labour or derived from some other source. It may have been the latter, and if so that circumstance would account for the allusions to loss of income by the Chief Baron, who of course spoke with reference to the facts before him. He is reported to have said, when rejecting evidence offered to shew the situation of the plaintiff with relation to her children as a foundation for enhanced damages of the character of those claimed in other classes of actions for mental suffering, that he had frequently expressed the opinion that the question was a pure question of pecuniary compensation, and nothing more, which was contemplated by the Statute. This he illustrated by pointing out that the richest peer of England who had married a lady enjoying a pension might bring an action for the loss of the pension by the death of his wife, while the poorest peasant, although his mental sufferings from the loss of his wife might be as great or greater, but who lost nothing by the death of his wife, was not entitled to sue. " All that is lost," he said " which is appreciable after the death of the party killed is the pecuniary loss sustained by his family ; and this Act enables them to recover that which the deceased would himself have sued for had the accident not terminated fatally. The framers of the Act never meant to give compensation to the parent for the mere deprivation of his son, or to the widow for that of her husband." Then he illustrated that proposition by supposing the case of the loss of the only child of a wealthy man. Sir F. Thesiger who was counsel for the plaintiff, observed : "In that view a widower would not be entitled to sue for compensation for the loss of the society and comfort of his wife;" and the Chief Baron answered : "Clearly not, unless her death is the cause of pecuniary loss to her husband." Counsel put another case of the death of a weak and sickly child who was a burden to his parents, and suggested that the framers of the Act intended to remove the anomaly which existed in the law, by giving a right of action in that case ; to which the Chief Baron's reply was : "It may be so, but I can only administer the law as I find it expressed in the Statute before me. It is my unalterable opinion that this Act is confined to compensation for pecuniary losses only, and I shall reject the evidence, inviting a bill of exceptions to my ruling." In charging the jury the Chief Baron explained the anomaly under the law as it had been, and said : "This statute proposed to correct this anomaly ; but it did not create any new ground of action. It only transferred to a man's family the right which he would have had if he had survived the negligence of the wrong-doer. The meaning of this enactment is this : If a man's life is valuable to his family by reason of his possession of an annuity, his family have now the right to say : 'We have lost the life on which this annuity hung,' and they may claim compensation for its loss, but nothing more. They cannot enter into the question of shock to their feelings. If a different view were to be adopted it would be difficult to say where the calculation of damages ought to stop. If, however, the mere pecuniary loss be set as the measure of damage, a rational construction would be put on the statute, which, it must be remarked, is limited to the case of wife, husband, parent, and child, excluding nephews and uncles and more distant relations who would in all probability not be dependent on the life lost. Acting on this view of the statute, the jury would say what damages they would award to the plaintiff, whose claim must be measured by such part of the income proved to

have been possessed by her husband, as they might think
she enjoyed during his life.   She had not made any claim
as required by the Act on account of her child, and her
condition with respect to her children could not be taken
into estimation."

There are four cases before Courts *in banc* reported in
1849 and 1850; *Dakin* v. *Brown*, 8 C. B. 92; *Reedie* v.
London and North-Western R. W. Co., 4 Ex. 244; *Wig-
more* v. *Jay*, 5 Ex. 354; and *Barnes* v. *Ward*, 9 C. B. 392;
in none of which was there any question of damages; but
in 1852, *Blake* v. *Midland Counties R. W. Co.*, 18 Q. B. 83,
was decided and settled the law on the footing acted on
four years earlier in *Gillard* v. *Lancashire and Yorkshire
R. W. Co.*, by Pollock, C. B.   The question was stated by
Coleridge, J., who delivered the judgment of the Court, to
be whether the jury in giving damages proportioned to
the injury resulting from the death of the deceased to the
parties for whose benefit the action was brought, were
confined to injuries of which a pecuniary estimate could
be made, or might add a solatium to those parties in
respect of the mental sufferings occasioned by such death.
That question he proceeds to solve by several arguments,
amongst others the improbability that the Legislature
would have thrown upon the jury such great difficulty in
calculating and apportioning the solatium to the different
members of the family, without some rules for their
guidance, and concludes by saying: " For these reasons we
are of opinion that the learned Judge at the trial ought
more explicitly to have told the jury that, in assessing the
damages they could not take into their consideration the
mental sufferings of the plaintiff for the loss of her husband
and that as the damages certainly exceeded any loss sustained by her admitting of a pecuniary estimate, they
must be considered excessive."

This decision has always been followed as decisive
against the right, under the statute, to any damages of a
merely sentimental character, or incapable of a pecuniary
estimate ; but it does not attempt any further definition of

damages of the latter class.   Subsequent cases afford
instances of what may be brought within the category.

In *Hicks* v. *Newport &c. R. W. Co.*, reported in a note at
p. 403 of 4 B. & S., Lord Campbell, in 1857, directed the
jury not to look to the wants of the family, but to the
loss they had sustained by their father's death, and to
deduct the amount of insurance money received from an
accident policy which fell in by reason of his death.

In the same year the case of *Bramall* v. *Lees*, 29 L. T., 111
and 166, in the Exchequer, may be usefully referred to as
illustrating the sense in which Pollock, C.B. used or understood the term " pecuniary loss."   In that case a father had
recovered a verdict of £15 for the death of a daughter 12
years old, who had never earned any money, but who
might, it was said, have got employment in a year or so in
a factory where she would have earned wages.   The verdict was moved against, and after consideration Pollock,
C. B., said : " It was a case tried by my Brother Crompton,
at Liverpool, and the Court thinks that if Mr. Knowles
desires to take the rule he may have it, not so much on
the doubt the Court entertains, as from the importance of
the question, and there having been undoubtedly a view
taken by the learned Judge which I believe he does not
now entertain.   But if Mr. Knowles thinks it worth while
to have the matter more fully discussed, the Court will
certainly grant a rule for that purpose.   Knowles, Q.C.—
If your Lordship pleases I will take the rule.   Whether
we proceed on it will depend upon consideration.   Pollock,
C.B.—I think it right not to grant you the rule without
distinctly stating to you that it does not so much arise out
of the doubt the Court entertains as the doubt which
undoubtedly the learned Judge who tried the cause did
entertain at the trial and after the trial, and also on
account of the importance of the question, and the general
matters connected with it, and the general administration
of justice upon the statute.   Knowles, Q.C.—I will keep
in mind what the Court has said, and whether your Lordship hears anything more of it or not will depend upon

consideration afterwards." It would seem that the rule
was not proceeded with, as the case is noted a month later
as "struck out." The Judge who had tried the case was
Crompton, J. He spoke of it during the argument of
Chapman v. *Bothwell*, the following year. His remarks
are thus reported in 4 Jur. N. S. at p. 1181—"*Bramall*
v. *Lees* (tried before me at the Spring Assizes at Liverpool
in 1857), which was an action by the father for the death
of a girl aged twelve years, who was at the time of her
death supported by her father, but it was said would, in
the course of a year or two have gone to work in a
factory and earned wages, a verdict was given for the
plaintiff for £15. On a rule for a new trial being moved
for, the Court of Exchequer, after a good deal of consideration, were of opinion that a rule ought not to be
granted. The Lord Chief Baron said that they would not
have granted it if the Judge at the trial of the cause had
not expressed a doubt, but at the end of the discussion I
was satisfied. The rule to shew cause was granted but
was not pressed." The same learned Judge again referred
to the case in the course of the argument in *Pym* v. *Great
Northern R. W. Co.*, 2 B. & S., at p. 763.

We have in *Franklin* v. *South Eastern R. W. Co.*, 4 H.
& N. 211, decided in May, 1858, another judgment delivered
by Pollock, C. B., which goes farther than any of the earlier
cases towards a definition of the pecuniary loss in respect
of which damages are recoverable under the statute. The
plaintiff there sued in respect of the death of his son, who
had assisted his father by doing some of his duty as light
porter at St. Thomas's Hospital, for which duty the father
was paid 3s. 6d. a week. The son earned wages at another
employment, but was not shewn to have contributed from
them to his father's support. Bramwell, B., left it to the
jury to say whether the plaintiff had a reasonable expectation, of any and what pecuniary benefit from the continuance of his son's life. The propriety of that charge was
discussed *in banc*, and Pollock, C. B., delivering the judgment of the Court, said : "The statute does not in terms

say on what principle the damages are to be assessed; and the only way to ascertain what it does, is, to shew what it does not mean. Now it is clear that damage must be shewn, for the jury are to 'give such damages as they think proportioned to the injury.' It has been held that these damages are not to be given as a solatium, but are to be given in reference to a pecuniary loss. That was decided for the first time *in banc* in *Blake* v. *The Midland R. W. Co.*, 18 Q. B. 93. * * It is also clear that the damages are not to be merely in reference to the loss of a legal right, for they are to be distributed among relations only, and not to all individuals sustaining such a loss; and accordingly the practice has not been to ascertain what benefit could have been enforced by the claimants had the deceased lived, and give damages limited thereby. If then the damages are not to be calculated on either of these principles, nothing remains except they should be calculated in reference to a reasonable expectation of pecuniary benefit, as of right or otherwise, from the continuance of the life. Whether the plaintiff had any such reasonable expectation of benefit from the continuance of his son's life, and if so, to what extent, were the questions left to the jury. The proper question then was left, if there was any evidence in support of the affirmative of it. We think there was. The plaintiff was old and getting infirm; the son was young, earning good wages, and apparently well disposed to assist his father, and in fact he had so assisted him to the value of 3s. 6d. a week. We do not say that it was necessary that actual benefit should have been derived, a reasonable expectation is enough, and such reasonable expectation might well exist, though, from the father not being in need, the son had never done anything for him. On the other hand, a jury certainly ought not to make a guess in the matter, but ought to be satisfied that there has been a loss of sensible and appreciable pecuniary benefit which might have been reasonably expected from the continuance of the life."

Dalton v. *South Eastern R. W. Co.*, 4 C. B. N. S. 296, was decided within a day or two of Franklin's case. That was also an action by a father as administrator to recover damages for himself and his wife for the death of their son. The deceased, who was earning good wages, had for seven or eight years been in the habit of visiting his father and mother, who were labouring people, once a fortnight, and taking them presents of tea, coffee, sugar, meat, &c., which, with occasional donations of money, averaged about £20 a year. There was a verdict for £80 for the father, and £40 for the mother, and a separate sum for funeral expenses and mourning. The latter sum was disallowed, and the verdict sustained as to the others. The judgment in Franklin's case, which the Court said was decided with their entire concurrence, being treated as disposing of the question.

Chapman v. *Rothwell*, 11 Jur. N. S., 180, decided in the Queen's Bench at the end of 1858, is the first reported English case in which the death of a wife was the cause of action. The plaintiff, her husband and administrator, claimed £200 damages in his declaration without averring pecuniary damage. There was a demurrer on that ground which was over-ruled by the court, consisting of Lord Campbell, C.J., and Wightman, Erle, and Crompton, JJ. No formal judgment is reported, but from remarks made during the argument, it is probable that the decision was merely that no averment of pecuniary damage was necessary in the pleading, the damage being a matter of evidence only.

In *Duckworth* v. *Johnson*, 4 H. & N. 653, decided in June, 1859, we have judgments delivered by Pollock, C.B., and by Barons Martin, Bramwell, and Watson, affiirming the doctrines laid down in *Franklin* v. *South Eastern R. W. Co.* and applying them to the case of a father who recovered £20 damages for the death of a son 14 years of age, who was not, at the time of his death, in any employment, but who had for two years and a half earned 4s. a week at Manchester, the father living at Liverpool. The learned Judges all agreed that if no damage were shewn a verdict for nominal damages could not be sustained, and that actual damage must be shewn ; but they all interpret that phrase by holding that evidence of a prospect of benefit sufficed ; and further that there need not be evidence given that the value of the boy to his father would be more than the cost of maintaining him, that being a matter of which the jury were able to judge. I do not stop to quote the remarks made, although they are instructive.

Cotton v. *Wood*, 8 C. B. N. S., 568, decided in 1860, deserves particular notice, because it was an action brought by the plaintiff as administrator of his deceased wife for an injury which resulted in her death. The only thing in question before the Court *in banc* was the proof of the negligence of the defendant. That was the only ground on which the verdict was attacked ; and the verdict was for £25, which was distributed, £10 to the plaintiff himself, and £15 for three children of the plaintiff and of the deceased. It was proved on the part of the plaintiff, that the deceased had by her industry contributed, to the extent of about 10 shillings weekly, towards the maintenance of the family. This is all the reported evidence on which the damages were estimated.

Pym v. *Great Northern Ry. Co.*, 2 B. & S. 759 ; 4 B. & S. 396, is an important case by reason of the further elucidation afforded by the judgments delivered of grounds on which estimates of pecuniary damage may be based, and because in it a Court of Error expressly affirmed the principle on which the statute was construed in the earlier cases. Unlike most of the earlier reported cases, in which the parties seeking compensation had been persons in humble life, and in several of which verdicts for comparatively small sums of money had been held to be excessive, this case related to the death of a gentlemen of large income, derived from an estate which upon his death passed by entail to his eldest son. By a settlement, a jointure of £1,000 a year had been settled on his wife, and £20,000 had been secured to the younger children on his death. He left eight younger children, all under twelve years of age

The jury awarded £1,000 to the wife and £1,500 to each of
the eight younger children. Those amounts the Court
considered excessive, having regard to the acceleration by
the death of the enjoyment of the moneys settled upon the
wife and children, and plaintiff's counsel assented to a
suggestion by the Court, to reduce the sums awarded to
the children to £1,000 each. It was expressly decided that
the condition that the action could have been maintained
by the deceased if death had not ensued, had reference,
not to the nature of the loss or injury sustained, but to the
circumstances under which the bodily injury arose, and
the nature of the wrongful act, neglect, or default complained of, and therefore the personal representative could
maintain an action for pecuniary loss, although that pecuniary loss would not have resulted from the accident to the
deceased if he had lived. Also that "as the benefit of education and the enjoyment of the greater comforts and con-
veniences of life depend on the possession of pecuniary
means to procure them, the loss of these advantages is one
which is capable of being estimated in money, in other
words, is a pecuniary loss." "We are not insensible,"
Cockburn, C.J., observed "to the argument *ab inconvenienti*, founded on the very serious consequences which
might ensue to a railway company in the event of a fatal
accident happening from negligence to an individual of
very large fortune; but we think this is rather for the
consideration of the Legislature, as to whether any limit
should be put to the liability, than for us. We see no
difference in principle between such a case as the present,
and that of a claim by the family of an artisan for the loss
of the advantages arising from the father's earnings, in
which case it is not doubted that the action may be maintained."

The judgment of the Court of Exchequer Chamber,
delivered by Erle, C.J., affirmed that of the Queen's Bench
on all the points.

In *Boulter* v. *Webster*, 13 W. R. 289 (1865) the jury
found that the father, who was plaintiff, had not sustained

any pecuniary damage by the death of the child who had been killed by the careless driving of the defendant's servant. It was argued in the Queen's Bench that a verdict for nominal damages might be entered; but the Court held that could not be done under this statute, the law not implying damage.

In *Springett* v. *Hall*, tried also in 1865, we have an instance of a new trial granted because the damages were too small. The report in 4 F. & F. 472, of the trial before Cockburn, C.J., informs us that damages were assessed at 40s. a verdict which the Lord Chief Justice characterized as being very unsatisfactory and evidently the result of a compromise. By a note in Fisher's Digest it appears that the 40s. was distributed, £1 to the widow and 10s. to each of the children, and that a new trial was ordered on the ground that the jury had shrunk from deciding the issue. The reference given is 6 B. & S. 477, but I do not find the case in that volume.

I am indebted to my Brother Burton for a reference to *Chant* v. *South Eastern R. W. Co.*, noted in the Weekly Notes for 1866 at p. 134. That was an action by a gentleman's gardener for the death of his wife. Owing to the plaintiff, who was the only witness on this part of the case, breaking down in the course of his examination, no evidence was given of the pecuniary loss sustained by him in the loss of his wife, but the jury found a verdict for £200. This was moved against in the Exchequer Chamber only on the amount of the damages, and it was urged in support of the rule that there was no evidence as to the pecuniary assistance rendered to the plaintiff by his wife. But the Court thought that in the absence of evidence to the contrary it must be assumed that she was a person of average health, industry and good character, that to a poor man such a wife gave a pecuniary assistance in keeping house, &c., and they declined to grant a new trial on account of excessive damages.

In *Read* v. *Great Eastern R. W. Co.*, L. R. 3 Q. B. 555 (1868) an action by a widow to recover damages for the

death of her husband, it was held that the action was
answered by a plea of satisfaction to the deceased in his
life-time ; because the party injured could not, in the
words of the statute, " maintain an action in respect thereof," after having received satisfaction.

There have been several cases in which the statute has
been applied in proceedings *in rem* in the High Court of
Admiralty. In three of these which happen to come in
this place in the chronological order I am pursuing,
questions of some interest respecting the parties contemplated by the statute were decided. In *The Guldfaxe*,
L. R. 2 A. & E. 325 (1868) the action was successfully maintained against a foreign ship owned by foreigners. In the
Explorer, L. R., 3 A. & E. 289 (1870) the persons in respect
of whose death damages were recovered were aliens and
not British subjects; and in *The George and Richard*, L. R., 3
A. & E. 466 (1871) it was adjudged that a child *en ventre
sa mere* was entitled to compensation for the death of its
father.

Rowley v. *London and North Western R. W. Co.*, L. R.
8 Ex. 221, which was before the Exchequer Chamber in
1873 on a Bill of Exceptions, is a case which ought to be
referred to as laying down important principles concerning
the mode of measuring damages, and the extent to which
annuity tables may be legitimately resorted to, but contains
nothing more directly touching our present inquiry.

I ought not to pass without notice in its order, a case
which I shall have occasion to refer to again : *Osborn* v.
Gillett, L. R. 8 Ex. 88 (1873) although it was not an
action under Lord Campbell's Act, particularly as it was
referred to in the Court below. The plaintiff claimed
damages for the death of his daughter and servant, caused
by the negligent act of the defendant's servant, whereby
the plaintiff lost the benefits and advantages which would
have accrued to him from her services, and was put to
expense in conveying her body to his house, and in respect.
of her burial. One plea was, that the deceased was killed
on the spot, so that the plaintiff did and could not sustain

any damage which entitled him to sue in this action for the acts complained of. To this there was a demurrer. It is not stated why the action was not brought under Lord Campbell's Act. It could not have been maintained under that Act for the funeral expenses. That had been decided in *Dalton* v. *The South Eastern R. W. Co.*, 4 C. B. N. S. 296, and again in *Boulter* v. *Webster*, 13 W. R. 289. And that the plaintiff may have been well advised in attempting to assert a right to damages at Common Law is apparent from the judgment in which Bramwell, B., with his accustomed force and ability, maintained that right against the opinions of Kelly, C. E., and Pigott, B. Lord Campbell's Act was brought into the discussion for the sake of the argument afforded by the declaration in the preamble that " no action at law is now maintainable against a person who, by wrongful act, neglect, or default, may have caused the death of another person ;" and by the omission of master from the list of persons for whose benefit the new remedy was given to the personal representative. But I do not think there is anything to be gathered either from the form of the action, or the language of any of the Judges who took part in the decision, that can fairly be regarded as bearing at all directly on the question now before us.

Bradburn v. *Great Western R. W. Co.*, L. R. 10 Ex. 1 (1874), was an action by a person injured, in which the defendants claimed to set off against the damages a sum received by the plaintiff on an accident policy. In rejecting this claim, the difference was pointed out between this case where the insurance money was paid in pursuance of a contract, and in consideration of premiums paid by the plaintiff, and a case like *Hicks* v. *Newport, &c., R. W. Co.*, 4 B. & S. 403, note, where the claim was under Lord Campbell's Act, and the insurance money came to the claimants by reason of the death, making them to that extent gainers by the event.

The cause of action in *Potter* v. *Metropolitan R. W. Co.*, 30 L. T. N. S. 765 in Q. B. ; and 32 L. T. N. S. 36, in the Exchequer Chamber, arose from injuries sustained by a

wife; but Lord Campbell's Act was not in question. The
curious feature of the case was that the wife herself, as ex-
ecutrix of her husband, brought the action. The point
decided was that the cause of action, being for breach of a
contract to carry safely, survived. The same point was again
decided shortly afterwards in *Bradshaw* v. *Lancashire and
Yorkshire R. W. Co.*, L. R. 10 C. P. 189, the injury there having been to the testator himself, occasioned by a breach of
contract by the defendants, and which injury ultimately
caused his death. Lord Campbell's Act was noticed in the
judgments of Grove and Denman, JJ., but only for the purpose of shewing that nothing in it prevented this action being
maintained by the executor for damage to the estate. This
decision was questioned by Mellor, J., in *Leggott* v. *Great
Western R. W. Co.*, 1 Q. B. D. 599, but was nevertheless
followed by him and Quain, J., who held that in that action,
which was brought by the administratrix for injury to the
personal estate of the deceased by the accident which caused
his death, the defendants were not estopped from denying
alleged facts connected with the accident, by their unsuc-
cessful defence of a former action brought by the same
plaintiff as administratrix, under Lord Campbell's Act for
the benefit of herself as his wife, and of his children.

Pulling v. *Great Eastern R. W. Co.*, 9 Q. B. D. 110, was
an action by an administrator to recover for medical
expenses incurred by the deceased in consequence of the
accident, and before his death. The reporter points out
in a note that the facts did not bring the case within Lord
Campbell's Act, an observation probably suggested by the
cases to which I have alluded when noticing *Osborn* v.
Gillett. The decision was that, as the action was founded
on tort and not on contract, the principle of *Potter* v.
Metropolitan R. W. Co., and *Bradshaw* v. *Lancashire and
Yorkshire R. W. Co.*, did not apply to enable the plaintiff
to recover.

Sykes v. *North Eastern R. W. Co.*, 32 L. T. N. S. 199,
(1875), is on the question of damages. The son, for whose
benefit the action was brought by the father, had worked

for his father for wages. It was held by Brett and Grove,
JJ., that there was not evidence of pecuniary loss, and
they therefore set aside a verdict rendered for £70, of
which £20 had been allowed for funeral expenses. Brett,
J., said : " There is no evidence that the plaintiff received
any pecuniary benefit from the continuance of his son's
life. The son was of full age and worked for fair wages,
the arrangements between father and son being purely
matters of contract," and Grove, J., said : " Lord Campbell's
Act was intended to compensate for the loss of a pecuniary
benefit which had been derived from relationship to the
person killed by the negligence of another. In *Franklin*
v. *South Eastern R. W. Co.*, 3 H. & N. 211, the father was
old and infirm, and the son assisted him in earning wages
from motives of filial affection. Here the father paid the
son the ordinary wages, and there is nothing to shew that
the son would not have left off working for his father if
he could have got better wages from anybody else."

In *Hetherington* v. *North Eastern R. W. Co.*, 9 Q. B. D.
160, the County Court Judge had nonsuited the plaintiff,
but it was held by Field and Cave, JJ., that there was
some evidence of pecuniary damage to go to the jury.
The evidence is set out and is very short. It was that of
the plaintiff and is thus noted : " The deceased was my
son ; he was 29 years old ; he gave me a portion of his
earnings when I wanted it ; I am nearly blind, and am
injured in my leg and hands ; my son used to contribute
to my support ; I am not so able to work as I used to be ;
I am fifty-nine ; my son was not married. *Cross-examined.*
—Five or six years ago I was out of work for six months,
and my son was very kind to me and helped me. *Re-
examined.*—He was always kind to me ; I have never had
money from him since."

Griffiths v. *The Earl of Dudley*, 9 Q. B. D., 357, decided
that a contract by a workingman with his employer, not
to claim compensation for injuries under the Employers'
Liability Act, 1880, bound the widow suing for damages
under Lord Campbell's Act; the principle being the same

acted on in *Read* v *Great Eastern R. W. Co.* L. R. 3 Q. B. 555.

In *Wilkins* v. *Day*, 12 Q. B. D., 110, in which case a husband recovered £100 damages for the death of his wife, the only question related to the obstruction of the highway by which the fatal accident was occasioned.

My immediate object, which is to follow the chain of English decisions upon Lord Campbell's Act, does not necessarily require any reference to cases decided in the Irish Courts. I may however refer to three of such cases, the reports of which I have seen. *Condon* v. *Great Southern and Western R. W. Co.*, 16 Ir. C. L. R., 415 (1866) was decided in the Exchequer. A son, aged 14, who had never earned any wages, but whose capabilities were valued at 6d. a day, lost his life by the negligence of the defendants. The probability that he would have enabled his mother to earn more, or would have devoted part of his earnings to his mother's support, was held to be evidence to go to the jury upon the question of damages; and it was held that the probability was increased by the past filial conduct of the deceased. This is the statement of the head note. The Court professed to follow, and did follow, the rule settled by English cases, the Chief Baron saying that it was established by a series of decisions, first, that in such an action the damages must be estimated with reference to pecuniary loss alone; and, secondly, that in estimating such pecuniary loss the jury are to consider, when the evidence warrants their so doing, the reasonable probability of pecuniary benefit accuring to the party claiming the damages, if the death of the deceased had not occurred. He also, in noticing an argument urged at the bar, gave it as the opinion of the Court, that there was no analogy between the small amount of service which may be sufficient in many cases to save a plaintiff from nonsuit in an action of seduction and the pecuniary loss which must be proved in an action on Lord Campbell's Act. In another Irish case to which I am about to allude, similar language was used. If what the learned Chief Baron meant was, that the pecuniary loss for which alone a plaintiff under Lord Campbell's Act can recover damages is to be estimated on a very different principle or theory from the exemplary or sentimental damages allowed to be given in an action of seduction, he merely laid down the law as settled by *Blake* v. *Midland Counties R. W. Co.*, 18 Q. B. 93, and invariably accepted ever since. But, if he meant that proof of acts of service, such as would suffice as evidence to avert a non-suit in an action of seduction would not be sufficient to leave to the jury as evidence of the probability of pecuniary advantage from the continuance of life, I think the proposition must be understood to relate only to cases where the only evidence to found an estimate of future probabilities consists of proof of services actually performed. Such cases may occur, though I should imagine but rarely.

The other two Irish cases lay down a rule which cannot be reconciled with that acted on in the English cases in which the plaintiff has recovered damages for the loss of a child who had never during its life been a source of profit, but may have always been a burden, and which is, I think, equally at variance with that on which the verdict in *Condon's Case* was sustained. It will further be noticed that the language of the judgments indicate that the English cases of this class had not been brought to the attention of the Court.

Bourke v. *Cork and Macroom R. W. Co.*, Ir. R. 4 C. L. 682, (1879) was an action by a father for the death of his son aged 14, who had been above the average in attainments, and had received special training and education at school to fit him for mercantile pursuits, and who would probably have remained for a couple of years longer. He was very strong and healthy, and a good, well conducted, industrious boy. The plaintiff was a spirit grocer and general merchant, and had the management of the local postal and telegraph office. He was carrying on a good business and in a respectable and comfortable position. In vacation time the deceased sometimes looked after the

assistants in the plaintiff's shop, but received no wages.
He was also occasionally employed in sending out tele-
grams, and was learning the telegraph instrument. He
was also sometimes useful on the plaintiff's farm. The
plaintiff deposed that his son, when he reached 16, would
have been put into the shop, where his services would
have been worth £20 a year; and that when he attained
21 his services would have been worth £100 a year. The
plaintiff, on cross-examination, stated that when his son
was at home for his vacation he kept him out as much as
possible, and gave him as much amusement as he could;
and that he carried on his business without assistance from
his son all the year round. It was held that there was
not evidence of reasonable expectation of pecuniary benefit,
Palles, C. B., saying that he was not aware of any case in
which a plaintiff recovered damages where he or she had
not been actually benefited by the child. "Many of the
cases," he said, "established that if there be this actual
benefit the jury are not limited in the amount of damage
to the benefit which actually was conferred, but may estimate the value of similar benefits which might reasonably
be expected to have been conferred during the continuance
of the life. But I am aware of no case in which, where no
benefits had been conferred, a verdict for the plaintiff was
sustained." Fitzgerald, B., concurred, and so also did
Dowse, B., who added—"I am inclined, however, to go
farther than he (the C. B.) has done, and to hold that in a
case of this description the plaintiff must fail, unless he
establishes, by evidence, that there was in existence at the
time of the death of the son, a state of facts in connection
with him, out of which pecuniary advantage arose, or had
formerly arisen, and was likely to again arise to the father,
and the continuance or renewal of which pecuniary advantage, the father might have reasonably expected had his
son not been killed. * * I think it the duty of this
Court to take care that actions under Lord Campbell's Act
do not become like actions of seduction, in which, on the
question of loss of service, fiction has taken the place of
fact."

In *Holleran* v. *Bagnell*, Ir. R. 6 C. L. 333 in C. P. D., Morris, C. J., again enunciated the rule that there must be definite "evidence of pecuniary advantage in existence prior to or at the time of the death, and this advantage must be a benefit to the plaintiff." There certainly was more reason in this case than strikes one as having existed in *Bourke's Case*, for setting aside the plaintiff's verdict, because the child killed was a girl of only seven years of age who had never done more than any such child always does in her home; and therefore the decision did not necessarily rest on the rule laid down by the Chief Justice.

The doctrine thus adopted by the Irish Courts may, I think, be fairly stated as being that no injury, within the contemplation of Lord Campbell's Act can result from the death ot one from whom no benefit had been received during his life. This is so far opposed to the tenor of all the English cases, and to the express decision in some of them, that it is obviously useless to look to the judgments of the Irish Courts for assistance, while we take those of the English Courts as our guide.

It may be truly said of the English decisions to which I have adverted that there is through them all the same principle of construction applied to the statute. Each fresh state of facts as it arose was dealt with, and furnished a further illustration of the working of the Act. The party claiming was held to be entitled or not to be entitled, the scale of compensation acted upon by the jury was approved or disapproved, in view ot the immediate circumstances: but in no case has it been attempted to decide by anticipation what are the limits beyond which the benefit of the statute cannot be claimed.

No case is precisely on all-fours with the present, so far as its facts appear, and there is certainly none by which it is expressly decided that claims like those we are dealing with cannot be maintained, nor is there any expression to be found, or any dictum, intimating that a claim in respect of the death of a wife or mother is to be judged by different rules from those applied to the loss of a husband, or father, or son.

We find no hint of such a construction of the law in such reports as we have of cases in which the death of a wife has been the cause of action.

The idea is not suggested by the language of the statute. " Parent" is the word used to describe mother as well as father; " child" includes girls as well as boys ; and the husband's right is given by the same words which enable a wife to recover.

There can be but one question: Is there before us evidence proper to be left to the jury that injury resulted to the husband of the late Mrs. Lett, and to her younger children, or to the husband *or* to the children, from her death ?

We have one thing very definitely settled, namely, that the injury intended by the Statute is not of the character of wounded feelings or affections or mental suffering. And Judges. while clearly distinguishing the kind of injury which is not intended, have given a kind of definition of what, in their view of the Act, is intended, and in so doing have adopted the word " pecuniary." Whether they call it " pecuniary injury" or "pecuniary loss," or contrast it with " pecuniary advantages" " pecuniary benefits," or benefits of which a " pecuniary estimate " can be made, the word " pecuniary" is used as the distinguishing term.

I daresay no better word could have been chosen ; but there is apt to be danger, when a new phrase is substituted for the words of a statute, of addressing our criticism to the interpretation of the supposed verbal equivalent instead of the language of the statute itself. I think this danger has not always been avoided in the present instance. Argument sometimes takes the direction of maintaining, not that the injury in question is merely sentimental and therefore outside of the statute, but that it is not " pecuniary" because there was to be no handling of money and is therefore not within the statute. I do not think the word " pecuniary " is used in this restricted sense, but, if it is, it is the wrong word. The principle of *Blake* v. *Midland Counties R. W. Co.*, 18 Q. B. 93 and the other cases is, that the statute is meant to give compensation not for mental injuries but material ones, loss of money or money's worth in a material and not in a sentimental sense. There is no decision which, rightly understood, proceeds in my opinion, upon a different understanding of the right given by the statute. On that principle it has with great uniformity been applied, in the cases I have cited, to claims by parents for the loss of children; by wives for the loss of husbands; and by children for the loss of their father.

There is no reason indicated by the statute why it should not be applied in precisely the same way when the husband claims in respect of the loss of his wife, and the children for the loss of their mother.

As far as the reported cases indicate, it has, without question, been so applied.

I have referred to four English cases of the kind: *Chapman* v. *Rothwell*, 11 Jur. N. S. 1180, which may not have afforded an opportunity for raising the question; *Cotton* v. *Wood*, 8 C. B. N. S. 568, where there clearly was the opportunity; as there was also in *Chant* v. *South Eastern R. W. Co.*, W. N. 1866 p. 134, and, as far as we can perceive, in *Wilkins* v. *Day*, 12 Q. B. D. 110.

The damages in *Cotton* v. *Wood*, were awarded in separate sums to the husband and children. The verdict was moved against, but not on this ground. If pecuniary injury means only the loss of money which would have come into one's pocket, it may of course be said that Mrs. Cotton earned 10s. a week; but there is not a word in the report to indicate that the decision would not have been the same on proof that she rendered to her husband valuable service in another form, as by saving money, or doing such things as the wife in *Chant's* case was assumed to do, and which another would not do without being paid. But the money was in law the husband's. It cannot weaken the authority so far as it touches the question of the children's share of the damages.

Legal right forms no consideration in these discussions. That is another point definitely settled by the decisions. That children dependent upon their father, or receiving benefits from him, could recover for his death no one disputes. For father substitute widowed mother, and it must be conceded that the law is the same. On what principle can a distinction be founded on the circumstance that the mother was not a widow? No distinction can be urged on any idea of legal rights or relations, for the benefits conferred by the statute do not depend on legal claims on the bounty of the deceased.

I have not been able to perceive any substantial distinction between the benefits which a man's children could reasonably expect from the continuance of his income if expended by himself as pointed out in *Pym* v. *Great Northern R. W. Co.*, 2 B. & S. 750, 4 B. & S. 396, namely, education and social advantages, and the same benefits, or benefits of the same class though perhaps less in extent, conferred by a father who employed his leisure in himself educating his family, or by a mother who rendered similar services. Nor do I see in what particular the claim of a wife for the loss of a husband who, as bread-winner for his family, provided the supplies for his household, differs from that of a husband for the loss of a wife whose housewifery gave those supplies additional value.

I do not overlook the fact that a great variety of considerations must enter into the estimate of the loss by the death of wife or mother; some of these were dwelt upon in the Court below, and possibly influenced the decision there by reason of the difficulty apparently inseparable from the inquiry. The character of the influence likely to be exercised by her over her children; the possibility, not always hypothetical, that their best interests might be better advanced by a stranger; on the part of a husband, the probability of his widowhood being of short duration; and many other such considerations would unavoidably present themselves. But similar contingencies have to be taken into account no matter which of the relationships enumerated in the statute happens to be in question. In fact the objection recalls the anomalous state of the law before the statute, which is justly denounced as a reproach to our jurisprudence, when because of the infinite value placed on human life no damages at all were given for its destruction.

It is, no doubt, the duty of the Courts to restrain jurors, as far as may be practicable, from awarding damages in excess of those proportioned to the injury for which damages are properly assessable ; and the Courts have, as a rule, been vigilant in this respect. We have, amongst the cases I have cited, several in which verdicts of no great magnitude were set aside as excessive. I have not always noted this circumstance when referring to the cases. We have examples of the same kind in our own Courts ; e. g., *Secord* v. *Great Western R. W. Co.*, 15 U. C. R. 631, *Morley* v. *Great Western R. W. Co.*, 16 U. C. R. 504 ; *Hutton* v. *Corporation of Windsor*, 34 U. C. R. 487, and other cases. But the liability of the power given by the statute to be abused cannot afford a valid argument against its legitimate exercise.

At Common Law a husband could maintain an action for the loss of his wife's services caused by the tortious act of another—(*Add.* on Torts, 4th ed., p. 922)—but he could not sue for the total deprivation of those services consequent on her death. *Baker* v. *Bolton*, 1 Camp. 493—" In a civil court " Lord Ellenborough told the jury in that case " the death of a human being could not be complained of as an injury ; and in this case the damages, as to the plaintiff's wife, must stop with the period of her existence."

This sentence expressed the anomaly which Lord Campbell's Act was passed to remove. It did not remove it in all cases, one case omitted being that of master and servant, as was pointed out in the judgment in *Osborn* v. *Gillett*, L. R. 8, Ex. 88, already cited. But one case included is, that of husband and wife, and the consequence of that is, that the law laid down by Lord Ellenborough in *Baker* v. *Bolton*, 1 Camp. 493, ceased, on the passing of

that Act, to be a reproach to English jurisprudence so far
as it restricted the husband's remedy for the loss of his
wife's services to the period which happened to intervene
between the injury and her death.   Under the statute he
acquired a right to damages of the same character, in
consequence of her death, as at common law he could
have recovered when they were caused by an injury
which disabled, but did not kill her.

The judgments delivered in *Osborn* v. *Gillett*, L. R. 8 Ex.
88, bear out this proposition.   Damages were sought in that
action for the death of the daughter and servant of the
plaintiff.   The action was not under Lord Campbell's Act;
and hence the common law right of master and servant was
all that was in question.   Bramwell, B., held that the
action lay; but Pigott, B., and Kelly, C.B., held the contrary, relying upon *Baker* v. *Bolton*, and upon the inference founded on Lord Campbell's Act, which recited the
law as it had stood, and then gave the new remedy to a
limited class of persons.   " The result is," Pigott, B., said
" in my opinion, that we are not at liberty to disregard the
law thus established so long ago, and expressly recognized
by the Legislature, nor in effect to add, by the decision of
this Court, another clause to Lord Campbell's Act;" and
Kelly, C.B., concludes his judgment by saying: " Such,
then, being the state of the authorities, I agree with my
brother Pigott, that we must leave it to the Legislature to
provide for a case like this, and that we ought not to take
it upon ourselves to create a new cause of action, which
would be to make and not to expound the law."

Had the case been for loss of the services of a wife
caused by her death, the exposition of the law as enunciated in these judgments, and under the statute which did
give a cause of action to the husband while it stopped
short of giving it to the master, must have been as contended for by the present plaintiff.

Now, bearing in mind that the right of action under the
statute does not depend on the legal rights existing between
the claimants and the deceased, as has been more than

once decided, we can apprehend the effect of the view I have just put, as illustrating one kind of injury for which the statute gives a remedy, namely loss of service ; an injury not resulting from the legal right of the husband to the services of his wife, but simply from deprivation of the benefits which would have been enjoyed, or might reasonably have been expected to result from those services, and therefore incident upon the children as well as upon the husband.

Benefits of that nature are of substantial value, and must be classed as " pecuniary advantages," if that term is comprehensive enough to include what, if my argument is sound, is clearly within the intention of the Act. If the term is not sufficiently comprehensive, then as I before remarked a better word ought to be chosen.

There has never been any hesitation in recognizing the right of a parent to recover under the statute for loss of the services of a child, or of a child or a wife to recover for the loss of the services of a father or husband. The right now asserted is placed by the statute on precisely the same footing ; and I have not been able to see, from any point of view, any satisfactory reason for questioning the right, either of the husband or the children of Mrs. Lett to recover for the loss of the services reasonably to have been expected from her if her life had been continued.

The amount of the damage is not complained of. I think the judgment of Mr. Justice Armour, in the Court below, puts the application of the statute to the facts of this case upon the proper footing, and that we should allow the appeal, with costs.

GALT, J.—After the best consideration I have been able to give to the law, as laid down by the numerous cases cited in the Court below, and by my learned Brothers, it appears to me that in actions under Lord Campbell's Act the right of the administrator to recover is based, not on the mental suffering, but on the material loss sustained by the persons on whose behalf the suit is brought. If I am correct in this view, surely a husband suffers a material loss by the death of his wife and if so, the amount of that loss is to be settled by the verdict of a jury.

In the case of *Wilkins* v. *Day*, 12 Q. B. D. 110, which is the last I have seen, the right of the husband was not even questioned. There was no evidence whatever of what may, be called "pecuniary," as distinguished from "material" loss.. As respects the children, there can be no doubt they sustain a material loss by the death of their mother, the amount of that loss is a question for the jury. It does appear to me to be an extraordinary state of the law to say that if a parent is rich the children sustain no loss because they inherit their mother's wealth, and if she is poor they have no claim, because she had nothing to bequeath. In my opinion the appeal should be allowed.

Rose, J.—The question for decision is, can a husband and his children recover damages against the defendants for the negligent killing of the wife and mother—she at the time of death being engaged as a prudent woman in taking sole charge of the household and housework, and disbursing to the best advantage the income earned by her husband, and looking after the physical, mental, and it. may be moral wants of her children.

Have the husband and children, or any of them, sustained any *injury* within the meaning of Lord Campbell's Act ?

There is no adverse decision directly in point.

It is said there is no decision in favour of the plaintiffs

It has been objected that if the decision is in favour of the plaintiffs, it will be adding another clause to the Act. If this is so, the plaintiffs must fail.

It is however not quite accurate to say there is no decision in the plaintiff's favour as will more fully appear. The words of the second section of the Act are " that every such action shall be for the benefit of the wife, husband, parent and child of the person whose death shall have been so caused and shall be brought by, and in the name of the

executor or administrator of the person deceased; and in
every such action the jury may give such damages as they
may think proportioned to the *injury* resulting from such
death to the parties respectively, for whom, and for whose
benefit such action shall be brought."

These words are also found in the third section of ch.
128 R. S. O.

It will be observed, that the persons to whom a right of
action is thus given are those who stand in such relation
to the deceased as might naturally and reasonably enable
them to expect assistance in any hour of necessity.

The claim in many of the cases would be founded entirely upon affection—in hardly any could it be said to be a
legal claim, *i. e.*, one that could be enforced by legal proceedings.

The word "injury" alone would certainly be broad
enough to include most cases, but it received a limited
meaning by judicial interpretation.

It was held in *Blake* v. *Midland*, 18 Q. B. 93, *not* to
include "mental sufferings." This was the *decision* in
that case. In reaching the conclusion the Court expressed
the opinion that the damages must be "confined to injuries of which a *pecuniary estimate* may be made," and this
opinion may be said to be the ground for the conclusion,
for it is stated "as the damages certainly exceeded any loss
sustained by her admitting of a pecuniary estimate they
must be considered excessive."

It is clear that the Court were more concerned to exclude
a solatium for mental sufferings than to give a comprehensive definition of all cases within the statute.

In the next case of *Franklin* v. *South Eastern R. W. Co.*,
3 H. & N. 211, the Court held the father (plaintiff) entitled
to recover £75 for the negligent killing of his son by the
defendants. The son was *of age* earning his own wages.
It is not said that he was living at home with his father or
that his father derived any *pecuniary* assistance from him
—the only assistance he received was that he, plaintiff, being light porter at St. Thomas's Hospital, and in the habit

of carrying up coals to the wards of the Hospital, for
which he was paid 3s. 6d. a week, and being ill, his son
" *had for some time past carried up the coals for him.*"

The learned Judge, Bramwell, B., left it to the jury to
say whether the plaintiff had a reasonable expectation of
any and what *pecuniary benefit* from the *continuance* of
the son's life.

On a motion to enter a nonsuit, the judgment of the
Court was delivered by Pollock, C. B., (it is not said who
were sitting, but the members of the Court at the time
were Pollock, C.B., Martin, Bramwell, Watson, and Channel,
BB.) The Chief Baron said: "The statute does not in
terms say on what principle the action it gives is to be
maintainable, nor on what principle the damages are to be
assessed, and the only way to ascertain what it *does*, is to
shew what it *does not* mean."

This, as I have pointed out, is apparently what the Court
were endeavouring to do in *Blake* v. *The Midland R. W.
Co.*, 18 Q. B. 93. He adds: "It is also clear that the damages are not to be given in reference to the loss of a *legal
right*, for they are to be distributed among relations only,
not to all individuals sustaining such a loss—and accordingly
the practice has been to ascertain what benefit could have
been enforced by the claimant had the deceased lived, and
give damages thereby. If then the damages are not to be
calculated on either of these principles, nothing remains
except they should be calculated in reference to a *reasonable expectation of a pecuniary benefit as of right or
otherwise from the continuance of the life.* * * *
The proper question then was left, if there was any evidence in support of the affirmative of it. We think there
was. The plaintiff was old and getting infirm, the son was
young, earning good wages, and apparently well disposed
to assist his father, and in fact he had so assisted him to
the value of 3s. 6d. a week. We do not say that actual
benefit should have been derived, *a reasonable expectation
is enough, and such reasonable expectation might well exist
though from the father being not in need the son had never*

done anything for him   On the other hand a jury certainly
ought not to make a guess in the matter, but ought to be
satisfied that there has been a *loss of sensible and appreciable pecuniary benefit* which might have been reasonably
expected from the continuance of life."

This case shews the opinion of the Court to have been
that :

1. The claim is not based on loss of a legal right, good
will and affection are its supports.

2. It must not be founded on injury to the feelings.

3. It must be founded on pecuniary loss.

4. The damages must be calculated in reference to a
reasonable expectation of pecuniary benefit.

5. It is not necessary to shew any benefit actually
received—

6. Or a present need of assistance—

7. Or a certainty of future need.

8. Evidence of good will is evidence upon which a
reasonable expectation may be founded.

9. Assistance in performing labour, the remuneration for
which goes to the claimant is pecuniary assistance.

10. Certainty of permanent pecuniary resource on the
part of the deceased need not be proved. Wages and
ability to earn them at the time of death constituted the
evidence in this case.

In *Dalton* v. *South Eastern R. W. Co.*, 4 C. B. N. S. 296,
Willes, J., speaks of *Franklin* v. *South Eastern R. W. Co.*
being decided " with our entire concurrence."

Duckworth v. *Johnston*, 4 H. & N. 653, lays down no
new principle but is interesting as illustrating the right of
a jury to estimate damages without distinct evidence of
value, drawing on their own common judgment to supply
the requisite information. The evidence disclosed that the
deceased son was earning 4s. a week which went into
the common fund, that the father bore the expenses of his
board, clothes, &c, No evidence was given as to the cost
which must of course be deducted to ascertain the loss
sustained. Pollock, C.B., said : " But as to that the jury

were better able to judge than we." Martin, B.: "It was argued that it ought to have been *proved* that the cost of boarding and clothing the boy did not exceed 4s. a week; but that was a question for the jury to determine."

In *Bramall* v. *Lees*, 29 L. T., pp. 82, 111, 166, a verdict in favour of the father was sustained. The deceased was twelve years of age—living at home—getting nothing, and pecuniarily a burden to her parents. It was said she might, in the course of a year or so, have gone to work in a factory near by, and taken back money as her earnings for the parents. The verdict was for £15, Pollock, C.B., having intimated to counsel for defendant that the Court entertained no doubt about the plaintiff's right to hold his verdict, the rule, although granted, was not taken out.

This case adds the further proposition which may be numbered.

11. The fact that the deceased was, at the time of death, a recipient of benefits, and could not be capable of rendering any assistance for some considerable time, does not entitle defendant to have the case withdrawn from the jury.

This case further illustrates the impossiblity of laying down any exact rules to guide juries in the ascertainment of the amount of damages.

Pym v. *The Great Northern R. W. Co.*, 2 B. & S. 759, is fully digested by Mr. Justice Armour, in the Court below. It gives an additional direction to the jury. On the trial Lord Chief Justice Cockburn told the jury that they "might take into consideration the loss of the advantages of superior education, social position, and personal comfort, of which the father's income, had he lived, would have secured the benefit and enjoyment to the family," &c. The same learned Chief Justice, in giving the judgment of the Court on motion to enter verdict for defendants or non-suit, said that "the loss of these advantages is one which is capable of being estimated in money," in other words as a pecuniary loss.

Proposition 12 may be stated thus:—The loss of the advantages of superior education, social position and personal comforts constitutes an injury capable of being estimated in money.

He also says, p. 768 : "We are not insensible to the argument *ab inconvenienti*, founded on the very serious consequences which might ensue to a railway company in the event of a fatal accident happening from negligence, to an individual of very large fortune. But we think this is rather for the consideration of the Legislature, as to whether any limit should be put to the liability, than for us." In the same case in the Exchequer Chamber, 4 B. & S. p. 506, Erle, C. J., says : " On the second point, also, Mr. Hawkins failed in his argument. He contended that the whole estate of the deceased passed at his death, to the class of relatives whom the Statute meant to protect, and as they got the whole estate among them, no loss was caused to them by his death. The remedy, however, given by the Statute is not given to a class, but to individuals; for by sect. 2, 'The jury may give such damages as they may think proportioned to the injury resulting from such death to the parties respectively, for whom and for whose benefit such action shall be brought.' This requires the jury to consider how each of the parties is situated, and how the interest of each is affected. If this is so, the younger children have lost by the death of their father."

This opinion is expressed, because the fund was resettled so as to give the younger children the right to share in only a portion of the income. It will be observed that they were, before the father's death, dependent upon his bounty ; that the fund, to a great extent after his death remained with the mother and eldest brother, and that it did not appear that it would not be still shared in common or that as a matter of fact, the children would have any the less the advantages, and yet, the Court upon counsel for the children accepting £1,000 for each of the children instead of £1,500 refused even to give a new trial.

Reference to *Sedgwick* on Damages 7th Ed. (1880), p. 544, 2nd Vol, will shew that in some of the States the damages are limited to $5,000:—this limit seems to apply only in case of death.

The case of *Hetherington* v. *The North Eastern R. W. Co.*, 9, Q. B.D., 160 (1882) is very like *Franklin* v. *South Eastern R. W. Co.*, 3 H. & N. 211, (1858), and shews that in the nearly quarter of a century which had elapsed since that decision the principles it laid down had not been shaken·

In this later case the evidence was as follows : "The deceased was my son ; he was twenty-nine years old ; he gave me a portion of his earnings when I wanted it ; I am nearly blind and injured in my leg and hands ; my son used to contribute to my support ; I work when I can ; I am not so able to work as I used to be ; I am fifty-nine ; my son was not married. *Cross-examined.*—Five or six years ago I was out of work for six months, and my son was very kind to me and helped me. *Re-examined.*—He was always kind to me ; I have never had money from him since."

Upon this evidence the County Court Judge ruled that there was no sufficient evidence of pecuniary injury, and nonsuited the plaintiff. A rule *nisi* had been obtained for a new trial on the ground of misdirection. In shewing cause, counsel for defendant said : "It was admitted by the father that the son was not contributing to his support at the time of his death, and had not in fact assisted him for five or six years. The mere relation of parent and child cannot give rise to the presumption that the child will give pecuniary assistance to the parent, and from the fact that five years before the son assisted his father pecuniarily no reasonable inference arises with regard to the probability of his doing so again."

The rule was made absolute without calling upon the plaintiff's counsel to support it.

Certain observations of Pigott, C.B., in *London* v. *Great Southern and Western R. W. Co.*, Ir. R. 16 C. L. 415, may be of assistance in ascertaining the province and powers of a jury in such cases. " As to the probable performance of those duties the jury were entitled to apply their own experience and knowledge of life, and to consider the habits of the peasantry of the country, and the probable amount of assistance and support which a widow might fairly and reasonably expect from a son."

Endeavouring to apply the principles to be gathered from the above cases :

First, as to the claim of the husband—The claim stands upon as high ground as by a father for the death of a son. We°have seen that assistance in the performance of labour, the remuneration for which goes to the father, is pecuniary assistance.

Does not a frugal, careful, loving wife, by attending to the household duties, disbursing the earnings of the husband with care and discretion, watching the servants to see that waste is not committed, repairing the clothes of husband and children so as to make them more lasting, and by a thousand and one other ways which will suggest themselves to the mind, render pecuniary assistance to the husband as certainly as if she went out from home and earned money and brought it into the common fund ?

Applying our common everyday knowledge of life, we know that a husband with a frugal, careful wife will have a neat comfortable home, a well spread table, cleanly, well-dressed children ; while another, with the same amount of income, who has lost his wife and has to trust his home and family to hirelings, will have a comfortless, untidy home, an ill-prepared table, and slovenly children, and run into debt. Is there room for doubt on such a question ? Would not the removal of such a wife be a loss to a man of " personal comforts," and constitute an injury which a jury can estimate in money ? The son performs labour which brings in money, and by the money the father secures personal comforts. The wife labours and manages the moneys brought in by the husband so as to provide for his personal comforts. Is there any real distinction ?

We are told you cannot measure affection in money, and the wife can be only looked upon as a person performing certain duties which may be performed by others, and

perhaps better performed. While affection, and its loss as
such cannot be measured, it is clear that affection is in most
cases arising under the Statute, the ground upon which is
based the reasonable expectation of assistance. What hope
would a father have of assistance from an unkind son who
had proven that he had banished all filial love? Apart
from the question of wages to be paid to a housekeeper, it
seems to me that it is affection which makes the services
of a wife of greater financial value to a husband, than the
services of a housekeeper.

In the judgment of Bramwell, B., in *Osborne* v. *Gillett*,
L. R. 8 Ex, 88, it is said that "it is obvious that the case of
master and servant raises a different question from that of
wife and husband." This language is referred to by the
learned Chief Justice of Ontario, presiding in the Court
below. I think we may draw a different meaning from it
to what he does.

Between master and servant, the only tie is that of service
rendered for hire or reward. While, of course, a good
servant may have an affection for his or her master, and
render willing service, a good master on the other hand
would take care to exact no service for which he gives no
remuneration. On the other hand while services are rendered by a wife to her husband and to her children, the
inducement is love and affection. What limit is there to
such service ? The limit is measured by the love and affection, and such a wife and such a mother, nerved by love,
renders service which money cannot buy, and the deprivation of which results in loss of personal comfort.

It seems to me, therefore, it may well be, that for the
death of a servant the master may not have an action, as
such service may be obtained for a similar wage, and yet a
husband may have an action for injury sustained in the
removal of a wife whose death may cause great loss and
injury. While *Osborne* v. *Gillett*, L. R. 8 Ex. 88, decides
that a master cannot recover for the loss of a servant by
death, it seems clear that it does not affect the consideration of this case.

The declaration was for loss of service, and burial expenses. It was by the father as master, not as administrator, nor under Lord Campbell's Act, nor was the line of cases which have been cited to us, referred to in any way. I am glad it does not control us in considering this case—as I may perhaps venture to say that the reasoning in Baron Bramwell's dissentient judgment is convincing to my own mind.

The father of a family discharging the duties of his position, must either have some one to take care of his children or take care of them himself. If he stays at home and takes care of them himself, he cannot go out and earn money for their maintenance. If, therefore, his wife stays at home and discharges the household duties and enables him to go out and earn money, does she not afford him pecuniary assistance as surely as the son who carried up the coals for which the father received remuneration? I think I may adopt the language of Bramwell B. in *Osborne* v. *Gillett* (p. 99):—" In this case it seems to me that the principle the plaintiff relies on is broad, plain, and clear, viz., that he sustained a damage from a wrongful action for which the defendant is responsible; that the defendant to establish an anomalous exception to this rule, for which exception he can give no reason, should shew a clear and binding authority either by express decision or a long course of uniform opinion deliberately formed and expressed by English lawyers or experts in the English law. I find neither."

The claim of a husband for loss of a wife is not a singular one in England.

In the cases, referred to in the judgment below of *Cotton* v. *Wood*, 8 C. B., N. S. 568; *Condliff* v. *Condliff*, 22 W. R. 325; *Evans* v. *Brend*, Law Times July 8th, 1882, the Courts had an oppportunity of stating that such an action could not be entertained, and yet we do not find any such question raised.

The want of authority is authority for the proposition for it seems to me with great deference that to hold in.

favour of the plaintiff will not be to add a clause to the Act, but that a contrary decision would be to declare that this case is one which is to be excluded from the provisions of an Act which is wide enough in terms to cover the case. It will be remembered that the decisions have not been to determine what cases are to be held as coming within the Act, but rather what cases are to be held as not . oming within the Act. Therefore, if actions were brought, as it appears they have been, to recover for the injury occasioned by the death of a wife, and the decision was in favour of her administrator, it probably would not excite attention or be reported. On the other hand, if the decision had been adverse, it would be another case determined not to be within the Act.

I think I am drawing the correct inference, because I find that in *Condliff* v. *Condliff*, which was an action by the son against the father for his portion of £5,000 recovered by the father as administrator of his wife—under Lord Campbell's Act—for the benefit of himself and his children, it appears that the defendants in the original action, *i. e.*, the South Eastern Ry. Co'y, *allowed judgment to go by default* of a plea, and the damages were ordered to be assessed but before the inquiry was made negotiations resulted in a consent order for £5,000.

It will be noted that the defendant company was the same company that was defendant in the early suit of *Franklin* v. *South Eastern R. W. Co.*, and *Dalton* v. *South Eastern R. W. Co.*

Reference to the report of *Evans* v. *Brend* shews that the facts were these: "The plaintiff's wife, a woman between fifty and sixty years of age, was crossing Endell Street at eleven o'clock, on the 25th of March, 1882, when she was knocked down by a hansom cab, and received injuries from which she died very shortly afterwards."

I would conclude from the report that the parties were in very humble circumstances as the husband was not represented by a solicitor at the inquest, and a certain person from the office of a legal firm " tapped him on the

shoulder and said, 'I am watching the case for you.'"
This appears to have been the mode of obtaining the
retainer, and we are not, therefore, surprised to find the
note of the case under the head "Speculative Actions."

It would seem as if such a case afforded the facts necessary to raise the questions raised here ; but if so they were
not thought of enough importance to merit reporting.

So also *Cotton* v. *Wood,* where the case went off on another
point and no discussion arose on the questions presented to
us for decision.

In the nature of things, actions by the husband for the
injuries sustained by the death of a wife, would be much
less frequent than by a wife for the death of a husband.

The observations of Pollock, C. B., in *Gillard* v. *Lancashire and Yorkshire R. W. Co.*, 12 L. T. 356, need not be
questioned. His words interweaving question and answer
are " Clearly a widower would not be entitled tc sue for
the loss of the society and comfort of his wife, unless her
death is the cause of a pecuniary loss by the husband."
This is not very accurate language, and in all probability
would not have appeared, but for the somewhat loose
manner which resulted from hurried answers given to
somewhat hastily put questions by counsel during the
argument. The exact question was : " In that view a
widower would not be entitled to sue for the loss of the
society and comfort of his wife ?" The answer " Certainly
not unless her death is the cause of a pecuniary loss by
the husband."

Is not the fair meaning " certainly not, but he may if her
death is, &c." This is consistent with all the cases and
leaves to be determined in each case, whether there is or is
not any pecuniary loss.

It would be clear that if a pension were lost by the
death of a wife there would be pecuniary loss. It is
equally clear that the poorest peasant " who may lose
nothing at all by the death of his wife cannot sue at all."

What the learned Chief Baron was desirous of excluding
was damages for wounded feelings. He says : "I think it

is utterly impossible for a jury to estimate any sum as a compensation for the injured feelings of the survivors." He also says : " I have frequently expressed this opinion," referring to similar language. It will be remembered that he presided in *Franklin* v. *South Eastern R. W. Co.*, and *Duckworth* v. *Johnston*, and from these his fully considered opinion may be gathered.

I am, therefore, of the opinion that whenever a wife is killed, and such facts as to her life and conduct and relation to her husband and his affairs are laid before a jury as enable a jury to bring to bear their common knowledge of the affairs of life, and to come to the conclusion, either that his income is lessened, or expenditure increased so as in effect to lessen his income, or that it is less likely that it will be frugally expended in such a way as to surround him with home enjoyments so that by her removal his personal comfort will be interfered with, in such a case the husband has given evidence of having sustained an injury within the meaning of the Statute, and the jury must be left to give such damages as they think proportioned to the injury sustained.

The principles I have endeavoured to ascertain from the decisions seem to me equally applicable to the claims of the children.

Bearing in mind that while affection is not to be estimated in money, and that without affection or good will it is difficult to find ground for the claim to rest upon ; it is clear that if a careful, loving mother is taken away from a family of children they must suffer an injury. We have seen that the jury may look at loss of personal comfort. Who will look so carefully after the children's personal comfort as an affectionate mother ? The money which she might expend upon herself is oftentimes placed aside to purchase needed comforts for her child. Who in the hour of sickness will watch with such self-sacrificing care, oftentimes giving her life to save her child's life ?

We have seen that the loss of the advantage of superior education may be considered, and I suppose also the loss of the advantage of education primary as well as superior.

Is it likely that any one will so well look after the training of a child as a thoughful, affectionate mother; see
that the school is regularly attended, and the home lessons
carefully prepared ?

The loss of social position may also be regarded. If a
child is well looked after at home, its person kept neat, its
habits watched, and its manners well formed, will not its
social position be advanced ? If the father's income is so
disbursed by the mother, as to enable her to procure for the
children greater comforts than if it were wasted, do they
not derive personal benefit ?

I quite agree that, to quote the words of the learned
Chief Justice in the Court below : " The differences between
a good and loving mother, and a careless, indifferent mother
would have to be considered;" but is that different from
considering whether a son is good and loving, or careless
and indifferent ? There may be many a case where the
children's temporal, and it may be eternal interests would
be advanced, so far as man can judge—by the death of a
mother ; but so there might be by the death of a father."
These are facts to be considered by the jury, and hence is
most pertinent the language of Pigott, C. B., above quoted,
that the jury were entitled to apply their own experience
and knowledge of life, and to consider the habits of the
class from which the parties were drawn.

The children might not at the time of death be in need
of any assistance, and yet according to the rules laid down
the jury are entitled to consider whether if the need
should arise they would have a reasonable expectation of
assistance.

With great deference I think the observation of the
learned Chief Justice that the jury would have to consider
" whether the care and training of the deceased parent
could not be obtained from some other source, much to the
advantage of the children," should be somewhat guarded.

In the event of it being shewn that the deceased parent
—say mother—was careful, and so performed household
duties as to minister most carefully to the personal interests

of her children, and that since her death they had not
been so comfortable for want of some one to guard these
interests ; could the jury be told that they must speculate
on the chances of a kind and attentive housekeeper, or an
affectionate step-mother being provided, any more than if
the deceased mother had been an annuitant, that they must
consider the chances of the father marrying a second wife
with a large annuity—or in case of an accident by which
a man was physically disabled from plying his trade—
could a jury be told that he might now be forced into
another business much more remunerative, and hence, in
all probability, he would suffer no injury, but the accident
would prove a blessing in disguise ?

Of course a jury would look at all the surrounding
circumstances, and if they felt there was no loss they
would say so, but if there was, then it would be no less a
present loss because among the chances of the future it
might prove a gain.

If one can recover damages for physical injuries which
incapacitate him in some degree from physical labour,
cannot damages be recovered for injury to the mental
being which renders the mind less active ? If, as is suggested in the *Tilley Case*, cited in the Court below, a person
under obligation to furnish a minor with instruction is
liable to damages for neglect of duty, and surely he would
be, is not the person who removes one who can best tutor
the mind and train the body liable in damages ? Are
there not times in the life of a girl when a mother's
watchful care and training are all important to not only
her mental and moral nature but also to her physical
being ? Is one who negligently deprives her of such a
guardian not to answer for it in damages ?

I refer also to the American decisions cited in the judgment of His Lordship the Chief Justice and Mr. Justice
Armour.

I think the facts in this case rendered it necessary to
submit the case to the jury, and that the learned Judge at
the trial could not have nonsuited. I think he could not

have withdrawn the consideration of the changed position of the children with reference to the mother's property. If the evidence had justified it, the jury might have found that the father would not have so bountifully provided for the children as the mother. I think the verdict in favour of the father and children justified by the evidence. I have been in some doubt as to the damages but by what rule can I be guided to enable me to say that they are excessive, and so excessive as to demand a new trial.

The jury are to determine the question, not I. They are to hear such facts as may be given in evidence, and to apply their own experience and knowledge of life, and to consider the habits of the family. How can I tell what information they derived from such knowledge and experience? They may have brought to bear knowledge I never had, and experience I could not obtain. How, then, can I interfere? If I did, what am I to suggest to be told to them at the next trial? If the case were sent down, and it happened that the jury incidentally learned the amount now awarded, and that this Court thought such amount excessive, and should ask for guidance to enable them to bring the amount within what would be thought just by the Court, what direction could be given? In my opinion the verdict must stand.

It does not, therefore, become necessary to consider the question stoutly argued by Mr. Osler, that the Court below, on a motion for new trial, had no power to enter a nonsuit. The other questions were disposed of in the Court below in the plaintiff's favour, and I think the decision as to them cannot successfully be attacked.

I am of the opinion that the appeal should be allowed, with costs; and the motion in the Court below be dismissed, with costs.

CAMERON v. BICKFORD.

Conflicting evidence—Reversing finding of Judge—Agreement for partnership—Onus of proof.

The learned Judge who tried the case, in which the evidence was conflicting and irreconcilable, rested his conclusion in favour of the defendant on the documentary evidence and the probabilities arising in the case. This Court, while not differing from the Judge as to the credibility of the parties or their witnesses, having come to a different conclusion on the whole evidence allowed the appeal and reversed the decision of the Court below.

In June, 1874, the plaintiff and defendant by writing entered into an agreement for supplying together the iron for the Grand Junction Railway, and providing for the division of the surplus or profits. No division of the profits was made and the defendant went on investing the receipts from that enterprise in other contracts, and the plaintiff claimed a like interest in them also, which the defendant denied his right to.

Held, that the onus of negativing such right of the plaintiff rested on the defendant, and having failed to negative his right to such share, the Court declared him entitled thereto, and directed a reference to take the accounts between the parties.

The fact that the plaintiff who had for some years acted as the legal adviser of the defendant, was appointed one of the directors of the railway company, at the same time that he claimed to be interested with the defendant in the contract for the construction of the road, formed no ground for the defendant refusing to account to the plaintiff for his share of the profits of the enterprise.

THE bill in this case was filed by Hector Cameron against Edward Oscar Bickford, on the 6th of July, 1881, setting forth that in 1874 the plaintiff and defendant agreed to enter into an adventure for their mutual benefit in the supply of railway iron required for the construction of the Grand Junction Railway from Belleville to the village of Hastings; and in pursuance of such agreement they entered into a contract in writing with Alphonso Brooks, the contractor for constructing the said railway, for the sale and supply to him of the iron required in the construction of said railway.

That by the terms of the agreement between the plaintiff and defendant the funds required for the purchase of the iron so to be supplied to Brooks were to be procured and provided by means of advances from banks; and after all moneys advanced and paid in order to secure such iron were paid out of the receipts, the profits were divisible between the plaintiff and defendant in the proportion of 80 per cent. to the defendant and 20 per cent. to the plaintiff.

The bill further alleged that large gains and profits had been derived from the adventure, and from sales and other dispositions of portions of the iron and rails procured for the purpose and on account of the adventure; but the same were received by the defendant, and no division was ever made thereof between the plaintiff and defendant in accordance with the terms of the said agreement; and without any such division having been made, the proceeds and profits of the said adventure were embarked in further enterprises for the mutual benefit of the plaintiff and defendant, eventually resulting in the acquisition of a very large and valuable interest in the said Grand Junction Railway, which interest was subsequently disposed of for a large sum, which was received and held by the defendant; and that after payment of all sums advanced and paid on account of such adventures and enterprises, and of all the necessary expenses connected therewith, there remained large gains and profits to be divided between the plaintiff and defendant, but the defendant neglected and refused to come to an account with the plaintiff for, or to pay over to him, his share of the said gains and profits.

The prayer was for an account of the gains and profits so arising or derived from the said adventures or enterprises; and that the defendant might be ordered to pay the plaintiff his share of such gains and profits and his costs of suit.

The defendant by his answer denied that he entered into the agreement alleged in the bill of complaint, and alleged that at and prior to the date of the alleged agreement the plaintiff was a practising barrister and solicitor in the Superior Courts of the Province of Ontario, and as such was disabled from entering into the alleged agreement, and defendant claimed that on this ground the same was invalid; and at the same time the plaintiff was defendant's

I cannot, therefore, take it to have been proved that this was an arrangement by which Mr. Cameron was to give all his professional services, and to receive the 20 per cent., the fifth part of the profits to be derived from this undertaking. In regard to the conduct of the parties, it is perhaps not of very much importance. The witnesses whom Mr. McCarthy has referred to—Mr. Hugel and Mr. Kelso and others—they state it was difficult, especially Mr. Kelso, said it was difficult to tell in what character Mr. Cameron appeared to be there : but he seemed to take a greater interest than a solicitor would ordinarily do ; but I do not think Mr. Hugel's evidence went to any greater extent than that; and, therefore, I am left to my own construction of that agreement, which appears in writing.

A most important matter, I also agree with Mr. McCarthy, is, what took place in June, 1878, and the whole case it seems to me, turns on that point. The plaintiff alleges in his bill that there was an express agreement by which the proceeds and the profits of the previous arrangement between them were carried into the new business, and that he was to share in a similar proportion the profits of the new business as he did in the old. That is expressly denied by the defendant, and there is nothing from which I can infer an agreement of that kind in the face of the denial by the defendant, and I think I cannot assume on the part of the plaintiff that any such agreement has been proved. Then I do not think, however, without an agreement of that kind—and in this I also agree with Mr. McCarthy—I do not think an agreement of that kind was necessary to enable the plaintiff to get the benefit of future dealings with the profits that had been invested in the business. I think the continuance of these profits in the business, either with or without the consent of the plaintiff, would have entitled him to a similar percentage in the profits upon his share of the capital invested; but his rights in that respect would depend entirely upon another question, and that is the payment of the $4,000 made in June, 1878. Was that a payment in satisfaction of the plaintiff's claim—the claim he now makes in this suit of the 20 per cent.—altogether irrespective of the costs he had charged against the defendant. Now the defendant positively and clearly asserts that there was that arrangement between them, that the $4,000 that he paid was paid in pursuance of that arrangement, that it was to be a settlement of the claims of the plaintiff up to that time. The plaintiff denies that, and the only question is, whether the circumstances subsequently arising between the parties lend a greater probability to the story of the defendant than they do to the story of the plaintiff. There are a number of circumstances which have been dwelt upon by counsel on both sides, and which have a considerable effect, in whatever light they are looked upon, in the decision of this question. We find, for example, in the first instance, that the conveyance by Bickford to Pardee, on the sale by Bickford to Pardee, Cameron was joined in the transfer. That was said to have been required by the solicitors of Pardee. At all events, Mr. Cameron's name appears there as a promoter, as a person interested in the contract, and as passing that interest to Pardee. His name does not appear in the purchase back from Pardee, and his name does not appear in any of the subsequent transactions between the parties in none of the subsequent transactions affecting the interest in this contract or iron does Mr. Cameron's name appear.

Then there is another very important circumstance, it seems to me, and that is the fact of Mr. Cameron asserting that he had no interest at the time the question was raised, as to whether he would sit upon the Board of the Railway in Hastings. Now I think that is the most important and material consideration; because, if Mr. Cameron's interest was such as he represents it to be—20 per cent. in the profits of that contract—then there is nothing plainer, it seems to me, than that that incapacitated him from sitting on the Board; and I cannot fancy Mr. Cameron could assume to believe, as a barrister of eminence and distinction here, that his interest at that time, though an equitable one, would not have prevented him from acting as director of the railway company. Why, the very position of the parties would have prevented him from acting as director of the railway company. Why, the very position of the parties would shew the impropriety of his doing so. According to his present allegation he was a contractor of the company, and he was also to be a director of the company, and I have always been under the impression that where a man's duty and interest conflict he ought to give up his interest; and if he takes this position, then the assumption is that he had not an interest conflicting with his position. The proceedings also in respect to the sale to McDougall & Cowan, all seem to me to be important. He deals with them, the papers all drawn as if Mr. Bickford was alone concerned; he never makes any assertion of interest to McDougall & Cowan; never claims anything from them—   *   *   *

I do not think there is any use of my detaining the consideration of the case for further investigation, or further looking at these matters, for it seems to me, on the very conflicting evidence that has been given, notwithstanding the very able argument on behalf of Mr. Cameron, that he has failed to make out a case here.

From this judgment the plaintiff appealed, and the appeal came on for hearing before this Court on the 3rd and 4th days of June, 1884.*

McCarthy, Q.C., and *Moss*, Q.C., for the appellant.
S. H. Blake, Q.C., and *J. Maclennan*, Q.C., for the respondent.

The additional facts, so far as relate to the question in issue and the points raised by counsel, appear in the judgment.

Present.—HAGARTY, C.J.O., BURTON, PATTERSON, and MORRISON, JJ.A.

October 20, 1884. HAGARTY, C. J. O.—I do not deem
it necessary to make any complete statement of the facts
of this case. It would be very long, and would not help
our decision. We all agree in the conclusion of the learned
Judge in the Court below, that the case must turn on the
one question, whether the defendant has or has not established that he made a settlement in full of the plaintiff's
claims in June, 1878. Up to that time the plaintiff had
an interest as alleged, and unless the settlement be established, he seems entitled to the account and relief asked.

The learned Judge notices the direct contradiction in the
evidence of the parties, and says : " The ultimate conclusion
I come to must depend in a great measure upon the documents produced and the probabilities of the case." He
considers the whole case turns on the point as to what
took place in June 1878. We will look at the relations of
the parties in the fall of 1877. The property had been
sold to Pardee & Co., and Pardee's notes had been given
for large amounts of the purchase money. He had been
applying for renewals of these notes and the plaintiff was
pressing for a realization on them. A long correspondence took place between the plaintiff and the defendant
beginning 29th October, 1877. The plaintiff claiming his
interest in the notes, the defendant denying any legal right
in the plaintiff, but that he always intended to deal liberally with him. The correspondence shews a clear insistance
on the plaintiff's part on his legal rights.

He speaks of $2,500 at least being then due to him for
costs. In one of the defendant's letters, November 13th,
1877, occur the words : " It is only when the ascertained
profit remaining after all advances, costs and charges are
paid, and the matter finally so closed that [it] can owe
you anything." The correspondence went on to December
29th, 1877. Bills of costs were rendered December 26th
to the defendant amounting to about $2,600.

On the 28th December, 1877, the plaintiff writes that
" I will not jump accounts at $5,000 as you suggested, more
particularly if you wish to include costs in that sum. The

amount fairly due to me, exclusive of costs, I estimate at
over $6,000 after deducting $4,000 for costs, but I am willing to abide by the letter of the agreement and the figures.
I do not ask you to pay me what is coming to me before
you receive it, but I want the amount ascertained," &c.

The defendant was about starting for England and the
plaintiff told him he must proceed at law.

We may refer to a statement of account by the plaintiff
called " the blue and red memo.," as furnished apparently
about this time.

A bill was filed by the plaintiff early in January, 1878,
setting out his claim and the sale to Pardee and Lloyd, and
the notes and payments given and made thereon and the
defendant's renewing, &c., against the plaintiff's wish;
claiming an account and a declaration of the plaintiff's
right to one-fifth of the profits, his costs and charges,
appointment of receiver, injunction against the defendant
dealing with the Pardee notes, asking payment thereout, &c.

The defendant answered this in England in February,
1878, insisting that the plaintiff's interest in prospective
profits was in lieu of all his professional services: that
he had offered, and was willing to pay all his costs if he
would give up his claim to profits, and that there were
not and would not be any profits.

The defendant returned in May, 1878. He and the
plaintiff met and appear to have made up their differences.
There was a good prospect of buying back the property,
with a large amount of other railway property, from
Pardee. They agreed to work the thing through (so the
plaintiff says), that they would make good profit in the
end, and divide up. The plaintiff agreed to this, and
nothing further was done in the Chancery suit.

Defendant swears, that soon after his return he made
a settlement with the plaintiff, who wanted to go to
England, and after some negotiations they agreed that the
plaintiff should accept $4,000 in settlement. He says the
plaintiff wanted this at once, but he refused until he had
finally arranged with Pardee.

This $4,000 was to be in addition to all he had before received, and in full of all claims against the defendant and the Grand Junction; and that this, counting previous receipts of $2,397, would leave to the plaintiff in all $6,397.

In his answer the defendant swore that he, being pressed by the plaintiff, "then paid him the sum of $5,500, which was taken in full discharge of all claims." In addition, he says the plaintiff was to be solicitor for the railway. As a matter of fact, the payments on the defendant's own shewing were not made till some months after the alleged settlement.

The plaintiff went to England in June, 1878, and returned about the 15th September. He says that before he went the defendant told him that if the matter was arranged with Pardee, he would send him some money to England.

The plaintiff, on the day he embarked, June 19th, 1878, received a telegram from the defendant: "Pardee here offers to accept nearly my terms; sorry you are going."

The plaintiff telegraphed in reply asking should he return. The same day the defendant replied:

"No need you should stop for this; it may take till your return. Yarker refuses it."

The final agreement was executed with Pardee on the 28th June, 1878. It states that all notes given by Pardee to the defendant and Cameron or either of them, or payable to them or either of them, be given up.

On the 5th August, 1878, the defendant by deed sells to McDougall and Cowan one-half share in all the property purchased from Pardee, for $68,909.

Five days after, on the 10th of August, the defendant telegraphed to the plaintiff in England: "Grand Junction convalescing; draw £150. Election fixed for the 19th prox. Return."

The plaintiff says he did not hear of the sale to McDougall & Cowan till 21st September, and then told defendant he had made a bad bargain, but defendant said the bank had forced him to sell.

Just as the plaintiff was leaving for England, 26th June, 1878, he made his note for $1500 to the defendant, or order; the latter indorsed and ultimately paid this.

On September 26th, 1878, the defendant gave the plaintiff a cheque for $1000; on October 10th, 1878, three cheques $500, $200, and $50. On this $50 the defendant wrote in the margin, "this is $4000." He says he wrote this in the plaintiff's presence. The latter distinctly denies ever seeing it.

By deed of the 1st June, 1881, the defendant and McDougall & Cowan sell the properties to the Grand Trunk Railway for about $832,500. It would appear that negotiations had been going on for some time, twelve months before, Mr. Cowan says. The plaintiff took a very active part in all these matters up to the last moment.

In October, 1878, the plaintiff was made a director on the railway board of the Grand Junction and North Hastings.

The defendant and McDougall & Cowan were contractors for the road. The plaintiff explains this by saying that in fact the directors were nominees of the contractors, and that it was a matter of no importance. The trustees and *cestuis que trust* were the same.

At the final arrangement with the Grand Trunk there is much discrepancy in the evidence as to what occurred. Mr. Cowan says that the plaintiff did not, to him, ever claim any interest in the road: that he complained that the defendant refused to act liberally with 'him: that the plaintiff did not open or complete the negotiations with the Grand Trunk, but "drew up the papers, kept us straight, and saw that everything was right."

He told witness at the settlement that he would accept $15,000 and costs: that the defendant had offered him a paltry $5,000 or $10,000.

The plaintiff handed Cowan a memorandum produced, stating bonus $15,000 and costs. Mr. Cowan thinks he offered for self and partner to give the plaintiff $5,000 and half his costs. The memorandum was not given to witness while the defendant was there. He could not say when it was given, or whether after the defendant had left for England.

The plaintiff in reply says that he made no claim on McDougall & Cowan except for their share of the costs, and said that anything they gave him beyond that was a bonus ; that the defendant offered him $10,000 in full of every thing, and at last said he would make it $14,000 ; that he, the plaintiff, made the memorandum for Cowan after the defendant had left for England, and after the plaintiff had filed this bill against the defendant and the others, and that he told them he would settle with them without prejudice to his claims on the defendant, and relieve them from further liability ; and the memorandum was made with that view.

At that time plaintiff claimed that for costs alone he was owed from $13,000 to $15,000.

The defendant says that at the final settlement the plaintiff was offered $10,000 and his costs. At page 90 of the appeal book he says : " I agreed to pay him all his costs of every kind and then we would give him a bonus of $10,000 in addition."

The present suit was commenced very soon after this.

It seems to me impossible to explain away the very serious discrepancies and contradictions apparent in the defendant's evidence. The learned Judge below notices them as not to be "laughed away." His evidence contrasts most painfully with his correspondence. We need only refer to his letter of March 20th, 1876, in which he states his representation to Mr. Crombie that the plaintiff's interest in the Grand Junction mortgage was worth $10,000, and then examine his statements on oath in this suit. His explanation of such matters as these can hardly satisfy the most lenient judgment.

Convinced as we must be, and as the learned Judge was convinced, of the existence of a real interest in the plaintiff, it must be borne in mind that the whole burden of proving that such interest was released and put an end to by the alleged payments in 1878, was on the defendant.

The proof of such release rests wholly on the defendant's own statement.

It is difficult to believe that after an acrimonious controversy as to their respective rights—after a suit brought to establish the plaintiff's claim, and a denial on oath of its existence, a keen man of business like the defendant would content himself with this alleged verbal agreement, without a word in writing to evidence its existence and only a number of cheques for unexplained sums of money produced as proof.

We can attach no importance to the memorandum placed by the defendant on the margin of the $50 cheque. The plaintiff emphatically denies all knowledge of it. We may repeat, it is hard to believe that a transaction so vitally important, so completely altering the positions of the parties, could have been so effected. We can understand it as taking place between two strong personal friends, each having full confidence in the honour and integrity of the other, but we can hardly accept it as probable after a law suit and a rather bitter controversy in which each impugned the other's veracity and fair dealing.

Apart from their respective assertion and denial, the transaction wholly fails to present the appearance of probability.

I am unable to attach the same weight as the learned Judge has done to the fact of the plaintiff acting as a director on the railway board after the alleged settlement.

It was thought that such a proceeding was a strong argument in favour of the belief that he had ceased to have any interest. The glimpses afforded by this case into the " inner life " of these railway boards, being in fact the mere creatures of the contractors for the road, do not suggest to our minds a very exalted estimate of the fastidiousness likely to be exhibited by a director actually, though not apparently, interested in the undertaking.

In fact, we might possibly deduce from it an argument or inference exactly opposite to that suggested by the defendant's counsel.

The plaintiff, a resident of Toronto, was transacting all
the legal business of the roads. His acceptance of a seat
on a board, meeting 120 miles off, might perhaps indicate
the existence of a stronger interest in the undertaking
than that of a mere professional adviser. But in whatever
aspect it is viewed, I cannot accept it as of much importance.

Then as to the lapse of time from say the close of 1878
to the negotiations for the sale to the Grand Trunk, which
seem to have begun early in 1880, and at first proved
abortive—say, perhaps, some eighteen months—it is urged
for the defendant that the plaintiff made no claim.

The plaintiff answers this by stating that there was
nothing to claim—that until there was a prospect of a
favourable sale of the roads it was idle for him to expect
any realization of his expected profit.

During that period we have not many communications
between the parties that throw much light on the dispute.

A letter from the defendant to the plaintiff dated July
5th, 1880, is curiously worded; assuming, as he swears,
that the plaintiff had no longer any interest, and was
merely acting as his and the railroad's legal adviser.

After complaining as to the largeness of the fees charged,
he says: " The fees you charged are only recognizable or
could be paid, as I have always told you, out of large
realized profits. They are not yet realized, so I contend
there is nothing due you, and in any other way than out
of realized profits, I shall only pay when I am obliged to.
Now I think you understand my view, and I have all along
known yours."

This letter was written after the first abortive negotiation for sale to the Grand Trunk.

There may be some explanation of it, but I cannot understand such language being used between solicitor and
client if the proper rate of legal charges was alone in controversy between them.

We have not in this case to differ from the learned Judge
in his estimate of the respective credibility of the parties,

and witnesses produced before him. His decision rests apparently on the documents produced and the probabilities of the case.

I am compelled to adopt a different conclusion from that at which he has arrived, and to hold that the plaintiff is entitled to substantial relief, and that an account be taken and payment-made as prayed.

BURTON, J. A.—I quite agree with the learned Judge below, that there is a conflict of evidence which it is quite impossible to reconcile, but I think the learned Judge has not given sufficient weight to the important circumstance, that the onus of proving the defence was upon the defendant, and if he has failed to make that out by evidence which is clear and satisfactory, the plaintiff's claim, which is evidenced by writing, has not been displaced, and he is entitled to the account which he seeks in this action.

Assuming it to have been open to the defendant to shew, contrary to the writing itself, that the share of the profits payable to the plaintiff was to include and be in satisfaction of his costs and charges, which could not have been in the contemplation of the parties at the time it was entered into, a question it is not now necessary to discuss, the learned Judge has found, and I think correctly, that the profits were not to be received in lieu of costs.

The defence, therefore, which the defendant sets up is, that a settlement was come to at a certain time, when the plaintiff agreed to accept the sum of $5,500 in full of all demands under the agreement or otherwise.

That arrangement, though sworn to by the defendant in his answer, was not sustained in evidence, but the defendant did endeavour to shew an arrangement by which the plaintiff agreed to accept the sum of $4,000 in full. It is denied by the plaintiff, and it is supported by evidence which is so unsatisfactory, that having regard to the rule which I have referred to as to the *onus probandi*, I should have had no hesitation as a Judge of first instance in holding that the defendant had failed to satisfy that *onus*.

I agree with the learned Chief Justice as to its being in the highest degree incredible that persons on the terms of these two parties, who had had very warm and bitter discussions in reference to this question, should have left matters open and left to depend upon a mere memorandum on a cheque. If such an arrangement as that now set up had in fact been made, what easier than to have expressed on the face of the cheque that it was in full of the sum of $4,000 agreed on, in full of all demands, and the indorsement of the cheque by the plaintiff would have been equivalent to a receipt.

But at least we should expect that such a settlement should be made out by the clearest and most explicit proof before we could hold the plaintiff's claim satisfied.

There may possibly be some mistake in the stenographer's notes, and I trust it is so, as he makes Mr. Bickford state in one part of his evidence (p. 59) "I gave him a cheque for $50 and to complete it he (that is Cameron) marked on the cheque: 'This is the $4,000.'" This is expressly denied by Mr. Cameron, and in fact it is admitted by Mr. Bickford himself in a subsequent portion of his evidence that it is not in Mr. Cameron's handwriting; but the statement itself is not accurate; the memorandum was not "This is the $4,000," but "This is $4,000."

The explanation given by the defendant is not of a character to confirm the settlement. He says that Cameron was asking $5,600, but that was subject to what had been paid. The sum paid, he says, was $2,397, so that all that Cameron was claiming, according to his account, was $3,203, and he offered to pay $2,500.

He at first speaks of the costs as being put in to swell the amount of this claim, in other words, I should have thought, as making up the claim to $5,600, but afterwards, when asked whether Cameron claimed $2,644.74 for costs in addition, says: "I cannot say he wanted all these costs;" but he says that Cameron handed in a memorandum of costs to that amount in addition to the $5,600; and he offered $2,500 in full; but he says that on the same day they came to a settlement for $4,000, which in addition to the $2,397 would amount to $6,397, in no way agreeing with the settlement relied upon in the answer.

Then, if this was a settlement in full, how is it recon-cilable with the defendant's letter of the 5th July, 1880 ? Why was the plaintiff as a mere solicitor to wait for his costs until the client had realized his profits ?   I can only say that, if we are doing any injustice to the defendant in holding his defence not made out, he has only himself to blame for it.   If he had adopted the ordinary business precaution of taking a receipt, no difficulty could have occurred.

He has not satisfied my mind judicially that the defence alleged is made out, and holding as I do that that *onus* was upon him, and has not been satisfied, I agree with the Chief Justice that the appeal should be allowed, and a reference directed to the Master to take the accounts in accordance with the prayer of the plaintiff's bill.

PATTERSON and MORRISON, JJ. A., concurred.

Appeal allowed, with costs.

NOTE.—The case has since been carried to the Privy Council.

BAKER v. THE GRAND TRUNK RAILWAY COMPANY OF CANADA.

Practice—Trial by jury—Nonsuit—Costs.

At the trial of a case with a jury, the Judge of the County Court at the conclusion of the plaintiff's evidence and without hearing any evidence on the part of the defendants, nonsuited the plaintiff. In the following term the Judge set the nonsuit aside and entered judgment for the plaintiff, claiming a right under the circumstances to do so. On appeal this Court, while satisfied with the ruling of the Judge on the legal liability of the defendants, set the nonsuit aside and ordered a new trial upon the facts, so as to afford the defendants an opportunity of adducing evidence : but, under the circumstances, refused them any costs of the appeal.

Rules 311, 312, 319, and 321 of O. J. Act, discussed.

THIS was an action in the County Court of the United Counties of Stormont, Dundas and Glengarry.

The Plaintiff claimed $200 damages for the loss of a horse, killed on the 8th June 1884, through the alleged negligence of the defendants in allowing a fence which divided their track from the field in which the horse was pasturing, to remain in a defective and useless condition.

Defence : not guilty by statute; on which the plaintiff joined issue.

The evidence established that the horse, when the accident occurred, was not grazing upon the plaintiff's own land, but upon a field which was part of a farm rented by one Lough, adjoining the railway track, and the real question in dispute in the action was whether the horse was lawfully in that field, and under circumstances which made the defendants liable.

The action was tried before Pringle, Co. J., and a jury. At the conclusion of the plaintiff's evidence, the learned Judge ordered a nonsuit to be entered, after which there was a discussion between Judge and Counsel as to the terms of the judgment. The following are the stenographer's notes of what occurred :

D. B. Maclennan, Q. C., for plaintiff. Will your honour take the opinion of the jury on the question of damages ?

W. Nesbitt, for defendants. We will take the responsibility of taking a nonsuit.

Maclennan, Q. C.—I want the opinion of the jury on the question of damages and what the bargain was. I think the opinion of the jury should be taken.

PRINGLE, J.—If I am right it will be useless. I don't think I ever had a case where I was so clear.

Maclennan, Q. C.—Certainly we are entitled to the opinion of the jury as to whether there was a bargain. There is no doubt there was an agreement. Your honour says it was not sufficient to make the defendants liable. That is a question of law. Why should that prevent your honour taking the opinion of the jury on the question they are to try? I will take the finding of the jury on your honour's charge.

PRINGLE, J.—Supposing you leave it in this way which will save all trouble; if I am wrong in my view of the law, allow me to assess the damages. They have been clearly proved at $150.

Nesbitt.—We will consent to that.

Maclennan, Q. C.—It is sworn to be more than that.

PRINGLE, J.—Well, I will assess the damages and consider the evidence.

Maclennan, Q. C.—If your honour is of opinion that the plaintiff has made out the case, you will assess the damages in term.

Nesbitt.—Let them move against the nonsuit; that is the simplest way.

PRINGLE, J.—I think I have the right, even on a motion for setting aside a nonsuit, to fix the damages.

Maclennan, Q. C.—Then it is subject to the plaintiff's moving to enter a verdict for him and assess the damages.

PRINGLE, J.—I think I have the right.

Nesbitt.—If your honour has the right, we have no objection.

PRINGLE, J.—I direct a nonsuit, with the right to the plaintiff to move in term to enter a verdict for him; the Judge to fix the damages if the plaintiff's motion succeeds.

Nesbitt.—Of course I don't consent to that.

At the next sittings of the County Court in term, Pringle, Co. J., set aside the nonsuit entered by him at the trial, and directed judgment to be entered for the plaintiff, assessing the damages at $150, and giving the plaintiff his costs.

From this judgment the defendants appealed.

The appeal came on to be heard on the 21st day of April, 1885.*

Wallace Nesbitt, for the appellants.

J. Maclennan, Q. C., for the respondent.

Present.—HAGARTY, C.J.O., BURTON, PATTERSON, and OSLER, JJ.A.

May 12, 1885. PATTERSON, J. A.—The question of law
decided by the learned Judge whose judgment is the subject of this appeal was the liability of the defendants to
the plaintiff for the killing of the plaintiff's horse which
had escaped on to the railway from an adjoining field of
one Lough.

I agree with the learned Judge that the horse was lawfully in that field, and under circumstances which make
the defendants liable to the plaintiff.

The facts shewn were that the plaintiff's horse or colt
was in the care of his tenant Gilliard who was bound by
his lease to take care of the plaintiff's cattle, and Gilliard
had an arrangement with Lough who had the adjoining
farm, that their young cattle should run together.   In
pursuance of this arrangement the line fence between the
farms was allowed to be down, and the plaintiff's colt was
with Lough's horses in Lough's field whence, along with
one of Lough's, it escaped, and both were killed.

These are the facts upon which a nonsuit was moved
for, the contention on the part of the defendants being
that, in order to entitle the plaintiff to recover, it was
necessary for him to have a special agreement or specific
license to have his horse in the field.

The learned Judge took the defendants' view, and nonsuited the plaintiff, declining to accede to the request made
by counsel for the plaintiff to take the opinion of the jury
as to the existence of an agreement; but after hearing
argument on the motion against the nonsuit he changed
his opinion, and gave judgment for the plaintiff.

I think he arrived at the correct conclusion.

The duty of the defendants, Consol. Stat. Can., ch. 66,
sec. 13, is to erect and maintain fences on each side of the
railway of the height and strength of an ordinary division
fence.   There are other provisions respecting openings,
gates, or bars in the fences at farm crossings of the road,
and cattle guards at road crossings, but the duty to fence
is imposed in the terms I have quoted.

The English statute 8 and 9 Vict. ch. 20, sec. 68, is less general in its language, enacting (I quote it from the report of *Dawson* v. *Midland R. W. Co.,* L. R. 8 Ex. 8) that a railway company shall make and maintain " for the accommodation of the owners and occupiers of lands adjoining the railway, sufficient fences for separating the land taken for the use of the railway from the adjoining lands not taken, and protecting such lands from trespass, or the cattle of the owners or occupiers thereof from straying thereout by reason of the railway."

Whoever could recover against a railway company under this English Act would *a fortiori* be entitled to recover under our Act.

In *Dawson's Case* the plaintiff had hired of the occupier of some land adjoining the defendant's line the use of a stable for his horse ; and it was arranged that the horse should be allowed to graze during the day in a field separated from the line by a fence. For this privilege no rent was paid. One night the horse escaped from the stable into the field, and thence through a defective fence on to the line, where it was run over and killed by a train.

It was argued that the plaintiff was not the owner or occupier of adjoining land, and that the horse was straying, and was not in the field with the owner's assent; but the Court held that the horse was upon the close with the license of the occupier, and that the defendants were liable.

The reasoning is in my judgment applicable to the facts before us ; and I think it is the same which has prevailed in the cases to be found in our own reports, particularly the latest one cited to us, *McAlpine* v. *Grand Trunk R. W. Co.,* 38 U. C. R. 446.

The defendants thus fail upon the substantial ground of their appeal , but they further complain that the learned Judge gave judgment for the plaintiff, assessing the damages at $150, in place of merely ordering a new trial.

There is an unfortunate want of distinctness in the short-hand writer's note of what occurred on the discussion of the motion for nonsuit. I should have gathered from

merely reading the notes that so long as the damages were
not put at a larger sum than $150, the defendants' counsel
was willing that the Judge should give judgment for the
plaintiff in case the law was decided against the defendants, but he refused to assent to the Judge assessing the
damages which, on the plaintiff's part, were claimed to be
more than $150. We are told, however, that no consent
was given on the part of the defendants to leave being
reserved to enter judgment for the plaintiff; and this is
quite consistent with the opinion expressed by the learned
Judge at the trial that he had power to dispose of the case
without consent, and with a certificate sent by him to the
registrar since the argument of the appeal to the effect
that he did reserve leave, and that on the argument of the
order *nisi*, which was moved (in one alternative) on leave
reserved, no objection was made to his finally disposing of
the action—nothing being said on the subject, as I understand him; but not stating that there had been any consent
at the trial to leave being reserved.

I therefore agree that there shall be a new trial if the
defendants really desire it; and I do not dissent from the
order for a new trial generally.

But I do not wish to be understood to decide that the
defendants are entitled as of right to have the whole case
opened again, nor even to hold that they are entitled as of
right to a new trial.

I do not affirm the contrary of either of these propositions; but I desire to leave myself free to consider the
effect of some of the rules under the Judicature Act, which
might perhaps apply in this case, when it becomes necessary to do so.

These rules are Nos. 311, 312, 319, and 321.

The peculiarity which distinguishes the case from many
others in which nonsuits have been granted is, that the
nonsuit was not moved on the ground that the plaintiff's
evidence failed to sustain his allegation of fact; but on
the ground that the fact proved by the evidence and
undisputed by the defendants, was not sufficient to entitle

the plaintiff to succeed. There would seem to be strong grounds for arguing that that fact, namely, the terms on which the plaintiff's horse was in Lough's field, was found or decided within the meaning of rule 312, which permits a new trial to be ordered on any question in an action, whatever be the grounds for a new trial, without interfering with the finding or decision upon any other.

If this had been the only issue of fact involved in the action, it would be hard to say that, after what passed, the Court had not before it all the materials necessary for finally determining the question in dispute, but must send the case back to a jury, notwithstanding the power given by Rule 321. Rules 311 and 319 are founded on the same principles as the others to which I refer.

But there are other issues of fact, such as the state of the fences and the quantum of damages, on which the defendants may desire the opinion of the jury; and, as I have said, I do not dissent from an order for a new trial generally. It should, however, be on the terms that the costs of the day and of the motion in the Court below shall be costs to the plaintiff in any event. But having regard to the fact that, while we decide the substantial matter of the appeal against the defendants we vary the order by giving a new trial, I am content to let the appeal be allowed, without costs.

OSLER, J. A.—This case was tried by the Judge with a jury and he dismissed it at the close of the plaintiff's evidence, saying he never had a case where he was so clear. It would have been better if the evidence for the defendants had been given, and the findings of the jury taken on the whole case, but having regard to the opinion expressed by the learned Judge, the defendants were in no respect to be blamed for accepting his decision: *Re Pincoffs*, 22 Ch. D. 312.

Upon the report of the evidence, which does not appear to me to be qualified in any degree by the learned Judge's subsequent certificate, I am not at all convinced that there was any consent that he should deal with the case after the dismissal otherwise than as by law he was authorized to deal with it. There was no reservation of any right, either to enter a verdict for the plaintiff or to assess the damages.

At the ensuing sittings of the Court the learned Judge came to the conclusion that he ought not to have dismissed the action and that on the evidence the plaintiff was entitled to recover. Instead however of directing a new trial he assessed the damages and directed final judgment for the plaintiff. In doing so I think, with great respect that he exceeded his power. If he had tried the case without a jury, I concede that he might have continued, as it were, the trial, might (and must) have received any evidence the defendants had to offer and could have assessed the damages and entered judgment for the party he might think ultimately entitled to succeed. But as the case was tried with a jury I think that in the absence of consent the only course open to him when he found that he ought not to have dismissed the action was to grant a new trial and send the case down to another jury.

He was not in a position to direct judgment for the plaintiff under Rule 321 (which indeed was not the judgment sought for) because he could not say that he had before him all the material necessary for finally determining the matter in dispute.

I agree that it is unfortunate that the last trial should be lost and the plaintiff be delayed, but I should consider it much more unfortunate if we were to do anything to countenance the idea that a defendant by accepting the decision of the Judge in his favour at the trial, loses the *right* to have the case tried by the proper tribunal if the Judge reverses his decision, or that by accepting a dismissal of the action at the close of the plaintiff's case he is to be taken to have admitted the facts for the purpose of any other disposition of the cause.

All difficulty might easily have been avoided at the trial

if the course now usually taken had been followed, viz., hearing all the evidence and taking the findings of the jury upon the facts and the damages, or putting the parties distinctly upon terms.

In *Herbert* v. *Park*, 25 C. P. 57-74, this Court on setting aside a nonsuit entered at the close of the plaintiff's case, directed the verdict to be entered for the plaintiff without sending the case down for a new trial, but that was expressly on the ground that leave to enter the verdict had been reserved at the trial.

In my view, looking at the course taken at the trial, I think the only thing we can do is to allow this appeal, and direct that the rule in the Court below shall be made absolute for a new trial generally without costs. We can not say that any terms shall be imposed under rule 312 or otherwise, simply because there has, as yet, been no finding or decision upon any question of fact, and the defendants are strictly within their right. It is not the case of granting a new trial as a matter of discretion as in *Townsend* v. *Hamilton*, 5 C. P. 230, where, after a second trial the Court granted a third trial as to one particular portion of the claim in the action, and as a condition of doing so, restricted the new trial to that part only, leaving the actual finding as to the rest undisturbed.

Upon the principal question I am of opinion that the learned Judge was right, for the reasons and on the authorities given in his judgment, and in those of my Brother Patterson. If the plaintiff's horse was lawfully on Lough's land, the company were as much bound to fence against him as against the owner.

I think the appeal should be allowed, without costs, and a new trial granted, costs to abide the event or to the plaintiff in any event.

HAGARTY, C. J. O., and BURTON, J. A., concurred.

MOOREHOUSE v. BOSTWICK.

Assignment—Partnership and separate creditors—Priorities.

On the dissolution of a partnership between L. and W., the latter
transferred all his interest in the partnership to L., who subsequently
became insolvent and assigned all his estate, including that part of it
which had formerly been assets of the partnership, to the defendant, in
trust to pay "the claims of his creditors ratably and proportionately,
and without preference or priority, recognizing such liens, claims, charges,
and priorities as the law directs."

Held, [reversing the judgment of the Court below, 5 O. R. 104] that
under the terms of the deed there was no priority between the separate
creditors of L. and the joint creditors of L. and W., all being creditors
of L., and that both classes of creditors were entitled to be paid *pari
passu.*

THIS was an appeal by the defendant from a judgment
pronounced by Proudfoot, J., on the 19th of January, 1884.

The action was brought by the plaintiff, on behalf of
himself and all others the separate creditors of L. A. Morrison, against the defendant, as assignee in trust for the
benefit of the creditors of L. A. Morrison, claiming priority
for the plaintiff and the other separate creditors of L. A.
Morrison over the joint creditors of L. A. Morrison and W.
J. Morrison.

A motion was made for an injunction to restrain payment over by the assignee of any portion of the trust
estate to the joint creditors until the separate creditors
were paid in full, and by consent of parties such motion
was turned into a motion for judgment, and thereupon
judgment was pronounced in favor of the plaintiffs, as
reported 5 O. R. 104, where the other facts are fully stated.

The appeal was heard on the 5th of February, 1885.*

J. H. Macdonald, for the appellant.

Moss, Q. C., and *F. E. Hodgins,* for the respondent.

The cases cited appear in the judgments and in the report
of the case in the Court below.

*Present—*HAGARTY, C.J.O., BURTON, PATTERSON, and OSLER, JJ.A.

March 3, 1885. HAGARTY, C. J. O.—It appears to me that the sole question for decision here must be, what is the legal effect of the assignment executed by Llewellyn Morrison to the defendant, declared to be made "for the purpose of paying and satisfying the claims of his creditors ratably and proportionately, and without preference or priority."

The plaintiff states that he has proved his claim before the assignee. Mr. Moss, for him, admits that he cannot impugn the deed in any way.

He asks the interposition of the Court for a direction to the defendant as to how he is to distribute the assets, claiming that he and the other separate creditors of the assignor are first to be paid out of his separate estate, and the creditors of the former firm of the assignor and his brother are to be in effect relegated to the proceeds of any joint effects or assets which were of said firm.

Some two months before the assignment, W. Morrison retired from the firm, assigning all his interest in the joint assets to Llewellyn, save and except two named claims of the firm, in which Llewellyn released his interest, W. Morrison binding himself to pay to Llewellyn a portion of each of the claims released to him, in one case absolutely, in the other contingent on recovery—the remaining partner indemnifying him as to the debts of the firm.

The law seems very clearly settled, as shortly defined in 2 *Lindley*, 4th ed., 1878, p. 1168, after noticing *Ex parte Ruffin*, 6 Ves. 119, &c.:

"It is therefore now beyond dispute that if a partner-ship is dissolved, and a *bonâ fide* agreement is come to between the parties, to the effect that what was the partnership property shall become the property of him who continues the business, and afterwards the firm or the continuing partner becomes bankrupt, that which was the partnership property cannot be distributed as the joint estate of the firm, but must be treated as the separate estate of the continuing partner. The creditors of the firm have no lien on its property which can prevent the partners from *bonâ fide* changing its character, and con-

verting it into the separate estate of one of them." * *
" The joint creditors of the firm cannot insist on its distribution as joint estate."

And the same subject is further discussed in 1 *Lindley*,
p. 655.

" It has frequently been held that agreements come to
between partners converting the property of the firm into
the separate estate of one or more of its members, and *vice
versa*, are, unless fraudulent, binding not only as between
the partners themselves, but also on their joint and on
their respective several creditors ; and that, in the event of
bankruptcy, the trustee must give effect to such agreements."

The subject is largely treated of in *Story* on Partnership,
secs. 97, 358-9, 361, 362, 371-3, 401. The authorities are
numerous, but the text-books give the results very distinctly.

The effect of this conversion of the joint assets into the
separate estate of the remaining partner does not, of
course, affect the right of the joint creditors to follow the
retiring partner and his estate; and the principle of such
a proceeding is well explained in the important case in the
Lords of *Kendall* v. *Hamilton*, 4 App. Cas. 504.

At the time of this assignment to defendant, the whole
of the former joint assets of the firm were the sole property
of the assignor. Although some of these assets still existed
in specie, it seems clear that the joint creditors had no
equity to claim their application to the prior payment of
the joint debts.

As against them, the partners had a clear right by a
bonâ fide transfer, to completely alter their character, and
place them in the exclusive ownership of the assignor.
They became as much his property as his previous separate
estate.

I find very great difficulty in believing, that as the joint
creditors have lost all right to be preferred as to what had
been joint assets, the former separate creditors of the assignor would be entitled thus to have the whole of his

assets from whatever source derived, so long as he held them
as his sole property, applied to the satisfaction of their claims
in priority to the joint creditors.

If previous to the assignment an execution had issued
against the firm, it would have, as against the property of
the remaining partner, effectually bound all his estate, and
would have had priority over a subsequent execution
against him alone by his separate creditor.   We must
bear in mind that this is not an administration suit, nor a
proceeding in insolvency to adjust the respective rights of
joint and several creditors.

It is a suit claiming the interference of the Court to
declare such respective rights and to direct the creditors'
assignee, the defendant, to distribute the estate in a particular manner.   It appears to me that all the plaintiff can ask
is to have the estate administered in accordance with the
trusts of the deed of assignment.

All the property dealt with by this assignment belonged
solely to him with no equities or liens attaching thereon,
in favour of any particular set of creditors.   He assigns
" for the purpose of satisfying the claims of his creditors,"
including, as we must hold, every creditor to whom he was
either solely or jointly indebted, certain lands and leaseholds mentioned in a schedule annexed, and also all goods,
chattels, personal estate, and effects on the premises
wherein he carried on business and being all the machinery,
plant, and general stock-in-trade of him the said debtor,
and also his furniture and effects situate &c., together with
all other goods, chattels, and personal effects of him where-
soever situate, and all book debts, &c., on trust to sell and
realize &c., and after paying all expenses &c., " to pay,
satisfy, and discharge all the debts and liabilities of him,
the said debtor to the said creditors ratably and proportionately and without preference or priority, *recognizing
such liens, claims, charges, and priorities as the law directs*
and the surplus (if any) &c., to hand over to him the said
debtor."

In the schedule were mentioned certain lands and lease-

holds, some that had been partnership property, and others
his separate property.

Then it is suggested, that under the words quoted the
assignee is empowered to distribute the proceeds of the
assets between the two classes of creditors, on the principle
urged by plaintiff.

This seems like begging the whole question.

The assignee, in my judgment, would not be warranted
on anything in the language of this assignment to take
any such course. It is an assignment for all creditors of
the assignor. The words used can only be read as referable
to any priorities, rights, or liens existing among the whole
body of creditors as a class, not as conferring any authority
to divide them into classes and appropriating the assets
first to one class and secondly to another class. The joint
creditors and the separate creditors neither have nor have
had, since the assignment on dissolution, any special equities or liens on the assets, as the interest of the former
joint owners therein was completely changed, and all
vested wholly in the remaining partner.

I think it impossible to give such an extended right to
the assignee under the words used.

My brother Patterson, in delivering the judgment of
this Court in *Mills* v. *Kerr*, 7 A. R. at 774-6, notices an
argument used to extend the right of the assignee to distribute the estate among classes of creditors under the
words, " so far as may be lawfully and properly done,"
and we held that such words could not extend, as contended, the otherwise plain meaning of the deed.

It may well be doubted, though we are not necessarily
bound so to decide, whether the assignor could have made
an assignment dividing the creditors into classes without
infringing our statute ch. 118. For myself, as at present
advised, I do not think he could have taken any such
course. All the assets assigned were his sole property.
All the creditors were his creditors, and I cannot see at
present his right to divide them into classes with pre-
ferences or priorities each over the other.

It is sufficient for me to say that the present plaintiff comes before us under the deed of assignment, and must be bound by its terms.

I consider those terms to be an assignment of all the estate then vested in the assignor for the benefit of all his creditors, without preference or priority, that there is nothing in the deed to warrant the assignee in dividing the creditors into classes, or dividing the assets into classes and paying one set of creditors before another set.

On this I rest my judgment, and think the appeal must be allowed.

As already suggested, we are not to consider the question as if, instead of the debtor having made this assignment, he had gone into insolvency, and the law had then to administer his estate. He has disposed of his estate by deed, and that deed is not impeached, and it appears to me we have nothing to do but to construe its provisions and see that its trusts are duly carried out.

The authorities are very numerous, but need not here be enumerated. I may especially refer to *Ex parte Dear*, 1 Ch. D. 514 (1876), where the principles are very clearly stated which distinguish it from *Ex parte Simpson*, L. R. 9 Ch. 572.

BURTON, J. A.—This case arose out of a motion for an injunction to restrain the trustee under a deed of assignment for the benefit of creditors, made by one L. A. Morrison, from paying or distributing any portion of the estate assigned, which was admittedly the assignor's separate estate, towards the payment of creditors of a partnership of which he was at one time a member, until all the separate creditors had been paid in full.

Mr. Moss very strongly contended that, as the debts contracted by the debtor when in partnership with his brother were joint debts, the same rule should be applied in making a distribution under this deed as would be observed in bankruptcy, or in the administration of the estate of a deceased partner, or the winding up of the affairs of a partnership in equity. I agree with him.

A partnership debt is not the separate debt of the partners, and a partnership creditor never had, and has not now, a right to maintain a suit or obtain a decree simply for the administration of the estate of the deceased partner: *Re McRae*, 25 Ch. D. 16.

It is true he might bring a suit against the representatives of the deceased partner and the surviving partner, and so obtain relief against the estate of the deceased partner; but there is no case in which a joint creditor has been allowed to obtain a decree for administration as a separate creditor; *Kendall* v. *Hamilton*, 4 App. Cas. 504.

Nor is the assertion, so frequently to be found in the books, that a partnership debt is in equity a joint and separate debt, correct except *sub modo*, that is to say, except in those cases where the remedy has been given against the assets of the deceased partner, upon the grounds stated in *Ex parte Williams*, 11 Ves. at p. 5.

As pointed out by Lord Hatherley, no case can be found in which a Court of Equity has held itself at liberty to turn a contract, at law joint, into a joint and several contract.

In the present case, upon the dissolution of the partnership firm, and a transfer of the effects to the continuing partner, the estate became his separate estate, and I do not think there can be the slightest doubt, notwithstanding the covenant which he entered into with his former partner, to indemnify him, and pay the debts of the partnership, that the creditors of the partnership could not prove upon his estate in the event of his insolvency, not having previous thereto accepted him as their sole debtor.

But I do not see how that helps the plaintiff. The assignor in this case is a debtor to the partnership creditors, who, it is true, were not bound to sue him alone, but had a right to sue both, and upon obtaining execution could levy upon the goods of either or both; but, as between himself and his former partner, it was his debt, and had he been sued alone an application on his part to have his co-partner joined could scarcely have been successful. We must assume that he intended to carry out his agreement with his partner honestly, and with that view, when he found himself obliged to make an assignment, that he would intend to provide for those debts which, as between himself and his partner, were to be considered as separate debts.

I do not wish to be understood as saying that, even apart from this consideration, the construction contended for by the plaintiff could be sustained, but under the facts in evidence it would scarcely lie in the debtor's mouth to say that these are not, under the circumstances, all his separate debts, and no distinction can be drawn between one class and the other I think, therefore, that the plaintiff fails in his contention, and the appeal should be allowed.

PATTERSON, J.A.—L. A. Morrison, being unable to pay his debts in full, by deed assigned all his property to the defendant upon trust to convert the property into money, and out of the proceeds " to pay, satisfy, and discharge all the debts and liabilities of him the said debtor to the said creditors, ratably and proportionately, and without preference or priority, recognizing such liens, claims, charges, and priorities as the law directs."

It happens that some of the creditors of L. A. Morrison, are creditors not of him alone, but of him jointly with another person, while to others L. A. Morrison is the sole debtor.

The plaintiff is one of the latter class, and he contends, on behalf of the whole class, that the trustee must first pay in full all these separate debts before paying any of the joint debts.

The proposition seems to me untenable.

Both classes of creditors are creditors of the assignor and come within the general words " his creditors " used to describe them in the assignment. The property assigned was the property of the assignor and entirely at his disposal, as is pointed out with perfect accuracy in the judgment in review.

To entitle the plaintiff to succeed, he has to maintain
that the law directs the recognition of some lien, claim,
charge, or priority, in favour of the class of creditors whom
he represents.

It is not contended that, if no assignment had been
made, any one of the joint creditors could have been prevented from seizing and selling under execution any part
of the property, whether the separate creditors were paid
or unpaid. No lien, claim, charge, or priority available for
that purpose is asserted ; but the argument is that because
the joint debts were contracted by Morrison and a partner
of his in the course of their partnership business, and the
former partner is still legally liable for them jointly with
Morrison to the creditors, although as between the partners they are the separate debts of L. A. Morrison, the law
directs the recognition of some lien, claim, charge, or priority in favour of the creditors who dealt with Morrison
alone, and not with his partnership firm.

Some of Morrison's property which he assigned to the
defendant had once been assets of his partnership; but
that is not a factor in the plaintiff's present contention, for
the reason that in the dissolution it became the absolute
separate property of Morrison, free from any equity in the
former partner to have it applied in payment of the debts,
because, although Morrison assumed the payment of them,
his partner and co-debtor was content with his covenant
to indemnify him, without retaining any charge or equity
in respect of the effects.

There being no equity in the partner, there is none which
can be asserted by the partnership creditors to be paid, in
priority to the separate creditors, out of the assets which
were once partnership assets. The decree now questioned
fully recognizes this doctrine, and indeed makes an extreme application of it, for, while it refuses to accord to
the joint creditors any priority over the separate creditors
in respect of what had been the joint estate, it does not
stop there, but postpones them to the separate creditors in
respect of that portion as well as of all the rest of the
property assigned to the defendant.

There is nothing in the terms in which the trust is declared to warrant a construction which leads to a result so unfair to the joint creditors.

I do not understand the deed to be intended to create any lien, claim, charge, or priority, that did not already exist. If they existed the assignor could not do away with them, and he directs the trustee to recognize them. The trustee would have been bound to do so without any express direction in the deed.

I think the judgment has been influenced by what appears to me to be the fallacy of treating the execution of the trusts of this deed as if the assignee was administering a partnership estate, in which there were joint debts of the firm and separate debts of the partners, and either some joint estate, or at least one solvent partner, and as if the rules applied in the English Bankruptcy Courts were to govern.

The practical effect is in this case to produce marked inequality among the creditors in place of distributing the estate *pari passu* among them.

I am satisfied that for the purposes of this deed there is no valid ground for making a distinction between different classes of creditors, and that, if the assignor had attempted by the terms of the deed to exclude the joint creditors from sharing *pari passu* with the others, the deed would have been so obviously framed to prefer one class to another that it could not have been supported under R. S. O. ch. 118, sec. 2.

I agree that the appeal should be allowed, with costs.

OSLER, J. A.—I concur in the result. I think the deed defines the trusts upon which the property is to be distributed by the assignee, and that we cannot go outside of its terms.

I do not desire, however, as at present advised, to intimate any doubt of the propriety of the decision in *Nelles* v. *Maltby*, 5 O. R. 263.

gage, it was on the faith of the representation that the lots allotted to him were equal to the others in size and value ; and that he never waived the objections agreeing to accept any two lots of less width than originally represented.

"In my opinion the plaintiff is entitled to judgment for $850, with interest thereon since commencement of the action, viz., the 18th September, 1883, and costs. It follows that the counter claim will be dismissed, with costs. The Master to tax common items but once."

The appeal was heard on the 15th and 16th days of March, 1885.*

S. H. Blake, Q.C., and *J. K. Kerr*, Q.C., for the appellant.

Moss, Q.C., for the respondent.

April 17, 1885. BURTON, J. A.—This is an action to recover the balance of a sum of money intrusted by the plaintiff to the defendant to be invested in the purchase of lands, and the nature of the authority itself is to be found in the receipt given by the defendant to the plaintiff on the 3rd February, 1882, in these words :

"Received from Mr. Henry Butterworth the sum of $1,000, to be invested in property in Manitoba, if the undersigned thinks it advisable, and if not, the above amount is to be returned to Mr. Butterworth."

The defendant did not pursue his authority, but purchased, or professed to purchase for his principal two lots in Portage la Prairie, for $1,400, upon which he had paid $850, leaving the balance of $550 to be paid, which was secured by mortgage on the property.

It is clear that the plaintiff was thus entitled to demand back his money, and had a complete cause of action at that time against the defendant.

But it is claimed that the plaintiff, on being advised of what his agent had done, ratified the transaction, and that he thereupon became bound by the act to the same extent as if he had originally authorized the purchase in that form.

* *Present.*—HAGARTY, C. J. O., BURTON, PATTERSON, and OSLER, JJ.A.

But to make such a ratification effectual, it must appear that the principal did so with a knowledge of all material circumstances, or with an intent to take all liability without such knowledge.

It was urged that the defendant should have taken the deed in the plaintiff's name, but this in itself would be no objection, if in truth the lots were purchased with the plaintiff's money, as there would be a resulting trust in his favor which would entitle him to enforce a conveyance from the defendant, but it is a piece of evidence which may shift the burden of proof, and which may be of importance when we come to consider the question of ratification.

It is far from clear I think upon the evidence that the plaintiff's money went into this purchase at all, nor is it at all clearly established that any two lots in particular were then selected and appropriated to the plaintiff, and it was, I think, incumbent upon the defendant to shew that when he took a conveyance of the ten lots in his own name it was under such circumstances that the plaintiff would have no difficulty in establishing that two of those lots were purchased with his money and were his in equity.

The plaintiff's statement is that the defendant said he had bought ten lots and he could have two of them if he wished, and that although he at first declined to take them he subsequently assented on the defendant agreeing to assist him in raising the money. If that be the true state of facts it would not assist the defendant as it was an agreement within the Statute of Frauds which has been set up in the pleadings.

What the defendant is bound to establish is that these particular lots were purchased with the plaintiff's money, and although that purchase was in excess of the authority, it was with full knowledge of all the circumstances ratified.

Assuming the first position to be established, viz., that these two lots were purchased for the plaintiff, he was not bound to accept them, and if he did accept, was it not upon the understanding that the lots were of equal size, and is

it not manifest that he would not have done so if it had then
been told him that they contained only the reduced
frontage ? In addition to which is the important fact that
before any intimation to the plaintiff that these lots had
been purchased on his account, the defendant had offered
them for sale at $1,000 without success, but this was not
communicated to the plaintiff.

The learned Judge has found that the plaintiff's money
was invested with the defendant's own in the purchase of
the ten lots, but he has not found that, at the time of the
purchase, any two specific lots were purchased for the
plaintiff—indeed he is of a contrary opinion, and therein
I agree with him.

The defendant's inequitable conduct in endeavouring,
after he became aware of the shortage, to force these lots on
the plaintiff until after action brought, when he agreed
to make up the deficiency from an adjoining lot, throws a
discredit upon the whole proceeding; and I think, upon
the finding of the learned Judge, that any ratification of
the plaintiff was based upon a representation that the lots
allotted to him were equal to the others in size and value,
a representation which was untrue in fact. The alleged
ratification therefore fails, and the plaintiff is entitled to
retain the judgment which has been given in his favour ;
and this appeal should be dismissed, with costs.

OSLER, J.A.—I think the judgment of my Brother Rose
is right, and should be affirmed on this short ground.

The plaintiff intrusted the defendant with $1,000 to invest
in lands. His duty was to invest in unincumbered lands.
Instead of doing so he invested it, according to his own
account, in two lots which were subject to a mortgage.
The plaintiff was not obliged to accept such lots and might
at once have demanded back the money he had entrusted
to the defendant. But on the representation of the
defendant that the lots were of a certain frontage, the
plaintiff was willing to accept them though incumbered,
in discharge of the defendant's obligation, and to incur
the liability to make the further advance.

Before the conveyance was tendered and this new proposal carried out, it was discovered that one of the lots instead of being thirty-three feet in front was only seventeen feet, whereupon the plaintiff declined to carry out the proposal, and brought this action. It appears to me that the defendant has no answer to the demand. He must shew a performance of the duty he undertook, or an agreement by which the plaintiff has become bound to accept something as equivalent to, or in satisfaction of it, and here he has shewn neither.

I see no reason for thinking that the findings of fact are wrong. I think they warrant the judgment.

HAGARTY, C. J. O., and PATTERSON, J. A., concurred.

JENKING V. JENKING ET AL.

Partition by County Court —Impeaching judgment—Practice.

Where proceedings for a partition in a County Court have been terminated by an order confirming such partition and nothing remains to be done by way of enforcing the judgment, such judgment cannot afterwards be impeached on the ground of fraud or deception practised on the Court otherwise than in resisting an action in which it is relied on, or by bringing an action for the express purpose of setting it aside.

THIS was an appeal by the defendant Joseph Alexander Jenking from the order of the Judge of the County Court of the county of Essex, dismissing the appellant's petition to vacate and set aside a certain partition of the lands and premises in question, made by the late Judge of the County Court of the county of Essex.

The facts are fully stated in the judgment on the present appeal, which came on for hearing on the 27th and 28th days of November, 1884.*

Marsh (Bethune, Q. C., with him), for the appellant.
Aylesworth, for the respondent.

December 18, 1884. The judgment of the Court was delivered by

OSLER, J. A.—This is an appeal from the Judge of the County Court of the county of Essex, dismissing the petition of the defendant Joseph Alexander Jenking to vacate and set aside a partition which had been made in the cause, together with the orders and reports on which the same was founded, as being a cloud upon the petitioner's title to the lands in question.

The case made by the petitioner, supported by his affidavit and that of one of his co-defendants, and of the plaintiff in the partition suit, is that the suit had been carried on in a manner and for a purpose entirely different from that for which it was instituted. That instead of procuring by means of it a confirmation of a voluntary

Present.—HAGARTY, C.J.O., BURTON, PATTERSON, and OSLER, JJ.A.

partition, which the several persons interested in the estate had theretofore made between themselves under a binding agreement and award in pursuance thereof, a new partition had been made different from the partition made by the award, which the parties never intended to alter or disturb. That these proceedings had been taken contrary to the instructions and without the knowledge of the plaintiff. That the petitioner, having been told by the plaintiff when the suit was instituted that its object was merely to confirm the original partition, relied upon that information, and did not answer or plead to the petition. That he never had any notice or knowledge that the suit was being made use of for any other purpose until the 31st August, 1883, when the surveyor, acting under the instructions of the Court, came upon his land and proceeded to plant stakes, &c., for the purpose of marking out the allotments &c.

The petition to set aside the proceedings was filed on the 27th of September following.

The proceedings in the suit appear to have been commenced in the usual way by a petition for partition, which bears date the 2nd April, 1879. In the judgment under review it is said, that there are two entries in the note book of the late County Judge relating to the suit from which it appears that the petition was presented by the plaintiff's solicitor on the 30th May, the appellant and the defendants Nelson, Mathilde, Thomas, and Shadrach Jenking being present: and that on the 9th June an order was granted for partition. The year in which these entries occur is not stated, but it is probably 1879, as the next proceeding entered is a copy of an order dated 10th June, 1879, allowing the petition, which is drawn up on reading the petition and affidavits of service thereof and of the notice for allowance on the defendants, and upon hearing the solicitor for the plaintiff.

From that time until the 26th February, 1883, a period of nearly four years, no other proceeding seems to have been taken in the suit.

On that day an order for partition was made, a copy of
which is returned with the other papers. This order purports to be drawn up on reading the petition, the affidavits
of verification thereof, affidavits of service of order allowing the same, and of all pleadings filed, and the consents
of Joseph Alexander Jenking, Nelson Jenking,.and George
Jenking, with the affidavits of execution thereof, and upon
hearing the consent of Mathilde Jenking given in her
proper person to the partition of the estate.

The order recites that the defendants Shadrach and
Thomas Jenking had pleaded to the petition, and that they
claimed by their answers no more of the lands sought to
be partitioned than they were each alleged by the petition
to be entitled to.

The real representative is then ordered to make partition between the parties.

Instructions bearing the same date as the order, and in
the usual form, were given by the real representative (the
County Judge) to a provincial land surveyor, as his assistant, as to the mode of making the partition.

On the 27th June, 1883, the surveyor made his report to
the real representative, setting forth therein a proposed
scheme of partition, prepared in accordance with the
instructions, differing from the partition which had been
formerly made in several particulars, adding one parcel to
the plaintiff's allotment, and taking away two which had
formerly been allotted to Joseph Alexander Jenking.

On the 14th July, 1883, the real representative, adopting
his assistant's report, reported this as the partition made by
him to himself, as the County Judge, and on the same day
the Judge made an order confirming such partition, and
declaring it to be final and effectual between all the parties
concerned. Further instructions were issued in pursuance
of the order (they bear date 11th July, sic,) to the assistant
of the real representative to mark out and plant posts, &c.,
to define on the ground the several allotments.

On the 31st August, 1883, the surveyor proceeded to act
on these instructions, and this, it is said, was the first

notice the defendant had that the rights acquired by him
under the former partition were interfered with by the
latter.

The facts stated in the affidavits filed in support of the
petition to set aside the proceedings were not denied or
explained, nor was any affidavit filed by the solicitor who
had the conduct of the proceedings, or by the parties to
the suit, other than the plaintiff, who have benefited by
the recent partition, and insist upon its validity.

These parties contend, in the first place, that no appeal
lies from the final judgment of a County Court in a
partition suit.

This question is not before us; the appeal is not from a
judgment of partition, but from the order refusing to set
aside or open up proceedings.

In *Furness* v. *Mitchell*, 3 A. R. 510, such an appeal
was entertained and allowed without objection, and I
cannot say that I have any doubt that it lies under section
6 of the Partition Act from the judgment of the County
Court, as well as from the judgment of the High Court,
when the suit has been removed by *certiorari* into that
Court.

Then it is said that no appeal lies from the order in
question. In my opinion it is a final, and therefore an
appealable order within the meaning of the 45 Vict. ch. 6,
sec. 4, which gives an appeal to this Court from any
decision or order "in any cause or matter, *disposing of any
right or claim*, provided always that the decision or order
is in its nature final and not merely interlocutory."

Lastly, it was argued that the Judge of the County
Court had no power to make such an order as the appellant asked for, and to set aside in a summary manner a
final judgment and proceedings in the partition suit. That
the remedy of the party was by appeal, if an appeal would
lie, or by a new action to impeach the judgment for fraud,
&c.

The case is a most peculiar one and we have to consider
exactly what it is the defendant complains of. It is
that, in a suit brought merely for the purpose of enforcing

or carrying out a partition which had already been made
by agreement and award between the parties, the Court
has, contrary to the intention of the parties, made a new
and a different partition of the estate. That the Court
has been moved to do this contrary to the actual instructions of the plaintiff in the suit, and *per incuriam* and by
the suppression and misstatement of facts, intentional or .
otherwise, on the part of the persons who had the conduct
of the proceedings. That, so far as the defendant had any
notice or knowlege of these proceedings up to the 31st
August last, he was under the impression and believed from
what the plaintiff in the suit had told him, that such proceedings were only for the purpose I have mentioned, and
for that reason only had not opposed them or answered
or pleaded to the petition.

The present learned Judge of the County Court held
that he had not power to set aside his predecessor's judgment in the partition suit, that even if he had the power,
the appellant had not shewn such facts as would entitle
him to the relief prayed, and that he would assume that
the former Judge had acted upon proper evidence and
materials before him in making the partition.

A suit for partition under the Partition Act would seem to
be a very futile proceeding, when there has been a partition
by agreement, which the parties do not intend to abandon,
since such a partition can neither be enforced nor set aside
by means of such a suit. Still, there is no reason why all
parties interested should not, if they wish to give the form
of law to their voluntary partition, join in such a suit and
take partition under it.

In this suit, which was instituted for such a purpose,
there has been, it is alleged, by deceptive fraud or *per
incuriam*, a miscarriage, and a new and original partition
has been made in disregard of the former, which was never
intended by those who set the Court in motion to be
given up.

I was at first disposed to think that the learned Judge of
of the County Court had authority to entertain the petition

presented to him by the appellant, and to set aside the partition made by his predecessor, on the ground that in the absence of any contradiction or explanation, such partition appears to have been obtained by something very like a fraud, or deception practised upon the Court, or at the very least that the Court was misled into making it by a mis-apprehension of what the parties really wanted.

In *Cocker* v. *Tempest*, 7 M. & W. 502, Alderson, B., said : " The power of each Court over its own process is unlimited ; it is a power incident to all Courts inferior as well as superior ; were it not so, the Court would be obliged to sit still and see its own process abused for the purpose of injustice. The exercise of the power is certainly a matter for the most careful discretion ; and where there are conflicting statements of fact, I agree that it is in general much better not to try the question between the parties on affidavit. The power must be used equitably ; but if it be made out that the process of the Court is used against good faith, the Court ought to interfere for the purpose of administering justice. The distinction between this power and that which is exercised by a Court of Equity in granting an injunction, is, that the injunction stops proceedings in another Court, this only in the Court in which the proceedings are."

In *Carr* v. *Royal Exchange Corporation*, 34 L. J. N. S. Q. B. 21-23, the Court, in the exercise of the power inherent in them to prevent the abuse of their powers, moulded and altered a judgment which had been entered and which was about to be enforced.

Abouloff v. *Oppenheimer*, 10 Q. B. D. 295, was an action on a foreign judgment, which was defended on the ground that the plaintiff had obtained it by practising a deception upon the foreign Court. This was held to be a good defence, upon the principle laid down in the *Duchess of Kingston's Case*, 2 Sm. L. C. 6th ed., 679. Brett, L.J., was of opinion that the same rule was applicable to an action brought on a judgment obtained in an English Court, other than the Court in which the action was brought.

Then he says, p. 305 : " There may be a difference where
it is sought to enforce by the process of a Court a judgment of that very Court, because, if that judgment has
been obtained by improper means, the objection does not
arise in a new action brought on that judgment, but it
arises with regard to the process of the Court to enforce a
judgment of its own. In a case of that kind it was, perhaps, formerly necessary to proceed in a Court of Equity
in order to get rid of the judgment, but I doubt whether
it was necessary, because, at least in my opinion, a Court
of Common Law would have, in the exercise of its own
jurisdiction, set aside a judgment procured from it by
deception."

These cases, however, do not assist the appellant, for
two reasons : (1) because the proceedings for partition in
the County Court are terminated by the order confirming
the partition, and nothing remains to be done or could be
done by way of enforcing the judgment, and (2) even if a
Court of common law could, as Brett, L. J., suggests, have
set aside a judgment obtained under similar circumstances,
the County Court has no original or common law jurisdiction. It has no authority but that which is set forth
in the Rev. Stat. ch. 101, and the case which has arisen
has not been provided for: *In re Knowles* v. *Post*, 24
U. C. R. 311, 313. So far as the County Court is concerned there is a final judgment of partition, which, if
obtained by means of fraud or deception practised on the
Court, can only be impeached in resisting an action in
which it is relied on : *Earl of Bandon* v. *Becher*, 3 Cl. &
F. 479 ; or by bringing an action for the express purpose
of setting it aside.

In *Flower* v. *Lloyd*, 6 Ch. D. 297, Jessel, M. R., held that
a new action, and not a motion in the original cause, was the
proper course, pointing out that all the jurisdiction of the
old Court of Chancery had been transferred to the High
Court of Justice, and quoting the passage from *Mitford's*
Equity Pleadings, 5th ed. pp. 112, 113, to shew what
that jurisdiction was in this respect: " If a decree has

been obtained by fraud it may be impeached by original bill, without the leave of the Court; the fraud used in obtaining the decree being the principal point in issue, and necessary to be established by proof before the propriety of the decree can be investigated. And where a decree has been so obtained the Court will restore the parties to their former situation, whatever their rights may be."

The judgment in the action afterwards brought between the parties in that case to impeach the former judgment for fraud is reported in 10 Ch. D. 327. I only refer to it for the purpose of observing that the doubts there suggested by James and Thesiger, L. JJ., as to the character of the fraud sufficient to sustain such an action were overruled or disapproved of by the Court in the case of *Abouloff* v. *Oppenheimer, supra.*

The case of *Gilbert* v. *Endean.* 9 Ch. D. 259, may also be referred to as shewing that a substantial question affecting the existence of a decree ought to form the subject of a new action between the parties, and not of a motion in the original cause. See also *Boswell* v. *Coaks,* 23 Ch. D. 302, 52 L. J. N. S. 465; *Merritt* v. *Shaw,* 15 Gr. 321. In the latter case Mowat, V.C., expressly held against the objection that the County Court was the proper *forum* in which to move to set aside the proceedings in partition.

On the whole we think the appeal should be dismissed.

I have not referred to the merits of the application, as indicated by the argument Mr. Aylesworth addressed to us on behalf of the parties who assert the validity of the judicial partition. If we thought the Judge had jurisdiction to set it aside on motion we should have felt much embarrassed by the fact that no affidavits had been filed in denial of the matters alleged by the appellant. They are such as certainly called for an answer of some kind, looking at the fact that the voluntary partition is not in any way impeached by the petition for judicial partition, which on its face seems to bear out the appellant's

statement that there was no intention of disturbing it.
No plausible reason is suggested why the partition of 1869
is invalid, or why the appellant should have been willing
to give up any rights he had acquired either under it or by
length of possession, and it is observable that the consents
of the appellant and other parties to the order for partition
and the affidavits of execution are not to be found among
the papers returned, nor is their absence accounted for.
Then the great and unexplained delay which took place
between the allowance of the petition and taking out the
order, nearly four years, and the fact that the subsequent
proceedings may easily have been carried on without the
knowledge of the appellant, make it very difficult to assume
anything in favor of their regularity, especially when we
find the plaintiff himself repudiating them.   We are
unwilling to suppose that the learned Judge was not aware
of the existence of some answer to, or defect in the appel·
lant's case, which has not been brought to our notice, as he
evidently entertained a strong opinion against the merits of
the application.   On the whole, the circumstances of the
case illustrate the justice and expediency of the rule that
a question of this kind should be investigated in an action
brought for the express purpose, rather than on a summary
application on affidavits.

McDonald v. Murray et al.

Agreement for sale of land—Payment of purchase money—Dependent covenants

By a contract for the sale and purchase of land the vendee agreed to pay $4,000, part of the purchase money, on the execution of the agreement (which was paid accordingly) and an additional portion of the purchase money was to be paid within sixty days thereafter, the balance remaining out on mortgage. After the expiration of the sixty days the vendor instituted proceedings to recover the amount agreed to be then paid, and at the trial, Cameron, J., directed judgment to be entered for the defendants with liberty to the plaintiff to bring a fresh action which, by an order of the Divisional Court, was set aside. (3 O. R. 573.)

On appeal, this Court (Hagarty, C. J. O., dissenting) discharged that order, with costs.

Per Burton and Patterson, JJ.A.—The agreement to convey the lands, and that to pay the money at the expiration of sixty days, were not mutual but dependent, so that the vendor before being entitled to recover the purchase money must shew that he was ready, willing and able to convey; and that the purchaser, until he did so, could not be called on to pay his money and rely on the ability of the vendor to convey the estate, or in the event of his being unable to do so, look to him for re-payment.

Per Rose, J.—Without determining that point expressly, the neglect and delay of the vendor to take the necessary steps to shew his title to the lands, part of which the vendor admitted was vested in one Y., were such as disentitled him to call for payment, and therefore that the finding of the Judge at the trial was correct.

This was an appeal by the defendants from the judgment of the Common Pleas Division, 3 O. R. 573, where the facts out of which the action arose are clearly stated, and came on to be heard before this Court on the 28th and 29th days of January, 1885.*

McMichael, Q.C., and *McCarthy*, Q.C., for the appellants.
S. H. Blake, Q.C., and *Holman*, for the respondent.

The authorities cited appear in the judgments, and in the report of the case in the Court below.

June 30, 1885. Hagarty, C. J. O.—In this appeal we have only to review the judgment of the Common Pleas Division on setting aside the nonsuit or dismissal at the first trial.†

Present.—Hagarty, C.J.O., Burton, Patterson, JJ.A., and Rose, J.

† Another appeal was pending from the judgment on the second trial.

The nonsuit or dismissal of the action at the trial was stated thus by the learned Judge: "That it appeared by the evidence and statement of claim that the action was for the recovery of purchase money on land, and that the time for completing the transaction on both sides had arrived before the commencement of the action, that it further appeared in evidence offered on behalf of thep laintiff that another person was part owner of the land, and that there had been no tender of a conveyance to defendant."

All that appeared as to the title was that McKilligan knew from hearsay that Daniel Young was a part owner of the property, that plaintiff McDonald told him so, and witness believed he was a part owner when the agreement was made.

Such a statement cannot, in my judgment, affect the right of the plaintiff to recover, unless we could hold that by the terms of the contract the duty was cast on the plaintiff to shew title or offer to convey before his right of action accrued.

The contract was as follows:—

WINNIPEG, Feb. 23, 1882.
Mem. of agreement between
(names of parties.)

The said McDonald sells, and the said Murray & Cuthbert agree to purchase lots, &c., at and for the sum of $60,000, payable as follows:—$4,000 to be paid at the signing hereof; $40,795 to be paid within sixty days from the date hereof, and the balance, $15,205, to be on mortgage at seven per cent.

J. B. McKILLIGAN,
for J. McDONALD,
J. MURRAY,
ROBT. CUTHBERT.

In *Pordage* v. *Cole*, 1 *Wms.* Saund. 319n, the agreement was under seal.

" 11th May, 1668.

" It is agreed between Doctor John Pordage and Basset Cole. Esq., that the said Basset Cole shall give unto the said Doctor £775 for all his lands with Ashmole House thereunto belonging, &c., &c. In witness whereof, we do put our hands and seals mutually; given as earnest in performance of this 5s., the money to be paid before Midsummer, 1668, all other movables with the corn upon the ground excepted."

The rule deducible from this case is, "if a day be appointed for payment of money or part of it, or for the doing any other act, and the day is to happen or may happen before the thing which is the consideration of the money or other act is to be performed, an action may be brought for the money, or for not doing such other act before performance, for it appears that the party relied upon his remedy and did not intend to make the performance a condition precedent, and so it is where *no time* is fixed for performance of that which is the consideration of the money or other act."

The effect of this rule is considered in *Mattock* v. *Kinglake*, (in 1839) 10 A. & E. 50. There the plaintiff sued the defendant as executor of S., deceased. By deed, S. agreed to sell and defendant to purchase for the sum thereinafter mentioned; defendant covenanted to pay on or before the 19th of February, 1825, as the consideration for such sale and purchase, the sum of £11, 206 with interest at five per cent. payable half yearly to the time of the completion of the purchase, S. allowing thereout the same rate of interest for so much of the purchase money as had been, or might be paid to him in meanwhile, defendant to pay for conveyance and stamp duty; averment that S. was always ready, &c., to perform his part of agreement, and did, in fact, offer to execute conveyance to defendant of all his estate and interest, &c. Defendant had always been in possession, &c., yet he did not pay as agreed, on or before said day though the purchase by defendant's default had not been completed before that day, and a large sum was still unpaid for principal and interest.

Plea that S. did not tender a conveyance. Demurrer.

Littledale, J., says, p. 56 : "A time being fixed for payment and none for doing that which was the consideration of the payment, an action lies for the purchase money without averring performance of the consideration. An action

for not executing a conveyance of the premises might
have been maintained by the defendant before the day of
payment; and in such action no allegation of payment
would have been necessary. The covenants are independent, and each has relied upon his remedy by action
against the other. It therefore differs from *Callonel* v.
Briggs, 1 Salk. 112 and from *Goodisson* v. *Nunn,* 4 T. R. 761,
Glazebrook v. *Woodrow,* 8 T. R. 366, and other cases."

Patteson, J : "*Pordage* v. *Cole,* is directly in point. We
must overrule it if we decide in favour of the defendant.
There is no express provision that the conveyance shall be
executed before payment, nor any reasonable intendment
that it was to be necessarily precedent to or concurrent
with it. The words 'completion of the purchase' which
furnish the only plausible argument in the defendant's
favour only mean payment of the rest of the purchase
money."

Lord Denman and Coleridge, J., agree.

I am wholly unable to point out or to understand any
substantial difference in favour of the defendant's contention
between the contracts in *Pordage* v. *Cole,* and in *Mattock*
v. *Kinglake* just cited, and the agreement before us, except
that the two first are on specialties and the last by parol.
This difference must surely be of no moment.

In *Wilks* v. *Smith,* 10 M. & W. 355 plaintiff agreed to sell
and defendant to purchase certain premises for £120,
which sum defendant agreed to pay on or before the expiration of four years from date, interest at five per cent.
half-yearly till paid. Mutual promises and averment that
two years interest had become due. General demurrer and
objections that no title was averred or shewn, and no readiness, &c., to convey.

Parke, B., p. 360. "No time is fixed for the sale, but a
time is limited within which the principal money is to be
paid with interest in the mean time. The consideration for
the defendant's paying the interest is the plaintiff's undertaking to sell the land, not the actual sale of it. The
plaintiff is not bound to do anything before the money is

paid. The rule as laid down in *Pordage* v. *Cole*, applies strictly to this case. No time then being fixed by the agreement for the conveyance of the land, it cannot be a condition precedent, nor can we imply that a conveyance was intended to be made before the interest was paid, else we should be supposing that the plaintiff intended to part with his estate before the money was paid, and such an intention certainly cannot be implied from the nature of the contract. It may be that no conveyance need be made till the principal money is paid, that is at the end of four years."

Alderson, B. " If there be two acts, one fixed in point of time, and the other not, the latter is not a condition precedent. Here the defendant relied not upon the plaintiff's performance, but upon his promise to perform."

It was noticed in the argument that the words in the present case are that the plaintiff "sells," not that he " agrees to sell." I do not at present see that any argument in favour of defendants' view can be drawn therefrom.

It may be that as plaintiff "sold " the defendants had the right at once to ask for a conveyance, they would then have the title subject to the subsequent payments, they would then have to pay the $40,000 by the time specified, and at the same time offer their mortgage for the residue of purchase money. If this be the proper reading of the contract the defendants might be in a position to rely on a defence that before the time appointed for payment, &c., they had tendered a conveyance for execution and that plaintiff refused to execute same, or that they had not title and could not convey the estate.

This would make the contract read, in consideration of plaintiff selling or conveying to us lots, &c., we agree to pay, &c.

The distinction is clearly pointed out between relying on the promise to do the act and the actual performance of the act.

In this view could the defendants resist payment of the

$40,000 at the stipulated time on the ground that the plaintiff had not completed the sale to them by deed ? If it was the defendants' duty to prepare the conveyance must they not prepare and tender it for execution before asserting or proving any default on the plaintiff's part in conveying.

Lord Kenyon's opinion is quoted in several cases as to the doctrine that the dependency or independency of covenants " must certainly depend on the good sense of the case." His language is guarded.

In *Campbell* v. *Jones*, 6 T. R. at p. 571, he says :—" If one thing is to be done by a plaintiff before his right of action accrues on the defendant's covenant, it should be averred in the declaration that *that thing was done*." He quotes Lord Holt : " Where there are mutual promises, yet if one thing be the consideration of the other, there a performance is necessary to be averred *unless a day is appointed for performance*." He proceeds, " the judgment of the Court must be in favour of the plaintiff, if upon the true construction of the deed a certain day be fixed for the payment of the money, and the thing to be done may not happen until after."

Lord Mansfield's words in *Jones* v. *Barkley*, 2 Doug. at p. 691, are sometimes quoted: "The dependence or independence of covenants is to be collected from the evident sense and meaning of the parties, and, however transposed they might be in the deed, their precedency must depend on the order of time in which the intent of the transaction requires their performance."

The language of Tindal, C. J., in *Stavers* v. *Curling*, 3 Bing. N. C. at p. 368, is much to the same effect. He says : " The question is to be determined by the intention and meaning of the parties as it appears on the instrument, and by the application of common sense to each particular case ; to which intention, when once discovered, all technical forms of expression must give way."

In *Roberts* v. *Brett*, 18 C. B. at p. 573, Jervis, C. J., says: "But, after all, that rule (the rule in *Pordage* v. *Cole*) only professes to give the result of the intention of the parties :

and where on the whole it is apparent that the intention is
that that which is to be done first is not to depend on the
performance of the thing that is to be done afterwards,
the parties are relying on their remedy, and not on the
performance of the condition; but where you plainly see
that it is their intention to rely on the condition, and not
on the remedy, the performance of the thing is a condition
precedent."

In the same case in Error, 6 C. B. N. S. 611, this view is
approved of by Bramwell, B., p. 634: "The rules laid down
in the notes to *Pordage* v. *Cole* are very excellent guides,
but not arbitrary tests," and he speaks strongly as to the
importance of observing "the obvious good sense of the
thing." The facts of that case were very clear for the
judgment arrived at, which was confirmed in the Lords.

In *Sibthorp* v. *Brunel*, 3 Ex. 826, the plaintiff owned land
which would be intersected by defendants' railway, the
defendants covenanted that within six months from the
passing of their Act, and before they should enter on plaintiff's estate, except to mark out the land, they would pay
the plaintiff £4,000 for the purchase of his land. Plaintiff
covenanted that on payment of the money and interest at
five per cent., after six months from the passing of the
bill to the day of payment of the money, he would convey
to the defendants, but the costs and expenses of deducing
title and the conveyance of the land should be paid by the
company, with other agreements by defendants; averment
that the Act had passed, general averment of performance
by plaintiff, lapse of six months, and nonpayment of the
£4,000.

Demurrer, that plaintiff ought to have averred his readiness and willingness to convey, and that the covenants to
pay and to convey were dependent.

Pollock, C. B., p. 828: There was a positive covenant to
pay at a specified time. *Mattock* v. *Kinglake* was expressly
in point. The rule in *Pordage* v. *Cole* may be the technical
one; but whether the language of these covenants be subject to a technical construction, or to their natural one, the
result will be the same—they are independent.

Parke, B.: "I am entirely of the same opinion. * * The words of the covenant upon which this action is brought are that the plaintiff shall pay the sum agreed *for the purchase* of the land; if they had been *upon*, or even *for*, *the conveyance* of the land, the defendants' argument might have been tenable, but they amount to a positive covenant to pay the money at a specified time."

In *Sugden*, V. & P. 14th ed., 239: "The true rule is, that it is not the employment of any particular word which determines a condition to be precedent, but the manifest intention of the parties: *Smith* v. *Woodhouse*, 2 New Rep. 233, * * although the purchase money is to be paid *as the consideration of such sale and purchase*, with interest *to the time of the completion of the purchase*, yet if a time is fixed for payment and none for the conveyance, an action for not executing a conveyance might be maintained by the purchaser before the day of payment, and an action by the seller for the money could be sustained, although he had not tendered a conveyance."

Dicker v. *Jackson*, 6 C. B. 103, adopts the rule in *Pordage* v. *Cole: Thames Dock Haven Co.* v. *Brymer* in Error, 5 Ex. 696, cites *Dicker* v. *Jackson*, and agrees with it, and that the rule is correctly laid down.

In *Marsden* v. *Moore*, 4 H. & N. 500, the acts of selling and of paying were held to be contemporaneous.

In *Bankart* v. *Bowers*, L. R. 1 C. P. at p. 489, Erle, C. J. (after *Pordage* v. *Cole* had been cited) said: "Where there is a contract by one party to sell an article, and by the other to pay for it, no time being named, it would be a strong thing to say that the buyer shall pay the money before he gets the consideration."

It is not necessary again to refer to the cases referred to in the judgment in the Court below.

The defendants would have to prepare and tender conveyances on such a contract as this. Something would have to be done on defendants' part of this nature. Their abstaining from doing anything up to the day appointed for payment, cannot (as I think) defeat the plaintiff's right of action.

I am of opinion that the grounds on which the nonsuit was entered are untenable, and that the judgment setting it aside and directing a new trial is right.

I have read all the cases referred to, and they confirm me in the opinion that the appeal must be dismissed.

I see no reason to hold that the plaintiff cannot, at the proper time, make a good title, nor that any real danger need be incurred by defendants in paying the money demanded. I see that our Court of Chancery in *Thompson* v. *Brunskill*, 7 Gr. 542, allowed a defendant who was sued for instalments of unpaid purchase money to bring his money into Court and obtain a stay of the legal proceedings till the title should be investigated. This was done on an allegation that the plaintiff had no title when bargain made and could not make title.

In addition to this, we have the formal offer made by the plaintiff on the argument that he is ready to consent to a reference of the title before the amount now sued for is paid over.

It appears to me that throughout all the cases the principle uniformly adhered to is, in the words of Littledale, J., that "a time being fixed for payment, and none for doing that which was the consideration of the payment, an action lies for the purchase money without averring performance of the consideration."

I do not purpose to discuss the wisdom or the unwisdom of the rule of law, so constantly adhered to. It is sufficient for me to adhere to it if it be law.

There is no doubt of the correctness of defendants' contention, if there be no time named for the conveyance or payment, or if the same time be appointed for both.

As it is I think the judgment below was right.

BURTON, J. A.—The plaintiff sues in this action, not for the purchase money of land sold and conveyed, but on an agreement, whereby the defendant agreed to pay the

balance of the purchase money over and above what was
to remain on mortgage ; averring that he had always been
ready and willing to complete the sale, and to execute
and deliver to the defendant a proper conveyance of the
lands, and that all conditions were fulfilled necessary to
entitle the plaintiff to recover.

Issue was joined on this allegation, and the plaintiff
failed to make out the affirmative of the issue if it was, in
fact, a material allegation.

The case may, therefore, be considered in the same way
as if the agreement had been set forth in the plaintiff's
statement of claim and the plaintiff had omitted this
allegation and the defendant had demurred. At the time
of pleading he seemed to consider that averment necessary
to his success, but he now takes a different stand, and
contends that the promise was a promise to pay at a
named day, wholly independent of the promise to convey
the estate, for which, he says, no day is named, and comes
therefore, within the first rule laid down by the learned
editor of Saunder's Reports in *Pordage* v. *Cole*, 1 *Wms.*
Saund. 319. n.

This depends upon the question of whether it can be
gathered from the agreement to have been the intention
of the parties that the payment of the money and the
conveyance of the land were to be concurrent acts or were
totally independant of each other.

If the former, the plaintiff was bound to tender a deed
or, at least, to aver and prove a readiness and willingness
which includes an ability or capacity to transfer the
estate ; and such a tender or ability was a pre-
requisite to the demand for payment of the sum sought
to be recovered.

For myself, I think, although it is not necessary for the
decision of this case, that he was bound to aver and prove
that he had executed and tendered a deed.

The agreement is in these words :—

" WINNIPEG, February 23, 1882.

" MEMORANDUM OF AGREEMENT between JOHN McDONALD, of the City of Winnipeg, Gentleman, and CAPTAIN JAMES MURRAY, of St. Catharines, and ROBERT CUTHBERT, of Toronto, Ontario.

" The said McDonald sells, and the said Murray and Cuthbert agree to purchase, Lots five (5) and six (6), Main Street, of Block three (3), Hudson Bay Reserve, at and for the sum of sixty thousand dollars, payable as follows : $4,000 to be paid at the signing hereof, $40,795 to be paid within sixty (60) days from the date hereof, and the balance, $15,205, to be on mortgage at seven per cent."

I do not at all dispute the authority or correctness of the rule I have referred to in *Pordage* v. *Cole*, 1 *Wms*. Saund. 319 n.

What we have to do is, to ascertain the true meaning of the parties to this agreement, and then say whether it falls within that or any other of the rules I have referred to.

In endeavouring to do this, we must discard as far as possible all rules of construction founded upon nice and artificial reasoning, and gather the intent and meaning of the parties from the instrument itself, and by our know-ledge of the ordinary affairs of life ; and, as Tindal, C. J., says in *Stavers* v. *Curling*, 3 Bing. N. C. 355, by the appli-cation of common sense to the particular case in hand.

Before proceeding to the consideration of this particular contract, I wish to refer to the opinions of one or two eminent authorities, one of them the late Lord St. Leonards, upon this question of construction. He says, *Sugden*, V. & P., 14th ed., 239 : " In agreements for purchase, the covenants are construed according to the intent of the parties, and therefore they are always considered dependent where a contrary intention does not appear."

And again p. 241 : " But an agreement to buy an estate and pay for it on a certain day implies that the seller is to convey the estate at the same time to the purchaser ; the one thing is to be exchanged for the other."

So, again, Mr. Dart, in his work at p. 958, lays it down : " As a general rule, the mutual engagements of the parties will be considered dependent on each other, and either must perform his liabilities before he seeks to enforce his rights under the contract. So that, on the one hand, the purchaser cannot in general sue upon the agreement without tendering a conveyance and the sum (if any) due, in respect of the purchase money and interest * * and, on the other hand, the vendor, if he sue only upon the agreement and not upon some security which he has taken for the purchase money, must have shewn a good title and have executed or offered to execute * * a conveyance."

So Mr. Leake, in his work on Contracts, p. 652: "In contracts for the sale of land, the conveyance of the estate and the payment of the purchase money are, in general, concurrent acts and dependent promises; whether a particular day be appointed for completion or not; and readiness and willingness to complete on either side is a condition precedent to a liability to complete on the other. Under such contracts an actual conveyance of the land is a condition precedent to the claim for the whole amount of the stipulated purchase money; so that if the purchaser refuse to complete and take a conveyance, the vendor, though he may claim damages for not completing, cannot claim the purchase money so long as he claims the property in the land."

Sir Wm. Anson, after remarking that some of the old cases on the subject turn upon very technical construction of terms, and after referring to the case of *Mattock* v. *Kinglake*, 10 A. & E. 50; where the covenants were held to be independent covenants, proceeds (*Anson* on Contracts), p. 286: "But upon the whole it may be safe to say that, in the absence of very clear indications to the contrary, promises, each of which forms the whole consideration for the other, will not be held to be independent of one another. A failure to perform the one will exonerate the promisee from a performance on his part."

These, then, being the general rules to be observed in gathering the intention of the parties, let us apply them to the present case. Had the agreement stopped at the words "sixty thousand dollars," it is quite clear that neither party could have maintained an action against the other without the performance, or an offer (coupled with the ability) to perform his part of the contract; the vendee would have been bound to tender the money and a conveyance, the vendor to tender a conveyance, or at least have averred his readiness and willingness to convey, before either could have actively asserted his right in a court of law. But the contract goes on, "payable as follows: $4,000 to be paid on the signing hereof;" that sum was payable immediately and the execution of the conveyance was not a pre-requisite to the calling for that payment. But it then proceeds: "$40,795 to be paid within sixty days from the date hereof, and the balance, $15,205, to be on mortgage at 7 per cent."

Applying the rules to which I have called attention, what was the manifest intention of these parties? Can it be reasonably doubted that what they meant was, there must be a deposit made at the time of sale as some security for the carrying out of this contract, which is to be closed in sixty days by the payment of the balance partly in cash and partly by security.

I venture to think that if the opinions of a dozen business men, taken at random in this city, were asked upon the construction of this contract in their view of it, there would not be a dissentient voice, applying the rule of common sense; and I venture also to think, that it is likewise in strict accordance with the rule which the eminent men I have referred to have laid down as the one to be adopted in construing contracts of this nature; and, I think, none of the cases to which we have been referred, when examined, are opposed to this construction of the contract.

In the case of *Sibthorp* v. *Brunel*, 3 Ex. 826, plaintiff had opposed the passage of a Railway Bill through Parliament, and he withdrew that opposition on the company consenting to pay him £4,000 within six months from the passing of the Bill, which was alleged, indeed, to be for the purchase of the land the company required, but which was to be paid at all events whether they took the land or not, and before the company should enter upon the land ; and the Court were unanimous in holding that it was clearly apparent, upon the face of the instrument, that the covenants were independent covenants.

The case of *Mattock* v. *Kinglake*, 10 A. & E. 50, referred to in that decision, was also the case of a covenant under seal, and, I think, when examined is only an authority for holding that, under the terms of the contract in that case, it was not a pre-requisite to the bringing of the action for the purchaser to tender to the defendant a conveyance.

The defendant covenanted there with the plaintiff, or rather with his testator, for this action was brought by the executor of the vendor, to pay before the 19th February, 1825, the sum of £11,206, with interest at 5 per cent. payable half-yearly to the time of the completion of the purchase, the vendor allowing thereout the same rate of interest for so much of the purchase money as had been or might be paid to him in the meanwhile, and the defendant agreed to pay for the conveyance, which has been held to be equivalent to a provision that he should get it ready : *Seaward* v. *Willock*, 5 East 198.

The plaintiff averred that he was always ready and willing to perform his part of the agreement, and did in fact offer to execute a conveyance and had put the defendant in possession. The declaration further averred that the defendant did not pay at the day named, although the purchase had not been completed before that day through the default of the defendant.

To this the defendant pleaded that the vendor had not tendered a conveyance, and that was demurred to.

The plea would appear, under the circumstances of that case, to have been clearly bad ; but the judgment proceeded on the ground that an action might have been maintained for not executing a conveyance of the premises the day after the agreement was signed without alleging payment ; that the covenants were manifestly independent, and that each party relied upon his remedy by action against the other, and therein distinguished the case from *Callonel* v.

Briggs, 1 Salk. 112, *Goodisson* v. *Nunn*, 4 T. R. 761, *Glaze-brook* v. *Woodrow*, 8 T. R. 366, and similar cases.

The language of Buller, J., in *Goodisson* v. *Nunn*, seems to me to be very apposite to the present case.

He says, p. 765: "The agreement was, that the plaintiff should sell his estate, and that the defendant should buy it. In the nature of the thing, therefore the two acts are to be done together. In *Kingston* v. *Preston*, 2 Doug. 689, Lord Mansfield said: 'The construction contended for is, that in spite of his teeth the defendant shall be obliged to give personal credit to the plaintiff; whereas the essence of the agreement was, that neither should trust the other personally.'"

In *Glazebrook* v. *Woodrow*, 8 T. R. 366, the Courts draw the distinction between such cases as *Campbell* v. *Jones*, 6 T. R. 570, and that case for they say there the instruction to be given was not to be, and in the nature of things, could not be performed at the same time, with the payment of money by the defendant, for which a certain time was limited, and Lord Kenyon, in his judgment adds, p. 370: "If we were to hold otherwise (that is to say that the covenants were not dependent) the greatest injustice might be done; for supposing in the instance of a trader who had entered into such a contract, that between the making of the contract and the final execution of it he were to become a bankrupt, the vendee might be in the situation of having had payment enforced from him, and yet be disabled from procuring the property for which he had paid."

The rule which has been referred to in the text books and the modern cases was plainly stated by Grose, J., p. 371, viz., "That the question of whether the covenants were dependent or independent must be collected from the apparent intention of the parties to the contract. There is certainly [he says] some confusion in the books on this subject, some of the older cases leaning to construe covenants of this sort to be independent, contrary to the real sense of the parties and the true justice of the case. But the later authorities convey more just sentiments, and the case of *Kingston* v. *Preston*, 2 Doug. 689, was the first strong authority in which they prevailed in opposition to the former."

It seems to me that the decision in *Marsden* v. *Moore*, 4 H. & N. 500, is decisive of this case. Bramwell, B., there lays down the rule which is founded on common sense, that if a man agrees to buy an estate and pay for it on a certain day, that implies that the seller is to convey the estate at the same time to the purchaser.

And Pollock, C. B., in distinguishing the case from *Pordage* v. *Cole, supra*, says, p. 504 : "It is essential to a contract of buying and selling that one shall pay, the other sell or convey. * * In such cases each party intends that the other shall perform his part and not to rely on a right of action."

Martin, B., p. 504 : "In order to see the meaning of this contract the parts of it should be separately considered. First, the plaintiff agrees to sell to the defendant a share in a mining sett for £250, and the defendants agree to purchase at that price. The sale and payment of the money are to be contemporaneous acts."

He then refers to the 4th and 5th rules referred to in the notes to *Pordage* v. *Cole*, and adds : "This particularly applies to the case of sales where the common understanding is that one thing is to be exchanged for another."

Bramwell, B., after referring to the grounds on which *Pordage* v. *Cole*, was decided, viz., that the Court assumed that there was no intention that the conveyance should take place on the day appointed for the payment of the money, proceeds, p. 505: "Assuming that to be so, the case is rightly decided ; but whether I should have so construed the agreement is another matter. Here the plaintiff agrees to sell, the defendants agree to purchase ; there is a clear present agreement for a future sale and payment. * * The sale and payment are to be contemporaneous."

I do not think this case can be distinguished in principle from *Marsden* v. *Moore*. It is, in my opinion, a stronger case in favour of the defendants; there was a present agreement for a future sale and payment; the money and the security are to be exchanged for the land; when is that to be ? Clearly at the time named, or it may be sooner, but whether on the extreme day named or sooner they are intended to be contemporaneous.

In accordance with all the rules I have referred to, that is the true construction to be placed on this agreement. That being so, neither party is entitled to sue without the performance of his part of the agreement. I think, therefore, the decision of the learned Judge at the trial was correct and ought to be restored.

Such cases as *Wilkes* v. *Smith*, 10 M. & W. 355, are clearly distinguishable. That was an action for the recovery of an instalment of interest on the purchase money. The vendor was not bound to convey until the day named for the payment of the principal money ; and it was manifestly unnecessary and would have been absurd to aver a readiness to convey as a condition precedent to enforcing payment of the interest.

PATTERSON, J. A.—This action is brought to recover $40,795, mentioned in an agreement which is in these words : [His Lordship here read the agreement as printed ante p. 111.]

The plaintiff, in his statement of claim, sets out the agreement, and avers that he has always been ready and willing to complete the sale and purchase and to execute and deliver to the defendants a proper conveyance of the said lands and premises, and that all conditions were fulfilled, and all things happened, and all times elapsed, necessary to entitle him to a performance of the agreement by the defendants on their part.

He admits payment of the $4,000 at the time of the making of the agreement, and complains of the non-payment of the $40,795, saying nothing as to the $15,205, and giving no reason why he makes no claim in respect of that sum.

The defendants in their pleading deny the alleged
agreement ; and also allege that the plaintiff has no title
to the land, and that he was not owner and cannot give a
good title to the defendants ; on which account they ask
to have the $4,000 paid back to them. They further make
charges of fraud, which it is not necessary now to state at
length.

At the trial before the present Chief Justice of the
Common Pleas, the greater part of the evidence given
related to the proof of the agreement, the original paper
happening to be in Winnipeg, and at length a copy was,
by consent, received in evidence. No evidence was given
on the charge of fraud, nor was any evidence given to
prove readiness and willingness to convey the land. It
seems to have been conceded that nothing had been done
from the time of the making of the agreement, when the
$4,000 had been paid, till the commencement of the action,
which was on the 8th May, 1882, two and a half months
after the date of the agreement. There were, however, two
facts proved by legal evidence. McKilligan, a witness for
the plaintiff, swore that the plaintiff told him that one
Daniel Young was part owner of the property: and the
defendant Cuthbert admitted that he had sold and conveyed his interest in it to one Fish, who, however, had not
paid him except by a promissory note which was
dishonored. Where the title to the land really was, was not
proved. The evidence was merely sufficient to shew, as
against the plaintiff, that Young was a part owner. No
title whatever in the plaintiff was shewn.

Upon this state of facts the learned Judge pronounced
the following judgment :

"It appearing by the evidence and statement of claim
that the action is for the recovery of the purchase money
of land, and that the time for completing the transaction
on both sides had arrived before the commencement of the
action ; and it further appearing by the evidence on behalf
of the plaintiff that another person is part owner of the
land ; and no tender of a conveyance to the defendants, or

to the defendant Murray, and the assignee of the defendant Cuthbert, having been made, I dismiss the action, with full costs, without prejudice to the plaintiff's right to bring a fresh action, or take any other proceeding that he would have had a right to take if this action had not been brought."

The Divisional Court of the Common Pleas Division having set aside that judgment and ordered a new trial, the defendants have appealed to this Court.

We are not at present required to consider the rights and remedies which would have been recognized and administered by a Court of Equity, on a bill filed by either party for specific performance of the contract. Those rights and remedies may of course be now asserted or pursued in the High Court of Justice; but the present action is not founded upon them. The plaintiff asserts a common law claim for payment of the purchase money of the land, and insists on his right to payment of that money notwithstanding that he has not conveyed, and is not able, as far as the evidence discloses, to convey the land to the defendants.

The question presented is the construction of the contract.

It is a question about which one would scarcely expect to find much difficulty.

When people bargain together, whether it is to barter one piece of property for another, or to exchange property for money, each party ordinarily expects to receive what he bargains for when he parts with what he is to give. If the intention is that either of them is to part with his property, and take his chance of the other afterwards performing his part, or paying damages for his default, it is not the ordinary transaction of sale or exchange, and when it is intended we may reasonably expect to find some express declaration of that intention.

I understand the view of the Court below to be that there was in this case such an intention; that the agreement to pay the large sum of $40,795 was independent of any agreement expressed or implied to convey the land; and that the defendants agreed to pay the money at the named day, not because they were, at or before that day, to receive the land, but because they, without further security than the implied promise of the plaintiff, relied upon his being able at some later time to convey the land, and upon his conveying it to them at that later time.

They would not even have the security of an equitable title to the land ; because, as the learned Chief Justice pointed out in delivering the judgment of the Court, it was not essential that the plaintiff should himself have any title to the land until the time arrived for the conveyance to the defendants.

No person, be he lawyer or layman, would, from reading the document without embarrassment from decisions or dicta, gather from it that the defendants were to pay more than the substantial deposit of $4,000, even if that sum was intended to be paid, without receiving something for their money beyond the word of the plaintiff.

The difficulty has arisen from the supposed application to this contract of one or more of the rules laid down by Mr. Serjeant Williams in his notes under *Fordage* v. *Cole*, 1 *Wms.* Saund. 548*, for determining when covenants are dependent, and when mutual or independent.

The purpose of rules of construction is to lead us to the real intention of the parties to the instrument. Fixed and technical rules must be cautiously applied; and we may sometimes require to resist a tendency, which is strongest when rules are well defined, to adopt a procrustean method of construction in order to make the contract fit the rules.

We find many words of caution uttered by eminent jurists with regard to contracts of the class of the one before us.

The case of *Thorpe* v. *Thorpe*, decided in 1701, is reported in 1 Salk. 171 ; 1 Lutw. 245 ; 1 Ld. Raym. 662, and 12 Mod. 455. The last mentioned report gives the judgment of Holt, C. J., at much greater length than any

*Ed. 1871.

of the others. I read a passage from the more condensed
report in 1 Ld. Raym. at p. 666.

"He considered then the reasonableness of the cases that
are founded on mutual remedies. And (by him) the
bargain of every man ought to be performed as he understood it; and if a man will make such an agreement, as to
pay his money before he has the thing for which he ought
to pay it, and will rely upon the remedy that he has to
recover the said thing, he ought to perform his agreement.
But, on the other hand, if his agreement was otherwise,
there is no reason that he should be compelled to give
credit, where he did not intend it."

In *Porter* v. *Shephard*, 6 T. R. 665, we find Lord
Kenyon saying, p. 668: "It has frequently been said, and
common sense seems to justify it, that conditions are to be
construed to be either precedent or subsequent, according to
the fair intention of the parties to be collected from the
instrument, and that technical words (if there be any to
encounter such intention) should give way to that intention."

Forty years later Tindal, C.J., in *Stavers* v. *Curling*, 3
Bing. N. C. 355, apparently following Lord Kenyon's phraseology, said, p. 368: "The rule has been established by a
long series of decisions in modern times, that the question
whether covenants are to be held dependent or independent of each other is to be determined by the intention
and meaning of the parties as it appears on the instrument,
and by the application of common sense to each particular
case; to which intention when once discovered all technical forms of expression must give way."

Passing on twenty years further to *Roberts* v. *Brett*,
18 C. B. at p. 573, we find Jervis, C. J., saying, with
regard to the first rule under *Pordage* v. *Cole:* "But,
after all, that rule only professes to give the result of the
intention of the parties; and where, on the whole, it is
apparent that the intention is that that which is to be
done first is not to depend upon the performance of the
thing that is to be done afterwards, the parties are relying

on their remedy and not on their condition; but where you plainly see that it is their intention to rely on the condition, and not on the remedy, the performance of the thing is a condition precedent." In the same case in the Exchequer Chamber 16 C. B. N. S. at p. 634, Bramwell, B., said: "I entirely agree with Jervis, C. J., that we are to ascertain the intention of the parties. The rules laid down in the note to *Pordage* v. *Cole*, are very excellent guides, but not arbitrary tests." And in the House of Lords, Lord Chelmsford (11 H. L. Cas. 354) added: "These rules are not proposed for the purpose of absolutely determining the dependence or independence of covenants in all cases, but merely as furnishing a guide to the discovery of the intention of the parties." Then he quoted Lord Kenyon's language from *Porter* v. *Shephard*. He had during the argument also referred to that of Tindal, C. J., in *Stavers* v. *Curling*.

From the judgment of Chief Justice Wilson, I gather that the reference in the contract to the mortgage for $15,205 was treated as indicating that the mortgage transaction was to take place *after* the payment of the $40,795, and thus pointing to a later date than the date fixed for that payment for completing the title.

Without conceding that the conclusion necessarily follows from the premises, I dispute the premises.

It is certainly anything but plain how this mortgage matter was understood by the parties to the contract. The words are, "the balance, $15,205, to be on mortgage at seven per cent." Had we been told that there was already a mortgage on the property for that amount, we should have understood the words to mean that the buyers were to assume the payment of it. But nothing of that sort being told us, I suppose the meaning must be that the buyers are to give a mortgage for the amount to somebody, *primâ facie* to the vendor; and the terms not being defined, the Court was doubtless correct in holding that they were to be in the discretion of the mortgagors.

But I cannot help thinking that the learned Chief Justice,

and the other learned Judges who agreed with him, assumed
too readily that the mortgage arrangement, whatever its
nature was to be, was to be later in point of time than
the payment of the $40,795. It is not expressly so stated
in the agreement, nor is it the necessary inference from its
being called a balance and mentioned last. The cash payment of $40,795, not being a round sum, but for a broken
amount, it might be not unfairly inferred that it was the real
balance after setting apart the other broken amount which,
for some unexplained reason, it was desired to leave on
mortgage.

There seems no sufficient warrant furnished by the
writing for holding affirmatively that the mortgage transaction was so clearly to occur after the sixty days that
the duty to make title and convey the land must have
been intended to be postponed till the later date. On the
contrary we may, without reasoning too astutely, find as
good, if not better reasons for the conclusion that it cannot
have been so intended. From what date was the seven
per cent. to be calculated? In the absence of express
mention of the date, we may take one of the two dates
referred to in the document, viz: the date of the signing of
it, and sixty days thereafter. Outside of these dates we
are in the region of mere guesswork. Then, if we assume,
as we may properly do, that the interest was not to run
before the date of the mortgage, and yet was to begin
from one of the two dates, we have no foothold for the
assumption that the agreement pointed to the making of
the mortgage at a later date than the sixty days, and
therefore cannot rely on the reference to the mortgage to
prove that the conveyance was not to be made within the
sixty days.

In my opinion we cannot attach to the reference to the
mortgage the significance which seems to have been attributed to it in the Court below. I think we may lay it out
of sight, and deal with the agreement as one by which the
time for the payment of the instalment now demanded is
fixed, while no time is named for the making of title or the
execution of the conveyance.

When an agreement simply declares that one shall sell
and another buy for a stated price, it is undisputed that
the conveyance and the payment are to be contemporaneous
acts; when we read an agreement in that form we find
nothing to indicate that either party meant himself, or
expected the other, to give without receiving. Why should
there be a difference when the time for payment happens
to be postponed to a fixed day, nothing being said in either
case, about the conveyance ?

The passages cited from text books by my Brother Burton are distinctly against the recognition of such a distinction, and I propose to shew that it is not supported by the
decisions of the Courts.

The plaintiff alleges that he was always ready and willing to convey, and the defendants traverse that allegation.

The Chief Justice in the Court below treats the allegation
as immaterial because, as he holds, the time for conveying
had not arrived until after the end of the sixty days, when,
if ever, the plaintiff's right of action accrued ; and because
the contract would be satisfied by his putting himself in a
position to give or procure a good title when the time came.

I think the time for conveying had arrived. On that
point I cannot take his Lordship's view of the contract.

But he further holds that, if the duty to convey was
not postponed, the averment of readiness and willingness
was all that was required, and that the issue on that
averment had not been tried, wherefore it was proper to
grant the new trial.

In connection with this he states the general rule of law
as being, in his opinion, clear that the plaintiff was not
obliged to tender a conveyance to the defendants, but
that it was the defendants' duty to prepare it and to
tender it to the plaintiff for execution.

Upon these points I am again unable to concur in the
views expressed, at least to the full extent.

The issue of readiness and willingness, (assuming it to
be material), was upon the plaintiff, and he gave all the
evidence he desired to give upon it, with the result which

I have already mentioned of stopping short of shewing in himself any right whatever to the land, while he shewed that Daniel Young was a part owner ; and while at the same time it was either shewn or conceded that no conveyance and been tendered by the defendants for execution, and that one defendant had resold to one Fish whatever interest he took under the contract.

The plaintiff's readiness and willingness, in which his ability is included, were disproved, or at all events he did not establish them, and therefore, if the issue was material, he was properly nonsuited, unless saved by the want of a tender of a deed by the defendants.

Now, accepting, for the sake of the present argument, the doctrine which may perhaps not be so free from doubt with us as it has come to be, in modern times, in England, that it is the purchaser's duty to prepare the conveyance and tender it for execution, the vendor is nevertheless bound to shew title. Before the purchaser can prepare a conveyance he must at least be informed who is to convey. Therefore the plaintiff cannot entitle himself to be paid for land which he has not conveyed, by the fact that no deed has been tendered, unless he shews performance on his own part by deducing title. Until title is shewn the defendants cannot be in default by not tendering a deed, and in the absence of such default, I find nothing in the agreement to justify the conclusion that the plaintiff can insist on payment of this money.

A considerable number of cases have been cited to us. Some of them will require more full examination than the others, the earliest being *Pordage* v. *Cole, supra,* which was decided in 1668, and the latest *Marsden* v. *Moore,* 4 H. & N. 500, nearly two hundred years afterwards.

Marsden v. *Moore,* being the latest case which has any very direct bearing on the questions before us, though not the latest that turned on the subject of dependent or independent covenants, it may be useful to discuss it first.

The plaintiff agreed to sell to the defendants one-fourth part of a mining sett for £250, and the defendants agreed

to purchase at that price. A company was to be formed
and registered, and the defendants agreed that as soon as
the company should be registered they would pay to the
plaintiff the £250. To an action to recover that sum the
defendants pleaded that the plaintiff had not any title to
the one-fourth part of the mining sett, nor any right or
title to convey the same; and that the plaintiff had never
been ready and willing to convey. These pleas were
demurred to, raising questions very much like those now
in discussion, and the judgments, which are not long, are so
apposite that I shall read them in full. Pollock, C. B., p. 503,
"We are all of opinion that the pleas are good and that
the defendants are entitled to judgment. The question
is, what did the parties mean by the agreement declared
on, whether each party is entitled to insist on performance by the other, without reference to his capacity to
perform his own part of the agreement. The plea sets
out an agreement by which ‘as soon as the company is
registered, with limited liability,’ the defendants agree to
pay to the plaintiff the sum of £250 ‘as hereinbefore stated’;
that is as the purchase of a mining sett. I do not think
that the reference to the uncertain period depending upon
the registration of the company brings the case within the
rule laid down in *Pordage* v. *Cole.* It is essential to a
contract of buying and selling that one shall pay, the other
sell or convey. On that ground this case is distinguishable
from *Pordage* v. *Cole.* In such cases each party intends
that the other shall perform his part, and not to rely on a
right of action. Therefore in the present case the plaintiff
is not in a condition to maintain the action."

Martin, B. "I am of the same opinion. I think that
the law is correctly laid down in *Pordage* v. *Cole.* In
order to see the meaning of this contract the parts of it
should be separately considered. First, the plaintiff agrees
to sell to the defendant a share in a mining sett for £250,
and the defendants agree to purchase at that price. The
sale and payment of the money are to be contemporaneous
acts. In the notes to *Pordage* v. *Cole* it is said, rule 4,

'Where the mutual covenants go to the whole consideration on both sides, they are mutual conditions, and performance must be averred;' and rule 5, 'Where two acts are to be done at the same time, neither party can maintain an action without shewing performance of, or an offer to perform his part.' This particularly applies to the case of sales, where the common understanding is, that one thing is to be exchanged for another. Then as to the other part, as soon as the company is registered the defendants agree to pay the sum of £250, 'as hereinbefore stated.' That does not convey to my mind that the defendants meant, if it should turn out that the plaintiff had no title, to take their chance of being able to recover back the £250 in an action for money had and received."

Bramwell, B. " I am of the same opinion. In the case of *Pordage* v. *Cole*, the Court construed the agreement as if it appeared on the face of it that there was no intention that the conveyance should take place on the day appointed for payment of the money. Assuming that to be so, the case is rightly decided; but whether I should have so construed the agreement is another matter. Here the plaintiff agrees to sell, the defendants agree to purchase; there is a clear present agreement for a future sale and payment. The subsequent part of the agreement merely postpones the time for performance; it does not alter the effect of the prior stipulation, which is that the money is to be paid upon the conveyance. The sale and payment are to be contemporaneous. The last plea is clearly good. As to the other plea there is more difficulty. The question is whether the defendant has sufficiently negatived the existence of such a title as would have enabled the plaintiff to convey the sett to the defendants. In the old days I think we should have said it was good in substance as an averment that there was no title."

Channell, B., " I entirely agree with the correctness of the propositions of law laid down in *Pordage* v. *Cole*. Whether they govern the present case depends upon the construction of the agreement. By the first part of the agreement the payment and conveyance are to be concurrent acts. The plaintiff is to sell and the defendant is to buy, a mining sett, at a price specified. Then is that altered by the subsequent part of the agreement? I think not. The true construction of the whole is, that the conveyance and payment are to be concurrent acts; but a provision is made as to the time at which the concurrent acts are to be done. The pleas are good traverses of that which is alleged in the declaration."

These judgments, I think, fully bear out the views I have attempted to express with regard to the contract we have to construe. The case seems to me as nearly as possible on all fours with the one we are considering, and to be decisive of it, so far as authority is required, unless it is so much at variance with other decisions as not to be relied on, notwithstanding its being of so much later date than the others. But I do not apprehend much difficulty in shewing that no other decision conflicts with it, though possibly *dicta* may be found wide enough to seem to conflict with the grounds on which it was decided.

The case chiefly relied on for the plaintiff is *Mattock* v. *Kinglake*, 10 A. & E. 50, decided just twenty years before *Marsden* v. *Moore*. It was an action of debt by the plaintiff as executor of Southwood. The declaration stated that the defendant was seised in fee of premises by virtue of a deed by which the Bishop of Winchester had bargained and sold the premises to Southwood to such uses as Southwood should appoint, and in default of appointment to the defendant in fee in trust for Southwood, his heirs and assigns for ever; that, by articles of agreement, Southwood agreed to sell and defendant to purchase the premises for the sum thereinafter mentioned; and defendant thereby covenanted with Southwood, his heirs and assigns, to pay to him or them, on or before the 19th February, 1825, as the consideration for such sale and purchase, £11,206 with interest at five per cent., payable half yearly, to the time of the completion of the purchase, Southwood allowing thereout the same rate of interest for

so much of the purchase money as had been, or might be
paid him in the meanwhile; and the defendant also agreed
to pay for the conveyance and stamp duty. Averment
that Southwood, in his lifetime, was always ready and
willing to perform his part of the agreement, and did, in
fact, offer to execute a conveyance to the defendant of all
his estate and interest in the premises; that the defendant
had, ever since the agreement, been in possession of all
the premises, and in receipt of the profits to his own use;
yet defendant did not, nor would pay, or cause to be paid
to Southwood in his lifetime the said sum and interest for
the same on or before 19th February, 1825; nor to plaintiff since Southwood's death. Plea that Southwood did
not tender any conveyance to defendant, to which plea the
plaintiff demurred. In support of the demurrer, counsel
relied on *Pordage* v. *Cole*, and the rules given by Mr.
Serjt. Williams for ascertaining the dependence or independence of covenants; and he argued that the duty to tender
a conveyance was upon the defendant and not upon the
vendor, and that the fact that the defendant was admitted
on the record to be already seised in fee of the legal estate
was alone sufficient to obviate the necessity of a tender,
or indeed, of any conveyance at all: and that the articles
of agreement, executed in the manner set forth, operated
as an execution of the power reserved to Southwood; so
that the whole estate, legal and equitable, was already in
the defendant. Manning, for the defendant, argued that
the case was distinguishable from *Pordage* v. *Cole*. Lord
Denman, C.J., p. 55: "None of the circumstances relied
upon by Mr. Manning are sufficient to shew that the acts of
payment and conveyance here were to be concurrent, or to
distinguish this case from *Pordage* v. *Cole* and the authorities
cited in the note to it. If, as is contended on the part of
the plaintiff, the legal and equitable estates are now united
in the defendant, he requires no remedy against the plaintiff which he has not already in his own hands. If not,
we cannot help him to a remedy which he has not secured
for himself by his contract." Littledale, J.: "A time

being fixed for payment, and none for doing that which was the consideration for the payment, an action lies for the purchase money without averring performance of the consideration. An action for not executing a conveyance of the premises might have been maintained by the defendant before the day of payment; and in such an action no allegation of payment would have been necessary. The covenants are independent, and each party has relied upon his remedy by action against the other. The case, therefore differs from *Callonel* v. *Briggs*, 1 Salk. 112, and from *Goodisson* v. *Nunn*, 4 T. R. 761, *Glazebrook* v. *Woodrow*, 8 T. R. 366, and other cases cited, where both acts were to be done at the same time, or on the same day." Patteson, J.: "*Pordage* v. *Cole* is directly in point. We must overrule it if we decide in favour of the defendant. There is no express provision that the conveyance shall be executed before payment, nor any reasonable intendment that it was to be necessarily precedent to or concurrent with it." Coleridge, J., "We must collect the intention of the parties from the whole instrument. It fixes with precision the time of payment, which is expressed to be the consideration of the sale and purchase, and contemplates the possible payment before that time.   *   *   The acts are clearly independent, within the rule correctly laid down by Mr. Serjeant Williams in the note to *Pordage* v. *Cole*, 1 Wms.' Saund. 320, note (4)."

The point actually decided, having regard to the facts admitted by the pleadings, was that under an agreement by which one person is to convey to another, no time for the conveyance being named, and the other is to pay the purchase money at a stated day with the interest in meantime, the purchaser having possession and receiving the profits to his own use, the purchaser cannot refuse to pay at the day fixed by his agreement, merely because the vendor, who has always been ready and willing to perform his part of the agreement, and has in fact offered to execute a conveyance to the defendant, who was bound by the agreement to pay for the conveyance, has not tendered any conveyance to the defendant.

In the case before us there was a great deal to be done by the plaintiff besides executing or tendering a conveyance. Not one of the important facts admitted by the plea in *Mattock* v. *Kinglake* is either admitted or proved by the present plaintiff. The decision does not, therefore, advance the discussion very far. The case is not relied on so much for the point decided as for the sake of the *dicta* of the Judges in the judgments which I have quoted and which seem to have been delivered at the close of the argument.

It may be questionable whether the decision depended upon any of the rules laid down in the notes to *Pordage* v. *Cole*. The only point raised by the demurrer was the same which in the following year was expressly decided in the Exchequer in *Poole* v. *Hill*, 6 M. & W. 835, namely, that when the title has been cleared up and nothing remains to be done but the execution of a conveyance, the purchaser cannot resist payment on the ground that no conveyance has been made, because it is his duty to tender the conveyance for execution; but the judgment of Lord Denman indicates that there were yet other sufficient grounds for the decision against the defence.

If the *dicta* are understood to mean that the mere fact of no time being named for the conveyance, while a day certain was fixed for the payment, makes it obligatory to hold that the parties intended that the money should be paid on the day whether or not the vendor had performed his part of the bargain, that doctrine is not reconcilable with *Marsden* v. *Moore*; and *Pordage* v. *Cole*, which seems to be the authority relied on, does not appear to me to be an authority for so general a proposition. But, after all, the learned Judges only profess to seek in the language of the instrument for the intention of the parties. Coleridge, J., says so in so many words, and Patteson, J., intimates the same thing when he alludes to reasonable intendment.

In *Marsden* v. *Moore* the Judges found, as I think we easily find in this case, a reasonable intendment that both parts of the contract were to be performed concurrently.

In *Pordage* v. *Cole* the action was debt upon a specialty by which it was agreed that the defendant should give to the plaintiff £775 for a property, 5s. of which was paid in earnest, and the residue was covenanted to be paid a week after the next midsummer. On demurrer it was " adjudged that the action was well brought without an averment of the conveyance of the land, because it shall be intended that both parties have sealed the specialty. And if the plaintiff has not conveyed the land to the defendant, he has also an action of covenant against the plaintiff upon the agreement contained in the deed, which amounts to a covenant on the part of the plaintiff to convey the land ; and so each party has mutual remedy against the other. But it might be otherwise if the specialty had been the words of the defendant only, and not the words of both parties by way of agreement as it is here."

I do not understand Mr. Serjeant Williams to profess to deduce the rules which he gives in his notes under *Pordage* v. *Cole*, or any of them, from the decision in that case, notwithstanding that he says that the ground of the judgment seems to be that which he puts as his first rule, because the money was appointed to be paid on a fixed day, which might happen before the lands were or could be conveyed.

In his notes, which were written some time before the close of the last century, he mentions the fact that almost all the old cases and many of the modern ones on the subject of dependent and independent covenants were decided upon nice and technical distinctions; and Lord Kenyon in *Goodisson* v. *Nunn*, 4 T. R. 761, denounced some of them as outraging common sense.

I take the decision in *Pordage* v. *Cole* simply to decide that because both parties had covenanted, as it was assumed they had done, therefore each had relied on the covenant of the other, and the covenants were independent.

It appears that the deed in that case did not fix a day certain for the performance of the vendor's part of the agreement, but I do not understand that circumstance to

have influenced the decision. I believe the decision would
have been the same if the same day had been named for conveying the land as for paying the money. There is not
a word in the judgment to indicate that it proceeded upon
any consideration but the one, viz., that the defendant had
covenanted, and that the plaintiff had covenanted also.
I think the whole scope of the decision was expressed by
Holt, C. J., when, referring to it in *Thorpe* v. *Thorpe*, 12
Mod. at p. 462, he said that "because a day certain was
appointed for the payment, though no assurance was made
of the house, &c., yet an action lay for the money."

The decision, thus understood, is certainly far from
recognizing some of the rules which in modern times are
perfectly well settled, *e. g.*, the rule that when no time is
named for either act, they are to be construed as intended
to be concurrent, and the same when the same day is
fixed for both acts. It is, however, consistent with what
I understand to be the doctrine that prevailed when
Pordage v. *Cole* was decided. I refer in support of this
opinion to two cases, one of which, *Peeters* v. *Opie*, Vent.
177, was decided in 1671, three years after *Pordage* v.
Cole, and the other *Trench* v. *Trewin*, 1 Lord Raym. 124,
twenty-five years later.

In *Peeters* v. *Opie* the struggle was to take the contract
out of the prevailing general rule, that the fact of there
being mutual covenants was enough to render one party
liable to an action before performance by the other.

The note of the case is as follows : "In an assumpsit the
plaintiff declares that there was an agreement between
him and the defendant, that he, the plaintiff, should
pull down two walls and build an house, &c., for the defendant, and that the defendant should pay him *pro labore suo
in et circa divulsionem, etc.*, £8, and that in consideration
that the plaintiff assumed to perform his part, the defendant assumed to perform his; and the plaintiff avers that
he was *paratus* to perform all on his part, but that the
defendant has not paid him the money. Hale, C. J. * *
'Now to shew this *pro labore* makes a condition

precedent, suppose the agreement to be in writing thus :
Memorandum, that J. S. agrees and promises to build,
and J. N. promises to pay him so much for his pains, it
cannot be taken but that the building must be precedent
to the payment. 'Tis the common way of bargaining, and
in common dealing men do not use to pay before the
work be done ; it would be inconvenient to give cross-
actions in such cases especially, since 'tis likely that the
workman is a poor man. 'Tis true if there be a time
limited for payment, which time may fall out before the
work or thing be done, there the doing it is not a precedent
condition, "*Twisden,* contra. ' There is no need of the averment, there being reciprocal promises, upon which the parties
have mutual remedies,' and relied upon the case, 1 Roll. 46.
Rainsford agreed with Hale. *Et adjornatur.*" P. 214.
" The case was moved again, and Hale held clearly, that
the promise being *pro labore* (though there was also a
counter-promise), did carry in it a condition precedent, viz.,
that the work should be done first. Twisden strongly to
the contrary. *Pro labore* (says he) is no more than would
have been implied if those words had been omitted ; then
'tis within the case of reciprocal promises. Hale was now
of opinion that the plaintiff's saying *paratus fuit et obtulit*
to do the work ; though he did not say, 'and the other
refused,' yet it was a sufficient averment after a verdict.
Wherefore, though they could not agree in the other matter, yet judgment was given for the plaintiff."

Trench v. *Trewin* is thus reported : " Covenant upon
articles of agreement between the testator Squire and the
defendant, by which it was covenanted and agreed between
them, that Squire should assign to the defendant his interest
in a house, &c., and that the defendant should pay to Squire
£30. The plaintiff assigns for breach, that the defendant
has not paid the £30, &c. The defendant pleads, that
Squire did not assign his interest in the house to the
defendant. The plaintiff demurs. And adjudged for him,
because these are mutual and independent covenants, and
the parties may have reciprocal actions ; and therefore the

plaintiff may bring his action before the assignment of the house. And the defendant has a remedy after, if the other party does not perform his part."

The judgments delivered in *Goodisson* v. *Nunn*, 4 T. R. 761, and in *Glazebrook* v. *Woodrow*, 8 T. R. 366, confirm my understanding of the decision in *Pordage* v. *Cole*, because, while in those cases there was a time fixed for performance as well as a time for payment, Lord Kenyon and the other judges who sat with him evidently understood that, when they held the covenants to be dependent on each other, they were departing from the canon of construction which would have been acted on in earlier times.

For these reasons, materially aided by the remark of Lord Bramwell in *Marsden* v. *Moore*, I am satisfied that *Pordage* v. *Cole* cannot safely be used as an authority for the general proposition on which the plaintiff relies.

I do not propose to comment on all the cases to which we were referred, although I have carefully examined them all. In most of them the points of distinction which render them only indirectly applicable, if applicable at all, are sufficiently obvious. It will, however, be proper to say a word with regard to some of them, particularly those referred to in the court below. Speaking of them generally, I believe there will be found no case, whatever was the form of the covenant or promise, in which the purchase money was recovered before conveyance when the title of the vendor was not either conceded or proved.

Roper v. *Coombes*, 6 B. & C. 534 I think was not cited to us. It was an action for money had and received, to recover back a deposit of £10 paid on an agreement made on the 31st of March, 1826, by the defendant to grant to the plaintiff a lease of a public house for 21 years from 29th September, 1826, in consideration of £1,000, of which £10 was paid down, £90 was to be paid on 13th April, 1826, and the residue on having possession. No time for granting the lease was expressly fixed by the agreement. The £90 was not paid on 13th April. On 20th April the plaintiff by his attorney required the defendant to exhibit

his title to the premises. The defendant on the other
hand called for payment of the £90 and insisted that he
was not bound to grant the lease, or to shew title, until
the 29th of September. Thereupon the plaintiff gave
notice that he would rescind the contract, and commenced
this action to recover back the £10.

It appeared that the defendant had not power to grant
a lease according to his contract at the time when the
action was commenced, which was before the 29th of
September. Lord Tenterden, C.J. p. 536: "The sole question
is, whether the plaintiff, at the time when the action was
commenced, had a right to rescind the contract. If he
had not, it follows that the defendant is entitled to maintain an action for the sum of £90, which was agreed to be
paid on the 13th of April. The contract, on the part of
the defendant, was to grant a lease on a future day not
specified. The plaintiff having agreed to pay £90 on the
13th of April did not do so; but, on that sum being
demanded, inquired what right the defendant had to grant
the lease. It was but reasonable that the party should
not pay so large a sum as £90 without knowing that the
defendant had power to complete his part of the contract.
No evidence of his right was then given; and at the trial
it was proved, on the contrary, that he had no such right
at that time. Under such circumstances I think that the
plaintiff was entitled to rescind the contract, and to sue
for the £10 which he had paid."

Lord Tenterden seems to have held the same views as were
expressed by Lord Kenyon in *Goodisson* v. *Nunn*, 4 T. R.
761, when he said, p. 764: "Suppose the purchase money
of an estate was £40,000, it would be absurd to say that
the purchaser might enforce a conveyance without payment, and compel the seller to have recourse to him, who
perhaps might be an insolvent person. The old cases,
cited by plaintiff's counsel, have been accurately stated;
but the determinations in them outrage common sense.
I admit the principle on which they profess to go: but I
think that the judges misapplied that principle."

In *Laird* v. *Pim*, 7 M. & W. 474 (1841), the defendant
had been let into possession under a contract to purchase,
and refused to pay.   The point in the case was the effect
of the allegation that the defendant had discharged the
plaintiff from performing his part of the agreement, and
that was held, on the authority of *Jones* v. *Barkley*, 2
Doug. 684, as equivalent to performance by the plaintiff
for the purpose of enabling him to recover damages for
defendant's breach of contract, which damages were not
necessarily the whole purchase money.   Parke, B., said,
p. 485 : " The distinction, which it has been attempted to
draw between this case and *Jones* v. *Barkley*, is no distinction at all ; it proceeds altogether on the ground, that there
two contemporaneous acts were to be done on a particular
day : but the case is just the same whether two contemporaneous acts are to be done at an indefinite time, or on
a specified day."

DeMedina v. *Norman*, 9 M. & W. 820 (1842).   It will
be sufficient to read the judgment of Alderson, B., which
puts in concise form the matters decided.

The action was for refusing to accept a lease.

" The second plea," the learned Baron said, p. 828, " takes
issue on an immaterial averment.   The declaration states
that before and at the time of the agreement the plaintiff
was legally possessed for the residue of a term of a certain
dwelling house ; now it is clearly immaterial to the right of
the plaintiff to recover, that he should prove that he had a
title to the lease before the demise to the defendant.   The
term might be merged in the fee, and so he might not be
possessed of it, but still he would be able to grant a lease.
There are many other suppositions in which the same
result would arise.   The averment in the declaration, is
therefore immaterial and the traverse insufficient.   The
third plea is also bad.   Then is the declaration good ?   I
think it is.   The averment of readiness and willingness to
let to the defendant includes the capacity to do so."

The vice of the third plea was that it was too large,
since it included the title of the plaintiff at the time of
the contract, and also at the time of the demise.

Wilks v. *Smith*, 10 M. & W. 355 (1842), was an action for interest. The declaration stated that the plaintiff agreed to sell, and the defendant agreed to purchase a lot of building ground for £120, which sum the defendant agreed to pay on or before the expiration of four years from the date of the agreement, with interest at five per cent. half yearly until paid. The declaration then alleged mutual promises, and that the four years had not elapsed, and that the £120 had not been yet paid ; and that £12 for two years' interest on £120 was due and unpaid.

The declaration was demurred to on the ground that it did not shew that the plaintiff had title, nor aver any ability or readiness or willingness on the part of the plaintiff to perform his part of the agreement. The decision was that it was not necessary to aver readiness and willingness to convey at every period of the contract, and that the defendant was bound to pay the interest. I call attention however to the remarks of Parke, Alderson, and Rolfe, B B., which seem to me to imply the opinion that the principal money could not have been demanded unless the plaintiff was prepared, concurrently with the payment, to perform his part of the bargain. Parke, B., said, p. 360 : " It is enough if he is ready and able to convey at the time when the title is to be made out. I also think that it is no objection that he has not averred that he had a title to the land. According to the terms of the agreement no time is fixed for the sale ; but a time is limited within which the principal money is to be paid, with interest in the meantime. The consideration for the defendant's paying the interest is the plaintiff's *undertaking* to sell the land, not the actual sale of it. The plaintiff is not bound to do anything before the money is paid. The rule, as laid down in the notes to *Pordage* v. *Cole*, applies strictly to this case. No time, then, being fixed by the agreement for the conveyance of the land, it cannot be a condition precedent; nor can we imply that a conveyance was intended to be made before the interest was paid, else we should be supposing that the plaintiff intended to part with his estate

before the money was paid, and such an intention certainly
cannot be implied from the nature of the contract. It may
be that no conveyance need be made till the principal
money is paid, that is, at the end of four years. The
question here is, whether or not the interest is to be paid
before the plaintiff has given up possession of the land. I
think it is, and that the conveyance is not a condition
precedent."

This language, so far as it relates to the principal money,
may not unaptly be applied to the contract before us. We
cannot imply that the conveyance was not intended to be
made, at latest, concurrently with the payment, else we
should be supposing that the defendant intended to part
with his money before he received the consideration, and
such an intention certainly cannot be implied from the
nature of the contract. It may be that no conveyance
needed to be made till the principal money was payable,
that is, at the end of the sixty days. The bearing of the
judgment seems strongly in support of my view that, at
the expiration of the sixty days, the duty to convey and
the duty to pay were concurrent, and that thus, by necessary intendment, the time for the performance of the
plaintiff's part of the contract was fixed.

Dicker v. *Jackson,* 6 C. B. 103 (1848), like *Wilks* v. *Smith,*
was an action for interest on the purchase money. The
plaintiff had, by his agreement, undertaken to deliver an
abstract and deduce a clear title within a month from being
required so to do. That time being therefore uncertain,
and one which might not arrive till after the day fixed for
the payment of the interest, it was held that the delivery
of the abstract and deduction of a clear title did not form
a condition precedent to the right to require payment of
the interest.

In *Thames Haven Dock Co.* v. *Brymer,* 5 Ex. 696 (1850),
Patteson, J., after quoting the first rule under *Pordage* v.
Cole, said, p. 710: "Applying this rule to the present case we
find the deed is dated the 22nd of April, 1841. The covenant of Bromley is to deduce good title to the premises

(not saying *when*), and, on or before the 25th of March, 1844, on payment by the company of £2,936 17s. 9d., to execute a proper conveyance. It is plain, therefore, that the execution of the conveyance and the payment of the money were intended to be concurrent acts. The day for the payment of the money could not happen before the thing which was the consideration for it, viz., the execution of the conveyance, was to be performed. The conveyance was to be prepared by the company. So far as regards the execution of a conveyance by Bromley, an averment of readiness and willingness on his part to execute it, if it had been prepared by the company, might be sufficient to entitle the assignees to maintain this action for not preparing the conveyance and paying the money; but the company contend that they could not prepare a conveyance until a good title had been deduced by Bromley according to his covenant; therefore that such deduction of title was necessarily a condition precedent. We are of opinion that they are right in so contending. The recitals to be introduced into the conveyance, and even the names of the persons who were to be parties to it, could not be known to the company with any certainty until the title had been deduced. Then follows the averment in the declaration, that Bromley and the assignees were ready to have deduced a good title, but that the company discharged Bromley and the plaintiffs, as such assignees, from deducing such good title as aforesaid, and from the execution of such conveyance as aforesaid," &c., &c.

Yates v. *Gardner*, 20 L. J. Exch. 327, adds nothing. There the defendant was to pay the purchase money on a day certain, which was more than six years before action, and the plaintiff was, upon payment of the purchase money, to convey, an agreement which, had there been nothing else, provided for concurrent acts, as pointed out by Patteson, J., in the judgment I have just read. But after the day fixed for payment, and within six years, the defendant signed an account stated in which he acknowledged the purchase money to be due as cash. He was not

allowed to resist payment on the ground that no deed had
been tendered.   The main question was the Statute of
Limitations.

Manby v. *Cremonini*, 6 Ex. 808 (1851). The plaintiff in consideration of £90 paid by the defendant at
the time of signing the agreement, and of the further sum
of £820 to be paid on the 1st of November then next,
agreed to sell to the defendant a messuage, and the defendant agreed to purchase the same and to pay to the plaintiff the residue of the purchase money on the 1st of
November then next, and that thereupon a conveyance of
the premises should be made to the defendant by all
proper parties, by and at the expense of the plaintiff. The
plaintiff agreed to deduce a good marketable title, and
there was a provision for payment of interest in case the
completion of the purchase should be delayed either by the
plaintiff or the defendant beyond the 1st of November,
the defendant being entitled to the rents and profits and
to the possession of the premises on and from that day.
It was held that the defendant was not bound to pay the
money on the 1st of November unless the plaintiff had
made out a good title, and unless the plaintiff was also
ready to execute a conveyance at his own expense.

Upon the whole I am of the opinion that the views of
the law enunciated in *Marsden* v. *Moore*, in place of conflicting with the earlier decisions, are in harmony with the
general current of authority, and that they relieve us from
any fear of violating settled rules of construction when
we give effect to what we cannot avoid feeling to have
been the real understanding of the parties to this contract,
by holding that the plaintiff is not entitled to demand
payment of the money now sued for without performing
his part of the contract by making a good conveyance of
the land, or at least deducing such title as will enable the
defendants to prepare and tender a deed for execution.
Until this is done it cannot be truthfully affirmed that the
plaintiff is ready and willing to convey. That issue was
for him to establish, and it was a material issue. Having

failed to establish it, he was properly nonsuited, and therefore this appeal should be allowed, with costs.

ROSE, J.—Upon the most careful consideration that I
have been able to give this case, I am unable to conclude
that it was the intention of the parties, as it may be drawn
from the agreement, that the plaintiff should be entitled to
enforce payment of the $40,795 without being ready, that
is able and willing, to convey the land, and that the
defendants should be left to rely upon their action to compel conveyance, or for damages in the event of the plaintiff
being unable to convey.

We are entitled to look at the circumstances surrounding
the parties at the time of making the contract. It appears
that the subject matter was land, the price of which was
rapidly fluctuating. It would have startled the defendants, if, immediately upon making the contract, they had
been told that they had bound themselves to pay the
money on the day named whether the plaintiff was or was
not ready and willing then to convey. They and all
parties well knew it was essential that immediately upon
paying the money the deed should be given, and that in
all probability the vendees would, before the day of payment, have sold their interest relying upon obtaining the
deed so soon as the money was ready.

I incline to the view that the defendants had a right to
call upon the plaintiff to make title immediately upon the
signing of the contract, and to obtain a deed reciting the
agreement to pay the $40,795, and cotemporaneously
with receiving the deed to give back the mortgage.

I do not gather from the conduct of the parties that
this was their intention, but it seems to me it was the
defendants' right, and that therefore the payment of the
$40,795 was to be made after the time for making title
and giving the deed.

It further seems to me it would have been the proper
course for the defendants at once upon the signing of the
agreement to have demanded an abstract and made requisi-

tions on title preparatory to the expiry of the sixty days, so that, when that day arrived, they would have been in a position to accept the deed, a good title having been shewn, or to reject it because no title had been shewn.

It does not become necessary to determine in this case whether, not having demanded an abstract, or availed themselves of the opportunity of investigating the title during the sixty days, they were in a position thereafter to demand proof from the plaintiff, he having sued for the instalment then due, or whether the *onus* was not then shifted on them to shew that the plaintiff had no title.

Amid such diversity of views as appears in this case, I desire to confine my opinion to the facts stated in the evidence so as to enable me to say whether in my judgment the nonsuit was right.

I therefore express no opinion as to the above question, because the plaintiff, as has been pointed out, has in the evidence furnished by him, appearing on cross-examination as part of his case, clearly shewn that one Mr. Daniel Young was, at the time of making the agreement and of the trial, a part owner of the property.

The plaintiff not only shewed no title to the property, but shewed title out of himself as to part. He does not state what part. For all that appears it may have been the greater part.

The plaintiff thus stood before the Court, asking that the defendants be ordered at once to pay $40,795, and at the same time he admitted that part of the property he sold for that sum never was his, and did not shew or suggest he had any control over it, or the power to command its conveyance to the defendants if the Court made the order for the defendants to pay.

On what principle of justice could the plaintiff hope for judgment on such a state of facts? Surely he could not expect any favour if he thus closed his case, not taking the trouble to inform the court as to how gross injustice would not be done in ordering the defendants to pay him for that which he had not, and did not even suggest he could obtain.

I observe that in the reasons against appeal it is stated
that plaintiff's counsel offered at the trial and before the
Divisional Court, and therein repeated his offer, if there
was any *bond fide* contention as to title, to have the money
paid into court until conveyance made and title shewn
to be satisfactory.

Such offer does not appear in the notes of evidence, but
assuming that it was understood to be made, it amounted
to nothing. If he had asked to have the trial postponed
to enable him to shew title, stating that his evidence
placed him in a false position, no doubt, on terms he might
have had the relief. Indeed the dismissal of the action
was without prejudice to the right to bring another action,
and so he had the privilege of shewing title or that he had
power to make or obtain a conveyance, if such power
existed.

But he asserted that on such evidence as it stood he had
the right to judgment, and, failing in so convincing the
learned judge at the trial, moved the Divisional Court.

I do not see how on such a state of facts he was entitled
to judgment, and therefore concur in holding that the
judgment of the learned judge at the trial was right and
must be restored.

I have not referred to the authorities, which I have
carefully considered, as they are so fully digested by my
learned Brother Patterson, who, as well as my learned
Brother Burton, states their general result.

I may be allowed to state my conclusion in almost the
identical words of Lord Tenterden, C. J., in *Roper* v.
Coombes, 6 B. & C. 534, found in my learned brother
Patterson's judgment. "It was but reasonable that the
defendants should not pay so large a sum [$40,795] with-
out knowing that the plaintiff had power to complete his
part of the contract. No evidence of his right was given
and at the time of trial it was proved, on the contrary,
that he had no such right, at least as to a portion of the
interest in the property." Under such circumstances I
think that the defendants were entitled to judgment.

And varying slightly the language of Lord Kenyon, in *Goodisson* v. *Nunn*, 4 T. R. 761, also cited. It would be absurd to say that the vendor might enforce payment of the purchase money without being in a position to give a deed and compel the purchaser to have recourse to him, who perhaps might be an insolvent person.

I agree that the appeal must be allowed, with costs.

Appeal allowed with costs, [HAGARTY, C. J. O., dissenting.]

THE GRIP PRINTING AND PUBLISHING COMPANY OF TORONTO v. BUTTERFIELD.

Patent—Infringement of patent—Want of novelty—Estoppel.

In 1882, one C. obtained a patent for what he called "The Paragon Counter Check Book," which, in his application, he stated to be "In a black leaf check book of double leaves, one half of which are bound together, while the other half fold in as fly leaves, both being perforated across so that they can be readily torn out, the combination of the black leaf bound into the book next the cover and provided with [a] tape across its ends ; the said black leaf having the transferring composition on one of its sides only."

In anticipation of procuring such patent, C. had, in January, 1882, sold one-half thereof to the defendant with whom he entered into partnership ; and on the 31st of July following, formally assigned such half interest to him, which, on a dissolution of such partnership four months afterwards, he re-assigned to C., who the same day assigned the whole interest to the plaintiffs.

Prior to such dissolution the defendant applied for and obtained a patent of what he called " Butterfield's Improved Paragon Check Book," which embodied several things claimed to be improvements on previous books, and defendant avowedly thereunder proceeded with the manufacture of books. The plaintiffs thereupon instituted proceedings to restrain such manufacture by the defendant, claiming the same to be an infringement of their patent, and at the trial of that action, Boyd, C., granted the relief prayed.

On appeal, this Court, while holding that the acts of the defendant amounted to an infringement of the patent granted to C., reversed the judgment of the Chancellor on the ground that such patent was void for want of novelty ; and that the defendant was not estopped by his conduct from shewing that the patent was void.

AN appeal by the defendant from the judgment of Boyd, C., of the 12th January, 1882.

The plaintiffs claimed under an assignment from one John Robert Carter, the original patentee, the exclusive right of making, using, selling, &c., an invention known as "The Paragon Black Leaf Check Book," and brought this action to restrain the defendant from infringing their patented right, by the sale of certain copying books and black leaf check books, and for damages.

The defendant also claimed to have a patent for an invention under which he made and sold a certain kind of black leaf check book, and which he contended was not an infringement or colourable imitation of the plaintiffs' patent, and he also contended that there was no novelty in the plaintiffs' patent.

By the seventh and eighth paragraphs of the statement of defence, the defendant alleged:

"That at the time of the issue of the patent assigned as alleged to the plaintiffs by said Carter, counter check books similar to those for which a patent issued to said Carter had been in use in the Province of Upper Canada, and in the Dominion of Canada, the user of said books having extended over a long period of years. 8. The defendant's patent is for a new and useful invention, of which he is the sole inventor, and not an infringement as aforesaid, or colourable imitation of the plaintiffs' or said Carter's patent."

The action was tried at Toronto on the 21st December, 1882, and judgment was pronounced in the plaintiffs' favour by Boyd, C., on the 12th January, 1883, as follows:

The relation of the two patents in this case appears to me to be substantially what is pointed out as an original patent and an improvement by Mr. Justice Crompton in *Betts* v. *Menzies*, 1 Ell. and Ell. at p. 1019: "Where there is an original patent and an improvement is made upon it, a patent may be taken out for the improvement, and then, by getting a license from the old patentee, the inventor may work the whole process. But I doubt whether this could be so in a case where the original patent was wide enough to include the subsequent improvement; where, in fact, the supposed improvement is but one of a great number of modes in which the old invention might originally have been carried out." An improvement must be something in addition to the first invention, which will not be the case if what is said to be invented amount to nothing more than a description of the best mode of applying the first invention. Now, here the single point of difference between the counter check-book made by the plaintiffs under their patent, and one of the kind made by the defendant, is, that the black carbon leaf is in the plaintiffs' bound into the book next to the upper cover, and in the defendant's it is bound into the book next to the lower cover. That is to say, instead of being fastened by binding at the upper side of the stubs, it is brought round and fastened by binding on the under side of the stubs. In the plaintiffs' specification the mode of fastening is described thus : " The black leaf is bound in with the other leaves, but next to the cover," and by the defendant's thus : " Bind the black leaf between the lower leaf of the book and the lower cover." The defendant says in his specifications he is aware of other books in which the black leaf is bound next to the upper cover, and proposes a different arrangement, presumably for the purpose of introducing his alleged improvements of the membrane at the back of the black leaf where it turns round the end of the stubs, so as to form a hinge, and the elastic fastening of the stubs. These improvements, it may be, are patentable, but the taking of all the rest of the plaintiffs' combination, and merely changing the point of attachment of the black leaf to the under instead of the upper cover is not justifiable : *Dudgeon* v. *Thompson*, 3 App. Cas. 34; *Harrison* v. *Anderston Foundry Co.*, 1 App. Cas. 574; *Sellers* v. *Dickinson*, 5 Ex. 312 ; *Cannington* v. *Nuttall*, L. R. 5 H. L. C. 205.

Neither party uses the tape which is described in the earlier patent. That, it seems to me, is an immaterial element, which, being rejected, still leaves the plaintiffs' patent as workable and useful as it is with the tape. The combination is the same in its working and its results with or without the tape. The books were made under the patent without the tape during the period of the defendant's partnership with the patentee, and he cannot be heard to say that the non-user or the rejection of this part destroys the patent or materially affects its combination of parts : *Chambers* v. *Crichley*, 33 Beav. 374. So far as I can judge upon the papers and the evidence the defendant is making substantially the same kind of books as the plaintiffs under their patent with some slight modifications, which may or may not be improvements, and as to which I have no evidence.

Copeland v. *Webb*, 11 W. R., 134, is an authority for the position that, under the old practice, the Court of Chancery might decline to interfere by interlocutory injunction where there was a contest to be determined between an earlier and a later patent for the same subject matter. The Court formerly would send such a matter to law to be tried there, but now everything is dealt with in the one suit, and I see no good reason for protecting a defendant any more than a plaintiff, who seeks to claim privileges under a patent if it appears that it covers the same ground as a prior patent.

The issue is raised here by the 7th paragraph of the statement of defence and the joinder of issue, whether the defendant's patent is an infringement of the plaintiffs'. It is not necessary to determine that, but if it were, and it appears that the two were for the same invention, there would be jurisdiction without more to declare the defendant's patent void : *Morgan* v. *Seaward*, 2 M. & W. 544, 561, and cases cited : *Saxby* v. *Hennett*, L. R. 8 Ex. 210.

Judgment is for the plaintiffs, as to the books similar to Exhibit " O," made by the defendant, with costs.

The appeal was heard on the 19th of February, 1884.[*]
The other facts in the case are fully stated in the judgment on the present appeal.

Moss, Q. C., and *Kingsford*, for the appellant. The plaintiffs did not, by their pleadings or evidence in the Court below, attempt to impeach the validity of the patent issued to the appellant, although they had express notice that he intended to rely upon it. They did not attack it, neither did they set up that such patent was void, as being in any way an infringement of that held by the respondents, nor did they seek to avoid it, or shew that the defendant was not working according to his patent, or was infringing in any way the plaintiffs' combination; and we contend that so long as the appellant's patent was not impeached, and it was shewn that, in manufacturing the books claimed to be an infringement of the alleged patent of the plaintiffs, he was working in accordance with his own patent, the plaintiffs were not in a position to succeed against him.

If the plaintiffs are right in their views their proper course was to impeach the defendant's patent by *scire facias*. Here it is shewn that the plaintiffs' alleged patent was simply for a combination, and their own evidence shews that they were disregarding their patent by not working their combination or making use thereof, and although the plaintiffs contend that while dispensing with the tape mentioned in their alleged patent they were using the black leaf spoken of in the evidence as a mechanical equivalent for such tape, yet the evidence shews that such black leaf was not a mechanical equivalent, but simply an omission of that element in the combination; that is, they omitted to use the tape which was intended to give their alleged patent its novelty, so that the plaintiffs could not rely upon their alleged patent, the same not being adapted according to their own evidence and admissions for the purpose intended. In other words the plaintiffs' alleged patent has been shewn to be void for want of novelty, and as such the alleged invention was incapable of being patented, and could not form the subject of a patent.

Cassels, Q. C., for the respondents. It is not necessary for the plaintiffs to impeach the defendant's patent by *sci. fa*, as contended for by the appellant. The defendant called no evidence, but relied on the case as shewn by the plaintiffs. The plaintiffs' patent is prior, in point of date, to that of the defendant, and the plaintiffs' case is established by the simple production of the patent referred to in the statement of claim, and which was assigned to the plaintiffs.

Such production proves the invention and the novelty, and in addition the plaintiffs established beyond doubt that the defendant was infringing upon their patent. It can form no justification for the defendant to establish that a subsequent patent has been issued patenting the invention claimed by the defendant. The plaintiffs have nothing to do with the patent issued to the defendant. Their case is established upon proof of their patent and that the defendant has infringed it.

The patent set up by the defendant as a justification for his wrongful act is not in any way one patenting the article manufactured by the plaintiffs. In the specifications of that patent, the article is described by what is claimed as an improvement in the binding of the book. The patent is for an improvement, and such patent does not justify the use by the defendant of the article patented to the plaintiffs.

Had the defendant obtained from the plaintiffs the right to use their invention he could then apply to such article his own improvement, but without such right the defendant is entitled to nothing more than the improvement, and cannot appropriate the invention of the plaintiffs. The non-user of the tape referred to is immaterial. It in no way affects the invention patented to the plaintiffs.

The defendant and Carter, the original patentee, when in partnership, manufactured books without the tape, and the defendant will not be allowed to raise the contention now put forward, namely, that he is not infringing. The defendant cannot be heard to deny the validity of the patent on the ground of want of novelty, there being no evidence whatever shewing want of novelty.

The authorities cited are mentioned in the judgment in the Court below.

September 5, 1884. PATTERSON, J.A.—The plaintiffs charge the defendant with infringing a patent which belongs to them by making and vending a particular kind of counter check book.

The patent asserted by the plaintiffs is one which was granted on 15th February, 1882, to one Carter, for an invention called the Paragon Counter Check Book.

Carter had, in January, 1882, in anticipation of the patent, sold half his interest in the invention to the defendant, and had formed a partnership with the defendant which lasted only six months. It was dissolved by deed dated 27th July, 1882.

After the issue of the patent, Carter had, on 31st March, 1882, formally assigned to the defendant the half interest in the patent; and the defendant, by a deed executed contemporaneously with the deed of dissolution, reassigned to Carter all the right, title, and interest in the patent which had passed to him by the deed of 31st March; and on the same day Carter assigned the patent to the plaintiffs.

The defendant obtained, on the 12th July 1882, a patent for another check book which he called "Butterfield's Improved Paragon Check Book." It embodies several things which are claimed to be improvements on the style of books previously in use. The plaintiffs do not of course, complain of the use of these improvements; but they say that they are merely additions to Carter's patent. Their complaint is of the use of the defendant's book as far as it infringes Carter's patent.

The learned Chancellor has found that there is an infringement, and I agree with him.

In Carter's specification he states the object of his invention to be to provide a check book, in which the black leaf used for transferring writing from one page to another need not be handled, and will not have a tendency to curl up after a number of leaves have been torn out. And he says it consists essentially of a black leaf check book composed of double leaves, one half of which are bound together, while the other half are folded in as fly leaves, both being perforated across so that they can be readily torn out; the black leaf being bound into the book next to the cover and provided with a tape bound across its end; the black leaf having the transferring composition on one of its sides only.

Then he thus states what he claims as his invention :

" In a black leaf check book of double leaves, one half of which are bound together, while the other half folds in as fly leaves, both being perforated across so that they can readily be torn out, the combination of the black leaf bound into the book next to the cover, and provided with the tape bound across its end, the said black leaf having the transferring composition on one of its sides only."

This combination, it will be observed, relates entirely to the use of the black leaf. It is to be used in a book, the character of which is not in other respects alleged to be novel.

The combination is of three things : 1st. The leaf is to be bound into the book next the cover ; 2nd. It is to be provided with a tape to use in turning it over ; 3rd. It is to have the black composition on one side only.

The result aimed at is, that the salesman using the book does not dirty his fingers as he would do if he handled the black leaf, or had to touch the blackened side of it ; and this use of the leaf, as well as the convenient employment of it in producing the duplicate entry, is facilitated by its position next the cover, instead of, as in some books, in the centre of the leaves, and by its being fastened in place of being loose.

It was found that the tape was unnecessary, because the fly-leaf could be used for the purpose of turning over the black leaf without touching it with the hand, and the books made by Carter and plaintiffs, under the patent, have therefore been made without the tape.

The book made by the defendant is essentially the same as Carter's book in the two particulars of the blackening of the leaf on one side only, and its position in the book. One of his improvements is in the mode of attaching the leaf to the cover. He does this by means of a thin membrane, which forms a sort of hinge connecting the leaf with the lower cover of the book, and which is also made to protect the stub of the check from being soiled by the leaf; but the position of the leaf, when in use, is next to the upper cover just as in Carter's patent, and the mode of using the leaf is precisely alike in both books.

But the defendant contends that even though he infringes the plaintiffs' patent he is not liable, for two or three reasons.

He alleges that he manufactures his books under his own patent, and he says that his patent is not an infringement of that of Carter, nor a colourable imitation thereof, or upon the principle thereof, save in some minor points of detail, as to which, he says, Carter was not the first inventor.

An argument was addressed to us on the subject of conflicting patents, and as to the necessity of proceeding by *sci. fa.* to impeach the defendant's patent, or at least for specifically pleading the objections to it.

But before the defendant can insist upon our considering those matters he is required to prove his allegations of fact concerning his patent, and this, I think, he has failed to do.

He claims as his invention three things:

First. A kind of type; *Secondly.* "The membrane hinge for a black leaf, the whole bound by an elastic band to the ends or sides of the lower cover as described, and for the purposes specified." *Thirdly.* A totalling sheet.

He may make and use all these things without by their use encroaching on the ground covered by Carter's patent. I do not see even a plausible pretence for saying that the defendant's patent by its terms assumes to protect him in respect of the acts of which the plaintiffs complain as infringements.

Then the defendant charges that the Carter invention was wanting in novelty; and further, that inasmuch as he has not used the tape, which is one part of the patented combination, he has not infringed the patent.

The plaintiffs urge that the defendant is estopped by the dealing between him and Carter from disputing the validity of Carter's patent.

I can find no good reason for adopting this position, whether we understand an estoppel to depend upon the relation between the parties or upon the effect of a deed.

In this case all that took place was, that Carter, having assigned to the defendant an undivided interest in the patent, the defendant retained it while they were partners, and upon the dissolution re-assigned simply what he had received, without giving any covenant and without asserting by recital or otherwise the validity of the patent. No case has been cited to us which, in my judgment, gives countenance to the assertion of an estoppel under such circumstances as these, and the judgment of Malins, V.C., in *Axmann* v. *Lund*, L. R. 18 Eq. 330, is very much against it. But even if there were better reasons than can be gathered from the nature of the dealings with this patent, for holding that the defendant, having once acquired from the patentee, and afterwards re-assigned to him a limited interest in the patent, had brought himself within the principles acted upon in cases like *Chambers* v. *Crichley*, 33 Beav. 374, so as to estop himself for ever from disputing the validity of the patent, it must be remembered that that was the patent for the combination of three things. What he now asserts is, that the combination of two of those three is not protected by this patent, because not a new and useful invention. He may be right, or he may be wrong in this assertion ; but he cannot be estopped from raising the question by any admission, express or implied, that the full combination described in the patent was a patentable invention.

To test the objection made by the defendant we must look again at the patent and specification from which I have already quoted the essential portions. One of the three features of the combination is, the leaving one side of the carbon leaf unblackened. I have not been able to satisfy myself that this feature contributes to the general result proposed by the specification. A leading object, as put forth, is, that the black leaf need not be handled. That desideratum was to be attained by the use of the tape ; and it is now said that the fly leaf can be used as an equivalent for the tape. If an equivalent, it of course effects the same purpose, viz., makes it unnecessary to handle the black leaf. If that leaf is not to be handled, it will not soil the hands, whether blackened only on one side or both. But as the leaf is fastened and the duplicate writing is produced by its lower side, there is no object in blackening the upper side. This is a sufficient reason for blackening one side only.

It is not so stated in the specification. No reason is there given, and the draftsman has even left it to be inferred that the leaf is to be bound in the book with the blackened side undermost. It seems impossible, without proceeding merely upon conjecture, to find a use in connection with the professed object of the invention, for the omission to blacken the upper side of the leaf; and, as I have just remarked, that omission is sufficiently explained by the circumstance that the carbon on the upper side of the leaf would have no office to perform. It has no more connection with the result than painting the side red would have.

We have thus one of the three things, namely, the tape eliminated altogether, its office being performed by using another thing, namely, the fly leaf, which was not new, and was not substituted in combination with the other things as an equivalent for the tape, but was a part of the book as it stood before the combination was devised.

We have in a second thing, namely, the omission of the carbon from one side of the leaf, an incident suggested by the absence of any use for blackening that side, but not anything that combines with the other things to produce the proposed result. That result would be produced if the leaf were blackened on both sides.

We have left only the third thing, namely the fastening of the leaf to the cover ; and this by itself, even if it were new, could not support a patent which is for a combination.

To uphold this as a patent infringed by the acts of the defendant, we must decide first that the attaching of the carbon leaf in a counter check book to the cover of the book is a patentable invention ; and, secondly, that it is protected by this patent.

There may not be distinct evidence, and I believe there is not, that books with the leaf so attached were made before Carter made them, though I rather think the specification concedes the fact ; but that is not what is claimed here. The patent has to stand for the combination of those things which the defendant has used, or it cannot, in this action, be asserted against the defendant.

Upon this ground, I think the plaintiffs fail, and that the result must be the allowance of this appeal, and the dismissal of the action. The costs must follow both events.

BURTON, and OSLER, JJ.A., concurred.

SPRAGGE, C.J.O., died before judgment was delivered.

The Cosgrave Brewing and Malting Company of Toronto v. Starrs.

Guarantee to a firm—Death of one partner, effect on surety—Notice to determine guarantee, effect of.

By an agreement under seal made in April, 1879, the defendant guaranteed to C. & Sons, or the members for the time being forming such firm, the price of any goods supplied by C. & Sons to one Q. to the amount of $5,000, and which he agreed should be a continuing guarantee. C. died in September, 1881, after which the sons who were named as executors in his will, carried on the same business under the like firm name until December, 1882, when the assets of the partnership were transferred to the plaintiffs, a joint stock company. Q. continued to obtain goods from the sons, and the plaintiffs since the formation of the joint stock company, until the Spring of 1883.

Meanwhile, and on the 5th of April, 1882, the defendant being dissatisfied with the manner in which Q. was conducting his business, wrote to the firm forbidding them to supply any more goods to Q. under such guarantee :

Held, (1) [affirming the judgment of Rose, J., reported 5 O. R., 189,] that such notice put an end to defendant's liability for any goods subsequently supplied to Q. ; but, *Held*, (2) [reversing the judgment of Rose, J.,] that the death of C. had not that effect, [Burton, J. A., dissenting.]

This was an appeal by the plaintiffs from the judgment of Rose, J. (5 O. R. 189).

The action was brought to recover $5,000 upon an agreement dated the 19th April, 1879, whereby Michael Starrs, the defendant, became security to Messrs. Cosgrave & Sons, brewers, for advances and sales of beer, &c., to be made to one Michael Quinn by Cosgrave & Sons. The statement of claim alleged that the business of Cosgrave & Sons had been assigned to the plaintiffs, and that at the date of the assignment Quinn was indebted to the firm in the sum of $5,000, which they claimed from the defendant.

One of the contentions raised by the defence was, that the defendant had notified the firm of Cosgrave & Sons on the 5th April, 1882, not to furnish Quinn with any more goods. This notice was admitted, but it was alleged by the plaintiffs that it had been withdrawn, and that the defendant had instructed the Cosgraves to continue to supply Quinn.

The action was tried at Toronto on the 18th and 19th days of January, 1884, before Rose, J., and a jury. The only question left to the jury was as to the alleged withdrawal of the notice. The jury said "We find that Mr. Cosgrave received no further instructions from Starrs to supply any more goods under the bond."

On the 21st January, 1884, the defendant moved before Rose, J., for judgment. The argument was then heard and judgment was delivered on the 19th February, 1884, in favour of the defendant.

The agreement in question and the points of law arising thereon, sufficiently appear in the former report, and the judgments delivered in this Court.

The appeal was heard on the 12th and 13th February, 1885. *

Osler, Q. C., and *Eddis*, for the appellants. Under no construction of the agreement entered into between the parties can Starrs be considered released from further liability on the death of Patrick Cosgrave, or by the transfer of the business to the plaintiffs, as the guarantee was given to the firm of Cosgrave & Sons, not only as then constituted by the particular individuals, but to the member or members for the time being constituting that firm, thus indicating that the agreement was intended as security to the business, notwithstanding any change in the membership of the firm, or in the ownership of the business.

We contend that the respondent was not at liberty to give the notice of the 5th April, 1882; and under any circumstances it could not put an end to the liability unless accompanied by an offer to pay what was then due from Quinn to Cosgrave & Sons; and in any event the appellants are entitled to judgment for what was due at the time such notice was given, and in that case there should be a reference to ascertain the amount.

Moss, Q. C., and *Aylesworth*, for the respondent. By the

*Present.—HAGARTY, C.J.O., BURTON, PATTERSON, and OSLER, JJ.A.

terms of the instrument in question the respondent was liable only to Patrick Cosgrave, John Cosgrave, and Lawrence Joseph Cosgrave, for goods supplied to Michael Quinn, by or on behalf of the three of them; and after the death of Patrick Cosgrave, which took place on the 6th of September, 1881, the liability of the respondent ceased, and did not extend to subsequent dealings between Quinn and the surviving partners, or either of them. Quinn's agreement extended only to purchases from the three Cosgraves, and the respondent only guaranteed the fulfilment of that covenant.

The evidence in the case, and the books of the appellants, as also those of the firm of Cosgrave and Sons, clearly establish that all goods furnished before the death of Patrick Cosgrave were paid for in full.

Besides, we contend that the appellants are not the assignees of the bond sued on, and are not entitled to maintain an action thereon. It was not disputed at the trial, and the books of the appellants clearly shew, that the account of Quinn, before and after the assignment to William James Douglas, the trustee of the appellants, was kept as one continuous account, and that, after such assignment, payments were made by Quinn, and credits given to him on the account which satisfied and discharged all items of the account prior to the giving of the notice of the 5th of April, 1882, and all items of the account prior to the assignment to the trustee.

Pease v. *Hirst*, 10 B. & C. 122; *Morss* v. *Gleason*, 9 N. Y. S. Ct. (Hun.) 31; *Mason* v. *Bickle*, 2 A. R. 291; *Hopkinson* v. *Rolt*, 9 H. L. Cas. 514; *Burgess* v. *Eve*, L. R. 13 Eq. 450; *Phillips* v. *Foxhall*, L. R. 7 Q. B. 666; *Harriss* v. *Fawcett*, L. R. 8 Ch. 866; *Wheatley* v. *Bastow*, 7 D. M. & G. 261; *Lloyd's* v. *Harper*, 16 Ch. D. 290; *Lindley* on Partnership, 3rd ed. p. 223, were referred to.

April 17, 1885. HAGARTY, C. J. O.—If I be compelled to accede to the result arrived at in the able and most careful judgment of my brother Rose, I feel that in all human probability I am defeating the real intention of the parties to the deed, as evidenced by the language used.

The Cosgraves, father and two sons, carried on business in Toronto as brewers, under the name and firm of " Cosgrave & Sons," and are so described as the parties of the first part. The defendant declares that he shall be " a continuing security to the said parties of the first part, or to the member or members for the time being constituting the said firm of Cosgrave & Sons ;" and his covenant with them is that he will " pay to the said parties of the first part, or to the member or members for the time being constituting the said firm of Cosgrave & Sons," for all ale, &c., to be sold from time to time " by the said parties of the first part, or the said firm of Cosgrave & Sons, or by any member thereof."

I think that in plain popular language the parties to this deed must have intended to continue this security beyond any such event as the death of one of the three persons composing the firm—the others carrying on the business as before.

It is suggested that what was in contemplation might be the case if a provision, sometimes to be found in copartnership deeds, providing that the death of a partner shall not operate as a dissolution ; and in such a case the words here used would have a due meaning attachable to them.

I cannot satisfy myself on this. Firstly, because the existence of any such provision, or of any written or other special partnership bargain between the Cosgraves was not shewn. Secondly, that as far as my experience goes I cannot think that the existence of any such provision could have reasonably influenced these contracting parties in using such words as we find here. What was meant then by such words as " members for the time being constituting the firm ?"

What was the " firm " in mercantile or popular phraseology ?

The Imperial Dictionary defines: Firm, " a partnership or house, or the name or title under which a company transacts business."

Wharton: " Firm—The name or names under which any house of trade is established."

Sweet's Law Dictionary (1882) : " Firm denotes, 1. The style or title under which one or several persons carry on business. 2. The partnership itself, that is the individual members forming the partnership."

He then quotes Lindley.

In Lindley (3rd ed.) vol. i., p. 213, it is said : " Merchants and lawyers have different notions respecting the nature of a firm. Commercial men and accountants are apt to look upon a firm in the light in which lawyers look upon a corporation, *i. e.*, as a body distinct from the members composing it, and having rights and obligations distinct from those of its members. * * Owing to this impersonification of the firm, there is a tendency to regard its rights and obligations as unaffected by the introduction of a new partner or by the death or retirement of an old one. Notwithstanding such changes amongst its members, the *firm* is considered as continuing the same ; and the rights and obligations of the old firm are regarded as continuing in favour of or against the new firm as if no changes had occurred * *. But this is not the legal notion of a firm. The firm is not recognized by lawyers as in any way distinct from the members composing it. * * The law, ignoring the firm, looks to the partners composing it ; any change among them destroys the identity of the firm ; what is called the property of the firm is their property, and what are called the debts and liabilities of the firm are their debts and their liabilities."

Mr. Lindley refers to the second edition of *Cory's* Practical Treatise on Accounts, which he calls "a valuable work, not so widely known as it should be."

Mr. Cory, at page 71, says : "The mercantile notion of a partnership is simply that it is a kind of corporation. The *firm* is always regarded as a kind of impersonification.

And though the Courts have not suffered traders to carry out the principle to its full and necessary extent, yet whenever the Crown or Legislature have established trading companies, such companies have always been impressed with the character of a corporation."

The subject is there very fully discussed.

In Lindley, (3rd ed.) p. 226, it is said : "A security given to a firm for advances to be made by it, is, upon a change of the firm, readily made a continuing security ; and a slight manifestation of intention on the part of the borrower that it should so continue will enable the new firm to hold the securities until the advances made by itself, as well as those made by the old firm, have been repaid."

I have read the very numerous cases cited and commented on by my learned brother Rose, and I fully recognize their authority. My difficulty is, to hold that they govern the case before us. No one of them contains words such as create the contest here. If we act on the law as laid down in the cases cited we give, in my humble judgment, no effect to the words here appearing. We must use the words, as I hold, in their mercantile and commercial sense, and as they would be understood by business men, such as the parties to this suit. I think they understood them and the use of the word "firm" as a kind of "impersonification," a business of a known nature, as suggested in Lindley and in Cory.

I have not met words of this character in many cases.

In *Ex parte Loyd*, 3 Dea. 305, the memorandum accompanying a deposit of title deeds stated it to be a security for the payment of the running balance which may be accruing "to you or any of you alone, or with any other partner or partners." Erskine, C. J., held that the argument that it did not extend the security to a change of the firm, was perfectly untenable, that it was evidently intended to apply to any state of the firm whether the number of partners increased or diminished. Cross, J., said : "It would be absurd to hold that the memorandum of deposit did not operate as a security to the four continuing partners."

I find words like these in a bond to partners in *Re Kensington*, 2 Ves. & Bea. 79, but Lord Eldon's judgment did not turn on them, but rather on the general effect of equitable deposits continuing on a change of partners where the advances continued to be made.

One of the cases often referred to was *Barclay* v. *Lucas*, cited in 1 T. R. 291n. This case has been more than once questioned, and can hardly be considered an authority.

But if the bond there had contained the words found in this agreement, would it ever have been questioned?

It was recited that the plaintiffs had agreed to take P. J. into their service and employ him as a clerk in their shop and counting-house, and the surety bound himself in £500, with a defeazance if P. J. should faithfully account and pay to the plaintiffs all sums that he should receive in their service. They were bankers and after this admitted another partner.

The Court held the surety liable for defaults after the admission of the new partner.

Lord Mansfield, C. J., Willes and Buller, JJ., considered it was the manifest intention of the parties that the liability should continue.

If after the words "account and pay to the plaintiffs," there had been our words, " or to the member or members for the time being constituting such firm," I think the authority of the case would never have been questioned.

In the case cited of *Strange* v. *Lee*, 3 East 484, 491, Lawrence, J., agreeing that the surety was discharged by the death of one of the partners, says: "A bond may be drawn * * for the obligor to be answerable not only to the present but to all future partners in the house; but that has not been done here."

Lord Ellenborough in the case cited of *Metcalf* v. *Bruin*, 12 East. 400, speaking of the bond given to the trustees for the Globe Company for the fidelity of a clerk, during his continuance in the service of the company, says p. 406:

"It must therefore have been intended to secure the faithful performance of the service to a succession of masters, who might from time to time constitute the company," and at p. 404 he asks, why may not the word company have been used in its popular sense?

The only question is upon the fair meaning of the words used in the obligation. We must put upon the word company "the sense in which the parties themselves used it." (p. 405).

The provision in the Imperial Mercantile Amendment Act, 19 & 20 Vict. ch. 97, sec. 4, is not copied into our statute. It is said, in *Backhouse* v. *Hall*, 6 B. & S, 507, by Lord Blackburn, that it does not alter the law of England. Its language, therefore, may be referred to.

Section 4 provides that a promise to answer for the debt of another made to a firm consisting of two or more persons, &c., shall not be binding in respect of anything done or omitted after a change in any of the persons composing the firm, or in the persons trading under the name of a firm, "unless the intention of the parties, that such promise shall continue to be binding notwithstanding such change, shall appear either by express stipulation or by necessary implication from the nature of the firm or otherwise."

I accept this as a statement of the law of England, as Lord Blackburn properly holds it to be, or, at all events, as he says, as following the decisions.

I am of opinion that the contract before us does, by express stipulation, prevent the ceasing of the obligation by the death of the one partner.

I agree with the judgment below that the obligation did not extend beyond the formation of the company out of the old firm and new shareholders into an incorporated firm.

The case cited of *Dance* v. *Girdler*, 1 B. & P. N. R. 34, is in point.

Groux's Soap Co. v. *Cooper*, 8 C. B. N. S. 800, cited in Lindley 225, qualifies this in the case of changes and amalgamations in companies under statutes, &c.

This view of the appeal compels me to consider the
effect of the notice found by the jury to have been given by
defendant 5th April, 1882, not to supply the principal with
more goods on his credit.

Patrick Cosgrave died in September, 1881 : the notice
was given 5th April, 1882, some seven months after the
death.

I think the law on this head has never been very clearly
settled. The latest case in which it has been discussed
seems to be *Lloyd's* v. *Harper*, 16 Ch. D. 290, (1880.)

The guarantee was not under seal, and it was held that
the death of the guarantor did not revoke it, as the consideration on which it was given operated once for all,
viz.: the admission of the surety's son as an underwriting
member of Lloyd's.

James, L. J., says, on the general question, p. 314: "It may
be considered equitable and right, that where a man is not
under any obligation to make further advances or to sell
further goods, a person who has guaranteed repayment of such
advances, or payment of the price of the goods, may say;
'Do not sell any further goods, or make any other advances:
I give you warning that you are not to rely upon my
guarantee for any further advances which you make or
any further goods you sell.' That might be in many cases
a very equitable view. It perhaps might be hardly equitable for a banker or merchant to go on making advances
after receiving a distinct notice from the guarantor that he
would not be further liable."

Cotton, L. J., (p. 315) speaks to somewhat the same effect,
but declines to decide it, as it was not then necessary.

Lush, L. J., says as to guaranteeing a running account
with bankers, or for goods supplied, p. 319: "There the consideration is supplied from time to time, and it is reasonable
to hold, unless the guarantee stipulates to the contrary, that
the guarantor may at any time terminate the guarantee.
He remains answerable for all the advances made, or all
the goods supplied upon his guarantee before the notice
to terminate is given ; but at any time he may say ' I put

a stop to this: I do not intend to be answerable any further, therefore do not make more advances or supply any more goods upon my guarantee.' As at present advised, I think it quite competent for a person to do that, where, as I have said, the guarantee is for advances made or goods to be supplied, and where nothing is said in the guarantee about how long it is to endure."

Lush, L. J., also says he fully approves of the decision of Bowen, J., in *Coulthart* v. *Clementson*, 5 Q. B. D. 42.

The guarantee there had a provision that it should continue till three months notice in writing. The surety died, and it was held that his death, with notice thereof, put an end to liability.

Bowen, L. J., says: p. 46 "In the case of such continuing guarantees as the present, it has long been understood, that they are liable, in the absence of anything in the guarantee to the contrary, to be withdrawn on notice."

Various explanations have been offered of this reasonable, though implied, limitation. The guarantee, as has been said, is divisible as to each advance, and ripens as to each advance into an irrevocable promise only when the advance is made. This explanation has received the sanction of the Court of Common Pleas in *Offord* v. *Davies*, 12 C. B. N. S. 748.

Whether the explanation be the true one or not, it is now established by authority that such continuing guarantees can be withdrawn on notice during the life-time of the guarantor, and a limitation to that effect must be read, so to speak, into the contract.

In *Offord* v. *Davies*, the guarantee was to secure the payment of bills to be discounted by plaintiffs for A. B. for the space of twelve months, to the extent of £600. It was held that it could be revoked during the twelve months as to bills not discounted before the revocation: see as to this case, *De Colyar*, 298.

As I have already said, the text writers do not speak with much certainty on the question: *De Colyar*, 297.

It is objected that this security being by deed cannot be discharged by notice.

I hardly think that this can be sustained.

Burgess v. *Eve*, L. R. 13 Eq. 450 (1872), is constantly referred to. In a contract of suretyship under seal the principal had misconducted himself and the surety sought to be relieved and the employers after notice still retained him. Malins, V. C., released the surety on paying up for all previous defaults.

He held that he had a clear equity to be relieved, and that it made no difference that the contract was under seal.

In *Phillips* v. *Foxall*, L. R. 7 Q. B. 666, a surety by an instrument not under seal was held discharged on an equitable plea that the principal had been guilty of dishonesty, not commnnicated by the plaintiff to the surety, &c.

The Court said, p. 677: "The discharge of the surety in the present case seems to us to arise rather out of the nature and equity of the contract between the parties than upon any assumed right of revocation."

It appears to me that in the case before us our deciding in favour of the defendant's discharge after notice must be considered as arising out of the equity of the case, and therefore not barred by any technical rule as to discharging a specialty by any lower document.

On the evidence here it seems that the notice was given by defendant apparently on discovering the true state of the principal's affairs, and the large arrears due to plaintiffs, coupled with the statements as to the principal's personal habits.

The relief to be given to him after or on this notice seems to me to arise as an equity to be released on a contract for supplies of goods furnished from time to time.

We must not omit to notice the distinction taken in the books between such a contract and a contract for the conduct of the principal who obtains a position of trust on the faith of the security, or in such a case as *Lloyd's* v. *Harper*, 16 Ch. D. 290.

On the whole, I have arrived at the conclusion that the reference must be as to the state of the account on April

5th, 1882, when the notice was given, and that defendant's liability then, and not till then, ceased; and that the appeal must, to that extent, be allowed.

BURTON, J. A.—It was possibly intended by the parties who prepared the agreement, which is sued on in this case, to extend the liability of the surety to any sale which might from time to time be made, not only by the persons who at the time of the making the agreement carried on business as brewers under the name, style, and firm of Cosgrave & Sons, but by any persons who might from time to time be admitted as members of the then firm, and associate themselves together, to carry on the business of brewers under that name. Such an agreement might of course be made, but it would require very clear language to warrant a Court extending the liability of a surety to that extent.

The firm then consisted of the father and two sons, and the death of any one of the partners would operate as a dissolution of the firm, unless there was an agreement to the contrary; but we all know that it is a very common thing to provide in articles of partnership that death shall not work a dissolution, but that the business shall be continued by the survivors, they making such compensation or settlement with the representative of the deceased partner as may be provided in the articles.

We have in this view one interpretation which might be placed upon the words which would give full effect to the instrument we are asked to construe.

The agreement is made between the three Cosgraves described as carrying on business as brewers under the name, style, and firm of Cosgrave & Sons, of the first part, Quinn, of the second part, and the surety, of the third part.

It recites an agreement that the parties of the first part should sell to Quinn, ale, beer, &c., on such terms as may be agreed on, and the surety shall be a continuing security to the parties of the first part, or the members for the time being constituting *the said firm* (not as shall be for the

time being members of that or any future firm carrying
on the business under that name, but such of the members
of the firm as shall for the time being constitute the same
firm) to cover and protect any sales now or hereafter
indefinitely to be made by the parties of the first part, or
any member or members of the said firm of Cosgrave &
Sons.

There is not a word here necessarily leading to the
inference that the surety's liability should extend beyond
the sales made by their firm, whether it consisted of the
three members then contracting, or such of their three
members as should still continue to be members of the firm
after the death or retirement of the others.

The next clause is equally consistent with the construction I have referred to; it refers to the security being a
continuing security *to the said firm.*

We then come to the principal debtor's covenant, which
is with the parties of the first part to pay for all the beer
*sold to him from time to time by the parties of the first
part* or any of them.

And then we come to the covenant of the surety, which
is that he will pay for *all such sales,* and that in default of
the principal paying for such sales, he will pay the parties
of the first part, or the members for the time being constituting the said firm of Cosgrave & Sons for all beer, &c.,
that shall from time to time be sold by the parties of the
first part *or the said firm* of Cosgrave & Sons, *or by any
member thereof,* to the party of the second part.

Now there is no doubt upon the general question that
every change in a partnership actually dissolves that partnership, and that all its prospective claims and liabilities
cease as to that partnership, and must have a new commencement in the new one. It is clear and undoubted
law that neither a new partner nor the executor of a
deceased partner can be joined in an action brought by or
against the original or surviving partner. A partner retiring remains liable to all the engagements entered into
before his retiring, and cannot reap any benefit or sustain
any injury from subsequent transactions.

There can arise no difficulty from such a state of the law; the suretyship continues good for all transactions entered into before the dissolution, and the new firm can, if they think it desirable, take a new security or discontinue the account.

There is also no doubt that parties might so frame their covenant as to extend to future partnerships, although there may be difficulties in working out such a covenant. A learned writer has suggested that it might be in this form: "With the partners then existing and the survivor or survivors of them and the executors and administrators of such survivor for the benefit of them and such of them as shall continue in the said trade, and for all other persons who may at any time hereafter become engaged in the said trade under the said style or firm."

But bearing in mind that in the absence of agreement to the contrary, the firm is dissolved by the death of one of its members, I find it very difficult to see how the construction attempted to be placed upon this agreement can prevail. If the partnership came to an end the parties who formed a new partnership upon the death of Patrick do not answer the description of the member or members constituting *the said firm*, they may be carrying on the same kind of business under the same style or designation, but they are not the same firm, as they are a new and distinct firm.

Reference was made to a case of *Barclay* v. *Lucas*, 1 T. R. 291 *n.*, but it may well be questioned whether that case was well decided, and much doubt is cast upon it by Mansfield, C. J., who delivered judgment in *Weston* v. *Barton*, 4 Taunt. 672. The plaintiffs who were bankers, took one P. J. into their service as a clerk in their shop and counting house, and the defendant entered into a bond for his fidelity. A new partner was subsequently admitted, and this was urged as an answer to a breach which occurred subsequently. The Court overruled the objection on the ground that it was a security to the house of the plaintiffs.

No doubt, where it can be clearly gathered that a mere change in the members of the firm is not to affect the liability of the surety, he will not be relieved; but making every allowance for the effect to be given to the language of this contract, does it mean anything more than what I have above suggested, and what was probably present to the mind of the draughtsman; if any of the partners die, and by the terms of the partnership the business is to be carried on by the survivors, this agreement shall continue with the then members of the firm?

If upon the death of Patrick, and the consequent dissolution of the firm, one son had continued the business of brewer at Toronto, and the other at Ottawa under the same name, but as distinct firms, could it be contended for a moment that either of them would be entitled, if he supplied beer to the debtor Quinn, to enforce this agreement? What difference can it make that the two are carrying on the business? It is not the same firm, or as surviving members of the same firm with whom the defendants contracted.

Such cases as *Pease* v. *Hirst*, reported in 10 B. & C. 122, are distinguishable, or, to speak more accurately, serve to illustrate the distinction which I have endeavoured to point out, viz., that although a bond or other instrument may be so framed as to comprehend future as well as present partners, that has not been done in the present case.

The instrument there in question was in the shape of a promissory note; all parties signing it appearing as principals, and the note was not confined to the present members of the firm, but was payable to them or order; all that the partners had to do when taking in a new partner was to indorse it to the new firm. It was evidently intended that it should continue from time to time to be an available security to such persons as afterwards constituted the members of the house, and being a negotiable instrument no further words were necessary to make the intention effectual than making it so payable.

In *Chapman* v. *Beckinton*, 3 Q. B. 703, Lord Denman remarked, p. 720: "We ought to be slow in extending by implication the meaning of words beyond that which they ordinarily bear in legal construction, in order to extend the liability of a surety."

In that case a partnership had been formed between the plaintiff, one W. Chapman, and Potts, in which Potts was to be the acting partner, and the bond there in question was conditioned that Potts, as long as he shall continue the acting partner "in the said trade" of the said co-partnership, should make a true account and pay the balance due to the plaintiff and Chapman.

The defendant was bound for the duration of the partnership in the said trade.

"If," the learned Judge remarked, p. 718, "the partners had wholly changed the nature of their business, it could hardly have been contended that the defendant's liability would have continued; and it can be with as little reason contended that it will continue beyond the duration of that co-partnership; but *the* co-partnership, in the ordinary sense of the term, was dissolved by the death of W. Chapman."

The partnership deed was in that case before the Court. It therein appeared that the partnership was to endure for twenty-one years; and it provided that if any partner, at the end of seven years, desired to retire, the covenants should cease as to him, and various other stipulations providing that a son or the executor of a deceased partner, might be taken into the concern for the remainder of the partnership, so that *inter se* there was no dissolution of the partnership either by death, or the introduction of new members in the manner provided for in the deed.

But the Court in construing the bond by which the liability of the surety was limited, held that as the condition of the bond was for the performance of something to be performed to Chapman and the plaintiff, with no mention of the survivor, assignee, or any other person, the safer construction was to give to the word "co-partner-

ship " its ordinary legal meaning limiting it, that is, in
duration to the period during which the same trade was
carried on by the same three original parties to the union.

That full effect was given to the intention of the parties
to the partnership deed by construing the stipulation in it
as to the introduction of new partners, and the carrying
on the same trade by the new firm as binding *inter se*
without intending to alter the legal consequences of such
change in the members of the firm.

The Court, therefore, held the surety discharged by
the death of one of the members, remarking that they did
not in the least question those decisions where it had
been held that in cases where the surety agreed that his
liability was not to be affected by a change in the members of the firm he would remain liable.

That case is an authority for holding that notwithstanding a stipulation in the partnership deed, as to the partnership continuing *inter se* in the event of the death of some
of the members on the introduction of new members, still
as regards the surety the partnership would come to an
end as regarded him, and his liability would cease in the
absence of clear words in the contract continuing such
liability to the firm carrying on the business.

If the deed of partnership in this case had contained a
provision that the partnership should not be dissolved by
the death of either of the partners, then I do not doubt
that the words here used in the agreement would have
been sufficient to continue the liability of the surety to
the remaining members of the firm, but not to a firm in
which new members had been introduced; but in the
absence of any such stipulation in the deed, the addition
of these words does not, in my opinion, assist the plaintiff.

The agreement was made with the three persons by
name describing them as constituting the firm of " Cosgrave & Sons." That firm came to an end, on the death
of Patrick; if there had been a stipulation that the security
should continue for the benefit of all persons who for the
time being may be carrying on the same business of

brewers under the same style or firm, I do not doubt that the responsibility would continue and he would have remained liable to the persons constituting the firm when the ale was supplied; but there is nothing from first to last in this agreement to shew that it would extend to such a case. The parties with whom the contract is made are designated by name, and it is limited to those individuals who were members of the firm at the time, if that firm had continued by the express stipulation of the partnership deed, notwithstanding the death of one of the members, then the words here used would continue the liability of the surety notwithstanding the death; but adopting the doctrine of Lord Denman, we should be slow to extend by implication the liability of a surety. This construction is fortified by the words of the covenant between the principal debtor and the three persons who were the other contracting parties. His covenant is to pay for the beer that may from time to time be sold to him by the parties of the first part, or any of them; whereas the liability of the surety is to 'pay for all beer that may be sold by the parties of the first part, or the firm of Cosgrave & Sons, or by any member thereof: that is, according to *Chapman* v. *Beckinton*, the then existing firm of Cosgrave & Sons, or any member thereof.

I refer also to *Pemberton* v. *Oakes*, 4 Russ. 154.

I do not think that the words here used, in the absence of evidence that there was any express stipulation in the articles of partnership that it should continue notwithstanding the death of any of its members, are sufficient to extend the liability of the surety to any goods furnished after the dissolution of the firm by the death of Patrick, and being of this opinion, I have not thought it necessary to consider the other points in the case, but think the judgment should be affirmed, and this appeal dismissed, with costs.

PATTERSON, J.A., agreed with the views expressed by Hagarty. C.J.O.

OSLER, J. A.—With deference to the opinions of my Brother Rose and my Brother Burton who take, as I understand, a different view of the meaning of the agreement, it appears to me to be reasonably plain that what the parties intended to provide for was the case of the death or retirement of one or more of the members of the firm of Cosgrave & Sons, and the continuance of the business by the remaining member or members in that name. In placing any other construction upon it I cannot think we are giving their ordinary meaning to the words which appear, first in the recital and afterwards in the operative part of the instrument, that the defendant " shall be a continuing security to the parties of the first part,"—that is the three persons named as such—" or to the member or members for the time being constituting the said firm." This language is broader and more comprehensive than is to be found in the instruments in question in any of the cases in which the surety has been held to be discharged by a change in the firm, and I think obliges us to hold in accordance with the authorities that the apparent intention of the parties was that the security should continue notwithstanding a change.

In *Strange* v. *Lee*, 3 East. 484-91, it is said: "A bond may be drawn * * for the obligor to be answerable not only to the present but to all future partners in the house."

In *Metcalf* v. *Bruin*, 12 East. 400, Lord Ellenborough, referring to *Barclay* v. *Lucas*, 3 Doug. 321; 1 T. R. 291 *n.*, says, p. 407: "A bond to A. cannot be extended to A. & B. unless the terms of the bond may be taken to explain such an intention. It may be even thought that there was greater difficulty in that case than in the present; but I only collect from it the principle on which it professes to proceed, which was the apparent intention of the parties at the time of entering into the compact to provide for a service to a changeable body carrying on the same concern."

And in *Backhouse* v. *Hall*, 6 B. & S. 507; 34 L. J. Q. B. 141, Mr. Justice Blackburn is reported in 34 L. J. Q. B. 144,

as saying: "Before the Mercantile Law Amendment Act it
had been well established that a guarantee was not a
continuing guarantee, so as to remain in force after
the death of a member of a firm to or for whom it
was given, unless it appeared by the terms of the instrument that it was the intention of the parties that it
should so continue. Now, when this intention appeared
by express stipulation in the instrument itself from the
terms used, as when the firm was named with the addition,
'and their successors,' there was no difficulty."

This is illustrated by the case of *Dance* v. *Girdler*, 1 B.
& P. N. R. 34. The bond there in question was conditioned to account to the obligees and their successors,
governors of the society of musicians. Sir James Mansfield, C. J., says p. 40: "The bond itself is inaccurately drawn;
being given to certain persons as governors of the society,
and their successors. The intention, no doubt, was that the
bond should be payable to those who should succeed the
obligees as governors. But this the law does not allow,
and the bond can only be considered as given to the twelve
obligees, and would ultimately have been payable to the
representative of the last surviving obligee. The condition also proceeds upon the same idea. But probably it would
not be deemed ineffectual on that account; and the condition would perhaps be construed to mean that the
collector should account to those persons who in future
should happen to governors."

To the same effect are the cases of *Ex p. Loyd*, 3 Dea.
305, and *Ex p. Kensington*, 2 Ves. & Bea. 79.

In *Weston* v. *Barton*, 4 Taunt. 672, it is said by Mansfield, C. J., p. 680, that the result of the cases was, "that
generally when a change takes place in the number of
the persons to whom such a bond is given, the bond no
longer exists," but it is manifest that he is dealing with the
question as one depending upon the construction of the
instrument in each particular case.

The cases of *Pemberton* v. *Oakes*, 4 Russ. 154, and
Chapman v. *Beckinton*, 3 Q. B. 703, were very much

relied upon by the defendant, as the articles of partnership
between the obligees in each of those cases contained provisions for the continuance of the firm notwithstanding the
death or retirement of a partner, and in the latter case the
obligor had notice of the terms of the partnership deed.
But the decision in each case expressly proceeded upon the
written language of the particular obligation into which the
party himself had entered, which by its legal construction
was held to extend only to the original co-partnership.

The case of *The University of Cambridge* v. *Baldwin*,
5 M. & W. 580, may be referred to for the purpose of
contrasting the language of the bond there in question
with the wider scope of that employed in the agreement in
the case before us. The bond recited that B. C. & J. had
been appointed agents for the sale of the books printed at
the University Press, and the condition was, that if B. C.
& J. and the survivor or survivors of them, and such other
person or persons as should at any time thereafter in partnership with them act as agents for the plaintiffs, &c.,
should duly account, &c., the bond should be void. J.
retired from the partnership; the other two carried it on
and the action was brought against the surety for their
default. It was argued and so held, that the states of things
contemplated under which the defendant was to be liable,
were, when a partner died or a new one was introduced, or
all carried on trade together, and that the retirement of a
partner was substantially different from all these. Lord
Abinger said, p. 586 : " The words of the condition are 'that
if the said B. C. & J. and the survivors and survivor of them,'
&c. If the words had been, ' or any or either of them,
or the survivors or survivor of any or either of them,'
that would have answered the plaintiffs' purpose, for it
would meet the case of one or more of these persons quit-
ting the partnership, or of one of them dying. But looking
at the precise words of this condition, the case certainly is
not brought within the terms of it."

I think, therefore, that the plaintiffs are entitled to
recover upon this agreement whatever sum may appear to

have been due to the 5th April, 1882, to the firm of Cosgrave & Sons as then constituted. That demand and the defendant's liability in respect thereof, I consider to be well assigned to the plaintiffs by the deeds of the 2nd October and the 13th December, 1882.

The case of *Dance* v. *Girdler*, already referred to, is a clear authority that the guarantee cannot, in any other respect, enure to the benefit of the plaintiffs, an incorporated company succeeding to, or taking over the business of the firm.

I concur with what has been said by the Chief Justice as to the effect of the notice in terminating the liability of the defendant.

The judgment of the Court below should therefore be varied by directing a reference to the registrar of that Court to inquire and ascertain what, if anything, was due to the firm of Cosgrave & Sons by Michael Quinn on the 5th April, 1882, and whether anything remains due in respect thereof. The costs of the cause and of the appeal should follow the result of the reference.

In the W. N. of March 28, 1885, p. 67 there is a note of a case of *Ashby* v. *Day*, in which Bacon, V.C., held that the death of one of several guarantors did not discharge the survivors, (*a*).

[This case has been carried to the Supreme Court.]

(*a*) Since reported, 52 L. T. N. S, 723.

MAGURN v. MAGURN.

Alimony.—Foreign divorce—Fraud—Domicile.

In an action for alimony the defendant relied upon a divorce granted on his own petition by the Circuit Court of St. Louis County, Missouri, where he then resided ; the wife (the present plaintiff) having made no defence thereto though notified of the proceedings. It appeared that the domicile of the husband at the time of the marriage and of the divorce was Canadian, though the marriage was celebrated at Detroit, and the wife was an American citizen. It was proved that the evidence of desertion by the wife as alleged by the husband, and on which the decree for divorce was founded, was untrue.

Held, that the decree, having been obtained on an untrue statement of facts, and for a cause not recognized by our law, could not be set up as a bar to the wife's claim for alimony.

Held, also, that the non-feasance of the wife in failing to appear or defend the action for divorce did not amount to collusion on her part so as to estop her from impeaching the validity of the decree made in that action.

Held, also, [affirming the decision of the Court appealed from, and following *Harvey* v. *Farnie,* 5 Pro. D. 153 ; 6 Pro. D. 35 ; 8 App. Cas. 43] that the jurisdiction to divorce depends upon the domicile of the parties, *i. e.,* of the husband, and that this being Canadian, the Missouri Court had no jurisdiction.

Per HAGARTY, C. J. O.—There is no safe ground for distinction between domicile for succession, and for matrimonial purposes, or a domicile by residence.

THIS was an appeal by the defendant from the judgment of Boyd, C., reported 3 O. R. 570, and came on to be heard before this Court on the 4th and 5th of February, 1885.[*]

S. H. Blake, Q. C., and *Millar,* for the appellant.

J. Maclennan, Q. C., and *C. R. W. Biggar,* for the respondent.

The facts appearing in the case and the authorities relied on, are all clearly stated in the former report and in the present judgment.

March 3rd, 1885. HAGARTY, C. J. O. — The main facts in this case may be said to be undisputed. The defendant, a domiciled Canadian and British subject, married the plaintiff in Detroit, United States. She sues

[*]*Present.*—HAGARTY, C. J. O., BURTON, PATTERSON, and OSLER, JJ.A.

the defendant for alimony. He sets up in defence a decree
of divorce dated 19th June, 1877, granted in the Circuit
Court of St. Louis County, State of Missouri. The plaintiff
answers that the decree was obtained by fraud and perjury
on defendant's part, on a false allegation of desertion by
plaintiff, and it was a fraud on the Court. She admits
that plaintiff by threats of taking her child from her, and
by promising to pay and allow her $50 a month induced
her to agree not to oppose his application for divorce.
She admits having been personally served with a copy of
the petition and notice of time of hearing. She did not
appear or make any opposition. She was living in Canada
at the time of service but had gone over to the American
side of the Niagara Falls by appointment to meet the
defendant.

The defendant's petition to the Missouri Court is dated
25th April, 1877. He states his marriage to plaintiff 14th
December. 1870: that he had lived with her as her husband until 26th April, 1876: that plaintiff had without
reasonable cause, disregarding her duties as his wife,
absented herself for the space of one year next before 20th
April, 1877: that he, defendant, had resided in that State
more than one year next before the filing of the petition,
having his domicile and place of business in the city of
St. Louis. He then swears that the facts stated in the
petition are true, and that the complaint is not made out
of levity, or by collusion, fear, or restraint between him
and plaintiff for the mere purpose of being separated
from each other, but in sincerity and truth for the causes
mentioned.

Proof was given of service of the petition and notice on
plaintiff.

June 12, 1877, there is the entry that plaintiff (the present defendant) comes, but defendant (now plaintiff) comes
not but makes default, and it is ordered that the petition
be taken against her as confessed. The decree is dated
June 19, 1877. After reciting the wife's default, &c., the
Court being satisfied that the plaintiff is an innocent and

injured party, it declares the marriage dissolved, and defendant restored to the rights of an unmarried person, &c.

In September of the same year defendant went through the form of marriage with another woman at Little Falls, State of New York.

The present plaintiff has always since borne her husband's name, and he continued paying her a monthly allowance for several years, down to 1881 or later.

We are at once confronted with the question whether a decree for divorce so obtained can be urged by the defendant. The marriage with the plaintiff is clearly proved; the defence rests on the sufficiency of this decree. It is shewn beyond dispute that it was obtained by fraud and false swearing, and that the Missouri Court was by defendant's untrue statements imposed upon.

The cause assigned was desertion by the wife. No such desertion as a Court could recognize had taken place. The whole proceeding was a contrivance of defendant to impose upon the Court, a method to obtain a colourable release from a distasteful union.

It is a waste of words to prove from authority that a decree so obtained would, if the application had been made in due time, on a disclosure of the facts, have been promptly reversed by any Court pretending to administer justice on any civilized basis. It is said to be irreversible after a certain lapse of time in the State in which it was granted.

How the defendant could have ventured to swear as he appears to have done in the foreign Court, can only be explained on the supposition that he could never have anticipated that his affidavit and the true state of facts on which it was based could ever again see the light.

We have thus a decree for divorce confessedly obtained on an untrue statement of facts, and for a cause not recognized by our law, urged as a bar to enforcing the claim of a wife against her husband.

If I rightly understand the defendant's evidence he does not admit there was any arrangement or collusion between

him and plaintiff as to her aiding in, or consenting to, or
not opposing his getting a divorce : that when she came
over from Toronto to Niagara and was served with the
petition, it was not by any arrangement with her, but that
he requested her to meet him there about some money
matters, and about their child.

Her account seems to be that she was induced not to
oppose his petition by threats to take her child away from
her, and he would pay her maintenance at so much per
month, telling her also that he could get a divorce in spite
of her.

In giving the judgment of the House of Lords, in *Lord
Bandon* v. *Becher*, 3 Cl. & F. 510, Lord Brougham cites
with approbation the vigorous language of Solicitor-
General Wedderburn, in the *Duchess of Kingston's Case*, 20
How. St. Trials, 355, 478 : "A sentence obtained by fraud
and collusion is no sentence. What is a sentence ? * * A
sentence is a judicial determination of a cause agitated
between real parties, upon which a real interest has been
settled.   In order to make a sentence there must be a real
interest, a real argument, a real prosecution, a real defence,
a real decision.   Of all these requisites not one takes place
in the case of a fraudulent and collusive suit.   There is no
Judge but a person invested in the ensigns of a judicial
office is misemployed in listening to a fictitious cause proposed to him : there is no party litigating : there is no
party defendant : no real interest brought into question :
and to use the words of a very sensible civilian on this
point, '*fabula, non judicium, hoc est; in scená, non in
foro, res agitur.*' "

Lord Brougham adds: " You may, either as actor or
defender, object to the decree, provided it was pronounced
through fraud, contrivance, or crime of any description, or
not in a real suit, or if pronounced in a real and substantial
suit between parties who were really not in contest with
each other."

The effect of an unreal or collusive recovery of a
judgment is fully discussed in *Girdlestone* v. *Brighton*

less any conclusion, that he ever lost that domicile or
acquired one in the United States. He marries in the
United States and the marriage as such would be sufficient
all over the world if in accordance with the *lex loci contractus*. But as to deciding whether the marriage so
legally contracted has legally been dissolved the determination seems to belong to the country of domicile. I cannot recognize any safe ground of distinction between
domicile for succession or for matrimonial purposes, or a
domicile by residence.

Harvey v. *Farnie* is a decision of the House of Lords in
1882, and if it covers and decides the legal question here
involved it seems useless to carry the discussion further
afield. The case was before the Court of Appeal, 6 Prob.
D. 35. The head note is: "The question of divorce is
not an incident of the marriage contract to be governed
by the *lex loci contractus*, but is an incident of status, to
be disposed of by the law of the domicile of the parties—
that is, of the husband."   -

If this be a correct statement of the law it is fatal to
this appeal. A domiciled Scotchman married in England
an Englishwoman. After marriage they went to live in
Scotland, and there after a couple of years the wife
obtained a divorce from the Scotch Court by reason of her
husband's adultery alone. After this he married again in
England. Divorce is not granted in England at the wife's
suit for adultery alone. After very full argument the
Court upheld the divorce as legally granted by the Scotch
Court where the husband was domiciled, although the
marriage was solemnized in England, and the divorce for a
cause not sufficient in England.

There are the judgments of three Lords Justices. I
only cite a few lines from that of James, L. J.: "But when
the domicile is the real *bona fide* domicile of the husband,
and consequently of the wife, the Court, the forum of the
country of that domicile is the forum which has to determine whether the status was originally well created, and
whether any circumstances have occurred which justify
that forum in deciding that the status has come to an end."

The case was again very fully argued in the Lords:

8 App. Cas. 43. Lord Selborne, C., says : "The present decision in the Court of Appeal is in accordance with international law and with the whole stream of sound authority. In such cases a Scotchman is in England considered a foreigner, and the Chancellor said that the words 'English marriage' are liable to two constructions, the contract of marriage performed in England is an English marriage, and a marriage performed with a domiciled Englishman is an English marriage."

I need only refer to one other case, *Gould* v. *Shaw*, also in the Lords, L. R. 3 H. L. 55 (1868) where the guiding principle of decision as to domicile governing the status is emphatically declared by Lords Hatherley, Chelmsford, and Westbury.

It may be well to quote a few lines from the judgment of the last mentioned Judge, bearing on a question started before us in argument, as to what could be said to be the law of Canada as to sufficient cause of divorce in the absence of any Court or general legislation on the subject:

" Until the recent Divorce Act, the law was administered by Parliament alone, and although the decision of Parliament was in the form of an Act or *privilegium*, and not of a judicial decree, yet the Act was granted upon evidence proving that the case came within the scope of certain established rules. This proceeding was in spirit a judicial, though in form a legislative Act. The justice of divorce was recognized, but no forensic tribunal was entrusted with the power of applying the remedy. But the law and practice of Parliament were well known, and in fact this House acted as a Court of Justice, it cannot therefore be correctly said that divorce, a *vinculo matrimonii* was contrary to the principles and institutions of this country. It follows that the validity of a foreign decree of divorce must be ascertained in the same manner and on the same rules by which the conclusive effect of other foreign judgments has to be determined."

I think the appeal must be dismissed.

Burton, Patterson and Osler, JJ.A., concurred.

purchaser for value without notice of plaintiff's lien if any such existed.

He also submitted that the plaintiff's claim rested on an alleged agreement respecting an interest in land which was not evidenced by any memorandum in writing as required by the 4th section of the Statute of Frauds. He cited *Kitchen* v. *Boon*, 24 Gr. 195; *McDonald* v. *McDonald*, 14 Gr. 133; *Dart's* V. & P., 5 ed., 923-6; *Fry's* V. & P. 2 ed. 223·

Moss, Q.C., for the respondent. The evidence clearly shews that plaintiff had advanced for the purchase of the land $160 more than Hiscocks, and the learned Judge who tried the case found that fact fully established, and the appellant was made aware of that fact when he applied to the respondent to join in the conveyance to him (Farr) of one half the lot, and Farr then promised to pay the amount claimed. Had it not been for such promise to pay, the respondent would not have executed the conveyance.

The respondent he contended was clearly entitled to the usual lien of a vendor for unpaid purchase money.

April 17, 1885. HAGARTY, C. J. O.—I agree with the conclusion arrived at by the learned Judge as to the effect of the evidence. It is clear that Hiscocks owed plaintiff a sum of $160. I also think that defendant was informed of this and also that plaintiff refused to join in the conveyance to him unless he was paid his claim. Defendant was to pay Hiscocks for the land and had in his hands notes to about $600 which Hiscocks had agreed to take in part payment. Hiscocks wanted cash, and it was agreed that defendant should arrange so as to pay cash. The learned Judge finds, on the conflicting evidence that it was agreed between Hiscocks, plaintiff, and defendant, that plaintiff's claim should be satisfied out of the fund in defendant's hands, as purchase money. I do not question that finding On the faith of this arrangement, Mr. Haverson acting for plaintiff if not for both plaintiff and Hiscocks, signs a memorandum to plaintiff that he will retain for plaintiff the $160 out of the moneys coming from Farr to Hiscocks·

This I think was done with defendant and Hiscocks's assent, and on the faith of this being so done plaintiff signed the deed, and would not otherwise have signed it, and without his signature a good title could not have been given to defendant.

I think these facts constituted a good equitable assignment to plaintiff, and was a good charge on the fund then in defendant's hands, whether consisting of the sale notes originally agreed to be taken in payment, or of cash to be paid in lieu thereof.

We had occasion to review this question of equitable assignment in *Goodall* v. *Mitchell*, 44 U. R. C. 398, and afterwards in appeal in this Court, 5 A. R. 164.

It is not necessary that such an assignment should be in writing: *Tibbitts* v. *George*, 5 A. & E. 107; *Gurnell* v. *Gardner*, 9 Jur. N. S. 1220; 1 *Fisher* on Mortgage, 81, when the intention of the parties is clear and sufficiently expressed. See notes to *Ryall* v. *Rowles*, 2 Wh. & Tud., at p. 776.

The bill here is framed to enforce a lien in favour of plaintiff on the land conveyed to defendant, and it was argued below and here, chiefly, if not wholly as a case of lien, and the learned Judge so decided it, and the decree is for a lien.

The bill sets out the arrangement made on the execution of the deed that the $160 was to be paid by defendant to plaintiff, and that defendant agreed so to pay, and plaintiff prays that defendant be decreed to pay him, and also asks the lien.

I am satisfied there was a good assignment of this money by what took place between the parties, and that defendant Farr was bound thereby, and must pay the amount to plaintiff.

I may refer to such cases as *Crowfoot* v. *Gurney*, 9 Bing. 372; *Wharton* v. *Walker*, 4 B. & Cr. 163; where the well known case of *Tallock* v. *Harris*, 3 T. R. 174, before Buller, J., is referred to. See also *Addison* on Contracts, 818, 821, and the cases there noticed.

The distinction is pointed out between an assignment without the assent of the holder of the fund, and the case where his assent is given.

The former case being only available in equity, the latter cognizable at law.

As Farr is admitted to be well able to pay, a personal decree would have been sufficient, but with a view to the costs of this appeal we have to consider the question of lien. It seems clear that Hiscocks would have his lien on the land sold to defendant for any unpaid portion of the purchase money. If he arranged with defendant to pay all or any portion thereof in payment of his debt to plaintiff, and the latter in consideration of such arrangement and defendant's promise to pay joined in the deed, it seems to me that the lien of Hiscocks as vendor would pass to plaintiff as the assignee of the money as unpaid purchase money : 2 Wh. & Tud. 321 states that the vendor's lien is assignable even by parol, citing *Dryden* v. *Frost*, 3 My. & Cr. 670, before Lord Cottenham.

The case is somewhat complicated, but supports that view.

There, Atkinson was trustee for the sale. Plaintiff Dryden, was his attorney also acting for the mortgagee, and Sharp, the plaintiff had possession of the title deeds. There was a sale, Atkinson vendor, and one Marr vendee. Plaintiff had a lien for costs of the sale. It was agreed between Atkinson and Marr that the plaintiff Dryden should have £100 of the purchase money.

Marr paid plaintiff £50 of this, and gave his note for the other £50. Lord Cottenham held that Marr the vendee could not, without paying the £50 to plaintiff have demanded the title deeds, and that plaintiff, had an equitable lien on them for the £50. He would have been entitled to retain the deeds against Atkinson, his client, until his bill was discharged.

He says, at p. 673: "It was contended that to give to plaintiff the benefit of the vendor's lien, for purchase money unpaid, would be contrary to the Statute of Frauds, as he could only claim by parol assignment from Atkinson the vendor. It is to be observed, however, that the lien for the benefit of vendor himself, as well as the lien by the possession of title deeds are not reconcilable with the principle of that statute, but that nevertheless equity gives effect to them, and that the plaintiff's title rests upon the latter as well as upon the former, for here we have the vendor and the purchaser to one or other of whom the title deeds must, after satisfying the mortgages belong, concurring in an agreement for the payment to the plaintiff, being in possession of the title deeds, of what remains unpaid of the purchase money." See also *Selby* v. *Selby*, 4 Rus. 336.

'In *Sugden*, V. & P. 653, it is said: ".If the seller agrees that the purchase money shall be paid to a third person, and the purchaser accordingly gives a note to that person for the amount, the lien on the estate will, it seems, go with the note," citing *Dryden* v. *Frost*, 3 My. & Cr. 670.

The case of *O'Donohoe* v. *Hembroff*, 19 Gr. 95, is not very fully reported. I gather from it that the defendant sold property for £2,000. For half he took a bond, and for the other half he took seven promissory notes from the vendee. He transferred some of the notes which came to plaintiff's hands. I presume that plaintiff filed his bill claiming a lien and for sale.

The memorandum of Mowat, V.C., is : " Declare lien to exist for purchase money. Master to take account of amount due on account thereof, and to whom owing," &c.

It seems to be assumed that the lien existed in favour of those to whom the vendor had assigned the notes representing the purchase money.

The case came up again in 20 Gr. 35, as to varying the decree, and it is spoken of as that of a creditor of a vendor of real estate, consisting of four parcels, claiming the benefit of a vendor's lien.

Again, in *Re O'Donohoe*, 23 Gr. 399, it is spoken of as a bill to enforce a lien, and a sale therefor being decreed.

I wish to express no opinion as to the existence of any right of lien in the plaintiff prior to the dealing that took place on the sale to the defendant.

I am of opinion that there was a good assignment for valuable consideration of this portion of the purchase money, sufficient to support a personal decree therefor against the defendant.

And as to the lien, I think it also passed to the plaintiff and that he is entitled to it to the extent of his claim as for so much purchase money. Hiscocks could have enforced it and the plaintiff is the assignee of his rights.

Since the foregoing judgment I find one of my learned Brothers thinks the evidence insufficient to establish a charge. I have again scrutinized it as closely as possible, and I wish to add the following to my reasons : I agree that it must be established with reasonable clearness that (1) Hiscocks agreed with Armstrong, that as the consideration for joining in the execution of the deed he should receive $160 out of the purchase money to be paid by Farr : (2) that this was communicated to Farr : (3) that Farr consented and agreed that such payment of $160 should be made to Armstrong out of the purchase money.

Haverson was acting for Hiscocks and also for Armstrong. Armstrong says that as to $120 part of his claim, it was first arranged that he was to be paid out of the first timber they cut off the lot. Then Hiscocks told him of the sale to Farr. They were to go down to Toronto to arrange the matter. Hiscocks first told him he would get the money out of money that Farr had paid in Toronto, and that it was ready for plaintiff. They came to Toronto and Armstrong saw Farr several times. They discussed the matter. Farr said he was not to pay cash, but notes. Haverson asked him to pay $200 in cash, and Farr then said he would pay cash : that Farr knew perfectly well of plaintiff's claim of $160, and that the money was to pass through Mr. Haverson's hands : that, but for that arrangement, the plaintiff would not have signed the deed, or let it out of his hands. Haverson signed the memorandum and gave it to Armstrong after Farr had promised to pay the money.

My brother Proudfoot asked this question: "Was there any arrangement between Farr, and Hiscocks, and yourself, that Haverson should get that money from Farr for you?" A. "Yes."

Armstrong admits that Farr was not present when he got this memorandum.

Again, at page 26, he says: "Farr knew I had this claim, and he promised before witnesses that he would pay this money in to me to pay me off the $160."

Haverson states that Hiscocks and Armstrong came to his office. Armstrong asked him for the money due him; witness said he had no money for Armstrong whatever. He then refused to sign the deed, and he complained of Hiscocks leading him to believe the money was there. They returned to the office with Farr, who said he was not bound to pay any cash. Armstrong would only sign if paid, and Farr said he would pay $200 cash to enable Hiscocks to settle with Armstrong. The latter took the deed up the country to get his wife to sign. Haverson advanced him $10 to pay his expenses.

After giving an account of the visit to Mr. Jackes's office, Haverson says the plaintiff and defendant were there, Hiscocks remained down stairs. "We left with the understanding that when the deeds were registered this $200 should be paid to me for Hiscocks, and I should deduct this money coming to Armstrong from the $200." He gave the memorandum to Armstrong. He says he never would have given the memorandum to Armstrong if he had not been satisfied the money would come to him.

The defendant Farr wholly denies these statements as to any agreement with the plaintiff as to his claim.

Mr. Jackes does not agree with Mr. Haverson as to an interview in his office.

I do not pretend to reconcile the contradictory evidence in this case. I think there is certainly evidence offered by plaintiff to establish what was necessary to create a valid assignment and charge on this purchase money to the extent of Armstrong's claim; and that Farr assented thereto, and agreed that money should be placed in Haverson's hands for that purpose.

The learned Judge adopted that view, with the witnesses all before him. I am not prepared to say he was wrong.

The impression left on my mind from a perusal of the evidence is, that his conclusion of fact is correct.

I think we should dismiss the appeal.

BURTON, J. A.—The statement of claim alleges that the plaintiff and one Hiscocks were tenants in common of a lot of land, and that he, the plaintiff, had paid at the time of the purchase $160 in excess of his share.

That in February, 1883, Hiscocks desired to sell the west half of the lot to the defendant for $1,500, and it was thereupon agreed that Hiscocks should release the east half of the lot to the plaintiff and that they should join in conveying the west half to the defendant, and that out of the purchase money the said sum of $160 should be paid to Hiscocks.

That the defendant had notice of this arrangement and was requested by Hiscocks and agreed with the plaintiff to pay it.

That the plaintiff and Hiscocks thereupon executed a conveyance of the west half to defendant.

That defendant pretends that he paid Hiscocks the whole of the purchase money and the plaintiff claims the payment of $160 and claims a lien therefor.

The defendant, in his answer, admits that he made an agreement with Hiscocks to purchase the half lot for $1,500, payable in a mare, &c., valued at $900, and certain notes which the defendant held to the value of $600.

At the negotiation for the sale Hiscocks represented that he had purchased the whole lot from Mr. Ball, and had sold an undivided interest to the plaintiff, and it was understood between Hiscocks and the defendant, that Hiscocks would release his interest in the east half to the plaintiff, and would procure the plaintiff to join with him in conveying the west half to the defendant, but there was no understanding either with Hiscocks or the plaintiff that the $160 should be paid by the defendant to the plaintiff.

The defendant denies knowledge of the alleged agreement. Pursuant to his agreement with the defendant, Hiscocks conveyed the west half to him, and he delivered the mare and the notes to the value of $600.

The plaintiff's evidence is not very intelligible, but this much is to be clearly gathered from it. That he came to Toronto at the request of Hiscocks to make a partition of the land in order to enable the latter to carry out a sale of the west half to the defendant ; that he positively declined to execute a deed until he was paid the $120 claimed to be due for excess of purchase money, and $40 money claimed for expenses or on some other account.

Hiscocks had told him before he went down that the $120 would be ready for him.

On arriving at Toronto he met Farr at Mr. Haverson's office, and then discovered that the money was not ready, and that by the agreement between Hiscocks and Farr the balance of the purchase money was to be paid in notes which he declined to take ; that Haverson then applied to Farr to see if he would not agree to pay $200 in cash, and that he finally assented to pay $200 by discounting a portion of the notes, and he adds that it was to go through Mr. Haverson's hands. At this time the money would necessarily have passed through his hands as he held the deed with instructions not to part with it till the payment of the money.

Mr. Haverson's account of the transaction is much clearer and more to be relied on than that of his client, who was manifestly illiterate, and gave his evidence in a confused way, and he informs us that Hiscocks first came to him on the 6th of February, and told him of the sale to Farr, and Haverson then informed him that it would be necessary to obtain Armstrong's signature, and he then prepared a deed which he handed to Hiscocks, who went up with it to Armstrong's to procure his signature, and in a few days returned with Armstrong, who asked him, Haverson, for his money, and appeared much surprised when he found it was not forthcoming, and refused to sign the deed, and they went away returning after a time with Farr.

Farr stated he was under no obligation to pay cash, and that he finally agreed to pay $200 in cash to enable Hiscocks to settle with Armstrong, and Haverson then gave the deed to Armstrong who returned home to get his wife's signature. Armstrong returned, and on the 23rd or 24th, Hiscocks signed it and Haverson took charge of it, to hold it as he says uutil the transaction was carried through. They went over to Mr. Jackes's office ; but that gentleman declined to allow his client to pay the money until the deed was registered, to which Armstrong demurred. Mr. Haverson states, but Mr. Jackes denies, that the latter offered to pay $200 into some bank, but Mr. Haverson adds that on the understanding that the transaction would be completed between Mr. Jackes and himself he felt there was no necessity for it, and they left upon the understanding that when the deeds were registered this $200 should be paid to him for Mr. Hiscocks, and he would then be in a position to deduct the plaintiff's $160 from it.

In this expectation, Mr. Haverson on his return to his office and without the privity of Hiscocks or Farr gave his client an undertaking to this effect :

"Mr. Richard Armstrong, I will retain out of the moneys coming from Farr to Hiscocks, $160 for you as you direct."

This was given to satisfy Armstrong so that he might return home and he then intended to do so, but having missed the train he afterwards abandoned the intention and determined to remain till the whole thing was closed.

This undertaking bore no date, and the plaintiff afterwards dated it by mistake the 24th March ; it is clear, however, upon the evidence, that it was given upon the 24th February, the same day on which the interview took place in Jackes's office.

I should here mention that Mr. Jackes denies the accuracy of Mr. Haverson's statement as to what occurred there, if that conversation was of any consequence as regards the matter in issue, which I do not think it was; but the correspondence which took place immediately afterwards is probably more to be relied on than the treacherous memories of the parties.

Bearing in mind that Haverson had at that interview parted with the deeds on which he relied for his client's security in order that they might be registered, and on the supposition that he was thenceforth relying upon the transaction being carried out between Messrs. Jackes and himself, we find him two days subsequently writing to that firm or one of the members of it thus:

"You can now send for certificates against Hiscocks and Armstrong and for taxes. *The money will of course be paid to me and not to Hiscocks.*"

On the same day Mr. Jackes writes back acknowledging it, and using this langugage:

"We do not understand, however, that there is to be any money paid, but the consideration is a mare and some notes."

To this Haverson sent no written reply, and a few days subsequently it was discovered that Hiscocks and Farr had arranged the purchase money between them without reference to the solicitors.

The learned Judge assumes, and the case was argued before us upon the assumption, that, as the plaintiff had, as one of the purchasers of the land, overpaid his portion of the purchase money, he would be entitled to a lien, for such over payment which would have to be repaid to him before he could be compelled to release his interest.

I do not so understand the law. By making such a payment he gains neither a lien nor a mortgage, because there is no contract for either; but the evidence does not satisfy me that there was such an over payment; $100 of the amount being for a balance due upon a former transaction, and $40 was a sum advanced long subsequently without any reference whatever to this purchase. I do not think that contention tenable, and no authority has been cited for it.

I was at first inclined to think, with the Chief Justice, that the case might be supported on the ground of there being an equitable assignment of an equivalent amount of the purchase money coming to Hiscocks, and that this had been assented and agreed to by the defendant; but a careful reperusal of the evidence has convinced me, much against my will, that such a state of facts is not made out as would enable the plaintiff to recover upon that ground. I say against my will, for I have a very strong conviction that the defendant, if inclined to act with ordinary fairness, might have saved the plaintiff from loss, although I think there is no ground upon which he can be made legally responsible.

Assuming that a valid, equitable assignment of the purchase money and the lien on the land can in a case like the present be created by parol, the Courts require in such a case the evidence to be clear and unequivocal. In *Gurnell* v. *Gardner*, 9 Jur. N. S. 1220, the evidence of the plaintiff was clear and uncontradicted, and the Judge was convinced that all the probabilities were in favour of the plaintiff's evidence.

Up to the time of the meeting in Mr. Jackes's office there was no necessity for any such arrangement. Haverson held possession of the deeds, and whether he was entitled legally to hold them or not, he claimed to hold them, and his client was perfectly safe.

The conversations which are narrated are matters which did not concern or affect the plaintiff or his lien, but relate to the mode in which Hiscocks was to raise the money to settle with the plaintiff.

The plaintiff and his solicitor were naturally indifferent how this was done so long as they held possession of the deeds.

The question was not raised or referred to in the judgment in the Court below, and we are therefore without the assistance of any finding of Court, and I am not surprised, after a perusal of the evidence, to find so careful and painstaking a counsel as Mr. Moss not pressing this upon us but relying upon the other ground.

The plaintiff merely speaks of Farr agreeing to pay Hiscocks $200 instead of notes. He says it was to go through Haverson's hands, but he does not say that Farr agreed that it should do so. It had at that time necessarily to do so, as Haverson held the deeds.

All that the learned Judge finds, as any one of us must have found upon the evidence, is that Farr had notice that the plaintiff claimed a lien, and if we could also find that that lien existed we should be bound to uphold the judgment, but the learned Judge has not found, and I am unable to find upon this evidence, that there was by reason of what occurred an equitable assignment of any portion of the purchase money of the sale between Hiscocks and Farr.

I do not feel the difficulty which the learned Judge experienced in accounting for Mr. Haverson giving the undertaking referred to.

It is clear to my mind that he gave it because he felt that when he parted with the deeds to Mr. Jackes he could rely upon the transaction being completed in that gentleman's office, and if it were he could safely rely on him.

I feel satisfied that the whole difficulty has occurred in consequence of the transaction not being carried out on strict business lines, but the whole evidence tends to convince me that there was nothing in the nature of an equitable assignment, and that we ought to be very guarded in giving effect to alleged parol contracts of that nature. It was the easiest thing in the world to reduce such an arrangement to writing if it existed.

It is attempted to be supported here by the vague and almost unintelligible statements of an ignorant man. His solicitor states the matter fairly enough, not substantially differing from the defendant, that the latter agreed so far to vary the original agreement, as to pay $200 in cash instead of notes to enable Hiscocks to carry it out, but the defendant denies that he made any other agreement, or any agreement with Armstrong, and the learned Judge in coming to the conclusion that Farr made some agreement, states his reasons for that conclusion, viz., that Haverson would not otherwise have signed the undertaking, for which other quite sufficient reasons are apparent. In addition to all which is the fact that no such claim was ever made before suit, or since; the transaction occurred in September, the plaintiff so far from asserting any such claim against the defendant proposed to put the criminal law in force against Hiscocks, and did not sue till the following March.

I do not regret that my learned brothers have seen their way to a different conclusion, as I am not satisfied with the conduct of the defendant, but I think we have made a stride to-day in support of parol equitable assignments far in advance of any decision either here or in England, which we may at some future day find inconvenient.

Haverson and Jackes I have no doubt acted in perfect good faith believing that the transaction would be carried out through them. Unfortunately the parties to the transaction when once they knew that the deed was executed and registered carried it out between themselves. Hiscocks of course knew that he was committing a fraud, and there is too much reason to fear that the defendant who might have prevented it was not much impressed with the immorality of the transaction but with that we have nothing to do, unless we can see clearly that there was an equitable assignment of this fund.

How far mere notice of an equitable assignment of only part of a fund without express consent of the debtor, would be operative, may some day come up for decision. It seems rather startling that a debtor should be subjected to distinct demands on the part of several persons, when his contract was one and entire. In the 11th Am. Ed. *Chitty* on Contracts, p. 1365, it is doubted, and a number of American authorities are cited in support of it.

In *Farquhar* v. *The City of Toronto*, 12 Gr. 186, the point does not appear to have been raised, and perhaps the question is not open under the decisions of our own Courts.

I do not think upon the evidence in this case that a payment by Farr to Armstrong would have released him from his debt to Hiscocks.

The point upon which we are deciding this case has not been argued. I do not say it is not open upon the pleadings although I have not the slightest doubt that the pleader had not the remotest intention in the 3rd and 4th paragraphs of his Bill to place his claim upon any such ground. It was evidently not discussed in the Court below nor referred to in the judgment, nor was it discussed before us beyond a faint allusion to it by counsel, in reply to a remark which fell from the Chief Justice, and it is not taken in the reasons against the appeal. The lien referred to in the three first reasons being the supposed lien of one tenant in common, by reason of an over payment, and the assumed vendor's lien referred to in the 3rd and 4th reasons, being based upon the theory that Farr was purchasing Armstrong's interest for which he had a lien. It is no where placed upon the ground that Hiscocks had a vendor's lien for the purchase money against Farr, and that he assigned a portion of it to Armstrong, such a point was never raised, and in my humble opinion is not tenable upon the evidence, and the appeal ought therefore to be allowed.

PATTERSON, J. A.—I do not propose to add anything to what has been said by his Lordship, the Chief Justice, upon the questions of law.

After a careful consideration of all the evidence, I am satisfied that the learned Judge at the trial had quite sufficient support in the evidence for the conclusions of fact which he expressed in the passages which I shall read from the report of his judgment.

"It is quite clear," he is reported to have said, "from Mr. Haverson's evidence that there was an interview between Farr and Haverson (*qu.* Hiscocks) and Armstrong

at his office, some time in the month of February, before
the close of the transaction : that Farr was informed then
that Armstrong would not convey his undivided interest so
as to give a separate estate to him, as a purchaser from
Hiscocks, without being paid the money that was due
from Hiscocks to him.   *   *   Well, Mr. Farr denies that
directly and distinctly. In opposition to that Mr. Haverson is supported by Mr. Armstrong, and I must say that
if it depended upon the evidence of Haverson and Farr
alone I would have no hesitation in accepting Mr. Haverson's statement of what took place; but being supported
by Armstrong the conclusion is obviously in favour of the
case made by the plaintiff that Farr was informed of this
claim by Armstrong, and that he would not convey unless
it was paid to him ; and I think that the action of Mr.
Haverson shortly afterwards is very strongly corrobora-
tive of Farr being made acquainted with that, and of the
further undertaking by Farr to pay the money himself or
to leave the money in Haverson's hands for the purpose
of paying off this claim.   *   *   It is impossible to come
to any other conclusion than that Farr did make some
arrangement of that kind."

These facts so stated, with the addition of one fact not
expressly mentioned here, but evidently taken as beyond
dispute, as upon the evidence it is, namely, that between
Hiscocks and Armstrong it was understood that Armstrong
was to be paid out of the purchase money, so that what
Farr was to pay to Armstrong or leave in Haverson's hands
for him, was the part of the purchase money which Hiscocks had appropriated to Armstrong, are in my judgment
sufficient to establish Armstrong's lien on the lands for
that amount.

I may refer, as briefly as I can, to the evidence as I
read it.

Mr. Haverson was solicitor for Hiscocks, and may be
said to have been solicitor also for Armstrong in this
matter.

Mr. Jackes was solicitor for Farr, but from his own
evidence would seem to have had nothing to do in the
transaction except seeing to the title, not being concerned
in the payments, and not even being informed by his client

of the change in the mode of payment from the sale notes to cash. This circumstance seems to me to go a long way to explain how he may have been unable to recall a conversation of which Mr. Haverson speaks very confidently, and in which the sincerity of Mr. Haverson's belief is borne out by the undertaking he gave to Armstrong and to Scholes to pay them money out of that which should come into his hands. The money in Mr. Haverson's mind was $200, which was the amount of cash which Farr was to pay, or the amount of the notes he was to discount. Speaking of the interview in Mr. Jackes's office, he says that Mr. Jackes offered to pay $200 into a bank, until the deeds were registered, but Haverson was content to take Mr. Jackes's word, and that he and Armstrong and Farr left the office with the understanding that the $200 should be paid to him for Mr. Hiscocks, and that from it he was to deduct the money coming to Armstrong. Now Mr. Jackes does not appear, even when giving his evidence, to have apprehended what was in Mr. Haverson's mind; for, when asked about the $200 matter, his answer is wide of Haverson's idea, and of the purpose for which the $200 was required.

" *Question :* Did you offer to retain any sum ? *Answer :* I did not ; I did not consider it necessary ; $200 even would be no security for a farm of $1,500. I told him that Farr was a responsible man, and he seemed satisfied with my statement."

Take with this kind of evidence, Mr. Jackes's letter of 26th February, 1883, where he states that he had not heard of the proposal to pay money, respecting which Mr. Haverson had on the same day written to him saying, "The money will of course be paid to me and not Hiscocks;" and we have but slight ground for surprise at finding, a year after the transaction that the conversation had not remained in Mr. Jackes's memory in the same way as in Mr. Haverson's.

Mr. Haverson's general account of the transaction, so far as the immediate question is concerned is, that Armstrong came with Hiscocks expecting the money to be ready, but finding it not forthcoming he refused to execute the deeds. They left Haverson's office, and returned with Farr. Then he says: " I remember stating to Mr. Farr that Mr. Armstrong would not sign this deed till he got his money. Mr. Farr stated that he was not under this agreement, bound to pay him any money whatever. Well, I said that so far as I was concerned I could not help it: it was a matter between themselves. Mr. Armstrong simply refused to sign this deed till this money was forthcoming, and Mr. Farr said he would pay $200 in cash. Q. Instead of the notes? A. Instead of a portion of them, for the purpose of enabling Hiscocks to settle with Armstrong, and I think they left the office, that would be before the 21st of February; then the deed was prepared," &c.

So far there was no idea of Armstrong parting with the deed, which he took home to procure his wife's signature to until he got his money.

Then followed the incident in Mr. Jackes's office, when it appeared that Farr would not pay anything until the deeds were registered. At that interview Mr. Haverson states that Armstrong and Farr were present. Hiscocks was not, as he remained on the street with his horse.

Mr. Armstrong's evidence puts in words some things that are not so expressly stated by Mr. Haverson.

Thus, speaking of the occasion in Mr. Haverson's office when Farr first agreed to give $200 in cash, he says the arrangement then was, that it was to go through Mr. Haverson's hands. This he repeats in answering "yes" to a question put by the Judge: "Was there any arrangement that Haverson should get that money from Mr. Farr for you?" And in another place he says that it was the arrangement made in Mr. Haverson's office that was renewed in Mr. Jackes's office.

There can, in my opinion, be no doubt that the learned Judge's findings are abundantly supported by the evidence, and I think it equally clear that they receive very strong support from the probabilities of the case.

I do not attempt an analysis of Mr. Farr's version of his dealings. I shall merely say that a perusal of his evidence leaves no misgivings as to the correctness of the learned Judge's appreciation of it when opposed to the other witnesses.

I agree that we should dismiss the appeal, with costs.

OSLER, J. A., concurred in dismissing the appeal.

Appeal dismissed, with costs, [BURTON, J. A., *dissenting.*]

BEATTY v. NORTH WESTERN TRANSPORTATION COMPANY
ET AL.

Incorporated company—Purchase from director of company, Ratification by stockholders—Trustees, &c.

J. H. B., one of the defendants, a director of the defendant company, personally owned a vessel "The United Empire" valued by him at $150,000; and was possessed of the majority of the shares of the company, some of which he had assigned to others of the defendants in such numbers as qualified them for the position of directors of the company, the duties of which they discharged. Upon a proposed sale and purchase by the company of the vessel "The United Empire" the board of directors (including J. H. B.), at their board meeting adopted a resolution approving of the purchase by the company of such vessel; and subsequently at a general meeting of the shareholders, including J. H. B. and those to whom he had transferred portions of the stock, a like resolution was passed, the plaintiff alone dissenting.

Held, (reversing the judgment of the Court below, 6 O. R. 300,) that although the purchase on the resolution of the directors alone might have been avoided, the resolution of the shareholders validated the transaction, and that there is not any principle of equity to prevent J. H. B. in such a case from exercising his rights as a shareholder as fully as other members of the company.

Per BURTON and OSLER, JJ.A.—In dealings of this nature the relative positions of the shareholders and directors are those of principals and agents, not those of *cestuis que trustent* and trustees.

THIS was an appeal by the defendant James H. Beatty, from a judgment of Boyd, C., pronounced on the 19th of

January, 1884, and came on to be heard before this Court on 10th, 11th, 12th, and 13th days of March, 1885. *

Robinson, Q. C., and *J. H. Macdonald*, for the appellant, *Maclennan*, Q. C., and *Marsh*, for the respondent.

The facts of the case and the authorities cited sufficiently appear in the report of the case in Court below; 6 O. R. 300, and in the judgments on this appeal.

April 17th, 1885. HAGARTY, C.J.O.—We must deal with this case as free from imputation of fraud or corruption. They are somewhat faintly suggested in the bill, but no attempt was made to prove them, and as I understand the parties on the argument, they were practically abandoned.

There are five directors, and they agree to purchase a steamboat from Mr. James H. Beatty, one of their own number, for a large price, equal to nearly half the capital of the company, to be used on the line of steamers run by the company, which was chartered (amongst other things) for the buying and selling of steamboats for transport, &c.

At a meeting of directors a by-law for said purchase was passed, James H. Beatty being present and joining in the proceedings. This was referred to a general meeting of shareholders, at which Mr. Beatty took the chair. After full discussion, all the 600 shares being represented except 5; the by-law was adopted by 306 votes against 289, a majority of 17. Of this majority 291 were votes on shares owned by Beatty. On his own votes he thus had a majority of two votes over all given against the by-law.

As against the company, I am satisfied that Mr. Beatty could not enforce this contract. This seems to have been conceded on the argument by the appellant. The authorities seem clear and uniform on that point. I think it is also reasonably clear that such a contract, voidable at the instance of the company, may (at all events in the absence of fraud) be ratified or validated by the company.

* *Present.*—HAGARTY, C. J. O., BURTON, PATTERSON, and OSLER, JJ. A.

The company here, who may be called the *cestuis que trustent* as against Mr. Beatty, are not before us as objecting. The objectors are the shareholders who were outvoted at the general meeting.

The difficulty is created by this peculiar position of the parties.

Primâ facie the company should be the plaintiffs on any question affecting its rights, and the Courts, if possible, will not interfere in their concerns.

The subject is discussed in Sir H. Thring's book, 4th ed. (1880), p. 92.

" The Courts will not interfere in the internal disputes of a company. A shareholder, therefore, cannot maintain an action on behalf of himself and others to set aside on the ground of improvidence or inexpediency an act of the directors sanctioned or *capable* of being sanctioned by a majority—nay, more, it would appear that he cannot be heard to object to any informality in the proceeding unless he has attempted to put the company in motion, and the company has refused to take cognizance of the matter. The question in such cases is, whether the company has power to do this act, and if it has the Court closes its doors against the complainant, and will not by an undue interference enable a recusant minority to throw obstacles in the way of a majority carrying into effect any scheme of which it may approve."

James, L. J., says in *Gray* v. *Lewis*, L. R. 8 Ch. 1035-1051 :

" I think it of the utmost importance to maintain the rule laid down in *Mosley* v. *Alston,* and *Foss* v. *Harbottle,* to which, as I understand, the only exception is where the corporate body has got into the hands of directors and of the majority, which directors and majority are using their powers for the purpose of doing something fraudulent against the minority, who are overwhelmed by them, as in *Atwool* v. *Merryweather,* L. R. 5 Eq. 464, when V. C. Wood under the circumstances sustained a bill by a shareholder on behalf of himself and others, and there it was after an attempt had been made to obtain a proper authority from the corporate body itself in public meeting assembled."

In *Menier* v. *Hooper's Telegraph Works*, L. R. 9 Ch. 350, a bill was upheld by a shareholder: the majority of the company proposed to benefit themselves at the expense of the minority. Lord Justice James says, it would be a shocking thing if the majority could divide the whole assets of the company and pass a resolution that everything must be given to them, and the minority have nothing to do with it.

Sir Geo. Mellish says, although it may be quite true that the shareholders of a company may vote as they please, and for the purpose of their own interest, yet the majority of shareholders cannot sell the assets of the company and keep the consideration, but must allow the minority to have their share of any consideration which may come to them.

In *Macdougall* v. *Gardiner*, 1 Ch. D. 21, James, L. J., says: " Nothing connected with internal disputes between the shareholders is to be made the subject of a bill by some one shareholder on behalf of self and others, unless there be something illegal, oppressive, or fraudulent—unless there be something *ultra vires* on the part of the company, *qua* company, or on the part of the majority of the company, so that they are not fit persons to determine it, but that every litigation must be in the name of the company, if the company really desire it."

The rest of his judgment is very instructive.

Sir Geo. Mellish says: "If the thing complained of is a thing which in substance the majority of the company are entitled to do, or if something has been done irregularly which the majority of the company are entitled to do regularly; or if something has been done illegally which the majority of the company are entitled to do legally, there can be no use in having a litigation about it, the ultimate end of which is only that a meeting has to be called, and then ultimately the majority gets its wishes. Is it not better that the rule should be adhered to, that if it is a thing which the majority are the masters of, the majority in substance should be entitled to have their will followed? If it is a matter of that nature it only comes to this, that the majority are the only persons that can complain that a thing which they are entitled to do has been done irregularly. Of course, if the majority are abusing their powers, and are depriving the minority of their rights, that is an entirely different thing."

In *Mason* v. *Harris*, 11 Ch. D. 97, 107, Sir Geo. Jessel says: "The rules applicable to the case are so well expressed in *Macdougall* v. *Gardiner* that I will not attempt to improve upon them. As a general rule the company must sue in respect of a claim of this nature, but general rules have their exceptions, and one exception * * is that where a fraud is committed by persons who can command a majority of votes, the minority can sue. * * If the majority were to make a fraudulent sale, and put the money into their own pockets, would it be reasonable to say that the majority could confirm the sale?" There the bill charged a fraudulent sale by the defendant, their managing director, to the promoters, which was approved by the company, charging that he possessed such a preponderance of votes that no steps could be taken within the company to remedy these acts. See also *Hazard* v. *Durant*, 11 Rhode Island 200.

The judgment of Wood, V. C., in *London and Mercantile Discount Co.*, L. R. 1 Eq. 277, largely supports the principle of non-interference with the powers of the company to manage its own affairs: *Morawetz*, sec. 390, et seq. 399 ; *Field* on Corporations, sec. 76.

I think it clear that the contract made with Mr. James H. Beatty was one which he could not have forced upon the company, and that if the latter chose to resist it the case would be clearly within *Aberdeen R. W. Co.* v. *Blaikie*, 1 Macq. 461.

I also think it clear that such a contract could be ratified and adopted by a vote of the majority of shareholders, and that there is nothing in this case to bring it within the well settled principles on which the Courts have declared

carrying a measure happens to hold a majority of the shares in the company. He can thus carry any measure *intra vires* the corporation. The same object could be effected by sale or assignment of his stock to various persons likely to adopt his views. We must refer to *Pender* v. *Lushington*, 6 Ch. D. 70, for the law in such cases.

There is no restriction apparently on the acquisition of a majority of shares in the hands of any stockholder, and it seems impossible for the Courts to interfere with the right of using these shares for voting purposes or to inquire into the motives actuating their owners, at all events so long as no fraud is practised and no illegal advantage sought to be obtained for the benefit of such majority at the cost and loss of the minority.

I fully agree in the judgment of the learned Chancellor in the view taken of the general impropriety and danger of dealings between any one in a fiduciary position and those whose interests he is bound to protect.

But I am unable to agree in the decision arrived at ; firstly, as I hold that the contract made as to this vessel was one that, although not binding on the company if resisted by them, was quite capable of being ratified and adopted by the shareholders ; and secondly, that I do not see our right to reject the votes on the shares held by the principal defendant, especially as they would be certainly available by a slight alteration in the form of the proceeding within the powers of the shareholders to adopt if they thought proper.

I think, therefore, that we must allow the appeal.

I am most anxious that nothing in the decision at which we have arrived should be considered as weakening or diluting (as it were) the salutary doctrines of equity that always govern dealings between directors or others in a fiduciary position and those whose interests they are bound to protect.

I do not think the case calls for any remark condemnatory of the motives of the principal defendant. I am

willing to believe that he was actuated by the honest
desire to promote the interests of the company. But I am
of opinion that the matter might have been conducted in a
much less objectionable manner—that he might have left
its decision to the rest of his co-directors, uninfluenced by
his presence or participation. Under all the circumstances I think we should not give the appellant the costs
of the appeal. The bill in the Court below should be dismissed, with costs.

BURTON, J.A.—The question raised in this case is an
important one, which has never before arisen in the
Courts of this Province, and before proceeding to its discussion it is as well to refer to certain propositions which
in my opinion have been settled by the decided cases.

Among these I think we may assume, notwithstanding
some expressions of very able Judges, that directors are
not trustees except in a qualified sense. They are the
agents of the company, *and of the company alone*—and as
regards the shareholders, they are merely trustees of the
powers committed to them, such as the powers of allotment
of shares, the power of making calls, &c.

I may perhaps be told that this is a question of words
merely, but in that I differ, holding that there is a very
broad distinction, and that it is important to bear this distinction clearly in view in the consideration of the case,
and I may on this' point refer to the remarks of Lord
Westbury in *Knox* v. *Gye*, L. R. 5 H. L. 656, where he
observed :

" The surviving partner is often called a ' trustee,' but the
term is used inaccurately. * * * There is not a more
fruitful source of error in law than the inaccurate use of
language. The application to a man who is, improperly and
by metaphor only, called a trustee, of all the consequences
which would follow if he were a trustee by express declaration—in other words a complete trustee * * * well
illustrates the remark made by Lord Mansfield that
in law is nothing so apt to mislead as a metaphor."

Clear definitions imply clear conceptions—clear conceptions imply the clear and logical thinking out of the problem one is called upon to solve.

I lay down, therefore, as the first of these propositions:

That the directors are agents of the company and of the company alone.

2nd. That unless there is something in the charter or deed of settlement of the company to prohibit it, any shareholder has a perfect right to vote at a meeting of shareholders upon any question, although he has a personal interest in the question opposed to that of the company ; and

3rd. That when there is no special provision to the contrary, the resolution of the majority of shareholders of an incorporated company duly convened upon any question within the powers of the company is binding upon the minority, and therefore upon the company.

I do not at all question the rule, which is one of universal application, that a director occupying a fiduciary position as agent of the company is precluded from entering into a contract in which he has or can have a personal interest conflicting, or which may possibly conflict with the interest of those whom he is bound by fiduciary duty to protect. I wish to state this in the broadest possible terms, and that it is immaterial whether the transaction is fair or not, and I wish further to state it as in my opinion clear law, that this rule applies even though the party whose act or contract is called in question is only one of a body of directors and not a sole director or manager. It is the duty of such a director to assist the company, and to give them the full benefit of all the knowledge and skill which he has on the subject, to get the article proposed to be contracted for at the cheapest possible rate, and therefore in such a matter his interest would be placed in conflict with his duty, and consequently whether he was a sole director or one of many can make no difference.

Such was precisely the case of *Aberdeen R. W. Co.* v. *Blaikie*, 1 Macq. 461, decided by the House of Lords in 1853, and whatever doubt may have existed previously to

that time, I apprehend no one at the present day, apart
from that decision, would entertain any doubt of that being
the law.

But that case goes only to this extent, that when a contract has been thus made by the company's agent for his
own benefit, when he comes to enforce it against the
company they have a right to say that is a contract not
binding upon us and we repudiate it, but that is very far
from solving the difficulties we have to grapple with in
this case. If a meeting of that company had been specially
called to consider that contract, and it had then been explained to them that it had been found impossible to effect
a contract with any persons on such favorable terms as
those offered by Mr. Blaikie's firm, but in consequence of
his position on the Board it was thought undesirable to
conclude it without taking the opinion of the shareholders,
and they had confirmed it by a majority, would it have
been competent to a dissatisfied shareholder to override the
majority and impeach the transaction? I will deal separately with the question of an interested shareholder's
voting. The point I am at present discussing is, whether
such a contract was or was not, or could or could not be
validated by a majority of the shareholders.

With great deference I take it to be perfectly well
established that such a transaction is at most voidable, and
that it may be affirmed by the conduct of the corporation
and *a fortiori* by an express ratification by a majority of
shareholders duly convened.

The duty of a trustee is distinct from fiduciary relationship—as agents of the company the directors are bound to
bring to the management of the company's affairs ordinary
skill, care, and prudence, but there is no rule which pro-
hibits companies and their directors from entering into
stipulations permitting the latter to have private and
personal interests in the companies' contracts, provided all
the attendant circumstances are made known.

The majority of an ordinary partnership have, apart
from express provisions while acting *bonâ fide,* full powers

over the operations and property of the firm, and can compel the concurrence of a dissentient minority, provided only they are fairly consulted and have an opportunity of expressing their objections. See the remarks of Lord Eldon, in *Court* v. *Harris*, T. & R. 496.

The same rule holds good with corporations, it being of course understood that what the corporation as a united whole cannot do, *a fortiori* a majority however great cannot do, but within the scope of the corporate affairs the majority not merely represent but actually are for most purposes the corporation. Contracts entered into and arrangements made or sanctioned by them are valid, notwithstanding the opposition or dissent of some of its members.

The broad rule is, that in all matters of purely internal economy the majority are supreme, and the courts will not interfere whether before, to prevent the doing of acts, or subsequently to relieve from the consequences thereof.

The principle is perfectly well established, and I may refer in illustration of it to such cases as *Lord* v. *The Governor & Co. of Copper Miners*, 2 Phi. 1740; and *Stupert* v. *Arrowsmith*, 3 Sm. & G. 176; *Kent* v. *Jackson*, 2 D. M. & G. 49; and the rule laid down in *Foss* v. *Harbottle*, 2 Hare 461, has never been departed from, although it has sometimes been misunderstood and extended to matters not properly within its application, such as refusing relief to individual shareholders when the act sought to be restrained was *ultra vires* or fraudulent. The principle laid down in *Foss* v. *Harbottle* was, that if the act though it be the act of the directors only, be one which a general meeting of the company could sanction, a bill by some of the shareholders on behalf of themselves and others to impeach that act cannot be sustained, because a general meeting of the company might immediately confirm and give validity to the act of which the bill complains.

And as the courts will not interfere in favour of the minority as against the majority, neither will they interfere in favor of the majority or the whole corporation, to reopen a question of internal management which has once been considered and determined upon by the corporation.

This, then, being a matter of mere internal management and admitted not to be tainted with fraud, it is manifest upon the authorities that the majority had power to deal with it.

Some doubt was suggested during the argument as to the statement to be found in the text books as to the second of my propositions, and some kind of intimation that, as is unfortunately too frequently the case, the text was not borne out by the authorities. Whatever foundation there may be for the general charge against text writers, I should hesitate long before including among them so able a jurist and writer as Lord Justice Lindley, and the cases which he cites for the proposition fully bear him out.

The first of these cases was *East Pantdu Mining Co.* v. *Merryweather*, 2 H. & M. 254. In that case the articles of association contained a prohibition against a director's voting in respect of any matter in which he had an interest, but it was held that notwithstanding that prohibition he was not debarred from voting at a shareholders' meeting, and no stronger case could be suggested for his not being allowed to vote than was presented in that case.

A bill had there been filed by some dissatisfied shareholders in the name of the company against one of the directors, seeking to set aside a sale in which he was interested on the ground of fraud.

A meeting of the shareholders was called for the purpose of ascertaining whether they would consent to the prosecution of the suit in the company's name, and the majority present at that meeting were in favour of the suit going on, but upon a poll being demanded they were outvoted by the votes of the defendant, although he was also a director, and the question then was, whether, as he was admittedly interested, his votes should be counted, and the Court held that notwithstanding his interest his votes must be counted, and therefore that the suit in which the alleged fraud would have been investigated must be discontinued. I do not very well understand one remark of V. C. Wood's, in giving judgment, that to discard the director's vote would be in effect to decide the question in the suit, as the effect of a contrary decision would simply have been to allow the suit to proceed upon the merits, but it is an express decision that although he had a direct personal interest in the matter he could not be prevented from exercising his right as a shareholder and voting on his shares.

Mr. Buckley and Sir. H. Thring in their works also treat it as settled law, and cite the same authority.

In that particular case a bill was subsequently filed by a dissatisfied shareholder on behalf of himself and all other shareholders, except'the defendant, against the two directors accused of the fraud and the company, and succeeded in setting aside the sale for the fraud which had been practised upon them by the two directors.

I apprehend, therefore, that there can be no question of the right of a shareholder to vote, notwithstanding his having a direct personal interest to serve opposed to that of the company. He is not a trustee for any one—he is not an agent for any one—he holds no fiduciary relations, and he is entitled to exercise his right as a shareholder, even though in doing so he is endeavoring to serve his own interest.

This right has been carried to what seems almost an extreme length in some of the English decisions, notably in *Pender* v. *Lushington*, L. R. 6 Ch. 70. There, although the articles of association provided that every member should be entitled to one vote for every ten shares at a general meeting, but should not be entitled to more than one hundred votes in all, it was held that a larger shareholder could transfer to nominees by him for the purpose of increasing his own voting power, and with an object alleged to be adverse to the interests of the company.

There can be no doubt from that and other cases to be found in the books that that is a rule sanctioned by courts of equity, although to a simple ' layman unversed in the mysteries of equity, it would have the appearance of a very harsh and unjustifiable proceeding towards smaller shareholders, who may have invested their money in the concern in reliance upon the assurance that no member should be entitled to more than one hundred votes.

If in the present case there had been a graduated scale of votes, and the defendant James H. Beatty not being a director, had in order to carry his object transferred his shares to persons in trust for him, and thereby increased his voting powers, that would have been a perfectly legal exercise of his right, and no Court could interfere with it. Here he has resorted to no such scheme, but has voted upon the shares which he held, and the sole question is, whether the accident of his being a director makes any difference.

Several cases have been cited by the learned Chancellor in his judgment, but I do not think any of them tend to shew that a shareholder's rights are, at all restricted or controlled from the circumstance of his being either President or Director of the company. I am satisfied no such case can be found, and the cases referred to by the learned Judge are not at all opposed on principle to the views I am propounding.

One of the cases so referred to is *The London Mercantile Discount Co.*, L. R. 1 Eq. 277, and was decided by the same learned Judge who decided the case in 2 H. & M., and it arose under the Winding-up Act of 1862: it decides, no doubt, that if the conduct of the majority amounts to a fraud upon or to undue influence with respect to the minority the Court will interfere, but it is also a very direct authority for the proposition that a shareholder, although a director, and although his own acts are impeached, can exercise his rights as a shareholder notwithstanding, as fully as any other shareholder, and the Vice-Chancellor suggested upon the application that it should stand over, to enable the sense of the company to be taken; but on the petitioners stating that there would be no object in that, as the directors had a controlling influence, he dismissed the petition, which would not of course preclude a shareholder from filing a bill to impeach the transaction on the ground of fraud; but upon the point of a director exercising his rights as an ordinary shareholder, the remarks of the learned Vice-

Chancellor are material. The Legislature has thought, he
says, that the shareholders should meet and regulate that
part of their own business as they would regulate any
other part of it, by the views of the majority ; and provided
the votes of the majority are given fairly and reasonably,
there is no ground whatever for the interference of the
Court. That, as I have said, was a case in which discretionary power was given to the Court to interfere with a
voluntary winding up, and the learned Judge proceeds
(p. 282) :

" At the same time no doubt it was foreseen that there
might arise cases of such decided undue influence, and such
a course of overbearing authority by those whose acts were
sought to be impeached, as would render it desirable that
the Court should interfere; and therefore, in such cases, there
was reserved to the Court the power of superintending a
voluntary winding-up by putting in force its coercive
jurisdiction, where any thing improper should be attempted
on the part of those who might endeavour to screen their
own actions by procuring a voluntary winding-up."

There, if the directors votes' had been deducted there
would have been a majority in favour of the winding-up
under the supervision of the Court.

Mason v. *Harris*, L. R. 11 Ch. 97, is also referred to, but
with great respect is an authority in favour of the appellant's contention.

In effect that was a contract by the defendant Harris to
sell and by the company to purchase a business. The
value of that business had been fraudulently and grossly
overvalued. It was alleged that the defendant as director
had appropriated cash bills belonging to the company, and
that the control of the company was in the hands of the
defendant, so that the plaintiff could not use the company's
name.

All these charges were admitted by the demurrer, and
the prayer of the bill was, that the agreement might be
cancelled on the ground of fraud, and that the defendant
should be ordered to pay back the money which he had
fraudulently appropriated. These being acts which the

majority could not sanction, and it being admitted on the pleadings that the defendant prevented the use of the company's name, it was held that one shareholder could sue on behalf of himself and others.

It was admitted that the company, strictly speaking were the proper parties to sue, but this came within the few exceptions which allow a deviation from that general rule.

Menier v. *Hooper's Telegraph Co.*, L. R. 9 Ch. 350, in fact affirms the proposition that the shareholders of a company may vote as they please and for the purpose of their own interests. In that case, however, it was held in accordance with the general rule, that a shareholder might file a bill to impeach a transaction which was *ultra vires*, and a fraud upon the shareholders other than those who profited by it. It was in fact an attempt by some of the shareholders to sell the assets of the Company, and put them into their own pockets.

Melhado v. *Hamilton*, 29 L. J. N.S. 364; is a case in which what was sought to be done was *ultra vires* of the company, that is the issue of preference shares, and therefore it was quite clear that a majority could not bind the minority.

In *Re Wedgewood*, 6 Ch. Div. 629, the consent of the court was required to confirm a resolution for a reconstruction scheme under the Joint Stock Companies arrangement Act, and the Court there held that the resolution must be passed *bonâ fide*, and without any sinister object, and that the act of one of the voters there upon a £25 debenture who was a debtor to the company for £35,000, and who had gone there for the purpose of relieving himself of that liability at the expense of another class of shareholders, could not be regarded as a *bond fide* exercise of his rights in favour of the company, but for his own interests, and as the Court had to judge whether that resolution had been properly passed, it refused under the circumstances to do so, stating that it was not different in principle from the decision in *Re Page* 2 Ch. Div. 223, where under a bankruptcy

proceeding creditors in value to the extent of three-fourths
had power to bind the minority. There, a bankrupt seeking
a composition,shewed by a statement of assets and liabilities
that he could pay four or five shillings in the pound,
but the statutory majority of the creditors agreed to
accept one shilling, and it was held that this was manifestly not a *bond fide* regard for the interest of the
creditors, but a mere favour shewn to the debtor, and the
registrar of bankruptcy having a right to decide whether
a resolution of creditors should be registered or not, and this
resolution being opposed, he very properly determined
that the creditors had exceeded their powers in making a
present to the debtor at the expense of the other creditors.
So, in the case then being decided, the Court held that some
of the majority were not acting under the statute *bond fide*,
having regard to the interests of the company but for the
purpose of exonerating themselves from a liability they
had incurred, and as remarked as to one of them, by a
course of conduct of a most improper description.

The case referred to by the Chancellor, of *Re Haven
Gold Mining Co.*, 20 Ch. D. 151, is, when properly looked
at, so far as the dictum of Sir George Jessel is concerned,
a strong authority in favour of the view that the shareholders here could ratify the transaction. He says, even
in the case of a fraudulent representation or fraudulent
representations in a prospectus, a company may, if they
think fit, waive the fraud and proceed with the bargain,
or they may vary the bargain on account of fraud, and
complete it with variations. As to that, the majority of
the company in general meeting assembled are the best
judges, but where the whole thing is gone the majority
cannot bind the minority to enter into an entirely new
speculation and it never has been so held.

The recent case also referred to by the Chancellor, of *In re
Pepperell*, 27 W. N. 410, does not appear to me to militate
against the views I have attempted to express, it was there
held that the husband of an administratrix filled a
fiduciary position, and could not purchase without the

assent of all the next of kin, but it was admitted that acquiescence on the part of the plaintiff would validate the sale.

Here, the defendant James H. Beatty occupied a fiduciary position towards the company : without its acquiescence, the transaction could be impeached, but with its consent signified in the usual way by a majority after due notice to all concerned the transaction was validated.

In many of those cases to which I have referred the majority vote was obtained by counting that of the interested party, who in many of them filled the position of director.

The contention of the learned counsel that such a vote though good in law was void in equity, has the merit of novelty, but is not supported by authority. The share-holder's vote is a right of property to be exercised in any way he thinks best, but there may no doubt be a distinc-tion, as illustrated in some of the cases I have cited, between such a vote and the vote of a creditor as a member of a class on whom is conferred by the Legislature the power of controlling the rights of the minority of that class. In the latter case, as has been well observed, there may be good ground for saying that the voter is entrusted with his vote in his character of a member of a class, and that he is bound to exercise it *bonâ fide* for the benefit of the class, including himself, and not for that of himself as opposed to the class.

It was, I thought, rather faintly urged that the company could only act through their agents the directors, and had no power at a general meeting to authorize a purchase of this nature. But it was very properly answered that the directors are appointed and entrusted with powers of management as a matter of convenience amounting almost to necessity, but that anything which the agents could do the principals could also do. I allude to it because some stress was laid upon the circumstance that the sale was actually made by the directors, the by-law passed, and the agreement for the purchase executed before the meeting of the shareholders. It is perfectly manifest that the whole thing was provisional and dependent entirely on its ratification by the shareholders, but assuming a view most favourable to the plaintiff, that the sale had been completed by the directors, and that its ratification by the shareholders had been an after thought, it is to my mind perfectly clear that being a pure question of internal management the shareholders had a perfect right to ratify the act or to treat it as an original offer and assent to and complete the purchase.

A court of equity regards the substance and not the mere form of the transaction; in the present case the majority have decided upon a certain course of action, which is *intra vires* of the company, and which so far as one can judge was absolutely essential to the continuance of the business of the company.

No case has been referred to in the Court below, nor cited to us on the argument of this appeal which would warrant us in fettering the hands of the majority, or in restraining them from carrying out what they believe to be most for their interest, from the mere circumstance that one of the parties interested in carrying out the sale is the largest shareholder, and makes his influence felt in a perfectly legitimate way at a meeting duly convened.

I have referred to the cases cited on the argument. and find none of them at variance with the views I have expressed, but do not think it necessary to allude to any of them specially, with the exception of *York, &c.* v. *Hudson*, 16 Beav. 485, because we were told that that case established that a confirmation to be valid must be by each and every shareholder. I do not at all question that in that particular case such a confirmation might have been necessary. There, a director in whose name for the benefit of the company a number of shares had been placed, sold them at a premium, accounting to the company for the par value of the shares, but putting the premium into his own pocket. The company brought a suit to compel him to account for this excess, and he had no answer to such a demand by

the company, but at p. 495 of the report, the Master of the
Rolls, intimates that it is not necessary to decide whether if
a meeting of shareholders had by a majority decided to make
a present to Mr. Hudson of this sum as a remuneration for
his services, that would be binding on the minority.   There
is nothing in that case to interfere with the general rule ;
that except in cases of fraud, or *ultra vires*, the shareholders
have full power to deal with all matters of internal management and domestic concern.

With the greatest respect for the opinion of the learned
Chancellor, I think there is no principle of equity to
prevent the defendant from exercising his rights as a
shareholder as fully as any other of the members of the
company, and that the appeal should be allowed, with costs,
and the bill dismissed, with costs.

PATTERSON, J. A., concurred in allowing the appeal.

OSLER, J.A.—I shall only add a very few words, having
had an opportunity of reading the opinion which has just
been delivered by my lord, in the reasoning and conclusion
of which I concur.

In the *Great Luxembourg R. W. Co. v Magnay*, 25
Beav. 586, which I refer to as an illustration of a number
of cases in which the rule is stated in a similar way,
the Master of Rolls, speaking of the duties and functions of a director of a joint stock company, says: "He
is in point of law not merely a director but he also
fills the character of a trustee for the shareholders, and he
is in regard to all matters entered into in their behalf to be
treated as an agent.   *   *   Therefore there attach to a
director, for the benefit of the shareholders, all the liabilities and duties which attach to a trustee and agent.   Accordingly if he enter into a contract for the company he
cannot personally derive any benefit from it.   *   *   *
There is no mode by which any species of sale or dealing
between the company and one of its directors can be made
valid and effectual, except by bringing the circumstances
attending it fully before a general meeting of the shareholders, and first obtaining their sanction to the transac-

tion." In the case before us the transaction was of that
character and the company might have repudiated it or
set it aside. But as it was not *ultra vires* the company,
it might have been sanctioned and adopted by the shareholders at a general meeting. At such a meeting the will
of the corporation is manifested, not by their agents the
directors, but by the corporators—the shareholders—themselves, each of whom, though he may also happen to be a
director or officer of the company and interested in the
contract or other matter under consideration, as for instance
his own continuance in or removal from office, has the
right to vote thereon in respect of his shares. The
distinction between the two positions of director and
shareholder is well pointed out by the Vice-Chancellor in
the case in 2 H. & M. 261 (n), "As to the management of
the company by the board, no director is entitled to vote
as director in respect of any contract in which he is
interested, but the case is different when he acts as one of
a whole body of shareholders. The shareholders of one
company may have dealings with interests in other companies and therefore it would be manifestly unfair to
prevent an individual shareholder from voting as a shareholder in the affairs of the company. At a general meeting his vote must be held to be good so long as he continues to hold his shares."

When, therefore, it is said that a director is trustee for
the shareholders, that must be understood in the qualified
sense, that he is so when he is acting as director of the
company, not in the broad and general sense in which a
trustee of property is trustee for his *cestuis que trustent*,
so that he cannot acquire it without the consent of each
and all of his beneficiaries. His right as a shareholder to
vote would otherwise be illusory, since *ex hypothesi* it is
only when there is a difference of opinion among the shareholders that it becomes necessary to exercise it. I may
quote the observations of James, L. J., in *Smith* v. *Anderson*, 15 Ch. D. 274, 275, although they were not made in reference to dealings between trustee and *cestui que trust*.
He says: "The distinction between a director and a trustee

is an essential distinction founded on the very nature of things. A trustee is a man who is the owner of the property and deals with it as principal, as owner, and as master, subject only to an equitable obligation to account to some persons to whom he stands in the relation of trustee, and who are his *cestuis que trustent*. The same individual may fill the office of a director and also be a trustee having property, but that is a rare, exceptional, and casual circumstance. The office of director is that of paid servant of the company. A director never enters into contracts for himself, but he enters into contracts for his principal, that is, for the company of whom he is a director, and for whom he is acting. * * That seems to be the broad distinction between trustees and directors."

According to the authorities which have been referred to, the will of the majority, even when that majority is ascertained by counting the vote of an interested shareholder, is the will of the corporation; *Gregory v. Patchett*, 33 Beav. 695; *Pender v. Lushington*, 6 Ch. D. 70; *Menier v. Telegraph Co.*, L. R. 9 Ch. 350, and, speaking generally, controls the minority in all matters relating to the internal economy and management of the company. And where the transaction is not *ultra vires*, and the company do not choose to attack it; but, speaking by the voice of the majority, adopt and confirm it; where the element of fraud or improper dealing is absent; *In re London, &c., Discount Co.*, L. R. 1 Eq. 277; *Lewis v. Gray*, L. R. 8 Ch. 1055; *Foss v. Harbottle*, 2 Hare 461, and where the majority are not by means of the transaction obtaining a benefit for themselves, or one of themselves at the expense of the minority, (29 L. T. N. S. 364, 6 Ch. D. 627,) it would seem that it cannot be impeached by a dissentient shareholder.

Several of the questions which have been argued before us in this case, and particularly the right of an individual shareholder to maintain the action, were discussed and considered by the late Chief Justice of this Court, in *McMurray v. The Northern R. W. Co.*, 22 Gr. 476.

I have to agree that the appeal should be allowed, but I think it should be without costs.

ELLIOTT v. BROWN ET AL.

Void conveyance by married woman—Possession contrary to the deed—
R. S. O. ch. 127, ss. 13 and 14.

In 1834 C. A., a married woman, purported to convey to one T., in
fee, the east half of a lot of land granted to her by the Crown, but the
conveyance was invalid by reason of the want of the usual certificate
by justices of the peace on the deed. T. never took possession, but in
1852, conveyed to H. through whom the plaintiff claimed. In or about
the year 1866, the two sons of C. A. went and resided on the west half
of the land upon the understanding and agreement with their mother
that they were to have the whole lot, but no conveyance was executed
to them until 1875. During the interval, however, the sons paid the
taxes on the whole property, and cut timber at times on the east half.

Held, (reversing the judgment of the Q. B. D., reported 2 O. R. 352) that
this was a sufficient "actual possession or enjoyment " of the east half
of the lot to prevent the operation of section 13 of R. S. O. ch. 127 (36
Vic. ch. 18, s. 12), by means of which such void deed would be rendered valid. OSLER, J.A., dissenting.

THIS was an appeal by the defendant John Kelly from
the judgment of the Queen's Bench Division, (2 O. R. 352).

The action was to recover possession of the east half of
lot No. 5 in the 13th concession of the township of
Hungerford, in the county of Hastings, and was tried at
Belleville before Senkler, Co. J. of Lincoln, (sitting for
Wilson, C. J.,) without a jury, when judgment was given
in favour of the defendants.

The Queen's Bench Division, (Cameron, J., dissenting,)
reversed the judgment at the trial and ordered judgment to
be entered for the plaintiff.

The facts are fully stated in the report of the case
below, and in the judgments on the present appeal, which
was heard on the 25th of November, 1884.*

G. D. Dickson, Q. C., and *G. H. Watson*, for the appellant.

G. T. Blackstock and *Wallbridge*, for the respondent.

January 26th, 1885. PATTERSON, J. A.—This is an
action to recover the east half of lot No. 5 in the 13th concession of Hungerford.

Present.—BURTON, PATTERSON, MORRISON, and OSLER, JJ.A.

The defendant Kelly limits his defence to the south half of the land claimed, and the other defendants defend for the north half only.

His Honour Judge Senkler, who tried the action, gave judgment for the defendants. That judgment was reversed by the Divisional Court of the Queen's Bench Division, Mr. Justice Cameron dissenting. This appeal is from the judgment of the Divisional Court, and is by the defendant Kelly only.

Catherine Allard was patentee of the lot. She joined with her husband in 1834 in executing a conveyance of the east half of the lot to one Terry, who conveyed to Howe, who conveyed to Davy. Davy died, and his interest was sold under a judgment against his administratrix to Perry, who on the 28th of April, 1871, conveyed to Francis Elliott. The plaintiff is widow of Francis Elliott and claims one undivided moiety of the east half of the lot by conveyance from one of the two sons and heirs-at-law of her husband.

The validity of this title depends on the effect of the deed of 1834 from the patentee to Terry. It was executed without the examination and certificate of freedom from coercion, necessary under the statute 1st Wm. IV. ch. 2, to give any validity or effect to the deed of a married woman.

Nothing, therefore, passed by any of the deeds which formed the chain from Mrs. Allard down to Francis Elliott or to the plaintiff, unless the statute passed on 29th March, 1873, which is now found in R. S. O. ch. 127, cured the defects of the deed of 1834.

The 13th section of that statute makes valid any such conveyance executed before 29th March, 1873, except in the cases mentioned in section 14.

That section provides for three cases in which the deed shall not be rendered valid. The *second* case is, when the conveyance from the married woman was not executed in good faith. We may leave this out of sight, as the *bonâ fides* of the deed of 1834 is not impeached, and confine our attention to the *first* and *third* cases or conditions.

The *first* is, that "nothing in this Act contained shall render valid any conveyance to the prejudice of any title subsequently to the execution of such conveyance, and before the said date, acquired from the married woman by deed duly executed and certified as by law required, unless actual possession or enjoyment of the real estate conveyed or intended to be conveyed by the prior conveyance has been had at any time subsequent thereto by the grantee therein, or those claiming by, from or under him, and he or they have been in such actual possession or enjoyment continuously for the period of three years before the said date, and he or they were at the said date in the actual possession or enjoyment thereof."

This is not the condition which comes directly in question in the present case, because Mrs. Allard did not execute any second deed of the land in question until after 1873.

The *third* condition is, that "nothing in this Act contained shall render valid * * any conveyance of land of which the married woman or those claiming under her is or are in the actual possession or enjoyment contrary to the terms of such conveyance."

The principle of the statute seems to be to give legal validity to those deeds which, though invalid for want of compliance with the law respecting conveyances by married women, have nevertheless been regarded and acted upon as if they were valid by the parties who made them; but to leave the defects uncured, when the understanding of the parties themselves was that the deeds were inoperative; and I take the *first* and *third* conditions of section 14 to define what is to be evidence of the recognition by the parties of the validity or invalidity of the deeds.

The *first* condition deals with the case where the married woman has made a second and valid deed. The two deeds are then in competition; and the statute seems to contemplate only a case where they have both been at least three years in existence, or where at all events the first one has been made for three years. Three years'

continuous possession by the grantee under the first deed
may fairly be taken to evidence the understanding that
the right is in the first grantee, the *bona fides* of whose
deed is one of the data, otherwise it would be avoided by
the *second* condition.

At all events the first grantee is asserting his right, and
the second grantee, if not intentionally acquiescing in the
assertion, has by his lack of vigilance enabled his competi-
tor to furnish the evidence which the statute requires.

Under which of the two conditions, the first or the
third, a case would come where the first and the second
deeds were both within the three years, or whether that
would prove to be a *casus omissus*, is a matter which will
have to be dealt with when it arises. The case of there
being no second deed is clearly contemplated by the *third*
condition : and under that condition the attitude of the
married woman, or those claiming under her, when the
statute takes effect, is that of repudiation of the conveyance or assertion of its invalidity. The statute does
not, in that case, assume to give to the deed an effect
which thitherto it had not possessed either in law or by
concession.

There is nothing in the statute which requires us to
attribute, or would justify us in attributing, to the Legislature an *ex post facto* interference with contracts which
had been understood and acted upon by the parties who
made them in accordance with their true legal effect ; nor
is there anything to require us to construe the words
" actual possession or enjoyment," with so great strictness
as not to be satisfied by such evidence as will shew with
reasonable certainty, under the tests prescribed in the
statute itself, how the transaction was really regarded and
treated.

Evidence which would prove possession under the
Statute of Limitations would of course always suffice ;
but there is no necessary analogy between the two statutes,
and the common position under the Statute of Limitations
cannot arise when the married woman or her second

grantee, being *ex hypothesi* the owner in fee by reason of
the invalidity of the first deed, takes possession by virtue
of the legal title and not as a wrongdoer.

If, therefore, Mrs. Allard was owner of the whole lot on
29th March, 1873, and was in actual occupation of any
part of it under her legal title to the whole, no person
being in adverse possession of any part of the lot, her possession would be actual possession of the whole lot. It
would not be merely constructive possession of any part,
such as would follow from her legal title in case she was
not in occupation of the lot at all. I understand the judgment of Mr. Justice Cameron to have been based on that
apprehension of the facts, and I believe the same thing
may be said of the judgment of Judge Senkler.

There is a good deal of difficulty however, in so collecting
the facts from the evidence.

Mrs. Allard was undoubtedly owner in fee of the east
half, because her deed to Terry was absolutely inoperative
to pass her estate. But her actual occupation, to the
particulars of which I shall presently refer, or at least any
occupation more continuous than the mere user of woodland for the ordinary purposes for which it is used, was
confined to the west half of the lot, and upon the evidence
we can scarcely hold that she owned the west half.

She tells us, in her evidence at the trial, that she had
conveyed the west half to one Power. It is not perfectly
clear from what she says whether that was before or after
the deed to Terry. That deed was in 1834. A year or
two later Terry told Mrs. Allard, as she says, that he had
been to look at the land, and that he would not live on it.
She does not say that he spoke of giving it up to her, and
the fact that Terry conveyed it to Horne in 1852 rather
goes to shew that he then thought it was his. In 1855 or
1856 Mrs. Allard and her husband went to see the land,
and were shewn it by Mr. Bowell, who lived on an adjoining
lot, and Mrs. Allard gave Mr. Bowell charge of the whole
lot, to protect it from trespassers. I shall read a few
questions and answers from her evidence on this part of
the case:

"Q. Did you or your husband go over the place? A. Yes. Q. Which one of you? A. My husband. Q. Did you leave it in charge of anyone? A. Yes; left it in charge of Mr. John Bowell: Mr. Bowell lives near there: I told Mr. Bowell to take charge of it, and if anybody troubled it to let me know. Q. Did you pay any taxes on it? A. Yes. Q. Can you tell from memory how many years you paid taxes on it? A. My son will tell that: I put him on it. Q. Before your son went on it, did you pay any taxes on it yourself? A. Yes; we paid some taxes on it before that.

THE COURT—Had you sold the west half at this time? A. No. Q. You still owned the west half? A. Yes.

MR. DICKSON.—Did you ever execute a deed of the west half to anyone? A. Yes. Q. Before you executed a deed to your son did you ever execute a deed of that lot to anyone—to Roger Power? A. Yes; to Roger Power. Q. Was that before or after the deed to Terry? A. It was before, I think."

On cross examination she was asked:

"Q. You did, you say, execute a deed to Roger Power? A. Yes. Q. Which half was that? A. The west hundred. Q. And before that you had given a deed to Terry of which hundred? A. The east hundred."

Counsel here changes the order of the two deeds from what Mrs. Allard had mentioned in her direct examination, and the witness answered the question, which had no reference to the date, without correcting him. The learned Judge at the trial says she stated in cross-examination, contrary to her former statement, that the Power deed was after the Terry deed; but what I have read is the only reference to it which I notice in the cross-examination, as the evidence is reported to us.

Mr. Bowell was also examined. I shall read a short extract from his evidence.

"Q.—About how many years ago would you say it was that they came there the first time? A.—I think it must be 24 or 25 years ago; I cannot say for a year or two. Q.—What took place then with regard to the lot? A.—They asked me if I would go and show them the lot. I told them yes. The next morning after breakfast Mrs. Allard and I started to go to the lot. Mrs. Allard got about half way across my pasture field, and she had to stop because the snow was up to her knees. Henry Allard went on with me. He asked me about a clearance that was on it called Power's clearance. I took him to that. He said ' why, he told us before he gave us the deed he had cleared five acres and built a house on it.' Said I, ' there is no house on the lot.' Power's clearing was on the west

half. Q.—Then did you go on the east half of the lot with him too? A.—
I did not. We went pretty well to the further end of the west half, and
then turned down and went to the edge of the swamp, because the east
half is all swamp, a very thick swamp that would puzzle anybody to get
through at that time, and we came along the side of it."

Then he spoke of the lot being left in his charge, that is
the whole lot, for the Allards did not tell him of the deed
to Terry of the east half; and he also mentioned an occasion
when a person was cutting timber on the lot, to whom Mr.
Bowell gave notice not to trespass. On cross-examination
he spoke again of Power's clearing, thus:

"Q.—Do you know when Power's clearing was made? A.—No. That
was long before I went into the woods. It was all grown up with young
trees and berry bushes. It was not cultivated at all."

The Terry title was indirectly mentioned by Mr. Bowell
when he spoke of the east half having been sold for taxes
to himself, and redeemed for the estate of Davy who had
taken under that title.

Mrs. Allard and Mr. Bowell were called on behalf of the
defendants. I think they are bound by her statement that
she conveyed the west half of the lot to Power, and on the
whole I gathered from her evidence, which seems to be
supported by Mr. Bowell's description of Power's clearance,
that the deed to Power was earlier than that to Terry.
When Mrs. Allard answered in the affirmative the Judge's
question if she had sold the west half at "this time," which
either meant the time she went to Mr. Bowell or some indefinite time when she says she paid taxes, I rather think
she must have alluded to having re-acquired the land from
Power, as her husband did when he spoke to Mr. Bowell
in the way that gentlemen mentions in his evidence which
I have read, and not that she meant to say she conveyed
to Power after that date.

The defendants do not seem to have appreciated the importance of proving this re-acquisition of the land by regular
evidence. Unfortunately for them, we have not even a
direct statement from Mrs. Allard that she did re-acquire it,
and can only surmise from what she happens to say, and

from what Mr. Bowell says was said by her husband, that possibly that may have been the fact.

What we know, then, is that in 1855 or 1856, Mrs. Allard, being owner in fee of the east half of the lot, and asserting title to the west half also, walked over the west half, or her husband did so, and Mr. Bowell on her behalf exercised some oversight over the lot, but without being in actual possession of it, until 1866 or 1867 when her sons, or one of them, went to live on the west half.

The two sons, James and John, had an arrangement or understanding with their mother that they were to take care of the lot, and she was to give it to them.

In pursuance of this they built a house on the west half and cleared some land, James living steadily there, and John living there also but not being always there. The young men had an understanding between themselves that the house and clearing, with the half lot on which they stood, should belong to the one who married first, who was then to assist the other one to clear as much land on his half lot. They agreed to divide the lot into north half and south half, because, as they state the reason, the east half was all swamp. I do not understand however that any actual division in the sense of separate occupation, took place until 1875, when James having married, their mother conveyed the south half to James and the north half to John, each of them paying her $50. In the meantime the statute had, on 29th March, 1873, come into force, and the question turns on the position at that date.

The bush land on the lot, which comprised the entire east half and part of the west half, had been used as woodland is ordinarily used by the owner of the farm on which it is, by cutting timber, rails, &c., as required, no distinction being made between the east and west halves, and by once selling a considerable quantity of timber off the east half. This last-mentioned transaction was after the sons were on the lot. It was a sale to a Mr. Wallbridge of timber for a mill. Mrs. Allard gave him the permission to cut, and James and John worked for him at the cutting.

The first attempt at taking possession under the Terry
title was by Francis Elliott, after he bought from Perry
in 1871.

In December of that year he had a line run by a surveyor between the east and west halves. This was
against the remonstrance of James Allard, who forbade
him and asserted title to the land in his mother; and
she had herself, as she tells us, given express notice to
Elliott, through his wife, before he had completed his
purchase from Perry, that the land belonged to her.

Elliott cut and drew away timber during the winter of
of 1871-2, and again during the winter of 1872-3. He
was clearly a trespasser at those times. Mrs. Allard brought
an action of trespass against him towards the end of
December, 1872. He filed an appearance in the action on
the 19th February, 1873, which shews that he was served
with the writ not later than that day, and ultimately, but
not till long after March, 1873, he settled the action and
paid the costs.

I do not know that much significance attaches to the
bringing of this action as a fact by itself. It was of course
an assertion of her right by Mrs. Allard, but it was not
necessarily an assertion of *actual* possession at any time,
or of possession either actual or constructive on the 29th
March, 1873. Elliott could not have resisted the action
successfully; and neither his admission of his want of title
when he committed the trespasses, which was merely an
admission of the truth, nor his paying for trespasses which
he found he could not justify, can have any bearing on the
question of the operation of the statute.

For the defendants it was contended before us that, in
some way, Elliott had estopped himself from disputing the
Allard title, and that the plaintiff who claims in privity
with him was likewise estopped. There is no foundation
for any such contention. Neither the defendants nor those
through whom they claim were led to change their position by any act or representation of Elliott; and his acts
or admissions, while creating no estoppel, were all consis-

tent with the true state of the title prior to 29th March, 1873, and do not touch the question of the possession upon that day, which is the one important fact.

The learned Judge who tried the action states it to be his opinion that Elliott did not cut timber on the lot later than the winter of 1872-3, and there is direct evidence, the reliability of which there is no reason to doubt, that he did not trespass after he was served with the writ.

I do not know that his assertion of title, or his unfounded dispute of the title of Mrs. Allard, are matters of any consequence; but there can be no doubt, as I understand the facts, that upon the day which we have to keep in view, viz., 29th March, 1873, Elliott was in no sense in possession of any part of the lot.

The question, however, still remains, was Mrs. Allard in actual possession or enjoyment of the east half upon that day contrary to the terms of her conveyance?

Before discussing this, there is just one other fact to mention, viz., that during the winter of 1872-3, while Elliott was cutting, James Allard was also cutting timber beside him on the east half of the lot.

The evidence can leave no doubt upon the mind that Mrs. Allard was distinctly asserting and insisting on her title to the east half of the lot, and that Francis Elliott was left in no uncertainty upon that point. We have not only the uncontradicted fact of her having as far back as 1855 given charge of the whole lot to Mr. Bowell, and the other fact of her having in 1866 transferred the charge of it to her sons under an understanding with them which embraced the entire lot, in accordance with which they had assumed actual possession; but we have her own evidence, which is not contradicted or impugned, that when she heard that Elliott was purchasing the east hundred acres she went to his house to see him, and not finding him at home, said to his wife, "He knows better than to buy it, that it belongs to me; you tell him I forbid him to buy it or cut timber on it." This was followed up by James Allard warning Elliott not to run the line, and forbidding him to cut timber, and afterwards insisting on himself cutting timber east of the line, and refusing to be deterred from so doing by Elliott; and finally by the action brought against Elliott.

If under these circumstances, the statute took the land from Mrs. Allard and gave it to Elliott, it had an effect which, if I have correctly interpreted the principle on which it was based, was foreign to the intention of the Legislature. It would, in that case, give to the deed of 1834 an effect which it had not possessed either in law or by the concession or recognition of the person by whom it was executed.

If Mrs. Allard's legal right, as it undoubtedly existed up to the passing of the Act, was taken from her, that result must have been due not to any want of apprehension of her right on her part, or want of actual and active assertion of it, but because her attitude with regard to the soil itself was not that which the statute made essential as evidence of her assertion of the invalidity of the deed of 1834, namely, actual possession or enjoyment contrary to the terms of the deed.

I am of opinion that the evidence required by the statute is afforded by the facts proved, and that the learned Judge who tried the action was right in holding that the deed of 1834 remained, as it had always been, invalid.

I think this appears, even if we regard the east half of the lot apart from its connection with the west half, as if e. g. the Allards had been living on an adjoining lot; but I by no means concede that the occupation, under the circumstances, of the west half, may not bear to an important extent, upon the question in dispute.

If we look at the east half by itself, we have not only the assertion of right to it, coupled with the indisputable legal title, all of which might be consistent with merely constructive possession; but we have also the actual occupation of it while cutting timber and exercising such acts of ownership as may be exercised over wild land, these

acts being ostentatiously done in opposition to the person who now disputes the existence of the actual possession, and we have these acts done by a person who was in
charge of the land for the owner of it, as caretaker (to
put the evidence in the way least favourable to the
defendants), and who lived close to it and constantly
watched it.

I take part of this language from the judgment of
Hagarty, J., in *Heyland* v. *Scott*, 19 C. P. at p. 172, where
he mentions the ruling of Draper, C. J., which had been
upheld by the Court of Queen's Bench in *Stoneburner* v.
Muttice, tried at Cornwall in October, 1867, in which the
evidence was that a person, claiming under a defective tax
title the whole of a wild lot, lived close to it and constantly
watched and guarded it from trespassers, using it himself
when required for cutting timber, &c. The same objection
was urged, the learned Judge states, and the same direction
in substance given to the jury, as in *Heyland* v. *Scott*,
the Chief Justice declining to rule that nothing but actual
enclosing and fencing would suffice.

The charge upheld in *Heyland* v. *Scott*, in which case,
however, part of the lot claimed was actually occupied,
was, " that if a person claiming title to a lot send a caretaker to live on it, and specially to protect the whole from
trespassers, and that if he do so accordingly, that such may
be a good legal possession of all so held and protected."
The law so laid down was approved and followed in several
cases—*e. g., Davis* v. *Henderson*, 29 U. C. R. 344, and
Mulholland v. *Conklin*, 22 C. P. 372. In *Harris* v. *Mudie*,
7 A. R. 414, my brother Burton remarked upon these cases ;
and while I do not understand him to disapprove of the
decision of *Heyland* v. *Scott*, upon the facts of that case,
he expressed the opinion that some of the later cases had
gone farther than was consistent with the true intent of
the Statute of Limitations, in extending the possession of
a trespasser on a lot to portions of the lot of which he had
no continuous occupation. I am not now entering at all
into that controversy. I concede, if necessary, that in

Stoneburner v. *Mattice*, and also in *Heyland* v. *Scott*, the defendants, who set up the Statute of Limitations against the legal title, had the benefit of a somewhat extreme view of the rule of evidence concerning the possession of wild land. The dispute touches only the extent, not the fact, of the possession.

We have no difficulty about the extent of the possession of Mrs. Allard who owned the land, if it existed in fact, and we have her possession in fact, or actual possession, proved by evidence of the same character and fully as strong and precise as that in the cases I refer to.

That there may be actual possession of wild land under section 14 of the statute which will prevent the operation of section 13 upon a conveyance of wild land, I take to be indisputable. If in this case there was not that actual possession, it is difficult to suppose a case in which it could be maintained. Enclosing the land would add nothing to what was actually done. When the question is raised under the Statute of Limitations by one who has entered without title, his fence, if he has erected one, may afford evidence of the extent of territory over which he asserts his possession, and may have presented visible notice to the person whom he dispossessed. There are reasons of weight given by Chief Justice Cameron in his judgment in *Harris* v. *Mudie*, why, in this Province where the land is divided and granted in defined lots or other parcels, the fencing may have less significance, or may be a less important feature of the evidence than sometimes supposed. Here we have acts done upon the ground which are as distinct assumptions of possession as well as of ownership as putting up a fence could be ; and we have as distinct notice given to Elliott of the extent, as well as the nature of the claim, as he could have had by seeing a fence round the whole hundred acres.

Then we must not overlook the alternative nature of the requisites of the statute. Actual possession is not required if there is actual enjoyment. Here again one must bear in mind that we are dealing with wild land. The evidence proves actual enjoyment and perception of profits of the land, of the nature of which wild land is capable. Elliott attempted to oust the Allards from that enjoyment, or to himself enjoy the land, by cutting timber. They not only continued their own use of the land, but by their action of trespass asserted their right to enjoy, in the shape of damages to be paid by Elliott, the timber which he cut and removed.

Some allusion was made in the Court below to Elliott disputing the possession. I have shewn that on the day to which our attention has to be directed his interference had ceased. But the statute says nothing of undisputed right. The question is, was Mrs. Allard on the 29th of March asserting her right by actual possession or enjoyment, contrary to the terms of her deed?

I think we should be bound to hold that she was, even if we look as I have been doing, at the east half of the lot, without reference to the west half.

But I am not prepared to hold that the west half can properly be excluded from the discussion.

The evidence of Mr. Bowell, as well as that of Mrs. Allard herself shews that she entered claiming to own the whole. She has, it is true, proved that she once conveyed away the west half, and has not proved that she re-acquired it. Her statement that she owned it when she gave Mr. Bowell charge, does not prove her ownership, but that statement coupled with her husband's statement to Mr. Bowell that Power had given them a deed, with what we know of the charge given to Mr. Bowell and the possession given to James and John Allard, sufficiently establish that the settlement upon the west half was made under an assertion of an existing right to the whole lot, not with the design of acquiring a title by twenty or forty years' possession to the west half of it.

We have in this circumstance, taken in connection with the other evidence of use and payment to which I have sufficiently referred, a state of facts which, if the question

was whether there was possession of the east half within
the contemplation of the statute of limitations, would be
as strong as those in the cases to which I have referred;
and then we have, in the actual ownership of the east half,
a fact which distinguishes the case from any other.

With these facts must always be taken the express notice
to Elliott, and his undoubted knowledge that the Allards
were claiming to be in possession of the whole lot, a knowledge which he must have had all along, but had beyond all
question when he was forbidden to run the line, and more
emphatically when he was served with the writ.

In my opinion the defendants proved that Mrs. Allard
was on 29th March, 1873, in the actual possession and enjoyment of the east half of the lot contrary to the terms of
her conveyance to Terry under which the plaintiff claims,
and that we should therefore allow the appeal, with costs,
and restore the judgment given at the trial.

BURTON, J. A.—I also agree in allowing the appeal and
restoring the judgment of the learned County Court Judge.

By the Act of 1873, the formality (usually a very useless one) of requiring a separate examination of the married
woman by Justices of the Peace, and a certificate by them
of her consent to make the conveyance, was abolished, and
she was allowed to convey her lands, provided her husband
joined in the deed, without any other formality than is
required by persons *sui juris*.

When passing a law of that nature it was apparently
thought reasonable that where deeds had been made by
married women previously without these formalities, but
had been acted upon as if they had been duly executed,
and had, in other words, been treated as valid by the parties
themselves, they also should be validated.

Perhaps no great injustice would have been done if the
law had been passed in this general form without any
exception, as the married woman in the great majority of
cases received a full equivalent for the lands which she
parted with; but however unnecessary such a protection to

married women may have been, that had been the policy of the law makers up to that time, and it was thought desirable to except from the operation of the enactment three classes of cases :—

1. Where the married woman had executed a subsequent valid conveyance, and the grantee under the defective deed had not been for three years in possession.

2. When the original deed was not obtained by the grantee in good faith, and

3. Which is the case with which we have now to deal, where the married woman is in the actual possession or enjoyment contrary to the terms of the defective deed.

It is obvious that under these exceptions there are many cases in which the married woman may have declined to recognize the validity of the deed, and yet it may have been validated under this enactment.

Assume the case of a grantee under such a conveyance having entered a few months only before the 29th March, 1873, when the statute came into operation, and an action pending by her to recover possession at that time ; I should suppose there could be no doubt that the grantee's title, which was invalid when he entered, would be validated by the statute, notwithstanding the pendency of the suit.

It is clear, therefore, that the mere determination of the married woman to take advantage of the defect in the deed is not sufficient, in itself, to prevent the operation of the Act, unless such determination is evidenced in the manner pointed out in the statute, that is, by actual possession or enjoyment of the land contrary to the terms of the defective conveyance.

In the case of cultivated lands, there would generally be no difficulty in ascertaining whether this condition had been complied with. If the possession was that of the married woman, or her tenant, the Act would not apply ; but the statute applies to 'every conveyance, and, in a great many cases, the land would be, even at the time of the passing of the Act, in a state of nature. What is meant by the actual possession or enjoyment of such lands? It cannot reasonably be held to mean building upon, clearing, and actually fencing any portion of it, and it cannot mean that, as to such lands, the exception shall not apply.

I agree, therefore, in thinking that the acts done by Mrs. Allard's sons in exercising open and notorious acts of ownership over the land in question, and appropriating the timber, was such a possession or enjoyment, contrary to the terms of the deed, as was sufficient to prevent the operation of the statute.

I think the appeal should be allowed.

MORRISON, J.A.—I concur in allowing the appeal.

OSLER, J.A.—If Catherine Allard or her assigns was or were on the 29th March, 1873, in the actual possession or enjoyment of the land contrary to the terms of the conveyance to Terry, the defendant is entitled to succeed, and the plaintiff who relies upon that conveyance will take nothing under it. The question therefore is, what is the meaning of that expression as used in the statute R. S. O. ch. 127, sec. 14, (36 Vict. ch. 18 secs. 12, 13)?

The 13th section validates generally all conveyances executed by a married woman before the 29th March, 1873, notwithstanding the absence of, or defect, or irregularities in the separate acknowledgment or certificate of her consent to convey her estate.

The 14th section excepts certain cases from the generality of this enactment. The first is, where subsequently to the void conveyance and before the above date, the married woman has made another conveyance duly executed and certified. In that case the void conveyance is not validated by the Act as against the latter, unless the grantee under the prior void conveyance has been in the actual possession or enjoyment of the land at, and for three years continuously next before, the said date.

Another exception is the case before us. The Act does not render valid any conveyance of land of which the married woman "or those claiming under her," is or are in the actual possession or enjoyment, contrary to the terms of such conveyance.

The actual possession or enjoyment which in the one case validates the void deed, in favour of the grantee against a later deed; and in the other prevents it from being validated as against the married woman herself, or those claiming under her, must in both cases be of the same character, though in the former it must have existed at and for a period of three years *continuously* (a word which strongly indicates an open undoubted possession) next before the date mentioned in the Act.

Where the married woman relies upon her possession, the Act evidently contemplates something more than the mere constructive possession, which the law attributes to the legal title which remains in her notwithstanding her conveyance. She must have not the possession merely, but the actual possession and enjoyment of the particular parcel of land embraced in the void deed.

The actual possession or enjoyment of the west half of a lot by building upon, fencing and cultivating it, would not in my opinion, for the purpose of this Act, be an actual possession or enjoyment of the east half, which had been intended to be conveyed by the void deed, though the legal title to the whole lot was in the same person (married woman). She always had the constructive possession or possession in law, contrary to the terms of the deed, but she must have had something more than that, in order to prevent the operation of the statute in its favour.

Upon the best consideration I have been able to give to the subject, I am of opinion, agreeing with the judgment of the Court below, that the actual possession or enjoyment required by the Act is not satisfied by occasional entries upon the land for the purpose of cutting timber upon it here and there, or by selling timber off it, or by what would have been mere isolated acts of trespass if done by one not having the legal title. There must be a possession in fact, by which I mean a possession visible

and apparent indicated by residing upon or clearing, improving, or cultivating either the whole or some part of
the particular lot or parcel of land mentioned in the deed:
McDonald v. *Lane*, 7 S. C'R. 462, 467; *Van Velsor* v.
Hughson, 9 A. R. 390, 407; *Thompson* v. *Burhans*,
79 N. Y. 93, 98; *Wolf* v. *Baldwin*, 19 Cal. 306, 314
(1861.); the latter case, which, making allowance for the
difference between city and farm property, appears to me
in its circumstances to run very close to the present, the
question being whether the plaintiffs had shewn that they
had such possession of the premises in controversy as to
entitle them to the benefits of what was known a- the
Van Ness Ordinance, by the 2nd section of which the city
of San Francisco relinquished all her right and claim to land
within her corporate limits with certain exceptions to the
parties in actual possession thereof by themselves or their
tenants on or before the 1st January, 1855, provided such
possession was continued up to the time of the introduction of the ordinance into the City Council, or if interrupted by an intruder or trespasser might have been re-
recovered by legal process. The Court, per S. J. Field, C.J.,
now one of the Justices of the Supreme Court, of the United
States, says, p. 314: "By actual possession, as the terms are
here used, is meant that possession which is accompanied
with the real and effectual enjoyment of the property. It
is the possession which follows the subjection of the
property to the will and dominion of the claimant to the ex-
clusion of others; and this possession must be evidenced
by occupation or cultivation, or other appropriate use,
according to the locality and character of the particular
premises. An enclosure, by an ordinary fence, of the premises, without residence thereon, or improvements or
cultivation or other acts of ownership, is, of itself insufficient. An enclosure of this character is by itself only the
declaration of an intention to appropriate and possess the
premises; it does not, unaccompanied with other acts,
constitute the *actual* possession which the ordinance contemplates." And Baldwin, J., says, p. 318: "No equivocal scrambling possession will do; but it must be a

possession so held and evidenced that, in the absence of
the Van Ness Ordinance, the party holding or claiming it
could, after the lapse of the legal period, invoke in his
behalf the Statute of Limitations, as against the holder of
the adverse title, if that holder were a private person. It
must, in other words, be an open, unequivocal, actual
possession, notorious, apparent, uninterrupted, and exclusive, carrying with it the marks and evidences of
ownership, which apply in ordinary cases to the possession of real property." This case was affirmed and
followed in *Davis* v. *Perley*, 30 Cal. 630 (1866.)

I thinkit was only a possession of that kind which the
Legislature intended to protect against her deed, if the
married woman had it when the Act came into force, or to
protect in favour of the deed against those claiming under
a later deed, if held by the grantee, under the former,
at and for three years continuously before that date. In
short I agree that it must be of the same character as that
which, in a case arising under the Statute of Limitations,
will ripen into a title to the whole of a lot by the possession
of a part for one who has entered upon a supposed or
defective title to the whole, the controversy as to which,
so far as this Court is concerned, is, in my judgment, concluded by the cases of *Harris* v. *Mudie*, 7 A. R. 414;
Shepherdson v. *McCullough*, 46 U. C. R. 573. See also
Hunnicutt v. *Peyton*, 102 U. S. R. 333, 368; *Steers* v.
Shaw, 1 O. R. 26. I don't think the expression "contrary
to the terms of the deed" cuts down the meaning of the
rest of the sentence. If but a single stick of timber had
been cut by Mrs. Allard that was contrary to the terms of
the deed; but neither that, nor cutting sticks of timber on
isolated occasions, or in every winter, would, in my view,
be having the actual possession at the time of the passing
of the Act. Upon the evidence, I see no reason to say
that the finding of the Court below is erroneous as to the
character of Mrs. Allard's possession in this respect. Apart
from her legal title, it would not have sufficed to maintain
trespass against an intruder upon the east half lot.

I think the appeal should be dismissed.

CORPORATION OF DOVER V. CORPORATION OF CHATHAM.

Municipal Act—Drainage by-law—Arbitration—Appeal.

Under the drainage clauses of the Municipal Act a by-law was passed by the township of Chatham, founded on the report, plans, and specifications of a surveyor to authorize the drainage of certain lands in that township. In order to obtain a sufficient fall it was necessary to continue the drain into the adjoining township of Dover. The surveyor assessed certain lots and roads in Dover, and also the town line between Dover and Chatham for part of the cost of the works in proportion to the benefit in his judgment derived by them therefrom. Dover appealed from the report on several grounds, and three arbitrators were appointed pursuant to the Act. At their last meeting they all agreed that the lands and roads in Dover were benefited by the work, but R. F., one of the arbitrators, thought $500 should be taken off the town line. W. D., another of the arbitrators, was of opinion that while the bulk sum assessed was not too great, the assessment on lands and roads should be varied, but that this was for the Court of Revision to do. A memorandum to this effect was signed by W. D. and A. E., the third arbitrator at the foot of which R. F. also signed a memorandum that he dissented and declined to be present at the adjourned meeting to sign the award "*if in accordance with the above memoranda.*" Later, on the same day, the two arbitrators, W. D. and A. E., met and signed an award determining that the assessment on the lands and roads in Dover and the town line should be sustained and confirmed, and also that on the town line between Dover and Chatham :

Held, (1) *per* HAGARTY, C. J. O., and OSLER, J. A., [affirming the judgment of CAMERON, C. J.,] that the award was bad (*a*) as formally sanctioning and confirming the particular assessments on lands and roads and the town line, instead of the aggregate amount assessed, the latter being the only award contemplated at the last meeting, at which all three arbitrators were present (*b*) : because one of the arbitrators had recorded his dissent from the adjustment or scheme of assessment, and yet by the award purported to sanction or affirm it.

Per BURTON and PATTERSON, JJ. A., *contra*, that the duty of the arbitrators was confined to ascertaining the correctness of the proportions payable by each township : that all other objections as to the amounts of the assessment were for the Court of Revision, and that the award did not substantially differ from the memorandum signed at the last meeting of the arbitrators.

Essex v. *Rochester*, 42 U. C. R. 523, and *Thurlow* v. *Sidney*, 1 O. R. 249, commented on.

Held, (2) that the report of the surveyor, incorporated in the by-law, sufficiently shewed the termini of the proposed work, and that under the circumstances it was not open to the objections that it did not expressly state that the work was to be constructed at the expense of both townships and in what proportions, and that it determined, in apparent disregard of section 554, that the work was to be kept in repair by Chatham at the joint expense of Chatham and Dover. OSLER, J. A., dissenting.

Held, (3) upon the true construction of the drainage sections of the Municipal Act, that when drainage works are extended and continued into an adjoining township beyond the limits of the township in which they are commenced, the roads in the former township and the town line are liable to be assessed in proportion to the benefits derived by them therefrom. OSLER, J. A., dissenting.

THIS was an appeal by the defendants, the corporation of the township of Chatham and North Gore, from the judgment of Cameron, J., reported 5 O. R. 325, where and in the present judgments the facts giving rise to the action, the points raised by counsel, and the authorities cited sufficiently appear.

The appeal came on to be heard before this Court on the 11th and 12th days of February, 1885.[*]

Pegley, for the appellants.
Robinson, Q. C., and *M. Wilson*, for the respondents.

April 17, 1885.   HAGARTY, C. J. O.—I think the arbitrators rightly decided not to enter into questions relating to the validity of the petition and the by-law.   What was referred to them under the statutes was the report of the engineer.

The report, plans and specifications are to be served on the head of the Municipality, sec. 538.   By sec. 540 they may "appeal therefrom," and it would seem that it is the only subject for their consideration.   The sufficiency of the by-law and the petition on which it is based can be left to the action of the courts on a proper application.

I also think that the report is not open to the objections as to not shewing a fixed point of commencement.   With the aid of the plans I think that is readily ascertainable. It also, I think, sufficiently fixes the amount to be assessed against Dover as to lots and roads, and we should not be too critical as to the possible inexactness of the language used, if the substantial meaning be clear enough.

Nor do I feel that we must hold the objection fatal that the surveyor could only go into Dover as far as was necessary to get sufficient outfall.   I am not prepared to hold that it appears that he has exceeded his reasonable right and duty in this respect.

I feel a great difficulty on one branch of the case.   At the last meeting of the arbitrators, according to the record

---

[*] *Present* : HAGARTY, C.J.O., BURTON, PATTERSON, and OSLER, JJ.A.

of their proceedings, they all agreed that Dover would be benefited by the work. Fleck considered that $500 should be taken off the assessment on the town line. The others held that the Dover lands and roads were benefited to more than the amount of assessment, and that it should be confirmed; but Mr. Douglas "holding that while the bulk sum assessed is not too great, the lands and roads and parts thereof so assessed should be varied, which it is competent for the Court of Revision to do. * * The arbitrators thereupon 'agree to confirm the assessment as above," &c.

They adjourn to four o'clock to sign the award, Fleck signing a memorandum that he dissents and declines to be present at the adjourned meeting to sign the award *if in accordance with the above memoranda.*

The other two meet and sign the award, determining "that the said assessment upon the lands and roads in Dover and the town line between Dover East and Chatham by the said McGeorge (the surveyor) be sustained and confirmed, as the said lands and roads in said township of Dover will be greatly benefited by the said work, and also the town line between Dover and Chatham."

It thus appears very clearly that the arbitrators on the face of this award sustain and confirm the assessments on lands and roads made by the surveyor; thus so far as in them lay giving their apparent full sanction and approval to his mode of assessment as to each lot and road.

At the same time it is equally clear that one of them thus declaring his assent to such assessment did not in fact approve thereof, but considered that it should be varied, and that the adjustment thereof should be left to the Court of Revision.

This raises a very important question whether arbitrators can so act, in plain language asserting that they confirm and sustain an elaborate distribution of assessment made by the surveyor, declaring at the same time that they do not think it correctly assessed or adjusted.

If the arbitrators considered that their whole duty was to fix a gross sum to be paid by Dover, and that the propriety and justice of the surveyor's adjustment of the amount on lands and roads was a matter with which they had nothing to do it seems to me that they should not have "sustained and confirmed" what the surveyor had done in that respect.

I am not prepared to say that this view was correct, and that the statute permits them to withhold their own judgment on this, and to refer the whole to the Court of Revision.

It is the report with its scheme of assessment and charge that is appealed against, and where a large sum is assessed against specified roads, and another against specified lots, I do not see how they can say that they have nothing to do with the distribution of the whole sum claimed, but only with its aggregate amount.

I think it would be perfectly proper for them to award that as to one or more of the roads assessed there was no benefit to be derived, or that as to lands in a named concession they would be wholly unaffected by the proposed drainage system.

It may be said that the various owners of lots charged are not present, or compellable or notified to attend, to assert their rights. That objection can hardly apply to the municipality, the owners of the roads, who are the actors in the matter of the reference.

We must bear in mind that we are not in this case required to lay down any hard and fast rule as to arbitrators being bound to inquire and adjudicate as to each specific lot or road assessed. What we have to deal with is, the proposition that an arbitrator can openly record his dissent from the survey or adjustment of assessment, and at the same time formally sanction and affirm it.

This becomes specially important when we find the third arbitrator leaving the others under the natural impression that no award would be made which would express that the assessment made by the surveyor on lands and roads should be formally sanctioned and affirmed. I do not think the memorandum imported more than that the amount of the assessment as a whole should be affirmed.

An award by respectable known arbitrators, fully approving of the surveyors detailed adjustment of the assessment, might have a strong effect in influencing the assessed landholders in deciding for or against appealing to the Court of Revision.

I do not think the decision of *Corporation of Thurlow* v. *Sidney*, 1 O. R. 249, has any effect on this case. There the assessment appears to have been made on specified lands in Sidney. The award sued on in the action made no reference to any lands benefited, nor did it contain any formal sanction or confirmation of the surveyor's report thereon, it merely declared that one of the drains proposed to be made would be no benefit to Sidney; that the other drains to be made would be a benefit to the corporation of Sidney, and that they should pay $300 "in full compensation on their part for the benefits they derive from the construction."

This award had no reference whatever to properties assessed, or as to properties benefited.

I do not hold, nor do I think the *Sidney Case* held that the arbitrators must necessarily specify each lot or road to be benefited. I think that a confirmation of the assessment on lands or roads as made by the surveyor in general terms would suffice, without specification.

Here, on the face of this award, I think we might support it against this objection assuming it to be an absolu e full confirmation of the surveyor's mode and amount of assessment.

But for the reasons above stated, I agree with my learned brother Cameron, that on this ground of objection, the award cannot be supported.

On the general merits of the award, I share with the learned Chief Justice his difficulty in seeing, on the evidence, how Dover was to be benefited by the proposed work, but

I share also his reluctance to interfere on that ground alone with the decision of the arbitrators, the more particularly as the dissenting arbitrator was willing to hold Dover benefited in a lesser sum than they awarded.

I am not prepared to adopt the view of one of my learned Brothers that the statute does not authorize the assessment of roads in the servient township.

I think a fair interpretation of the several sections points to a different result.

BURTON, J. A.—This is an appeal against a judgment of the present Chief Justice of the Common Pleas Division, setting aside an award made under the authority of secs. 540, 541 of the Municipal Act, R. S. O. ch. 174.

The grounds of appeal taken against the award, and urged before the learned Judge, and renewed before us, are very numerous.

The first of these, which, if well taken, is fatal to the award, is that by signing a memorandum on the last day of the sitting of the arbitrators, when they met to decide as to the award, they were *functi officiis*; and that the formal award, signed after adjournment for a few hours in order to its preparation, is null and void.

I do not think there can be anything in the objection. The arbitrators apparently signed minutes of all their meetings, and what took place on this occasion was nothing more than a minute of their proceedings, and is not distinguishable from an ordinary memorandum of instructions from the arbitrators to a solicitor to prepare a formal award, for the purpose of putting in legal form the conclusion at which they had arrived.

On this occasion two of the arbitrators came to a certain definite conclusion, which was to form their award; the third dissented, and intimated that if the formal award was to be in that shape he must decline to sign it, and would not be present at the adjourned meeting to sign it.

The meetings for deliberating on the conclusion to be arrived at were over, the conclusion had been arrived at

and an hour fixed for signing the award agreed upon, at
which the third arbitrator might have been present had
he chosen.

It would be carrying this beyond any of the decided
cases if we were to hold their award bad on that ground:
see *White* v. *Sharp*, 12 M. & W. 712.

If the award signed differs in any material respect from
the minutes, then it would undoubtedly be bad.

It is said that the award differs from the minutes
because Mr. Douglas whilst holding with the other arbitrators that the amount assessed by the engineer was not
too great, thought that the proportions should be varied
so as to distribute the amount in a different proportion
between the lands and the roads which it was competent
to the Court of Revision to do.

I think the view taken by Mr. Douglas was the correct
one, viz., that if any of the parties or the municipality
complained of the assessment *inter se*, the proper course
was to appeal to the Court of Revision after the by-law
determining the assessment had been introduced, and that
it was a matter with which the arbitrators were not concerned, that their duties were confined simply to ascertaining the correctness of the proportions payable by each
township, and therefore there is no want of concurrence
between the arbitrators, and no deviation from the minutes.
The first and second objections, therefore, in my opinion,
fail.

But it is said that the award actually signed differs
from the conclusion arrived at, inasmuch as it professes to
confirm the assessment made by the surveyor upon the
roads and lots, and parts of lots referred to in his report
in the several proportions mentioned by him ; if that be
so I quite agree with the Chief Justice that it cannot stand,
not only for the reasons mentioned by him, but because
they would be exceeding their authority in dealing with a
matter with which they had no power to deal, but I am
unable to come to the conclusion that it is open to that
objection ; so to hold would be to ignore what appears to

have taken place before the arbitrators when the counsel for the township of Chatham strongly urged the arbitrators to consider only the bulk sum whilst the counsel for Dover objected to that, and wished them to consider the propriety of the several assessments which they declined to do, holding that they had no jurisdiction, and to ignore the express admission of the parties in whose aid the construction is also invoked who not only deny that construction, but object to the award on the ground that it should have dealt with these matters—this is the objection in their own words :

"Because the findings or awards do not set forth or show or assess or charge every road, lot or portion of lot according to the proportion of benefit the same, in the opinion of the arbitrators, derives or will derive from the proposed work, while it is clear therefrom that the arbitrators did not confirm or intend to confirm the different particular assessments." And because to place such a construction upon the words in the face of the evidence, and the express admission of the parties would be to violate the principle constantly acted upon by the Courts to support where possible the validity of the award, and to make every reasonable intendment and presumption in favour of its being a final, certain and sufficient determination of the matters in issue.

We come then to the more serious objections upon which the learned Chief Justice of the Common Pleas Division has come to the conclusion that the award cannot be upheld.

The chief of these objections was as to the sufficiency of the surveyor's report. I do not profess to have much practical knowledge in such matters, but I am unable to appreciate the objections to the report. The plan and profile in connection with the report appear to me to be intelligible enough. I find no difficulty in understanding their meaning, and I apprehend therefore that a body of practical men, such as these municipal bodies are usually composed of, with a knowledge of the locality, would have

no difficulty in understanding them, and the line is staked
out on the ground.   But is it framed in compliance with
the requirements of the statute ?

The surveyor is required by section 529, to examine the
proposed works, and to furnish plans and estimates, and
he is to make an assessment of the real property to be
benefited, stating as nearly as may be the proportion of
benefit to be derived from the deepening or drainage by
every road and lot, and portion of lot.

By section 534 he is authorized when necessary to continue the deepening or drainage beyond the limits of the
municipality to continue the survey and levels into the
adjoining municipality until he finds fall enough to carry
the water beyond the limits of his own municipality.

In what respect does this report fall short of the legal
requirements.

It contains an estimate of the cost of the work, giving
the cost in detail of each station of sixty rods in extent,
from the place of commencement on the Prince Albert
road to the town line between Chatham and Dover, and
thence, as shewn on the profile and plan, to section 239,
from which point there is, as I understand, little or no fall,
so that the profile necessarily stops here, whilst the other
plan seems to me to indicate with sufficient clearness the
direction and extent of the proposed deepening.   I think
that the estimate is in compliance with the requirements
of the statute.

He then proceeds to assess the lands in proportion to
the benefit derived.

I am unable to see in what way he has failed in his
duty in that respect.

As I understand the Municipal Act and its provisions in
reference to these drainage powers (dealing at present with
works within the limits of the municipality, and where the
adjoining municipality is not benefited), the council is
empowered, on receiving such a report, to pass a by-law for
borrowing the required amount, and for assessing upon the
real property to be benefited a special rate sufficient for

the payment of the loan, and interest to be levied as other
taxes are levied, by a rate on such real property, including
roads held by joint stock companies or individuals, and for
determining what real property will be benefited, and the
proportion in which the assessment should be made on the
various portions of the lands benefited.

In practice the councils on the adoption of the survey-
or's report, provisionally pass a by-law assessing the property reported by him to be benefited in the proportions
mentioned.

This by-law must be published for at least four weeks
before its final adoption, and complaints may be made to
a Court of Revision to sit not earlier than twenty and not
later than thirty days from the first publication of the by-
law.

Any party interested in the property assessed may complain either of over charge in the case of his own property
or undercharge of any other person's property, or that
some property has been wrongfully omitted, and the Court
of Revision has power to vary the rolls, and in case of
such variation to adjust the entire assessment so that the
aggregate amount shall remain the same as if there had
been no appeal, subject to a further appeal to the County
Judge.

This then being the general scheme we come to those
cases in which it becomes necessary to extend the works
beyond the limits of the municipality in which it originated.

In such cases the surveyor is to determine and report to
the council whether the deepening and draining shall be
constructed and maintained wholly at the expense of the
municipality which initiated the work, or at the expense of
both, and in what proportion, and he is in such case to
charge the lands to be benefited by the works.

The council proposing to do the work is therefore to
serve the head of the other municipality with a copy of
the report, plan and specifications of the surveyor, and
unless appealed from as provided in a subsequent section,

that report becomes binding on the municipality, and if
not appealed from the council is bound to raise the sum
mentioned in the report.

The council may, however, appeal within twenty days
from being served with the report to arbitrators, one to be
named by themselves.

Proceedings are then suspended until the arbitrators
make their award, but upon an award being made the
municipality is bound to pass a by-law to levy the amount
fixed by the award in the same manner and with the same
formalities as in the case of a by-law for drainage works,
wholly confined to the first municipality.

The persons then assessed have within the same period
after the first publication of the by-law as above referred
to, power to appeal against their assessment or against the
omission of other lands from the assessment with the same
incidents in ordinary appeals. It seems clear, therefore,
that the only question with which the arbitrators have to
deal is the gross amount charged against the municipality,
and it is manifestly proper that that should be so as they
have no power to place omitted persons on the roll, and
their doing so without notice to the parties interested
would be violating an elementary principle. Mr. Douglas
was therefore perfectly correct in his view of the law and
the objection to the award on the ground of want of concurrence in the two arbitrators falls to the ground.

But it is said that the report is bad inasmuch as the
surveyor did not expressly state the proportions in figures
to be borne by each as one-eighth or seven-eighths, or
whatever the true proportion might be.

I cannot help thinking that this is far too hypercritical
a rule to apply to such proceedings. I think we may
very fairly invoke the maxim of *id certum est quod certum
reddi potest.*

The surveyor states the gross amount at $10,196, and
then reports that when completed it is to be kept in repair
by the municipality of the township of Chatham, at the
joint expense of Dover and Chatham, and of the lands

assessed for the work ; the said municipalities and lands
paying in the same relative proportion as for the work
herein reported on. No one can fail to see that in Chatham
the lands other than those belonging to the municipality
were assessed to pay $5679 00

The municipality itself.......... 3038 00

_____

$8717 00

Leaving as Dover's proportion.... 1479 00

_____

$10196 00

If these documents are to be scrutinized with such exact-
ness as this the drainage system may be as well abandoned,
for no by-law could be sustained.

I think it is not open to the parties upon this application to raise any question as to the sufficiency of the
petition—that may be open upon an application to quash
the by-law, if defect there be, which is not apparent.

A good deal was said about the injustice of Dover being
made to pay for new bridges, but it is founded on a misapprehension, it is not called upon to pay for the bridges.
The bridges however form necessarily part of the projected
works, and are included in the estimate of the total expenditure required, but Dover pays not for the bridges but
for the benefits that work confers on its roads and lands.

I agree with the learned Chief Justice, that we ought
not lightly to interfere with the finding of the arbitrators
as to the amount and in his remarks that "a knowledge
professed by the arbitrators of the locality may enable
them to see benefits which we do not," and that "he would
therefore on the mere question of the amount of benefit
defer to them." And we find that the Dover arbitrator
merely objected that it was $500 only in excess of what
he was willing to award.

In the case of _Essex_ v. _Rochester_, there were several
municipalities interested, and the main question was,
whether in the event of an arbitration being necessary it
was not necessary that all the municipalities interested

should be parties, inasmuch as a reduction of one amount might result in increased burdens upon the others, it is not necessary to express any opinion upon that point ; but if I understand Chief Justice Wilson's language correctly, he entertains the same view which I have expressed, namely, that both townships, that is the one originating the work and the one benefited by it, must before the work is proceeded with pass the necessary by-laws, that due notice must be given, and that all parties have the opportunity to appeal if they desire it, and upon such appeal can complain of any omission and the roll can be corrected accordingly.

A point has been taken by one of my learned Brothers that there is no power under the statute to assess the roads in the servient municipality. The question was not dealt with by the learned Judge below; nor was it expressly taken in the motion against the award, except as applying to lands in Dover generally. The only reference to the roads is to be found in the 10th objection, which seems to admit the right to assess the roads, but complains that no facts, circumstances, or opinions are shewn upon which the right to assess them arose. If, however, no such power is given, we are bound to give effect to the objection whenever taken.

But although roads are not specially referred to in sec. 579, which provides that the surveyor is, where necessary, to make plans and specifications of the work to be constructed, and charge the lands to be benefited by the work, as provided therein, it is necessary to read it in connection with the other clauses and the general scheme designed under it.

So read, we find that when the drainage is confined wholly to the one municipality, the surveyor is required to make an assessment of the real property to be benefited, and we find that this term is intended to include roads as lands, as he is required to state the proportion of benefit to be derived therefrom by every road and lot, or portion of lot.

The council in the same connection are required to
assess the real property to be benefited, real property
being there also declared to include roads; and by sec. 13
to determine what real property will be benefited, no
reference being made to roads, and the proportion in which
the assessment should be made on the various portions of
lands so benefited; but the assessment so made is subject
to appeal to the Court of Revision, which, taken in connection with the first portion of sec. 570, clearly gives a
right to complain that roads have not been assessed for
their proper proportions.

Which is further shewn by subsec. 15, which provides
that if the assessment is varied, the Court or Judge shall
vary *pro rata* the assessment on the other lands and roads
benefited as aforesaid.

When we come to sec. 577, where the works, though
confined to one municipality, benefit lands in an adjoining
municipality, or greatly improve a road lying in such
adjoining municipality, or between two or more municipalities, then the engineer is to charge the lands so benefited, or the roads which are improved, with such proportion of the cost as he may deem just.

And in such a case the council of the municipality
making the improvement is to serve the head of the municipality whose lands are benefited with a copy of the report,
and unless appealed from it is binding on the council, and
they are bound to pass a by-law to raise the sum in the
same manner, and with such other provisions as provided
by section 570. It is clear, therefore, that when the work
is confined to one municipality, but benefit is conferred
upon lands or roads in another, the council of that other is
bound to pass a by-law to raise the amount estimated by
the surveyor.

It would be strange if where the work is continued into
that other, and lands or roads there are benefited, no provision were made for assessing them in the same manner.

I confess I see no difficulty in extending it to both cases,
and the language would have to be very clear which would

exclude the roads in the one case, and include them in the other. There would be no object in serving the head of a municipality into which the works are continued unless that municipality was alleged to derive some benefit from them. It is therefore contemplated that where such benefits are derived, the real property benefited, whether it consists of lands or roads, should be charged subject to the same right of appeal as provided in other cases.

The words of section 579 are general, and give power to the surveyor to charge the lands to be benefited by the work as provided therein. Taken in connection with the other sections, I do not think any other fair construction ought to be given to them than to hold that in all cases under this Act, where lands or roads are benefited, they are to contribute to the sum fixed by the surveyor in the proportion decided by the councils of the municipality within which they lie.

From what I have said it will be seen that I think *Sidney* v. *Thurlow*, 1 O. R. 249, was not correctly decided, and Chief Justice Cameron, although he took part in that decision, seems inclined now to that view.

I do not think that any sufficient grounds have been shewn for setting aside the award, and I am therefore of opinion that this appeal should be allowed.

PATTERSON, J. A.—It is at first sight a little puzzling to decide which of the three statutes to follow.

The Act of 45 Vict. ch. 26, which was passed on 10th March, 1882, made some material amendments of the drainage clauses of the Municipal Institutions Act, R. S. O. ch. 174. These were embodied in the Municipal Institutions Act of 1883, 46 Vict. ch. 18, which was passed on 1st February, 1883, and that Act further amended one of the enactments which we have now to refer to by omitting from the new section 580, some important words which were in the corresponding section 538 of the revised statutes.

The proceedings now in question began before the passage of the Act of 1882, and continued after that of 1883 was in force. The most convenient course will be to take the Act of 1883. It was in force before section 580 was acted on ; and if its provisions are not identical with those of the revised statutes in respect of anything which was governed by the revised statutes, the distinction can be noticed.

The first step in proceedings to procure drainage work, under these clauses is, under sec. 70, a petition of a majority in number of the owners of the property to be benefited in any part of any township. &c., for the deepening of any stream, creek or watercourse, or for the draining of the property (describing it).

I read this as in R. S. O. ch. 174, sec. 529, omitting the amendments made in 1882.

The petition may thus be for draining property not yet provided with a drain, or for improving existing drainage by deepening. I do not see any satisfactory reason for confining the term watercourse to natural watercourses. The duty of the surveyor, when drainage is asked for, is to examine the locality proposed to be drained ; and when deepening is asked for his duty is to examine the stream, creek or watercourse. This distinction, which is made in section 570 and preserved in the other sections, apparently treats the whole subject as covered by the two conditions, viz., that in which there is no existing drainage, natural or constructed ; and that in which there is some drainage, though insufficient.

In this case the petition was, as recited in the by-law, "that the Little Bear Creek drain be deepened and enlarged from the Prince Albert road to Chatham and Dover town line ; and as much further as the engineer deems expedient to make the said drain an efficient outlet."

The drain is an artificial drain till it reaches the town line, where it joins a natural watercourse called Little Bear Creek. The whole is, in my opinion, embraced in the term " watercourse," as used in the statute, and is properly the subject of a petition for *deepening*.

I agree with the learned Judge in the Court below that there is a conspicuous absence of accuracy in the documents before us. The by-law recites that the council procured an examination of *the locality proposed to be drained* to be made by a surveyor, which was not the appropriate action on a petition for deepening; but this would seem to be an error in drawing up the by-law, because the surveyor reports that the work he was instructed to do, and what he did, was to examine the drain and make a survey of Little Bear Creek.

Sec. 570 authorizes the council also to procure plans and estimates to be made of the work, by the engineer or surveyor, and an assessment of the real property to be benefited by such work, stating as nearly as may be, in the opinion of the engineer or surveyor, the proportion of benefit to be derived therefrom by every road and lot or portion of lot.

Before giving attention to the surveyor's report on these matters, let us look at some other provisions of the statute which operate when, as in this case, the work extends from one municipality into another.

Sec. 576 authorizes the surveyor to continue the levels into the adjoining municipality until he finds fall enough to carry the water beyond the limits of the municipality in which the deepening or drainage commenced.

Sec. 577 deals with a different case from that now before us; but for the sake of its bearing on the construction of other clauses I shall read it in full.

"When the works do not extend beyond the limits of the municipality in which they are commenced, but in the opinion of the engineer or surveyor aforesaid, benefit lands in an adjoining municipality, or greatly improve any road lying within any municipality, or between two or more municipalities, then the engineer or surveyor aforesaid shall *charge the lands to be so benefited,* and the corporation, person or company whose road or *roads are improved,* with such proportion of the cost of the works as he may deem just; and the amount so charged for roads, or agreed upon by the arbitrators, shall be paid out of the general funds of such municipality or company."

Sec. 578 requires the surveyor to determine and report to the council by which he was employed whether the work shall be constructed and maintained solely at the expense of such municipality, or whether it shall be constructed and maintained at the expense of both municipalities, and in what proportion.

Sec. 579 authorizes him, where necessary, to make plans and specifications of the works to be constructed, and charge the lands to be benefited by the work as herein provided ; and by sec. 580, "the council of the municipality in which the deepening or drainage is to be commenced shall serve the head of the council of the municipality into which the same is to be continued, or whose lands or roads are to be benefited without the deepening or drainage being continued, with a copy of the report, plans, specifications and estimates of the engineer or surveyor aforesaid ; and unless the same is appealed from as hereinafter provided it shall be binding on the council of such municipality."

It will be convenient in discussing these sections to use the terms "assessment" and "charge," as they are used in the sections, to denote the surveyor's apportionment among the lands, &c., of the cost as he estimates it ; but we must not take those words to imply that his act creates any liability to pay. As far as the individual lots or their owners are concerned, the liability depends on a by-law of the municipal council to which the surveyor's report is only preliminary ; but the adjustment of the proportion in which each of two municipalities shall contribute depends on the report, subject to appeal.

Now, while it is clear from the provisions I have quoted that the duty of the surveyor to assess the property to be benefited is not limited to the property in the municipality by which he is employed, but extends to property benefited in another municipality, whether the work is continued into the other municipality or not, a question has been raised as to the right to charge such other municipality in respect of the improvement of its roads. It is contended on the part of Dover that the only liability with which it can be charged is in respect of lots or parts of lots which may be benefited ; that if in any case a municipality in which the drain does not commence can be charged in respect of the improvement of its roads, it is only, under section 577, when the drain is not continued into its territory ; and that at all events no charge can be sustained in respect of the town-line road between Dover and Chatham.

It must be admitted that the language of the statute is not so precise or so consistent as to leave this contention without some support. I think, however, that on a fair reading of the different sections on the subject, the intention to base the liability to contribute on the improvement to roads as well as on the benefit to lots or parts of lots is reasonably clear, and that no distinction can be made between a municipality deriving benefit from a drain continued into it, and one which the drain benefits without being continued, and that a road on a township line ranks with ordinary township roads.

Under sec. 577 the liability for roads in cases where the works do not extend beyond the limits of the municipality where they are commenced, but greatly improve the roads of another, is created in express terms ; and township lines are also expressly included. The words are "greatly improve any road lying within any municipality, or between two or more municipalities." The engineer or surveyor is to charge " the corporation, person or company whose road or roads are improved."

Finding thus the liability put beyond question, as I take section 577 to do, in a case where the drain is not continued into the municipality which it benefits, the intention of the Act will naturally be assumed, in the absence of some insuperable indication to the contrary, to make the liability the same when the benefit is derived from a work which is continued into the municipality.

Whatever difficulty there is arises from the use of the word "lands" in section 579 without the addition of an express reference to roads.

If this clause had to be construed without the aid of others, and particularly if we found the word "lands" consistently used to signify farm lands only, or lands other than roads, there would be much force in the objection to its being here understood to include roads, even in the face of the impossibility to assign a good reason for applying a different rule to benefits derived from a drain on one side of a township line, from that applied when the drain was on the other side of the line.

But the section is not to be read by itself. When it directs the surveyor to charge the lands to be benefited by the work *as provided herein,* we turn to sec. 570 which explains what is meant by the surveyor charging the lands. That section authorizes the council to procure certain things from the surveyor. Sec. 579 directs the surveyor, when necessary, to do some of the same things. These are described in sec. 570 as "an assessment of the *real property* to be benefited by such work, stating * * the proportion of benefit to be derived therefrom by every *road and lot* or portion of lot." Here the term "real property" obviously includes roads as well as lots. The word land is not used, but I take it to be synonomous with real property : and in fact we find the words used interchangeably in this very section, in sub-sec. 5, when it is said that a by-law may be passed "for determining what real property will be benefited by the works, and the proportion in which the assessment should be made on the various portions of lands so benefited." That this word lands, as here used, includes roads is further evident when we notice that the appeal to the Court of Revision which is given by sub-sec. 5 to owners of property assessed, for undercharge or omission of any other property clearly enables them to complain that the roads are not made to bear their due share of the burden.

Section 580, while it may seem at first sight not to bear on the construction of the word lands, as used in the preceding section, because it only speaks of roads in describing a municipality of the kind dealt with in sec. 577, " whose

lands or roads are to be benefited without the deepening
or drainage being continued " into it, really helps to shew
that the lands of sec. 579 include roads. The report, &c.,
are to be served on the head of the council of the municipality into which the deepening or drainage is to be continued. We cannot give these words their full literal
meaning without construing them to require the service to
be made on a municipality which may derive no benefit
whatever from drainage works which happen to be continued into it in order to find a fall to carry off the water
from the municipality above. In such a case the lower
municipality does not contribute to the expense, and
therefore the mandate which in its literal terms would
require the purposeless service to be made, must be
restricted by something else. We find that in the following words, "*or* whose lands," &c; and the meaning,
though far from being skilfully expressed, evidently is
that the report is to be served on the municipality whose
lands or roads are to be benefited by the deepening or
drainage whether the work is continued into it or is not so
continued.

Then we have the sections respecting the passage of a
by-law to raise the money named in the report or fixed by
arbitrators, and regulating the appeal to arbitrators, which
nowhere suggest that the liability is to be within narrower
limits when the drainage works are continued than when
they stop before crossing its border, or, being wholly within
a lower municipality, benefit its lands and roads by providing an outlet for its waters; and we have a very strong
confirmation of my view in section 587.

Secs. 584 and 587 lay down rules for the maintenance of
drainage works. The general *rule, under section 584, is
that each municipality is to do the repairs within its own
limits, though not necessarily at its own expense; and
section 587 throws the expense as well as the duty wholly
on the municipality making (the work in any case where
it has not been continued into any other municipality. or
wherein *the lands or roads* of any such other municipality
are not benefited.

If the drain benefits the lands or roads, the liability to contribute to its maintenance is here plainly enough asserted without distinction between a drain continued and one not continued.

It would certainly be better if the statute was so worded as to plainly and fully express what is meant; but, construing it as it stands, I do not think the objection to the power to charge the township of Dover in respect of its roads, including a moiety of the township line ought to prevail.

It is objected that the surveyor did not, as directed by section 578, report whether the work should be constructed and maintained solely at the cost of Chatham, or whether it should be constructed and maintained at the expense of both Chatham and Dover, and in what proportion. Let us see what he did. He reported that the drain will greatly benefit lands in both townships. He estimated the whole cost at $10,196. He said, "I assess the cost of the work as in the annexed schedules." And he made a schedule of assessment on lands and roads in Chatham, and another schedule of assessment on lands and roads in Dover, apportioning to each lot and road a certain amount, the aggregate being $10,196.

These amounts did not represent the cost in each locality, but the proportionate benefit. The details of the cost are given. There was included $1,236 for bridges and incidental expenses, leaving $8,960 for excavation alone. Of this, the sum of $4,710 was to be spent in Chatham and $4,250 in Dover. The surveyor stated, though not in his report, that $450 of the cost of bridges was for bridges in Dover. That would make the actual outlay in Dover $4,700. Adding up the amounts placed against lands and roads in Dover, it comes to $1,479, that is to say $279 in lands, $200 in roads other than the township line, and $1,000 for the moiety of the amount charged against the township line road.

Thus while $4,700 was to be spent in Dover, the proportion of benefit for which it was to pay was $1,479

The schedules moreover have headings stating that the assessment was for benefit.

I think it is sufficiently shewn that the cost of construction was to be borne by the two townships in the proportion of $1,479 by Dover, and $8,717 by Chatham.

It was argued that the proportion is not properly stated; and the suggestion that the ratio, e. g. $\frac{7}{8}$ and $\frac{1}{8}$, should be expressed seems to have met with some favour in the court below.

We have the fractions in effect stated with perfect accuracy, viz., $\frac{1479}{10196}$ and $\frac{8717}{10196}$, but that cannot be necessary.

There would seem to have been some doubt of this, because in 1882, the rule was enacted which is now sub-section 7 of section 570, that "the proportion of benefit to be derived from any works by different parcels of land or roads may be shewn by the engineer or surveyor by placing sums of money opposite such parcels and roads, and it shall not be deemed to have been necessary to state the fraction of the cost to be borne by each parcel or road."

This applies in principle, if not literally, to assessments between townships; but, as I have said, every such assessment must in effect state the fractions, each assessment being a numerator, the total cost the common denominator, and the sum of all the fractions making the unit of the price.

The report provided in express terms for the maintenance of the work by Chatham at the joint expense of Chatham and Dover, and of the lands in those municipalities "assessed for the work herein reported on; said municipalities and lands paying in the same relative proportion as for the work herein reported on."

The surveyor here seems to have overlooked the terms of section 578, which do not empower him to say who shall maintain the work, but only to say at whose expense it shall be maintained, and also section 584, which casts on each municipality the duty of maintaining the work within its own limits in the proportion determined by the engineer or arbitrators.

We need not decide what effect, if any, the unauthorized direction that the one township shall do the whole work of maintenance at the joint expense of both may have, because we are dealing only with the arbitrator's award, and no objection to the report on this ground was raised by the notice of appeal to the arbitrators, which notice is by section 603, sub-section 4, required to state the grounds of appeal. The award cannot be held bad for failing to correct an error of which no notice was given.

I am not sure that I fully appreciated a part of the argument in which it was insisted that in some way Dover was wrongfully compelled by this report to contribute to the expense of enlarging some bridges. Making or enlarging bridges may certainly be a necessary incident of constructing or enlarging drains, and an unavoidable cause of expense. Dover is called on to pay only a small sum in proportion even to the money to be spent in that township.

The objections to the report, plan, and profile for want of definiteness do not strike me as having any substantial foundation. There may be room for a charge of want of mathematical precision, but I see no reason to suppose that they failed to convey all the information that was necessary to enable the officials of Dover to understand exactly what was proposed to be done. The course of the drain from Prince Albert road to the middle of lot 32, west of Baldoon street, is traced on a plan which must be familiar to all the persons concerned. The profile shews the depth of excavation, or the fall, at stations numbered from 0 to 239, when the fall ceases, and it shews that the drain crosses the town line at station 135. The report estimates the cost at so much per rod for each space of ten stations or sixty rods, running to station 240, or six rods, costing $18, beyond what is on the profile.

So far there is not much room for objection.

But then there is a note on the profile, "continue 300 rods farther clearing bars and timber;" and an item in the estimate, "clearing out bars below 240, $350; and another item, "clearing and logging to a width of 100 feet in Dover $300." I am not sure that any argument is founded on this last item. The surveyor explains in his evidence that it refers to work to be done eastward, or up stream, and not below station 240.

The objection to the clearing out of the stream below 240 which was put on the ground of that kind of work not being mentioned in the statute, if it ever would have had force, can have none since the passing of 40 Vict. ch. 26, three weeks after the date of the report, and over a year before it was communicated to the head of the Dover council, and which enacted that the provisions of R. S. O. ch. 174, sec. 529 should extend to (amongst other things) the removing of any obstruction which prevents the free flow of the waters of any stream. This is now in section 570.

Another objection to the report is, that the engineer or the council of Chatham had no authority or right to continue the proposed deepening or drainage farther into Dover than sufficiently to find fall enough to carry the water beyond the limits of Chatham.

I have not been able to lay my hand on the proof of any facts in support of this objection. The evidence of two surveyors, McNab and Macdonell, seems rather to suggest that the work should be carried farther than proposed on account of the creek being obstructed.

It would only be upon very satisfactory evidence that the Court would interfere with the judgment of the surveyor entrusted under the authority of the law with the duty of determining how far it was necessary to extend a drain.

My examination of the report leaves me satisfied of its sufficiency.

Upon receiving the report the council, if it is of opinion that the proposed work or a portion thereof would be desirable, may (section 570) pass by-laws for providing for the proposed work or a portion thereof being done, and *inter alia*, (5) for determining what real property will be benefited by the works and the proportion in which the assessment should be made on the various portions of lands so benefited, and subject in every case of complaint by the owner or person interested in any property assessed, (whether of overcharge or undercharge of any other property assessed or that property which should be assessed has been wrongfully omitted to be assessed) to proceedings for trial of such complaint and appeal therefrom, in like manner, as nearly as may be, as on proceedings for the trial of complaints to the Court of Revision under the Assessment Act.

(10) The Court of Revision is to sit not earlier than twenty nor later than thirty days from the day on which the by-law was first published.

(10) Trial of complaints is to be had in the first instance by and before the Court of Revision of the municipality in which the lands or roads lie ; and (13) the appeal from the Court of Revision shall be to the Judge of the County Court of the county in which such municipality is situate.

Sec. 572. Before the final passing of the by-law it is to be published for four weeks in a newspaper, and directions are given touching notice of application to quash the by-law, or in place of advertisement, notices may be sent to owners of lands, and the final passage is not to be for three weeks after the last notice is served.

The appeals to the Court of Revision and County Judge are apparently contemplated to take place before the final passing of the by-law, though that would seem scarcely possible if the extreme times are insisted on. This appears from a provision in section 570 (15), for readjusting the whole assessment when the proportions are disturbed by any assessment being varied, and a direction in section 571 (2), that in that event the by-law before being finally passed shall be amended to correspond with the alteration made by the Court or Judge.

I have already read section 580, which provides for service of the report, &c., on the head of the *quasi* servient municipality.

35—VOL. XI A.R.

The direction of section 581 is, that "The council of such last mentioned municipality shall within four months from the delivery to the head of the corporation of the report of the engineer or surveyor, as provided in the next preceding section, pass a bylaw or by-laws to raise such sum as may be named in the report, or in case of an appeal, for such sum as may be determined by the arbitrators, in the same manner and with such other provisions as would have been proper if a majority of the owners of the lands to be taxed had petitioned as provided in section 570 of this Act."

Now reading this section along with section 578, under which the engineer or surveyor fixes the proportion in which each municipality is to provide for the expense of construction and maintenance ; and with sections 580 and 581, which shew that the documents to be communicated to the servient municipality are the reports, &c., of the engineer or surveyor, not the by-law of the council; and with the provisions of section 570, which make the liability to pay the assessment depend on the by-law of the council, not on the engineer's report; and which leave the council at liberty to depart from the engineer's opinion, both as to what real property will be benefited by the works, and the proportion in which the assessment should be made on the various portions of lands so benefited ; and give the appeal to the Court of Revision from the by-law and not from the report; it seems perfectly manifest that the servient municipality is in no way affected by the engineer's detailed assessment of its lots and roads, but is bound only by his apportionment of the aggregate amount between the two municipalities. That amount it distributes by its own by-law among its lands and roads, in the same manner and with the same incidents of appeal to its own Court of Revision, and to the Judge, as the other municipality. Each may avail itself to what extent it pleases of the engineer's details ; those details will doubtless, as a matter of practice, be in most cases adopted and followed in the by-law; but the statute leaves both municipalities alike free to vary them.

I now come to the questions respecting the award.

By section 582 the council of the municipality into which the work is to be continued, or whose lands or roads are to be benefited without the work being carried within its limits, may within twenty days from the day on which the report was served on the head of the municipality, appeal therefrom to arbitrators.

This appeal being between the two municipalities, the only question between them being the proportion of the expense which each is to pay, and those aggregate amounts and not the engineer's opinion of the relative benefit to be derived by the several lots or roads, being all that in the absence of an appeal becomes binding, the appeal from the report is simply an appeal against the aggregate charge' upon the municipality.

The council of Dover appealed.

It was of course quite regular, upon the appeal, to attack the legal validity of the report as well as to criticize the judgment of the engineer in his estimate of the proportionate benefit to be derived by each municipality from the proposed work.

There were three arbitrators, Fleck, Merritt, and Douglas.

An award was made by the two last named gentlemen.

It recited the appointment of the surveyor by the municipal council of Chatham, and that he had reported t.) the council that it would be necessary to extend the drain from the Prince Albert road to a little beyond Baldoon street in Dover East, and that the drain would greatly benefit lands in both the townships Chatham and Dover East, and that he assessed and charged the lands to be so benefited in Dover East the sum of $279, and certain roads in Dover East $1,200; and then after further reciting the formal proceedings in the appeal to the arbitrators, proceeded thus: "First, we order, award, and determine that the said assessment upon lands and roads in the said township of Dover East and West, and the Town Line between the said township of Dover East and West and the township of Chatham and North Gore by the said McGeorge, be sustained and confirmed, as the said lands and roads in the said township of Dover East and West will be greatly benefited and improved by the said work, and also the said Town Line road between the said municipalities of Dover and Chatham. And that the said appeal be and the same is hereby dismissed, and that the several grounds mentioned in the notice of appeal have not been sustained."

I think I have dealt with all the grounds set out in the notice of motion against the award which were founded on objections to the report, except one which impeached the fairness of the charge of $2,000 for the improvement of the road on the township line.

Mr. Fleck, the dissenting arbitrator, thought $1,000 would be enough. I think the evidence for leaving it at $2,000 is stronger than that for reducing it, which consists entirely of an opinion expressed by Mr. Macdonell, a surveyor. How the $1,000, if deducted, should be distributed, and whether Dover's half of the deduction should not still be allotted to Dover, or what Mr. Fleck's view on this part of the question was, or whether he considered it at all, are matters which are left in obscurity. Mr. Macdonell would not have reduced the total assessment of Dover, he would only have rearranged the distribution.

It is impossible to say that the arbitrators erred in not giving effect to this objection.

A question of some importance is raised by the first ground taken against the award, which reads thus:

"That after the execution of the first finding or award, the said arbitrators were *functi officio*, and had no authority or power to make or execute the second or final award made by Merritt and Douglas, and the said final award was made in the absence of Fleck, and without discussion, and was not according to the decision arrived at even by the two arbitrators who signed the final award."

What is here called the first finding or award was a memorandum signed by the three arbitrators, which I shall read, omitting the passage respecting the costs on which nothing at present turns:

" The arbitrators have considered it best to decide against the legal objections and to decide against Mr. Wilson's contention, leaving him to bring them before the Court, if he thinks proper.

" The arbitrators all agree that Dover will be benefited by the work, Mr. Fleck holding that on the evidence offered $500 should be taken off the assessment on the town line road, the other arbitrators holding that lands and roads in the township of Dover are benefited to more than the amount of assessment, and that it should be confirmed, but one of the arbitrators—Mr. Douglas—holding that, while the bulk sum assessed is not too great, the lands and roads and parts thereof so assessed should be varied, which it is competent for the Court of Revision to do.

" The arbitrators thereupon agree to confirm the assessment as above.

" Mr. Fleck declines to sign the award.

" Arbitrators now adjourn till 4 p.m., this day, to sign the award at same place.

" A. E. MERRITT,

" WM. DOUGLAS.

" Dissenting as above stated from the decision of the majority arbitrators, I decline to sign any award, and also decline to be present at the adjourned meeting to sign the award if in accordance with the above memoranda.

" R. FLECK."

I do not think the appellants have anything to gain by insisting on this being an award and not merely a memorandum from which the award was to be prepared.

If this is an award we have merely to consider whether or not it is valid as against the objections. If the formal award agrees with this, and the objection that it was made after the arbitrators had become *functi officiis* were to prevail, the effect would only be to throw us back on this memorandum as the operative award.

But if the formal award does not agree with this, there is the fatal objection to it that it was made in the absence of one of the arbitrators who had no notice of any meeting except one for the purpose of signing a different award, and then if we still concede to the appellant that the

memorandum is itself an award, the task of considering
its validity remains.

It is clear from the terms of the memorandum that it
was not intended to be the award.

After the best consideration I have been able to give to
the matter, I am of opinion that the award does not differ
from the memorandum; but before giving my reasons for
this I shall read the next objection, which is thus expressed: "That said findings and awards do not set forth
or shew or assess or charge every road and lot, or portion
of lot, according to the proportion of benefit the same in
the opinion of the arbitrators derives from, or will derive
from the work, while it is clear therefrom that the arbitrators did not confirm or intend to confirm the different
particular assessments, but only the total sum charged
against Dover:" and with these objections I shall consider
another which is not taken in the notice of motion, but
which was given effect to in the Court below, namely, that
the memorandum shews that the two arbitrators who joined
in the award were not agreed as between themselves.

The answer to these three objections is contained in the
proposition which I have sufficiently elaborated, that the
subject of the reference was not the distribution of Dover's
contribution among the various roads and lots, but was
the liability of Dover to pay $1,479 of the estimated cost
of $10,196. The two arbitrators were agreed upon that,
although they might not have agreed upon the apportionment of it.

The arbitrators had, in my view, no jurisdiction to deal
with the apportionment.

It is shewn by an affidavit filed by the appellants in
support of their objection that this question of jurisdiction
was expressly argued before the arbitrators; and that they
were pressed by counsel for Dover to consider the apportionment, counsel for Chatham contending that they
should deal only with the bulk sum charged to the township; and that the majority of arbitrators decided that
the consideration of the apportionment was only for the
Court of Revision for Dover.

I may add to what I have said on that subject, though I may be only repeating my observations in another form, that the soundness of the decision of the majority is confirmed by considering that this adjustment of the taxes on the lots or roads, if they had attempted to make it, would manifestly have bound no one, but would have been nugatory.

The council would have still had, under section 581, to pass a by-law. In that by-law it would have been their duty, under section 570 (5) to determine what real property would be benefited by the works, and the proportion in which the assessment should be made on the various portions of lands so benefited, and this would have been subject to appeal to the Court of Revision. There is no place, amongst all the machinery, for an adjustment of the assessment by the arbitrators to fit in, and there is no office for it to serve.

I believe the learned Judge in the Court below was inclined to the opinion which I have expressed upon this branch of the case, but considered himself bound by the decision in *Thurlow* v. *Sidney*, 1 O. R. 249. I think the functions of the Court of Revision were not sufficiently considered in that case, and that an erroneous view was taken of the purpose of the arbitration and the duties of the arbitrators.

If the Act in force when *Essex* v. *Rochester*, 42 U. C. R. 523 was decided, had been like the present Municipal Institutions Act, I should have said that a similar misapprehension had prevailed in that case. I allude to a passage in the judgment of Wilson, C. J., at p. 541, when he says:

"I think then, the arbitration on the subject of the assessment should have been an arbitration which included all those bodies which were interested in the work, and that all those who are assessed are interested until the respective proportions of assessment have been definitely fixed upon each one of them. There may still be a further difficulty in some cases, if it can be shewn that some body or person who has not been assessed should have been assessed as a body or person that will be benefited by the work. That fact may come out in the course of the arbitration, and how is such body or person to be made a party liable to assessment? Must the engineer or surveyor amend his report, and make a different redistribution of the respective assessments, or may the arbitrators report that fact as a matter to be settled preliminary to their proceeding further with the reference, and have the new body or party brought into the arbitration? The statute has not provided for such a case."

The case is, as I have shewn, provided for by the present law, not by referring the distribution to the arbitrators but by making it the province of the council in passing the by-law, under section 581 "in the same manner, and with such other provisions as would have been proper if a majority of the owners of the lands to be taxed had petitioned as provided in section 570 of this Act." The corresponding section at the date of *Essex* v. *Rochester*, 42 U. C. R. 523, was section 456 of the Municipal Institutions Act of 1873, and curiously enough it had the word *without* where we now read *with*. The section was altered from section 10 of 35 Vict. ch. 26, one of the alterations being the introduction of the words "*without* such other provisions as would have been proper," &c. It thus forbade the very thing which is now enjoined, namely the determination by the by-law of what real property would be benefited and the proportion in which the assessment should be made on the various portions of lands, &c., subject to appeal to the Court of Revision.

The award disposes of the matter over which the arbitrators had jurisdiction, and disposes of it in the way noted as agreed upon in the memorandum. The reference to Mr. Douglas's idea that while Dover was not charged too much, the amount should be differently apportioned by the court of Revision is outside of the subject of the reference, and is, I think, properly to be understood as a note of the same fact which the appellants have proved by Mr. Wright's affidavit, namely, that the arbitrators were of opinion that their functions did not embrace the revision of the details of the assessment.

One objection of which notice is given alleges defects in the by-law of Chatham. I have shewn that, as I read the statute, Dover is not concerned with that by-law.

My conclusion is, that the award is good; and that we should allow the appeal, with costs.

OSLER, J. A.—We have again to consider the obscure and difficult sections of the Municipal Act relating to drainage by-laws.

The case was one in which it became necessary to continue the works beyond the limits of the township which originated them, into an adjoining township. An arbitration took place between the municipalities as provided by the Act, out of which the present litigation arises.

Three different cases appear to be contemplated by the Act. The first where the works and all benefits to be derived therefrom are confined to the originating municipality. The second, which is the case we have to deal with, where it is necessary to continue the works beyond the limits of that municipality in order to find fall enough to carry the water beyond such limits; and the third where, though the works do not extend beyond its limits, they may benefit lands in an adjoining municipality or greatly improve any road lying within any municipality or between two or more municipalities.

We may pass over the initiatory stages of the proceedings, the petition and the provisional by-law, confining our attention for the present to the action of the surveyor and his report on which the by-law is based and against which the appeal to the arbitrators was taken. We may assume that he meant to assess against lands in Dover $279 and against roads in that township, and the townline $1,100, in all $1,379, and will now turn to the statute and endeavor to ascertain what he was authorized to do.

The case is one in which one municipality is exercising or assuming to exercise, jurisdiction in another municipality.

Section 284 of the Municipal Act, enacts that the jurisdiction of every council shall be confined to the municipality the council represents except where authority beyond the same is expressly given.

Section 576 provides that when ¡it is necessary to continue the works beyond the limits of the originating municipality, the surveyor may continue the survey and levels until he finds fall enough to carry the water beyond the limits of the former.

That is what the surveyor did here, but section 576 by itself would give him no power to assess the adjoining municipality, or any lands or roads therein. The power to enter it is given for a special purpose and would be exhausted when that purpose was accomplished. Though its exercise proved beneficial to lands or roads in that municipality something further is needed to authorize their assessment.

The next section (577) is material to be noticed, as it defines with some precision what is to be done in the third of the cases I have alluded to. This section is distinctly limited to the case where the works do not extend beyond the limits of the municipality in which they were commenced, but, in the opinion of the surveyor, benefit lands in an adjoining municipality, or greatly improve any road lying within any municipality, or between two or more municipalities. In that event he is to charge the lands and the corporation, person, or company whose roads are improved with such proportion of the cost of the work as he shall deem just; and the amount so charged for roads, or agreed upon by the arbitrators (who are here mentioned for the first time) is to be paid out of the general funds of the municipality or company. In the case which arises under this section it will be seen that provision is expressly made for assessing both lands and roads; but we have to look further for the power to assess anything outside of the originating municipality in the case before us.

Section 578, which requires the surveyor to report, &c., as to the proportion in which the expense of the works shall be borne, may refer to the two preceding sections, if any such power can be found; if not, its effect is plainly confined to sec. 577.

Section 579 enacts that the surveyor shall make plans and specifications of the works to be constructed, and charge the lands to be benefited by the works as provided herein. These directions would seem to be unnecessary unless it was intended thereby to confer the power to assess lands benefited in the municipality into which the work is continued; no power to do so is given elsewhere in the Act, and this section does not authorize the surveyor to assess or make any charge in respect of the roads of that municipality, a power which, as I have pointed out, is expressly given in the case which arises under sec. 577 ; and also where the works and benefits arising therefrom are confined to the originating municipality.

I do not think there is anything in the Act which warrants us in holding that the expression "lands to be benefited," in section 579 must there have the meaning "lands and roads."

In section 570 we have the term "real property" with the meaning "road and lot or portion of lot." In sub-sections 3, 5, and 6 of that section the same term means merely lots and *private* roads. Sub-section 7 speaks of the different parcels of "land or roads" benefited. Sub-section 9, "lands and roads" benefited. Sub-section 10 refers to the trial of complaints before the Court of Revision of the municipality in which the "lands or roads" lie. And sub-section 15 speaks of the "property" which is the subject of appeal and "other lands and roads benefited."

The distinction between the cases provided for by sections 576 and 577 is observed in sections 580 and 582, which relate to the appeal from the report, and speak of the municipality into which the work is to be continued *or* whose lands (meaning probably the lands in which) *road* or *roads* are to be benefited without the work being carried on within its limits. These sections harmonize and are not inconsistent with the two cases provided for, though it may be doubted whether a distinction was intended to be made between the case where the drainage is *from*, and that where it is *into*, an adjoining municipality. I think, however, upon the best consideration I have been able to give to the question, that such a distinction does exist, and that in the latter case the surveyor is not authorized to assess anything upon the roads of the adjoining municipality. The express authority by which in one case the originating municipality exercises powers in the adjoining municipality, under section 576 is subject to limitations which do not exist in the other under section 577.

If this view is correct the award was rightly set aside, as the arbitrators should have given effect to the first part of the eighth reason of appeal, viz., that the report does not shew any facts or circumstances upon which Dover could be legally assessed for the roads in that township or for the town line.

As regards the assessment for the town line there is moreover a peculiar reason for its disallowance. Even if it be conceded that roads in an adjoining municipality may be assessed when the works are continued therein, it seems clear that roads *between* two municipalities can only be assessed in the single case provided for by section 577 (the only section which refers to roads of that description,) viz., where the works do not extend beyond the limits of the municipality in which they are commenced, but improve any road lying within any adjoining municipality, or between two or more municipalities. On the other hand, if, upon the true construction of the Act, a proportion of the cost of the work may in such a case te assessed upon the town line, there seems to me an insuperable difficulty in the way of bringing it before the Courts of Revision of the townships, and the matter would be one for the arbitrators to deal with, and this they have not done.

With regard to the duty of the arbitrators in hearing
and disposing of the appeal and the form of the award,
which professes to confirm the assessment in every respect,
I concur with what has been said by my lord on that part
of the case.

I think also that the the surveyor's report is at least
technically defective in the following particulars : (1) In
not shewing one of the termini of the proposed work. It
gives the cost of 240 stations separately, but in profile plan
incorporated or referred to in it, the last station is omitted.
(2) In not stating as expressly required by section 578,
that the work is to be constructed at the expense of both
municipalities, and in what proportion. I think the Act
intended that the report should distinctly state the proportion, and should not leave it to be inferred or spelt out
from a comparison of the amounts assessed against each
municipality as the present cost of the work. The surveyor
is, by sub-sec. 7 of sec. 571, relieved from stating the proportion of benefit to be derived from the work by each
particular lot or parcel of land, but the fact that he is
thus excused in one case, only emphasizes his duty in the
other. (3) In reporting and determining that the work is
to be kept in repair by Chatham at the joint expense of
Chatham and Dover, and of the lands assessed therein.
Section 584 enacts that each municipality shall maintain
and keep in repair that part of the drain within its own
limits. The words " until otherwise provided for," in that
section, relate to the proportion of the expense which each
is to bear, and which it would seem may, in some not very
comprehensible way, be altered or re-arranged by the
surveyor or arbitrators after the completion of the works.

It is possible that to these objections or some of them
no effect would be given if raised for the first time after
the works had been completed and money expended under
the by-law. The Courts would strive to uphold as far as
possible what had been done.

But it is extremely necessary that the very extensive
powers which have been entrusted to municipalities in

these matters should be exercised with care and some
degree of accuracy. If not so exercised they merely lead
to embarrassment and litigation in the future. In such
circumstances it is better that proceedings which offend as
these do against the plain directions of the Act should be
set aside or quashed before further expense is incurred
under their authority.

For these reasons I am of opinion that the appeal should
be dismissed.

The Court being equally divided, the appeal was dismissed, with costs.

[The case has since been carried to the Supreme Court.]

CLOUSE v. THE CANADA SOUTHERN RAILWAY COMPANY.

Railway crossing—Under-crossing, verbal agreement for—Re-valuation of land.

When the defendants, the Canada Southern Railway Company were locating their road, an agent was employed by them for the purpose of obtaining the right of way from the several land owners along their line of road, and amongst others the agent purchased such right of way across the plaintiff's farm for a sum which the plaintiff swore was much less than he would have accepted therefor, in consequence of the agent agreeing that a certain crossing underneath the railway where trestle work was to be constructed, should be continued permanently.

Several years afterwards the company desiring to make an alteration in the construction of the road by substituting a solid earth embankment for the trestle-work, proceeded to effect such alteration, when the plaintiff instituted proceedings to restrain the company from destroying or interfering with the crossing.

Held, [varying the judgment of PROUDFOOT, J., 4 O. R. 28,] that the plaintiff was not entitled to such crossing in perpetuity, but that under the circumstances there should be a new valuation of the lands conveyed to the company, and if the parties could not agree on the amount or the mode of ascertaining it, a reference for the purpose should be made to the Master.

THIS was an appeal by the defendants from the judgment of Proudfoot, J. (4 O. R. 28.)

The action was brought for damages, and for an injunction restraining the defendants from obstructing and hindering the plaintiff in his use and possession of certain under-crossings under the line of the defendants' railway, which passed through the plaintiff's farm.

The facts appear fully in the former report, and in the present judgments.

The appeal was heard on the 18th and 19th of February, and again, in consequence of the death of Spragge, C. J. O., on the 23rd October, 1884.*

Cattanach, for the appellants.

Osler, Q.C., and *Plumb*, for the respondent.

December 18, 1884. HAGARTY, C. J. O.—The case made by the plaintiff must, I presume, stand or fall on his ability to establish a binding contract on the part of the railway company to grant to him a right of way under the track.

Present.—HAGARTY, C.J.O., BURTON, PATTERSON, and OSLER, JJ.A.

I do not think he has made out a case for reforming the deed in fee simple, which he gave to the company, by inserting in it the agreement or covenant he now insists was part of the bargain. We could not do this except on evidence of undoubted force and clearness.

I am not at all satisfied that, if we should so reform the instrument, we should be carrying out the true bargain between the parties.

The agreement for the sale of the land is dated 23rd January, 1871, and is silent as to crossings. The deed was executed 16th March, 1871, and is equally silent.

The plaintiff's case is, that on execution of the agreement, he wished to have the crossings provided for, as verbally agreed, but that Tracey, defendants' agent, assured him that a writing was unnecessary, and that the law would compel defendants to build and maintain the crossings.

Nelson Boughner is subscribing witness to the agreement and deed. He understood they had agreed with Tracey for three level and two under-crossings besides the money consideration. He said: "The agreement was drawn up and witnessed by me; do not remember when it was drawn up; do not think at the time the bargain was concluded. I know it was understood by me and others that the statute would protect, and that there was no need of a bargain about the under-crossing. I think Tracey also thought this."

Plaintiff swears that after the bargain as to crossings he spoke of having papers signed, and they said there was no need of it, as the statute provided for it. "I think Mr. Tracey told me this, and lawyer Duncombe told me the same."

His son says that Tracey said we were to locate the crossings and the law would compel them to make them; that writings were not necessary; that Tracey said they were going to build a bridge seventeen feet high, and plaintiff might as well have the crossing as not.

Tracey was employed by defendants to obtain the right of way. He had discussions with plaintiff who asked at first $1,100 or $1,200 for the land required, and they talked about the crossings to be allowed.

It was intended to cross this part of plaintiff's land by a trestle bridge, and Tracey admits he told plaintiff that there was a chance for him to pass under, and discussing the price urged upon him that he would have that chance. He denies that he made that any part of the consideration. He made an entry in his book produced: " Settled with Clouse,—he can have one pass under bridge."

Plaintiff finally consented to accept $662.

Tracey swears he had no authority to bind the company to give an under-crossing; that he did not so undertake for them, or intend so to do. He thinks he told the company's engineers about plaintiff having this crossing.

Ragatzki was the engineer in charge of that section. Plaintiff says that when the bridge was being built he spoke to him and told him of his bargain that he was to have the crossing on the west side of the creek, and Ragatzki directed the men so to place it.

Boughner confirms this. He says Ragatzki spoke to him asking him as to plaintiff's bargain. Witness went with him to the place, and he gave instructions to the workmen to make it as plaintiff directed. Plaintiff claimed it was to be made so as a load could pass under.

The plaintiff had the use of this crossing for some eleven years.

The defendants insist that the trestle bridge was merely a temporary way for economy sake, and they always intended to fill the ravine in when they could afford it.

I think we can have no difficulty in ascertaining what really did take place. The plaintiff was demanding a large price for the land required. The agent, Tracey, was trying to beat down the price. Certain level crossings were agreed on. The plaintiff was pointing out the loss he would sustain by severance at the ravine, or depressed portion of his land. Tracey meets this by pointing out that the road would

Court, from the circumstances it has created, and the relations it has formed, that they are only consistent with the assumption of the existence of a contract the terms of which equity requires, if possible, to be ascertained and enforced."

The case seems to stand thus. The agreement and the deed consequent thereon are absolute in form. The agent through whom the defendants acquired the land from the plaintiff made the memorandum in his book that he had " settled with Clouse—he can have one pass under bridge."

It may fairly be assumed that he communicated this to his superiors.

Then as to the acts done, standing by themselves, and the user, they seem to point clearly to at least one fact, that the defendants acceded to some agreement or understanding that plaintiff should have this passage under their bridge so long as it was there. Their making, or allowing to be made, the slight alterations required for such passage, assists materially that view.

But the plaintiff, to succeed in his main contention, must prove an express or binding implied contract to afford him a perpetual subway under the railway.

I find great difficulty in holding, or believing on the evidence, that the company ever so agreed, or had any intention of so agreeing, or directly or indirectly authorized the purchaser of the right of way, or any of their officers, to consent to such an arrangement.

It could not be pretended that they undertook always to keep a trestle bridge there, and would never exercise the common right of replacing it by a solid embankment, a practice so general in the progress of a railway adventure. The cost of subways for vehicles through an embankment was and is always a costly matter, and it seems most unlikely that over every ravine or local depression, so numerous in a long line of railway, any company would bind itself for ever to grant and maintain underground farm crossings.

On the whole, I am unable to agree with the judgment of the Court below.

At the same time, I think it appears in evidence that the plaintiff accepted a reduced price for his land, under the belief that he was always to have an underground crossing.

I think that under the prayer for such further or other relief as the nature of the case will admit, we may hold that he is entitled to open the valuation of the land conveyed to the railway company, and to have it estimated how much (if anything) he is entitled to receive as additional compensation for the permanent closing of his crossing.

If the parties cannot agree on the amount or the mode of ascertaining it, we direct a reference to the Master.

I do not think there should be any costs of the appeal to either party.

Further directions and costs, other than of the appeal, reserved till after the reference.

BURTON, J.A.—The order complained of in this case was pronounced on the 26th November 1882, and directs that the defendants, their servants, workmen, and agents be for ever restrained from interfering with, hindering, or obstructing the plaintiff in his possession, use, and enjoyment of the under-crossing under the line of the defendants' railway, on land owned by the plaintiff.

I see no reason to doubt the correctness of the learned Judge's finding that the plaintiff in his negotiations with the railway did originally ask a larger sum than he eventually agreed to accept, and that he was influenced in accepting that reduced amount by the consideration that he was promised, in addition to the over-crossings, an under-crossing at this particular spot, and that the evidence of the plaintiff and his witnesses in that respect is confirmed by the memorandum made at the time in his book by the right of way agent.

But I do not think the evidence warrants. the conclusion at which the learned Judge arrived, that Tracey had any authority to bind the company by an agreement to give a perpetual under-crossing, or that he ever advised the company of his having done so.

The mere user of the way, so long as the trestle bridge stood, would not necessarily convey to the company any intimation that he claimed any greater right than that of using it during that condition of things, not in perpetuity.

The evidence to fix the company with the knowledge is, that when the bridge was being constructed the plaintiff found the uprights were being placed in such a position that he would have to cross the creek in order to use the way, and he went to the resident engineer and represented to him what his bargain with Tracey had been, and the engineer said if that was the bargain he would alter the position of the bents or uprights of the bridge ; but the chief engineer testifies that the resident engineer had no authority to alter the plans, although he would naturally, as he says, locate the exact spot where the bents were to be put.

He also shews that these bridges were not intended to be permanent, but were put up at the time to save the expense of embankment.

How then could the company be affected in this way with any notice that the plaintiff claimed this right permanently to enjoy the crossing? If, therefore, the agent had no right originally to bind the company, and there is nothing which subsequently occurred which can be regarded as a ratification of his act, the decree as based upon a concluded agreement for a perpetual under-crossing ought not to be allowed to stand.

But, assuming this all to be so, the right of way agent had authority to fix the compensation, and if, as part of this compensation, the landowner was induced to accept this under-crossing so long as the trestle bridge stood, there would seem to be no reason why he should not claim further compensation, if he is now to be deprived

by the act of the company of what formed a part of the
original compensation, in other words, why he should
not claim now, what presumably he might have claimed
if this concession had not been made, and, although he has
not prayed for it specially, I think we are justified in
varying the decree by making a declaration, that the
granting of the injunction shall be without prejudice to
any course which the defendants may be advised to take
in reference to ascertaining the additional compensation to
which the claimant may be entitled by reason of their
depriving him of the privilege hitherto enjoyed.

PATTERSON, J. A.—This appeal has been argued on the
part of the defendants the railway company as if the
plaintiff's right depended on his ability to establish a
contract made by and binding upon the company.

That appears to me a mistaken apprehension of the
relative position of the parties.

The railway company applied, in 1870 or 1871, to the
plaintiff for the land necessary for the construction of
their railway across his farm. Their plans shewed that it
was to be carried across at a higher level than part of
his land.

His farm would be unavoidably injuriously affected by
the construction of the railway across it, and the injury
from dividing the farm by an embankment would obviously
be greater than from merely crossing on the natural level
of the land.

The plaintiff shews that he demanded $1,000 or $1,200
for the purchase money of the land to be taken and the
resulting damages ; but, coming to an understanding with
the defendants' agent respecting some level farm crossings,
and it being represented to him that, in place of an embankment, the design was to carry the road on trestle work
across the low land, which would afford him access, under
the railway, from one part of his farm to the other, he
moderated his demand and accepted $650. He signed a
paper, which is under seal, dated 23rd January, 1871,

agreeing to sell and convey to the company so much of his lot as was taken by the company for its line of railway, containing $7\frac{21}{100}$ acres, for $650, " being the price of the said land and all damages in respect thereof, and allow the company to take possession at once for the purpose of prosecuting the work of grading." The price of $650 is shewn upon the document itself to be made up of $540.75 for the price of $7\frac{21}{100}$ acres of land, and $109.25 price of damages.

A deed was afterwards executed by the plaintiff and one Abraham Clouse and their respective wives, conveying the $7\frac{21}{100}$ acres of land to the company, in which deed the expressed consideration is $662. I believe there is no explanation of how the $662 was arrived at, and I do not think it is of importance to know how it was. In my view of the rights of the parties, the giving of the deed is not a material fact. The deed does not relate to the damages for injuriously affecting land which was not taken. The fact which I think should govern the decision is that the sum of $109.25, which is all that was paid by way of compensation for damages, apart from the price of $75 an acre, which was to be paid for the land taken. was paid for such damages as the farm would suffer from a railway carried across on trestles, and not for such a complete severance as would result from a solid embankment.

Let us look at the provisions of the law as we find them in Consol. Stat. Can. ch. 66, which is the statute that applies to this company.

Section 5 establishes the general principle that "for the value of lands taken, and for all damages to lands injuriously affected by the construction of the railway in the exercise of the powers by this, or the special Act, or any Act incorporated therewith, vested in the company, compensation shall be made to the owners and occupiers of, and to all other persons interested in, any lands so taken or injuriously affected."

Section 9 defines the powers of the company, including under 2dly the power to purchase any land necessary for the construction of the railway; and under 4thly and 6thly, the power to make, carry, or place the railway across or upon the lands of any corporation or person on the line of the railway or within a certain deviation; and to make, complete, alter, and keep in repair the railway with one or more sets of rails or tracks to be worked by the force and power of steam, or of the atmosphere, or of animals, or by mechanical power, or by any combination of them.

Section 10 requires surveys and levels to be made and taken of the lands through which the railway is to pass together with a map or plan thereof, with other particulars, and gives the right to any person to resort to copies, which are to be deposited in public offices named.

And section 11 deals with "Lands, and their valuation."

The provision numbered 5thly is, that after one month from the deposit of the map or plan and book of reference and from notice thereof in a newspaper, application may be made to the owners of lands or to parties empowered to convey lands, or interested in lands which may suffer damage from the taking of materials or the exercise of any of the powers granted for the railway, and thereupon agreements or contracts may be made with such parties touching the said lands or the compensation to be paid for the same or for the damages, as to the mode in which such compensation shall be ascertained, as may seem expedient to both parties.

7thly prescribes the kind of notice which is to be served upon the land owner. It is to contain, amongst other things, a description of the lands to be taken, or of the powers to be exercised with regard to any lands, describing them, and a declaration of readiness to pay some certain sum as compensation for such lands, or for such damages; is to be accompanied by the certificate of a sworn surveyor, that he knows the land or the amount of damage likely to arise from the exercise of the powers; and that the sum offered is in his opinion a fair compensation for the land and for the damages.

And, by 29thly, upon payment or legal tender of the compensation the agreement vests in the company the power forthwith to take possession of the lands, or *to exercise the right, or to do the thing for which such compensation has been agreed upon.*

For the sake of distinctness I quote these enactments without referring to the provisions for cases where the parties do not agree upon the amount of compensation.

In this case there were not the formal notices, &c., which the statute points out. The arrangement was verbally made between the plaintiff and the agent delegated by the defendants to bargain with land owners for the amounts to be paid them for the price of the land taken, and for the damages in respect of lands injuriously affected. But, although not put formally in writing, the evidence leaves no doubt as to the character of the damages for which the compensation was arranged ; or to use the words of the statute *the right* proposed *to be exercised,* or *the thing* proposed *to be done,* for which the compensation was agreed upon, is made very plain.

If the plaintiff and Tracey, the defendants' agent, had set out fully in writing what was understood at the time, it is clear from the evidence of both of them that they would have said that the plaintiff was to be compensated by the $109.25 for the injurious effect upon his farm of a railway which he could cross at stipulated places on the level, and which was carried over the hollow on trestles, under one at least of which he could pass.

This would have been substantially the same thing as if the negotiation had begun, at arms' length, with a notice that the company proposed to exercise the power given by those parts of sec. 9 which I have quoted, by making and carrying the railway across the plaintiff's farm on the trestles and with the level crossings, and with an offer of compensation based on the probable injury from that construction.

I do not, as it is needless to say, suppose it to be usual for railway companies to give notices with such details. I imagine the notice will usually be more general; but, when in the course of a negotiation some demands of the land owner are acceded to, and a corresponding limitation placed upon the proposed exercise of the power, the result is the same as if the notice had originally been in the shape of the ultimate agreement; and the right which becomes vested by payment of the compensation is only the right to do the thing for which the compensation has been agreed upon.

This line of argument is not met to my apprehension by suggesting that the company, as owner in fee of the land which it takes, may use that land for what purpose it pleases. I do not understand the company to have a right so absolute as that suggestion would assume. The right to use it for the construction and working of the railway is derived from the statute, which gives immunities which an individual owner would not enjoy at common law, and the same statute which gives the powers forbids the exercise of them until compensation has been made for the damages estimated as likely to be done to lands which they may injuriously affect. The maxim *sic utere tuo ut alienum non lædas* applies to the company except so far as the statute interferes; and that interference is made conditional on payment of compensation.

In this case I think the proper conclusion is, that the company in 1871, or whenever the railway was constructed, exercised all the power with reference to this plaintiff's farm for which they paid him compensation. They did the thing for which the compensation was agreed upon.

If they desire, as they now do, to exercise the further power of constructing their road in a different manner which will affect the plaintiff's farm more injuriously, I do not see anything to hinder them from taking steps under section 11 to acquire the right by ascertaining and paying the appropriate compensation. Until they do so, however, it appears to me that an injunction may as properly be issued, as it would have been to restrain them from doing the first injury until they had paid compensation for it.

This view of the case which I have presented, and which I think is correct, involves no hardship upon the railway company, while it only does justice to the farmer by protecting him from injury for which he has not been compensated.

Upon any other construction of the statute it would not be a very easy matter to say how the company could be prevented from obstructing any farm crossing which was not secured by deed to the farm owner.

Ever since the alteration of the word " and " to " at " in section 13, as noticed in *Brown* v. *The Toronto and Nipissing Railway Co.*, 26 C. P. 206, which alteration was made in 1859 in the Consolidated Statute, Chap. 66, many years before the incorporation of the defendants' company, there has been no statutory obligation upon railway companies governed by that statute to construct or maintain farm crossings. They are now to make their fences " with openings, gates, or bars therein at farm crossings of the road, for the use of the proprietors of the land adjoining the railway; " but the right to farm crossings must depend on something not here provided for. They may of course be secured by direct stipulation evidenced by the deed of the Company, but I doubt if that proceeding has often, if it has ever, been resorted to. It is more likely that the matter has entered into the computation of compensation for the severance of the farm; and the facilities afforded in the way of crossings, or in other words the limitation submitted to by the company of its power to construct and work the railway across the farm, will have mitigated the injury to the farmer and lessened the price paid by the company. When this is the case, as it is in the present instance expressly proved to have been, it does not strike me that we are required, or that we should be justified in treating the obligation of the company, or the right of the farmer, as resting on the contract of the company to do something or to refrain from changing the state of things, as contended for by the present appellants.

The right of the plaintiff is to have the state of things which has existed for the last ten years maintained, unless and until the company shall proceed under the statute to acquire a right to do what they now propose to do.

I have looked at the authorities cited to us, and at others which are collected in *Redfield* on Railways, and *Hodge* on Railways, on the subject of compensation. The law, which was very fully discussed in *Croft* v. *London and North Western R. W. Co.*, 3 B. & S. 436, under the Lands Clauses Consolidation Act, 1845, 8 & 9 Vic. ch. 18, sec. 68, seems to me to bear out the view I have taken of the principle to be applied to the present case. The decision there was that damages must be assessed, once for all, in respect of injuries which were foreseen or ought to have been foreseen as likely to result from the works; and that the occurrence of greater damage than had been anticipated did not give a right to maintain an action against the company. The work there in question was a tunnel, which caused more injury to the plaintiff's property than had been expected by him when the compensation had been fixed; but that was not owing to any change in, or addition to, the works originally proposed. The distinction was clearly pointed out between damages which were, or ought to have been, foreseen, and damages which could not be ascertained at the time of the inquiry. Of the latter class I take the damages to be against which the plaintiff is in this case contending, resulting, as they would, from work not contemplated by him, and of a different character from that with respect to which his compensation was arranged and paid.

Todd v. *Metropolitan District R. W. Co.*, 24 L. J., N. S. 435, is to the same effect.

In *Re Ware*, 9 Ex. 395, an award was objected to on the ground, amongst others, that nothing had been given for damages to certain pieces of land which, it was alleged, would certainly be flooded by the canal works there in question. This was answered by an affidavit that no injury had yet arisen. Pollock, C. B., said, p. 402:

"If any injury should hereafter arise, Mr. Ware will be entitled to compensation under the 68th section, which is expressly provided to meet such a case as this."

This case is referred to in both the others which I have cited, and the expression of the Chief Baron seems to have been treated as made with reference to some unforeseen damages.

Clarke v. *Manchester, Sheffield and Lincolnshire R. W. Co.*, 1 J. & H. 631, may be referred to as an instance in which an interlocutory injunction was granted to restrain a company from proceeding with works by which the rights of parties with whom they had contracted might be injured.

There is a case in 18 Pickering 443, *Ruel Morse*, petitioner, before the Supreme Judicial Court of Massachusetts, which is worth noting as an instance in which part of the compensation for the severance of land by a railway embankment was to consist of something done by the company to make the severance less injurious. The commissioners in that case had awarded that the company should make a culvert through the embankment, and also pay $500. The petitioner was dissatisfied, and had his damages assessed by a jury at $600. The question on which the costs depended was, whether this was a larger award than that of the commissioners. It was not decided that the commissioners could have compelled the company to make the culvert; but as the company might have accepted the award, the Court refused a *mandamus* to compel the commissioners to render judgment for the $600 and costs.

The acceptance of that award would have put the company very much in the position of these defendants, when the plaintiff reduced his claim to the amount estimated as the damage to be caused by the railway constructed as represented.

I do not know that the injunction in the form ordered by the decree to restrain the defendants from forever interfering with the plaintiff's under-crossing would necessarily prevent their taking fresh steps under the statute to entitle themselves, by paying compensation, to exercise further powers by making a solid embankment; but to avoid question, it will be better to vary the order so as to restrain such interference unless and until compensation shall have been made as the statute directs.

OSLER, J. A.—By section 13 of the General Railway Clauses Consolidation Act, 14 & 15 Vict. ch. 51, it was enacted that fences should be erected and maintained on each side of the railway with openings, or gates, or bars therein, *and* farm crossings for the use of the proprietors of the lands adjoining the railway.

The same provision in similar terms was contained in the railway legislation of the State of New York; Laws of New York, 1848, sec. 42; *Ib.*, 1850, 233, sec. 44. It was held in many cases both in our own Courts and those of the United States, that an obligation was thereby imposed upon the company to make the crossings, and in the case of *Wademan* v. *The Albany and Susquehanna R. R. Co.*, 51 N. Y. 568, the New York Court of Appeals held— overruling on this point *Wheeler* v. *Rochester, &c., R. R. Co.*, 12 Barb. 227—that it was the right of the company to determine where the crossing should be located, but that regard must be had to the convenience of both parties, and that such a location must be made as would not subject the proprietor to needless and unwarrantable injury. A similar construction had already been placed upon our statute by our Court of Common Pleas in *Burke* v. *The Grand Trunk R. W. Co.*, 6 C. P. 484. See also *Reist* v. *The Grand Trunk R. W. Co.*, 6 C. P. 421, *S. C.* 15 U. C. R. 355.

Where, however, the expense of making the crossing was greatly disproportionate to the value of the land and to the value of the crossing to the proprietor. the Courts would not enforce the statutory obligation, but awarded compensation in damages in lieu thereof: *Clarke* v. *Rochester, &c., R. R. Co.* 18 Barb. 350; *Wademan* v. *The Albany, &c., R. R. Co.*, 51 N. Y. 568.

When the statutes were consolidated in 1859 a change
occurred in sec. 13, which, in Consol. Stat. Can. ch. 66, sec.
13, now reads thus: "Fences shall be erected and maintained, &c., with openings, or gates, or bars therein *at* farm
crossings of the road, &c.," for the use of proprietors of the
lands adjoining, thereby, as it is contended, limiting the
obligation of the company to that of making and maintaining fences with openings, &c., therein at farm crossings.
Whether there should be farm crossings or not was thus
left to be the subject of special agreement between the
proprietor and the railway company. If they would not
give him any, his claim for compensation for severance
would be proportionately increased. The authority for
this alteration in the language of the Act is not known.

It seems probable that the word "at" was at first substituted for "and" by mere inadvertence, as section 14 was
retained in the Consolidated Act, which enacts, as did its
predecessor in the earlier Act, 20 Vic. ch. 35, sec. 1, that
the provisions of section 13 shall not be construed to confer
any rights to farm crossings upon those proprietors *who
had formerly received compensation from the railway
company for the severance of their farms.* And if crossings
were to be subject of agreement or of compensation only,
it is not quite apparent why the provision as to maintaining
gates, &c., should have been retained, since one might as well
form the subject of agreement as the other. The altered
form of the section has however been adopted in all subsequent railway legislation, and in *Brown* v. *The Toronto
and Nipissing R. W. Co.*, 26 C. P. 206, it was held that
under the section as thus altered, no liability was cast
upon a railway company to make or maintain farm
crossings. The plaintiff's right to the crossing in question
depends therefore entirely upon agreement.

I was at first disposed to think, having regard to
Tracey's memorandum and the evidence of what was done
by the company in the construction of the bridge, that we
might hold that there had been a part performance of the
agreement on which the plaintiff relies sufficient to take it

out of the Statute of Frauds. Further consideration, since the second argument of the case, has led me to doubt the correctness of my first impression, and I am forced to the conclusion that we cannot, consistently with the principle enunciated in *Maddison* v. *Alderson*, 8 App. Cas. 467, hold that the acts of part performance relied upon are so exclusively referable to an agreement for a permanent under-crossing at the trestle bridge as to entitle the plaintiff to specific performance. I think the effect of the evidence on this point is fairly stated in the judgment of my lord, and we ought of course to be satisfied beyond any reasonable doubt, before finding the existence of an agreement, which may so trammel the company in the management and construction of the road as to bind them forever to maintain a crossing at any particular point. It is however quite clear that the use of the under-crossing was taken into account in fixing the amount of the compensation or damages for severance, and it is not inconsistent with the evidence that the crossing was to continue only so long as the company maintained a trestle bridge at this point. But if they desire to build a close embankment and thereby complete the severance of the plaintiff's farm, that is something for which they have not paid him compensation, and I think they must take the proceedings to ascertain and pay it before disturbing the existing state of things. I agree with the views which my Brother Patterson has expressed on this part of the case, and think the decree should be varied in accordance with his suggestion, and that the appeal should be dismissed.

ERWIN v. CANADA SOUTHERN RAILWAY COMPANY.

Railway crossing—Written agreement for under-crossing—Re-valuation of land.

The agent of a railway company while engaged in obtaining the right of way agreed with one S., through whom the plaintiff claimed, for the right of crossing his property, and S. executed an agreement to convey to the company $4\frac{17}{100}$ acres of his farm for that purpose in consideration of $1,650; such agreement before being executed having had indorsed thereon a memorandum that S. should " have liberty to remove for his own use all buildings on the said right of way ; and it is also further agreed that in the event of there being constructed on the same lot a trestle bridge of sufficient height to allow of the passage of cattle, the said company will so construct their fence to each side thereof, as not to impede the passage thereunder."

The company did construct a trestle bridge which the plaintiff as well as S. whilst owner of the lot continued to use, for the purpose of passing under the railway from one portion of the farm to another for upwards of ten years, when the company determined to convert the trestle bridge into a solid embankment :

Held, that the company were at liberty so to change the bridge, but that the plaintiff was, as in *Clouse* v. *The Canada Southern R. W. Co.*, (ante p. 287) entitled to a re-valuation of the land conveyed.

BURTON, J. A., dissenting, who thought the plaintiff had under the circumstances failed to establish any claim for relief.

THIS was an appeal by the defendants from the judgment of Proudfoot, J., of the 4th of April, 1883.

The action was brought to restrain the defendants from interference with the plaintiff's use of an under-crossing or cattle-pass under the defendants' railway where it crossed the plaintiff's land in the township of Townsend, and for damages. The facts of the case, with such exceptions as are noticed in the judgments on the present appeal, are similar to those in *Clouse* v. *The Canada Southern R. W. Co.*, 4 O. R. 28, and ante p. 287.

The cause was heard by Proudfoot, J., upon motion for judgment upon the pleadings, affidavits, and part of the evidence taken in *Clouse* v. *The Canada Southern R. W. Co.*, and judgment was given in favor of the plaintiff.

The appeal was heard at the same time as the appeal in *Clouse's Case*, the same counsel appearing for the parties respectively.

December 18, 1884. BURTON, J. A.—I think we must hold, as in Clouse against the same defendants, ante p. 237 that no authority has been shewn in Tracey to grant a permanent undercrossing; but it differs from that case in this, that the parties have reduced their agreement to writing, and the then owner of the land appears to have been very particular that all the stipulations for his benefit should be embodied in the agreement.

The original agreement was silent as to the crossing, and when the deed was executed the owner required a further memorandum to be indorsed on the agreement in these words :

"It is further agreed, and it is to be taken as part of the within agreement, that the within named Smith shall have liberty to remove for his own use all buildings on the said right of way ; and it is also further agreed that *in the event of there being constructed on the said lot a trestle bridge* of sufficient height to allow of the passage of cattle, the said company will so construct their fence to each side thereof, so as not to impede. the passage thereunder.—Dated September 26th, 1871."

So that if the company had decided at that time, as they were at perfect liberty to do, to substitute embankment for trestle work, they could have done so without rendering themselves in any way liable to the landowner in consequence. The agreement is quite consistent with the evidence of Tracey and the chief engineer of the company, that the former had no authority to make bargains agreeing to grant permanent undercrossings.

The company had no objection to the use, by parties interested, of the vacant spaces under the trestle work for the purpose of a crossing, so long as the trestle work remained; but that is a very different thing from debarring themselves for all time from substituting a permanent embankment for trestle work.

I think in this suit no case for compensation has been established. The landowner obtained at the time all that he asked, and the compensation would appear to have been large. I think that the agreement indorsed correctly described the understanding of the parties, and no case for a reformation of the contract has been made out.

The question as to the Statute of Limitations was disposed of during the argument.

We have not been furnished with the learned Judge's reasons for his judgment, but if they proceeded, as is alleged in the reasons against the appeal, upon the construction of the agreement, I must respectfully differ from the conclusion arrived at, as it merely contemplated that the owner of the land should have that right only in the event of the trestle bridge being built; and I think it not an unfair corollary to that proposition that, upon its being removed and a permanent structure substituted, the right should cease.

I think we ought to hold that the plaintiff has failed to establish any claim for relief, and that his bill should be dismissed, and this appeal allowed, with costs.

PATTERSON, J.A.—We are unfortunately without any findings of fact, or statements of the opinion of the learned Judge from whose decree this appeal is brought.

The formal decree declares that, *upon the true construction of the agreement* in the statement of claim referred to, the plaintiff is entitled to the use, occupation, and enjoyment of the under-crossing in the pleadings referred to.

The allegation in the statement of claim is that Smith, the plaintiff's predecessor in title, should convey to the company $4\frac{17}{100}$ acres of land, and that the company should pay him $1,650 and should provide an under-crossing or cattle pass under the railway, and should keep and maintain it for all time for the use of Smith his heirs and assigns.

It is not alleged that any such agreement as this was put in writing. The evidence of it is given by affidavits, the principal witness being a son of Smith, who says the arrangement was made by him with a Mr. Boughner who was acting for Mr. Tracey, the agent of the company, and with Mr. Tracey himself.

The agreement is thus stated by him :

4. It was finally agreed upon between me and the said John Avery Tracey, on the twenty-fifth day of September, one thousand eight hundred and seventy-one, that my said father should convey the land required by the defendants, amounting to four acres and seventeen hundredths of an acre, upon the terms and conditions following, that is to say, the defendants were to pay my father one thousand six hundred and fifty dollars; my father was to be at liberty to retain possession for five years of the wood-shed in the rear of his house and the ground upon which it stood, and was to have a passage of five feet in width between the said wood-shed and the railway fence, and *at a water-course crossing the right of way, it was agreed that a cattle-pass should be constructed for my father's use under the defendants' line of* railway, if there was sufficient height to admit of the passage of cattle, but *that in any event* a passage should be constructed to be used by *sheep and hogs*, and my father was to be at liberty to remove for his own use all buildings upon the land sold to the defendants for right of way.

A sister of this deponent states the agreement in the same way.

Mr. Boughner makes an affidavit in which he puts the agreement respecting the under-crossing without the qualification by which the others say it might have been merely sufficient for the passage of hogs and sheep. The paragraph of his affidavit reads thus:

4. At a very early period in the negotiations for the purchase of said right of way, it was agreed that, as a part of the consideration for the same, said James H. Smith should have an under-crossing under the defendants' railway to be built across said lot, to be used by him as a cattle-pass. This and all the other terms of the agreement were settled without much difficulty except the one point as to the amount of the money consideration to be paid to said Smith, which remained in dispute until the month of September, one thousand eight hundred and seventy-one, when a sum was finally agreed upon, and the bargain closed without any change as to the agreement relative to the cattle-pass.

Mr. Tracey made no affidavit, but it was agreed that his evidence and also that of a Mr. Finney, given in the case of *Clouse* v. *Canada Southern Railway Co.* should be read in this case.

Smith's name is not mentioned in that evidence, nor is Erwin's name mentioned except for a purpose unconnected with this claim. Tracey speaks with reference only to *Clouse's Case.* He says he made no bargain with Clouse for crossings: that on three or four occasions he made bar-

gains for under-crossings by special instructions of Mr.
Courtwright : that he had no authority to make bargains
about under-crossings without special instructions : and
that when the subject of crossings was brought up, during
the negotiation with Clouse, he remarked that the law
gave them all necessary crossings, and they would get all
necessary crossings.   He said also that the cases where he
made special agreements along the line were few, and the
agreements were reduced to writing.

Mr. Finney's evidence does not touch the question of the
bargain.

There was a special agreement reduced to writing, and
executed by Tracey.   It was taken to Smith's house when
Tracey, accompanied by Boughner, and by Mr. Kingsmill
the company's solicitor, went to pay him his money, and
procure his conveyance.   Neither of the two last named
gentlemen was able to state from recollection what then
occurred, but Mr. Smith's son and daughter state that their
father objected that the document did not mention his
right to remove some buildings from the land he was conveying, nor the cattle pass.   Thereupon a supplementary
clause was indorsed by Mr. Kingsmill, and Mr. Smith
executed the deed and accepted the money.

The agreement as originally prepared was in these words:

The Canada Southern Railway Company, by John Avery Tracey their
duly constituted agent for the purchase of right of way, do hereby agree
with James H. Smith, the owner of lot twelve in the ninth concession of
Townsend, his heirs and assigns, as follows :

The said Smith having sold to the said company the right of way over
lot number twelve in the ninth concession of the township of Townsend,
containing four acres and seventeen hundredths of an acre, at and for the
price of one thousand six hundred and fifty dollars. and having given a
conveyance to the said company for the same.   It is hereby, notwithstanding such conveyance, agreed between the said parties that for the
period of five years from the date of this agreement the said Smith, his
heirs and assigns, shall have possession undisturbed by the said railway
company of the wood-shed and the ground on which it is erected at the
rear of his house and on the right of way so conveyed, and the fence of
the said railway shall be so constructed as to leave a passage of at least
five feet wide for the use of the said Smith, his heirs and assigns, between
the said wood-shed and the railway fence, and the said fence shall run

from a point five feet south of the south-easterly corner of the said wood-shed in a straight line to the south-westerly corner of a barn now standing on the fence line of the said railway, and shall so remain during the space of five years as aforesaid.

And it is hereby agreed that the said company shall give such further assurance as may be deemed necessary to carry out this agreement, which is hereby declared part of the consideration for the said conveyance.

Dated September 26th, 1871.

J. AVERY TRACEY. { SEAL }

WITNESS, NICOL KINGSMILL,
Secretary.

And the clause indorsed was as follows: [His Lordship here read the memorandum as set forth by Burton, J. A., ante p. 807.]

It is shewn that the railway was carried upon trestle work across the depression in Smith's land, and he had a passage for his cattle under it, though not at the place at first proposed. The railway fences were adjusted with reference to this passage, and Smith, and Erwin after him, had the use of it for over ten years, until recently interrupted by preparations of the company to make a solid embankment.

The learned Judge, who tried *Clouse's Case* and this case delivered a judgment in the former in which, although he makes no allusion to this case, I think we may infer that he was to some extent influenced by the opinion that a farm crossing having once been established, the company is bound to maintain it. That was the effect of the Railway Clauses Act, 14 and 15 Vict. ch. 51, sec. 13, and it was so held in many cases. But under the law as found in C. S. Can. ch. 66, sec. 13, which has always applied to this company, I do not understand any such duty to be created.

As I apprehend the rights of railway companies and farmers under the present law, the right to have a farm crossing and all questions as to its maintenance are matters depending on the terms settled when the right to cross the farm is given.

I need not repeat what I have said on this subject in *Clouse's Case.*

There was evidently, in the present case, an understanding that Smith was to have a crossing, sufficient for cattle to pass, or at least sufficient for sheep and hogs. I infer this, not only from the direct evidence of the son and daughter and of Mr. Boughner, but also from Mr. Tracey's statement that he assured Clouse that the law gave a right to all necessary crossings, an opinion which, whether well founded or not, certainly went as far as to concede that he was to have crossings if required; and which, expressing his idea of the law, may reasonably be assumed to have been conveyed to Smith as well as to the other people with whom Tracey dealt for what is called the right of way.

This is not met by any evidence but the clause indorsed on Smith's deed, which, it is argued, gives the right only as contingent upon there being and continuing to be a trestle bridge of sufficient height to allow of the passage of cattle.

If we had not this memorandum, I should conclude from the other evidence, on the same view of the law as I expressed in *Clouse's Case*, and on a somewhat similar apprehension of the facts, that one of the factors in the computation of the compensation for Smith's damages, was the use of a farm crossing for his cattle; and that a crossing having been enjoyed by him, which enjoyment was properly referable to the rights retained by him, a state of things had been established which the company could not alter to his prejudice without making adequate compensation.

I do not find in the written memorandum anything necessarily in conflict with this understanding. In its terms it relates only to the making of the railway fence, which was to be constructed so as not to impede the passage under the trestle, if the bridge should be of sufficient height to allow the passage of cattle. This would, of course, imply no agreement to construct or maintain a trestle bridge; and if we had to look to this document alone for the agreement the plaintiff might fail. But, if my construction of the law in *Clouse's Case* is correct, the question is not whether there is an enforceable agreement of an executory character, but what was the basis on which the compensation was computed.

Now taking into account Mr. Tracey's opinion, as he expressed it to the farmers, that they had a right by law to necessary crossings, an opinion which, we cannot doubt, was also entertained by the person he bargained with, it would not be reasonable to conclude that the right to a crossing of any kind was understood between him and Smith to depend on the accident of the height of the trestle.

Smith seems to have had a preference for an under-crossing, and even to have been willing to put up with one through which only sheep or hogs could pass, though Mr. Boughner does not seem to have recollected that concession; and I have no doubt that all parties had reasonable ground for believing that the trestle work would be made, as in fact it was made. If made, the crossing was to be under it. It is called a bridge in the memorandum, and the evidence shews that it was intended and spoken of that the crossing was to be under the road when it was carried over a stream. It was changed, as is shewn by the company's officer, and was given to Smith at a different place, not under *the bridge*, if that term referred only to the locality of the stream.

I think the under-crossing now in question was not the one in the minds of the parties when the memorandum was written, but that it was one provided for Smith by reason of the understanding that he was to have a crossing, and that, if the trestle work permitted. he was to have it under the railway.

Upon the same grounds as those on which my opinion in *Clouse's Case* proceeded, I think the company cannot deprive the plaintiff of a crossing without making him compensation : and that the crossing he now enjoys being that which was in contemplation, or that which the company, with Smith's assent, substituted for the one by way of the stream which was in contemplation when the com-

pensation was fixed and accepted, the *status quo* ought not
to be disturbed until the further compensation is made.

It is alleged in the statement of defence that the defendants have notified the plaintiff that they will furnish
him with a good and suitable level crossing over their line,
but that the plaintiff insists upon having the under-crossing maintained. The plaintiff amended his statement of
claim to meet some allegations of the defence, and takes
no notice of the offer of a level crossing, but reiterates
his claim to hold the under-crossing in fee by virtue of his
ten years' user

The claim under the Statute of Limitations is too fanciful
to deserve serious discussion. There can be no pretence
that the company has ever been dispossessed, or has ever
discontinued the possession of land which supports the
roadway, which has always been in use by their trains and
kept in repair by their servants.

If it is of importance to the company to construct the
proposed embankment, and if they can, as suggested in
their defence, accommodate the plaintiff with a level crossing, that circumstance will be proper to consider in estimating the compensation to which he may be entitled.
The injury from closing his present crossing would obviously be only the difference of value to him between the
two crossings for his cattle.

There is more room for doubt in this case than in *Clouse's
Case*, probably because the facts are not so satisfactorily
brought out; but I do not see sufficient reason for saying
the decree is wrong. It should, however, be varied in the
same manner as the decree in *Clouse's Case*.

HAGARTY, C. J. O., and OSLER, J. A., concurred with
PATTERSON, J. A.

TOWERS v. DOMINION IRON AND METAL COMPANY.

Sale by sample—Inspection—Place of delivery—Defects in quality—Cross-action.

The defendants agreed with one W., who stated incorrectly that he was acting as broker for the plaintiff, for the purchase by sample of a quantity of cotton waste at 1¼ cents per lb., to be delivered at St. Catharines. In reality W. was selling for his own benefit, as he arranged to purchase the waste at one cent a pound. Instead of inspecting the goods at St. Catharines, the defendants requested W. to consign them to their house in Cincinnati, U. S., which the plaintiff did by direction of W. The plaintiff, at the request of W., made out a bill of lading in the name of the defendants and drew on them for the price at 1¼ cents per lb., which draft was accepted by the defendants, the plaintiff paying W. his profit in cash. On the goods reaching Cincinnati, an inspection took place when they were found greatly inferior to the sample. The defendants rejected the goods but refused to return them to the plaintiff at St. Catharines, although he was willing to accept them there. In an action on the bill of exchange,

Held, [affirming the judgment of SENKLER, Co. J.] that the defect in quality formed no ground of defence, that the plaintiff's contract was to deliver the goods at St. Catharines, where the inspection ought *primâ facie* to have taken place, and that the only redress of the defendants was by cross-action.

This was an appeal from the judgment of his Honor Judge Senkler of the County Court of the County of Lincoln, discharging an order *nisi* to enter judgment for the defendants in an action tried before the learned Judge with a jury, in which he had entered judgment for the plaintiff on the findings of the jury.

The action was upon a bill of exchange for $329.18, drawn by the plaintiff on, and accepted by the defendants.

The defence was that the bill was accepted for the price of certain goods sold to the defendants by the plaintiff, according to sample, and that the goods were not according to sample, and had not been accepted.

There was a further defence that the defendants' acceptance of the bill was without value or consideration.

The facts may be shortly stated thus: The defendants, a firm of merchants in Toronto, told one Wright, with whom they had been in the habit of dealing, that they required some cotton waste, and if he could get any to bring them a sample. A few days afterwards Wright brought a sample which he said the plaintiff, a merchant in St. Catharines, had for sale, and for which he wanted 1¼c. per lb. in St. Catharines. The defendants agreed to take it if equal to sample. Wright told them he was only getting his brokerage from Towers, and the defendants supposed they were dealing with him as a broker, and buying from the plaintiff.

The plaintiff on the other hand, who had also been in the habit of dealing with Wright, said he had sold the waste at one cent per lb. to Wright himself, as he had always done, and Wright swore that he bought the stuff on his own account, having in fact sold to the defendants at 1¼c. before doing so.

As to the bill. The plaintiff was to be paid by Wright in cash, but at his request he charged the goods to the defendants, and drew upon them for the price Wright had sold them for, paying Wright the difference (¼c.) in cash. This was because Wright did not wish them to know that he had only paid one cent per lb.

As to the goods it was alleged in the statement of defence and proved in fact that they were to be delivered to the defendants f. o. b. at St. Catharines. Defendants at first wanted them sent to Toronto, but afterwards directed Wright to ship from St. Catharines to their branch house in Cincinnati. They were forwarded there in accordance with Wright's instructions.

The bill of lading with draft attached was sent to the defendants. A witness, Leo Frankel, said he was present when Isaac Joseph one of the defendants asked Wright, "What if stuff does not amount to sample?" Wright said, "You accept draft, and if stuff does not come to sample, Towers will allow the difference."

On arrival at Cincinnati the goods were found not in accordance with sample. The defendants did not return them, nor did they return or offer to return the bill of lading.

The plaintiff offered to take back the goods if the defendants would return them to St. Catharines. This they refused to do.

No place for inspection was mentioned. There was no evidence that they could not have been inspected at St. Catharines.

The jury found in answer to questions put to them:

1. That the goods did not correspond with the sample.
2, 3. That they were not absolutely valueless, but were worth one cent per pound.
4. That Wright was not Towers's agent for sale of the goods, but
5. That he represented himself to the defendants as being such.
6. That it was to the plaintiff whom the defendants looked to make good any loss they might sustain.

On these findings, judgment was entered for the plaintiff for the amount of the bill, with interest and costs.

The defendants subsequently moved to set this judgment aside, which on the 6th of October, 1884, was refused, with costs.

The defendants thereupon appealed to this Court, and the appeal came on for hearing on the 18th of March, 1885.*

Allan Cassels, for the appellants, contended that the respondent was estopped from denying that the contract made by him was to deliver the goods to the railway company at St. Catharines, as carriers, for the purpose of carrying them to the appellants' firm at Cincinnati; and that the bill of lading accompanying the draft was sufficient assent to this contract, on the part of the respondent; and, also, that although there had been such an acceptance of the goods by the appellants, as to take the case out of the Statute of Frauds, still as the goods were sold by sample, there was no such acceptance as to deprive the appellants of their right on inspection of the goods after reaching Cincinnati, to reject them on the ground that they were not equal to sample.

Present.—HAGARTY, C. J. O., BURTON, PATTERSON, and OSLER, JJ.A.

Osler, Q. C., and *Towers*, for the respondent.   To entitle the defendants to succeed in their defence, they must shew a total want of consideration.   Here the goods having been delivered at St. Catharines and no rejection of them made or the bill of lading returned, there had been in fact an absolute assignment and delivery to the appellants, and the retention thereof by them and of the bill of lading was a sufficient consideration to entitle the respondent to recover on the bill of exchange.

Even assuming that Wright acted as agent for the plaintiff, the right, if any, of the defendants to succeed, is upon an implied warranty ; but as they had contented themselves with an express warranty upon the part of Wright which they relied upon, their remedy was against him, and against him alone.   But, however, that may be, the answer of the jury that Wright was acting, not as the agent of the plaintiff, but in his own interest in making the sale, is conclusive against the defendants : *McMaster* v. *Gordon*, 2 C. P. 16 ; *Grimoldby* v. *Wells*, L. R. 10 C. P. 391, were referred to.

April 17, 1885.   HAGARTY, C. J. O.—I think this appeal should be dismissed.

It appears to me that on the evidence before us we ought to hold that the plaintiff's contract was to deliver the goods at St. Catharines : that if the defendants desired an inspection for the purpose of exercising their right to reject as not being in accordance with sample, it ought to have taken place at St. Catharines : but that the defendants by accepting the draft for the price accompanied by the bill of lading or shipping bill, assumed the complete ownership of the goods : that, in the language of the case of *Street* v. *Blay*, 2 B. & Ad. 456, so often referred to, the property became indefeasibly vested in them, and that they retained no right to revest it in the plaintiff because it was not equal to sample.

In *Mondel* v. *Steele*, 8 M. & W. 858, the view as expressed by Parke, B., at p. 870, was that such absolute acceptance does not interfere with their right to seek for damages in consequence of the inferiority of the article to the quality represented. This was not the case of property with internal faults or hidden defects not discernible by ordinary examination. Bales of cotton droppings could be examined and samples taken from each, as far as we can see, without any great difficulty.

Joseph, the defendant, speaks of putting in his arm and taking a sample from the bags. He says: "The goods were bought at St. Catharines; delivered there to be shipped to Cincinnati."

If defendant's argument be sound, then if he had directed them to be shipped at St. Catharines to New Orleans or Jamaica, he would, at either of the latter places, have the right to reject and notify the plaintiff that they were there at his risk, &c.

The law seems clear that if vendees have the right to reject at the agreed on place of delivery, they are not bound to return the property to vendor, or to place it in neutral hands: *Grimoldby* v. *Wells*, L. R. 10 C. P. 391; *Lucy* v. *Mouflet*, 5 H. & N. 229; *Cutter* v. *Powell*, 2 Sm. L. Cases, (Ed. 1879).

The case of *Heilbutt* v. *Hickson*, L. R. 7 C. P. 438, seems the fullest in its treatment of the question. It is cited at length in Benjamin on Sales, 851 (4th Am. Ed. from 3rd English, 1883). It arose on a contract for large quantities of shoes for the French Army, which were rejected as containing paper, &c., in the soles, a defect not visible without opening each shoe.

The delivery was to be at a wharf in London for shipment to Lille, inspection and payment to be in London on delivery.

Some question as to this defect arose in London, and the vendors wrote to the vendees that they would take back all shoes rejected by the French authorities at Lille, in consequence of paper being found in the soles.

At Lille a large quantity was rejected by the French. The Court held that the vendors were liable; that the ven-

dors' letter must be treated as a new contract adding fresh
terms to the original contract, and upon the proper construction of the whole bargain, the vendees were entitled to throw
the shoes on the vendors' hands both at Lille and at the
London wharf.   Bovill, C. J., and Byles, J., held that but
for the letter the vendees could not have rejected them,
having accepted and dealt with them as their own property.   Brett, J., held that apart from the letter, the
vendees could return them at Lille, inasmuch as the London
inspection was insufficient by reason of a latent defect for
which the vendors as manufacturers were liable, and that
the shoes were rejected immediately upon an opportunity
occurring for discovery of such defect.   The judgments in
that case are very instructive.

The case is very fully commented on by Mr. Benjamin,
and accepted as declaring the law on the subject.

In *Grimoldby* v. *Wells*, L. R. 10 C. P. 391, Brett, J., re-
affirms his views.

I am strongly of the opinion that the only remedy in
the case before us must be by cross-action.

In no other way can injustice be avoided.   The price
agreed to be paid was one and a quarter cent, the jury
found the value was one cent.   The property lies at Cincinnati in the railway stores, and the bill of lading apparently is still in the vendees' hands.

I think the appeal must be dismissed.

BURTON, J.A.—I agree in dismissing the appeal, and
affirming the judgment of the Court below; but I am of
opinion that a great deal of foreign and irrelevant matter
was introduced into the case, both in the Court below and
in the argument before us, and that stripped of these sur-
roundings, the case is a very simple one.

The only contract made by the plaintiff was that
entered into with Wright, that is, for the sale of a certain
quantity of cotton droppings at one cent per pound
deliverable at St. Catharines.

Wright contracted to sell the same cotton that he was purchasing to the defendants, but he falsely represented to them that he was acting as the agent of the plaintiff.

Having effected this sale at one and a quarter cent, he returned to the plaintiff and concluded his purchase, and whilst mentioning his re-sale, carefully concealing the fact that he had professed to do so as agent for the plaintiff, but on the contrary, making another false representation to the plaintiff that he had sold on his own account, and desiring the plaintiff in effect to discount the paper he was to receive and pay him his profit out of the proceeds in cash.

This is what it in effect amounted to, the mode in which it was carried out was by Towers shipping, at Wright's request, to the defendants' order upon their accepting a draft of the plaintiff for the purchase money.

To speak of this as an adoption of Wright's contract would be a confusion of ideas. The plaintiff never learned that Wright had assumed to act as his agent, and that material ingredient being wanting, there could of course be nothing in the shape of a ratification of a contract which he had never heard of, what he did suppose was that Wright resold the goods to the defendants, and to oblige Wright, and believing his representation he sent the goods to the defendants upon their accepting the bill.

Apart from this acceptance, there was no privity between the plaintiff and defendants.

If the sale to Wright and that to the defendants had been at three months, and upon a similar state of facts to those I have recounted, the plaintiff had sent the goods to the defendants, he could not have recovered the price from them, but would have had to look to his original vendee.

It is quite true that the defendants, believing the representation of Wright followed by the shipment to them by the plaintiff, not unnaturally supposed that he was the seller and they were the immediate purchasers, but their supposition upon the subject cannot affect the rights or

liabilities of the defendants, all that can be said is that a
fraud was practised upon them by Wright, but the plaintiff was not responsible for that fraud.   Wright was not
originally authorized to make the sale as the agent of
plaintiff, nor did the plaintiff ratify the assumed agency
subsequently.

A fraud was practised upon both plaintiff and defendants, but the plaintiff did nothing to enable Wright to
commit the fraud, and cannot be affected by any representation made by him.

The result is, that there is no answer to the plaintiff's
action on the bill, and the appeal should be dismissed, with
costs.

OSLER, J. A.—I am of opinion that the judgment should
be affirmed.   Mr. Cassels argued, and the point was probably intended to be taken by the second reason of appeal,
that the contract was to deliver the goods to the defendants' firm in Cincinnati, U. S.

If this were so, it would no doubt be a very important
fact as bearing upon the right of the defendants to inspect
and reject the goods there.

No question, however, was raised about it at the trial, I
suppose because it is negatived by the defendants in their
statement of defence, and by the evidence.   For the same
reason the learned Judge refused to entertain it in term,
and we can give no effect to it now.

In the third reason of appeal it is said that the bill of
lading which accompanied the draft sued on shewed an
assent on the plaintiff's part to such a contract, that is, to
deliver in Cincinnati.   As to this, it can only be said that
no point of that kind was made at the trial or in term.
The bill of lading was not put in, and we can know
nothing of its terms beyond the fact that it was a document of title to the goods under which they were sent on
to Cincinnati, where the defendants afterwards had possession of them.   It need not necessarily be inconsistent with
the contract proved.

It is clear that there was a delivery to the defendants at St Catharines, and an acceptance and receipt by them there in sending the goods forward to Cincinnati, sufficient to make a binding contract within the Statute of Frauds : *Currie* v. *Anderson*, 2 E. & E. 592. But an acceptance and receipt sufficient for that purpose, does not necessarily preclude the purchaser from objecting to the quality of the goods as not answering the contract, and the case turns upon the question, whether the defendants having thus sent them forward were at liberty to inspect and reject them at Cincinnati.

We need not discuss any questions not argued before us as to the position of the parties arising out of the double sale, first at 1¼c. by Wright to the defendants, ostensibly but not really, as agent for Towers ; and the second at one cent. by the latter to Wright, as to which see *Cundy* v. *Lindsay*, 3 App. Cas. 459 ; and *Hamet* v. *Letcher*, 41 Am. 519, 37 Ohio St. 356.

The case was properly treated by the learned Judge as if the plaintiff was the seller of the goods to the defendants. They believed that they were dealing with him, and it does not lie in his mouth to say that they were not, since at Wright's request he charged the goods to them and drew on them the bill in question, in order to conceal the traces of Wright's conduct in the matter. Nor do I think it necessary to consider whether the acceptance by the purchaser of a draft for the price of the goods after an acceptance and receipt sufficient to satisfy the statute, would affect his right to reject them. I do not see how the effect of that can be greater than actual payment of the price, which does not exclude it.

I am of opinion that as the place of delivery was St. Catharines, that was *primâ facie* the place for inspection. The goods were at the railway station there, and there is no evidence that they could not have been conveniently and effectually inspected there before the defendants had them sent on to Cincinnati. In such circumstances, we should require very strong and convincing proof of the intention, and agreement of the parties that the purchaser was to be at liberty to take the goods from the place of delivery, having ample opportunity for inspection there, to a foreign country, subjecting them, as in this instance, to charges for freight and duty nearly equal to their price, and then, in the absence of the vendor, inspect and reject them.

In *Heilbutt* v. *Hickson*, L. R. 7 C. P. 438, Brett, L. J., says (p. 456) that a contract for sale by sample "always contains an implied term that the goods may, under certain circumstances, be returned ; that such term necessarily contains varying or alternative applications, and among others the following, that if the *time* of inspection *as agreed upon* be subsequent to the time agreed for the delivery of the goods, or if the *place* of inspection *as agreed upon* be different from the place of delivery, the purchaser may upon inspection at such time and place, if the goods be not equal to sample, return them *then and there* upon the hands of the seller."

He then proceeds to shew that the time and place of inspection *may be* different from the time and place of delivery, if inspection at the latter place be ineffectual by reason of a latent defect in the article for which the vendors as manufacturers were responsible, or by any other wrongful act of the vendors.

In *Grimoldby* v. *Wells*, L. R. 10 C. P. 391, the vendor and purchaser lived about nine miles apart, and the goods were sent part of the way in the vendor's cart, and then transferred into one belonging to and sent by the purchaser for the purpose of using them. They were inspected on their arrival at the purchaser's residence, and rejected because the bulk was not equal to sample. Brett, J., said : " Here there is a contract for the sale of goods, and by agreement they are to be delivered before a fair opportunity for inspection arises ; for it cannot properly be said that it would be reasonable to hold the defendant bound to examine them when they were delivered to him at halfway of the journey." See also *Campbell* on Sales, p. 388

These cases may suffice to shew that there is nothing in the agreement, or in the circumstances of this case, to take it out of the general rule that inspection must be had at the time and place of the delivery of the goods.

If Cincinnati could be treated as the place of delivery, it would seem from the evidence of Frankel, already referred to, as if the defendants had accepted the bill and waived the right to reject the goods, relying upon Wright's assurance that if they did not equal the sample, Towers would allow the difference. They have not counter-claimed for it in the action, and from the course taken at the trial the learned Judge thought he ought not to permit them to amend, and left them to their cross action. I think we cannot interfere with his decision.

Appeal dismissed.

DOYLE v. BELL.

Dominion Election Law—Penalties—B. N. A. Act—Property and civil rights.

The jurisdiction of the Provincial Legislatures over "property and civil rights" does not preclude the Parliament of Canada from giving to an informer the right to recover, by a civil action, a penalty imposed as a punishment for bribery at an election.

The Dominion Elections Act 1874, by sec. 109, provides that all penalties and forfeitures (other than fines in cases of misdemeanor) imposed by the Act shall be recoverable, with full costs of suit, by any person who will sue for the same, by action of debt or information, in any of Her Majesty's Courts in the Province in which the cause of action arose, having competent jurisdiction.

Held, that this enactment was valid.

THIS was an appeal from a judgment of the Court of Common Pleas refusing to disturb a verdict recovered by the plaintiff against the defendant in an action for penalties under the Dominion Elections Act, 1874, 37 Vict. ch. 9; reported 32 C. P. 632, where the facts giving rise to the action are clearly stated.

The appeal came on to be heard before this Court on the 11th of December, 1884.*

H. J. Scott, Q.C., for the appellant.
Osler, Q.C., for the respondent.

The authorities cited appear in the report in the Court below and in the present judgments.

December 18, 1884.   HAGARTY, C. J. O.—I think this appeal should be dismissed, and the judgment of the Common Pleas affirmed, for the reasons given by that Court.

In the argument before us a very wide proposition was advanced as governing this case, viz.: that the Dominion Parliament could not pass any Act by which an action of debt, or anything in the nature of a civil proceeding at the suit of an individual in our Courts for the recovery or enforcement of a penalty was created: that "civil rights"

*Present :—HAGARTY, C. J. O., PATTERSON, MORRISON, JJ. A., and ROSE, J.

were exclusively within the jurisdiction of the Local Legislatures, and that the creation or enforcement of a liability like the present trenched upon that exclusive jurisdiction.

If this be correct, the Dominion Parliament is powerless to create or enforce any civil liability to penalty as to damages in civil proceedings in Provincial Courts over the wide field of their legislation on the numerous subjects entrusted to their exclusive jurisdiction, such as, the regulation of Trade and Commerce, Navigation and Shipping, Banking, Customs and Excise, Weights and Measures, Bills of Exchange and Notes, Bankruptcy and Insolvency, Patents, Copyright, and many others.

They cannot enact that there can be any pecuniary penalty recoverable by one person against another for a violation of anything ordered or prohibited, or that an action will lie, or damages be recoverable, for infringement of a patent or copyright, or that lands can be expropriated for public works, or any other right or privilege which they have the exclusive right to grant or confer.

I am wholly unprepared to assent to any proposition so startling or so destructive to the due and necessary exercise of the legislative functions of the General Government. I cannot see how, in discussing legislative powers as to " civil rights," it can be in any way necessary to argue that the right to enforce a penalty at suit of an individual touches the admittedly exclusive right of our Legislature over " property and civil rights in the Province."

It can hardly be said that it is a civil right in the defendant to commit bribery, but it is argued that a civil right is involved in making him liable to pay money to another person in a civil action. I think this is a strained and unnatural construction.

It was urged by Mr. Scott in his very able argument, that granting the right of Parliament to make all necessary provisions to enforce purity of election, they could have fully effected such purpose by their undoubted right to enforce it by the Criminal Law ; that they might legally effect the same object by information at suit of the

Attorney General, and therefore there was no reason for their conferring the right to sue on an individual.

I think their right to do as they have done here cannot be measured by our view of the necessity of such a proceeding. Such a power existed at and before Confederation. I do not believe there is anything in the Confederation Act limiting their power on such a subject.

I am also of opinion that, granted the existence of the power to impose the penalty, it can be properly recoverable in our Courts.

Nor do I see any encroachment on the subject of civil procedure. An action of debt for a penalty seems still to be brought in our Courts under local statutes. We had one before us within the last two months, and such actions are so described in our local election law (a).

It is unnecessary to discuss the right of our Legislature to alter or prescribe a new form or course of procedure in our Courts for the recovery of penalties.

The general subject of the right of Parliament to deal with subjects specially allotted to them by the Federation Act, and to enforce their enactments by civil as well as criminal proceedings in the Provincial Courts, is very fully discussed in *Valin* v. *Langlois*, 3 S. C. R. 1; and also in the Privy Council, 5 App. Cas. 115.

I think the appeal must be dismissed.

PATTERSON, J. A.—The Dominion Elections Act, 1874, by section 92, declares that any person offending against the provisions in that section made against bribery shall be guilty of a misdemeanor, and shall also be liable to forfeit the sum of $200 to any person who shall sue for the same, with full costs of suit. Section 109 provides that all penalties and forfeitures (other than fines in cases of misdemeanor) imposed by the Act shall be recoverable with full costs of suit, by any person who will sue for the same by action of debt or information, in any of Her Majesty's Courts in the province in which the cause of

(a) *Garrett* v. *Roberts*, 10 A. R. 650.

action arose, having competent jurisdiction; and in default
of payment of the amount which the offender is condemned to pay, within the period fixed by the Court, the
offender shall be imprisoned in the common gaol of the
place for any term less than two years, unless such fine
and costs be sooner paid.   Then section 110 contains some
rules of pleading or procedure " in any action or suit given
by this Act."   Section 111 declares that " in any such civil
action, suit or proceeding as last aforesaid, the parties to
the same and the husbands or wives of such parties respectively shall be competent and compellable to give evidence
to the same extent, and subject to the same exceptions as
in other civil suits in the same Province ; but such evidence
shall not thereafter be used in any indictment or criminal
proceeding under this Act against the party or person
giving it"; and sections 114, 115 and 116 contain further
provisions on the subject of pleading and evidence in these
actions.

This action is brought to recover several sums of $200
each, for as many offences alleged to have been committed
by the defendant against the provisions of section 92.
The plaintiff recovered a verdict and judgment for two
penalties of $200 each, with full costs of suit.

This appeal is from the refusal of the Court of Common
Pleas to disturb the verdict or the judgment.

The only question which has been argued before us is
the very important one of the legislative jurisdiction of the
Parliament of Canada.

The contention on the part of the defendant is, that in
giving an action to an informer to recover the penalty in
a civil action, the Parliament has overstepped the jurisdiction conferred upon it by the B. N. A. Act.

One argument in support of this contention was based
upon the existence, in section 109 and the sections following it to which I have alluded, of provisions touching procedure and evidence in civil actions.   It was urged that
this was a clear violation of the division No. 14 of section
92 of the B. N. A. Act, which places amongst the classes of

subjects, in relation to which the Provincial Legislature is given exclusive power to make laws, procedure in civil matters in the Provincial Courts.

This position struck me as being a formidable one, and I still think so. The action to recover a penalty by an informer is clearly a civil action, and not a criminal proceeding. That was solemnly decided more than a century ago in *Acheson* v. *Everett*, Cowp. 891, which was an action of the character of the present action, to recover a penalty for bribery under 2 Geo. II. ch. 24, sec. 7; and this quality of the action is expressly recognized in the words which I have just read from section 111.

But when we look attentively at the proceedings before us, it is apparent that the objection founded on section 109 and the later sections does not properly arise for decision. The plaintiff's statement of complaint does not contain the allegations authorized by sec. 110, "that the defendant is indebted to him," &c.; the action does not purport to be an " action of debt or information;" and I gather from the judgment of the learned Judge who tried the action, which is reported in 32 C. P. at p. 633, that he did not act upon the evidence which section 115 assumes to make sufficient, but required and received other evidence of the writ and return. I notice also that he gave judgment only for the amount of the verdict and costs, without imposing any term of imprisonment under section 109.

There is nothing before us, either in the form of the action, or the conduct of it, or the judgment, which requires support from anything beyond what is found in section 92. That section declares the offender liable to forfeit the sum of $200 to any person who shall sue for the same, with full costs of suit; and the plaintiff states his cause of action in those terms, and asks for nothing more than that section entitles him to ask.

The technical aspect of the question, which we thus get rid of, may hereafter require consideration in some action for penalties which are not given to the informer except by force of section 109. Such *e. g.* as those imposed by sections 47, 72, 84, and 91, and perhaps others. At present we have to deal with the broader inquiry whether the jurisdiction of the Provincial Legislature over "property and civil rights in the Province," assigned to it by division No. 13 of section 92 of the B. N. A. Act, excludes the power of the Parliament of Canada to give the right to an informer to recover, by a civil action, a penalty imposed as a punishment for bribery at an election.

I do not think this subject has been so directly touched by any of the decisions upon the B. N. A. Act as to relieve us from the duty of considering it on principle.

Any argument founded upon the inevitable interference with property and civil rights by the Parliament, in the exercise of its exclusive legislative authority over the large class of subjects enumerated in section 91, seems to me entirely beside the present discussion; and, without venturing an opinion as to how far civil rights created by Dominion legislation ought to be left for their enforcement to the remedies and procedure provided by the Provincial Courts under Provincial laws, or how far such remedies and procedure may be prescribed by Parliament, I think the fullest power in connection with such matters might be conceded to the Parliament, without necessarily involving the right to give a civil action to a private individual as a mode of punishing an offence.

The two subjects have, to my apprehension, no analogy.

We are indebted to Mr. Scott for the citation of all the cases in which questions under the B. N. A. Act, at all resembling those now raised, have been discussed.

One important decision which is relied on for the plaintiff is *Valin* v. *Langlois*, 3 S. C. R. 1; 5 App. Cas. 115. We have a series of able and exhaustive judgments delivered by the Judges of the Supreme Court, to which it would be instructive to refer; but I prefer to confine my attention to that of the Judicial Committee, delivered by Lord Selborne, not because it adds materially to the others, but because the matter is presented in one judgment only. The subject of the decision was the power of the Parliament of Canada to commit the trial of election petitions to Provincial Courts. That power was affirmed on distinct grounds which I need not stay to notice. The decision did not involve any question similar to that now raised. The question was, the jurisdiction to deal in the mode adopted with the general subject of the trial of controverted elections. Part of the reasoning of the Lord Chancellor was founded on the 41st section of the B. N. A. Act, which declared that until the Parliament of Canada should otherwise provide, all laws in force in ' the several Provinces at the union, relative to certain specified matters, should respectively apply to elections of members to serve in the House of Commons for the same several Provinces. If this reasoning bears at all on the present controversy, it is capable of being appealed to by the defendant, because the matters specified do not include the punishment of corrupt practices; and Mr. Scott did so use section 41 in his argument before us. On the whole, I do not regard the case of *Valin* v. *Langlois*, as very directly aiding us at present.

I think the same observation may be made with respect to the other decisions upon the Act, without stopping to particularize them, with the exception of *Hodge* v. *The Queen*, 9 App. Cas. 117. The principles laid down in that case respecting the construction of the power given the Provincial Legislatures, by No. 15 of section 92, to impose punishment by fine, penalty, or imprisonment, for enforcing any law of the Province made in relation to any matter coming within any of the classes of subjects enumerated in that section, are, in my opinion applicable in the present case.

"Under these very general terms," it was said by Sir Barnes Peacock, "it seems to their Lordships that there is imported an authority to add to the confinement or restraint in prison that which is generally incident to it 'hard labour;' in other words, that 'imprisonment' there means restraint by confinement in a prison with or without its usual accompaniment, 'hard labour.'"

The prevention of corrupt practices at elections is a neces.
sary incident of the power to regulate the mode of election
of Members of Parliament.   The legislative jurisdiction of
the Dominion Parliament with respect to election of
members of that body is beyond dispute.   One exercise of
that jurisdiction was the subject of the contest in *Valin* v.
Langlois.   The forfeiture of money to be sued for and
recovered by an informer with full costs of suit, as a
punishment for bribery at elections, has, ever since the
passing of 2 Geo. II. ch. 24, more than 150 years ago, been
part of the system of legislation on this subject in England.
It was so in this Province before Confederation, and as
far as we are informed, was so in the other Confederated
Provinces.

We have in these considerations abundant reason for
regarding the provision as a recognized, if not an absolutely necessary incident of the authority to deal with the
subject of elections, and one which can reasonably be
assumed to have been in the contemplation of the Imperial
Legislature as accompanying the right given, whether by
express terms or by necessary implication, to the several
Provinces and to the Dominion respectively, to regulate
the election of members of their respective Legislatures.

Mr. Scott urged with force and with truth, that penalties
of this class, inasmuch as they differ from ordinary punish-
ments for crimes by being placed beyond the control of
the Crown and removed out of the reach of the leniency
which, in proper cases, is extended to persons who may
have broken some law, are of a different class from
those of the criminal law, which is specially assigned to
the Dominion Legislature.   This consideration would have
weight if it were necessary, in order to support the jurisdiction, to treat the punishment in question as an ordinary
punishment for crime.   But when the power to award the
punishment is found, not in the jurisdiction over crimes as
such, but in the authority to legislate concerning the conduct of elections, the argument loses its force. The question
becomes one of policy rather than of legislative juridiction.

But after all it may be questionable whether the creation of this right of action is properly to be regarded as an interference with property or civil rights in the Province.

I do not propose to enter upon a discussion of the meaning or extent of those words as used in section 92　For our present purpose it is unnecessary to do so.

We have now the assistance of several decisions of the Privy Council, in which the duty is enforced of reading the B. N. A. Act, and particularly these sections 91 and 92, as embodying a scheme of general legislation, and not to be construed in a narrow sense or without reading one part of the Act or the section with another. Amongst these decisions are : *L'Union St. Jacques de Montreal* v. *Bélisle*, L. R. 6 P. C. 31 ; *Dow* v. *Black*, L. R. 6 P. C. 272 ; *Citizens Ins. Co.* v. *Parsons*, 7 App. Cas. 96 ; *Russell* v. *The Queen*, 7 App. Cas. 829 : *Valin* v. *Langlois*, 5 App. Cas. 115 ; *Hodge* v. *The Queen*, 9 App. Cas. 117.

The principle of these decisions requires us to be cautious before treating as an enroachment upon the legislative jurisdiction over property and civil rights, every enactment by which a right or a liability cognizable in a Civil Court is created.

I agree that it is proper to dismiss the appeal, with costs.

Morrison, J. A., concurred.

Rose, J. — It clearly appears from the decisions in *Valin* v. *Langlois*, 3 S. C. R. pp. 1-89, and *Peek* v. *Shields*, 6 S. C. R. 639, and cases therein referred to, that as to subjects within the exclusive jurisdiction of the Dominion Parliament, that Parliament has the power to make such enactments as are necessary whether the same interfere with civil rights or not, and also the power to provide all necessary procedure to be adopted to enforce such rights.

It further appears that Local Legislatures have the right to prescribe procedure in civil matters only in respect of such matters as by the B. N. A. Act were placed under the exclusive control of the Local Legislatures. Mr. Scott therefore was driven to argue that the clause providing for recovery of a penalty as sued for in this action, was not the exercise of a *necessary* power, and hence *ultra vires* the Dominion Parliament.

I do not understand by the use of the word necessary, as found in various decisions and text books, that it is meant to lay down the doctrine that to bring within the powers of the Dominion Legislature any provision of an enactment respecting a subject within the exclusive jurisdiction of such Legislature, and which provision might affect civil rights, it must necessarily appear that without such provision it would be *impossible* to carry into effect the intentions of the Legislature, or that probably no other provision would be adequate. On the contrary, it seems to me that if such provision might, under certain circumstances, be beneficial and assist to more fully enforce such legislation, then it must, at all events, on an appeal to the Courts be held to be necessary, that is, necessary in certain events. Surely the Legislature must be allowed some, and in my opinion, a very wide discretion as to the mode of enforcing its own enactments. It cannot be that the Courts are to sit in judgment on the exercise of such discretion and dictate to the Legislature whether they shall adopt this or that mode, because in the opinion of the Courts one mode is the more convenient or better, or at least as well adapted to effect the purpose of the Legislature.

It was not contended before us that the provision in question might not be beneficial, it was contended, however, that criminal proceedings might accomplish the same purpose.

When it appeared that a similar provision is to be found in the legislation on this subject prior to Confederation, also in the legislation on the same subject in other Provinces and in Great Britain, it seemed to me the argument as to want of necessity failed. The evidence to the contrary is too clear and strong to enable the Court to interfere. I certainly cannot take upon myself to declare unnecessary what so many Legislatures have declared necessary.

I agree that the appeal must be dismissed.

Appeal dismissed, with costs.

PETRIE v. GUELPH LUMBER COMPANY ET AL.

STEWART v. THE GUELPH LUMBER COMPANY ET AL.

INGLIS v. THE GUELPH LUMBER COMPANY ET AL.

Action for deceit—Company—Prospectus—Directors—Misrepresentation.

The defendants other than the company being directors of the defendant company, made certain representations concerning the affairs of the company, which they believed to be true, but which were not in fact correct, and procured the plaintiff and others to take stock in the company.

Held, affirming the judgment of the Court below, 2 O. R. 218, in an action to recover back the amount of the subscriptions paid by the plaintiffs, and to remove their names from the list of stockholders, that the defendants were not liable.

PATTERSON, J.A., *dubitante.*

THIS was an appeal from a judgment of the Chancery Division, dismissing the action of the plaintiffs, reported 2 O. R. 218, where and in the present judgments the facts giving rise to the action, and the authorities cited, are fully set forth.

The appeal came on to be heard before this Court on the 24th and 27th days of October, 1884.*

McCarthy, Q.C., and *Plumb,* for the appellants.
Robinson, Q.C., and *Cassels,* Q.C., for the respondents.

January 26th, 1885. BURTON, J. A.—The main facts are stated in the judgment of Mr. Justice Ferguson from which this appeal is brought.

It is an action which used to be called an action on the case for deceit, but although it has become more usual than formerly to bring this action in the Chancery Division of the Court, I apprehend that it must be decided on the same principles as the old Common Law action of deceit, and that there is no such thing even since the Judicature Act, as one learned Judge has expressed it, as an equitable action of deceit.

*Present—*HAGARTY, C.J.O., BURTON, PATTERSON, and OSLER, JJ.A

There is a good deal of confusion in the text books and even in expressions attributed to learned Judges as to what is a sufficient misrepresentation to constitute an actionable wrong, arising to some extent from the difference which formerly existed between the rules of Courts of Equity and Courts of Common Law, a difference which since the Judicature Acts no longer exists, and to a still greater extent from a failure sometimes to examine and ascertain precisely the nature of the case in which the expressions were used.

It was never necessary in a Court of Equity in order to set aside a contract obtained by material false representations, to prove that the party who obtained it knew at the time when the representation was made that it was false.

It was held that a man should not be allowed to retain a benefit from a statement which he now admits to be untrue, even although at the time he made that statement innocently, believing it to be true.

Whatever distinctions however formerly existed between Courts of Law and Courts of Equity, are now removed, and as pointed out in *Redgrave* v. *Hurd*, 20 Ch. D. 1, the rules formerly existing in Equity are to prevail, and the Master of the Rolls, who was one of the Judges who delivered the judgment in that case, refers to the judgment of Lord Cairns in *Reese River Mining Co.* v. *Smith*, L. R. 4 H. L. 64, as setting forth clearly the doctrine of equity. That noble Lord had used this expression in that case, (p. 79): "If persons take upon themselves to make assertions as to which they are ignorant whether they are true or untrue, they must in a civil point of view, be held as responsible as if they had asserted that which they knew to be untrue."

These words taken alone would seem to countenance the view which has been urged in this case that they would apply to an action of this nature, but the question there was as to the right of the respondent to repudiate his shares, a right to rescind.

That it was the view of the Master of the Rolls, and the learned Judges who sat with him, that the language would not extend to an action, in the nature of an action for deceit, is manifest. not only from their language in *Redgrave* v. *Hurd*, but from the express decision upon the point by himself in the case which immediately follows in the same volume of the reports, *Smith* v. *Chadwick*, 20 Ch. D. 27, and the expressions in *Arkwright* v. *Newbold*, 17 Ch. D., 301, but also from the expressions used by Lord Cairns himself, who was one of the Judges who delivered judgment in *Peek* v. *Gurney*, L. R. 6 H. L. 377, where the Lord Chancellor distinguishes such an action from such cases as *Burrowes* v. *Lock*, 10 Ves 470, and *Slim* v. *Croucher*, 1 D. F. & J. 518, and says, (p. 390): "It is a suit instituted to recover damages from the respondents for the injury the appellant has sustained by having been deceived and misled, by their misrepresentations, and suppression of facts, to become a shareholder in the proposed company, of which they were the promoters. It is precisely analogous to the common law action for deceit. There can be no doubt that equity exercises a concurrent jurisdiction in cases of this description, and the same principles applicable to them must prevail both at law and in equity." And Lord Cairns in the same case (p. 403): "Mere non-disclosure of material facts, however morally censurable, however that non-disclosure might be a ground in a proper proceeding at a proper time for setting aside an allotment or a purchase of shares, would in my opinion form no ground for an action in the nature of an action for misrepresentation. There must, in my opinion, be some active misstatement of fact, or, at all events, such a partial and fragmentary statement of fact, as that the withholding of that which is not stated makes that which is stated absolutely false."

We have it then that before the Judicature Act Courts of Equity had concurrent jurisdiction, but that the same principles would prevail in the trial of such an action wherever brought, and we find the same learned Judges who admitted that the rules of equity as regards the rescission of contracts were hereafter to prevail in all Courts, declaring that an action of deceit is a common law action, and must be decided on the same principles whether it be brought in the Chancery Division or any of the Common Law Divisions, and I cannot do better than quote the words of Sir George Jessel as to what he thought it necessary to establish in a case of this kind in *Smith* v. *Chadwick*, 20 Ch. D. at p. 44, viz., that the party had been induced to act "by means of representations which were material, which were false in fact, false to the knowledge of the defendants, or as to which at all events they made statements although they knew nothing about the facts that is, statements made so recklessly as that in a Court of Law they would be in the same position as if the statements were false to their knowledge." But in such an action (p. 45), "even though the statement may be untrue, yet if it was made in good faith, and the defendant had reasonable ground for believing it to be true, the defendant will succeed."

I have already pointed out that Lord Cairns could not have intended his remarks in *Reese River Mining Co.* v. *Smith*,, to apply to an action of this kind, and I desire to shew that the language of Lord Justice Knight Bruce in *Rawlings* v. *Wickham*, 3 Deg. & J., at p. 313, which is sometimes quoted to shew that knowledge is not material, must be qualified by confining it to the subject with which that learned Judge was dealing. He says in one passage: "He joined in a representation which was not true, and for every purpose of pecuniary liability the case is the same, as if he had known that it was not true." But below he says. "He became, however, for every purpose of this suit, answerable for a misrepresentation of such a nature as to vitiate the contract." The suit being in effect one to rescind the contract.

After considerable fluctuation of opinion in the Common Law Courts in England, they settled down finally to the conclusion in 1860, that it was established by the case of *Collins* v. *Evans*, 5 Q. B. 820, and other authorities, that to support an action for false representation, the representation must not only have been false, in fact, but must also have been fraudulently made; *Childers* v. *Wooler*, 2 El. & El. 287.

The cases seem to go fully to this length, that there is no actionable wrong in a representation which, though untrue in fact, is believed to be true by the person making it, even if the belief is not held upon reasonable grounds, but the presence or absence of reasonable grounds is relevant and important, for determining whether the belief was really entertained.

In 1867, the case of *Addie* v. *Western Bank of Scotland*, L. R. 1 Sc. App. 145, came before the House of Lords. The Lord President, in his charge to the jury, had told them that if the case should occur of directors putting forth in their report statements of importance in regard to the affairs of the bank, false in themselves, and which they did not believe, or had no reasonable ground to believe to be true, that would be a misrepresentation and deceit.

Exception was taken to this direction and overruled, and in support of the exception the case was put of an honest belief being entertained by the directors of the reasonableness of which it was said the jury upon this direction would have to judge, but the direction was upheld, Lord Chelmsford remarking, (p. 162) : "Supposing a person makes an untrue statement, which he asserts to be the result of a *bonâ fide* belief of its truth, how can the *bona fides* be tested except by considering the ground of such belief?" He does, indeed, go further, and says: "If an untrue statement is made founded upon a belief which is destitute of all reasonable grounds, or which the least enquiry would immediately correct, I do not see that it is not fairly and correctly hcaracterized as misrepresentation and deceit."

But LordCranworth thought the charge went too far, and said (p. 1868):

"I confess that my opinion was, that in what his Lordship thus stated he went beyond what principle warrants. If persons in the situation of directors of a bank make statements as to the the condition of its affairs which they *bonâ fide* believe to be true, I cannot think they can be guilty of fraud, because other persons think, or the Court thinks, or your Lordships think, that there was no suffi-

-cient ground to warrant the opinion which they had formed. If a little more care or caution must have led the directors to a conclusion different from that which they put forth, this may afford strong evidence to show that they -did not really believe the truth of what they stated, and so that they were guilty of fraud. But this would be the consequence, not of their having stated as true what they had not reasonable ground to believe to be true, but of their having stated as true what they did not believe to be true."

I shall accept as sound law the statements made in the Court of Appeal by the Master of the Rolls: *Smith* v. *Chadwick*, 20 Ch. D. at p. 45 (*et seq*).

1. That in an action of deceit, even though the statement be untrue, yet if it was made in good faith, and the defendant had reasonable ground for believing it to be true, the defendant will succeed.

2. Or it may be, that although the means of knowledge were in the hands of the defendant, yet the matter was minute and required a careful examination, and there may have been reasonable grounds for the defendant to believe that this statement was true, although he had those means of knowledge in his possession. The defendant, in such a case, would also be entitled to succeed.

And, assuming, though not accepting as law (except as evidence tending to show that the defendant did not in truth believe), that a statement made recklessly is equivalent to a statement made knowingly, how does this case stand upon the evidence ?

It was contended, and no one, I think, reading the evidence in this case can come to any other conclusion than that arrived at by the learned Judge who heard the case, that the partners in this unfortunate concern had no intention to deceive or defraud, but, on the contrary, that they were acting honestly, and intended fairly to represent things as they were, and that if the judgment of the learned Judge is to be reversed, and an adverse decision given against them, it must not be on the ground of dishonesty, but on the ground of reckless carelessness of whether the statements were true or not, which is sometimes treated in Courts of Law as equivalent to fraud in its consequences; and in that connection I must refer to the remark of that able Judge and keen observer of what was going on around him, the late Sir George Jessel, in a somewhat similar case: *Smith* v. *Chadwick*, 20 Ch. D. at p. 46, that " that circamstance has a material bearing in construing the documents, because, if you once arrive at the conviction that the persons who made the representation intended to act honestly, I think, if you have any doubt or hesitation as to the meaning of the terms, the rule prevails that you presume things were done rightly."

The first ground of misrepresentation relied on is in reference to the proposed purchase of new limits, and as to which the plaintiff states his objection thus in his reasons of appeal:

1. " Because the defendants, other than the Guelph Lumber Company (limited), hereinafter called the company, who were the promoters, and the then intending and afterwards actual directors of the said company, represented and promised in and by the prospectus in the bill of complaint and statements of claim set forth, on the statements contained in which the plaintiffs were entitled to rely, and did in fact rely, when they subscribed shares of the preference stock of the said company; that the said company was desirous of purchasing additional timber limits, and that the issuing of the preference stock was with that object; and that the whole of the proceeds of the same would be used for the purposes of the new company; whereas the evidence shows that neither the old company nor the new could have entertained the idea of being able to purchase additional timber limits, nor, in fact, was the money subscribed for preference stock or any of it so used, but was applied, as the defendants admittedly knew it must be applied, in liquidating the debts of the old company, then practically insolvent; and that such untrue representations and promises by the defendants in their position as promoters and directors of the said new company as aforesaid, made with the knowledge which they each and all had, or were bound to acquire, renders them liable to the plaintiffs for the relief they seek."

Admitting that the language of the prospectus is to be taken most strongly against the promoters, it is quite capable of the interpretation placed upon it by them. It was true, in fact, as the lands were purchased provisionally upon the faith that money would be obtained in this way, and the plaintiff admitted on his examination that he did not complain on that ground, and so far as the Petrie action was concerned, the first ground was abandoned on the argument.

On his examination he is asked :

Q. The prospectus states that there were 222½ square miles of limits, and you have made no cause of complaint in your bill as to the quantity ? A. No.

Q. And you don't new complain on that head ? A. I don't know that there is anything to complain of.

Q. Your objection is to the quantity of timber alleged to exist on these limits ? A. Yes.

Q. You don't know of your own knowledge ? A. No.

Q. Your complaint isn't of the quantity of acres but the quantity of timber contained on those acres ? A. Yes.

And again :

Q. Now, to go back to this question of timber limits, and what was represented, etc., do you think now that the number of acres and the quantity of timber on it was wrongly stated ? A. I don't know but what the acres may be nearly right.

Q. Do you pretend to say now that the quantity of timber is wrongly stated in that prospectus ? A. Yes, I think so.

Q. How was it wrongly stated ? A. Over-estimated; I couldn't tell you how much.

But as that ground is raised in the other suits also I may as well refer to it.

I think that the fair reading of the prospectus is, that the limits to be acquired were limits already contracted for, and formed part of the 222½ square miles referred to in the prospectus.

The language used in that part of the prospectus, is:

The timber limits of the company *inclusive of the recent purchase* consists of 222½ square miles, and are estimated to yield 200 million feet of lumber.

So that the complaint would seem to be rather that the quantity of timber was over-stated in the prospectus.

And in connection with this I refer to the 4th reason of appeal which reads thus :

"Because the defendants, other than the company, took as their basis of valuation for the purpose of making, in the year 1877, the statement of their then assets in gross, in the next preceding paragraph referred to, a valuation made in the year 1875 by one Wadsworth, which shows them to have owned 12,100 acres of pine timber, purchased from settlers, estimated at 2,500 feet of timber per acre, or, in the aggregate, 30,250,000 feet of timber, valued to produce $45,375 clear profit; whereas the prospectus in question admits that in 1877 there only remained 4,500 acres of pine timber, and that although, therefore, a reduction should been made in the statement of gross assets of 7,600 acres, or 19,000,000 feet of timber, or $28,500 clear profit thereon, yet no such reduction was made, nor was a reduction made as should have been made for 14,000,000 feet of timber, or $21,000, Wadsworth's estimated profit thereon admittedly cut off the limit between 1875 and 1877."

This is of course rather startling, if borne out by the evidence.

Wadsworth does not refer to the extent of the limits, but estimates the quantity of timber on the limits which the company then owned

At............................. 43,560,000 feet.
And on 12,100 acres of settlers' land at 30,250,000 feet.
                                         ──────────
In all. .... 73,810,000 feet.

The prospectus deals with the new limits as well as the old, but refers to 4,500 acres only of pine timber purchased from settlers.

There is evidence to shew that between 1875 and the date of prospectus the defendants had been cutting timber to a considerable extent—in the memorandum handed in by the plaintiff's solicitors this is stated to be 20,000,000 feet, but according to Mr. Guthrie's evidence, not so much; he places it at 14,000,000, of which 3,000,000 were cut on settlers' lands. I do not think that it is of any great consequence on which they were cut, except as regards the amount of Government dues, as to which there was for some time a difference, although subsequently the dues were reduced to a uniform rate of 75 cents per thousand feet, whether upon settlers' lands or on ungranted lands.

I do not think that in an action of this kind we should assume, in the absence of evidence, that there only remained 4500 acres of timber on settlers, lands if there is any other reasonable solution.

The only direct evidence there is upon the subject is that of Macdonald, a gentleman of considerable experience apparently as a wood-ranger, and who was employed by these gentlemen shortly before the issue of the prospectus to inspect the company's property and prepare a plan of it.

He did prepare a plan, including the new purchase, which shewed that within the limits there were 122½ square miles which he estimated would yield 22,000,000 feet of lumber, and he then noted, exclusive of 4,500 acres of settlers' lands outside the limits—this would seem to indicate that a portion of the settlers' lands were within the limits —that, at least, would appear to be a fair inference in the absence of any evidence to the contrary.

The second objection is, that the defendants made a representation that "they would even at the then low prices, be able to pay a handsome dividend on the ordinary as well as on the preference stock, and that their timber was so situated that it could be got out and floated to the mill at a small expense, and that the estimated yield was 200,000,000 feet of lumber, yet the evidence shews that the defendants could have reasonably had no expectation of paying a handsome or any dividend upon the ordinary or preference stock, and that their timber was not so situated that it could be got out and floated to the mill at a small expense, and that the yield of lumber could not reasonably be estimated at nearly 200,000,000 feet."

The whole of this, with the exception that their timber was so situated that it could be got out and floated to the mill at a small expense, consists of mere matter of opinion and not of matter of fact, and cannot be treated as a fraudulent representation—if for no other reason that these are matters in respect of which different men will be of different minds, and there is no evidence to disprove the mere statement of fact as to the situation of the timber.

The principal grounds relied on, and those most pressed
upon us during the argument, consist of the representations
referred to in the 3rd and 4th reasons of appeal, and which
are thus stated : "That the interest of the defendants,
other than the company, in the assets of the old company
were worth $140,000 over liabilities, and had been trans-
ferred to the new company at $105,000, all taken in paid
up stock."

The statement in the prospectus is :—

The interest of the proprietors of the old company in the
assets, estimated at about $140,000 over liabilities, has
been transferred to the new company at $105,000 all taken
in paid up stock—to my mind a very vague and meaning-
less statement not calculated to mislead anyone. It may
mean anything or nothing. If, for example, the fact had
been that the estimated assets amounted to . . $1,140.000
Whilst the liabilities amounted to   1,000,000
                                                 _____
Leaving an apparent surplus of . . . .$ 140,000,
no one in his senses would regard that, in the circumstances as disclosing an available surplus at all, inasmuch
as a very trifling fall in the value of the timber would
sweep away the surplus and leave a large deficiency.

Whereas if the assets had been $142 000
The liabilities. 2 000
                                                        _____
Leaving the same estimated surplus of $140 000
any one could see at a glance that there was something
substantial to rely on.

In truth there was an error in the accounts from which
the estimate of the surplus was made up ; the parties had
before them an estimate of the assets, partly made up from
a report of Mr. Wadsworth, two years previously, to a loan
company to whom the Guelph Lumber Company had made
an application for a loan, giving a very full and detailed
account of the mill and the other premises connected with
it, but in which he admits that his examination of the
limits was not of a searching character, stating, however,

at the same time, his opinion that the situation of the mill must render the working of it profitable to the proprietors when the present depression in the lumber trade was overcome. The other property was valued by Mr. Maclean the manager at the mill, making a total of $333,374.00.

The liabilities, made up chiefly by Mr. Guthrie, were put down at $196,000.00, which left an apparent surplus of $137,374.00.

Mr. Guthrie states that he then put down everything that he thought was owing, but he subsequently discovered that he was mistaken to, at least, the amount of $15,400, and possibly more. It was, however, clearly established that to the extent of $15,400 the liabilities had been under-estimated.

At the same time it is in evidence that Maclean thought Wadsworth's valuation too low—the mill very much below the mark, and that the quantity of lumber was under-estimated as well as the expenditure for improvements; and when it is borne in mind that this valuation was made for a company for which Wadsworth acted as valuator, it is reasonable to assume that, in the discharge of his duty he did not over-value.

Mr. Guthrie, in his evidence, states that the valuation of the assets was, under the circumstances, necessarily only an estimate, and that they considered that, if they made a reduction of about 25 per cent., they would be quite sure that they were not over-estimating them in the representation to the public; but persons issuing such a statement are answerable, not only for what they had in their own minds, but for what any one might reasonably suppose to be the meaning of the words they have used.

The question here is, however, not whether the plaintiffs could successfully on the discovery of the actual facts on which the estimate was based have come to the Court for a rescission of the contract. It is quite possible that they would have been entitled to that relief. I quite concede that upon such an application it might be no answer to say that the plaintiffs were wanting in ordinary caution and prudence in not making further inquiries.

The plaintiffs furnished us with a statement of assets and liabilities, as they compute them, which is not, I think, strictly accurate.

They take Wadsworth's estimate of the quantity of the lumber.

At	73,000,000	feet.
And they then deduct, as admitted they say, to have been cut since	20,000,000	"
	53,000,000	
And they add to it the the subsequent purchase of	6,000,000	"
	59,000,000	"
They deduct, however, a further quantity of	19,000,000	"
for the supposed deficiency on 7600 acres of settlers' lands to which I have already referred; leaving only	40,000,000	"
as the quantity of lumber left on the lands included in Wadsworth's valuation, which they say was worth only 70 cents per m, or,	$30,000.00	

Now, I find no evidence whatever of there being a cut of 20,000,000 in the interval. Mr. Guthrie, in his evidence, places the total cut at 14,000,000, of which only 11,000,000 came off the limits valued by Wadsworth, and there is no allowance made for the reduction of the encumbrances referred to by Mr. Wadsworth of $1.50 dues, subsequently reduced to 75 cents.

Mr. Guthrie points out that in making their estimate, they first deducted

Lumber and logs at the mill........ $ 6,750.00

He then estimates that in the two years 11,000,000 were cut on lands within Wadsworth's limits, and 3,000,000 on settlers' lands, which, at the estimated value of $1.50, would amount to 21,000.00

Making a total of........ 27,750.00

But the lumber when valued by Wadsworth was subject to Government dues of $1.50 a thousand, subsequently reduced to 75 cents. This, therefore, on the timber remaining on the land had to be first taken off, and amounted to .. 23,000.00

Leaving .... $ 4,750.00

The sum deducted.

I cannot say that the plaintiff has succeeded in convincing me that there was anything wrong in the estimate made by the defendants based on the Wadsworth report.

Without entering into the minute calculations presented to us on the argument, the value of the timber was to a great extent a mere question of opinion, and as the evidence has failed to satisfy the Judge of first instance that there was any fraud on the part of the defendants, I do not think that we could safely or reasonably, on the material before us, come to different conclusion on this the most material branch of the case.

It is to be regretted that greater care had not been taken, but unless we can be satisfied that the defendants did not really believe what they stated, and so that they were guilty of fraud, the plaintiff's case in my opinion fails.

A great deal of evidence was given of the subsequent condition of the company's affairs, from which the Court is asked to infer that it was in an insolvent condition, and these defendants must have known it. We ought not to lose sight of what the issue was, and what the plaintiffs had to make out before they were entitled to recover. That issue being that the statements in the prospectus were false to the defendants' knowledge, as before explained, and that they were made with the view to the plaintiffs acting upon them, and they did so act upon them ; but it must, I think, be clear that this kind of evidence is wholly unreliable for that purpose, when one takes into account the fluctuations in the value of everything which goes to make up the expenditure in such a business as this, as well as the returns, and the manner in which the books were kept at the mills, which cannot be better described than in Mr. Davidson's letter referring to them, viz: " It is almost impossible to arrive at any intelligent conclusion as to the assets and liabilities of the company at any given time further back than 1879."

If I were to hazard an opinion as to the cause of the want of success of the company, I should attribute it to a very great extent to the inexperience of the manager and his subordinates, in a time doubtless of great depression, but I think it would be contrary to sound principles to decide this case upon any other evidence than what is shewn to have been the actual state of things existing at the time the prospectus was issued.

The objection raised in the 5th reason of appeal does not appear to me tenable. Assuming that it had been shewn that the promoters had undertaken to take back these plaintiffs' preference stock on the terms suggested, that might or might not furnish a good ground of action for breach of that agreement, but furnishes no ground for charging the defendants with deceit.

Nor do I think that any effect can be given to the objection that certain facts came to the knowledge of the defendants, after the issuing of the prospectus, and before the alleged allotment, I do not think there was any allotment or that any allotment was necessary, the subscription was absolute when it was made, besides I think it clear that these subsequent facts, which might if known at the time, have falsified the prospectus, cannot be relied on in an action for deceit, which is based on the assumption that the statements were then known to be untrue.

And for a similar reason the subsequent dealings with the property cannot affect the question really involved in this action, which is, put in any way it may be, whether the defendants have been guilty of fraud. There may be an appropriate remedy, if they have abused their trust, but that is a very different matter from holding them guilty of fraud.

But there is another and a distinct ground upon which I think the learned Judge would have been justified in finding as he did, that assuming the statement as to the value of the assets to be untrue, the plaintiff must shew that he was deceived by it, and acted upon it to his prejudice.

These parties resided in the same town, and were well acquainted with each other. The plaintiffs, who were men of business, knew that the defendants were recommending the investment with a view to getting some benefit or advantage to themselves, and I do not think that we should be too ready, when a business turns out disastrously, to listen to statements that parties were induced to enter into an important contract by misrepresentations, unless made out by very clear and distinct evidence.

My reason for this doubt is that on Mr. Petrie's first examination he stated that he was told that the prospectus was issued by Guthrie, Hogg, and Ferguson, but at first says that he cannot say that he looked at it, afterwards he qualifies this by saying that " he read it as carefully as a person would in a hurry of business," and does not state that he relied upon that in taking the shares, whereas he does admit that knowing the parties did influence him to some extent.

I find no express statement that the representation of the value of the assets over the liabilities formed any inducement, or that he took any steps to inform himself as to the extent of the liabilities, and I am satisfied that the plaintiff made his investment on the confidence he placed in the defendants, not in their prospectus, and on the general belief that the business was a good thing and likely to be successful, but I go upon the more general ground that it has not been established that the defendants made a fraudulent statement, even assuming that recklessness in making a statement could be sufficient to support an action of the kind the basis of which is fraud and deceit.

If I am correct in assuming that the plaintiffs were not induced by the statements in the prospectus to take the stock, that disposes of the action against the company also, but I am not disposed to quarrel with the learned Judge's finding that the subsequent action of the plaintiffs precludes their application to rescind.

I am of opinion, therefore, that the judgment of the learned Judge was correct, and should be affirmed, with costs.

HAGARTY, C. J. O.—The leading questions of fact on which our decision must turn, have been stated so clearly by my brother Burton as to not make it necessary for me to repeat them.

The action is an action for deceit resulting in the plaintiff's damage.

The law governing it is, I think, sufficiently clearly established, and it can hardly be stated more favourably for the plaintiff.

Citing Buller, J., Lord Blackburn says in *Smith* v. *Chadwick*, 9 App. Cas. at p. 195: "The foundation of this action is fraud and deceit in the defendant and damage to the plaintiffs."

In *Eaylesfield* v. *Londonderry*, 4 Ch. D. 693, James, L. J., says (p. 711): "The representation must be wilful and fraudulent. Whether the fraud is supposed to be a fraud on the Court as distinguished from a moral fraud or not, there must be a wilful and fraudulent statement of that which is false to maintain an action of deceit."

Lord Cairns: " I apprehend it to be the rule of law, that if persons take upon themselves to make assertions as to which they are ignorant whether they are true or untrue, they must, in a civil point of view, be held as responsible as if they had asserted that which they knew to be untrue:" *Reese River Mining Co.* v *Smith*, L. R. 4 H. L. at p. 79.

In *Arkwright* v. *Newbold*, 17 Ch. D. 301, Cotton, L. J., says (p. 320) : " It is a common law action in which it is necessary to prove that a statement had been made which, to the knowledge of the person making it, was false, or which was made by him with such recklessness as to make him liable just as if he knew it to be false."

James, L. J., (p. 329) : " We cannot accede to the suggestion * * that the persons issuing a prospectus are liable to an action of deceit, because they do not mention a fact coming to their knowledge before the allotment of shares which falsifies a statement in the prospectus."

We must always bear in mind the marked distinction, between a suit to rescind a contract for misrepresentation, as in *Reese River Mining Company* v. *Smith*, and the action for deceit.

At the close of the very elaborate and excellent argument on this appeal, I entertained a strong impression that the case made against the defendants, did not go far enough to make them liable, and that the decree below was substantially right.

A perusal of the voluminous evidence, and papers in the case has confirmed that impression.

My conclusion, is that the defendants believed honestly in the substantial truth of the main facts stated in the prospectus.

Then it is urged that they made the statements recklessly, and are therefore liable as if they knew them to be false.

Bad faith seems to me to be essential to success in this action.

An assertion of a fact, of the truth of which a man knows nothing, with a view to its being acted on by another, is, in my judgment, inconsistent with good faith in the assertor.

It is made recklessly with an unfair and improper disregard of truth or falsehood, and is therefore made *mald fide.*

I do not consider the defendants to be open to the charge of reckless assertion.

They may have been unduly and incautiously sanguine, but they were not without strong and plausible grounds, from their point of view, in believing what they asserted as to the value of their assets.

The assurances of their manager Maclean, the unimpeached report of Wadsworth some 18 months before, the opinion of Edgar, and of McDonald, the woodranger, cannot be overlooked.

Maclean may have been a bad manager, and deficient in keen judgment, but I am not prepared to hold him guilty of intentional misrepresentation.

In the case of directors of public companies, it seems impossible to hold that unless they knew the true facts of their own personal knowledge that they are necessarily to be held guilty of reckless assertion, or of bad faith.

In the great majority of such cases they must, from the nature of the case, depend on information derived from managers, agents, and others.

They are not to be absolved from gross carelessness and negligence in the performance of their duty. Every case must be judged on its own merits and circumstances.

Lord Bramwell says, in *Smith* v. *Chadwick,* 9 App. Cas. p. 203: " The defendants have sworn that they were told by Hannays, who were respectable people, people to be trusted, that the actual rate of production was such that it was over one million a year, and that they believed it, and in addition to that, one of them has given the convincing proof of his sincerity, that he staked £5,000 upon it, which he has lost. * * The question here is, not whether they should be in any way punished for most improvident and rash statements (more than one) in the prospectus, but whether we are satisfied that this particular statement was a fraudulent, as well as what it was to my mind, an untrue statement * * An untrue statement as to the truth or falsity of which the man who makes it has no belief, is fraudulent; for in making it, he affirms he believes it, which is false."

Lord Cairns says, in *Peek* v. *Gurney* L. R. 6 H. L. at p. 403: "I will not dwell upon the words that the terms made, 'in the opinion of the directors cannot fail to insure a highly remunerative return to the shareholders.' That was a reference, not to fact, but to opinion: and, strange as it may appear to us now, looked at by the light of subsequent events, I am not satisfied that this statement as to the opinion of the directors was not perfectly consistent with the opinion which they really held."

In this celebrated case there was the fatal feature of improper concealment, viz, as to the "arrangement deed," besides the proved hopelessly insolvent state of the business.

In the case before us there has been a minute, and, we may fear most costly investigation of the accounts, and we have as the result a mass of most contradictory evidence as to the real value of defendants' assets.

It is easy now to argue in the light of subsequent events that the business was actually insolvent when the prospectus was issued. The business was of a highly speculative character, its success or failure depending so much on the fluctuations of the lumber market.

If a season like 1880 had followed 1877 we may well assume that the affairs of this ultimately unfortunate company would have presented an appearance far different from that of 1878.

On the whole, I concur in holding that the appeal must be dismissed, with costs.

PATTERSON, J. A.—The learned Judge in the Court below spoke without exaggeration when he said that the volume of evidence adduced before him was so great as entirely to preclude the idea of his giving even a synopsis of it in his judgment; and the view which he took of the law as applicable to the charges against the defendants made it sufficient for the purpose of his judgment to allude in a very general way to the leading facts without stating his views of the details which have been discussed before us, as they were also discussed before him. In many, indeed in most of those details the facts have to be deduced from calculations and estimates not always free from intricacy, and we have in some instances figures given by witnesses on opposite sides, and given in different ways by different witnesses on the same side, as foundations for inferences as to values and prices and cost of production, those inferences being of facts which are of material importance. Under these circumstances, and not having the assistance of any findings of fact upon these matters of detail, by the learned Judge before whom the evidence was given, we have a task of unusual difficulty in the attempt to master the facts from which we are asked to draw the inferences upon which the contest has to turn. For my own part I feel by no means sure that I have accomplished the task very successfully.

The result of the opinions formed by the members of the Court is, that the judgment in favour of the defendants will not be disturbed. I am not displeased with that result, because I am quite satisfied from perusing the evidence that the defendants are not properly chargeable with intentional deception or actual fraud in procuring the subscriptions to the stock of the company; but I take no share of the credit of working out that result, because I have not been able to satisfy myself as fully as I could desire, that the case is one to which the doctrines which govern ordinary actions for deceit are in all respects applicable.

I think the case may not improperly be regarded as one in which representations, untrue in themselves, were made by the defendants to induce the plaintiff to do something by which the defendants were to be personally benefited; and I am not satisfied that in such a case any fraudulent design, or a knowledge that the statements were untrue, or even that recklessness of the truth or falsity which is equivalent to fraud, is required to be proved. The inclination of my opinion is the other way. On principle I do not see why such proof should be necessary, and I have not so read the authorities as to convince me that I am wrong.

It may be questionable whether this form of the question properly arises, because it has not been found as a fact that the plaintiff was induced to subscribe to the preference stock by any one of the representations which he now alleges to have been untrue; and, although there is evidence enough to support a finding, there are considerations on the other side.

In the statement of claim as originally filed the gravamen of the charge is a fraudulent scheme and conspiracy, of which the incorporation of the company was one of the overt acts, and the object of which was to make the plaintiff and others the prey of the defendants; and in the complaint as amended the broken promises of the prospectus are as much relied upon as the misstatement of facts.

The evidence entirely fails to reach the charge of conspiracy; and, when it is examined to ascertain what it does establish, it is not a matter of course to hold that the plaintiff's deposition made it more plain than his complaint that his decision to subscribe was influenced by reliance upon any one, or upon all, of the representations of facts, as distinguished from the sanguine anticipations set forth in the prospectus, or that in fact he paid very much attention to that document.

Were it necessary to decide this question of fact, I should probably find in favour of the plaintiff, as I assume, from a remark made by the learned Judge in the Court below, he would have done. But as the fate of the appeal does not depend upon my opinion, I prefer not to come to a final decision upon it.

It is made clear, and I believe is not denied, that the defendants who constituted the unincorporated partnership called The Guelph Lumber Company, were personally liable for a very large sum of money to one or more banks,

and that one immediate purpose to which the money paid
for the preference stock was to be applied was the payment of those debts. This relief from their personal
liability is what I refer to as the benefit they were to
derive from the subscriptions which were made on the
faith of their representations. It is not so announced in
the prospectus. On the contrary, there are two statements
which, though in separate parts of the prospectus, it seems
proper to read together, and which convey a different
assurance. These passages read thus : " The above company
being desirous of securing additional timber limits, and
opportunity for doing so advantageously being offered by
the low state of the lumber market, have decided to issue
a limited quantity of preference stock. * * The interest of
the proprietors of the old company in its assets, estimated
at about $140,000 over liabilities, has been transferred to
the new company at $105,000, all taken in paid up stock,
and the whole of the proceeds of the preferential stock
will be used for the purposes of the new company."

This statement that the proceeds of the new stock were
not to go to pay old debts, with the reason connected with
it that the old assets so much exceeded the liabilities,
strikes one as one of the most persuasive representations in
the whole prospectus, and nothing could well be more
distinct; yet we have, in relation to it, a cause for hesitation before finding as a fact that the plaintiff was deceived
by the prospectus, for he shews by his own evidence that
he was told, before he subscribed, that the money was to
go to reduce the bank account, as well as to go towards the
purchase of the new limits.

I shall, however, assume, for the purpose of the reference
I have to make to the question of law, that the plaintiff
was deceived by representations which were untrue, but
which were believed to be true by the defendants, who
made them in order to induce the plaintiff to act upon them,
and in order that they might derive benefit from his act.

The point was taken in the Court below and is thus
mentioned by the learned Judge in his judgment: "The
plaintiff's counsel argued, however, that there is no distinc-

tion between moral fraud and legal fraud as applied to this case, because the effect here has been to benefit these defendants; that where the party making the representation derives a benefit, or where a duty rests upon him towards the other party, there is no difference between what is called *legal fraud* and moral fraud; and that wherever fraud gives a right to rescind the contract an action can be maintained; adding that a part is bound in equity to make good the injury arising fromyhis fraud. and that this is tantamount to the action of deceit."

And he decided against the contention, referring to language used by James, L. J., in *Eaglesfield* v. *Marquis of Londonderry*, L. R. 4 Ch. D. 711, where he says : "Whether the fraud is supposed to be a fraud in this Court as distinguished from moral fraud or not, there must be a wilful and fraudulent statement of that which is false to maintain an action of deceit;" and he also quotes from the judgments of Cotton, L. J., and James, L. J., in *Arkwright* v. *Newbold*, 17 Ch. D., at pp. 320 and 317, where the distinction is pointed out between the principles upon which a common law action of deceit is maintainable, and those on which a Court of Equity acts in setting aside a purchase or a contract obtained by misrepresentation of a fact, or by means of the concealment or suppression of a fact which the Court thinks ought to have been stated.

These cases the learned Judge cites, referring also to *Silverthorn* v. *Hunter*, in this Court, 5 A. R. 157, not as stating new doctrines, but as being recent cases. But, with great respect, I venture to think that they do not touch the point. I do not understand the question to be the existence of any distinction between legal and moral fraud. The liability for misrepresentation, whether it arises because of actual fraud, or from the duty to make no statement in a matter in which one is interested without first ascertaining it to be true, if I am right in supposing such a distinction to exist, is a common law liability; and although the principles on which it rests may run parallel with, or may include the rules on which in equity a contract will be set aside, it is not necessary to treat the two systems as involved one with the other, nor yet to regard them as

contrasted or opposed to each other. In *Eaglesfield* v.
Londonderry, the plaintiffs had bought £10,000 of preference stock from one Savin, induced as they alleged by a
misrepresentation concerning that stock contained in the
certificates issued to Savin by the defendants as directors
of the company. Jessel, M. R., held that the directors were
liable in equity, even though an action for deceit could not
have been maintained against them. That was the proposition which was combated by James, L. J., in the Court
of Appeal. The judgment proceeded on the view of the
facts that the plaintiffs had not purchased upon any representation, but had really bought from Savin quite irrespec-
tively of the certificates. No question of interest arose,
the action not being against Savin who was the person
benefited by the sale. Nor did any such question arise in
Arkwright v. *Newbold*. There, Mr. Justice Fry had decided
for the plaintiff, upon grounds which the Court of Appeal
considered applicable only to an action to set aside a contract, not to an action of deceit. The remarks of the Lords
Justices were addressed to this topic and to point out that
an action of deceit was governed by the same principles
whether brought as of old in a Common Law Court, or
brought now in the Chancery Division; and they decided
the case on the ground that there had been no misrepresentation.

Silverthorn v. *Hunter* was also free from any such
question as that now in discussion.

Taylor v. *Ashton*, 11 M. & W. 401, has the appearance
of being an authority against the proposition I am supporting. It was an action against directors of a banking
company for false and fraudulent representations in a
report concerning the state of the bank which it was
alleged were calculated to induce people to buy shares.
The charge to the jury was objected to. Parke, B.,
delivering the judgment of the Court refusing a rule *nisi*
to set aside a verdict for the defendants, said : "It was
contended by Mr. Knowles that it was not necessary moral
fraud should be committed in order to render these persons

liable; for that if they made statements for their own benefit, which were calculated to induce another to take a particular step, and if he did take that step to his prejudice in consequence of those statements, and if such statements were false, the defendants were responsible though they had not been guilty of any moral fraud. From this proposition we entirely dissent; because we are of opinion, that, independently of any contract between the parties, no one can be made responsible for a representation of this kind unless it be fraudulently made. This is the doctrine laid down in *Pasley* v. *Freeman*, where, for the first time, the cases on this subject were considered." * * But then it was said, that in order to constitute fraud, it was not necessary to show that the defendants knew the fact they stated to be untrue; that it was enough that the fact *was* untrue, if · they communicated that fact for a deceitful purpose; and to that proposition the Court is prepared to assent. It is not necessary to shew that the defendants knew the fact to be untrue; for if they stated a fact which was true for a fraudulent purpose, they at the same time not *believing* that fact to be true, in that case it would be both a legal and a moral fraud.

In 2 *Smith's* L. C. 8th Ed., p. 90, it is said that in the passage, "true for a fraudulent, &c," the word "true" is printed for "untrue." No authority is given for the correction, and the report in the Law Journal (12 L. J., N. S., Ex. 369) agrees with the regular report.

The reporters append to this judgment a reference to *Moens* v. *Heyworth*, 10 M. & W. 147, and looking at that case the law certainly seems to be laid down somewhat differently. Lord Abinger, C.B., says (p. 155): "The fraud which vitiates a contract and gives the party a right to recover, does not in all cases necessarily imply moral turpitude. There may be a misrepresentation as to the facts stated in the contract, all the circumstances of which the party may believe to be true. In the case of a contract for the sale of a public house, if the seller represented by mistake that the house realized more than in fact it did, he would be defrauding the purchaser and deceiving him, but that might arise from his not having kept proper books or from non attention to his affairs; yet as soon as the other party discovers it an action may be maintained for the loss consequent upon such misrepresentation, inasmuch as he was thereby induced to give more than the house was worth. That action might be sustained upon an allegation that the representation was false, although the party making it did not know at the time he made it that it was so." I am not sure whether I am quite correct in understanding Parke, B., to hold the same view. In one place he says: " I think it essential that there should be a moral fraud, and indeed all the cases show that it is, though the word *legal* fraud is used. That is a description of fraud not of so grave and serious a character, that is to say, a representation made without any private view of benefit to the party making it * * In this case the plaintiffs must prove a representation by words or acts, of that being true which was known to the defendants to be untrue ; as in the case of *Polhill* v. *Walter*, in which a party had falsely represented that he was authorized to accept a bill by procuration ; so also in *Foster* v. *Charles*, where the allegation of the party was by a false representation of character. In both cases there was not any deliberate intention to deceive, yet it was called a fraud, though it was not of so grave a character." Alderson, B. gives an illustration of how fraud may be committed by telling the truth, by relating the anecdote of a very eminent ambassador, Sir Henry Wotten, who, when he was asked what advice he would give to a young diplomatist going to a foreign Court, said, " I have found it best always to tell the truth, as they will never believe anything an ambassador says, so you are sure to take them in." He does not say that such a course would be actionable deceit.

There are further reasons for not regarding the opinion expressed by Parke, B., in *Taylor* v. *Ashton*, as an authority of weight against my view. In *Thom* v. *Bigland*, 8 Ex. 725, he said : " It is settled law that, independently of duty, no action will lie for a misrepresentation unless the party making it knows it to be untrue, or makes it with a fraudulent intention to induce another to act on the faith of it, and to alter his position to his damage. This appears from the cases of *Evans* v. *Collins*, 5 Q. B. 820, and *Ormrod* v. *Huth*, 14 M. & W. 657, which have perfectly settled the law on that point." In 1 Smith, L. C., 8th ed., p. 186. it is said that the passage, " or makes it with a fraudulent intention," should be corrected by changing *or* into *and*, and by striking out the word *fraudulent;* referring to a note in 9 Ex. 726, where the misprint of "or" for "and," is noticed, but nothing is said of the word "fraudulent." The Law Journal report agrees with the regular report. (22 L. J. Ex. 240.)

To clearly understand the full scope of this judgment one would require to know what was in the learned Baron's mind when he spoke of duty which might create liability without scienter ; but when we refer to the two cases he cites, we find that in *Ormrod* v. *Huth,* which was an action for misrepresentation of the quality of goods sold by sample, the decision was that in the absence of actual fraud, the rule of *caveat emptor* applied; and that in *Evans* v. *Collins,* the distinction made by the party making the representation having an interest in it was expressly recognized.

Evans v. *Collins,* 5 Q. B; 804, was an action by a sheriff against an attorney. The sheriff had one John Wright in custody under a *Ca. Sa.* The defendant had a *Ca. Sa.* for a client against another John Wright, and his clerk, who was found by the jury to have had authority, told the sheriff that the defendant John Wright was the same as the man in custody, who was thereupon detained by the sheriff, and for that detention the sheriff had to pay damages for which he brought this action against the attorney. The Court of Queen's Bench held the defendant liable on the principle of *Humphreys* v. *Platt,* 5 Bligh. N. S. 154. "One of two persons," Lord Denman said, p. 819, "has suffered by the conduct of the other. The sufferer is wholly free from blame ; but the party who caused his loss, though charged neither with fraud nor with negligence, must have been guilty of some fault when he made a false representation." This judgment was reversed in error. Counsel referred in argument (p. 820) to the fact that in *Humphreys* v. *Platt* the party making the representation got a benefit by it, and to *Chitty* on Contracts where the decision in *Adamson* v. *Jarvis,* 4 Bing. 66, is supposed to rest on this ground ; and Tindal, C. J., while he distinguishes the case from *Humphreys* v. *Platt* on a different ground from that taken by counsel, says with reference to the doctrine of *Pasley* v. *Freeman* and the cases which followed it: "Neither again can this case be distinguished from the others on the ground that the defendants had an interest in the representation they made, and that it was information given for their own benefit; for they could have had no interest in stating the John Wright who was then in actual custody to be the defendant against whom the writ was issued if he was not so; on the contrary," etc.

In *Evans* v. *Edmonds*, 13 C. B. 777, fraud was pleaded to an action on a bond—not the general plea, but an allegation of specific facts. A verdict having been rendered for the defendants upon evidence which proved a gross fraud, the plaintiff moved for judgment *non obstante veredicto* for want of an allegation of scienter in the plea. The plea was held good after verdict. Maule, J., thus stated the law: "I conceive that if a man having no knowledge whatever on the subject, takes upon himself to represent a certain state of facts to exist, he does so at his peril; and if it be done either with a view to secure some benefit to himself or to deceive a third person he is guilty in law of a fraud, for he takes upon himself to warrant his own belief of that which he so asserts."

Rawlings v. *Wickham*, 1 Giff. 355, 3 Deg. & J. 304, is an instructive case for our present purpose. The bill was to rescind a contract of partnership by reason of misrepresentations in a statement presented to the plaintiff during the negotiation for his entrance into the banking firm. There had been three partners, Bailey, Wickham, and another who was retiring and whose place the plaintiff was to take. Of the three, Bailey alone was an active partner, and he was also a practising solicitor, the principal conduct of the banking business being entrusted to the chief clerk, in whom the utmost confidence was placed, but who was found to have appropriated to his own use the moneys of the bank to a very large extent. The statement which was presented to the plaintiff by Bailey, Wickham joining him in doing so, represented the balances due customers as being £11,000, when in truth the amount was £26,000.

As I understand the facts, the actual and intentional fraud in this was chargeable to the clerk; and Bailey, although he ought to have known the state of the books, relied on the clerk and adopted his statements without having himself a design to deceive the plaintiff, and the difference between Wickham's position and that of Bailey consisted merely in the latter being the partner whose active connection with the business made it more his duty, as between himself and his partners, to be acquainted with the details of the business; while his position being known to the plaintiff, the plaintiff would naturally take his presentation of the statement to be an assurance that he knew it to be accurate. The fraud was not discovered till after the death of the clerk. The plaintiff brought an action at law against Bailey and Wickham for deceit. Wickham died before declaration, and the plaintiff recovered against Bailey a judgment for £11,800 damages; and then, not being able to realize the amount, he filed a bill against the representatives of Wickham to rescind the contract of partnership on account of the misrepresentation, and for a return of his £2,500 and indemnity against the debts of the concern and he obtained a decree from Stuart, V.C., which was affirmed by the Lords Justices Knight Bruce and Turner. It would be interesting, and might perhaps aid us at present to know the views of the law and the facts on which the judgment at law against Bailey was obtained, particularly whether his personal good faith was admitted, inasmuch as his position seems not very unlike that of the present defendants. As far as one may judge from the references to that action in the reports of the suit in equity, having regard also to the fact that the action was begun against Wickham as well as against Bailey, and to the absence of any hint that Wickham would not, if he had lived, have been held equally liable with Bailey, I see no reason for supposing that moral fraud on Bailey's part was the ground of the recovery, or that it was held to exist farther than as it may have been inferred from his negligence in omitting to verify the figures he placed before the plaintiff. The case is, I think, reported more fully in 5 Jur. N. S. 278, than in the regular report. Sir J. L. Knight Bruce thus refers to the partners (at p. 280): "Was there any excuse, was there any apology for Mr. Bailey? There was none. He was a professional man, he was the active partner, personally managing the affairs, and personally attending at the place of business. He (Sir J. L. Knight Bruce) would in the most pointed manner say that it was his duty to have known what the books contained. Beyond a doubt he was a party to these gross misrepresentations. On the other hand, Mr. Wickham was an inactive partner, he attended at the bank occasionally only; he did not interfere with the customers, nor did he meddle with the books or know anything of them. But still he was a partner— a partner though inactive; not a sleeping partner, but one who had a right to examine the books, and had power to make himself acquainted with the whole circumstances and state of the business; and between himself and a partner whom he was seeking to introduce it was his duty to know the real condition of affairs. But what was the fact? Whether with acquaintance or with lack of acquaintance with the affairs of the bank, it was proved that he joined with Bailey in the assertion of these misrepresentations, in producing the statement of accounts alluded to, and alleging it to be an accurate account of the position of the bank. It was plain that he ought not to have asserted that which he did not know to be true. If he did not know, it was his duty to have said, ' It may be true or not; I have a good opinion of Bailey and Gattrill (the clerk); I don't know the facts, you must ascertain for yourself.' But he did not say so; he joined in the assertion that an utter falsehood was the truth; and in the position in which he stood with relation to the plaintiff, he (Sir J. L. Knight Bruce) was clearly of opinion that he was as much personally liable as if he personally had known the falsehood of what he asserted. It was plausibly urged that even if Wickham had made statements consistent with the facts, the plaintiff would nevertheless have acted as he did, having confidence in Bailey. But this was only conjecture, and the Court was not at liberty to speculate on what did not happen. The plaintiff ought to have had the choice which such a statement would have given him. He had therefore the joint assertion of Bailey and Wickham for every purpose of this suit, though he did not say for every moral purpose; not as implicating Wickham in any delinquency beyond that which would arise from neglect of his business, and omitting to state what he ought to have done as to his knowledge of what was the real condition of the bank. He became, therefore, answerable for the misrepresentations, and the contract was vitiated." Sir G. J. Turner said (5 Jur. N. S., 'at p. 281): "The delivery of this document by Wickham to the plaintiff could not be considered in any other light than as a representation made by Wickham to the plaintiff that the concern was debtor only to the amount of £11,000, whereas the real amount was upwards of £26,000. At best it was a representation by Wickham of a fact of which he knew nothing whatever, whether it was true or not. But that the representation must have formed a material inducement to the plaintiff to purchase a share of the business could not be doubted. It turned out that that representation was false. This was no moral fraud. Wickham did not know that the amount was inaccurate; but as the representation made by him was untrue, there was legal fraud, and the consequence was that the estate of Wickham must be held answerable for it." In *Peek* v. *Gurney*, L. R. 6 H. L. at p. 294, Lord Chelmsford, discussing the liability of the estate of a deceased debtor to damages in an action of deceit, referred to *Rawlings* v. *Wickham*, and after a short allusion to the nature of the suit and to the facts, said: "It may be doubted whether, looking to the nature of the suit, the rule of *actio personalis, etc.*, applied. At all events the question was never raised, and the Lords Justices held that the action brought against Bailey, which was urged as an objection to the suit, did not free the estate of the deceased from his liability in equity where alone the estate could be reached, but that whatever might be obtained under the judgment in the action against Bailey should go in relief of Wickham's estates."

We are not interested at present in the question of the survival of the cause of action, but I think the remark I have just quoted may be fairly taken to recognize the decree in *Rawlings* v. *Wickham* as being essentially the same thing as the common law judgment against Bailey; and the decree and the reasoning of the

Lords Justices who affirmed it, may, as I also think, be
fairly regarded as placing the liability under a state of
facts very much resembling those before us, upon a principle which applies in actions like the present one.

The Reese River Silver Mining Co. v. *Smith,* L. R. 4
H. L. 64, was an application to remove a name from the
register, and possibly the rule of law stated by Lord Cairns,
that " If persons take upon themselves to make assertions
as to which they are ignorant whether they are true or
untrue, they must in a civil point of view be held as responsible as if they had asserted that which they knew to
be untrue," may not have been intended to have any wider
application than to the jurisdiction then being exercised.
The language is, however, very general.

In *Redgrave* v. *Hurd,* 20 Ch. D. 2, the plaintiff sought
specific performance of a contract, and the defendant succeeded in avoiding the contract for misrepresentation. I
shall not at present read any part of the judgments on
that branch of the case. The defendant had also counter-
claimed for damages. That part of the case was disposed
of by Jessel, M.R., saying: " We consider that it fails so
far as damages are concerned, because he has not pleaded
knowledge on the part of the plaintiff that the allegations
made by the plaintiff were untrue, nor has he pleaded the
allegations themselves in sufficient detail to found an
action for deceit."

Smith v. *Chadwick,* 20 Ch. D. 27 ; 9 App. Cas. 187, was
an action for deceit in representations contained in a prospectus. The action was against the agents of the vendor,
not against any one for whose benefit the representations
were made ; and the decision was that the plaintiff had
not been misled. It may, therefore, be said that any
enunciation of the law was not necessary for the decision
and that, at all events, the point I have now in view was
not in the minds of the Judges. But it will not be out of
place to quote some of the remarks made in the Court of
Appeal and in the House of Lords. Jessel, M.R., remarked
that, without repeating at full length what he said in a
recent suit, alluding to *Redgrave* v. *Hurd,* he thought the

Law was clear. "A man may issue a prospectus," he said, "or make any other statement to induce another to enter into a contract, believing that his statement is true, and not intending to deceive ; but he may through carelessness have made statements which are not true, and which he ought to have known were not true, and if he does so he is liable in an action for deceit; he cannot be allowed to escape because he had good intentions and did not intend to defraud. * * Again in an action for deceit, even though the statement may be untrue, yet if it was made in good faith, and the defendant had reasonable ground for believing it to be true, the defendant will succeed. Finally, it is not every misstatement although untrue, and although untrue in a sense to the defendant's knowledge, that will do. It may be that the misstatement is trivial, so trivial as that the Court will be of opinion that it could not have affected the plaintiff's mind at all or induced him to enter into the contract ; or it may be that although the means of knowledge were in the hands of the defendant, yet the matter was minute, and required a careful examination, and there may have been reasonable grounds for the defendant to believe that this statement was true, although he had those means of knowledge in his possession, in that way also he would be entitled to succeed."

In the opening remark of the Earl of Selborne in the House of Lords, the general rule of law is very happily expressed in these words : " My lords, I conceive that in an action of deceit like the present, it is the duty of the plaintiff to establish two things ; first, actual fraud, which is to be judged of by the nature and character of the representations made, considered with reference to the object for which they were made, the knowledge or means of knowledge of the person making them, and the intention which the law justly imputes to every man to produce those consequences which are the natural result of his acts ; and secondly, he must establish that this fraud was an inducing cause of the contract, for which purpose it must be material, and it must have produced in his mind an erroneous belief, influencing his conduct."

Lord Blackburn made some observations which I shall not now quote, but which may sometimes be usefully referred to when a practical question which often presents itself both in the Divisional Courts and in this Court has to be dealt with, viz : the extent to

which in reviewing the findings of a Judge, the Court
should be confined to the considerations which are appropriate when the verdict of a jury is moved against;
and Lord Bramwell, after alluding to the fact which he
thought apparent, that the defendants believed the statement they made to be true, one of them giving convincing
proof of that by himself staking £5,000 which he lost—an
incident which has something of a counterpart in the present case—went on to say : "The question here is not
whether they should be in any way punished for most
improvident and rash statements (more than one) in the
prospectus, but whether we are satisfied that this particular statement was a fraudulent as well as what it was to
my mind, an untrue statement. I am not satisfied of that.
Let me not be misunderstood. An untrue statement as to
the truth or falsity of which the man who makes it has no
belief is fraudulent, for in making it, he affirms he believes
it, which is false."

In *Peek* v. *Gurney*, L. R. 13 Eq. 79 ; L. R. 6 H. L. 377,
the bill prayed for a declaration that certain statements put
forward by the directors of the company in a prospectus
were so put forward with a view to deceive and mislead
the public, and the plaintiff as one of the public, and contained misrepresentations and suppressed important facts,
&c., and *inter alia*, that the defendants the directors were
jointly and severally liable to the plaintiff to indemnify
him against the loss he had sustained and might sustain in
consequence of his having become a member of the company. The plaintiff was not an original allottee of shares but
had purchased from one of the original allottees. The case
was decided against him in the House of Lords, on the
ground that the representations of the prospectus had not
been made to any but those who were invited to apply for
and receive allotments of shares, to which class he, being
only a transferee of shares, did not belong. Strictly
speaking, it may therefore perhaps be said to have been
unnecessary to decide whether or not the defendants would
have been liable to the parties who subscribed for shares
on the faith of the truth of the prospectus. Still, one can

hardly venture to class as *obiter dicta* the valuable and
exhaustive discussions of the law and facts bearing upon
that subject by Lord Chelmsford and Lord Cairns. A
good deal of discussion turned upon the liability for
mere concealment or non-disclosure of facts. In connection with that question Lord Chelmsford pointed out
that the suit was precisely analogous to a common law
action for deceit. It will be remembered that the action
was earlier than the passing of the Judicature Act.
Lord Cairns also discussing the same topic, made use of
language which is often quoted without reference to the
connection in which he used it, saying : " There must in
my opinion 'be some active misstatement of fact, or, at all
events, such a partial and fragmentary statement of fact.
as that the withholding of that which is not stated makes
that which is stated absolutely false." Another passage of
his judgment is not inappropriate to some of the facts
before us. Referring to an acquittal which had taken
place on a criminal charge, he said (p. 409) : " My lords, I
must say that so far as I understand the case I entirely
agree with the result at which the jury arrived in that
proceeding ; and strange as it may appear, I think there is
a great deal in the papers before your lordships to show
that the gentlemen who formed this company were themselves, judging by the extent to which they embarked their
means and continued their property in the concern, labouring under the impression that this transaction, disastrous
as it ultimately turned out, had in it the elements of a
profitable commercial undertaking ; and, so far as motive
is concerned, they may be absolved from any charge of a
wilful design or motive to mislead or to defraud the public.
But in a civil proceeding of this kind all that your lordships have to examine is the question : Was there or was
there not misrepresentation in point of fact ? And if there
was, however innocent the motive may have been, your
lordships will be obliged to arrive at the consequences
which probably would result from what was done."

Joliffe v. *Baker*, 11 Q. B. D. 255, should be referred to
both because it is one of the most recent cases on the subject, and because the discussion turned to some extent on
the interest of the defendant in the representation in ques-

tion. The defendant having advertised a property for
sale, said amongst other things, in reply to a letter of
inquiry from the plaintiff, that it contained "in all three
acres," giving also other particulars. The plaintiff bought
the property and took a conveyance of it; and afterwards
discovering that the area was only a trifle over two acres
and a quarter, brought the action to recover compensation.
The contract, made after the representation complained of,
described the property as "containing by estimation three
acres or thereabouts," and it was so described in the conveyance. In fact the defendant had himself taken it by the
same description, and he believed the description as to the
acreage to be correct. The main point in the case is not
one which directly concerns us. It was held that in the
absence of actual fraud an action for compensation could
not be maintained 'after conveyance. Watkin Williams,
J., delivering a judgment in which Cave, J., concurred, and
to which A. L. Smith, J., added only a few words, discussed
the question at considerable length and with much vigor.
He disapproved of the decision of Fry, J., in *Hart* v.
Swaine, 7 Ch. D. 42, and that of Jessel, M. R., in *re Turner
and Skelton*, 13 Ch. D. 130. Fry, J., had said (7 Ch. D. 46):
"The defendant took upon himself to assert that to be true
which has turned out to be false, and he made this assertion for the purpose of benefiting himself. Though he
may have done this believing it to be true, the result
appears to me to be that which is expressed in the judgment of Maule, J., in *Evans* v. *Edmonds*," then reading
the passage I have already quoted, and continuing: "That
is to say, the defendant having taken upon himself with a
view of securing a benefit to himself to assert that the
property was freehold, has in the view of a Court of law,
committed a fraud. The same principle is laid down by
Turner, L. J., in *Rawlings* v. *Wickham*, where he says: ' If
upon a treaty for purchase, one of the parties to the contract
makes a representation materially affecting the subject
matter of the contract, he surely cannot be heard to say that
he knew nothing of the truth or falsehood of that which he
represented, and still more cannot be allowed to retain any

benefit which he has derived if the representation he has
made turns out to be untrue.   It would be most dangerous
to allow any doubt to be cast upon this doctrine.'"   In
allusion to this judgment Sir Watkin Williams (11 Q. B. D.
259) said : " It is certainly unfortunate that the language
of *Evans* v. *Edmonds* should have been cited as an authority
for the proposition that there can be an actionable legal
fraud in the absence of moral fraud, because *Evans* v.
Edmonds was a case of the most flagrant fraud and
treachery to be found in our books."   And then after
noticing the facts of *Evans* v. *Edmonds* he said: " The
objection after verdict was obviously frivolous and absurd,
and the observations of Maule, J., in answering it were
conceived in a vein of the keenest irony and satire, when
he said that a person might make such a representation
fraudulently, as the jury found, consistently with his not
knowing it at the time to be false, which was not averred."
As to this I may venture to say that I find no trace in the
report of *Evans* v. *Edmonds* of the motion for judgment
non obstante being dealt with in the very unusual spirit
which the learned Judge ascribes to Mr. Justice Maule,
either by resort to irony or satire, or by the still less
probable importation into the discussion of the details of
the evidence on which the jury founded their verdict.
The learned Judge also deals with *Rawlings* v. *Wickham*
by suggesting that "Whatever may have been the language
of the judgment, the decision rests and may be supported
upon the sound, broad foundation of the well known
principle of law, that every partner undertakes and
engages for the fidelity of his co-partners in the execution
of matters within the scope of the authority conferred
upon them; and all that could be decided in that case was
that Wickham, even though an innocent partner, could not
escape from the consequences of the fraudulent misrepresentation of his partner in a transaction which he had
authorized him to carry out, and there was no necessity to
resort to any doctrine of fraud."   Now, setting aside the
consideration to which I have adverted, and which the
learned Judge does not appear to have noticed, that the
so-called fraud of Wickham appears to have been exactly
of the same nature as that of his partner, as far as
Rawlings was concerned, the actual fraud being that of

Gattrill, the clerk, the suggestion that the decision can be explained or supported on the grounds of the agency implied between partners is to my mind more than questionable. The opinions for which principally I cite the case were certainly not influenced by any such views; and if we could adopt the suggestion it would seem to involve a matter of contract, like a warranty, a result which the defendants in the present case might find fully as formidable as the charge they have to combat. Discussing then the representation concerning the quantity of the land, and the contention that, as it was made by the defendant for his own benefit, fraud need not be found, the learned Judge pointed out that there was no fraud; and that, even were the representation a warranty, the warranty was not broken, because it was true that the land had been estimated to contain about three acres. He made further remarks upon the law, from which I shall read a short extract: " I adopt," he said (p. 270), "with regard to that expression (legal fraud) the words of Lord Bramwell, in *Weir* v. *Bell* 3 Ex. D. 243, where he says: 'I do not understand *legal fraud*. To my mind it has no more meaning than legal heat or legal cold, legal light or legal shade. There never can be a well founded complaint of legal fraud, except where some duty is shown and correlative right, and some violation of that duty and right. And when these exist it is much better that they should be stated and acted on, than that recourse should be had to a phrase illogical and unmeaning with the consequent uncertainty.' Armed with this authority of Lord Bramwell, I reject the phrase 'legal fraud,' as distinguished from 'moral fraud' and deceit, as wholly inapplicable and inappropriate to legal discussion, and I simply ask the question in the present case: Do the facts disclose a case of fraud? and I reply unhesitatingly that they do not. Perhaps it is scarcely necessary to add that there can be no doubt that if a man affirms something as a positive fact concerning which he has no knowledge whatever, knowing neither whether it is a fact or not, and does so intending to induce another person to act upon it as a fact, and for his own benefit, regardless of whether the fact is so or not, then that is the strongest possible evidence of fraud in the plain meaning of the word, because by the hypothesis, he could not have known that to be true as a fact which he pretended to know and which he represented that he knew to be a fact. Still even in such a case as that, the fraudulent element must be found to exist *as a fact*, and cannot be adopted as a mere *inference of law.*" This saving proposition is not readily distinguished from the dictum of Maule, J., in *Evans* v. *Edmonds*, the use of which by Fry, J., was caviled at by the learned Judge, or from the position attributed by Turner, L. J., to the testator of the defendants in *Rawlings* v. *Wickham.*

We may concede, without hesitation, the propriety of what is suggested by Lord Bramwell in such graphic language in *Weir* v. *Bell*, and drop the term " legal fraud" as one which does not accurately describe the quality of the acts or omissions or conduct to which it is usually applied, provided we do not go farther than that suggestion warrants, as almost seems to have been done in the passage I have just read from the judgment in *Joliffe* v. *Baker*, and assume that when we give up the name we get rid of the thing itself. Lord Bramwell, while he objects to the phrase as inexpressive, throws no doubt on the right of action for the violation of any duty or of its correlative right.

I had not intended to refer to any others of the numerous cases in which untrue representations have been in question, except by merely noting *Harvey* v. *Wallace*, 16 U. C. R. 508, because I do not think they throw much light upon the point in discussion; but having the report of *Weir* v. *Bell* before me, I may call attention to the judgment of Cotton L. J., not with the idea that it differs in any respect from his opinion in *Arkwright* v. *Newbold*, which is quoted in the judgment we are reviewing, but as giving an instance in which he holds a person bound by a fraudulent representation although he had no actual knowledge of the fraud. "It is true," he says, " that Mr. Bell did not see the prospectus, but in November, whilst he was abroad, he learnt from an advertisement in a newspaper that a prospectus had been issued, and though that advertisement did not contain the statements of the pro-

pectus which have been found to be fraudulent, it gives
the summary of the prospectus, which ought to have put
Mr. Bell on inquiry, knowing as he did the actual state of
the company, as to the contents of the prospectus. He
certainly knew that the debentures would be applied for
in reliance on the statements contained in the prospectus,
and in my opinion it was his duty to ascertain what those
statements were. He neglected this duty. Had he looked
at the prospectus he would have seen that material statements were untrue. It is well established that in an action
of deceit a defendant may be liable not only if he has made
statements which he knows to be false, but if he has made
statements which in fact are untrue, recklessly, that is
without any reasonable grounds for believing them to be
true, or under circumstances which shew that he was
careless whether they were in fact true or false." Bramwell and Brett, L. JJ., and Cockburn, C. J., differed from
Cotton, L. J. as to liability of the defendant Bell, who
alone out of several defendants had appealed, and the immediate grounds of the decision do not bear directly on
the question now before us. The judgment of Bramwell,
L. J., mainly consists of a rejoinder to a judgment delivered
in *Barwick* v. *English Joint Stock Bank*, L. R. 2 Ex. 269,
by Willes, J., who had disapproved of the judgment of
Bramwell, B., in *Udell* v. *Atherton*, 7 H. & N. 172; but
Cockburn, C. J., in whose judgment Brett, L. J. concurred,
alludes to the subject of the defendants obtaining a benefit
from the representations, which must be my excuse for
reading a remark of his. After noticing the facts as they
applied to the defendants other than Bell, one fact being
that on their own authority they applied a considerable portion of the money received for shares to the discharge of
their own pecuniary claims on the company, which claims
the company had no other means whatever of satisfying;
and mentioning, that one defendant, Barnet, who had been
absent during the transactions, and was ignorant of all
that was done in the interval of his absence, inclusive even
of the fact of the payment of the amount due to him from
the company, the money having been paid to his agent in
his absence, having retained the money when the facts

came to his knowledge, stood on the same footing with the rest ; and after some references to the law of principal and agent, he continued : " If, therefore, the case of the defendant Bell, with which we alone have to deal—as it is only against the decision of the Court below in his favour that the present appeal has been brought—had been undistinguishable from that of the other defendants, I should not have felt warranted in affirming the decision. But his case differs from that of the other defendants in two most important particulars. First, that though a party to the receipt of the plaintiff's money he does not appear to have been at that time acquainted with the real state of the company's affairs, and thus aware of the falsehood of the statements contained in the prospectus ; secondly, that none of the money actually came into his pocket." And again, after alluding to Bell's deposition denying knowledge, &c., " I cannot, therefore, say that he was guilty of fraud in receiving the plaintiff's money on behalf of the company ; and, as has been already stated, he derived personally no benefit from the receipt of it."

I take it to be the law, and I think my opinion is borne out by the cases to which I have referred, that it is the duty of a person who desires, for his own benefit, that another shall do something, and who, in order to induce him to do it, represents to him any fact, to take care that he states it truly, or if he is himself only taking it on trust as represented to him by some one else, to so state it.

If damage is sustained in consequence of reliance upon such a representation which turns out to be untrue, I do not see on what principle of justice the person who is innocent and who has not been careless should be the one to bear the loss. I further think that authority is afforded by the whole tenor of the decisions for maintaining an action for damages for the misrepresentation.

The technical name of the action may be of little consequence. If there is, in the language of Lord Bramwell in *Weir* v. *Bell*, " a well-founded complaint," for the violation of any duty or its correlative right, the action to enforce that complaint may be called by whatever name will sufficiently describe it, in case the term " fraud," or

" deceit" should, on logical or critical grounds, be held to be
as inappropriate as he deemed " legal fraud" to be in the
position it had so long and not unusefully occupied.

But if it be considered indispensible to call the action
an action of deceit and to allege and prove fraud, I
apprehend there is enough in these cases to warrant us
in holding a person guilty of deceit who puts forward a
statement of a fact which is or ought to be within his own
knowledge, inviting action upon it for his own benefit, and
under circumstances calculated to amount to an assertion
that he knows the fact to be as stated, when he has not
taken pains to verify it.

If a statement thus taken on trust and repeated without
inquiry, though in other respects in good faith, by one who
seeks and obtains a benefit from it, turns out to have been
fraudulently made by his informant, so that there is actual
fraud committed by some one, the case would come very
nearly if not literally within some of those which I have
cited, yet the consequence to the man who parts with his
money on the faith of the representation and loses it, and
the neglect of the duty of the man who makes the representation and gains by it to ascertain that what he states
is true, are the same if the statement is simply untrue.

I am inclined to the opinion that the principle of the
liability in such a case is not different from that acted
upon in Courts of Equity when they set aside a purchase
or a contract obtained by misrepresentation and compel the
restoration of whatever has been gained by means of it,
without requiring proof of actual or moral fraud; and when,
as in *Rawlings* v. *Wickham*, they even give indemnity not
limited by the gain which resulted from the contract. To
quote the language of Jessel, M. R., in *Redgrave* v. *Hurd*,
20 Ch. D., at p. 13 : " Assuming that fraud must be shown
in order to set aside a contract, you have it where a man,
having obtained a beneficial contract by a statement which
he now knows to be false, insists on keeping that contract.
To do so is a moral delinquency. No man ought to take
advantage of his own false statement."

This is I think only to the same effect as some of the views expressed in *Weir* v. *Bell,* and I have already quoted even more distinct language used by the Lords Justices in *Rawlings* v. *Wickham.* I may also refer to the judgment delivered by Wilde, B., for himself and Pollock, C. B., in *Udell* v. *Atherton,* 7 H. & N. 172, as putting the liability in an action for deceit, when the defendant gained a benefit from the representation, upon the same ground on which in equity he would be compelled to restore what he had received. Bramwell, B., and Martin, B., whose nonsuit was moved against, took a different view of the liability of the defendant in the case, and as I have remarked before, their opinion was criticized in *Barwick* v. *English Joint Stock Bank,* by Willes, J., without convincing the learned Baron who delivered it that he was in error.

I have already quoted language of Lord Abinger, in *Moens* v. *Heyworth,* 10 M. & W. 155. The same doctrine is laid down by Alderson, B., in *Smout* v. *Ilbery,* 10 M. & W. 9, 10, where in delivering the judgment of the Court, he says: " It is a wrong to state as true what the individual making such statement does not know to be true, even though he does not know it to be false, but believes, without sufficient grounds, that the statement will ultimately turn out to be correct. And if that wrong produces an injury to a third person who is wholly ignorant of the grounds on which such belief of the supposed agent is founded, and who has relied on the correctness of his assertion, it is equally just that he who makes such assertion should be personally liable for its consequences."

Now, referring to what I have already said with reference to the facts and evidence in this case, I have only a few words to add. If it were satisfactorily established that material representations of facts were contained in the prospectus issued by the authority of the defendants; and that the plaintiff was induced to part with his money by relying upon those statements of fact, and by understanding and relying upon them as assertions of the defendants themselves, without inferring and believing from his knowledge of the defendants personally and of the limited

extent to which the conduct of the business was in their
hands, and of the character of the business which required
skill and experience to qualify one to judge of details of
value, &c., that the statements were only put forward as
estimates in which the defendants had confidence, but of
which they did not profess to have personal knowledge;
and that by reason of things not being as represented the
plaintiff lost his money; my present opinion is, that I should
be prepared to hold further that the representations were
made with a view to the benefit of the defendants, and
that they were liable to make good the plaintiff's loss.

These preliminary facts have, however, not been found
either at the trial or by any view of the evidence on which
in this Court we are agreed; and for reasons partly already
explained, I do not take so strong a view of the evidence
in favour of the plaintiff, as to induce me to dissent from the
judgment dismissing the appeal. I am content, therefore,
to concur in that judgment with the explanation I have
given of the reasons for which I do not quite agree with
my learned brethren upon the law governing actions of
this kind.

I have had immediate reference in what I have said to
Petrie's Case ; but whatever is said of his case applies with
at least equal force to those of Inglis and Hunter and of
Stewart.

OSLER, J. A.—I have had an opportunity of reading the
judgment of my Brother Burton, and, agreeing with the
views expressed by him as to the evidence and the law
applicable to the facts and the nature of the action, do not
think it necessary to say more, than that in my opinion,
the decree is right, and that the appeal should be dismissed.

McKenzie v. Dwight.

Deceit—Representation of opinion—Rescission—Dominion Land Acts—
Mounted police force—Land warrant.

The plaintiff upon the assurance of the defendant that a land warrant
issued to one of the North-West Mounted Police Force would entitle
the holder to 160 acres of Dominion lands, and which warrant on its
face expressly stated that the party was entitled to 160 acres, purchased
such warrant from the defendant for $312.00. In consequence of vari-
ous Acts of the Legislature and orders in Council, lands in the North-
West territory, which at the time this warrant was issued, were held
for sale at $1, were increased to $2 per acre, so that on the presentation
of the warrant to the proper officer, the plaintiff would only be credited
with $160 on the purchase of land at the established price. The defen-
dant was not aware of this change. In an action brought by the plaintiff
the Queen's Bench Division held that he was not entitled to recover
back his purchase money as having been obtained by misrepresentation.
On appeal, this Court being equally divided, the appeal was dismissed.

THIS was an appeal by the plaintiff from a judgment of
the Queen's Bench Division, reported 2 O. R. 366, where
and in the present judgments the facts are fully stated,
and the authorities cited are mentioned.

The appeal came on to be heard before this Court on the
21st of November, 1884.*

McCarthy, Q. C., for the appellant.
McMichael, Q. C., and *Pearson*, for the respondent.

January 26, 1885. BURTON, J. A.—If this is to be treated
as an action of deceit, I must hold upon the grounds so
fully discussed in the recent case of *Petrie* v. *Guelph*, *ante*
p. 336, that on the findings of the jury in this case the
action cannot be maintained.

But it is contended that the plaintiff has done nothing
to disentitle himself to rescind the contract, and that
although in an action for deceit it would be necessary to
shew that the representation was false, and false to the
knowledge of the defendant, or under such circumstances
that the jury might draw the inference that he did not
believe it to be true, which the jury have not found, the

* *Present.*—BURTON, PATTERSON, MORRISON, and OSLER, JJ.A.

findings of the jury are sufficient to entitle the plaintiff to
a rescission of the contract.

The law upon the subject is well settled that it is not
necessary in order to set aside a contract obtained by
material false representations to prove that the party who
obtained it knew at the time that the representation was
made, that it was false, because a man is not allowed to
get a benefit from a statement which he now admits to be
false, if the other contracting party has done nothing to
disentitle him to rescind, and is in a position to place the
person he contracted with in *statu quo*.

But a misrepresentation to be material should be in
respect of an ascertainable fact as distinguished from a
mere matter of opinion, or as to the legal effect of a document, for the law in general is equally within the knowledge of all, and therefore a representation or statement of
mere matter of law, although erroneous, will not in general
be a sufficient ground for imputing fraud.

The findings of the jury must be read in connection with
the evidence and the Judge's direction to them, and I am
unable to find that there was any such direction as would
clearly convey to their minds the distinction between
representation as to matters of fact, and as to the legal
effect of the warrant the defendant was negotiating.

The learned Judge treats the evidence of the plaintiff
and defendant as not substantially differing. I think the
plaintiff in his evidence carries the case further than is
admitted by the defendant.

The plaintiff himself seems to have had some doubt as
to whether such a warrant would entitle the holder to more
than its value at one dollar per acre, to which he says the
defendant answered: " No, that thing was binding on the
Government for 160 acres of land, not he thought in Manitoba, but in the North-West territories."

On cross-examination he said that the defendant had
made inquiries and he was positive the defendant swore it
was his first transaction: that he had no knowledge on the
subject, but he admits that he did tell the plaintiff that

he could get 160 acres of land, giving as his reason "because the assurance was written on the face of the instrument," but he might not get it in Manitoba.

Asked about making that statement without any knowledge, he replies: "Except what I had on the face of it. I had no knowledge otherwise, whatever. I had not taken the trouble to make inquiry."

In this respect he is contradicted by the plaintiff. Bounell says that what he told the plaintiff was that all he knew about it was that some said it was worth $160, others, that they sold at $500.

The learned Judge appears to have considered that the representation was made in reference to the legal effect of the document, for he says this comprehends within its terms the affirmation of fact by the defendant that there were then lands subject to sale at one dollar per acre, which seems to assume that apart from that implied affirmation there was no express representation to that effect.

But whether there was evidence of any such express statement, or whether it is to be inferred from the representation alluded to by the learned Judge, I conceive that it was of the most vital importance that the attention of the jury should have been specially directed to what constituted the affirmation of fact, and their finding asked for upon it.

If that question had been expressly left to the jury and found against the defendant, I think the matter would have been concluded upon that branch of the case by that finding; but that question was not submitted except in the general way I have mentioned, and the jury have not found, nor were they required to find, that the defendant represented as a matter of fact that there were then Dominion lands open for sale at one dollar per acre.

The learned Judge in his charge refers to the representation which the defendant admits he made, which was that the warrant would entitle the holder to 160 acres of land.

That was the representation which he asked the jury to decide about. Was that representation made or not? to

such an inquiry there could be but one answer, but can
any one say that if they had been asked, did the defendant represent as a fact that there were then Government
lands open at one dollar per acre, they would have answered
that question in the affirmative.

Neither that question nor the falsity of the representation was left to the jury; the learned Judge held, as a
matter of law, that the warrant did not entitle the plaintiff
to call for 160 acres of land.

I think that upon these findings coupled with the direction, there was no sufficient ground established for the
rescission of the contract, and there ought to have been a
new trial to take the opinion of the jury upon the point.

I do not agree with the *ratio decidendi* in the Divisional
Court. Their decision proceeded in my view upon a mis-
reading of the language of the 30th section of the Act of
1881, passed to take the place of the repealed section of
the Act of 1879, under which the class of lands mentioned
in the land warrant ceased to exist, and the price was left
to be regulated entirely by the government, although they
were prevented from selling at less than $1 per acre.

But I think the case has not gone to the jury with such
a direction as would enable them clearly to understand the
distinction between a representation upon a matter of fact
and a matter of mere opinion.

The Court is equally divided, and therefore the judgment stands ; but in my opinion no sufficient evidence
was given that the Crown would not on a proper
application perform this contract. All that we know is,
that since the passing of the regulations referred to in the
evidence, the officers of the department refuse, as they
must necessarily refuse, to grant lands upon them ; but
the Act of 1881 does not prohibit the government from
selling lands at $1 per acre, and I think we should assume
that good faith will be kept by the Crown with the parties with whom these contracts have been made. I think
at present it has been assumed rather than proved that
the government has refused to recognize them, and that

upon a proper application grants would be made, and the regulations altered with that view ; but it has not been affirmatively established that the Government have repudiated the contract.

PATTERSON, J. A.—This action is brought to recover back from the defendant the sum of $312, being the amount paid by the plaintiff to the defendant for a certificate or Mounted Police land warrant, on the ground that the plaintiff was induced to buy the certificate from the defendant and to pay him the money by a misrepresentation. The plaintiff also asks for interest upon the money from the time of payment. The misrepresentation is charged in the statement of complaint as having been made fraudulently and with knowledge that the statement was untrue ; but the charge of actual fraud of that character is not pressed.

The certificate is in these words :

DOMINION OF CANADA,

No. 0297.   *Department of the Interior.*

It is hereby certified that under the Orders in Council of 27th November, 1876, and 16th May, 1879, authorizing free grants of land to certain constables and sub-constables, for service in the North-West Mounted Police, constable Phileas B. Brunette is entitled to locate one hundred and sixty acres, being one certain quarter section, upon any of the Dominion lands subject to sale at one dollar per acre.

Recorded in the Dominion Land Office.

A. RUSSELL,
For the Surveyor-General.
J. S. DENNIS,
Deputy Minister of the Interior.

Given under my hand and seal of office,
this second day of August, 1880.   [SEAL.]

NOTE.—This certificate may be located at any of the offices of the Dominion lands, by the owner, or by returning it with his request to that effect endorsed thereon, specifying the province and land district in which he wishes the location made, it will be located for him. Should he locate it himself he must fill up and sign the following application :

18	Locate this certificate in the quarter
To the Agent of Dominion Lands, at	of section , Township, Range, Meridian. (Attested) *Agent Dominion Lands.*

The transaction between the plaintiff and the defendant was in March, 1882, more than a year and a half after the date of the certificate.

The representation on which the complaint is founded is charged in the statement of complaint as being that the certificate would entitle the plaintiff to 160 acres of land in the Province of Manitoba, or the North-West Territories of Canada, free from settlement duties, and exempt from taxation for five years from the date of location, and that the plaintiff could locate the same at any time.

In his statement of defence the defendant gives the following very different version of the matter:

4. The defendant during the negotiations told the plaintiff that he had been informed that the said certificate was good for one hundred and sixty acres of land, but that the plaintiff would have to ascertain for himself as to the conditions of such information, and the defendant produced the said certificate to the plaintiff to enable him to ascertain for himself, and the plaintiff made the purchase in reliance upon his own judgment and the result of his own enquiries and investigations, and not upon any statement or representations whatever of the defendant.

The issues were tried before Mr. Justice Armour, with a jury. Written questions were submitted to the jury, and answered as follows:

First—Did the defendant represent to the plaintiff, in order to induce him to purchase the scrip, that it would entitle the plaintiff to 160 acres of land? Ans. Yes.

Second—Did the plaintiff purchase the scrip on the faith of such representation? Ans. Yes.

Third—Was such representation true or false? Ans. False.

Fourth—Did the defendant, when he made such representation, know it to be false?—or, did he believe it to be true?—or, did he make it without knowing that it was true or false, with the intention that it should be relied upon? Ans. He made the statement without knowing that it was true or false, with the intention that it should be relied upon.

The answer to the third question was given in accordance with his Lordship's direction as a matter of law that the certificate would not bring 160 acres of land, but only $160 on account of such land as the holder of it might purchase from the Dominion Government.

The direction was based upon evidence given by an officer of the Department of Public Lands, and upon orders of council and the statutes concerning Dominion lands.

Upon the findings of the jury, judgment was given for the plaintiff for $322.27.

In the Divisional Court, Mr. Justice Cameron concurred with the Chief Justice in reversing that judgment, Mr. Justice Armour dissenting.

This appeal is from the judgment of the Divisional Court.

The judgment proceeded, as I understand from the remarks of the learned Chief Justice as reported in 2 O. R. at p. 383, wholly upon the opinion that the certificate "entitled the holder of it to 160 acres of land, and not merely to a credit of $160 in money on any purchase of Dominion lands," and that, therefore, when the "defendant represented to the plaintiff that the document would entitle him to 160 acres of land, the representation was proper and such as he could properly make." I am here quoting from the judgment without reading the remarks made in support of the opinion.

The reversal of the judgment notwithstanding the finding of the jury that the representation was false, was in accordance with the course taken at the trial, the learned Judge there directing the jury to answer the question upon the view of the effect of the warrant which he then stated, telling them that if the Court should hold that the warrant entitled the holder to 16 acres of land, the action would fail.

At the date of the warrant, 2nd August, 1880, and for eight or nine months after that date, there were Dominion lands subject to sale at $1 per acre, and the holder of the warrant might, so far as I can perceive, have during that time obtained 160 acres of the lands of that class. But when the defendant sold the warrant to the plaintiff, there were no Dominion lands for sale at less than $2 per acre.

The statutes and orders of council bearing on the question
have been very fully noticed in the judgments in the Court
below, particularly in that of Mr. Justice Armour. My
references to them may therefore be comparatively short.

The Mounted Police force was established by the Act of
1873, 36 Vict. ch. 35, (D).

The 17th section of that Act authorized the Governor
in Council to make a free grant not exceeding 160 acres to
any constable or sub-constable of the force, who, at the
expiration of three years of continuous service in the force,
should be certified by the Commissioner of Police to have
conducted himself satisfactorily, and to have efficiently
and ably performed the duties of his office during those
three years.

Nothing was said in that statute of a certificate or warrant being given to the constable ; but in the Public Lands
Act of the preceding year, 35 Vict. ch. 23,(D.) regulations had
been made, by sections 23 to 26 inclusive, concerning warrants issued by the Minister of Militia and Defence for
military bounty land grants; and these regulations were,
by an order in council of 27th November, 1875, made
applicable to the warrants to be granted to constables.

In 1879 the Acts respecting the Mounted Police were
consolidated by 42 Vict. ch. 36, (D.) which however made no
change in the provision for grants of 160 acres to the constables of the force.   The Act of 1873 had placed the force
under the control of the Minister of Justice ; but in 1878
it had, under a power given by the statute, been transferred
to the Department of the Interior.   The consolidating Act,
which received the royal assent on the 15th May, 1879,
placed the force in the Department of the Interior ; and
by an order in Council, made 16th May, 1879, apparently
without noticing the new statute, the Minister of the
Interior was authorized to sign land warrants for service
in the North-West Mounted Police.   This order refers also
to that of the 27th November, 1876, which directed the
assigning or locating of such warrants to be regulated in
all respects by the provisions of sections 23 to 26, both

inclusive, of the Dominion Lands Act, 33 Vict. ch. 33, a
direction which, I have no doubt, retained its force notwithstanding the repeal of the Act by 42 Vict. ch. 31 (D.), which
also was passed on the day before the order in Council, and
which consolidated the laws relating to Dominion lands,
re-enacting the sections relating to military bounty warrants.

Under the authority thus shewn the warrant was issued;
and, according to its tenor, it entitled the holder to 160
acres of lands of a particular class, namely, those subject
to sale at $1 per acre.

The power to restrict the right to lands of a particular
class has not been questioned; and, having regard to the
terms of section 17 of 36 Vict. ch. 35 (D.), or the equivalent
section 10 of 42 Vict. ch. 36 (D.), it could not be successfully disputed. It is not properly a restriction, because
the right arises only from this document.

The Act 35 Vict. ch. 23, sec. 29 (D.), and also the Act 42
Vict. ch. 31, sec. 30 (D.), declared that "Unappropriated
Dominion lands, the surveys of which may have been duly
made and confirmed, shall, except as otherwise hereinafter
provided, be open for purchase at $1 per acre;" and orders
in council, made after its passing, fixed the price of lands
in belt E at $1.

Thus there was an extensive class of lands from which
the 160 acres might have been selected: but, by 44 Vict.
ch. 16 (D.), passed in 1881, a new section 30 was substituted
for the section of that number in the Act of 1879. The
new enactment was that "Unappropriated Dominion lands,
the surveys of which may have been duly made and confirmed, shall, except as otherwise hereinafter provided, be
open for purchase *at such prices, and on such terms and
conditions regarding settlement or otherwise, as may be
fixed from time to time by the Governor-in-Council:*
provided that no such purchase shall be permitted at a
less price than $1 per acre:" with other provisos similar
to the original section, but not affecting the matter in
discussion.

By the effect of this statute, the class of lands mentioned
in the warrant ceased to exist. Lands were no longer, in
the words of the warrant, "subject to sale at $1 per acre,"
or at any other price except such as should be fixed by
Order in Council; and the first order which followed the
statute, viz., that of 25th May, 1881, fixed the lowest price
at $2 per acre. Later orders have varied the price of
different classes of lands, but have not made any lands
subject to sale at a lower price than $2.

This was the state of the regulations which the plaintiff
alluded to when he spoke in his evidence of asking the
defendant whether the warrant was not good for only
eighty acres, and when, as he says though the defendant
does not admit it, he was assured it was good for 160.

When it was held in the Court below that the warrant
entitled the person who held it in March, 1882, to 160 acres
of land, I cannot help thinking that the attention of the
learned Judge, who formed that opinion cannot have been
sufficiently directed to the terms of the warrant which
gave, not a right to purchase 160 acres by paying $1 per
acre, but a right to a free grant of 160 acres of lands subject to sale at $1 per acre, and to the force of the statute
of 1881; or that, at all events, that statute was to some
extent misapprehended.

It is at this point that, with the greatest respect for both
those learned Judges, I feel compelled to differ from them;
and it may therefore be proper that I should state the view
to which my opinion is opposed in the words of his Lordship the Chief Justice, as they are reported at p. 383 of
the volume. After a rapid glance at the prior legislation,
he said: "44 Vict. ch. 16, in amendment of the Act of 1879,
sec. 4 amending sec. 30 of the Act of 1879, says that unappropriated lands surveyed shall be open for purchase, &c.,
provided no such purchase shall be permitted at a less price
than $1 per acre. Even without the light thrown on it by
the Statutes and Orders in Council, &c., it appears to me
very plain that this certificate or land warrant entitles the
holder to 160 acres of land, and not merely to a right to a

credit of $160 in money in any purchase of Dominion
lands. * * At the date at which it was granted the
the Government held abundance of land at the declared
price of $1 per acre, and the Act cited of 1881, a year after
the certificate, speaks of land open for purchase at $1 per
acre."

This passage expresses the reading of the statute which
seems to me to have influenced the judgment, and which I
take to be a mistaken reading. I do not understand the
new section 30, which is contained in section 4 of the Act
of 1881, to speak of land open to purchase at one dollar
per acre. Reading the whole section, including the portion
passed over by his Lordship in his extract from it, I understand it to speak of land as being open to purchase only
at the price and on the terms and conditions to be fixed
by the Governor in Council, and to refer to one dollar per
acre only for the purpose of forbidding the fixing of any
lower price.

The directions at the foot of the warrant may supply a
not unapt means of testing the operation of the warrant in
1882. The holder could not possibly fill in the blanks
with a meridian, range, township, or number of quarter
section in which lands were subject to sale at one dollar
per acre, because in 1882 there were no lands answering
that description. His warrant did not entitle him to
make an arbitrary choice of locality and demand 160 acres
there. He had to ascertain where lands of the class
specified were to be found, and he discovered that while
such lands had existed from 1873 till 1881, they had
ceased to exist in the latter year.

It may make no difference in this action whether the
cesser was by reason of the act of the executive or of the
Legislature, but the fact may be noted that it was the
latter. Now, I apprehend that to justify the representation that the warrant would entitle the plaintiff to 160
acres of land, it must be made out that he could obtain the
land in the mode directed by the document itself, and that
if it should appear that he had reasonable grounds for

maintaining a petition of right to enforce an allotment of 160 acres, while at the same time he could not obtain the land according to the tenor of the warrant, the charge of misrepresentation would not thereby be answered.

The bargain was not for a doubtful right, or one which could only be asserted by litigation; and the representation had no relation to an abstract or possible right of that sort. On this topic I may refer, without repeating them, to some remarks which I made in delivering judgment recently in *Burns* v. *Young*, 10 A. R. 215.

I am of opinion that the finding of the jury that the representation was false is not open to objection, and that therefore the plaintiff is entitled to retain his judgment, unless some of the other objections are valid.

I shall refer to the objections *seriatim* as I find them stated in the reasons against the appeal.

No. 1 is, that any representation made by the defendant must be construed with reference to the terms of the certificate that Brunette was entitled to locate 160 acres upon any of the Dominion lands, subject to sale at $1 per acre.

The representation was that the plaintiff, as assignee of Brunette, was in 1882 entitled, &c., and it was made in view of the question raised touching the recent legislation and the plaintiff's apprehension that he might only get 80 acres, or, in other words, be allowed only a credit for $160.

No. 2: that Brunette is not shewn not to be entitled to 160 acres, but the contrary; therefore no action for fraudulent misrepresentation or rescission.

I have already stated my opinion that the question is the right under this warrant, not the possible existence of a different contract with the Crown.

No. 3: that the only representation was that it was good for 160 acres when the Government set apart land at $1 per acre.

This is answered by the jury's finding, and any different finding would have been against evidence.

No. 4: that the finding of the jury, if the proper construction has been placed upon it by Mr. Justice Armour,
is wrong.

I do not understand this objection; and we are not
asked to give a new trial ; nor should we order one upon
the materials before us.

No. 5 : if the representation involved the affirmation
that there were lands subject to sale at $1 per acre, the
same reasoning would prove a contract on the part of the
Government that the Government had such lands, and so
there was no misrepresentation.

My answer to No. 2 applies also to this objection. But
the objection confounds two things which are distinct, viz.,
the effect of the warrant when it was made, when, if it
implied a contract that there were lands to satisfy it, it
implied nothing but what was true, and the representation
thirteen months later, which was untrue.

No. 6: I pass over for the moment.

No. 7 : that the representation was at most only as to a
matter of law.

I do not think this objection well taken. The plaintiff
may be assumed to be bound to know the law. It is not
necessary to consider closely whether the rule applies,
because there is enough in his evidence to shew that he
did know the law; or at least that he had been informed
that the statute which fixed the price of $1 per acre was
no longer in force. He does not put his information in
those words, but he lets us know that he had been told
that the certificate might be good for only 80 acres. Now
we know the law, and that in 1882, it made the price of
the public lands depend on the action of the Governor in
Council. If there were, in March, 1882, lands subject to
sale at $1 per acre, that could only have been by virtue of
an Order in Council, which is a matter of fact and not of
law.

Then as to objection No. 6, that there was no bad faith.
I take the fact to be as so stated, qualified only so far as
the last answer of the jury may qualify it, that he made

the statement without knowing whether it was true or false, with the intent that the plaintiff should act upon it: and I add another fact, which in this case is one of those palpable facts that no one would think of asking the jury to find formally, that the action intended was to be for the benefit of the defendant, who was getting $312 for what he had just bought for $205.

I have so recently discussed the law on this subject at quite sufficient length, in *Petrie* v. *Guelph Lumber Co.*, *ante* p. 336, that I shall not now do more than refer to that discussion, and particularly to the cases of *Rawlins* v. *Wickham*, 1 Giff. 355; 3 D. & J., 304; and *Redgrave* v. *Hurd*, 20 Ch. D. 1. I single out those cases, because, while I remain of opinion that under the circumstances of this case, an action of deceit would have lain at common law, those circumstances clearly bring it within the equitable jurisdiction to rescind the contract and order restitution. Mr. Justice Armour in his judgment makes a long and very apposite extract from the judgment of Jessel, M. R., in *Redgrave* v. *Hurd*, which, I believe, I did not introduce into my judgment in *Petrie* v. *Guelph Lumber Co.*, and to which I now refer without reading it.

I am of opinion that we should allow the appeal, with costs.

MORRISON, J. A.—I agree, with much doubt, in reversing the judgment upon the grounds mentioned in the judgment of my Brother Patterson.

OSLER, J. A.—The statement of claim alleges (1) that the defendant offered to sell the certificate in question to the plaintiff, and in answer to questions stated that the certificate would entitle the plaintiff, if he purchased it, to 160 acres of land in Manitoba or North-West Territories; and (2) that he then assured the plaintiff that he was quite familiar with such certificates, and knew of his own knowledge from past experience that the plaintiff would be enabled with it to procure from the Government of

Canada 160 acres of land at any time; (3) that the plaintiff relied upon these representations solely, and would not have bought the scrip if he had not believed that the possession of it would have entitled him to 160 acres, as the defendant well knew when he offered it for sale and made the representations; (4) that the fact is, as the defendant well knew when he made the representations, that the certificate did not entitle the plaintiff to 160 acres of land, but only to be credited in the books of the Dominion Lands office with $160 on account of any purchase he might make of Dominion lands, &c.; (5) the defendant made said representations knowing the same to be false, and with intent to defraud the plaintiff.

The statement of defence denies allegations 2 and 3 of the statement of claim : alleges that the defendant did not, on any occasion, assure the plaintiff that he would be enabled by means of the certificate to procure 160 acres of land from the Government : alleges that he told the plaintiff during their negotiations that he had been informed that the certificate was good for 160 acres, but that the plaintiff would have to ascertain for himself the correctness of such information, and the plaintiff relied upon his own judgment in making the purchase.

The action is in form an action for deceit, the allegation being that the defendant's statements were falsely and fraudulently made. The only relief, however, which the plaintiff asks seems in effect to be a rescission of the contract. As the material evidence on the question of the actual representation made by the defendant is very brief, I shall extract it.

One Bonnell, the defendant's partner, first spoke to the plaintiff about selling the scrip, and about an hour afterwards the defendant came to the plaintiff with it. The plaintiff read it, and asked defendant if he was sure everything was all right.

"Q. What did you do, and what did he do? A. I asked him if he was sure that it was not only eighty acres you could get for this, as I had been told the Government only took this for $1 an acre ; and he said no, that thing was binding on the Government for 160 acres."

The plaintiff could not give the defendant a decided answer at that interview, and the latter gave him until twelve o'clock to make up his mind. He then endeavoured to make inquiries about the scrip, but the person he wanted to see was absent. Then he went to the defendant's office with Bonnell. There they had a discussion as to the thing being all right, and the money was handed over. He was asked :

"Q. Did anything further pass between you than what you have stated? A. No; nothing, except that Dwight assured me several times I could get 160 acres of land for that scrip; that the way I would proceed would be to find out what unlocated land I wanted, then send the scrip to the nearest land office to the land, stating that I wanted certain lots located in my name, and that it would be done."

Subsequently the plaintiff, on endeavoring to get the land, received a letter from a land agent in Winnipeg, named Ruttan, stating that the warrant was not worth more than $160: that it would not buy a Government quarter section; but that it would apply on Government land to the extent of $160. He shewed this letter to the defendant, and told him the scrip was not what he had held it up to be.

" The defendant said he could not help it; I ought to look to the government, not to him ; I said to him, did you not tell me that I could get 160 acres of land for the scrip ; says he, I did, and believe that you could : That was all he said."

On cross-examination he said :

"Q. What was the falsehood he told you? A. The falsehood? why, he sold me a document purporting to be good ; he told me that the document—the document that he sold me—would get 160 acres of land in the north-west, and it did not get it.

Q. Did you read the document? A. I read the document.

Q. Didn't you think that entitled you to locate 160 acres of land? A. I read through that, 'for sale by the Dominion Government, at a dollar per acre: I did not know whether they had any for sale at a dollar per acre.

Q. Assuming that there were lands for sale at a dollar an acre in the hands of the Dominion Government, didn't you understand that certificate entitled you, the holder of it, the person to whom a lawful transfer had been made, to locate 160 acres of land? A. I did think that.

Q. Did you ask the question whether there were any lands for sale at a dollar an acre? A. I made the remark there might not be any for sale at a dollar an acre—and how about it then?

Q. To whom did you make that remark? A. Mr. Dwight.

Q. You knew that was so? A. I did not know for positive, however; but I thought so : I thought that because land was worth more in the north-west at that time; that was the only reason; I had heard the Government were selling lands at two dollars an acre; I had heard of the constable's bounty warrants, but had never seen them before; I made the remark, I thought lands in the north-west were two dollars an acre, and very likely more; that I would only be able to get 80 acres; I said that to Dwight, I am positive.

Q. Was it before or after you came out of the office he made the statement to you that you considered a lie? A. Both before and after.

Q. In what language? A. I cannot remember the exact words, except that I specially asked him if he was sure I could get 160 acres for it, and he said he was sure I could.

Q. What words did he use in saying he was sure? A. He said he had made all necessary enquiries.

Q. And what? A. that he was positive."

The defendant in giving evidence said that this was his first purchase in land in any speculation whatever, and his first sale.

His examination proceeded :

"Q. Now, the plaintiff says you said you did not think he would get land in Manitoba; do you remember saying anything about that? A. He asked me that at the time ; and I do remember saying I did not think he could get land in Manitoba, but he would get it in the Northwest Territories, I made certain because all the land there was not taken up.

Q. Did you give him that statement, that he might locate it anywhere? A. No sir; I told him he could get 160 acres—that is all.

Q. At which conversation was that, the first or second. A. That was the first conversation ; at the second conversation I had very little to say to him."

On cross-examination—

"Q. Tell me the conversation? A. I went into the room   * * shewed him the scrip, he looked it over ; one of the questions was, can you only get 80 acres of land for it? I said that is contradictory of the face of it, read it for yourself, the Government cannot go back of that ; he did not think they could. I said to him, there it is plain on the face of it ; he took it, and said he wanted to go out of the room to see somebody in reference to it ; he took it out, and was gone three or four minutes, and came back again ; I do not think he said anything then to me about it, except he said when he went away he was acquainted with a

civil engineer who knew all about these things ; I told him at the time
I understood he could get it located, and free from settlement duties and
taxes for a period of five years.

Q. You represented to him that would be a great advantage? A. I
told him I had heard that.

Q. You also said he would get 160 acres? A. I am positive I told him,
because the assurance was written on the face of it; but that he might
not get it in Manitoba ; that is the result of what I told him.

Q. You were speaking with regard to that, without any knowledge?
A. Except what I had on the face of it; I had no knowledge of it otherwise whatever ; I had not taken the trouble to make enquiry at the constituted authorities about it.

Q. You assumed to tell him he would get 160 acres in the north-west,
although you did not know one way or the other ? A. I thought decidedly he would ; that was given by the Government, and they had to
recognise that."

There was other evidence which in view of the findings
of the jury it is not necessary to refer to.

I think the case entirely fails as an action of deceit.

The answers of the jury must be read in connection
with the learned Judge's charge and with the evidence.

The defendant does not deny that he said to the plaintiff that he could get 160 acres from the government on
the warrant, and the jury found that he represented to the
plaintiff that it would entitle him to 160 acres.

But as to the falsity of that statement, they were told
that the representation was false *as far as the law was concerned;* that the plaintiff could not get 160 acres on the
scrip, "and so in fact the representation would be false,
that is, a representation that was not true :" and they were
further told that if the Court should afterwards determine
as a matter of law, that the scrip did entitle the holder to
160 acres the action would fail. Having been thus direct
ed, that part of the case was taken out of their hands,
and they answered the 2nd question in accordance with
the direction of the Judge, that the representation was
false, *i. e.,* that it was an untrue statement of the law and
nothing more. They were not required to find, nor did
they find that the defendant represented as a matter of
fact that there were then Dominion lands for sale at $1
per acre, and if they had been asked that question, I do
not think they would or could have so found.

Then they were asked the further question whether the defendant when he made the representation knew it to be false, or believed it to be true, or whether he made it without knowing that it was true or false with the intention that it should be relied upon, and they answered that he made it without knowing that it was true or false with the intention that it should be relied upon.

In order to judge of the effect of this answer we must see how the jury were directed upon the point. They were told:

"In the first place, do you think the defendant, at the time he made the representation, thought it was a false representation? Did he know that warrant would not bring 160 acres of land to the holder? The only evidence about that is this, the defendant himself says he knew nothing about it one way or the other that he never read the orders in council or regulations, and knew nothing about it in one way or the other."

And again:

"Then there is the other branch of the question, did he make the representation without knowing whether it was true or false, with the intention that it should be relied upon? You may not be able to find he made the representation knowing it to be false; and you may not be able to find he believed it to be true; but, did he make it, without knowing it to be true or false. He himself tells you he knew nothing at all about it. He did not know anything about what the Government would take that warrant for. Again, he knew nothing at all except what he saw on the face of the warrant. There will be very little difficulty in answering that question, if he himself swears he did not know whether the representation was true or false. Then, did he make the representation, with the view of inducing the plaintiff to purchase? I tell you as matter of law, that land warrant will not bring 160 acres of land; it will only bring what Mr. Goodeve says it will bring, $160."

The learned Judge was asked, but he declined, to submit the further question, whether the representation was made recklessly or carelessly without proper inquiry.

Looking at the direction given to the jury on the last branch of the last question, and at the evidence already quoted, it is manifest that the case was left to them as to that, on the defendant's evidence; and that the finding amounts to nothing more than that the defendant stated his belief as to the legal effect of the warrant. The jury are told there will be little difficulty in answering the question if the defendant himself swore that he did not

know whether the representation was true or false. His
evidence is certainly to that effect, but it cannot be dis-
severed from the explanation he gave with it, namely, that
the assurance (that he would get 160 acres) was written
on the face of the document.

"Q. You assumed to tell him ¡he would get 160 acres in the North-
West although you did not know one way or the other. A. I thought
decidedly he would; that was given by the Government; they had to
recognize that."

In the report of the trial, as it appears upon the appeal
book, the plaintiff's counsel is represented as saying, before
the jury were addressed, that all that was sought was
rescission, and that he did not care to press the case of
fraud. On the argument, however, we were informed that
the case ultimately went to the jury on the other question,
and it was strongly urged that the representation made by
the defendant was as to the practice of the office—what
the land office were in the habit of doing, as a matter of
fact, with regard to these warrants. I think neither the
evidence nor the findings of the jury justify that contention.

As I read them, there is no false or fraudulent representation of any matter of fact by the defendant. I do
not think any member of the Court below took a different
view. Therefore, as I have said, the action fails as an
action of deceit. My Brother Armour, in his dissenting
opinion, treated the case as one for rescission because the
defendant had, by implication, affirmed as a fact that there
were Dominion lands for sale at $1.00 per acre. But that,
as I have observed, was not a question left to, or passed
upon, by the jury. The only false statement found by
them was an untrue statement of the legal effect of the
document. If either a false affirmation of a material fact
or a fraudulent statement of a matter of law, e. g., as to
the legal effect or meaning of the warrant, had been found
by the jury, the plaintiff would have made out a case for
rescission of the agreement: but I think the action fails
on this ground also. *West London Commercial Bank* v.
Kitson, 13 Q. B. D. 360 ; *Rashdall* v. *Ford*, L. R. 2 Eq. 750 ;

Beattie v. *Lord Ebury*, L. R. 7 Ch. 777 ; *Reese River Silver Co.* v. *Smith*, L. R. 4 H. L. 64 ; *Redgrave* v. *Hurd*, 20 Ch. D. 1, 12, 13 ; *Cooper* v. *Phibbs*, L. R. 2 H. L. 150-170 ; *Hirschfeld* v. *London, &c. R. W. Co.*, 2 Q. B. D. 1 ; *Kennedy* v. *Panama, &c. R. W. Co.*, L. R. 2 Q. B. 580.

If I could regard the warrant as conferring simply a right to a credit ot $160 on a purchase of Dominion lands, I should be disposed to accede to Mr. McCarthy's argument that there was such a fundamental error, as it has been called, as to the very thing agreed to be bought and sold, that the purchaser would be entitled to rescission on the principle laid down in such cases as *Kennedy* v. *The Panama, &c., R. W. Co.*, L. R. 2 Q. B. 580-587.

Lord Blackburn there says, p. 587 : "Where there has been an *innocent* misrepresentation or misapprehension it does not authorize a rescission unless it is such as to shew that there is a complete difference in substance between what was supposed to be and what was taken, so as to constitute a failure of consideration."

Here both parties believed themselves to be dealing with a right to 160 acres of land, not with something representing the purchase money of that or a lesser number of acres according to a fluctuating price per acre.

But I entirely agree with the Chief Justice in the Court below as to the meaning of the warrant : that on its face it appears to entitle the holder to 160 acres, and not merely to a credit of $160.

It may be that existing Orders in Council stand in the way of the power of the holder to locate lands as a matter of routine, in accordance with the warrant, without making a special application to the Governor in Council to vary or relax such orders in favour of warrants granted previously to their passage. Or he may even be driven to present a petition of right, to obtain what it appears to me the warrant entitles him to.

But as the case now stands upon the evidence, and the findings of the jury, I think we can only dismiss the appeal.

GAGE v. CANADA PUBLISHING COMPANY.

Trade name—Injunction—Fraudulent use by one of his own name—Sale of article bearing name—Partnership—Future use of name in same manner.

The plaintiff and defendant Beatty, carried on business as partners from 1st May, 1877, to 28th August, 1879, during which time Beatty prepared a series of headline copy books, published as "Beatty's System of Practical Penmanship," but spoken of as "Beatty's Head Line Copy Books" and "Beatty's Copies," from the sales of which large profits were realized by the firm. At the date last mentioned Beatty having sold his interest to the plaintiff for $20,000, retired from the firm, the most valuable asset thereof being the series of copy books. Subsequently, and in the year 1882, Beatty, at the instance of his co-defendants, the publishing company, in consideration of a royalty to be paid to him, and with the express purpose of enabling the company to publish a copy book to be called "Beatty's" prepared another series of headline copy books differing only to a colourable extent from the former series. The title of the new series was "Beatty's New and Improved Head Line Copy Books," the name "Beatty" being printed conspicuously on the cover; and the books were in such a form and cover as to lead the public to believe that they were the books published by the plaintiff, and it was shewn that the plaintiff's business was injured by the sale of the new series.

Held, [affirming the judgment of FERGUSON, J.,] that the conduct of the defendants in publishing the new series was illegal, inasmuch as by simulating the plaintiff's books, they deprived him of the profits he would otherwise have made; and that he was entitled to a perpetual injunction, restraining defendants from issuing, advertising, publishing or selling, or offering for sale the books called "Beatty's New and Improved Head Line Copy Books" in and with its present cover, or in any other form of cover calculated to lead persons to believe that it was the plaintiff's book

THIS was an appeal by the defendants from a judgment pronounced by Ferguson, J., reported 6 O. R. 68, where the facts giving rise to the action are clearly stated; and came to be heard before this Court on the 4th, 5th, and 6th days of June, 1884.*

Robinson, Q. C., and *Davidson*, for the appellants, the Publishing Company.

Moss, Q. C., for the appellant, Beatty.

S. H. Blake, Q. C., and *Lash*, Q. C., for the respondent.

The points raised and authorities cited appear in the former report and in the present judgment.

Present.—HAGARTY, C.J.O., BURTON, PATTERSON, and MORRISON, JJ.A.

September 12, 1884. HAGARTY, C. J. O.—On the 1st of May, 1877, the plaintiff and Beatty entered into partnership under the firm name of Adam Miller & Co. Articles were executed declaring that they became partners in the business of publishing, booksellers, stationers, and dealers in fancy wares at Toronto, for five years, unless sooner dissolved by death or notice.

The capital was to consist of the then present capital of the late firm of "Adam Miller & Co.," and the parties to be interested and own the same in equal proportions. The lease of the late firm to become joint property. Parties entitled to profits equally, and at the annual stocktaking to be carried to their respective capital accounts, and thereafter be treated as capital. No portion to be withdrawn till amounting to $35,000. Each partner to get $1,000 annually as a salary.

The partnership continued to the 28th August, 1879, on which day a deed of dissolution was executed in consideration of $20,000 paid or to be paid to him by the plaintiff Gage, stated to be the value of the share of Beatty in the property, stock, and credits of the partnership, and of an indemnity against liabilities the defendant Beatty "releases all his interest in the property, lease, stock, credits, and business of the partnership to said W. J. Gage, with power in the name of Beatty, his executors, &c., to recover and give receipts for the same premises."

The plaintiff claims that a large part of the business consisted in the manufacture and sale of " Head Line Copy Books " for use in the public schools &c., and that when the partnership was formed, and during its continuance, defendant Beatty designed certain head line copy books of great value, one of the chief assets of the business.

That the books were sold and known as " Beatty's Head Line Copy Books," and large sums were spent in advertising and in obtaining a reputation for them.

That on the dissolution the plaintiff paid Beatty $20,000, and the price paid was chiefly so paid on account of the purchase of Beatty's interest in the copy books : that it was understood and agreed that the plates and copies of the copy books, and the right to manufacture and sell the same were to be the property of the plaintiff, and that but for acquiring the sole right to make and sell the same he would not have paid any such amount.

That the word "Beatty" as applied to said books was a valuable asset of the firm, and had been the trade mark of the firm, and the right to use that name was an asset of the firm.

That the defendants, the PublishingCompany, and Beatty, colluded together to get up and manufacture headline copy books, and have advertised the same as "Beatty's New and Improved Head Line Copy Books," and sell the same to persons who buy under the belief that they are the plaintiff's headline copy books, &c., and that this is done to obtain the advantage derivable from the known value attaching to Beatty's Head Line Copy Books owned by the plaintiff, which value has resulted from the large amount spent by plaintiff in advertising the said books, praying that defendant be restrained (1) from infringing on plaintiff's trade mark.

2. From advertising said books in such a manner as to lead the public to believe they are the plaintiff's copy books.

3. For damages and other relief.

For defence, the Publishing Company deny any knowledge of the plaintiff issuing copy books entitled "Beatty's Head Line Copy Books," or of the business relation of the parties.

The knowledge of any trade mark of the plaintiffs, and that the copy books, or the word "Beatty" could not form the subject of a trade mark.

They deny all fraud, collusion, &c., to issue books designed to mislead the public so as to believe that they are the plaintiff's books.

That the plaintiff was well aware, for a long time, of their intention to issue such books, and their valuable preparations therefor, and was guilty of *laches*, &c., in delaying to take proceedings.

The defendant Beatty claims that the terms of dissolution are contained in the deed produced, denies that he ever agreed that the plaintiff should have exclusive use of his name as a trade mark, and that he would not have agreed to a dissolution if he supposed or believed he was to give up the right to prepare and publish other copy books, or to the use of his own name therewith : that he never knew of the plaintiff's design to register the name "Beatty" as a trade mark, and that it was not a proper subject for a trade mark : that the books prepared by the defendants are an entirely distinct series from those of the plaintiff, and not based on or copied from them; and denies collusion and bad faith.

During the partnership—16th March, 1878—the firm of A. Miller & Co. registered under the Copyright Act of 1875, a declaration that the firm were proprietors of the books called "Beatty's" Head Line Copy Books in nine numbers by S. G. Beatty, published by the firm. During the partnership the work prepared by Beatty was always published under the name of "Beatty's system of Practical Penmanship." But it seems that in speaking of it, it was often called "Beatty's Head Line Copy Books."

In March, 1878, we find the Public School Board recommending their adoption in the schools as "Beatty's Head Line Copy Books."

Plates were engraved for the work. It became most extensively used, and very large profits realized by it. On the dissolution, after some bargaining, Beatty retired and received $20,000 for his interest. The plaintiff swears that the right to this work he considered most valuable, and but for his belief that he was to have it he never would have given Beatty so large a sum. Beatty denies this.

The dissolution took place August, 1879. After that the name of Adam Miller & Co. was changed to W. J. Gage & Co., and on 26th August, 1881, the latter firm registered under the Act of 1879, a specific Trade Mark which consists of the name "Beatty" in connection with Beatty's Head Line Copy Books.

The Canada Publishing Company, defendants, seem to have been established after dissolution of the Adam Miller & Co. firm. Mr. Campbell was the manager. The business before incorporation was carried on by "James Campbell & Son."

When Beatty retired from the firm it would seem that he had no idea of remaining in any business of a like character, and he went into some drug business.

The dealings between Mr. Campbell and Beatty are described fully in the judgment of Ferguson, J. There seems to be no doubt, on the evidence, that the company desired to bring out a book to compete with the plaintiff's book. I need not repeat the letters and conversations which led to the agreement finally concluded. I think we must find that Beatty was fully aware of the company's views on that point. Up to the summer of 1882 they had dealt simply in the sale of the books purchased from plaintiff under the name of "Beatty's Copies."

During the negotiations for partnership it is clear that the defendants anticipated or found some difficulty with plaintiff.

In the agreement dated 15th March, 1882, Beatty agreed to prepare for them a "series of not less than nine head line copy books to be known and called 'Beatty's New and Improved Series of Head Line Copy Books,'" to be the sole absolute property of the company. Beatty to prepare the head lines for the series, carefully revise the proofs, and superintend the engraving of the plates. He bound himself not to prepare any other series of the head line copy books, nor allow his name to be used in connection therewith. Also, that he has not entered into any previous agreement whereby he has abridged his right and deprived himself of the right to make the agreement; also that if by any action based on the copyright of the series of copy books under the title of "Beatty's Improved System of Penmanship," the publication and preparation of the therein named copy books be restrained, the parties shall equally bear all costs and damages awarded and his royalty to cease.

Before this he was fully aware that plaintiff objected, and denied his right to make any such agreement.

This action was brought in June, 1882.

The principal point insisted on below and before us was, that Beatty could not publish or put his name to any book or work in the nature of a copy book, to depreciate the value of the property bought from him at the dissolution.

Plaintiff admitted there was no similarity in the covers of the books beyond the use of the name "Beatty."

From the voluminous evidence given at the hearing I come to the conclusion that although the books are not alike in appearance, yet that both being popularly called "Beatty's Copy Books" and being generally asked for by that name, the last publication was sometimes given and accepted, and was calculated to interfere very clearly in the sale of plaintiff's books. The subject of the two was the same, the name of Beatty gave the known value to each, and the last one published, professing to be on a revised and improved principle by the same author, would naturally induce a preference on the buyer's part.

The defendant stands on his strict legal right to do as he has done.

I think that the plates and the work itself published by Adam Miller & Co. was, at the time of dissolution, the property and assets of the firm, and, as such, became wholly vested in plaintiff by the deed; and that the possession and right of publishing such work as it then stood formed a substantial ground of consideration between them, and that but for its existence and continuance with plaintiff, he would not have paid so large a sum to Beatty for his interest in the joint estate.

It was, as I understand, conceded in argument and held in the Court below that nothing turned on either the Copyright Act or the Trade Mark Act, and that the decision must turn on the general law. A great number of cases were cited, English and American, and certain governing principles seem of general acceptance. Apart from contract, it is clearly held that no man has a right to

put anything in the market in such a shape as to induce
the public to purchase it or to take it as goods of another.

That if any one have obtained a reputation for his goods
which have been placed in the market in a well known
form, and are known by such form or appearance, a man will
be restrained from imitating such form or appearance so
as to induce the public to buy them as the goods of the
other.

Lord Kingsdown's words are often quoted(*Leather Cloth
Co.* v. *American Leather Co.*, 11 H. L. at p. 538): "The
fundamental rule is, that one man has no right to put off his
goods for sale as the goods of a rival trader."

Westbury, L. C., declares the rule of interference to be
based on the ground of property, not on that of fraud, dif-
ferring from *Croft* v. *Day*, 7 Beav. 84, and agreeing with
Millington v. *Fox*, 3 M. & Cr. 338.

James, L. J., in *Levy* v. *Walker*, 10 Ch. D. 447, says:
"It should never be forgotten in these cases that the sole
right to restrain anybody from using any name that he
likes in the course of any business he chooses to carry on
is a right in the nature of a trade mark, that is to say, a
man has a right to say, 'You must not use a name whether
fictitious or real—you must not use a description, whether
true or not, which is intended to represent, or calculated
to represent, to the world that your business is my business,
and so, by a fraudulent misstatement, deprive me of the
profits of the business which would otherwise come to me.'
That is the principle, and the sole principle on which this
Court interferes. The Court interferes solely for the purpose of protecting the owner of a trade or business from a
fraudulent invasion of that business by somebody else.
It does not interfere to prevent the world outside from
being misled * * The plaintiff can only proceed on the
ground that, having established a business reputation under
a particular name he has a right to restrain any one else
from injuring his business by using that name."

See *McAndrew* v. *Bassett*, 10 L. T. N. S. 442, per Lord
Westbury; *Fullwood* v. *Fullwood*, 9 Ch. D. 176; *Hudson*
v. *Osborne*, 39 L. J. Ch. 79.

This case has also to be considered as matter of contract.

I do not consider it is of importance to notice the argument as to the absence of "good will" in the deed of dissolution.

The property, which plaintiff seeks by this suit to protect, passed to him as we think by that deed as far as Beatty's interest in it was concerned.

Beatty appeared to have fully consented to the work being issued in his name, and was aware of the value attached to his name as the author or compiler, and of the great success the work had obtained, and its large value to the firm.

A stranger could be restrained from issuing a work or compilation so framed as to pass for that issued by the plaintiff, or likely to induce the public to accept it as plaintiff's.

It is insisted that Beatty could still less take such a course and, as it were, derogate from his own grant.

It would certainly seem that the claim against him must necessarily be stronger, as he has been paid for the property now sought to be protected.

In *Ward* v. *Beeton*, L. R. 19 Eq. 207, the defendant had been a bookseller and publisher, and owned a work called "Beeton's Christmas Annual."

Plaintiff purchased the whole of his copyright stock and business property, and the defendant afterwards entered into an agreement with the plaintiff, to the effect that he was to devote his attention to developing plaintiff's publishing business, &c., and that the plaintiff might use his name for present or future publications, &c. The annual was published in defendant's name for years, then they quarrelled, and he refused to prepare it. Plaintiff arranged with another person to prepare the Annual, and the defendant then advertised that he had nothing to do with it, and was preparing another Annual under another name. Plaintiff filed a bill to restrain the defendant from announcing that he was interested in any other annual, book, or publication, or that the use of his name by the plaintiff in Beeton's Annual was unauthorized, and asking accounts, &c.

The Court said (p. 216): "What is the meaning of purchasing "Beeton's Christmas Annual?" Did it mean that they could not call it "Beeton's Annual" unless Beeton superintended the publication, or approved of the contents? It would have been just the same as if they had bought Blackwood's Magazine, or Fraser's Magazine, or any publication known by a particular name. It does not certainly mean that the person whose name it has borne is to continue to be connected with it * * it is perfectly clear in my mind that they acquired the right to publish this publication as "Beeton's Annual," although Beeton might not have continued to have any connection with it whatever. * * When you sell a newspaper, it is not merely the right to sell a number of it, but continuing to publish it from day to day," &c.

Of course in that case there was the express agreement that plaintiff might use defendant's name, but I think if a property of that character had obtained and was always known by a specific name and such property was sold, the name would be considered as part of the bargain.

If Gage and Beatty had been druggists or chemists, and for some time had dealt in an article which had a great sale and high character as "Beatty's Dyspeptic Pills," I think under a deed of dissolution framed as here, Gage could have continued selling them under the same name, and that Beatty could not interfere, or attempt to sell pills representing them as the true article, or to pass them off as if sold by plaintiff.

In the absence of any sale for value of his interest in the article, defendant could after dissolution sell the pills as his own under the old name. See such cases as *James* v. *James*, L. R. 13 Eq. 421; *Burgess* v. *Burgess*, 3 D. M· & G. 896.

Metzler v. *Wood*, 8 Ch. D. 606, 610, cited in the Court below, is an instructive case. At a sale of partnership property of D'Almaine & Co., plaintiffs purchased a work called *Hemy's Royal Modern Tutor for the Piano;* another work, "Jousse's Royal Standard Piano-forte Tutor," was bought by defendants. Hemy's work had been written for D'Almaine & Co., but not registered so as to secure copyright. It went through several editions, and after being bought by the plaintiffs was revised for them by Hemy.

Afterwards the defendants employed Hemy to prepare a revised edition of Jousse's work, an old work published fifty years before, once in high repute, but then almost unknown. This revised edition was printed mostly from the original plates, with some additions and some few alterations, and was brought out as "Hemy's new and revised edition of Jousse's R. S. Piano-forte Tutor," and the word "Hemy's" was printed both on title page and cover in much larger letters and was more conspicuous than any other part of the title. It was proved that the title was calculated to deceive.

Malins, V. C., and the Court of Appeal held that plaintiffs were entitled to the injunction asked.

James, L. J., says (p. 610): "There is really no question of law in the case, no question of the right of a man to the use of his own name, or anything of the kind. No such question arises as whether Mr. Hemy had sold his name, like a man selling his shadow. The simple question is: Did the defendant dishonestly pass off his work as the work of the plaintiff? That really is the sole issue. * * There was nothing to prevent Mr. Hemy from employing his talents in revising and bringing out a new edition; but, having done so, instead of the defendant bringing out his work as 'Jousse's R. S. P. Tutor: new edition, revised by Hemy,' he brings it out with Hemy's name at the top, and in the largest type, even larger than in the other, as 'Hemy's new and revised edition of Jousse's R. S. P. Tutor.' * * There is evidence * * that persons wanting to get the plaintiffs' work might have the defendant's given them without detecting the difference."

Thesiger, L. J., says (p. 614): "I may say that I attach some importance to the mode in which the republication of this work of Jousse's came about.

It is obvious to my mind that the defendant was minded, if he could, to make use of Hemy's name in order to get some piano-forte tutor into the market, because the conversation between him and Mr. Hemy commenced by suggestions on defendant's part, that he should publish in a new and revised form, not Hemy's work itself, but a sequel to the 100th edition, as it was called, of 'Hemy's Royal Modern Piano-Forte Tutor.' * * * Obviously, whatever was the suggestion of defendant, it was one which Mr. Hemy considered was not a proper suggestion, and it was in consequence of that, that Mr. Hemy suggested there should be a new edition of Jousse's work. I agree with the Vice-Chancellor in thinking that there is nothing in the work itself of which the plaintiffs had a right to complain." He then agrees as to the deceptive nature of the title page, &c., &c.

These latter remarks are very applicable to the case before us.

The present case is peculiar. It is not the ordinary case of defendant offering an article of merchandise in such a guise as to deceive the public into the belief that it is the production of another. It is the production of a work professing to be a distinct work from that which is the plaintiff's property, or an improved edition thereof. The defendant's work in its title distinctly refers to the previous work by name: "New and improved Head Line Copy Books by S. G. Beatty, author of 'Beatty's Practical Penmanship.'"

It seems to me that it is erroneous to call this a representation that defendant's work is the work which is the property of the plaintiff. It professes to be either a distinct work therefrom, or an improved work preferable thereto. It is as if he said: "I wrote a book called Practical Penmanship, which plaintiff publishes. I now produce a work on the same subject called, 'New and improved Head Line Copy Book.' I offer it to the public as a much better book, and a great improvement on the book I composed for plaintiff."

The plaintiff objects to this on two grounds : first, that defendant cannot lawfully publish any book on the same subject as his book under the well known name of "Beatty," which gives it its chief value. Second, that even if he could do so in producing a substantially different book on that subject, that the book he has put forth is substantially the same book with certain colourable variances and alterations : that, in effect, it is the old book, which is the property of plaintiff, dressed up in a colourable guise to commit a fraud on plaintiff and to destroy his property, purchased by him from defendant.

The learned Judge below (p. 343) says : " The book was put upon the market and furnished to others to be sold by them, and exhibited to the public for sale in such a form and manner as to deceive people into the belief that the one book was the other book." The case does not strike me exactly in this light. It seems to me to be as I have suggested.

He was also of opinion " the preparation of the book was, I think, part of the scheme, and I incline to the opinion that on the merits the so-called novelties and improvements are mere colourable changes."

If the learned Judge was correct in the last opinion, I think the plaintiff was entitled to the interference of the Court.

In that view the form of injunction would probably require to be modified so as to prevent what appears to me to be the true mischief, viz., the issuing of a book professing to be a new and improved work by Beatty on penmanship or on head line copy-books, while substantially the same as the work sold for value to the plaintiff.

As to the alleged differences between the two works, we must consider the subject.

It is not like a legal or scientific treatise on a subject varying with the decisions of judicial authorities or with the increased enlightenment or information of the world. It is on a subject of a *quasi* mechanical nature, and as no new theory as to the means of teaching children to write

is attempted to be broached, nothing is easier than to
make a vast number of apparent changes in words or
expressions, or to lessen the number of books in a course,
&c.

What we have to look at in this branch of the case is,
Is the defendant's work substantially a different work, not
merely in name, or garb, or frame-work, or is it, as the
learned Judge finds, that the changes are merely color-
able ?"

I think he had ample grounds for believing that the
production of the new work was clearly an attempt by
the Publishing Company and defendant Beatty to get over
the supposed legal difficulty, and issue a book in Beatty's
name, which would profitably supersede in the market the
valuable work which belonged to the plaintiffs. In this
connection the words of Thesiger, L.J., already cited from
Metzler v. *Wood,* may be referred to.

In dismissing this appeal I wish to guard myself from
deciding a question of very grave importance.

It is this. A man in partnership with another publishes
a valuable work on a legal or scientific subject in his own
name, such as Manual of Scientific Invention, Handbook
of Electricity, The Judicature Acts, Municipal Manual.
Such a work attains popularity and the firm derives much
profit from its publication and it becomes a most valuable
asset. After some time there is a dissolution, the author
retires as here, receiving his share of the agreed on value
of the assets.

After several years the work in question falls behind the
requirements of the time. New facts appear in the investigations of science. Legislative and legal decisions have
materially changed or modified the doctrines and principles
laid down in his treatise.

I am not prepared to express an opinion that he is not
at liberty to publish either a new edition of the old work
under the old name, or under a new name, bringing it
forward to the line or up to the level of the improved
knowledge or culture of the period ; nor can I hold that if

he do so it can only be for the profit and benefit of the old partnership. When such a case arises it must be dealt with on its special facts and merits.

I uphold the decision appealed from on the particular grounds hereinbefore stated.

BURTON, J. A.—I concur in the result, without committing myself to everything which the learned Chief Justice has stated in the able judgment just delivered. I agree that the judgment below should be affirmed.

PATTERSON, J. A., agreed with the view of Burton, J. A.

HAGARTY, C. J. O., intimated that Morrison, J. A., who was unable to be present, although he had not committed his views to writing, had not been able to concur in the result.

Appeal dismissed, with costs [MORRISON, J. A., dissenting].

[The case has since been carried to the Supreme Court.]

CAREY v. THE CITY OF TORONTO.

Sale of lots by plan—Streets and lanes shewn on plan.

The mere fact of the owner of lands selling them in lots according to a plan shewing streets and lanes adjoining the several lots does not bind him to continue such streets and lanes, unless a purchaser is materially inconvenienced by the closing of any of them.

The defendants, the City of Toronto, announced a sale by auction of city lots, the advertisement stating that "lanes run in rear of the several lots." A plan of the land shewing the streets and lanes was exhibited at the sale, and was incorporated in the contracts of purchase. At such sale the plaintiff purchased a lot situate on the north side of Baldwin street, which lot abutted on a lane running from east to west; a lane also ran in rear of other lots situate on Huron street, all of which were bought by the defendant M., such lane joining at right angles the lane in rear of the plaintiff's lot. The lane in rear of the lots on Huron street was subsequently closed.

Held [reversing the judgment of FERGUSON, J., 7 O. R. 194], that, as the plaintiff had ready access to the streets by the lane on which his lot abutted, he could not prevent the city from closing up other lanes on the property.

THIS was an appeal by the defendant Alexander Macdonell, from a judgment pronounced by Ferguson, J., reported 7 O. R. 194.

The action was brought by Patrick F. Carey against the Corporation of the City of Toronto, and Alexander Macdonell, seeking to have a lane in rear of certain lots on Huron street, Toronto, leased by the defendant corporation to the defendant Macdonell re-opened, it having been closed by Macdonell. The defendants William Henry Bennett, and James Arthur Bennett, were added as parties by order of the Court, they being mortgagees of the plaintiff's leasehold interest in a lot on Baldwin street, Toronto. The plaintiff leased this lot from the City Corporation, and it ran back to a lane running east and west at right angles to the lane which had been closed up, and which the plaintiff sought to have re-opened.

The action was tried before Ferguson, J., at Toronto, on the 1st day of June, 1883.

The judgment was in favour of the plaintiff, ordering the defendant Macdonell to remove the fence across the lane in question within thirty days, and restraining him from in any way closing up the lane; it gave the plaintiff costs against the defendants Macdonell and the City Corporation and the defendants, Bennett, costs against the defendant Macdonell.

The facts are more fully set out in the report of the case in the Court below.

The appeal came on to be heard before this Court on the 2nd day of February, 1885.*

Robinson, Q.C., and *Moss*, Q.C., for the appellant.
S. H. Blake, Q.C., and *Caswell*, for the respondent.

The authorities cited appear in the judgments.

March 10th, 1885. HAGARTY, C. J. O.—The conditions of sale professed to apply to " Property described in advertisements and posters relating to same, dated April 20th, 1881." They contain nothing further bearing on the present matter.

The advertisement announced a sale by auction of three sets of lots, respectively, on Huron street, Cecil street, and Baldwin street, giving the size of each lot.

It is stated below : " Lanes run in rear of the several lots. For further particulars apply at city hall, where plans and diagrams of the several properties can be seen."

The plan in the city hall, and produced at the sale, shewed the three parcels to be sold and the space behind the lots purchased by the defendant MacDonell, as "lane to be opened."

A man who is about to sell a corner of his estate may exhibit a plan of the whole estate, in order to shew the situation of that part which he is about to sell, but is he on that account to have his hands forever tied up from the enjoyment and use of all other parts of the estate ; and is he to preserve it in exactly its present state ?

Per Lord Cottenham, *Squire* v. *Campbell*, 1 My. & Cr. 459.

Peacock v. *Penson*, 11 Beav., 355, is as to the general disposition of the property as shewn on the plan, and as to alterations which might attract an occupancy and population entirely different from that which would have been produced by acting on the plan proposed and held out at the sale.

In *North British R. W. Co.* v. *Tod*, 12 Cl. & F. at p. 731, Lord Cottenham said : " In *Squire* v. *Campbell.* I thought it my duty to review all the cases tha thad occurred * * for the purpose, if possible, of establishing a rule which might be a guide on future occasions when similar cases should occur, and I found that certainly, what had been very much the opinion of the profession in this country, namely, that the parties were bound by the exhibition of such plans, had met with a very wholesome correction by the doctrine laid down by Lord Eldon and Lord Redesdale in the case of *Heriot's Hospital.*"

In *Randall* v. *Hall*, 4 D. & Sm. 343, the Vice-Chancellor, Knight Bruce, held there was no clause in the particulars and conditions of sale providing that any lot was to have rights of way beyond the road adjoining it and leading into the nearest public highway. He could therefore only give him a right of way over the road adjoining the lots he had purchased, and thence by the nearest road to the highway. Sug. V. & P., 25, discusses the subject and cites the cases. Referring to *Fewster* v. *Turner*, 6 Jur. 144, he says, " An accurate plan does not amount to more than a view of the property, as said by the Vice-Chancellor."

But in that case easements were claimed over other lots marked on the plan, and, as said in the Vendors and Purchasers, " The case is open to observation." He adds, " it proves that a man should expressly stipulate for the easement exhibited on the face of a plan as enjoyed with property he proposes to purchase."

If this had been a case in which the vendors were seeking to compel the plaintiff to accept a conveyance by which he would lose the benefit of this lane opposite to the lot

he had purchased, I think he would probably have successfully insisted on proof of what took place at the sale,
and proof of his purchase in reliance on the plan, and of
having the use of such a lane and its importance and value
to him. Such cases as *Beaumont* v. *Dukes,* Jacob 422.

Myers v. *Watson,* 1 Sim. N. S., 523, is a very important
case.

In 1 Dart. 121; " So on a sale or lease of building ground
the exhibition on the plan of intended roads and other
improvements on adjacent land, does not bind the vendor
or lessor to make or extend such road or improvement, nor
entitle the purchaser or lessee to a grant of a right of way
over any road so laid down on the plan, except such as
form the direct means of communication with the nearest
highway," citing *Randall* v. *Ball,* and adding in a note to
it: " But *quœre* whether the vendor refusing to grant a
right of way at any rate over such road as might eventually be made could enforce specific performance."

Mr. Dart then notices the decision in *Peacock* v. *Penson,*
already mentioned in this judgment. At p. 120 he says,
" When a plan of an estate is attached to or accompanies the
particulars and is incorrect, it will be a material consideration with the Court of Equity whether the purchaser was
thereby misled ; but if accurate, it is merely tantamount
to a view of the property."

Fry, 408, may be also referred to. He states the effect
of the decisions. He notices *Nurse* v. *Lord Seymour,* 13
Beav. 254. " Where a plan was referred to in the contract,
and used as a description of the property in question, and
on this plan the measurement and width of the street were
marked, but there was nothing in the contract which
distinctly pointed to that part of the plan as binding the
parties, Lord Langdale held that it did not form part of
the contract so as to entitle one party to relief against an
encroachment on the width of the street."

I notice a remark of Kelly, C. B., in *Espley* v. *Wilkes,* L.
R. 7 Ex. 298: " It is expressed in the lease that there
were to be streets then made, or afterwards to be made,

and though it is possible that a covenant might be implied that new streets should then be made, there is nothing in the lease to bind the lessor to make them public streets, or to dedicate them to the public, and it was competent for him to make them into private streets for the use only of the lessees of the houses to be built upon the land demised."

I notice this in connection with the argument that the lanes marked on the plan here were only intended as for the use of the lots abutting on them and not as public highways.

In this connection we may notice in Mr. Justice Gwynne's judgment in *Rowe* v. *Sinclair*, 26 C. P. at p. 244, that "street" is synonymous with a public way or road in a town or city, a main way, in distinction from a lane or alley, citing the Imperial Dictionary.

In two cases cited, *Rossin* v. *Walker*, 6 Gr. 619 and *Cheney* v. *Cameron*, Ib. 623, in which language is imputed to the learned Judges as favourable to the plaintiff's contention, the facts of the cases as reported do not require for their decision language so wide as is reported to have been used by Esten, V. C.

No map or sketch in the principal case is given, but as far as I can understand the statement it does not present a state of facts resembling those now before us.

The learned Vice Chancellor says : " We have decided in this Court that when a map or plan is exhibited as a particular of sale, presenting on its face roads, streets, squares, and other advantages and attractions, and purchases are made according to and on the faith of it, he cannot afterwards divert the ground appropriated to such use to other purposes, although he may not be bound to make or construct all the roads, streets, and squares, and other things of the same sort which the map exhibits." This may be quite correct up to the circumstances of the decision in *Peacock* v. *Penson*, 11 Beav. 361, already noticed, and at the same time be inapplicable to the case for judgment.

We have had cases such as *Regina* v. *Rubidge*, 25 U.
C. R. 302, decided on our registry law. But the case before
us must, I think, be decided without reference to them.
The plaintiff's claim rests wholly on contract.

When the contract of purchase was made, there was no
registered plan in existence The first registration was
three months later, and the plan then placed on record did
not shew the lane in question, which had then been conveyed to the defendant MacDonnell as part of the lots
leased to him.

The only use of a reference to the Statutes would be
perhaps to shew the view of the Legislature in the earlier
Act, permitting the owner, after registration, to have a new
survey made, and the former plan partially cancelled,
subject to the proviso, that no part of any street would be
altered or closed, on which any lot of land sold in the
original division abutted, or which connected any such
sold lot with, or afforded means of access therefrom to the
nearest public highway.

In the Revised Ontario Registry Act, cap. 111, following
31 Vict., cap. 20, sec. 77 ; 39 Vict., cap. 25, sec. 4, it is declared that the registered plan shall not be binding unless
a "sale has been made according to such plan or survey,"
and in all cases amendments may be ordered at the
instance of the person registering, by order of one of the
courts, &c., on hearing the parties.

In the Revised Ontario, ch. 146, the Surveyors' Act, it is
declared that the owner may cancel and alter, with the
proviso, that no part of any street or streets shall be
altered or closed on which any lot sold abuts, or which
connects any such lot sold, with the nearest public highway,
24 Vict., cap. 49, sec. 1.

This idea or principle in the Statutes seems to me to
indicate the true *ratio decidendi* in a case like the present.
The provision in the existing Registry Act, allowing an
alteration by the Court or Judge, after hearing the parties
on terms, seems to clash with the principle here insisted on
by the plaintiff, viz., that, by his contract of purchase he
is enabled as of right, to preserve the plan intact.

If the plaintiff's argument be sound, his equity to have this lane preserved will apply to all the leaseholders of the lots exhibited on the plan.

The plaintiff is at the south-east corner of the block on the plan. The leaseholder at the north-west angle on Cecil and Huron streets must have also a like equity as to this lane. If the rule be sound it must apply equally to a plan of lots on a block of an acre, and to a plan of lots on a block of 30 or 50 acres, and once the principle of confining the right to streets or lanes abutting on the lot sold, or affording to it access to the nearest highway is abandoned, I see no way of escaping from holding that every purchaser of a small lot at the farthest point of the plan has an equity to insist on a rigid non-interference by the owner with every street and lane shewn thereon.

On the argument I was impressed by the idea that a plan used as here could not be altered. An examination of the authorities forces me to a different conclusion.

I think the plaintiff's right is confined to the maintenance of the lane in rear, on which his lot abuts.

There is much force in the view taken by some of my learned Brothers, that the plaintiff has materially affected his position by the course he has taken in accepting his conveyance.

He has accepted a lease, dated 19th May, 1882, and this lease describes the property as " Lot No. 10, on north side of Baldwin street, according to registered plans Nos. 352 and 380." When he took the lease the estate in this lane had been vested for the term in MacDonell nine months previously, and in accordance with a registered plan not shewing the lane claimed.

It is not easy to understand the course taken by the corporation, except on the ground that it is a corporation, in registering another plan on the same day they execute the lease to the plaintiff, again shewing the lane, as a lane " to be opened," accompanied by the curious declaration that the plan shewed the manner in which they had "dedicated and set apart the rear 20 feet of lots 11 to 15 inclusive, for the purposes of a public lane."

It is to be presumed that this very original method of dedication must have been made under oblivion of the fact that the city had already vested this portion of land in the defendant MacDonell for a long term, and that it was then fenced in as part of his land.

Perhaps it was meant as a promise, that whenever the land re-vested in the city they would so dedicate.

As is said in the authorities, if a purchaser desire to insure his obtaining the benefit of streets or roads shewn on the plan, but not abutting on his parcel, he ought to insist on a contract to that effect.

I think the appeal must be allowed, and the action dismissed, with costs; no costs of appeal to either party.

BURTON, J. A.—The complaint is in effect in the nature of an action for the specific performance of a contract alleged to have been entered into by the defendants, the city of Toronto, with the plaintiff, and of which the defendant MacDonell had notice, and two questions arise: one whether the plaintiff has established any such contract as alleged, and if so, whether, by taking a lease, as he has done, he has now placed it out of his power to claim any other or higher rights than are granted to him by the lease?

First, then, as regards the original contract of purchase:

The lot in question, with others, was, on the 18th May, 1881, offered for sale by the proprietors, the city of Toronto at public auction.

An advertisement of the sale had been previously posted and circulated through the city, that these lots would then be put up for sale, and in referring to the particulars of the advantages to accrue to purchasers, after describing the lots by numbers, as shewn upon the plan, it is stated that the sizes of the lots, above given, are to be read as being according to said measurements, "more or less," followed by these words: "*Lanes run in rear of the several Lots.*"   A plan or diagram was exhibited at the time of the sale, and the purchaser was required to sign a memorandum of purchase at the foot of the conditions of sale, which referred to that plan in these words:

" I hereby agree to purchase the property described in the plan hereto annexed, and marked A, as lot No   , on the   side of   Street, subject to foregoing conditions of sale, for the sum of   per foot frontage on   Street,"

There is nothing material to the present question in the conditions of sale, and the inquiry resolves itself into what was meant by the the contract, which undoubtedly embodies in it by reference, the plan which was produced at the sale.

That plan shewed lanes in rear of all the lots intended to be sold, but in this particular block they formed, in fact, one continuous lane running from Huron street in rear of the lots on Baldwin street, the full depth of the block.   Thence northerly, in rear of the lots on Cecil street, to Huron street.

The defendant MacDonell purchased all the lots between the two side lanes fronting on Huron street, and the plaintiff Carey purchased lot 10 the extreme easterly lot on Baldwin street, facing the lane in rear of MacDonell's lots, though this is, in my opinion, of no importance, as if he has a right to claim, as he is doing in this action, it was a right common to all the other purchasers in that block, and possibly, if the plaintiff's contention be carried to its full extent, common to all purchasers of any lots shewn on the plan.

The defendant MacDonell having no necessity for the lane in rear of his lots, and fearing that it would, in fact, be a nuisance to him, applied to the city for permission to close it very shortly after his purchase, and it would appear that, probably, in consequence of some doubts having been expressed as to the power of the city to do so, he, a few days subsequently, wrote a letter offering to indemnify them against any claims which might be made by other lessees.

Accordingly, on the 9th June, 1881, the city prepared and registered a plan of the property, in accordance with the provisions of the Registry Act, extending the lots, pur-chased by MacDonell, to the rear of the block; but in order to reduce to a minimum the inconvenience to the purchasers of other lots, the city reserved from the lease an additional four feet in rear, making the side lane therefore in rear 25 feet wide, to the depth of 20 feet, and upon this plan so registered, the lease to MacDonell and all the others with the exception of that to the plaintiff and another, were granted.

Some months after the granting of the lease to MacDonell, although he had apparently objected, from time to time, to the Solicitor, Carey made his first formal remonstrance to the city authorities against the lane being closed, and the publication of this protest in the newspapers led to Mr. MacDonell's writing to the Council, and to an investigation before the Property Committee of the Council, which led to their giving instructions for the preparation of a new plan professing to dedicate the rear 20 feet of the lots in question, for the purpose of a public lane' which plan they caused to be registered in the Registry Office as plan No. 380; a more useless and illusory proceeding it is almost impossible to conceive.

But this is the way in which a committee of the Council proposed to correct the action of the corporate body, in making and registering a plan, and granting leases in accordance with it.

It may be that under the terms of the contract with the plaintiff he may have been entitled to enforce the opening of the lane both against the city and MacDonnell, but it is manifest that as between the city and MacDonnell, to whom they had made a lease of this property, this attempt by the committee or the council itself was as nugatory as it was ill advised.

The defendant MacDonell then sent in a formal petition to the Council, reciting the facts and intimating his inten-tion to make an application to a Judge to make an alteration in the plan filed, and asking to use the name of the corporation if necessary for the purpose.

This action was, however, instituted before any action was taken upon the petition, and it was after the bringing of this action that the defendant MacDonell gave a bond to the city, with the double object of indemnifying them against the costs of such an application to change the plan and the expenses of the action.

The Court below has made a decree against the city, and the defendant MacDonell, ordering the lane to be opened, and the appeal is against that decision.

Apart from the consideration that the contract at the time of the commencement of this action was no longer executory, as to which I have something presently to say, the first question is, what was the contract upon which the plaintiff is entitled now to call for the interposition of a court of justice ?

I think that the true construction of the contract read with the plan is, that there are and were intended to be lanes in rear of each of the lots which it was proposed to sell, and that it did not oblige the city to keep open lanes shewn upon the plan not answering the description. If, for instance, the lots on Baldwin street alone had been sold, I do not think that the city would have precluded itself from selling the remainder of the property in one lot, leaving, of course, a lane 20 feet wide in rear of the Baldwin street lots.

I do not think the plaintiff's case can be carried any further than if the lot had been described as lot number ten, together with the use of the lane in rear thereof, as shewn by a certain plan, the plan could then have been referred to as shewing the dimensions of the lot and the width of the lane; but would not have conferred upon the grantee the use of other lanes shewn upon the plan.

There is nothing in the particulars or conditions of sale providing that the purchaser of any lot shall have any rights of way except over the lane immediately in the rear of it, and the plan is only of importance as defining the position and dimensions of the lots and showing these lanes, and did not, in my opinion, impose upon the vendor the obligation to make good the whole of that plan to the purchasers.

But assuming that the plaintiff could have filed a bill whilst the contract was still executory, can he do so when that contract, whatever it was, has been carried into execution by the lease itself, which contradicts what is alleged by the plaintiff to have been the agreement? The lease describes the land demised as lot 10, according to a certain plan which shews no lane in rear of the lots leased to MacDonell; it is true it refers to another plan and professes to give whatever rights the Corporation could transfer under it, but it is clear that the attempt as they describe it to dedicate to the public a portion of the defendant MacDonell's property was *ultra vires*, they could not thus derogate from their own grant, and nothing under the lease to the plaintiff passed so far as this lane was concerned.

It is not alleged that by mistake or fraud one of the terms of the original agreement was omitted from the lease. On the contrary, it was well-known to both the contracting parties that a lease had been granted to MacDonell of what had at one time been intended to be kept open as a lane, and the plaintiff, instead of taking the ground that the corporation had no power to divert it from the original purpose, and filing a bill to have his contract carried out according to his construction of it, takes a lease under the very plan which shews the alteration, and now wishes the Court to read the instrument as if an additional term had been inserted, on the ground that such additional term formed part of the original agreement, which cannot be done unless fraud or mistake be shewn as a ground for reformation.

The contract for the lease no longer exists. The plaintiff has chosen to accept as a fulfilment of the contract a lease according to plan 352. And a further provision in lieu of what he originally contracted for under plan 380. In other words, he accepts the easement which the corporation profess to have the power to grant under the so called dedication of part of the defendant MacDonell's land without by-law or compensation.

There is nothing, so far as has been disclosed in this case, which would have warranted the corporation in applying to set aside or reform the lease to MacDonell, as having been obtained by fraud, mistake or misrepresentation, some of the members of the corporation seem to have disapproved of it, and they had sufficient influence to induce the Council to stultify itself by attempting to dedicate land it no longer owned, and to grant the right to use that land to the plaintiff. I think that nothing passed by that grant, and the plaintiff having, as he admits, taken his lease not by means of any deception practised upon him, but because he desired to raise money on it, cannot now fall back upon the original contract which was merged in the deed.

In *Palmer* v. *Johnson*, and cases of that kind, the acceptance of a conveyance does not bar the vendee's right to sue for a breach of an express agreement in the contract for sale, whereby compensation was to be granted in case of deficiency or variation between the premises mentioned in the particulars and conditions of sale and those conveyed. The taking the conveyance leaves that collateral and independent contract untouched. The taking the deed does not cover the whole ground of the preliminary contract.

But in a case like the present, where there is an executory contract which is to be carried out by deed afterwards executed, the real completed contract between the parties is to be found in the deed, and you have no right whatever to look at the contract though recited in the deed, except for the purpose of construing the deed itself, as said by Lord Justice James, in *Leggatt* v. *Barrell*, 15 Ch., D. 309 : "You have no right to look at the contract, either for the purpose of enlarging or diminishing, or modifying the contract which is to be found in the deed itself."

I agree with the learned Judge below, and indeed it is a self-evident fact that it would be a material advantage not only to the owner of lot 10, but to the owner of all the lots on Baldwin street, to have the lane continued through behind the defendant's lots ; but that is not the question we have to deal with, which is simply what was the contract between the parties and what are the rights of the plaintiff after accepting a deed as in fulfillment of the contract.

For the reasons I have endeavoured to explain, I think the plaintiff not entitled to recover, and I think it is to be regretted that after the pecuniary compensation offered, and the expression of willingness on the part of MacDonell to make even greater concessions in the way of widening the lane, the plaintiff should have embarked in this unneighborly and expensive litigation. I think that the appeal should be allowed and, perhaps, for the reasons stated by the Chief Justice, without costs, although I see no sufficient grounds for departing from our usual practice, and the action should be dismissed, with costs of the defendant MacDonell, who ought also to be relieved from the payment of the costs to the Messrs. Bennett, which should be paid by the plaintiff.

The corporation of the city of Toronto have contributed more than their quota to this unfortunate litigation, and should receive no costs.

PATTERSON, J. A.—I have no doubt that the plaintiff ought to fail in this action, and that this appeal should be allowed.

The question is, what was his contract with the city ? And I answer that his contract was to lease a lot running from Baldwin street to a lane.

The error which, in my opinion, influenced the judgment appealed from, arose chiefly from attaching too much significance to the exhibition of the plan or sketch of the proposed division of the " Bowes property," which was exhibited at the auction.

The advertisement stated that "lanes run in rear of the several lots."

It also referred intending bidders for further particulars to "the City Hall, where plans and diagrams of the several properties can be seen," but this did not point specially to lanes, nor was notice concerning the use of the lanes left to depend on what might appear on those plans or diagrams. There was the separate intimation, "lanes run in rear of the several lots."

The advertisement referred to many lots, and the plan or diagram shewed twenty-five lots on the east side of Huron street, laid out in three tiers, and nine lots on the west side of Huron street, laid out in two tiers, besides some other lots. These diagrams corresponded with the terms of the advertisement, by shewing a lane at the rear of each of the lots affording access to and from public streets, the lanes in rear of the thirty-four Huron street lots leading to that street; but the notice, to those who read it was distinctly that what was offered was a number of lots, each of which ran from a street to a lane.

The plaintiff has a lane from the rear of his lot to Huron street, and there is evidence which accords with knowledge common to most people who know the city, and shews that on the score of width and convenience, he has nothing to complain of, but that the lane compares very favourably with most lanes in the city.

Unless there is something to give a legal right to every lessee of one of the lots to have all the lanes shewn on the diagram kept open, merely because they were shewn on the same paper on which his lot and the lane in rear of it were delineated, I can perceive no foundation for his claim. He has, to use the language of Knight Bruce, V. C., in *Randall* v. *Hall*, 4 Deg. & S., 343, the right of way over the road (lane) adjoining the lot he has purchased, and thence by the nearest road to the highway.

"It was perfectly wild," Lord Eldon remarked in *Feoffees of Heriot's Hospital* v. *Gibson*, 2 Dow, 301, "to say that the mere exhibition of a plan was sufficient to form a binding

contract." Other cases cited to us contain strong authority
against giving the plan greater effect than as one of the
factors from which the contract is to be deduced, e. g., the
language of Lord Cottenham, in *Squire v. Campbell*, 1 My.
& Cr., 459, and again in *North British Railway v. Tod*,
12 Cl. & F., 752, and of Lord Langdale, in *Nurse v. Lord
Seymour*, 13 Beav., 270.

On the footing of the contract as it stood immediately
after the plaintiff signed the memorandum at the foot of
the conditions of sale, on 18th May, 1881, I think he has
all he bargained for, which was "the property described in
the plan hereto annexed and marked A, as lot No. 10, on
the north side of Baldwin street," and he has the easement
of a way by a lane which is shewn on that plan.

That plan was not then and never was registered. The
contract is therefore unaffected by any statutory provision
concerning the registration of plans

When, a year later, the plaintiff took his lease from the
corporation, the lot was described as lot 10, according to
the registered plans numbers 352 and 380.

These two plans had, in the meantime, been prepared
and registered by the city corporation, the earlier one at
the instance of the defendant MacDonell, and the later one
at the instance of the plaintiff. No. 352 shewed the lanes
which are now actually on the ground, and shewed the lots
11 to 15, which are those leased to MacDonell, including in
them the space which the plaintiff now claims to have
opened as a lane.

No. 380 is said by the plaintiff in his evidence to be
identical with the plan exhibited at the auction; but it
really differs materially from that plan, if I correctly
understand what it was. The difference is not so much in
the tracing of the lots and lanes, though in that respect it
does differ where it cuts off a corner of each of MacDonell's
lots, 11 and 15, instead of leaving the side lines of those
lots of equal length, as in the character given to the lanes
This plan 380 is certified, under the common seal of the
city, by the Mayor and Treasurer, to represent correctly

the manner in which they have "dedicated and set apart the rear 20 feet of lots 11 to 15 inclusive, for the purposes of a public lane."

The corporation of the city, like any other owner of land, could of course dedicate part of it to the public, and I suppose section 67 of the Surveyors' Act (R. S. O., ch. 146), applies to a lane so dedicated, and makes it a public highway, not merely a private road over which the occupants of certain lots have a right of way.

But it is plain that the corporation, having leased lots 11 to 15 inclusive to Mr. MacDonell, could not dedicate any part of those lots to the public in derogation from his title.

Therefore the words "lane to be opened," which on this plan are written upon the twenty feet strip, must refer to an intention to open it at some future time, when Mr. MacDonell's term shall have expired or been determined.

This dedication of the lane was the sole purpose of the registration of plan 380, as appears from the certificate, and from the recognition of plan 352 which is involved in the reference to lots 11 to 15, which, as laid down on that plan, extended back to the boundary line of the city's property.

By section 82, sub-sec. 2 of the Registry Act (R. S. O., ch. 111), all instruments affecting the land shewn on plan 352, executed as the plaintiff's lease was after the filing of that plan, were to conform thereto, and the Registrar was to keep an index of those lots by the numbers shewn on the plan.

The reference in the plaintiff's lease to plan 380 cannot have had any effect as descriptive of the lot, which was fully described by the reference to plan 352, and operated merely as an express intimation to him that he would have the benefit of the dedication of the 20 feet as soon as Mr. MacDonell's term was at an end.

It therefore does not aid him at present.

OSLER, J. A.—The defendants, the City of Toronto, offered for sale by public auction, leaseholds of certain building lots as described upon a plan of the property which they had caused to be prepared for the purpose of the sale.

These lots were laid out in three ranges ; a range of ten lots fronting on the north side of Baldwin street, with a lane shewn in the rear, 20 feet wide, running from the east side of Huron street ; another range of ten, fronting on the south side of Cecil street, with a lane shewn in the rear, 20 feet wide, running from the east side of Huron street ; and, between the lanes in rear of the other ranges, a third range of five lots, fronting on the east side of Huron street, also with a lane in the rear, 20 feet in width, which lane was connected at each end thereof, with the other two, so that upon the plan it appeared as a continuous lane round the three sides of the centre range.

At the auction, the defendant MacDonell became the purchaser of the five lots fronting on Huron street, and the plaintiff of lot No. 10 on Baldwin street, this lot being on a line with the lane in the rear of the defendant's lots.

Subsequently, the defendant MacDonell in good faith, and conceiving that he, as purchaser, of the five lots, was the only person interested in the lane in rear thereof, and not desiring to have such a lane opened, procured the officers of the corporation to prepare and register a plan of the whole block without such lane, which was then taken into and formed part of his lots.

On this plan, which was registered on the 9th June, 1881, as No. 352, the ends of the lanes at the rear of the other ranges were made 25 feet in width and a small triangular piece taken off the lower end of the defendant MacDonell's lots, which adjoined these lanes, for the convenience of turning carts, &c.

The lease to MacDonell was executed on the 14th June, 1881, the lots being described as situated on the east side of Huron street, according to registered plan, No. 352.

At the time when all this was done, as the learned Judge by whom the case was tried has found, the defendant MacDonell " had full notice and knowledge of the plaintiff's purchase, the terms of it, his contentions and his rights, whatever they were."

The plaintiff was not a party and had not in any way assented to the alteration of the plan. He refused to accept a lease in accordance with it, insisting upon his alleged right to have the lane opened in rear of the defendant's lots.

After some time, and when he had threatened to enforce this right by litigation, the property committee of the Council caused a new plan of the block to be prepared, corresponding with that which had been produced at the sale, except that it shews the corners of the defendant MacDonell's two lots taken into the lane as on plan 352. The plan is certified by the mayor and treasurer of the corporation, under the city seal, as follows: "We hereby certify that this plan represents correctly the manner in which we have dedicated and set apart the rear 20 feet of lots 11 to 15, inclusive, for the purpose of a public lane."

It was registered on the 19th May, 1882, and the plaintiff's lease was completed on the same day, the lot being described therein as lot No. 10, on the north side of Baldwin street, according to registered plans, 352 and 380.

Both leases are perpetually renewable for terms of 21 years.

The lane in question, having been fenced in and kept closed by the defendant MacDonell, this action was brought, and the substantial relief claimed, is that the lane may be opened up and maintained, as shewn on the plan by which the lots were sold, and on plan 380.

It was argued in this Court, though not, I think, with much confidence, that the plaintiff was estopped by having taken his lease, describing the lot by reference to the two plans, 352 and 380, but assuming for the present that he was entitled by his contract, or by the general law to the right he claims in respect of the lane in the rear of Mac-Donell's lots, I am obliged, with great respect, to say that I cannot think he has done anything to waive it or to estop himself from asserting it. His case is, that as be-

tween himself and the defendants, he could have compelled
the city to execute a lease in accordance with their contract, and that nothing that was done by them at the instance of their co-defendant would have affected that right;
that the city have done no more than they were bound to
do in giving him his lease according to a plan which
shews a lane in rear of MacDonell's lots, and that having
got what he contracted for, the defendants ought to be restrained from obstructing the lane. His action is not, as I
understand the pleadings, in any sense for specific performance of his contract or rectification of the lease ; it is
in assertion of the alleged right acquired under it, a right
unaffected by anything attempted to be done by the defendants in derogation of it.

His contention, in short, is, that he had the right, by his
contract, substantially to what the defendants have professed to convey to him by the lease, and it is only if that
contention is wrong in point of law that he can be affected
by plan 352.

The first inquiry therefore is, what were the terms of
the contract ? They are found in the advertisement, the
plan, the conditions of sale, and the memorandum signed
by the purchasers.

The latter is as follows : " I hereby agree to lease the
property described in the plan hereto annexed, and marked
A, as lot No. 10, on the north side of Baldwin street, subject to foregoing conditions of sale, for the sum of $1.30
per foot frontage, per annum, on Baldwin street."

The conditions of sale are entitled " conditions of sale,
leasehold interest in property, described in advertisements
and posters relating to the same, dated 20th April, 1881."
The only condition necessary to refer to is the first.

" A leasehold interest for the term of twenty-one years,
renewable at a valuation upon the usual terms contained
in city leases (a form of which is produced,) is offered for
sale, and all bids shall be at a frontage rate per foot, per
annum, upon the lots offered as the same appear upon the
plan or survey produced."

The material parts of the advertisement are the following, so far as relates to the lots purchased by the plaintiff and the defendant, MacDonell.

" Leases will be offered for twenty-one years, renewable, of the following valuable lots, owned by the City of Toronto, and situate as under, that is to say :
"Huron street (between Cecil and Baldwin streets.)

No. on Plan.	Size.
1 Lot........11..........21 ft. 8 in. x 194 ft. 6 in.	
4 Lots ......12 to 15 ....Each 21 ft. 9 in. x 194 ft. 6 in.	

Situation.	Reserve per Foot.
East side of Huron Street......................$1 00	
Do. Do. 1 00	

Baldwin street (running east from corner of Huron street.)

9 Lots.....2 to 10....   Each 21 ft. x 120 ft....
North side of Baldwin street, East of No. 1....$1 25

The above properties will be virtually equivalent to freeholds.

Lanes run in rear of the several lots.

For further particulars, apply at the City Hall, *where plans and diagrams of the several properties can be seen.*"

The next question is, whether the plaintiff under this contract aquired any right to or interest in any lane shewn upon the plan other than the one in the rear of the range of lots on Baldwin street ?

The plan is, by reference, unquestionably incorporated into the contract to some extent, and if the case was to be determined by considerations of convenience, or of the inducements which probably operated upon intending purchasers of lots as laid out on this plan, it cannot be denied that the right contended for is of great importance to the plaintiff, and if the defendants were at liberty to refuse it, I have very little doubt that they could not have forced the purchase upon him : *Myers* v. *Watson,* 1 Sim. N. S., 523.

That, however, is not the question here.

In the *North British R. W. Co.* v. *Tod,* 12 Cl. & F., 730, Lord Cottenham says : " If a contract or an Act of Parliament refer to a plan, to the extent that the Act (or contract) refers to the plan, and for the purpose for which the Act or contract refers to the plan, undoubtedly it is part of the contract, or part of the Act ; about that, there is no dispute. A contract or an Act of Parliament either does not refer to the plan at all, or it refers to it for a particular purpose."

In the case before us, each of the ranges of lots on the plan exhibited by the vendors, fronted upon one of the public streets or highways of the city, and the object was to give access to the same, or another highway from the rear of such lots. This object would be accomplished in the case of the ranges on Baldwin and Cecil streets, by a lane along the rear opening into Huron street, and that is what is expressly stated in the advertisement and shewn on the plan, and, consequently, in the contract which embraces them.

In view of the cases of *Randall* v. *Hall*, 4 D. G. & S. 343 ; *Feoffees of Heriot's Hospital* v. *Gibson*, 2 Dow. 301, and *Squire* v. *Campbell*, 1 My. & Cr. 459, there is, I must own, great difficulty in holding that as regards the purchasers of lots on Baldwin and Cecil streets, the reference to the plan conferred anything more than the right to a lane in the rear of the range on which the lot was situated, or that it can be treated as incorporated in the contract to any greater extent or for any other purpose than to identify the lots, and shew the lane in the rear of each.

Having regard to the principle which the authorities I referred to seem to establish, though the facts to which it was applied, are not in any of them on all fours with those in the present case, the rule would appear to be too broadly laid down in the cases in the 6th vol. of Mr. Grant's Reports. With those cases, however, before him, both of them decisions of the full Court, I think my Brother Ferguson could not have decided otherwise than he did, and I must add that I have felt a doubt which is not entirely removed, partly as to whether we are giving due effect to sect. 84 of the Registry Act, R. S. O., ch. 111, which seems to recognize the law as laid down in those authorities, and enacts that in no case shall a plan or survey, *though filed and registered*, be binding on the persons filing or registering it unless a sale has been made according to such plan ; and partly upon the question of the contract, having regard to the scheme of the survey and sale of the lots, and the fact that the lane shewn upon the plan is a continuous one in rear of the three ranges entering from and returning upon the same street, and that the purchaser of any lot on the Baldwin and Cecil street ranges, would see by the plan that a purchaser of a lot on the Huron street range (all being put up and offered for sale on the same occasion), would probably be entitled as a matter of necessity to have the whole kept open.

The same necessity cannot, however, be said to exist in the case of purchasers of lots on the former ranges. Each sale was distinct, and as regards sec. 84 of the Registry Act, it has been expressly held in this Court in the case of *Morton* v. *St. Thomas*, 6 App. R. 323, that it was not intended by the Registry Act, either to alter the relative rights of vendor and purchaser, or to confer any additional or other right upon the public than they would have had under a sale made in accordance with an unregistered map or plan.

I am compelled to concur in allowing the appeal. I cannot help saying I do so with regret, as I think the plaintiff has not been well used by the city, and that in entering upon this litigation he was doing no more than most people would have supposed they were justified in doing, to assert a valuable right believed to have been acquired.

WANSLEY V. SMALLWOOD.

Appeal for costs—Disclaimer—Practice.

J., one of the defendants, had bid for and had became purchaser of a lot of land sold, under the provisions of the R. S. O. ch. 216, by certain parties claiming to be trustees of the Colored Wesleyan Methodist Church, whose. proceedings in respect of such attempted sale were impeached in the action to which J. was made a party defendant, although he avowed his willingness to withdraw from the purchase, and by his answer disclaimed all interest in the result of the suit, and alleged that no effort had been made by him to have the sale carried out, as he was aware that the same would have to be first confirmed by the members of the said church. At the trial judgment was pronounced setting aside the sale, and ordering the defendants generally to pay costs.

Held, [varying the judgment of the Court below], that under the circumstances a formal disclaimer was not required, and J. was ordered to be paid his costs of the appeal, but the action in the Court below was dismissed as against him, without costs.

Per OSLER, J. A.—The rule as to an appeal on the question of costs appears to be this, that if in making the order complained of there has been any violation of principle, or the Court has proceeded on a wrong general rule, or if the discretion of the Court has been exercised upon any misapprehension of fact, a Court of Appeal will interfere but not otherwise.

THIS action was instituted in the Court below by Francis Wansley and William Turner, sole surviving trustees of the property therein referred to, on behalf of themselves and all other members of the Coloured Wesleyan Methodist Church in Toronto who should contribute to the expenses of the action, against Thomas Smallwood (since deceased), Richard Wallace, William Thomas, and George Jackson.

The statement of claim set forth, amongst other things, that on the 7th day of July, 1838, a religious congregation or society of coloured Methodists, in the city of Toronto, purchased the property therein referred to, and thereupon took a deed thereof in the words following: (The deed set out was dated 9th July, 1838, and was a conveyance under the 9 Geo. IV. ch. 2, of a parcel of land containing one-tenth of an acre, in the city of Toronto, to Wilson R. Abbott and four other trustees appointed under the statute by a religious congregation of Methodists, and conveyed the land to them as such trustees by the name of "The Trustees of the Coloured Wesleyan Methodist Church in

Canada Chapel and Burying Ground in the City of Toronto," to hold to the said trustees and their successors forever, for the site of a chapel, &c., for the use of the Coloured Wesleyan Methodist Church in Canada.)

The statement of claim further stated: that the defendants other than Jackson made some agreement among themselves to sell the property, and in January, 1883, advertised it for sale by auction, without any right whatever, and on the 14th of February sold it by auction to Jackson: that a meeting was called by the plaintiffs when they heard of the proposed sale, Jackson not having been let into possession, nor having paid any purchase money; and at a meeting held on the 22nd of the said month of February, it was resolved by the members of the said congregation not to sell the property: and the plaintiffs submitted that the proposed sale was entirely unwarranted and illegal, and should be set aside, and prayed relief accordingly.

The defendants, other than Jackson, filed a statement of defence which is not material here.

The defendant Jackson filed a separate statement of defence, setting up as stated in the judgment that he had not any interest in the suit.

The motion on further directions came on before Proudfoot, J., on the 6th day of February, 1884, when the plaintiffs were declared to be the sole trustees of the property in question, and the surviving defendants were ordered to pay to the plaintiffs their costs of the action.

Jackson thereupon appealed to this Court, and the appeal came on to be heard on the 19th of March, 1885.[*]

S. Richards, Q.C., and *Caswell*, for the appellant. It is true that Rule No. 428, O. J. A. provides that costs shall be in the discretion of the Court, and sec. 32 provides that no order as to costs only, which by law are left to the discretion of the Court, shall be subject to appeal, except by leave of the Judge, which had been refused, still we contend

[*] *Present.*—HAGARTY, C.J.O., BURTON, PATTERSON, and OSLER, JJ.A.

that the case is appealable under sec. 37. Sec. 32 does not prevent an appeal in cases where the decision has been upon a question of principle, and not of discretion. Here it is shewn that the appellant never had claimed to have any interest in the property, and consequently he was not a necessary party to the suit. At the time of the alleged sale by auction at which Jackson bid, the power to sell such property was governed by R. S. O. ch. 216.

It is nowhere stated or shewn that the assent of the congregation, or the sanction or approval of the County Court Judge had been obtained, as required by the Act or had even been applied for.

The statement of claim calls it merely a "proposed sale," and the plaintiffs allege that the congregation had refused assent to the sale, and that Jackson had never been let into possession, nor had he paid any purchase money, and that the other defendants had not been able to get him to carry out the purchase.

The appellant never had or acquired any interest in the property, or any right which he could enforce, and he was unnecessarily made a defendant; and the well established rule is that a party unnecessarily made a defendant is entitled to his costs: *Morgan* on Costs, 2nd ed. 118.

Jackson's statement of defence is to all intents a disclaimer. A disclaiming defendant, if brought to a hearing, is entitled to be dismissed, with or without costs, according to the form and extent of his disclaimer: *Morgan* on Costs, 2nd ed. 115. A disclaimer of all interest "in the matters in question in the suit," or "in the object of the suit," or "in the result of the suit," is in effect the same in each case, and is in each case a sufficient disclaimer.

The appellant, in his statement of defence, in effect says that he does not claim anything adversely to either party, that is, to the plaintiffs or the other defendants, and submits to the Court making such order as it thinks fit. The case is not unlike *Moet* v. *Pickering*, 8 Ch. D.

372, where the Court held the defendant entitled to his costs.

Here the appellant is not shewn to have done any act whatever further than bidding for the property at a public auction sale; and no act whatever is shewn which would give a Judge any discretion to order him to pay the plaintiffs' costs, and, according to the rules and principles by which Courts are governed in deciding as to costs, the action should have been dismissed as against the appellant; with or without costs. On the whole facts appearing in this case, Jackson should have been ordered to receive his costs.

Walter Read, for the respondents. The judgment appealed from is right. The question of costs was one in the discretion of the Court, and hence no appeal lies without leave. The giving of costs was, and seems to be governed by the conduct of the parties in the action.

The appellant was properly ordered to pay costs because, by his conduct and in the answer he had filed, and by appearing at the trial and not asking to be dismissed, but asking a reference and all through the reference contesting the title of the plaintiffs as trustees, he had so wrongly acted that the Court rightly exercised the discretion of ordering him to pay costs, and the exercise of that discretion is not appealable.

The plaintiffs had a right to costs against the appellant. He was a necessary party to the suit, having acquired some right or title to the property by its having been knocked down to him at the sale in question. Had he abandoned the purchase, it might have been that no costs would be given against him: but the only reasonable construction to be put on his defence is, that he claimed whatever right he had acquired at the sale. He did not at any stage of the action ask to be dismissed. On the contrary, he contests it all through. The plaintiffs could not dismiss as against him, he not having abandoned his rights.

The other defendants had a perfect right at any time to say they elected to carry out the sale. The 7th section of the Act merely says they shall not be compelled to do so; but on their doing so the appellant's right of purchase could be exercised. Such right in fact never had been lost.

The learned Judge below held it was not a full disclaimer, but merely a qualified one. This is the fair construction to be placed on it. *Moet* v. *Pickering,* cited by the appellant, is not a parallel case. There, a third party, a wharfinger, was held entitled to costs, as he had fairly stated he had no claim but that to which he was entitled, namely, his lien for charges.

In this case the appellant had no right whatever. It was not his bidding that was wrong; it was his subsequent conduct in attempting to both approbate and reprobate the contract.

Witt v. *Corcoran,* 2 Ch. D. 69; *Re Clements,* 46 L. J. Ch. 375, 381; *Re The City of Manchester,* 5 Pro. D. 221; *Dicks* v. *Yates,* 18 Ch. D. 76; *Metropolitan Asylum District* v. *Hall,* 5 App. Cas. 582; *Harpham* v. *Shackleton,* 19 Ch. D. 215; *Butcher* v. *Pooler,* 24 Ch. D. 273; *Re Primrose,* 23 Beav. 594; *Mitford's* Ch. Pl. 381, were referred to.

April 17, 1885. BURTON, J. A.—The contest in this case is substantially between the rival trustees of a Church, or between two sets of people who claim to be trustees; and the defendant Jackson has been brought into the litigation in consequence of his having become the purchaser at public auction of a property belonging to the church which the defendant trustees advertised for sale, and attempted to sell at the auction in question.

We see by the statement of claim that the sale was made under the provisions of the R. S. O. ch. 216, by the 7th, 8th, and 9th sections of which the trustees are under no obligation to carry out the sale, if in their judgment an adequate price is not obtained, nor does it even then become a binding contract unless approved of by the congregation, or by the Judge of the County Court.

The plaintiffs admit that it has never been so approved of, and the defendant trustees allege that they were not satisfied with the price bid.

Mr. Richards therefore contended that Jackson was not a necessary party to the suit, as the bid under the circumstances amounted to nothing more than an offer for the property; it was not like a contract which either party could enforce; and that Jackson never had any estate or interest in the land.

The necessity for making him a party is not very apparent, as an injunction could have been obtained against the defendant trustees to prevent their carrying out any sale, and in the decree which was actually made, the sole question dealt with was, to decide that the plaintiffs and not the defendants were the trustees of the property, and no order was made in reference to the sale to Jackson, but he, as well as the other defendants, was ordered to pay the plaintiffs' costs, and this appeal has been brought by Jackson against this portion of the decree.

It is objected that this is an appeal for costs only, and cannot be brought without the leave of the Judge, which has not been obtained, and it was properly admitted that this was so, unless it can be brought within the class of cases where an appeal has been allowed inasmuch as the decision involved some question of principle.

It is said in this case that the learned Judge proceeded upon the ground that the defendant ought to have disclaimed in proper form all interest in the property, and that the pleading is not in proper form. It reads thus:

" The defendant Jackson says he has no interest in this suit other than as a purchaser at the said sale, and that it is immaterial to him whether the same is carried out or not, and that he does not know the other defendants in the matter, he being only a bidder at such sale, therefore he disclaims all interest in the result of this suit, and no effort has been made by him to have said sale carried out as he was aware that the same would have to be first confirmed by the members of the said church."

If the defendant had disclaimed all interest in all matters in question in this suit that would have been sufficient, but it is said that as he only disclaims any interest in the result of the suit, it is insufficient, although he sets up no claim either for costs or for any other relief.

The first question that suggests itself is, whether it is a case in which any disclaimer was necessary at all.

As Vice-Chancellor Page Wood remarked, in *Maxwell* v. *Wightwick*, L. R. 3 Eq. at p. 211 : "Where a person by any solemn instrument, or by the act of law, becomes invested with an estate, the plaintiff is not obliged to make any application to him in order to ascertain whether he claims any interest or not, but is entitled to a disclaimer from him if he claims no interest in the subject matter of the suit."

Here the defendant Jackson had no estate or interest, as is apparent from the plaintiffs' statement of claim, and no formal disclaimer could therefore have been necessary, and so far as I can see could serve no useful purpose. Any disclaimer by him could not operate to relieve him from an obligation to complete the purchase, if the congregation and trustees elected to hold him to it.

In cases where parties have an estate or interest in the land which has to be got rid of, as for instance a subsequent incumbrancer in foreclosure suits, the plaintiff has a right to their formal disclaimer on record, but he has even then to be careful not to make persons parties who had no interest or had ceased to have an interest.

In *Earl of Cork* v. *Russell*, L. R. 13 Eq. 210, it was held that after the passing of the 27th and 28th Vict. ch. 112, previous to which time a judgment creditor had a lien on the land and was therefore a necessary party to a foreclosure suit, judgment creditors who had not issued execution had no interest in the land, and it was improper therefore to make them parties. And the question then arose as to their right to costs, and it having been shewn that they had before suit written to disclaim any interest in the property, they were held entitled to costs.

The Master of the Rolls had, previously to this decision
in *Mildred* v. *Austin*, L. R. 8 Eq. 220, held that judgment
creditors who had not lodged executions were proper
parties, and in the case I am now referring to, in 13 Eq., the
learned Vice-Chancellor said as to such defendants in the suit
then before him, as they had been made parties in accordance
with a decision of one of the Judges, the plaintiffs were
justified in the course they had taken, and he could not
make them pay the defendants' costs. He then proceeded
to deal with some defendants who had at one time been
subsequent mortgagees, but had assigned their mortgages,
and as to them he said, there was the further question
whether the disclaimer they had put in was sufficient.

It was in these words, (p. 216) : " We have not and do not
claim, and except during the time when we held the before
mentioned mortgage,   *   *   we never had, or claimed to
have, any right or interest in any of the matters in question ;
and we disclaim all right, title, and interest, legal or equitable,
in any of the said matters ; and if we had been applied to
by the plaintiff before the filing of the bill we should have
disclaimed all such right, title, and interest."   And he held
that having disclaimed in that form, they were entitled to
their costs, and he added : "I think they are also entitled
to their costs on principle—that a man being made party
to a Chancery suit in respect of a matter in which he has
no interest, should not have to pay costs."

It does not appear to me, therefore, a case in which a
disclaimer was required, and the course which the defendant took was to admit the facts stated in the plaintiffs'
claim, viz. : that he was a purchaser under the circumstances there mentioned ; that he claimed no other interest
in the suit than that ; that he had made no effort to have
the sale carried out ; and that it was immaterial to him
whether it was or was not carried out ; and did not ask for
costs.

A formal disclaimer being in my opinion unnecessary,
the answer appears to me to state the facts candidly, and
as Jackson had no interest in the estate, to disclaim any
interest in the suit, and to submit to the decree of the
Court.

In *Moet* v. *Pickering*, 8 Ch. D. 372, Lord Justice James said, (p. 374) he thought it was not the practice of the Court, or the reasonable justice of the case, to make the party pay the costs because the counsel representing him claims a little more than he is entitled to.

The defendants there, who were wharfingers, said in their answer that they submitted to any order which the Court might think fit to make " *upon their costs, charges, and expenses of this action being paid or provided for.*"

" That," he goes on to say, " is merely matter of language. Every person in this country, when engaged in litigation, must submit to what a Court of Justice orders him to do. In this case, they say, ' We will do what you tell us if you do so and so.' The real meaning of that is, ' We do not claim any thing adversely to the plaintiffs, or Pickering,(the defendant.) Let the Court settle the matter between the parties who are in dispute. We have nothing to do with it. We do not raise any objection to the Court doing any thing as between them it may think right.'"

In that cause the Vice-Chancellor had ordered the defendants to pay the plaintiffs' costs, but the Court of Appeal held not only that they were not liable, but that they had done nothing to disentitle themselves to the costs of the action. In the Court below the Judge said he would have given the defendants their costs if they had not opposed the claim of the plaintiffs in the suit; that they had not only claimed their costs, but a lien for their charges in priority to the plaintiffs' lien.

Here the defendant Jackson made no claim whatever, and the plea put in was treated as a disclaimer and withdrawal from the action, for on the case coming on for hearing a decree was made in the presence of counsel for *both* parties, not *all* parties, but the *litigating parties*, for a reference to ascertain which of those two parties were trustees of the property.

Upon the reference, the Master states that he was attended by the solicitors of *both* parties, that is the two parties that were still engaged in the litigation, and he found the one fact submitted, viz., who were the trustees, and on the decree upon further directions, that was the only question adjudicated upon except the costs.

I find it difficult to distinguish this case in principle from *Moet* v. *Pickering*. This defendant was an innocent purchaser; he submitted to do whatever the Court thought proper, and ought, in my humble judgment, to have received his costs. We are not, however, now called upon to deal with that, but we are asked to reverse so much of the decree as orders the defendant to pay them. I adopt L. J. Thesiger's remarks in that case, p. 377, that "I can see no ground in principle, and none upon authority, for saying that that (order) is right;" but I go further, and say that the defendant was not a proper party defendant, because the bid at the auction, taken in connection with the statute, amounted at most to an offer to purchase, and no party is properly a defendant to a suit from the mere circumstance of his having offered to purchase: but assuming even for the moment that he is properly made a party, upon what principle is an order made against him for costs? As a rule, where no account, payment, conveyance, or other relief is sought against a party, but the plaintiff requires him to answer a bill, the costs are payable by the plaintiff.

In the *Wharfingers' Case* (*Moet* v. *Pickering*), they had no interest in the suit, although they set up a claim for their charges, and were ordered to pay the costs; the Court relieved them, and went further and gave them their costs. Here an innocent bidder at an auction sale states the fact of his so bidding, and although he did not go through the unnecessary form of submittting his rights to the Court, he makes no resistance to the suit, made no claim adversely either to plaintiffs or defendants, and made common cause with neither. If *Moet* v. *Pickering* is well decided, it justifies the decision which, in my opinion, we ought to give in this case, viz.: to allow the appeal, with costs, and dismiss the bill as against Jackson, without costs.

OSLER, J. A.—I think this is a case in which an appeal lies against the order making the defendant Jackson pay the costs of the action, for we can see that it was not made merely in the exercise of the discretion of the learned Judge below, but because he was of opinion that the disclaimer was insufficient. In the first reason against the appeal, it is said that the defendant had been properly ordered to pay the costs, because of his misconduct in contesting the plaintiffs' title as trustees at the trial and throughout the reference. This, however, as it appeared on the argument before us, he had not really done, and if the order proceeded at all on the assumption that he had, it was a misapprehension of the fact, and would be appealable on that ground also. The rule as to an appeal on the question of costs appears to be this, that if in making the order complained of there has been any violation of principle, or the Court has proceeded on a wrong general rule, or if the discretion of the Court has been exercised upon any misapprehension of fact, the Court of Appeal will interfere, but not otherwise: *Re Silver Valley Mines*, 21 Ch. D. 381; *Re Gilbert*, 52 L. T. N. S. p. 8; *Cooper v. Vesey*, 20 Ch. D. 611; *Johnstone v. Cox*, 19 Ch. D. 17; *Ex parte Wainwright*, 19 Ch. D. 140, 152; *Dutton v. Thompson*, 23 Ch. D. 278; *Butcher v. Pooler*, 24 Ch. D. 273; *Krehl v. Burrell*, 28 Sol. J. 48; *Re Bradford*, 50 L. T. N. S. 170.

If we had to dispose of the case upon the question of the technical sufficiency of the disclaimer, we could not in my opinion say that the judgment was wrong, as the disclaimer does not in substance or form comply with what the practice requires: *Daniell's* Ch. Pr. 629, 631, Forms 525, 526; *Story's* Equity Pleadings, 8th ed., 1870, secs. 838, 843, 844; *Earl of Cork v. Russell*, L. R. 13 Eq. 210; *Ford v. Chesterfield*, 16 Beav. 516.

Nor am I prepared to accede to the argument that the defendant Jackson is not a proper party to the suit, which would of course be a good reason for not ordering him to pay the costs: *Earl of Cork v. Russell, supra; Cooper*

v. *Vesey*, 20 Ch. D. 611. The general rule is thus stated
in *Story's* Equity Pleadings, 8th ed., 1870, sec. 77 : "All
persons legally or beneficially interested in the subject-
matter of the suit should be made parties ; or if the
expression be deemed more exact and satisfactory   * *
all persons who are interested in the object of the bill are
necessary and proper parties." And see *Calvert* on Parties,
pp. 10, 12, 13.

The object of this suit was to have it declared that the
plaintiffs and not Jackson's co-defendants were the trustees of the church property. His position was this : he
had been a bidder at the sale, and the property had been
knocked down to him. Having regard to the provisions
of the Act R. S. O. ch. 216, secs. 7, 8 and 9, he probably
could not, have compelled specific performance against
the vendors, but inasmuch as they might, if they really
were the trustees, have been willing to carry out the sale
by procuring the sanction of the County Judge and his
approval of the deed, I cannot say that he had not such
an interest in the object of the suit, and the success of his
co-defendants, as to render it proper that he should be made
a party, not only that he might have an opportunity, if he
desired it, of supporting their title, but to prevent the
attempted sale from being carried out.

The case is not one in which a disclaimer, strictly so
called, was the appropriate pleading. There was no
reason why the defendant should not have said, "If my
co-defendants are really the trustees, I am ready and willing to adhere to my offer, if they choose to accept and
carry it out. But as I know I cannot compel them to do
so, it is a matter of indifference to me whether they are
declared to be the trustees or not." All that he could do
to relieve himself from liability to the costs of the suit,
(his conduct in bidding at the sale being entirely innocent)
was to stand indifferent between the two sets of rival
claimants, not making common cause with or assisting
either of them, and this, I think, it sufficiently appears
upon the pleadings, which on motion for decree must be
taken to state the facts, that he has done.

Therefore in the absence of anything to shew misconduct on his part, either in relation to the facts of the case
or the conduct of the litigation, as for instance by casting
in his lot with and supporting the contention of his co-
defendants, there seems no reason or principle why he
should have been ordered to pay the costs of the action.
The case of *Moet* v. *Pickering*, 8 Ch. D. 372 ; 26 W. R.
637, cited by Mr. Richards, seems a good deal in point.

I think the action should have been dismissed against
this defendant at the original hearing, without costs, and
probably we should not have heard of this appeal if
this view had been presented to the Chancellor, instead of
the appellant consenting to a reference and to the costs
being reserved ; or if the same view had been presented
to my Brother Proudfoot, when the case was before him.
The appeal must however be allowed.

HAGARTY, C.J.O., and PATTERSON, J.A., concurred.

Per Cur.—*Appeal allowed, with costs, and the action in
Court below dismissed as against Jackson, without costs.*

EDGAR AND WIFE v. THE NORTHERN RAILWAY COMPANY.

Negligence—Railway Company—Invitation to alight—Finding of jury.

Where, after calling out the name of the next station, a railway train was slowed up on approaching and passing it, but was not brought to a full stop, and the plaintiff, who had purchased a ticket for that station, received injuries on alighting there :

Held, that there was evidence of an invitation to alight, and that it was for the jury to say whether she had acted in a reasonably prudent and careful manner in availing herself of it.

THIS was an appeal by the defendants from the judgment of the Queen's Bench Division, 4 O. R. 201, discharging an order *nisi* for a nonsuit or a new trial in an action for damages for injuries sustained by the female plaintiff in jumping off the defendants' car at a station called Lefroy, on the defendants' line of railway, while the train was in motion, and in which a verdict was given at the trial in favour of the husband for $200, and of the wife for $100.

The appeal was heard on the 3rd day of December, 1884.*

The facts are fully stated in the report of the case below and in the present judgment.

Boulton, Q. C., for the appeal. There was no negligence on the part of the appellants, and even if there was it was not the cause of the accident, which was occasioned by the negligence of the female plaintiff. No person is justified in jumping from a moving train simply to avoid inconvenience : *Lewis* v. *The London, Chatham, and Dover R. W. Co.*, L. R. 9 Q. B. 66 ; *Siner* v. *Great Western R. W. Co.*, L. R. 3 Ex. 150 ; 4 Ex. 117 ; *Davey* v. *London and South Western R. W. Co.*, 11 Q. B. D. 213.

Pepler, contra, referred to *Robson* v. *North Eastern R. W. Co.*, 2 Q. B. D. 85 ; *Bridges* v. *North London R. W. Co.*, L. R. 6 Q. B. 377 ; L. R. 7 H. L. 213 ; *Cameron* v. *Milloy*,

14 C. P. 340; *Radley* v. *London and North Western R. W. Co.*, 1 App. Cas. 754; *Lax* v. *The Corporation of Darlington*, 5 Ex. D. 28; *Slattery* v. *Dublin, Wicklow, and Wexford R. W. Co.*, 3 App. Cas. 1155; *Clayards* v. *Dethick*, 12 Q. B. 439; *Haldan* v. *Great Western R. W. Co.*, 30 C. P. 89.

December 18, 1884.   BURTON, J. A.—The learned counsel for the plaintiffs laboured almost to a wearisome length, if I may say so without offence, a point which can admit of no question at the present day, namely, that if there is any evidence from which negligence may be inferred, it is for the jury, and not for the Judge, to deal with the question.

I do not attach any importance to this being an action for negligence.   In this, as in all other cases, there is always a preliminary question for the Judge, namely, whether from any given state of facts there is any evidence on which the jury could properly find the question in favor of the party on whom the onus of proof lies.   If there is not, the Judge ought to withdraw the question from the consideration of the jury.   In an action of this nature the Judge must say whether upon the whole facts in evidence negligence can legitimately be inferred, the jury have to say, in case the Judge rules that there is evidence from which it may be so inferred, whether it ought to be inferred.

If, for instance, in the present case, the defendants having undertaken to carry the plaintiffs upon their railway from Toronto to Lefroy, had passed that point at full speed without stopping, they would have been guilty of a breach of contract with the plaintiff; but if the plaintiff under those circumstances had attempted to jump from the railway carriage to the platform at the Lefroy station, and had thereby injured herself, the duty of the Judge would have been not to allow the case to go to the jury, because there would in such a case be no evidence from which negligence on the part of the defendants leading to the plaintiff's injury could be inferred; the plaintiff would have brought the injury upon herself by her recklessness;

or if, as I supposed was the case here at the commencement of the argument, the plaintiff had attempted to alight from the train before it had come to a stand still, and thereby caused the injury to herself, the Court would have been equally bound to withdraw the case from the jury, because there would have been nothing from which negligence on the part of the company could be legitimately inferred. But, when investigated, the facts in evidence here present a very different case. It was the duty of the defendants safely and securely to carry the passengers to Lefroy, and afford the ordinary and reasonable facilities for alighting at that point. From the evidence it appears that the train was not brought to a stand still at all, or for so short a period of time as to afford passengers no opportunity of leaving whilst it was not in motion, and that the company's servants intended therefore to afford no other means of alighting than by jumping from the train whilst passing the station at a reduced rate of speed.

I think no Court could properly say, under such a state of facts, that there was not evidence from which negligence might have been inferred, and it was, therefore, a case in which the jury were properly required to say whether it ought to be inferred.

I do not think that *Bridges* v. *The North London R. W. Co.*, L. R. 6 Q. B. 377, and L. R. 7 H. L. 213, in the House of Lords, important decision as it was, established any new principle, nor do I consider that any new principle has been established in any of the more recent cases to which we have been referred, so as to take from the Judge the duty and responsibility of determining as to the existence or non-existence of evidence fit to be determined. It simply affirms a proposition which is indisputable, that when such evidence exists the jury must be allowed to decide as to its weight and value.

In the present case I think there was clear evidence from which negligence might be inferred, and that the jury was the only tribunal, therefore, to deal with it, and the jury having found negligence the only other point was whether the question of contributory negligence was properly dealt with.

The learned counsel for the defendants might, perhaps, well have complained if the learned Judge had held that there was no evidence for the jury upon that point, but he can scarcely contend that it was any more competent for the Judge to declare affirmatively that the plaintiff was guilty of negligence than he was entitled to do so as regards the defendants' negligence ; both are questions of fact to be disposed of by the jury, if the facts are of a nature from which negligence may legitimately be inferred.

I am of opinion that it was a case which could not have been withdrawn from the jury, and that the appeal should be dismissed, with costs.

PATTERSON, J. A.—The train having slowed, but not stopped, at Lefroy station, it may properly be held that the only facility afforded, or intended to be afforded, to the passengers for alighting was the slackening of speed to the extent to which that was done. The duty of the company to the passenger was to afford reasonable facilities for alighting with safety, and by reason of neglect of that duty the accident to the female plaintiff happened, unless she herself contributed to it by negligence on her part. The jury negatived contributory negligence, and, having regard to the fact that Lefroy station was the place to which the defendants had contracted to carry her ; that by slowing the train they intimated that passengers were to alight ; and that from the fact that the train did not wholly stop, the inference that the invitation was only to alight when the train stopped is rebutted ; the finding against contributory negligence is clearly justified.

If the plaintiff had, as it is suggested she ought to have done, relied on the contract to allow her to alight at Lefroy, and kept her seat until the train stopped somewhere else, she would have to meet the contention that it was her own fault for not alighting when invited to do so. Her reply would of course be that she could not be sure of being able to alight with safety, because the train did not wholly stop.   She would, in short, be involved in the same contest respecting the fulfilment or non-fulfilment of the duty to afford facilities for alighting with safety as she is now engaged in.

The announcement that the next station was Lefroy does not strike me as having much significance.   As a statement of a fact, it conveyed nothing new to the plaintiffs; and as a statement that it was intended that certain passengers should get off the train at that station, it gave no more information than what was contained in the contract evidenced by the ticket.   But taken in connection with the slowing of the train without stopping it, it is, as far as it goes, a bit of evidence consistent with the position taken by the plaintiffs.

I think the case was one for the jury, and that we ought not to interfere with the judgment, but should dismiss the appeal, with costs.

OSLER, J.A.—I think there was evidence of negligence on the part of the appellants which could not properly have been withdrawn from the jury.

If there had been nothing but the calling out of the name of the station, I should have been of a different opinion.   That of itself was not an invitation to the passengers to alight.   But when it is coupled with the fact that the train slowed up as it approached and was passing the station, never coming, as the jury have found, to an absolute stand, but gradually increasing in speed, no attempt being made, so far as the evidence discloses, on the part of the officials to prevent any of the passengers for that station from getting off the train there, I think there was evidence of an invitation to those passengers to take such means of alighting as the company was providing for them.

It was not suggested by the defendants at the trial that the train had been slowed up for any other purpose, and it was then for the jury to say whether the plaintiff had

acted in a reasonably prudent and careful manner in getting
out when she did, and availing herself of such means of
doing so as the defendants were offering her. They turned
out to be attended with danger to which she ought not to
have been exposed, and as the jury did not find that she
acted unreasonably, it is just that the defendants should
bear the consequences of their neglect of the precept to
"hasten slowly."

I refer to *Lax* v. *The Corporation of Darlington*, 5 Ex.
D. 28; *Robson* v. *North Eastern R. W. Co.*, 2 Q. B. D.
85, and to the judgment of Kelly, C. B., in *Siner* v. *Great
Western R. W. Co.*, L. R. [3 Ex. at p. 155, which appear
to me to be very much in point as applied to the circumstances of the present case.

MORRISON, J. A., concurred.

Appeal dismissed, with costs.

———

BELL v. ROSS ET AL.

Insolvent Act, 1875, secs. 84, 85, 86—Creditor valuing security— Election by assignee.

When an assignee in insolvency elects, under sec. 84 of the Insolvent Act, 1875, to allow a creditor to retain, at a valuation, the property which he holds as security for his debt, the creditor becomes a purchaser at that valuation, freed from any right or equity to redeem on the part of the insolvent or his estate.

Where the secured creditor has valued his security for the purpose of proof, the policy and express language of the Insolvent Act, 1875, require that the decision of the assignee shall be promptly made.

A formal resolution of the assignee allowing the creditor to retain the property is not necessary. Therefore where the assignee had ample means of knowing the value of the assets before the creditor proved his claim and valued his security in January, 1879, and where no meeting of creditors was held after that date till the 30th of July following, and the estate was sold without any reference to the security; and where nothing further was done by the assignee until the 13th October following, when he wrote to the creditor : ·· Your claim as filed shews a balance over security of $3,091.13, but Mr. Leitch [the purchaser of the estate] disputes your claim to any dividend, on the ground," &c., it was

Held, that the assignee had signified his election to allow the creditor to retain the security, and his abandonment of any right to redeem it for the estate.

THIS was an appeal by the defendants from a judgment pronounced by Proudfoot, J., on the 12th September, 1883.

The action was brought by Andrew Wilson Bell, assignee in insolvency, under the Insolvent Act of 1875, of the joint and separate estates of Alexander McDougall and Samuel McDougall, against James G. Ross and Robert Campbell, for the redemption of certain timber limits which had been assigned by Samuel McDougall to the defendant James G. Ross, by an instrument absolute in form, but alleged to be in reality a mortgage, and transferred by Ross to his co-defendant Campbell absolutely, for valuable consideration.

The defences raised and the material portions of the evidence are fully set out in the judgments delivered in this Court.

The action was tried at Ottawa on the 11th and 12th days of September, 1883, before Proudfoot, J., who pronounced judgment in favour of the plaintiff, declaring him

entitled to redeem as against both defendants, and giving
the defendant Campbell relief over against his co-defendant Ross for the amount paid by Campbell.

The appeal from this judgment was heard on the 30th
January, 1885.*

McCarthy, Q. C., for the appellant Ross.
Maclennan, Q. C., for the appellant Campbell.
Robinson, Q. C., for the respondent.

March 3rd, 1885. BURTON, J. A.—The plaintiff, who
was the duly appointed assignee of the joint and separate
estates of Alexander McDougall and Samuel McDougall,
brings this action, claiming that previously to, and at the
time of the insolvency, Samuel McDougall was owner of
a timber limit on the Bonnechere, subject to a mortgage to
the defendant Ross, to secure certain advances made by
him to the firm by an instrument which, though absolute
in form, was intended to operate as a mortgage.

The claim further alleges that about the 1st of February,
1879, the defendant Ross improperly assumed to sell the
limit to the defendant Campbell, who had notice of the
plaintiff's title ; and prays for a declaration that the
plaintiff is entitled to redeem, upon payment of what, if
anything, is found to be due after charging the defendants
with the timber cut and converted.

The defendant Ross, in the second, third, and fourth
paragraphs of his answer, states facts which appear to me
to be decisive of this suit without reference to the other
questions raised.

The statement is briefly : That the firm were indebted to
him in a large sum, and that Samuel was also so indebted
in a further sum.

That in order to obtain the advance which constituted
the firm's debt, Samuel transferred the timber limit in
question as part security for such advances, for which the
defendant also held other securities.

Present—HAGARTY, C.J.O., BURTON, PATTERSON, and OSLER, JJ.A.

That when he proved his claim in the insolvency proceedings, he did, pursuant to the provisions of the Insolvent Act, place a value on the said limit, and merely
proved for the difference after deducting the value placed
on the limit, and that he was allowed by the creditors'
assignee to retain the limit at the valuation placed thereon,
and he then became the owner and entitled for his own
benefit.

Some discussion was raised as to whether there had been
any election by the assignee, with which portion of the
case I will deal hereafter; at present I propose to deal with
the legal question only, assuming for this purpose of the
argument that the creditors and the assignee had, by
resolution and in the most formal manner, consented to
the retention of the security.

This depends upon the construction to be placed on
sec. 84 of the Act of 1875.

The portions material to this inquiry are :—

If a creditor holds security from the insolvent or his
estate, or if there be more than one insolvent liable as
partners, and the creditor holds security from one of them
as security for the debt of the firm (which is this case), he
shall specify the nature and amount of such security in his
claim, and shall therein on his oath put a specified value
thereon.   And the assignee under the authority of the
creditors may either consent to the retention of the property constituting such security, or on which it attaches,
by the creditor, at such specified value, or he may require
from such creditor an assignment or delivery of such
security or property at an advance of 10 per cent. on such
specified value, to be paid by him out of the estate so soon
as he has realized such security, *in which he shall be bound
to the exercise of ordinary diligence*, and in either of such
cases the difference between the value at which the security
is retained or assumed and the amount of the claim of
such creditor shall be the amount at which he shall rank
and vote as aforesaid.

Here is a case in which the creditor did hold in security the property of one of the insolvents. What course could the creditor take? He could of course, if the security was ample to cover his claim, stand outside the insolvency proceeding, and realize his claim by sale of the premises, but if it were not ample, as in the case before us, he could only prove his claim at all by placing a value on his security.

The creditors or the assignee had then the option of allowing the proving creditor to retain the property at the value placed upon it, or of taking it themselves at the advance. Whenever the assignee elects to allow the creditor to retain the property, what, looking at the whole scheme of the Acts, does it mean? Surely it must mean that he becomes a purchaser out and out at that valuation, freed from any right or equity to redeem on the part of the insolvent or his estate.

The original debt for which it was pledged is *pro tanto* discharged, it no longer stands as security for it, but has, with the consent of the creditors and the assignee, been accepted in satisfaction of it.

In the English Bankruptcy Act it is expressly provided that if a secured creditor proves he must assess the value of the security and prove only for the difference. But then the Act in terms provides that if he realizes less than the value so assessed it is his loss, whereas if he realizes more he is bound to pay the surplus over to the estate. It does not appear to be altogether an equitable provision, and as Lord Blackburn remarked in *Société Générale de Paris* v. *Geen*, 8 App. Cas. at p. 619, it seems like what is popularly expressed by the phrase, " Heads I win, tails you lose."

Our Legislature has acted upon what I cannot help regarding as a fairer plan, it has not allowed the creditor arbitrarily to fix a value, and then become the purchaser at his own valuation, but has provided that the creditors or the assignee for them may allow him to do so, or may themselves take it at a certain increase over that valuation

It is said that the formal assent of the assignee of the separate estate of Samuel McDougall was necessary. It seems, in the present case, to be answered by the fact that the same person, the plaintiff in this proceeding, was assignee of both estates, but I do not think that any such consent can be required under this section of the Act.

The one partner had pledged his property for the joint debt; on the insolvency the creditors of the firm were the parties to say whether the secured creditors should retain it or not, and if they had elected to do so they might have taken it at an advance. A question might possibly have arisen whether, upon realizing from it and paying the secured creditor the amount at which he had valued it and the advance, the surplus, if any, would belong to the joint creditors or the separate creditors of Samuel. It is not necessary to express any opinion upon that point. But in the event which has happened, it seems to me that the election of the assignee not to take it, vested the property absolutely in the creditor, freed and discharged from all equity or right to redeem.

In the present case, Samuel, in connection with one Bell, had made an assignment in insolvency on the 31st August, 1877.

The assignment of the estate of A. & S. McDougall was not made until the 31st October following, and the plaintiff was the assignee under both assignments; but for the purpose of testing the strength of the plaintiff's contention, let us assume that some third party had represented Samuel's estate under the first insolvency.

If, under such circumstances, the security, instead of being general as it is here, had been to secure £5,000, the property covered by it being somewhat greater in value, and he had valued his security at its face value, and the creditors had taken it at an advance of ten per cent. or £500, could the assignee of Samuel have claimed to redeem? If so it would be on payment of the original debt and interest, and the creditors would lose the £500. If not, has he any different right when the secured creditor is allowed to retain the property? I cannot think there is any distinction between the thing retained and the thing

transferred, it means in both cases the property covered by
the security, and the assent of the creditors or the assignee
operates as a statutory release.

The separate partner and his assignee must be held to
have known, that, when he pledged his separate property for
a joint debt, he placed it in the power of the joint creditors
to deal with it in the case of insolvency. The assignee of
Samuel had a right, no doubt, before the insolvency of A.
& S. McDougall, to redeem the property, but whenever that
insolvency intervened the rights of all parties were left to
be dealt with by a domestic forum, if the creditor chose to
submit his rights to that forum by proving his claim and
asking to rank on the estate.

It is to be regretted that more precise language had not
been used in this section, and the assignee expressly
authorized, if he assented to the retention of the property,
to release the insolvent's equity of redemption, but that
must be the effect of the creditor being allowed to retain ;
why should the creditor, after valuing his security and the
assignee assenting to his retaining it at that valuation, be
driven to file a bill of foreclosure against the very party
who has given that assent ? Such a proceeding would be
contrary to the whole spirit of the insolvency legislation
which contemplated that as far as possible the whole
matter should be worked out by means of the machinery
there provided.

The construction I am placing upon these words, is, I
think, confirmed by the 85th section, which provides that
if the security consists of a mortgage upon real estate or
upon ships, *the property mortgaged shall only be assigned
and delivered* to the creditor subject to all previous mortgages.

The whole section seems to be founded on the idea that
the former rights of the mortgagor were extinguished and
gone, and that upon the creditors or the assignee electing to
allow the secured creditor to retain the property nothing
further was required to perfect his title than a delivery of
the property, if in the possession of the assignee, or an

assignment. The former section makes no reference to either assignment or delivery, but simply to the retention of the property or effects constituting the security, or on which it attaches, by the creditor ; but whether assignment or delivery be requisite, the scheme of section 85 appears to be that the title of the secured creditor shall not become absolute until he has assured and bound himself to pay all the previous mortgages or charges, and secured the same upon the property in the same manner, and to the same extent, as the same were previously secured thereon.

This he could not be in a position to do, unless, simultaneously with its being done, the whole estate were vested in him.

The mode of proceeding is probably founded to a great extent upon the law of Quebec, as it has been not the practice with us to deal in this summary way with interests in real estate.

But it is manifest that to do complete justice to the insolvent's estate, the creditor could not be allowed to retain the property at his valuation of his interest in it without relieving the estate of the previous encumbrances, and so we find it declared that thereafter the holders of such previous mortgages shall have no further recourse or claim upon the estate of the insolvent. In other words, the secured creditor as a condition to his obtaining the property is to get the holders of those prior encumbrances to accept his personal obligation in lieu of the insolvent's liability, and to secure that obligation by a mortgage or mortgages on the property.

But that no rights of the mortgagor or his assignee were intended to be recognized is further manifested by the concluding portion of the section which does not require their consent, but, nevertheless, expressly provides that if there are any mortgages or charges subsequent to those of the secured creditor, the consent of such encumbrancers shall be obtained, although having an estate in the land, they are not required to release, but their consent in the same way as the assent of the assignee appears to be all that is required to perfect the title of the secured creditor.

But it is said that the assignee never made any election.
There was no necessity for a formal resolution to that
effect. The defendant Ross, having proved his claim in
the only way he is allowed by law to prove it, had done
everything that was required of him to entitle him to be
placed on the dividend sheet.

Section 86 declares that upon such a claim being filed,
it shall be the duty of the assignee to procure the
authority of the inspectors or of the creditors at their first
meeting thereafter to assent to the retention of the
security, or to require an assessment, and if any meeting
of inspectors or of creditors takes place without deciding
on the course to be adopted in respect of such security, the
assignee shall act in the premises according to his discretion
and without delay.

The claim was proved in insolvency in January, 1879,
and there was a meeting of creditors on the 30th July,
1879.

There had been a meeting of the creditors of Samuel
McDougall, at which the inspectors moved that the assignee
be authorized and empowered to convey the necessary title
of certain property mortgaged by Samuel to the Bank of
British North America, and also to all other parties who
have mortgages on land from Samuel McDougall. It may
perhaps be urged with some reason that this was a mere
authority to do so if in their discretion they deemed it
desirable to do so, and not having executed such release,
no inference unfavourable to the present claim should be
drawn from that circumstance.

But a meeting of the joint creditors took place on the
30th July, when no action was taken, and on the 13th
October following, in reply to a letter from Ross asking
for a dividend, the assignee advised him that at that meeting the creditors had resolved to sell out the estate to
Robert Leitch, he agreeing to pay ten cents on the $ of
their claims in four months, and then proceeds: "Your
claim as filed shews a balance over security of $3,091.13,
but Mr. Leitch disputes your claim to any dividend, on the

ground that you have some goods in your hands more than sufficient to pay it."

But this letter recognized in the most explicit way the right of Ross to retain his security which had been valued at $4,000, thus reducing his claim to the sum of $3,091.13, for which he had sums collocated on the dividend sheet.

This would seem to be as unequivocal a declaration of the election of the assignee to allow the creditor to retain his security as could well be made, and according to well settled principles, if a man once determines his election, it shall be determined for ever.

It is clear also that having parted with the estate to a purchaser, he could no longer deprive the creditor of his security.

I think therefore that there can be but one conclusion upon the evidence, that apart from the delay in acting upon the defendant's claim, which would in itself under the words of this enactment be almost conclusive evidence of his election, (see *Clough* v. *London and North Western R. W. Co.*, L. R. 7 Ex. 26, 35,) the letter by the assignee to the defendant shews beyond all question that the assignee had elected to the retention of the security, and if so, to vest the property absolutely in him.

If this be the proper construction to place upon the statute, it becomes unnecessary to consider the other points which were discussed in argument.

I think, for the reasons I have mentioned, the plaintiff had no right to redeem, and the appeal should be allowed, with costs, and the bill dismissed, with costs.

OSLER, J. A.—In the case of *Deacon* v. *Driffill*, 4 A. R. 335, the late Chief Justice Moss, thus stated the effect of sections 84 and 106 of the Insolvent Act: " The combined effect is to enable the secured creditor to assume any one of three positions. He may stand outside the insolvency proceedings, and realize upon his security in any manner the general law authorizes. * * He may release his security, and prove in the Insolvent Court for the amount of his claim as an unsecured creditor. He may come into

the insolvency proceedings and value his security, and
then whether the estate take it at the valuation and 10
per cent. additional, or permits him to retain it, he may
prove for the excess of his claim beyond the valuation."

In the present case the defendant Ross assumed the
last position. He filed his claim with a valuation of his
security, and the question is, what, upon the proper construction of the Act, it then became the duty of the
assignee to do? Section 84 says that he may under the
authority of the creditors' take one of two courses. He
may (1) either consent to the retention by the creditor of
the property or effects which constitute the security at the
specified value; or, (2) may require from the creditor an
assignment or delivery of such security, property, or effects
at an advance of 10 per cent. on such specified value. If
he adopts the latter course he must pay the creditor the
specified value with the additional 10 per cent out of the
estate so soon as he has realized the security, in doing
which he is bound to the exercise of ordinary diligence.

Then section 86 points out what action is to be taken
by the assignee, enacting that it shall be his duty to procure the authority of the inspectors, or of the creditors at
their first meeting after the claim and valuation have been
filed, to his taking one of the two courses required to be
taken with regard to the security by section 84 ; and further, that if any meeting of inspectors or creditors takes
place without deciding on the course to be adopted, the
assignee shall act according to his discretion and without delay.

Section 85 deals with the case where there may be prior
or subsequent incumbrances to that of the particular
secured creditor whose claim may be in question. Nothing
turns upon it here, the defendant Ross being apparently
the only incumbrancer. In the judgment delivered at the
hearing, my Brother Proudfoot is reported as saying: "It
was the right of the creditors after that," that is after the
filing of the claim, "to determine whether they would take
the security, whether they would redeem the security by
advancing ten per cent. or allow Ross to retain it. Now,

I cannot think that under the Insolvent Act that was intended to be determined by their silence one way or the other.   If the creditors did not choose to act through the assignee, then the creditors (I think the learned Judge must have said the claimant) had the right to act and say, what will you do ?   Mr. Ross could have come in at any time and said, will you redeem me ? or shall I keep this security ? and upon that application to the creditors, I suppose that probably silence then might have been fatal to any right."

I think that this language hardly describes the position of the secured creditor with entire accuracy.   When his claim is filed, the duty at once devolves upon the assignee and creditors to determine what course they will take, and the secured creditor must be looked upon as from that time forward demanding and awaiting their action. The statute does not in a simple case of this kind, however it may be in a case arising under section 85, require anything further to be done by him, if he is not to be asked to assign his security.   The other alternative is the consent to its retention, which is not required to be expressed in any particular way, and may, I think, well be evidenced by conduct and silence on the part of the assignee and the other creditors.   The effect of the secured creditor being allowed to retain his security, or of his taking an assignment or delivery of it from the assignee, is, in my opinion, upon the proper construction of the 84th, 85th, and 86th sections, to make him the owner of it out and out, so that it becomes from thenceforth irredeemable by the assignee or the debtor.   In this respect our Act differs from the English Bankruptcy Act and Rules of 1869, in which it is expressly provided that in bankruptcy and liquidation by arrangement, if a surplus is realized by the creditor it shall go to the trustee.   The same thing happens in the case of a composition: the debtor gets the benefit of the surplus: *Couldery* v. *Bartrum*, 19 Ch. D. 394 ; *Société Générale de Paris* v. *Geen*, 8 App. Cas. 606 ; *Bolton* v. *Ferro*, 14 Ch. D. 171.

When the secured creditor has valued his security for the purpose of proof, the policy and the express language of our statute require that the decision of the assignee shall be promptly made, and it is evidently of the first importance both to the creditor and to the estate, that it should be so, not only because of the extreme reluctance with which a creditor is permitted in changed circumstances to re-value his security, but because the consequences of delay, where, as here, the property is of fluctuating and speculative value and precarious in its nature, may be such as to deprive the creditor on the one hand, and the estate on the other, of the benefit of the security.

In the case before us, the assignee had the opportunity for nearly eighteen months before the defendant Ross proved his claim, of making himself acquainted with the value of the assets of both estates ; and I think the fact is not without significance, as indicating the creditors' views of the values of the insolvent's incumbered property, that at the first meeting held on the 1st November, 1877, the assignee was directed to convey the necessary titles to all parties who had mortgages on land from Samuel McDougall.

The claim was proved and the security valued in January, 1879, and the inference from the assignee's letter of the 9th January, 1879, acknowledging its receipt, is very strong that the timber limit in question was not regarded by him as having any value in it for either of the estates. His subsequent inaction confirms that view, for his duty, if he thought there was anything in the limit above the defendant's valuation, clearly was to have called a meeting of the inspectors or creditors to advise him what he should do. No meeting was ever called for that purpose, though one was called for the 30th July to consider the question of selling the estate to Leitch. No directions were given as to the limit at that meeting, and then the duty was cast upon the assignee himself to act in the premises at his discretion and without delay. Still he did nothing but to complete the sale to Leitch, and to declare

a dividend, ranking the defendant on the dividend sheet
for the amount of his proof.

On the 13th October he wrote to the defendant advising
him of the sale to Leitch, and of the dividend to be paid
upon the claims: "Your claim" he adds, "as filed shews
a balance over security of $3,091."

Bearing in mind the ample means of knowledge the
plaintiff had always possessed of the value of the limit,
and having regard to his letter of the 9th January, 1879,
the subsequent delay between that date and the first
meeting of creditors after filing the proof, the sale of the
estate without any reference to the security, and the
further delay till the 13th October, I am clearly of opinion
that the defendant Ross was entitled to regard that letter
as a distinct intimation, if anything further was necessary,
of the plaintiff's consent to his retention of the security
and abandonment of any right to redeem it for the estate.

For these reasons, I am of opinion, with great respect,
that the appeal should be allowed, and the action dismissed
against both defendants.

HAGARTY, C. J. O., and PATTERSON, J. A., concurred.

Appeal allowed.

DANIELS V. THE GRAND TRUNK RAILWAY COMPANY.

Railway company—Defect in fences—Liability for killing animals on track.

Sheep belonging to the plaintiff escaped from his premises on to the highway, and from thence owing to defects in the fences of the defendants into lands of theirs, whence they strayed on to the railway track where they were killed by a passing train.

Held, (reversing the judgment of the County Judge) that the defendants were not liable for the loss, the sheep not being lawfully on the highway.

THIS was an appeal from the County Court of the county of Brant.

The action was brought to recover damages for the loss of certain sheep killed on the defendants' railway, in consequence, as was alleged, of the defendants' neglect to keep their fences in repair.

The jury assessed the damages at $114, and, on their answers to questions submitted to them by the learned Judge, judgment was entered for the plaintiff.

The defendants afterwards obtained an order *nisi* to enter a nonsuit or judgment in their favor, which after argument was discharged. From that judgment the present appeal was brought.

The material facts were as follow: The plaintiff was the owner of two farms, consisting of lots numbers two and three in the fourth concession of the township of Blenheim, through which the defendants' railway passed.

These farms were separated by a side road, which crossed the railway by an overhead bridge.

Adjoining the railway track, and in one of the angles formed by its intersection with the side road, there was a parcel of land, part of lot number three, about ten acres in extent, the property of the company, which were used by them as a gravel pit. This parcel was fenced off from the plaintiff's land in lot number three, but not from the railway track; and the fence along that part of it which fronted on the side road, and was opposite the plaintiff's farm (lot number two) on the other side of that road, was out of repair.

The plaintiff's sheep were being pastured on lot number two. They escaped through a gate, which somebody had left open, into the side road, and from thence through a defect in the defendants' fence, about ten or fifteen rods north of the overhead bridge, into their land above described. From thence they strayed on to the track where they were killed by a passing train.

A by-law was proved, No. 248 of the township of Blenheim, for restraining and regulating the running at large of certain animals. It provided that no horse, mare, colt, filly, or gelding; no bull, ram over five months old; no boar or swine of any age, or any other animal known to be breachy, should be allowed to run at large in the township.

The defendants offered no evidence, and the jury found: (1) That the gravel pit was in common "with the rest of the track without any dividing fence, but used only for the purpose of a ballast pit;" And (2) that the sheep were killed by reason of their escaping on the defendants' railway track through the defects of the defendants' fences.

The appeal came on to be heard before this Court on the 5th December, 1885.*

Woods, for the appellants.
Hardy, Q.C., for the respondents.

The authorities cited are mentioned in the judgments.

January 13th, 1885.   OSLER, J. A.—Upon the evidence the plaintiff's case is, that the railway runs alongside the highway, and that his sheep got into the defendants' lands immediately from the highway, through a defect in the fence between those lands and the highway. It is not alleged that the defendants were negligent in managing their train, the only charge is, that they omitted to keep the fence in repair. Their contention is, that the statute does not bind them to fence against a highway when it runs alongside the railway, or if it does that the duty is a qualified one, and that if the plaintiff's sheep were not lawfully on the highway he cannot recover, even if the fence was out of repair.

In *Ricketts* v. *The East and West India Docks,&c.,R.W.Co.,* 12 C. B. 160, it was held that the liability of the railway company under the Railway Clauses Consolidation Act, 8 & 9 Vict. ch. 20, sec. 68, to make and maintain fences, was not more extensive than the ordinary common law liability of a person who is bound by prescription or special obligation to do so for the benefit of the owner or occupier of the adjoining land. The well known passage from *Dovaston* v. *Payne,* 2 H. Bl. 527, 1 Wms. Saund. ed. 1871, p. 560 n. is cited, " No man can be bound to repair for the benefit of those who have no right. Therefore the plaintiff cannot recover for the damage occasioned to his cattle by their escape from the adjoining close through the defect of the defendants' fences, unless the plaintiff had an interest in that close, or a license from the owner to put them there ; or, if they escaped from an adjoining highway, unless they were lawfully using the highway."

In *McLennan* v. *The Grand Trunk R. W. Co.*, 8 C. P. 411, and *McIntosh* v. *The Grand Trunk R. W. Co.*, 30 U. C. R. 601, *Ricketts' Case* was treated as laying down a rule of construction applicable to our own statute, C. S. C. ch. 66, sec. 13. That construction was recognized by this Court in *Douglass* v. *The Grand Trunk R. W. Co.*, 5 A. R. 585 ; and it is now well settled that the statutory obligation to fence imposed upon these defendants by that Act can only be taken advantage of by the adjoining proprietor, or by one who is in occupation of the lands of such proprietor with his license or consent. See also *McAlpine* v. *Grand Trunk R. W. Co.*, 38 U. C. R. 446.

The question then is, whether a highway running alongside a railway can be treated. as regards one lawfully occupying or using it, as the lands of an adjoining proprietor so as to make it compulsory upon the railway company to erect and maintain fences between their track and such highway.

The learned Judge in the Court below was of opinion that such a case was within the Act though not provided for in express terms. He says : "I think that *the public,* lawfully using the highway, have the same rights as adjoining private proprietors, *and that they are, in fact, as to the highway the adjoining proprietors thereof,* so far as to impose on the railway company the duties of fencing between their line and the highway."

This is the construction which was placed on section 68 of the English Act, in the case of *Manchester, &c., R. W. Co.* v. *Wallis,* 14 C. B. 213, which was not cited to the learned Judge, or on the argument of the appeal. We may assume, for the purpose of the present case, but without deciding it, that our Act admits of a similar construction ; but I cannot agree with the learned Judge in treating the company's obligation in this particular as unqualified and unlimited, as it is with regard to cattle guards at road crossings : *Huist* v. *Buffalo and Lake Huron R.W. Co.,* 16 U. C. R. 299 ; and as it was under the Act on which *Fawcett* v. *The York and North Midland R. W. Co.,* 16 Q. B. 610, and *Renaud* v. *The Great Western R. W. Co.,* 12 U. C. R. 408, were decided. Where the duty is absolute, to fence at all events, the company cannot say that the cattle were not, as against them lawfully on the highway. But that is not this case, which is distinguishable from the cases I have just referred to, and which are relied on in the Court below, on this ground. The duty to fence the highway, if it exists, cannot be put higher than the duty to fence as against an adjoining proprietor. The next question therefore must be, whether the sheep were lawfully on the highway when they escaped into the defendants' land, for, if they were not, the defendants were under no greater obligation to fence against them than against cattle trespassing on the land of any other adjoining proprietor.

The plaintiff relies upon the township by-law as by implication giving the sheep a right to run at large. This point is not noticed in the judgment below, though it is assumed, and I think properly so, that they were unlawfully at large as against the municipality.

The by-law, while expressly enacting that certain animals shall not run at large, does not expressly permit sheep to do so.

In *Crowe* v. *Steeper*, 46 U. C. R. 87, the question was as to the defendant's right to impound the plaintiff's cattle which had strayed from the highway into the defendant's land through defect of his fences. The plaintiff relied upon the township by-law by which other kinds of cattle were prohibited from running at large. The Court say, p. 91 : " If the municipality choose to exercise the powers given to them by the Legislature to regulate the running at large of cattle, they must do so in reasonably express terms and not merely by implication. By the common law, if these cattle stray from the high road into the land of another and do damage there, the owner is responsible therefor, irrespective of any question of fencing : see *Mason* v. *Morgan*, 24 U. C. R. 32. And by our own statute law already cited, R. S. O. ch. 195, it is pointedly declared that such is the law till varied by by-law. • • It can only be by a strained application of the maxim, *Expressio unius est exclusio alterius*, that we can hold that a directing that a horse or a pig shall not be allowed to run at large necessarily allows any other animal so to do."

The case of *Jack* v. *Ontario, Simcoe, and Huron R. W. Co.*, 14 U. C. R. 328, is noticed, where the Chief Justice, Sir John Robinson, so ruled at the trial, and the point was expressly decided in the same way in *McLennan* v. *Grand Trunk R. W. Co.*, 8 C. P. 411.

I think the by-law does not help the plaintiff, and the case must therefore depend upon the use the animals were making of the road. They had the right to pass and repass, or to be upon it for some particular object, but not to stray upon it. I think the only inference the evidence admits of is that they were straying there. They had escaped into it from the owner's field and were wandering there, not in charge of any one, or for any particular purpose, when they got through the defendants' fence. The case of *Manchester, &c., R. W. Co.* v. *Wallis*, 14 C. B. 213, is much in point. There, as here, the cattle had escaped from the highway on to the track of the railway and were killed.

The Court say, p. 224 : " Were, then, the cattle · · at the time they were killed, the cattle of the owners or occupiers of the adjoining land—the highway ? We think they were not. · · Whilst cattle are passing along a highway, the owners of such cattle · · are strictly occupying the highway. If, therefore, whilst passing along the road, they stray into an adjoining field, the owner of that field cannot distrain them, damage *feasant*, if he was bound to keep up the fence against the road : but, if, instead of passing along the road, the cattle had strayed there, they might, if they escaped into the adjoining close, be distrained damage *feasant*, notwithstanding the owner of that close was bound to repair the fence between his close and the road, because the cattle were wrongfully on the road, and the owners were not occupying it so as to cast any obligation to repair upon the distrainor."

It was held that the respondents were not occupying the road with their cattle which strayed on the road, and that therefore there was no obligation on the railway to fence against them.

I am of opinion that we must arrive at the same result in this case for the same reasons, and allow the appeal (a).

HAGARTY, C.J.O., BURTON, and PATTERSON, JJ.A., concurred.

Appeal allowed, with costs.

_____

(a) See also *Baker* v. *Grand Trunk R. W. Co.*, *ante* p. 68.

THE CORPORATION OF THE COUNTY OF BRUCE v. McLAY.

Registrar—Dismissal during the year—Liability for excess of fees—Notice of action.

Where a registrar of deeds was dismissed before the expiration of the year, having received in fees an amount in excess of that specified in the statute, (R. S. O. ch. 111, sec. 104.)

Held, (affirming the judgment of the Queen's Bench Division, 30. R.23), that he was bound to return and pay over to the treasurer of the municipality a proportionate amount of such excess, although not in office at the time prescribed by the statute for making his return ; but,

Semble, that the treasurer could not maintain an action for such fees before the 15th of January, the day named in the Act for the registrar sending in his return.

Held, also, that the defendant was not entitled to notice of action.

THIS was an appeal by the defendant from the judgment of the Queen's Bench Division, 3 O. R. 23, affirming the judgment of Galt, J., at the trial, in favour of the plaintiffs.

The defendant was registrar of the county of Bruce, and during the year 1882 was discharged from office. The plaintiffs brought this action for the recovery of the proportion of the amount of fees received by him up to the time of his dismissal in excess of the amount allowed to be retained by him pursuant to R. S. O. ch. 111, sec. 104.

The appeal was argued on the 21st day of November, 1884.[*]

The facts stated and the authorities cited are referred to in the report of the case below and in the present judgments.

Robinson, Q.C., for the appellant.

D. W. Ross, for the respondents.

December 18, 1884. BURTON, J. A.—Notwithstanding Mr. Robinson's very ingenious argument, I think that the judgment of the Divisional Court was right, and must be affirmed.

For many years before the passage of the 35th Vict. ch 27 (O.), the registrars were required to furnish either to the Legislature or to the executive a statement of all fees and emoluments received by them by virtue of their office; and by the Act of 1868 they were required to·make a return under oath to the Lieutenant-Governor on the 15th January in each year, of all the fees and emoluments during the preceding year.

Up to the time of the passing of the Act I have referred to, 35th Vict. ch. 27, in 1872, the registrar received to his own use all the fees and emoluments of his office, but a very considerable change was effected by it. After it came into operation the registrar was only entitled to retain to his own use, absolutely, those fees and emoluments up to the amount of $2,500.

Of the fees and emoluments received above that amount, he was entitled to retain a certain per centage, and no more.

In the events which have happened in the present case, the registrar held in his hand, in addition to the sums he was entitled to retain for his own use, some $1,700 for the use of some one else.

Nothing is said as to who is the party entitled until we come to the 7th section, and there we find a declaration that the party entitled to the excess over and above the sums which the registrar was entitled to retain to his own use, is the treasurer of the county for the use of the municipality.

As I read this, it is in effect a declaration that the moneys from time to time received by the registrar, in excess of those which he was authorized to retain for his own use, were the property of the treasurer of the county for and on behalf of the municipality. These moneys always were the moneys of such officer, although he probably would not have been entitled to maintain a suit for them before the 15th January.

This Act is now to be found incorporated in the Registry Act R. S. O. ch. 111, secs. 98-105, inclusive.

It is not necessary, I think, to consider whether, when a registrar has ceased to fill the office before the 15th January in any year, he could be compelled to send into the

Lieutenant-Governor a duplicate of the return required under section 97; but there can be no sound reason why he should not be bound to pay over at that time the moneys which he has always held, not as his own, but as a mere custodian for the municipality, or its treasurer.

I agree with Mr. Robinson that the language of the Act can neither be extended beyond its natural and proper meaning in order to supply omissions or defects, nor strained to meet the justice of the particular case; but we are not called upon in this case to do so. The same Act which declares that the registrar, of the fees received, shall retain so much and no more to his own use, provides that he shall pay over the excess on a certain day to a named officer; it does not say that he shall only be required to do so if still in office. There might be a loss to the municipality in the event of a change in the office of registrar during the year in case each of the officers received $2,500, and no more; but I apprehend that if each of them received a larger sum they would each be liable to pay to the treasurer of the municipality the proportion of fees received beyond what they were entitled to retain. I see no difficulty in giving that meaning to the statute, whilst the construction contended for would in the case of a registrar resigning his office at any time anterior to the 31st December, or even the 15th January, leave him in possession of funds to which he had no claim, but which he had all the time held for the use of the municipality.

As to notice of action, it is contended that the defendant is entitled to the protection given under R. S. O. ch 73, which provides that no action shall be brought against any one fulfilling any public duty for any thing by him done in the performance of such public duty until one month after notice in writing.

It seems very difficul indeed to see how such a case as this can be within the statute.

The 1st and 13th sect ns seem to shew very conclusively that such an action as this was not contemplated; the first of these sections provides that the action shall be an action on the case, expressly alleging that the act was done maliciously and without reasonable or probable cause; the other for the tender of amends.

In the case referred to by Mr. Robinson of *The Midland R. W. Co.* v. *The Withington Local Board*, 11 Q. B. D. 788, the language of the Act was much wider; it was "for any thing done, or intended to be done, or omitted to be done under the provisions of this Act."

There is nothing in the last point urged as to proceedings on the covenant being a condition precedent.

I am of opinion that the appeal must be dismissed.

OSLER, J. A.—The group of sections 98-105 in R. S. O. ch. 111, is taken from 35 Vict. ch. 27, the preamble of which recites that the income derived from fees in certain registry offices is excessive, and that it is "expedient to make some provision in the premises." These sections must be read together with section 92, which regulates the fees allowed to be taken by the registrar for services specified.

He is entitled to retain to his own use all the fees received by him in each year up to $2,500. After he has received that sum, the amounts he is entitled to retain are ascertained by reference to a sliding scale, which gives him a fixed and definite proportion of 90 cents of every $1 received by him up to $3,000, 80 cents up to $3,500, and so on for every additional $500 until a minimum of 50 per cent. is arrived at. Then what disposition is made of the surplus?

The 97th section provides that the registrar shall make an annual return to the Lieutenant-Governor on the 15th January in each year of all fees received by him up to the 31st December of the previous year; and the 107th section requires him to transmit to the treasurer of the county, &c., *of which he is registrar*, a duplicate of that return, and also to pay to such treasurer for the uses of the municipality such proportion of the fees received by him during the preceding year, as he is not entitled to retain to his own use.

It is argued that, because the Act says " Each registrar shall make the return to the treasurer of the county of which he is registrar," and shall pay " such treasurer" the surplus, he is not liable to pay it, if he ceases to be registrar before the time when he is required to make the return.

It is also contended that there can be no apportionment of the surplus fees for any part of a year.

I do not think there is any real difficulty in the construction of these sections of the Act. They must all be read together, and with reference to the supposed grievance intended to be remedied. The test of the plaintiffs' right to maintain the action is: to whose use did defendant receive the excess of fees ?

The Act makes an apportionment of every single dollar received by him after a certain amount, as and when he receives it. One part he is entitled to retain to his own use. To whose use does he receive the residue ? Clearly, as it seems to me, to the use of the municipality. It is not as if the Act had made an apportionment of the receipts of the year as a whole. All that is done is to delay the accounting for and payment over of the excess until the 15th January. It is not the return which ascertains the right of the municipality to the excess, for it cannot be argued for a moment that they are bound by any return, however inaccurate or fraudulent, the registrar chooses to make, or that he can deprive them of the excess by making no return at all. I agree with the reasons given in the judgment of the Court below for holding that the defendant, notwithstanding his dismissal before the end of the year, is liable to account for the excess of fees received by him.

In the case of *The County of Hastings* v. *Ponton*, 5 A. R. 543, though not a decision upon the question involved in the present suit, I find an observation in the judgment of the Court (p. 545) which I am content to adopt as expressing the meaning of the Act, viz., that to the extent to which the defendant received such excess of fees, he received it only for the purpose of paying it over to the plaintiffs.

I think he cannot evade or escape that duty by setting up either his resignation or dismissal during the year.

As to the necessity for notice of action, a point strongly urged upon us; it has been held in *Harrison* v. *Brega*, 20 U. C. R. 324, and *Ross* v. *McLay*, 40 U. C. R. 83, that a registrar is a public officer within the meaning of the Act to protect justices of the peace and other officers from vexatious actions, section 20 of which enacts that, so far as applicable, the whole of the Act shall apply for the protection of every officer and person mentioned in the said section, that is, every officer or person fulfilling any public duty, for anything done in the execution of his office as therein expressed, that is, for anything done in the performance of a public duty, whether such duties arise out of the common law, or are imposed by any statute: *Hodgins* v. *Corporation of Huron and Bruce*. 3 E. & A. 169, 173.

The section relied on is the 10th, which requires that one month's notice of the intended action shall be given.

It is not always easy to determine whether what is complained of in such an action is an act done in the execution of the office, or a mere omission or *nonfeasance*. If it is strictly the latter, the defendant is not entitled to notice: *Harrison* v. *Brega*, *supra*; *Ross* v. *McLay*, 40 U. C. R. 83.

The object of the provision requiring notice is said by Lord Blackburn in *Selmes* v. *Judge*, L. R. 6 Q. B. 724, 727, to be, " to protect persons from the consequences of committing illegal acts, which are intended to be done under the authority of an Act of Parliament, but which by some mistake, are not justified by its terms, and cannot be defended by its provisions."

The Act has been construed liberally in favour of defendants, and the length to which the Courts have gone in extending the rule to what at first sight appear to be cases of mere omission, is seen in *Wilson* v. *The Mayor of Halifax*, L. R. 3 Ex. 114, where the defendants were sued for a negligent omission to erect a fence between a foot-path and a post. The continued non-performance of a supposed duty was treated as "a thing done or intended to be done" under the Public Health Act. Kelly, C.B., said (p. 119): "It is now settled by authority, that an omission to do something that ought to be done in order to the complete performance of a duty imposed upon a public officer under an Act of Parliament, or the continuing to leave any such duty unperformed, amounts to an act done or intended to be done within the meaning of these clauses requiring notice of action." And see *Moran* v. *Palmer*, 13 C. P. 528.

So in cases like *Jolliffe* v. *Wallasey Local Board*, L. R. 9 C. P. 62; *Davis* v. *Curling*, 8 Q. B. 286; *Newton* v. *Ellis*, 5 E. & B. 115, where the cause of action arises from what Coleridge, J., in the latter case, calls a complex act, the defendant having done something not of itself illegal or improper, such as placing a temporary obstruction on the highway for the purpose, or in the course, of repairing it but omitting to secure protection for the public, notice of action is necessary.

In *Jolliffe* v. *The Wallasey Local Board*, *supra*, L. R. 9 C. P. at pp. 86, 87, Brett, L.J.,says that the rule established by judgments in former cases is this; "where a man is sued in tort for the breach of some positive duty imposed upon him by an Act of Parliament, or for the omission to perform some such duty, either may be an act done or intended to be done under the authority of the Act, and if so done or intended to be done the defendant is entitled to a notice of action."

The cases of *Waterhouse* v. *Keen*, 4 B. & C. 200; *Charrinton* v. *Johnson*, 13 M. & W. 856, 864; *Selmes* v. *Judge*, L. R. 6 Q. B. 724, and *The Midland R. W. Co.* v. *The Withington Local Board*, 11 Q. B. D. 788, are cases of another class. They shew that the substance of the action will be regarded, and though it may be in form an action to recover a debt, yet if it is substantially founded on a tort committed or threatened *colore officii*, as for instance an action to recover back money exacted by means of an illegal rate or toll or demand, notice of action must be given. There is no case, however, which decides that the mere non-payment of a debt, which has not originated in some wrongful act, omission or demand of the defendant, is an act done by him within the meaning of the Statute, so as to make a notice of action for such debt necessary.

The case of *The Midland R. W. Co.* v. *The Withington Local Board, supra,* was pressed upon us as laying down a more comprehensive canon of construction than had hitherto been applied, to our Act, at all events. The facts were, that the defendants had given the plaintiff notice to perform certain works. On their refusal to do it the defendants did it and charged the plaintiffs with the cost, supposing that they were exercising rights conferred upon them by the Public Health Act, 1875. This was found to be a mistake, and the plaintiffs, who had paid the money in compliance with the defendants' demand, now sued to recover it back. It was held, following the principle of the decisions in *Selmes* v. *Judge* and *Waterhouse* v. *Keen, supra,* that the defendants were entitled to notice of action under section 264 of the Act, which enacts that no action shall be brought "for anything done, or intended to be done, or omitted to be done, under the provisions of the Act" until after a month's notice of action. Brett, M.R., said (p. 794): "I incline to think that the draftsman of the section had his mind directed to actions of tort; it rather applies to actions sounding in damages; but the question is, what is the meaning of the whole section? I am prepared to say that it applies to everything intended to be done or omitted to be done under *the powers of the Act.* It has been urged that the section does not apply when the action is for money had and received and the *tort is waived.* I think that view too narrow; and I am of opinion that wherever relief is sought in respect of anything done or omitted to be done under an intended exercise of the powers of this Act, this section applies."

The other members of the Court, Lindley and Fry, L. JJ., placed their judgment on the ground that there had been an unlawful taking of the plaintiffs' money under the statute, which was "an act done" within the meaning of the section. The actual decision, therefore, as applied to the circumstances of the case, goes no further than former cases have gone in defining what is an "act done" within the meaning of similar enactments; and while I see no difficulty in applying these decisions, so far as they have gone, to cases arising under our own Act, it must not be overlooked that the whole scope of the latter Act indicates much more clearly than the English Act does, that it is intended to apply only to actions of tort, or arising out of tort.

For example, apart from section 264, which speaks of "an act done or intended or omitted to be done, under the provisions of the Act," language on which the Master of the Rolls lays some stress, the limitation of time for bringing an action under that Act is six months from the "accruing of the cause of action:" whereas under section 9 of our Act, it is six months next after the "act complained of was committed." One Act speaks of tender of amends simply; the other, section 13, of tender of amends for the injury complained of, and sections 14 and 15 refer to the "damages" to which the plaintiff is entitled. I lay no stress upon section 1 of our Act, which declares that the action is to be an action on the case as for a tort, because that is immediately followed by the provision that the declaration shall allege that the act complained of was done maliciously, and without reasonable and probable cause, which is, of course, quite inapplicable to many cases clearly coming within section 20.

The claim in this action is essentially different from that in any of the cases which we have been referred to. It is for a debt pure and simple, payable without any previous demand. If notice of action is necessary, it follows that the action must also be brought within six months from the time when the debt became payable.

I am therefore of opinion that the Act does not apply to a demand of this nature, and (2) that its non-payment is a mere act of omission or *nonfeasance,* and so cannot be treated as an act done under the powers, or in exercise of the powers of the Act. I refer also to *Venning* v. *Steadman,* 9 S. C. R. 206, 218, 235.

PATTERSON, and MORRISON, JJ.A., concurred.

Appeal dismissed, with costs.

PROCTOR v. MACKENZIE ET AL.

Practice—Ca. sa.—Fixing bail.

Held, [reversing the judgment of the County Judge,] that proceedings to fix bail cannot be maintained on a writ of *ca. sa.* which is made returnable immediately after the execution thereof : for such purpose it is necessary that the writ should be returnable on a day certain. [HAGARTY, C. J. O., dissenting.]

THIS was an appeal by the defendants from the judgment of Sinclair, County Judge of the county of Wentworth, refusing to set aside a verdict and judgment obtained by the plaintiff in an action in the County Court of that county, against the defendants as special bail for one John Mackenzie.

The other facts are fully stated in the judgments.

The appeal came on to be heard on the 3rd and 4th of December, 1884.*

Mackelcan, Q. C., for the appellants, contended that the writ of *ca. sa.* on which the action rested was void, as having been issued contrary to the statute, which enacts that no person shall be liable to be arrested for costs the amount of which was, together with the debt, indorsed on such writ, not specifying what was for debt and what for costs, which it should have done according to the rules of Court. The writ was also improperly made returnable after execution, and the same had never been executed, therefore it could not be returned so as to fix the bail. In order to do so the writ should have been made returnable on a day certain ; consequently there was not such a valid return as would entitle the plaintiff to maintain this action.

W. F. Walker, for respondents. The fact that the costs of the action against John Mackenzie were included in the amount that was indorsed on the writ was not such an objection as invalidated the writ. Had the defendant been arrested, and had he paid or tendered the amount exclusive

of the costs, a question then might have been raised as to
the legality of continuing him in custody for the excess
which consisted of costs. The object of the plaintiff in
that action being merely to fix the bail, all that was necessary was, that the writ should remain in the sheriff's hands
for the prescribed time.

Clark v. *Woods*, 2 Ex. 395; *Corbett* v. *Johnston*, 11 C. P.
317; *Mortimer* v. *Piggott*, 2 Dow. 615; *Meyers* v. *Ken-
drick*, 9 Pr. R. 363; *Kemp* v. *Hyslop*, 1 M. & W. 58;
Levy v. *Hamer*, 5 Ex. 518; *Beattie* v. *McKay*, 2 Ch. R. 56;
Cochrane v. *Eyre*, 6 U. C. R. 289, 594; *Gore Bank* v. *Gunn*,
1 Pr. R. 323, were referred to.

January 13, 1885. HAGARTY, C. J.:O.—This is an action
against the defendants as special bail for one J. McKenzie.
Judgment was given for plaintiff in the County Court of
Wentworth, and the defendants appeal.

The statement of defence sets out a *ca. sa.* against J.
McKenzie, which is in the form prescribed by the rules
made on the passing of the C. L. P. Act of 1856, returnable
immediately after the execution thereof. It is tested 16th
July, 1883, and is to satisfy $182.71 recovered for debt and
costs.

Endorsement to levy that amount and interest, and $10
for costs.

Defence states that said writ is null and void, being
issued contrary to R. S. O. ch. 67, sec. 3, declaring that no
person shall be arrested for non-payment of costs.

That defendants could not be lawfully rendered liable in
such a suit in accordance with the terms of the indorse-
ment.

Plaintiff replies that the said writ was duly sued out
and delivered to the sheriff to be executed and duly
returned by him before this action commenced: that J.
McKenzie was not found in his abiliwick, as by writ and
return of record appears; and prays inspection, &c.

Joinder of issue.

At the trial the record, writ, and return were produced.

It appeared that the writ was received by the sheriff on the day of the teste, 16th July, 1883, and was returned on 21st July, 1883.

It was objected that the judgment appeared to be for damages $119.71, and costs $62.94: that plaintiff should have set out (I presume, in this *ca. sa.*) how much of the judgment was really for costs, because that was a substantial part of the judgment.

Judgment was reserved, and afterwards a rule was taken out to set aside the verdict, &c., on the law and evidence, on the ground that the *ca. sa.* and return were void for the reasons set forth in the statement of defence.

The learned Judge decided against the bail in a well considered judgment. I find he notices (for the first time apparently) that it was urged that the *ca. sa.* should have remained in the sheriff's hands eight days instead of four, to fix bail. He decides that four days are sufficient under the well established rule.

In the reasons for appeal it is urged that the writ never became returnable as it had never been executed by defendant's arrest: that it should have been made returnable on a certain day, and no valid return. There should have been eight days between teste and return. It is also urged on the main ground, as to being in effect an arrest for costs.

I do not propose to enter into a discussion of the question whether the whole amount of debt and costs can be properly claimed on a *ca. sa.* It is unnecessary for the decision of the case before us, as we agree in holding that the original defendant could have been legally arrested on that writ, as the debt recovered was over $100. On a motion to reduce the endorsement of claim or to allow new bail on the *ca. sa.* for the debt alone, the whole question could have been tried and decided. The present defendants by the recognizances undertook that their prinpal should pay the costs and condemnation money, or render himself, &c., or they would do it for him.

He has not so paid it, and has not rendered himself.

I fully agree with the learned Judge below that the writ was not void.

The late Sir James Macaulay, says, in *Baker* v. *McKay*, 1 Ch. Rep. 75-6 : " There is no application to reduce the levy, so that if the arrest be legal to any extent, and the *ca. sa.* therefore is valid, it must fail, though it may be excessive," citing authorities, amongst them 5 Wm. 4, ch. 3, sec. 2, it shall not be lawful to take execution against the body of any person upon a judgment recovered for costs only, and in any case in which the judgment shall not be rendered for the sum of £10 or upwards, exclusive of costs.

In *Beattie* v. *McKay*, 2 Ch. R. 59, Draper, C. J., on an application by bail to set aside a *ca. sa.* on the grounds that there were not fifteen days between teste and return, and that it did not lie in the sheriff's hands four days before return day, says : " The principal could not have moved to set aside the writ on the ground that it had not lain four days in the sheriff's office. As to him this was no irregularity, and if he had been taken or rendered on the writ, he would have been regularly, as far as that is concerned, in custody, the authorities are quite clear that the four days are exclusive, and therefore the irregularity secondly complained being established in fact, the defendants are entitled to succeed on that objection.

As to the four days, 2 Salk. 599, 2 Saund. 72, a *ca. sa.* to charge bail must lie four days exclusive in the sheriff's office. This is also declared to be the practice in *Cork* v. *Brockhurst*, 13 East 592, and see 1 Archb. 886.

As to the teste and return days. Draper, C. J., says, in *Beattie* v. *McKay*, that there need not be fifteen days between teste and return—that whatever doubt existed before our Act, 12 Vict. ch. 63, there is no doubt now.

I hardly see how this statute affects the question.

Under the C. L. P. Act of 1852 rules were made by the Judges in England. Rule 74: " Writs of *ca. sa.*, for the purpose of outlawry on final process, or to fix bail, must be made returnable on a day certain in term, and may be so returnable on any day in term, and it shall be sufficient for either purpose that there be eight days between teste and return."

Rule 75 further provides that a *ca. sa.* to fix bail shall have eight days between teste and return, and must in London and Middlesex be entered four clear days in sheriff's office.

Then the Imperial Act of 1854, sec. 90, provides that writs of execution to fix bail may be tested and returned in vacation. To which is added a note in *Markham's* C. L. P. Acts, p. 197. "This enactment seems to have been made to remedy what was probably an oversight in Rule 74, 1853, which provided that these writs should be returnable on a day certain in term."

Our C. L. P. Act, 1856, has a like clause, 273: "Writs of execution to fix bail may be tested and returnable in vacation.

But I can find no rule of Court as in England—rules 74 and 75—amongst the rules made by the Judges, under our C. L. P. Act. These rules seem intentionally omitted from our rules.

Our Act also, sec. 272, directs that every writ of *ca. sa.* shall be tested the day it issues, and remain in force two months.

A form is given of a *ca. sa.*: "We command you that you take, &c., * * have the body before, &c., immediately after the execution hereof to satisfy," &c.

The absence of any rule, like 74 in the English rules, in our practice creates some difficulty. It seems to me that we must consider that the *ca. sa.* to fix bail must be in the form prescribed for all *ca. sa.'s*, and that there can be no distinction, such as is required by the English rules. Therefore that it is not necessary that it should be returnable on a day certain.

It must lie four days, clear juridical days in the sheriff's office its teste, of course being the day of issue. If this view be correct all objections as to teste and return are disposed of. I am inclined to think that objections of this kind should be disposed of as matters of practice on motion, and not by way of plea.

I do not think the Judicature Act allows matters to be pleaded in bar which, as matters of practice have hitherto always been disposed of by motion.

No question appears to have been raised at the trial, or in the rule to set aside the verdict as to teste, or return, or the necessity of the return being on a day certain.

From the language of the judgment, I gather that on the argument of the rule it was objected that the writ should have been eight days instead of four in sheriff's hands.

In the reasons of appeal appears for the first time the point as to a day certain.

I think the appeal fails on all the grounds taken. The bail could have rendered their principal, if not on the writ before action, but in the time usually allowed after.

My learned Brothers take a different view of the law. I must say that I think the profession might well have considered that they should adopt the form of *ca. sa.* presented by the rules of Court as apparently a form of general use without any exceptions.

I especially regret that all remedy against the bail should be thus lost, and instead of a just debt being recovered, a heavy amount of costs exceeding the amount in dispute be incurred by the plaintiff, and on a point, as far as I can see first taken by the defendants in their reasons of appeal.

BURTON, J. A.—It is not, I think, necessary in this case to express any opinion upon the point so strongly urged by Mr. MacKelcan upon the argument, that no person can be arrested for costs, even though those costs form part of a judgment recovered for debt and costs, because, assuming his argument to be well founded, the writ was not therefore void, but might have been amended so as to confine it to the debt.

On the lodging of the writ which was issued with the sheriff, the defendant in the original suit could have rendered himself in discharge of his bail, and upon application would have obtained his discharge on payment of the debt, if that really be (contrary to the practice of the profession for over a quarter of a century) the correct view of the law.

Whether the *ca. sa.* should or should not be returnable on a day certain may admit of some question. I have always entertained the opinion myself that it was the correct practice to make it returnable on a day certain, and it is the course I should myself have pursued if called upon to take proceedings to fix bail since the passing of the C. L. P. Act; but even assuming that to be the proper form of proceeding, the question arises, whether the objection is now open to the appellant, or whether it should not have been taken by motion, as was the case in *Kemp* v. *Hyslop*, 1 M. & W. 58.

I have no doubt that unless a change has been made by the recent legislation in fusing law and equity, that any objections to the sufficiency of the writ, by reason of there not being the requisite number of days between the teste and return, or its not lying for the requisite time in the sheriff's office, must be the subject of motion and cannot be raised by plea.

The omission to place a *ca. sa.* in the sheriff's hands at all, or placing there a writ which is void, is a different matter, and can no doubt be pleaded, but the distinction is very clear.

I endeavoured to point out, in *Harvey* v. *Harvey*, 9 A. R. 91, that mere matter of practice is not pleadable, although I admit that if something is required by statute or by contract to be done as a condition precedent to the bringing of the action, then the omission to do that act, although a mere matter of practice in one sense, can be pleaded.

Thus the omission in that case to lodge a *fi. fa.* and procure a return of *nulla bona* would have been properly the subject of a plea.

And in the present case, an omission to lodge a *ca. sa.* would have been pleadable. The condition of the recognizance is, that the defendant shall pay the costs and condemnation money or render himself; and, inasmuch as the object of the recognizance is to secure to the plaintiff in the action satisfaction of his judgment, it has always been construed with reference to that object.

If the plaintiff sues out a *fi. fa.* and makes his money there is an end of the matter, and therefore the condition has been held to be satisfied if the defendant render within a certain time after the plaintiff has notified his intention to have execution against his person, and as long ago as the 38th Eliz. it was held that the render required in the recognizance was intended to be a render upon process awarded. The suing out of the process therefore is not as pointed out in *Sandon* v. *Proctor*, 7 B. & C. 800, a matter required by any rule or practice of the Court, but by the recognizance, and on that ground it is a good plea that no *ca. sa.* issued.

That a mere irregularity in the writ, or an omission to lodge the writ for the requisite time could only be taken advantage of by motion and not by plea, I may refer to *Tidd's* Practice, vol. 2 p. 1182; and to *Ball* v. *The Manucaptors of Russell*, 2 Lord Raymond, 1196, where it was held that although the *ca. sa.* was bad for irregularity, there being only five days between the teste and return and would have been set aside on motion, it could not be raised by plea: *Elliott* v. *Lane*, 1 Wil. 334.

Cherry v. *Powell*, 1 D. & Ry. 50, where the point raised by the plea was the lodging of the writ for the requisite time in the sheriff's office, the Court held that being a mere matter of practice, though essential to the fixing of the bail, it was not arguable that it could not be pleaded but must be raised by motion; and the Court then refers to *Dudlow* v. *Watchorn*, 16 East 39, and distinguishes it on the ground that the writ was issued to the wrong county, and was not such a writ as would give the defendant searching in the proper sheriff's office any information. See also *Campbell* v. *Cumming*, 1 Burr. 1187, where the *ca. sa.* was made returnable in vacation: *Chomley* v. *Veal*, 2 Lord Raymond, 1096.

I do not think that any change has been made in this respect by the legislation referred to. No doubt it is intended that a litigant shall be able to obtain now in one and the same Court the relief which he was sometimes driven to obtain in another ; but the bail were always enabled to obtain in the one Court the relief to which they were entitled, it was simply a question of how it should be obtained, they were never driven to file a bill in equity to obtain the relief, but they could not set up mere matter of practice by plea, although they might by an application on motion set aside the proceedings if they were irregular.

If, therefore, this is to be regarded as a mere irregularity, I think it is not open to the defendants to raise the question by plea, but if there has been no substantial compliance with what the recognizance requires then the defence is open upon the record, and although apparently not much depended upon in the Court below it is raised in the reasons of appeal, and we are I think bound to give effect to it.

That objection is in effect that the writ of *ca. sa.* not being made returnable on a day certain has been returned before it was returnable, the defendant not having been taken upon it, and the two months fixed by the statute as the period during which it shall remain in force not having expired at the time the return was made.

The difficulty that the bail would experience with a writ issued in this form is, that on going to the sheriff's office they find a writ not returnable on a particular day, and they know that until the return day they are entitled to render their principal in discharge of their obligation. How are they to know that the sheriff will take upon himself to make a return after the expiration of four or any other number of days, at the instance of the plaintiff? Might they not rather assume from the circumstance that no day is named, that the plaintiff intended to extend to them the indulgence of rendering their principal during the entire period that the writ remained in force ?

In *Kemp* v. *Hyslop*, 1 M. & W. 58, Lord Abinger says, if no Judge's order had been made to return the writ of *ca. sa.* there can be no question that the bail would not have been fixed, for the writ of itself would not have been returnable and until then the bail are not liable. He goes on indeed to say, "and indeed it never would have been returnable at all until the principal had been taken, and then the bail would have been discharged by the act of taking the principal."

I incline to think, although it is not necessary in this case to decide, that if the writ had remained in the sheriff's hands until the expiry of two months from its date and had been then returned, that would be sufficient to fix the bail.

It is singular how little is to be found in the books on this subject, since the alteration in the form of the writs, and the plaintiff's solicitors in this case might not unreasonably have felt themselves justified by the form of pleading given in *Bullen & Leake's* work on pleading, in adopting the course they have done, but I have come to the conclusion, not however without some fluctuation of opinion, that no writ was duly issued in this case, such as by law is required, with a return day named up to which time the bail could render, and that it is therefore properly the subject of a plea, and is open to the appellant on this appeal.

I think that we must allow this appeal, and dismiss the action as premature.

PATTERSON, J.A.—This action is upon a recognizance of bail, whereby the defendants undertook that if John Mackenzie should happen to be convicted at the suit of the plaintiff in a certain action then depending in the County Court of the county of Wentworth, he should satisfy the costs and condemnation money or render himself to the custody of the sheriff of the county of Wentworth, or that they would do it for him.

The statement of defence begins with a plea of *nul tiel record* which is untrue; and then goes on to allege that the judgment recovered was for $119.77, and $62.94 costs: that no valid *ca. sa.* was sued out against John Mackenzie and returned into Court: that a writ which is set out and no other was issued, setting out a *ca. sa.* for $182.71 for debt and costs, tested 16th July, 1883, returnable immediately after execution, and indorsed, "*ca. sa.* to fix bail: Mr. Sheriff, levy the whole $182.71 and interest thereon at six per cent. per annum, from the 20th day of October, A.D. 1882. Also $10 for this and former writ, your own fees and incidental expenses:" That the *ca. sa.* was null and void having been issued contrary to R. S. O. ch. 67 sec. 3, which enacts that no person shall be liable to arrest for non-payment of costs; That the indorsement was also in violation of the terms of the statute; and that the defendants could not lawfully have rendered their principal under that writ or in accordance with the indorsement thereon.

A reply was filed in which the plaintiff avers that the writ was duly issued, but which adds to the allegations of fact only the allegation that the *ca. sa.* was delivered to the sheriff to be executed, and returned *non est inventus.*

The evidence adds the further fact that the *ca. sa.* was delivered to the sheriff on 16th July, 1883, and returned on 21st of same month.

The learned Judge of the County Court decided against the defence, and Mr. Mackelcan has renewed his objections on this appeal.

The objection founded on the direction in the writ to take the body of the defendant for the costs as well as for the debt recovered is clearly no defence to this action.

If the defendant had been rendered or arrested, and then detained for the costs after satisfying the debt, the question of the right to arrest for the whole judgment, including the costs, when the original debt is over $100, would come up. At present it is not necessary to express any opinion upon it, because the writ cannot be said to be void, even if the costs were improperly included. It would be simply issued for too much, and a mistake of the kind is always amendable: *Laroche* v. *Wasbrough*, 2 T. R. 737; *Monys* v. *Leake*, 8 T. R. 416, note; *McCormack* v. *Melton*, 1 A. & E. 331; *Evans* v. *Manero*, 7 M. & W. 463; *Englehart* v. *Dunbar*, 2 Dowl. P. C. 202; *Bradley* v. *Bailey*, 3 Dowl. P. C. 111.

A more serious question is, whether the bail can be charged upon this writ, which is returnable only upon execution, and which has been returned without being executed, or, in other words, before it was, according to its tenor, returnable.

Other questions, touching the time the writ ought to lie in the sheriff's hands, &c., have been raised, and upon them arises the preliminary question whether they can be raised by plea, or only by motion, as being merely matters of practice. I do not, at this moment, propose to discuss this preliminary question, or to inquire how far our present practice is necessarily governed by the rules that were imperative in former times when, as pointed out by Buller, J., in *Donelly* v. *Dunn*, 2 B. & P. 45, the defendant, in such an action as this, was called upon to state a legal defence upon record, not merely to say that he had an equity in his favour—these matters of practice belonging, as he explained, rather to the equity side of the Court.

The question of there being a proper writ and a proper return to fix the bail was always, as I understand the law, a proper subject for plea, though it may have been also one which might be raised by motion to set aside the proceedings on the recognizance.

In *Dudlow* v. *Watchorn*, 16 East 39, the plea was, that no *ca. sa.* was *duly* sued out, returned, and filed according to the custom and practice of the Court, to which the plaintiff replied shewing a writ of *ca. sa.* into Middlesex, and the defendant rejoined that the venue in the action against the principal was in London. The rejoinder was held not to be a departure, because the allegation of the plea that it was *duly* issued referred to the purpose for which it professed to be issued, that of charging the bail, and was equivalent to saying that no *ca. sa.* was sued out in the manner required by the practice of the Court to charge bail. Lord Ellenborough said : " We must take notice of the practice of the Court in a case like this, where it is the very subject matter of dispute, and is put in issue. For what purpose is the issuing of the *ca. sa.* at all in this instance, except as a matter of practice ?" and Bayley, J., said : "Alleging that no writ of *ca. sa.* was duly sued out and returned or filed, &c., means that it was not so sued, returned, and filed as to enable the plaintiff to charge the bail ; and if it be shewn not to have issued according to the practice of the Court for that purpose, it is shewn not to have been duly issued," &c.

In *Sandon* v. *Proctor,* 7 B. & C. 800, the plea to a *sci. fa.* on recognizance of bail was no *ca. sa.* duly issued, lodged, and returned. Replication *ca. sa.* issued and returned *non est inventus.* Rejoinder that the *ca. sa.* did not lie in the sheriff's office four days. On demurrer, the rejoinder was held bad as pleading a mere irregularity. Bayley. J., in distinguishing the objection from that to a *ca. sa.* itself, said : " It seems to me that the obligation to sue out a *ca. sa.* results by law from the terms of the recognizance. The language of the condition of the recognizance is, ' if the principal shall not pay the damages or render himself.' The latter words, ' or render himself' have been construed to import that the principal is to render in discharge of his bail only when the plaintiff has, by suing out a *ca. sa.* intimated an intention to take the body of the plaintiff. If the plaintiff elects to proceed by *fi. fa.* or *elegit* the bail are not bound to render the principal ; so if the principal die before the *ca. sa.* is returnable, the bail are discharged, because they are not bound to render the principal before the return day of the *ca. sa.*"

The same doctrine as to the bail not being bound to render the principal before the return day of the *ca. sa.* is stated also by Holroyd and Littledale, JJ. The latter points out that the recognizance does not require that the *ca. sa.* shall remain in the sheriff's office four days exclusive of the return day and an intervening Sunday; and that an allegation that it has not remained for that time in the sheriff's office shews that the party has broken a rule of Court, but not that the condition of the recognizance is satisfied.

The recognizance in the present case is in the same form as that in *Sandon* v. *Proctor*, and, after as full an investigation of the subject as I have been able to give it, I see no reason to suppose that the law with us is not the same as stated by Bayley, J., and the other Judges in that case, namely, that the bail are not bound to render their principal until the return day of the *ca. sa.*; and that for this reason the writ must be returnable on a day certain, and be in the hands of the sheriff on that day. I do not say for how many days before that day, because I am at present only discussing the necessity for its being returnable on a day certain.

In England it was enacted by 3 and 4 Wm. IV. ch. 67, sec. 2 that "all writs of execution may be tested on the day on which the same are issued, and be made returnable immediately after the execution thereof." While this was the law, and before the Common Law Procedure Act, under which rules, which I shall notice, were made, the case of *Kemp* v. *Hyslop*, 1 M. & W. 58 was decided. A judgment having been obtained on a trial at *nisi prius*, in the vacation, against the principal, a *ca. sa.* was sued out on 14th August, returnable immediately after the execution thereof, and on the same day was lodged at the sheriff's office and entered in the public book. On the 12th of September a Judge's order was made for the sheriff to return the writ in six days. It was served on him on the 14th, and he returned the writ the same day *non est inventus*. Proceedings were thereupon had against the bail. A Judge made an order to set them aside, being of opinion that the bail were not regularly fixed. That order was affirmed by the Court.

Lord Abinger, C. B., said: "If no Judge's order had been made to return the writ of *ca. sa.* there can be no question but that the bail would not have been fixed; for the writ itself would not have been *returnable*, and until then the bail are not liable; and, indeed, it could never have been returnable at all until the principal had been taken, and then the bail would have been discharged by the act of taking the principal." He then discussed the power of the Judge to make the order to return the writ, which was questioned, and expressed the opinion that, admitting the order to be legal on one of three grounds suggested, it could not have the effect of altering the time at which the writ was returnable; and that, if it had such effect, the bail could not be fixed till they had notice of it. He expressed a doubt whether bail could be fixed at all, except by process of *ca. sa.* in the old form, and suggested that it would be well in future to avoid question by issuing the *ca. sa.* in the old form, returnable in term, in those cases where it was intended to proceed against the bail.

Then, in England, came the rules of Hilary Term, 1853, made under the Common Law Procedure Act, 1852. Rule 72 provided that every writ of execution may be made returnable on a day certain in term. This seems to have made it optional to make the writ returnable on a day certain in term, or immediately on execution: *Drake* v. *Gough*, 1 Dowl. N. S. 573.

Rule 74 was that "writs of *capias ad satisfaciendum* for the purpose of outlawry on final process or to fix bail must be made returnable on a day certain in term, and may be made so returnable on any day in term; and it shall be sufficient for either purpose that there be eight days between the teste and return." The latter part of this rule shortened the time necessary between the teste and return of a *ca. sa.* to fix bail or proceed to outlawry which, at common law, was fifteen days, and had been so left by the statute 13 Charles II., St. 2, ch. 2, sec. 6, which made the fifteen days unnecessary in the case of other writs of *ca. sa.* or *fi. fa.*

Rule 74 was in one respect varied by the C. L. P. Act 1854, sec. 90, which enacted that "writs of execution to fix bail may be tested and returnable in vacation," leaving the requisite of the day certain untouched.

We have not, in this Province, followed very closely the steps of the Imperial law-givers, either judicial or parliamentary, though we have probably attained the same result.

We have no statute directly declaring that writs of execution may be made returnable immediately upon execution; nor have we ever had a Rule of Court like that part of the English rule 72, which I have quoted, nor like rule 74. The place of these enactments is, however, supplied by the forms of writs prepared by our Judges under the Common Law Procedure Act of 1856, in which they are made returnable immediately after execution, and by the provisions contained in sections 189 and 192 of that Act with a variation of section 189, in the consolidation of the. C. L. P. Act, C. S. U. C. ch. 22, sec. 272.

Section 189 of the Act of 1856, following section 124 of the English C. L. P. Act. 1852, declared that all writs of execution should remain in force for one year and no longer unless renewed. This in England placed a limit upon the duration of the writ, which, under the Act of 3 & 4 Wm. IV. ch. 67, was in force till executed, whatever length of time might elapse before that was completely effected, and even though the judgment creditor died in the interval: *Ellis* v. *Griffiths*, 16 M. & W. 106; *Jordan* v. *Binches*, 13 Q. B. 757. With us it extended the life of the writ, which before that had been bounded by by the return day. In consolidating the C. L. P, Act, sec. 189 became section 249, and writs of *ca. sa.* were excepted from the class of executions to which it applied; and, by section 272, writs of *ca. sa.* were to continue in force for two months from the day of issue and no longer, and were not renewable, a new Judge's order for arrest being made necessary. We now have section 249 of the C. S. U. C. ch. 22, represented by section 11 of R. S. O. ch. 66; section 272 by section 53. Section 192 of the C. L. P.

Act of 1856, which was copied from section 90 of the
English C. L. P. Act 1854, and was section 274 of the
C. S. U. C. ch. 22, now declares, in section 54 of R. S. O.
ch. 66, as it did in the other statutes that " writs of execution to fix bail may be tested and returnable in vacation;"
thus obviously recognizing the continued necessity for
making a *ca. sa.* issued for the purpose of fixing bail
returnable on a day certain. Up to the passing of the Act
of 1856 the writ was returnable in term. The statute
altered the law in that particular, without dispensing with
any other requisite.

If it had been intended to vary the conditions on which
the liability of the bail depended, as laid down in the cases
which I have cited of *Sandon* v. *Proctor* and *Kemp* v.
Hyslop, we should doubtless have found it so expressly
enacted.

It may not be out of place to remark, notwithstanding
that I am not discussing the other requisites of the writ,
such as the time between the *teste* and return, that, having
regard to the terms of the Statute of Charles II., and to
the absence of any rule like the English rule 74, it may be
prudent for practitioners to let the time be at least fifteen
days.

My conclusion is, that the bail in this case were not
fixed, and that this appeal should therefore be allowed,
with costs, and the action dismissed, with costs.

OSLER, J. A.—I desire to express no opinion on the
point whether in any circumstances a defendant may be
arrested for costs which form part of a general judgment
for debt or damages, and costs.

If the debt is beyond the arrestable amount, the writ of
ca. sa. cannot be void merely because costs are also included.
That would at most afford a ground for a motion by the
defendant to reduce the sum for which he had been arrested,
or for the bail to claim a reduction of the amount for
which they would otherwise be liable on the recognizance

to pay the costs and condemnation money, a question which is not before us on this appeal.

What we really have to determine is, whether the proper proceedings have been taken for the purpose of fixing the liability of the bail.

At the time of the passage of the Common Law Procedure Act, 1856, a *ca. sa.* to fix bail was returnable, as were other writs of execution, on a day certain in term. There must have been eight days between the teste and the return day: *Beattie* v. *McKay*, 2 Ch. R. 57; *Kymer* v. *Sydsert*, 4 M. & S. 636; *Harr.* C. L. P. Act, p. 278, 2nd ed. And it must have lain for the last four of those eight days, exclusive of the day of lodging it and the return day, in the sheriff's office: *Harr.* C. L. P. Act, 378; *Potts* v. *Baird*, 7 P. R. 113.

Under the 16 Vic. ch. 175, sec. 6, it must have borne teste and been dated on the day of its issue instead of being as formerly, tested as of some day in term: C. L. P. Act, 1856, sec. 189, R. S. O. ch. 66, sec. 53. I think that continued to be the recognized and prevailing practice, although it is arguable that when writs came to be tested on the day of issue it was no longer necessary that there should be eight days between the teste and the return, which, in practice, was a mere fiction when writs could be tested of a day previous to that in which they were actually issued. Possibly it would be sufficient to issue it in time to lodge it in the sheriff's office for the four clear days before the return day: *Beattie* v. *Taylor*, 2 P. R. 44, which however was not the case of a *ca. sa.* to fix bail. Then, what change was introduced by the C. L. P. Act 19 Vict. ch. 43?

The 189th section (C. S. U. C. ch. 22, sec. 249) provided that every writ of execution should remain in force for one year from the teste and no longer if unexecuted, unless renewed, and the 192nd section enacted that writs of execution to fix bail might be tested and *returnable* in vacation.

It is manifest from these two sections, and also from the fact that section 33 of 7 Wm. IV. ch. 3, C. S. U. C. sec.

248, R. S. O. ch. 66, sec. 9, (the latter part of which provides that it shall still be necessary in order to charge bail to sue out process of execution into the particular district,) was left unrepealed, that a distinction was intended to be maintained between ordinary writs of execution and an execution to fix bail. The former were not to be returnable at any particular time, short of their actual execution; and they might be executed at any time while they were in force during the first, or by renewal during the second year from the teste. No return day therefore was required for such writs beyond the day of their actual execution or expiration. But with regard to writs of execution to fix bail, it was otherwise. By the law of the land, not merely by the practice of the Court, bail were not bound by their recognizance to render the principal before the return day of the *ca. sa.*; *Sandon* v. *Proctor,* 7 B. & C. 800; *Hinton* v. *Acraman,* 2 C. B. 369; *Kemp* v. *Hyslop,* 1 M. & W. 58, 64; and therefore if a *ca. sa.* to fix bail was in force for a year and renewable, and made returnable like other writs immediately after the execution thereof, *ex vi termini* bail would either not be fixed until the expiry of a year from the teste of the writ, or would be discharged by its execution, that is to say, by the actual personal caption of their principal. A special return day was therefore necessary, and is, in my opinion, required by the very terms of the section, which provides that such writs may be *returnable* in vacation. That implies a return day different from the return after execution. The case of *Kemp* v. *Hyslop,* 1 M. & W. 58 is a strong authority that bail cannot be fixed by a writ in this form.

That case arose under the Imperial Act, 3 & 4 Wm. IV., ch. 67, sect. 2 of which provided that all writs of execution might be tested on the day on which the same were issued, and might be made returnable immediately after the execution thereof. A writ of *ca. sa.* having issued returnable in that way and having remained in the sheriff's hands a for considerable time unexecuted, a Judge's order was made pursuant to 2 Wm. IV. ch. 39

sec. 15, directing the sheriff to return it in six days.
On the day on which the order was served upon him
he returned the writ *non est inventus*, and proceedings
were thereupon taken against the bail. These proceedings were set aside. It was held that though the
order was a legal one for the purpose of compelling the
sheriff to notify by his return what he had done with the
writ, it could not have the effect of altering the time
at which the writ was returnable, or if it had, that
bail could not be fixed until notice of it had been given
to them, or at least until it had been lodged in the sheriff's office four clear days before the time at which it
made the writ returnable.

A doubt is expressed which seems to intimate the
opinion of the Court, whether bail *can* be fixed at all
except by process of *ca. sa.* in the old form. The cases of
Lewis v. *Holmes*, 10 Q. B. 896, and *Levy* v. *Hamer*, 5 Ex.
518, which decided that proceedings to outlawry cannot be
founded on a *ca. sa.* returnable immediately after the
execution thereof, are also distinctly analogous in principle.
See *Beattie* v. *Taylor*, 2 P. R. 44.

Writs of execution with us were not made returnable
immediately after the execution thereof expressly by any
statute, as in England, but the reasoning of these cases is
not less applicable on that account.

The 189th section of the C. L. P. Act in effect made
writs, other than writs of execution to fix bail, so returnable, and the forms of writs framed by the judges,
and appended to the Reg. Gen. H. T. 1857 run in that way,
Harr. C. L. P. Act 1st ed. p. 537, n. (*a*), 2nd ed. p.
445, note. A form of *ca. sa.* is given, returnable immediately after the execution thereof, appropriate to a
ca. sa. other than a *ca. sa.* to fix bail. No form is expressly
provided for the latter, but that it was not supposed that
these forms would meet every case is evident from Rule
169 Harr. C. L. P. Act, 2nd ed. p. 704, which provides that
they " may be used in cases to which they are applicable
with such alterations as the nature of the action, the

description of the Court, the character of the parties, or the circumstances of the case may require."

The C. L. P. Act in the Con. Stat. U. C. ch. 22, and the Act respecting arrest and imprisonment for debt, the provisions of which are now found in the R. S. O. ch. 66, ss. 9, 11, 53, 54, and ch. 67, s. 7, only emphasized the distinction between the writ of *ca. sa.* issued where the defendant had not been held to special bail, and the writ of execution to fix bail, merely providing, in the former case, that the writ, which can now only be obtained on a Judge's order specially granted for that purpose (R. S. O. ch. 67, sec. 7), shall be in force for two months only, and shall not be renewed, and requiring a new writ to be issued on a new affidavit after that time (ch. 66, sec. 53); but in the latter case that the writ may issue without an affidavit (ch. 67, sec. 7), and (under the heading "Writs of execution to fix bail") that they may be tested and returnable in vacation (ch. 66, sec. 54). I am, therefore, of opinion, as I may say I have been ever since I had occasion to examine the question in the case of *Potts* v. *Baird*, 7 P. R. 113, though it was not raised by the bail in that case, that the bail cannot be legally fixed by a writ of *ca. sa.* returnable immediately after its execution.

Such a writ is not irregular, as the plaintiff may desire to take the body. The bail could not move to set it aside, and they undoubtedly might, if they had notice of it, render their principal upon it. But inasmuch such as they are not bound to render before the return day, and such a writ is not returnable before execution, which *ipso facto* discharges them, it is not a writ appropriate to the case; and as the question is not one merely of the practice of the Court, but of what is required by the law of the land, in order to fix the bail, I think the objection though it might have been taken by motion to set aside the proceedings, may also be raised on the pleadings as a defence to the action. The right to do so does not, in my judgment, depend in the slightest degree upon anything to be found in the Judicature Act.

I think the appeal should be allowed.

Appeal allowed, with costs : [HAGARTY, C. J., *diss.*]

HOGG V. MAGUIRE.

Will, validity of—Establishing prior will— Uncorroborated evidence of beneficiary.

The testator, by his will made in June 1880, gave the bulk of his property to the plaintiff, his sister, with whom, in the autumn before his death, he had quarrelled, and it did not appear that she saw him again before he died. The defendant, another sister, claimed under a second will made an hour or two before the testator's death. The evidence shewed that the testator was a very determined man, and not easily influenced; that he was suffering from excessive indulgence in drink; that he latterly spoke in very bitter and offensive terms of the defendant, and had frequently said that she should have nothing; that he had frequently, and as late as a few days before his death, stated that if he died everything was arranged and that the plaintiff would get his property. Shortly before his death the defendant had him brought to her house. On the night of his death the physician in attendance told defendant that if anything was to be settled it should be done at once. A solicitor was sent for to draw a will. The defendant instructed him before he saw the testator, and upon her instructions the will was drawn, which gave the bulk of the property to the defendant, and a bequest of $1,000 to the plaintiff. This the solicitor read over to the testator and asked him if he approved of it. He made a sign of dissent. The defendant urged the testator to give the plaintiff the $1,000, but (as the defendant stated) he said $10 was enough for the plaintiff. The solicitor thereupon went away leaving the will with the defendant, and during his absence it was signed.

The evidence of various witnesses for the defence was conflicting as to the incidents which happened during this time and until the testator's decease; and while they all spoke of the testator's unwillingness to give the plaintiff more than $10, there was no evidence, other than that of the defendant, of his desire to give her the bulk of his property or to make any disposition of it.

Held, reversing the judgment of Proudfoot, J., that the second will could not be established on the uncorroborated evidence of the defendant, and the prior will was declared to be the testator's last will.

THIS was an appeal from a judgment pronounced by Proudfoot, J., establishing a will alleged to have been executed under the circumstances stated in the judgment, by Edward Brown, of the city of Toronto, moulder, whereby he devised to the defendant the bulk of his property; and came on to be heard before this Court on the 26th and 27th of November, 1884.*

Robinson, Q.C., for the appellant.

S.H.Blake, Q.C., and *Francis*, for the respondent Maguire.

Lash, Q.C., for the respondents Brown.

Present.—HAGARTY, C.J.O., BURTON, PATTERSON, and OSLER, JJ. A

The circumstances giving rise to the action and the authorities cited appear in the judgment.

January 13th, 1885.   HAGARTY, C. J. O., delivered the judgment of the Court.

This is an appeal from a judgment of Mr. Justice Proudfoot, in which he pronounced in favour of a will made in defendants' favour by one Edward Brown.

Plaintiff claiming under a prior will, appeals.

Edward Brown died on Monday, April 17, 1882.

On 3rd June, 1880, nearly two years before his death, he made his will leaving all his property to plaintiff, his sister, Isabella Hogg, subject to legacies, $200 to Mary Maud Brown, payable at twenty-one; if dying previously to revert to plaintiff, and $100 to his sister Margaret.

No question arises as to the validity of this will.

He was a moulder by trade, aged about thirty-six at his death, owning some houses. He was for some time very intemperate in his habits, working steadily at times, and then drinking heavily.

He is described by most of the witnesses on both sides as a man of a very determined turn of mind, and likely to have his own way.

In the fall before his death he had some quarrel with plaintiff, who lived with him, and they parted, and she does not appear to have seen him alive again. It is proved that she spoke very bitterly of him, and declared she would never go near him, &c.

He was dangerously ill in January before his death, but rallied, and appears to have resumed work in Toronto. He boarded with Patrick McNicol, a tavern-keeper.

He was taken ill about Tuesday, April 11th, and was attended by Dr. Fisher until the Sunday following. They had great difficulty in keeping him in the house, and he got out on Friday, and was brought home in a very bad state. He was suffering from pneumonia, in addition to either delirium tremens or something very like it.

On Monday morning McNicol obtained an order from
Dr. Fisher to have him admitted to the hospital as they
could not keep him.

The defendant Mrs. Maguire, also his sister, lived in
Toronto, on Teraulay street. The terms on which she and
deceased lived will be noticed hereafter; they do not
appear to have been very friendly.

McNicol thought that he had better see defendant
before taking deceased to the hospital, and went up on
the Monday morning to see her. She said not to take
him to the hospital, but to bring him to her house, and she
would take care of him. To induce deceased to go to
defendant's, McNicol told him that she was ill, and asked
him to go and see her. He agreed; they went, and she
received him kindly. McNicol says he did not at first seem
willing to remain; said he must go to his work. Defendant urged him to stay, saying they would give him every
attention.

Doctor Cassidy visited him about noon; he found him
with pneumonia, in a very low condition. He was
rational—no delirium—thought him in danger. He was
called in again about nine that night. He told defendant
that he was dying, and advised her to send for a clergyman
and some one to arrange his affairs. The doctor considered
him intelligent and in a rational condition; cannot say he
asked him any questions distinctly; he seemed to know
him. When the doctor told Mrs. Maguire what he advised,
deceased asked her what he had been saying to her. He
seemed anxious to hear what the doctor had said. The
doctor considered the deceased capable of making a will.
He then left. He told the defendant she had no time to
lose; that if she wished anything done it must be done
that night. She asked would not to-morrow do; the
doctor said that would be too late. The doctor says he
died from asthenia, as he thinks—failure of heart power.
He left him at a quarter past nine. He died at a quarter
to twelve, midnight. Doctor Cassidy said that, from his
appearance when he left him, his consciousness might

probably last for two hours longer, and he might have
possession of his mental faculties till the last moment, or
shortly before his death; that he formed that opinion
without speaking positively. He did not see him again
alive. He was then sinking rapidly; thinks as he left
deceased put out his hand to him as to shake hands; the
process of dissolution had begun; he heard the death
rattle in his throat; this was from the accumulation of
phlegm in the throat, and was apparently noticeable for
many hours before he died.

Mr. Wardrop, a solicitor, was sent for, and came about
half past nine. Before seeing deceased, Mrs. Maguire gave
him what she represented as deceased's instructions as to
his property. He sat down, and from them he prepared
a short will. By this he left all his real and personal
property to defendant, his sister, in trust to pay his sister,
Isabella Hogg, the plaintiff, $1,000; to his niece Maud
Brown, $200; to his brother John, $100; to his sister Margaret, $25; to Polly and Maggie Carlton, $25 each; and to
Walter Carlton, $20; residue to defendant.

Mr. Wardrop states he then went up with her to the
bed room. He said: "This is the will prepared for you
from instructions received from Mrs. Maguire." Deceased
said nothing, raised his eyes and looked at witness. He
thought him conscious. He then read the will slowly over
to deceased; he thought he was following the reading.
Asked him if he approved the will; he made no answer;
moved his head as if in dissent; witness asked defendant
how this was, and stepped back and she took his place at
the bed side. She said: "Edward, you said you would before
this gentleman came. You know Bella is very poor and her
children won't or can't do anything for her; remember she
is your sister." Deceased muttered some sounds, witness
could not understand what they were. Defendant turned
to witness who said: "What is the matter?" She said:
"He only wants to leave Bella $10." He left the room.
She said she thought he would sign it from what he had
said to her before. He says, on being asked why he did

not take instructions direct from deceased, that defendant told him he would not be able to understand deceased, or would have difficulty in understanding him.

He says he thought deceased was conscious. did not suspect that he was not; his voice was like mumbling, plenty of voice, but defect in articulation. He was breathing hard with great difficulty, there was a gurgling continually, what is called death rattle.

Before he left he saw the elder Cullen, and gave him directions how to have the will executed. Mr. Wardrop must have left the house not before twenty minutes past ten p.m.

We now turn to Mrs. Maguire's account of the transaction.

She says that after the doctor had told her to have his affairs settled, she spoke to deceased, saying: " I suppose you have heard what the doctor said ? " He said, yes. She asked, was there a will. He said, no, it was destroyed. She asked, should she send for a lawyer. He assented. Wardrop came; she asked deceased should he come up. He said : " No, I will tell you and you can explain it." He said $10 was enough for Bella. Witness urged him to leave her $1,000, as she was poor. He said $10 was enough, the way she had treated him; then he spoke of the little girl, Maudie Brown, and he said he would leave her $200, the same as he had left in the will he had destroyed. She said she had never seen that will or heard what was in it. She then suggested his brother John, and urged him to leave him something. He considered, and then said, leave him $100, and $25 to Maggie, Mrs. Grey; then she suggested Mrs. Carlton's children, and he said $25 to Polly and $25 to Maggie. I said: "Edward, what will you do with the balance ? " He said : " You pay my debts and the balance goes to you." I said : " Leave the balance to some one else." He said : " No; you pay my debts, and the balance goes to you."

She again urged him to give Mrs. Hogg $1,000 and before she left he consented.

She gave the particulars to Mr. Wardrop who drew out the will.

They went up; Wardrop read the will to deceased, and asked was he prepared to sign it. He said: "No;" I said: "What was the objection?" He said: "Bella; I think $10 is enough for her." She then went down; so did Wardrop. She came up with some beef tea; he took it. She again urged him to leave Bella $1,000. Harry Cullen was then in the room. After that she said nothing further to him about the will. She did not know till between two and three in the morning that the will had been signed.

No one was present when she gave the instructions to Wardrop.

When her son, John Maguire, came home, she told him to go up and do the best he could for Bella, that all deceased wanted to give her was $10.

She remembers Mr. Jones coming about half an hour before the death; this would be after the signing of the will. She made no enquiry as to whether it had been signed or not. While Jones was there she asked deceased his age. He said: "Thirty-six." She said: "Don't you think you are thirty-seven or thirty-eight?" He said: "No, only thirty-six."

Three other persons were called by defendant as present at the execution of the will.

Henry Cullen was there at seven p.m. Deceased was then quite rational, recognized him and spoke to him by name; was there when Doctor Cassidy came; heard latter advise defendant to have his business affairs settled, and to send for a clergyman. Witness went away on an errand, and on his return found Wardrop reading the will to deceased. Deceased objected, saying he would only leave Bella $10, that was enough; she should get no $1,000. Defendant told him to try and leave her $1,000, as she was poor. He said: "The way she treated me, I will give her no more than $10." Witness stood by the door; did not hear all the will read. They left the room. Defendant came last and asked deceased to give Bella the $1,000. He made the same answer as before. William Cullen, his father, then came in and asked deceased, were his worldly affairs settled. Deceased said, no. The father said: "Well, are you ready to settle them?" Deceased again objected; said he would leave Bella $10. Father told him to try and do what Mrs. Maguire wanted him to do, and he would do what was right. Father coaxed him two or three times, and at last he consented. Father brought over the will and wrote the name, "Edward Brown," and deceased put his mark, and the witness Henry Cullen and John Maguire signed as witnesses. Deceased asked, had he put his cross all right. Deceased understood perfectly that it was the will read over to him by Wardrop. He was sensible till death. Remembers that Jones came in fifteen or twenty minutes after the will was signed. Thinks that deceased recognized him: that deceased said: "Good bye, Doctor," when Dr. Cassidy left him; after father had urged him to do as defendant wished him to do, he asked: "Are you ready to sign your will?" Deceased nodded his head. Father had previously written deceased's name to will. Deceased nodded again, when father asked, was he prepared to execute it. John Maguire, he says, also pressed deceased to leave the money to Mrs. Hogg.

Defendant knew that the will was signed shortly after; is sure she was told of it; one of them told her; heard some one telling her the will was signed; this was between eleven and twelve p.m. Witness does not remember the contents of the will; did not hear it all read.

William Cullen, his father, came about ten p.m. Deceased was quite conscious. Witness asked him if his affairs were settled. Deceased said: "No." Again asked him was he inclined to do so, and after a couple of minutes, having asked him again, he said: "Yes." Witness does not know what objection deceased had to sign the will. Witness brought will over; told him distinctly, and made him understand this was the will the lawyer had read to him; and deceased fully understood it. Witness never read the will, and says he wrote, "Edward Brown," after deceased had put his mark. Deceased took the pen, and witness steadied it for him. After this Jones came in. Witness heard defendant ask deceased how old he was. Deceased said, thirty-six; she said she thought he was thirty-seven; he said : " No, thirty-six." Deceased nodded his head to Jones. He says he did not urge deceased to sign ; he said nothing, " with the exception of something I might have said about Mrs. Maguire; there might have been a word used about Mrs. Maguire, that that was the will she wished him to sign."

John Maguire, defendant's son, (rather deaf), swore he came home about ten p.m, from the country. Defendant told him of the will and that deceased only wanted to leave Bella $10, and asked him to go up and see deceased. He did so, and urged deceased to consider how poor she was, and to leave her $1,000. Deceased said $10 was enough for Bella, she will get no $1,000 : that I did not know how badly she treated him. Witness went out and came back again and asked deceased had he reconsidered what he said. Deceased said : " Yes." William Cullen brought over the will and said : " This is the will the lawyer read to you." They assisted him to sit up; he put his mark, and they witnessed it. Deceased understood it. Witness says W. Cullen did not persuade him to sign while witness was there.

James Maguire, defendant's husband, swore he heard Wardrop read the will and heard deceased say (when defendant asked what he objected to): " Bella, $10 is plenty." This he said so that anybody could hear. Deceased was quite sensible. Witness heard them talking that the will had been signed between eleven and twelve o'clock. William Cullen told him. Witness thinks there would have been no difficulty in deceased instructing a lawyer and telling him what he wanted: that he had his senses and spoke loud enough, not low, and he could be heard; no difficulty in understanding what he said.

As to the feelings of deceased towards the plaintiff, Alexander Carlton, a brother-in-law of deceased, stated that early in the winter before his death, deceased told him he was going to make a will. Witness said he had heard he had already made one. Deceased said, yes, he had made a will—it is no good—he left all to the one side, to the Hogg family, except a trifle to Maguires, to Billy's young one. He said: "I'll make a will, and the Hogg family shall never get a dollar:" that he wanted to leave Billy's young one $500, and witness's Polly and Billy, and three or four others, and whatever was left he intended to leave to his brother Johnny. He said he had destroyed or burned his will. Another time he said he would leave Mrs. Hogg nothing; they were all one as near to him as the other; that the Hoggs had robbed him right and left.

William Jones was called by plaintiff; he had been out that day in the country with John Maguire; came back at half past ten; went to the house about eleven; found Maguire and H. Cullen with the deceased, who seemed to be dying; heard the death rattle; never spoke. Defendant was there and asked deceased if he knew Jones; he said nothing; heard defendant say, turning to deceased, it was too bad for a young man of his age to go that way at thirty-six; did not hear her ask him his age, and swears deceased did not speak or answer while he was there; witness saw him die.

The first will made in June, 1880, was proved; it was drawn by James Banks, who stated that deceased used to ask him on several occasions whether he had got his will. Witness would answer that he had it. That the last occasion of asking was four or five weeks before death.

William McKen, a witness to this will, says he several times heard him speak unfriendly as to defendant; that she was avaricious, mean, &c.

Margaret Gloynes used to wash for deceased. He brought his washing to her about a week before his death; he seemed very sick and sat down; said he was trying to wean himself from drink; witness said her brother-in-law had dropped off with drink. Deceased said: "If I was to drop on your floor the corner is Bella's;"—that she had toiled for him between six and seven years, and no one had looked after him except what she had done for him. This corner was next door or two to where witness then lived, and was deceased's property.

In the preceding summer she had heard him, when in liquor, say that he would not leave defendant the value of his shirt.

Thomas Johnston said that about April, 1881, he heard deceased say he had made his will, that he had not many to leave his property to, that it was in favour of Mrs. Hogg, except $200 for his brother George and some young woman. That he often heard him speak of defendant not friendly but not maliciously. He said he would sooner have a black snake after him than defendant.

Thomas Green said on the Friday before he died he saw deceased very ill. Witness said, " You ought to be home in bed ; if you don't you will be in the cemetery soon." He said : " If I do every thing is all right, any how." Witness asked : " What do you mean, is it in regard to property ?" He said : " Yes, that is settled, that was settled long ago." Before that deceased had told him he had made a will in favour of Mrs. Hogg, and mentioned about some legacies. One time deceased told him the reason he made the will in Mrs. Hogg's favour was that Mrs. Maguire should not receive anything of it. He was talkative about his property.

John Ryan swore, that in March next before his death deceased told him he had made a will giving most of his money to Mrs. Hogg, $500 or $250 to his brother's child, and the rest to her. Again on another occasion in January before his death. He was living at McNicol's on one of the occasions ; he said he would give Mrs. Maguire nothing.

Wm. J. Gibson often heard deceased speak against Mrs. Maguire in language not fit to be repeated. He said Bella was his favourite, and she was to be the one to get his property in case of accident, and the rest would not get a little bit of it.

John Sanderson said that two or three weeks before his death he asked deceased if he had made his will ; he answered, yes, it was all right, it was fixed, and there would be no dispute over it. He used to speak hardly of defendant, and call her names, not nice expressions. About a year before his death he heard him say he would never enter her house.

There was a good deal of medical testimony as to the probabilities of men affected as deceased was, retaining their faculties to the last hour of life.

The facts in evidence are peculiar. The deceased two years before his death made his will in favour of the plaintiff, Mrs. Hogg. He had a quarrel with her some six months before his death.

But with the exception of Alex. Carlton's evidence, and the expressions said to have been uttered by him the night of his death, there is nothing to shew any intention on his part to alter this will.

On the contrary, a number of witnesses, down to the Friday before his death, testify to his stating on several occasions that he had made his will in favour of the plaintiff, and that she would have his property.

The witnesses on both sides agree that he was a very determined man.

Banks, who drew his will and had it in keeping, proves that down to four or five weeks before his death he had asked him had he the will.

No witness, not even Carlton, testified that he had ever spoken of his sister, the defendant, as an intended object of his bounty. Carlton said he told him he would leave the residue to his brother John. On the contrary, there was a good deal of evidence of expressions of dislike on his part as to her.

It need hardly be said that the claims urged by defendant as to the last will require the most careful consideration by the Court.

She took the alleged instructions from the deceased. Beyond the alleged expressions as to plaintiff, in the last two hours of his life, that $10 would be enough for her, there is no evidence whatever from the lips of the deceased that Mrs. Maguire was to take the bulk of his property, or even to have any benefit under his will.

When Mr. Wardrop came the defendant was his only instructor as to deceased's views. Her witnesses state that deceased was quite capable of giving instructions himself, and that there was no difficulty in understanding him. The solicitor had no talk with him. He read the will and asked, did he approve—all he got was a sign of dissent. Then he heard defendant remonstrate with deceased, urging him as to "Bella," the plaintiff, and told witness he only wanted to leave plaintiff $10. Witness said his voice was like "mumbling." She had previously told Mr. Wardrop that he would not be able to understand, or would have difficulty in understanding deceased, when she gave him the instructions.

Mr. Wardrop, therefore, can give us little, if any, insight into deceased's testamentary wishes or capacity.

His description of deceased's inarticulate "mumbling" is strangely at variance with the account given by defendant, the Cullens, and her son, as to his ability to talk and converse.

It is further to be noted that none of those present during these last few hours of life heard anything whatever from deceased as to his disposal of his property beyond the expressions hostile to the plaintiff. They all profess ignorance of the contents of the will.

When Wardrop was reading the will, Henry Cullen standing at the door, says he heard deceased object as to "Bella." Wardrop standing at the side of the bed could not hear him say anything beyond "mumbling."

Harry Cullen says that his father, William Cullen, coaxed deceased several times to sign the will, telling him to do what Mrs. Maguire wished him to do, and that would be right, and at last deceased consented.

William Cullen swears he did not coax him at all.

Mrs. Maguire declares she did not know the will had been signed till between three and four in the morning. This most unlikely statement is directly contradicted by

Henry Cullen, who says he heard her told of it shortly
after it was signed.

After the execution of the will the defendant says
deceased in answer to her question, told her his age.
One of the Cullens corroborates this. Jones, who was
present, contradicts it, declaring that she made the remark
about the age, but deceased never said anything.

It was urged in argument in favour of the truthfulness
of the defendant's statement as to the instructions that, as
she knew nothing of the contents of the other will, the
deceased must have told her of some of the legacies.

There were two legacies, $200 to Mary Maud Brown,
$100 to his sister Margaret. The later will has this legacy,
$200 to Mary Maud Brown, and $25 to his sister Margaret. It has seven legacies, the former only two. The
only similarity as to legacies is that to Mary Maud. She
told all these legacies verbally to Mr. Wardrop, as she
says from deceased's instructions.

The only matter of remark is the $200 legacy. It is
clear from the evidence that deceased was often talkative
as to his disposition of his property, and, judging from the
whole complexion of the family relations, it is difficult to
believe in the absence of all knowledge of this unfortunate
man's disposition of his property.

If I rightly understand the learned Judge, whose decision is now in appeal, he seems to place his judgment
wholly in the position of an ordinary case of disputed fact,
and that if he found against the validity of the will set
up by the defendant, he must hold her and several of her
witnesses as guilty of perjury. He does not much discuss
the very peculiar questions arising as to a will so prepared.

I think we have to look at the validity of this will as
depending almost wholly on the testimony of the defendant herself. No other witness can give us any evidence
as to the testator's desire or intention to give her any part,
much less the bulk of his property. On this, the main
point of the case, her evidence seems to be without any
direct corroboration.

Substantially it is a claim to the bulk of a deceased man's estate resting almost wholly on the evidence of the claimant. Before parties to suits were admitted as witnesses there would have been no evidence in the present case sufficient to establish this will.

The general rule of law may be very fairly gathered from the judgments of the late Lord Wensleydale in the Privy Council in such cases as *Baker* v. *Batt*, 2 Moo. P. C. 317 ; *Barry* v. *Butlin*, Ib. 480. In the former case, it is said (at p. 321) : "There is also another principle upon which the Court below has acted, and which has long prevailed in the Ecclesiastical Courts, which is this,—that if the person benefited by a will, himself writes or procures it to be written, the will is not void, as it would have been by the civil law; but the circumstance forms a just ground of suspicion, and calls upon the Court to be vigilant and jealous, and requires clear and satisfactory proof that the instrument contains the real intention of the testator."

Again, in the latter case, at p. 482 : "If a party writes or prepares a will, under which he takes a benefit, that is a circumstance that ought generally to excite the suspicion of the Court, and calls upon it to be vigilant and jealous in examining the evidence in support of the instrument, in favour of which it ought not to pronounce unless the suspicion is removed, and it is judicially satisfied that the paper propounded does express the true will of the deceased." After correcting some false impressions as to the law requiring—*as a matter of law*—any special manner of proof, he says, (p. 486): " Their Lordships wish it to be distinctly understood, that entirely acquiescing in the propriety of the rule, so qualified and explained, they should be extremely sorry if anything which has fallen from them should have the effect of impeding its full operation."

In *Mitchell* v. *Thomas*, 6 Moo. P. C., at p. 150, it is said that their Lordships were unanimously of opinion that the law so laid down by Mr. Baron Parke is the law, and should be strictly adhered to.

Scouler v. *Plowright*, 10 Moo. P. C., at p. 445, again refers to this as the law, that, " Where a will has been prepared for the testator by the party principally benefited by it, and executed under his supervision, proof, if the circumstances are suspicious, must be given that the testa-

-tor was cognizant of the contents of such will, and executed it freely without undue control."

In *Fulton* v. *Andrew, L. R.,* 7 H. L. 448 (1875), Lord Cairns (p. 461) quotes Baron Parke's rules at length as declaring the law. Lord Hatherley (p. 471): "There is one rule that has always been laid down by the Courts having to deal with wills, and that is, that a person who is instrumental in the framing of a will, as these two persons undoubtedly were, and who obtains a bounty by that will, is placed in a different position from other ordinary legatees who are not called upon to substantiate the truth and honesty of the transaction as regards their legacies. It is enough in their case that the will was read over to the testator and that he was of sound mind and memory, and capable of comprehending it. But there is a further onus upon those who take for their own benefit, after having been instrumental in preparing or obtaining a will. They have thrown upon them the onus of shewing the righteousness of the transaction. Now, how did these persons discharge this onus in the present case? They only discharged it by themselves giving evidence before the jury of the reading over of the will, and they were the only persons who did give that evidence."

In that case the jury had found for the capacity of the testator, and for the will as to all parts except the residuary clause, which gave the residue absolutely to the executors; they found that the testator did not know and approve of that clause.

The Judge of the Court of Probate, after these findings, admitted the whole will to Probate, making a rule absolute to enter verdict for plaintiff. On appeal to the Lords, his decision was reversed; and it was directed that probate should be granted of the will omitting the residuary clause.

In *Sugden* v. *Lord St. Leonards,* 1 P. D. 154, the celebrated case of the lost will, Miss Sugden's evidence as to its contents was accepted, though she was largely interested. The general rule, however, seems to have been freely acknowledged. Her evidence was fully corroborated as to large portions of the will. Sir James Hannen says, (p. 177): "Miss Sugden's position is exceptional; of her integrity there can be no doubt; that has been stated with even greater force by those who represent the defendants than by the learned counsel who represent Miss Sugden herself."

On appeal, Sir George Jessel says, (p. 244): "We have the gratification of knowing, in deciding this case, that there has been no question raised as to the credibility of Miss Sugden, and this appears to be an answer to that assumed danger which might apply to other cases in allowing such proof as this to establish wills. The present case has, in my opinion, nothing to do with a case where the credibility of the witness is contested."

In *Hill* v. *Wilson*, L. R. 8 Ch. at p. 900, Sir W. James discusses the law, shewing the danger of allowing evidence, unless corroborated, to charge the estate of a deceased person. His language is very strong. In that case there was apparently no imputation on the witness' integrity.

Re Finch, 23 Ch. D. 267, is a very strong case. In an administration a widow tried to prove her right to certain property as having been made a gift to her by the deceased. Mr. Justice Kay held that the surrounding circumstances furnished corroboratory evidence.

In appeal his decision was reversed by Jessel, M. R., Baggallay, and Lindley, L. JJ.

Sir George Jessel, says, (p. 271): "I cannot find that any body ever laid down the law or the doctrine that the rule that a claim against a dead man's estate should be supported by something more than the uncorroborated testimony of the claimant is confined to gifts. * * It is a rule of prudence that, sitting as a jury, we do not give credence to the unsupported testimony of the claimant, with a view, no doubt, of preventing perjury, and with a view of protecting a dead man's estate from unfounded claims. It is not a rule of law, but it is a question to be decided by a jury, although the Judge must recommend the jury not to trust the uncorroborated evidence; but still if they did I do not know that any one could interfere with their verdict. But where we are sitting here as a jury *we apply that rule to ourselves*."

The language of the other Lord Justices is very strong. There was no imputation on the integrity of the witness·

In *Hegarty* v. *King*, 5 Ir. L. & Ch. 249, Warren, J., at p. 253, cites Sir James Hannan's language from an unre-

ported case of *Cooper* v. *Penrose*, as to the burden of proof
cast on a person situated as is this defendant.　He also (p.
252) cites the same learned Judge's language in another
unreported case of *Gardiner* v. *Palmer:* "'When a man drew,
himself, without the assistance or knowledge of any other
person, a will in his own favour, he invited suspicion, and
it lay upon him to establish, by the clearest evidence that
should bring home to the minds of the jury conviction
beyond a doubt, that the will was not his will, but the will
of the deceased person.'　Clear evidence was given by the
witness in that case in favour of the will, but the jury
did not believe him.　The Judge said he entirely concurred
with the verdict, and the will was condemned."

This case, *Hegarty* v. *King*, was affirmed in appeal, 7
Ir. L. & Ch. 18, by Lord O'Hagan, C., and Deasy, and
FitzGibbon, L. JJ.　Lord O'Hagan says, (p. 20): "It
is now too clear for controversy that if there be a testamentary disposition in favour of a particular person,
and if the will containing it was prepared by that person
without the intervention of any faithworthy witness, or
any one capable of giving independent evidence as to the
alleged testator's intention and instructions, the duty of
establishing that disposition by plain and coercive proof
is cast upon the man who propounds such a will for his
own benefit; the presumption is against its validity, and
the gravest suspicion is attached to it, which must be
removed before the will can be confirmed, either by the
finding of a jury or the ruling of a Judge in a Court of
Justice.　This salutary principle is adopted in many
cases, if indeed cases were wanting to support a doctrine
so needful to be steadily sustained in the interest of society
and for the prevention of fraud."

Many other cases might be cited, but the foregoing are
clear as to the general rules governing cases like this.

I have read the evidence in this case with the greatest
care of which I am capable.　I think it discloses a case of
the gravest and most painful suspicion.

If my learned Brother who tried this case had merely to
decide between the amount of credit to be given to one set
of witnesses over another set, I would feel very strongly
my reluctance to interfere with his superior advantages as
the trial Judge.

I cannot but feel, however, that the principles to be gathered from the authorities as to Mrs. Maguire's position and evidence do not appear in the judgment as applied to her.

The decision seems rested on the idea that the learned Judge could not give effect to the objections urged against her, " without treating the evidence of four or five witnesses as being deliberate perjuries."

I think a larger question is involved in the decision of the case. It is unnecessary in my view to hold that the witnesses other than the defendant were committing perjury; and as to her evidence, it is not necessary to stigmatize it in any offensive language.

It is clear to me that she has voluntarily placed herself in a position requiring her to give us " plain and coercive proof" (as said in one of the cases) that the paper produced is not merely her will, but the intelligent act of her deceased brother.

As already remarked, there is no proof whatever beyond her own oath of any intention or desire on his part to leave all or any property to her.

The evidence of the witnesses who testify to his strong objections to benefit his other sister, the plaintiff, gives no corroboration to his alleged will in favour of defendant.

He had another sister besides the two litigants and a brother, besides many nephews and nieces, and the defendant's only witness to prove an intention to leave the residue to another than the plaintiff, testified to his intention to give it to his brother John.

As to his capacity at the time of execution, I think the gravest doubts must be entertained.

No test whatever seems to have been applied by any of the witnesses to ascertain what he desired to do with his property, beyond the remarks hostile to plaintiff. We all know the value, or rather the no value, of general statements as to a dying man's mental capacity, unless the persons expressing a favourable estimate shew us on what that estimate is based.

Mr. Wardrop's evidence is, to say the least of it, very suggestive as to the apparent capacity of the dying man. We have heard all about the state to which, by disease and dissipation, he had been reduced.

His will was apparently executed within an hour of his death, at the strong solicitation of some of the witnesses to do as the defendant wished him to do.

On the whole, I come to the conclusion that the defendant who seeks to establish this will, fails to do so by such proof as a Court should accept.

It is impossible to overrate the vast importance of preserving unimpaired those well settled legal principles as to the disposition of the estates of deceased persons.

The present case is, to my mind, one that loudly calls for their strictest application.

The appeal must be allowed, and the will of the 30th of June, 1881, be established and declared to be the last and only will and testament of the said Edward Brown; and that the paper writing of the 17th of April, 1882, and the letters probate thereon issued, be declared null and void, and be delivered up to be cancelled and rescinded; and that the defendant Elizabeth Maguire be restrained from collecting or interfering with the estate of the said Edward Brown; and be ordered to account and pay over what portion of the said estate she may have received.

Kelly v. Imperial Loan and Investment Company et al.

Mortgage of lease—Renewal of term, Irregularity in—Purchaser with notice—Power of sale—Execution of power.

In a mortgage of leasehold premises, the *habendum* was as follows: "To hold to the said mortgagees, their successors and assigns, for the residue now unexpired of the term, and every renewal term, save and except one day thereof." The mortgage contained a power of sale to be exer·cised in default of payment, without notice. The mortgagor, K., assigned his equity of redemption to O'S., in trust to pay off the mort·gage, but O'S., after renewing the lease for a term of twenty-one years in his own name, reconveyed to K. without paying off the mortgage. The mortgagees, with knowledge that the beneficial interest was in K., filed a bill for foreclosure against O'S. alone, and O'S. filed an answer and disclaimer, stating his position as above, but ultimately withdrew his disclaimer and consented to a decree for foreclosure. After decree and final order of foreclosure, the mortgagees sold to D., reciting in their conveyance the foreclosure proceedings, and making no mention of the power of sale. D.'s solicitors accepted the title after searching the foreclosure proceedings.

Held, that the decree so obtained was invalid, and that D. had notice of and was affected by the irregularity, and was not protected as an innocent purchaser for value without notice.

But, *held*, that the power in the mortgage authorized a sale of the renewal term, and that the conveyance to D., though not purporting to be made in exercise of the power, was nevertheless a valid exercise of it, and as the sale was made in good faith and was not a disadvantageous one, the decree for redemption pronounced by Proudfoot, J., was reversed.

This was an appeal by the defendants from a judgment pronounced by Proudfoot, J., on the 7th November, 1882.

The plaintiff brought the action seeking to set aside a decree and final order of foreclosure of a mortgage made by him to the defendant company on the 7th August, 1875, the sale of the mortgaged premises made by them to the defendant Damer after foreclosure; and to be permitted to redeem.

The action was tried at the Toronto sittings, in November, 1882, and the material facts are as follow.

The plaintiff, being the owner of certain leasehold premises on the corner of York and King streets, Toronto, under a lease for twenty-one years, dated the 1st July, 1857, containing a covenant for perpetual renewal, mortgaged the same on the 7th August, 1875, by demise for th residue of the term, less one day, to the defendant company; the *habendum* being as follows: "To hold to the said mortgagees, their successors and assigns, for the residue now unexpired of the term of years thereby created, and every renewal term, save ard except one day thereof." The mortgage contained a power of sale " of the said lands and term ot years," in default of payment, without any notice to the mortgagor, and at the discretion of the mortgagees.

On the 7th September, 1876, Kelly assigned the said premises to D. A. O'Sullivan absolutely, for a nominal consideration, in trust to enable him to raise money to pay off the mortgage.

In January, 1877, the company and Kelly leased the premises to one Scully for five years. O'Sullivan was made a party to the lease, but did not execute it. Kelly soon afterwards removed from the Province, leaving no certain address, and in about a year the tenant failed, and the premises became vacant.

In July, 1878, O'Sullivan, not having heard from Kelly, renewed the ground lease in his own name for twenty-one years from the 1st July; and not having succeeded in procuring a loan or fulfilling the object of the trust, and the company threatening proceedings on their mortgage, he became anxious to get rid of his responsibility, and on the 15th November, 1878, executed a deed purporting to reconvey his interest in the property to Kelly, absolutely.

On the 21st November, 1878, the company, who knew that O'Sullivan had no beneficial interest in the property, filed a bill against him to foreclose the mortgage, simply setting forth the mortgage, and alleging that he was entitled to the equity of redemption.

On the 28th November, O'Sullivan filed an answer and disclaimer, stating fully his connection with the property, and renouncing all interest in it, and further as follows: " Before the filing of the bill and on the 15th day of November, 1878, I wrote to the said Kelly that the company had written me that they were about to take proceedings to foreclose the property, and stating that he could have it back in his own name at any time he applied for that purpose, and by deed of the same date I reconveyed the property to the said Kelly."

The plaintiffs' solicitor, it was alleged, had threatened to file a replication and go to trial, contending that there had been no effectual delivery of this reconveyance, and O'Sullivan, being apparently in doubt as to the point and averse to incurring costs, ultimately agreed to withdraw his disclaimer, and appeared in Court and consented to a decree, which bore date 14th January, 1879, and was drawn up on hearing counsel and on reading the pleadings and proceedings in the cause. A final order of foreclosure was made on the 15th May, 1880.

In September, 1881, the company agreed to sell the property to the defendant Damer for $20,000, which was less than the amount of their claim.

About a week after their acceptance of his offer, and some time before the contract was completed by conveyance, the plaintiff, according to the defendant Damer's evidence, notified him not to purchase the property, as he had an interest in it.

Damer had not, at this time, paid any portion of the purchase money.

The title was examined by his solicitor, who searched the proceedings in the foreclosure suit, and read O'Sullivan's answer and disclaimer, but completed the purchase, relying upon the decree and final order.

On the 1st October, 1881, the company executed a conveyance to Damer, by which, after reciting the original lease ; the assignment thereof to Kelly ; that Kelly had on the 7th August, 1875, assigned the same and all his interest therein by way of mortgage to the company ; that he had subsequently assigned all his interest to O'Sullivan, whose equity of redemption therein had been foreclosed by the final order of foreclosure of the 15th May, 1880 ; that in pursuance of the covenant for renewal, Northcote, the original lessor, had, on the 1st July, 1878, executed a lease of, and demised the lands to O'Sullivan for twenty-one years, and the said lease, term, and premises had become vested in and were then lawfully held by the company; and that the assignee had agreed with the assignors to purchase the lease and premises, the company granted, &c., to Damer " the said parcel of land and all other the premises comprised in and demised by the said in part recited indenture of lease, together with the said indenture of lease, and the right of renewal thereof," &c. *Habendum* to the assignee for and during the residue of the said term granted by the said indenture of lease, and the estate, term, right of renewal, if any, and other interest of the assignors therein.

The instrument contained the usual covenants for title, right to convey, and further assurance.

The learned Judge held (1) that the decree and final order of foreclosure were void as against the plaintiff; that O'Sullivan could not be treated as a trustee within G. O. Chy. 58, 61, Rule 95, O. J. Act, for the purpose of representing him; and that even if he could be so treated, yet that the reconveyance had been executed before the filing of the bill, and therefore the plaintiff was at that time the owner of the equity of redemption and the proper party to the action, of which the company had notice.

(2.) That the sale to the defendant Damer could not be supported as an exercise of the power of sale in the mortgage, as it did not profess to be made under the power, but under the title gained by means of the foreclosure suit.

(3.) The plaintiff was entitled to redeem subject to Damer's right to compensation for improvements.

The appeal was heard on the 15th and 18th days of February, 1884.*

Moss, Q.C., for the appellants the company. O'Sullivan was the only necessary party to the foreclosure proceedings, for the document which purported to be a reconveyance to the respondent was never delivered and is inoperative.

Present.—SPRAGGE, C.J.O., BURTON, PATTERSON, and OSLER, JJ.A.

The respondent was aware of the foreclosure proceedings before the final order, and is bound by his own laches. Even if the foreclosure proceedings were properly set aside, the sale can be sustained as a sale under the power in the mortgage to the company. A mere recital in the deed to th: effect that a final order of foreclosure had been obtained does not prevent the deed from operating as a valid exercise of the power of sale. The title is not weakened by the foreclosure.

Cassels, Q.C., and *A. C. Galt*, for the appellant Damer. It is not shewn that Damer had notice of any defect in the foreclosure proceedings. Even if those proceedings were defective, the appellant Damer is entitled to protection as a purchaser for value without notice. The alleged reconveyance to the respondent was never registered, but the deed to the appellant was registered, and the appellant should have the benefit of the registry laws. The appellant Damer can rely upon any right or title the company had, and if the foreclosure proceedings were defective, the power of sale was not extinguished, and the deed to the appellant Damer was a valid exercise of such power.

Plumb and *Wallace Nesbitt*, for the respondent. The foreclosure proceedings were irregular and void against the respondent, who had no notice thereof and was not a party. The appellants the company, when assuming to sell the property in question, only professed to deal, and only did deal with it by virtue of their title acquired under the foreclosure proceedings, and these having been found to be defective, they cannot as a mere after-thought be heard to say that they transferred the property to Damer by the exercise of a power of sale which they did not exercise, and which they were not in a position to exercise.

The authorities cited are referred to in the judgments.

September 5, 1884. BURTON, J. A.—The point upon which I have hesitated in coming to a conclusion that we could properly reverse the judgment in this case, was, as to whether the sale could be upheld under the power of

sale, for I agree in the view taken in the Court below, and
by my learned Brothers, that the foreclosure proceedings
will not support it.

I have been unable to find much authority on the subject of the exercise of a power of sale pure and simple;
but in reference to the execution of powers generally, it
may now be considered perfectly well established, notwithstanding opinions and decisions at one time to the
contrary, that an express reference to the power is not
requisite, but the intention may be gathered from other
circumstances, as by a reference to the property which is
the subject of the power, or from the instrument affecting
to deal with property in such a manner that the deed cannot have effect except by the exercise of the power.

In *Bennett* v. *Aburrow*, 8 Ves. 609, Sir William Grant
said (p. 615) it was always a question of intention whether
the party meant to execute the power or not. "Formerly,"
he said, "it was sometimes required, that there should be
an express reference to the power. * * The intention
may be collected from other circumstances; as * * that
a part of the will would be wholly inoperative, unless
applied to the power."

It is not necessary therefore to deduce from the instrument an intention that the power shall be executed.

If it appear from the instrument that the party intends to do the act, which act can only be done by an
execution of the power, and cannot be done by means
of any estate which the party possessed, the law will
consider such act as an execution of the power.

This doctrine is clearly laid down in *Wade* v. *Paget*,
1 Br. C. C. 363. In that case a person had an exclusive
power to dispose of an estate among certain objects. On
the marriage of one of the children, he joined in a
settlement in which it was recited that he was seized
in fee. He was not seized in fee, but inasmuch as the
deed would have been *wholly inoperative, except by an*
execution of the power, it was held to be an execution
of the power, although the party intended to pass the

estate by virtue of the interest, and not in the execution of a power.

To the same effect is a case decided by the Lord Chancellor of Ireland, *Irwin* v. *Rogers*, 12 Ir. Eq. 159, where a person had executed a settlement, reserving to himself a power of revocation. In making his will he forgot the fact of the existence of the power, and in that will he recited that he had been induced to execute the settlement by fraud, and directed his trustees to take steps to defeat it, and then disposed of the property included in the deed. The Lord Chancellor held that, although the testator did not intend to execute the power, as he had manifestly forgotten it, yet, as he clearly intended to devise the property, and as that intention would not otherwise take effect, the will amounted to an execution of the power to revoke the deed.

If this had been a deed in general terms without any recital, I should have thought it clear that the sale could be referred to the power.

The doubt that I felt for some time was caused by the recital of the mortgagees having become absolute owners in fee by foreclosure of the premises, which at one time were the subject of the power, a state of things inconsistent with the continued existence of the power; and, although they were mistaken in that view, still the deed did not become wholly inoperative, but did pass their interest as mortgagees, and therefore it could not be said that the deed was wholly inoperative.

I think we have a right to complain of having received no assistance from counsel on this branch of the case, and I may say that I approached its consideration with the impression that the execution of the power of sale could not, under these circumstances, be invoked in aid of the defendants, but upon further consideration I have arrived at the conclusion that the case is not distinguishable in principle from some of the cases I have referred to. The mortgagees intended to sell the absolute interest, not a partial interest. And, although in some of the earlier cases it was decided, in the quaint language of the reports of that day, " that where according to the way the parties intended the conveyance would have no effect at all, that there it should pass another way. Yet, when the conveyance would have *some* effect, though not *all* that was intended by the parties, then it should pass no other way than the parties designed; the more recent decisions declare that though the deed should have some effect but not all intended there, to the end that the main design should be attained, the estate shall pass in another way than the parties intended."

As this absolute sale of the entire interest was the main design which all parties had in view, and as this could only be carried out by the exercise of the power, I think that we are bound in accordance with the authorities to hold that the mortgagees must be presumed to have intended to execute it.

In the case of *Carver* v. *Richards*, 27 Beav. 488, the Master of the Rolls, says (p. 496): "If it can be shewn that the intention of the donee was not to execute the power, then certainly it does not take effect." And then quotes Lord St. Leonards to the same effect, " that it is the intention which governs, and that, if the intention be not to execute the power, the power is not executed; but if the intention be to pass the property by all the means in the power of and at the disposal of the donee, then still the property passes and the appointment will take effect, even though the existence of the power under which it operates was not present to the mind of the person who exercised it, that is to say, to the mind of the person who endeavors to pass the property."

" I admit," the Master of the Rolls proceeds to say, "that this leads to very nice distinctions, and that it may very often be extremely difficult to distinguish or define the limits between an intention not to execute a power, and the case of no knowledge of the existence of the power; in which case, strictly speaking, there is no intention to execute it, while in the former there is an intention not to execute it."

The facts from which such intention and such absence of intention are to be inferred, may very often run very near to each other, and possibly lead in some cases to very nice, and perhaps technical, distinctions, but this principle appears to me to be very cleaily established by the cases.

Upon whom was the onus of establishing that it was not the intention of the mortgagees to execute the power ? If it had been a voluntary deed, I think they would have been bound to shew that intention. Where the sale was for value, the person executing it is understood in equity to engage with the person whom he deals with to make the instrument as effectual as he has the power to make it. See remarks of Lord Redesdale in *Blake* v. *Marnell*, 2 Ball & B. 35.

That case was afterwards carried to the House of Lords, 4 Dow. 248.

I have, therefore, come to the conclusion that it must be presumed in the present case, that the mortgagees in selling the absolute interest in the term intended to avail themselves of every means in their power to carry out that object and keep faith with the purchaser, and that the sale may thus be upheld, if the power applied to the renewal term.

Upon this point I have felt considerable doubt, but after much consideration, I have come to the conclusion that the sale comes within the power, and may be sustained for the reasons which are stated by my Brother Osler.

I think, therefore, that we ought to allow the appeal, with costs.

OSLER, J. A.—The questions to be determined are : (1) Whether the decree and final order of foreclosure in the action against O'Sullivan were regular.

(2) If not, whether the defendant Damer is affected by any irregularity or invalidity in the proceedings.

(3) If he cannot rely upon a title acquired by his co-defendants under the foreclosure, whether their convey-ance to him can be upheld as an effectual execution of the power of sale in their mortgage.

The instruments which have been executed by the parties, in dealing with the reversion of the original term and the renewal, are singularly inappropriate, but on the authority of *Marshall* v. *Frank*, Gilb. 143, and *Roe* v. *Archbishop of York*, 6 East, 86, and similar cases, the deed from Kelly to O'Sullivan, and the re-conveyance from O'Sullivan to Kelly, though purporting to convey the fee, may operate in the one case by way of assignment of the grantor's reversion and equity of redemption in the original term, and in the other by way of assignment of the renewal and equity of redemption subject to the company's rights as mortgagees.

The first question depends mainly upon whether there was a complete execution and delivery of the re-conveyance from O'Sullivan to Kelly, before the commencement of the foreclosure suit. If there was, he, and not O'Sullivan, was the owner of the equity of redemption ; and he, not O'Sullivan, should have been the defendant in that suit.

The learned Judge finds as a fact upon the evidence, and I agree with him, that the re-conveyance was completely executed before the filing of the bill. It bears date the 15th November, 1878, and appears on the face of it to be formally sealed and delivered in the presence of an attesting witness. It was urged that the language of the answer was equivocal, as it merely states that the property was reconveyed by deed "bearing date the 15th November," and that it may really not have been executed until after that date. That, however, is evidently not the impression intended to be conveyed by it, nor, looking at the whole paragraph, do I think it is fairly open to such a construction. From Mr. O'Sullivan's evidence it is pretty clear that at the trial he had, to use his own language, "no recollection different from what the papers shew themselves." Looking at the fact that the deed bears date on the day he wrote to Kelly to tell him he could have the property back in his own name at any time he applied for it, and that he was then anxious to relieve himself from further responsibility, and to avoid a threatened law suit, I think there is no sufficient reason for assuming that the

deed was not executed on the day it bears date, but on
some other day, subsequent to the filing of the bill. It is
true that it remained in the grantor's possession, but there
is nothing in the evidence to lead us to infer that it was
not intended to have effect from its execution according to
its legal operation, whatever that might be; and we therefore cannot infer from that fact alone that it was not
delivered as it purports to be: *Doe d. Garnons* v. *Knight*,
5 B. & C. 671; *Xenos* v. *Wickham*, L. R. 2 H. L. 296, 309;
Hope v. *Harman*, 11 Jur. (Q. B. 1846) pp. 1097-1100;
Watkins v. *Nash*, L. R. 20 Eq. 262; *McDonald* v. *Mc-
Donald*, 44 U. C. R. 291.

The last case is said to have been reversed on appeal.
The decision of the Court of Appeal is not reported, but it
must have proceeded upon some other ground than the insufficiency of the delivery of the deed there in question.

The foreclosure suit was thus wrongly constituted, and
the mortgagees had notice of the defect. Instead, however,
of making the present plaintiff a party, and, as it might
almost be inferred, to avoid the trouble and delay of doing
so, their solicitor seems to have persuaded Mr. O'Sullivan
and himself that there had been no effectual delivery of
the deed, and that the former had better consent to a
decree notwithstanding his answer. "I stated to Mr.
O'Sullivan that I did not think the conveyance had been
executed prior to the time of the bill, and Mr. O'Sullivan
neither admitted nor denied it; and I said: 'As you have
been unable to get any address of Kelly, I don't consider
the deed has been delivered;' and he said: 'I think that is
so too;' and I said: 'If that is your idea, I don't see why
you should not consent to a decree;' and he said he would
come up some Wednesday and would consent to the
decree." The witness then describes what took place in
Court: "Mr. O'Sullivan hesitated backwards and forwards,
and the Vice-Chancellor became impatient, and told him
he had better make up his mind what he would do; and
after some consideration we came to the conclusion that
the deed was not delivered, and he gave his consent to the
decree."

A decree thus obtained, is clearly invalid and not binding on the plaintiff, as the learned Judge has held.

I agree with him also that it is impossible to hold that there was here such laches on the plaintiff's part, or evidence of an intention to abandon the property, as to justify the Court in refusing to set aside this invalid decree, and denying redemption, on the principle applied by the learned Chief Justice of this Court, in *Skae* v. *Chapman*, 21 Gr. 534, and *Kay* v. *Wilson*, 24 Gr. 212. The circumstances of those cases were most peculiar, and in both of them, assuming that the Court had power to refuse redemption, it was, to use the language of the Chief Justice, just to refuse it, and would have worked injustice to grant it. I may refer on this point to the recent case of *Martin* v. *Miles*, noted in 19 C. L. J. 316, not yet reported.*

The defendant Damer, however, contends that the decree and final order being regular on their face, he was not bound to inquire into the regularity of the prior proceedings, and is not affected by any error therein.

The cases of *Gunn* v. *Doble*, 15 Gr. 655; *McLean* v. *Grant*, 20 Gr. 76; and *Shaw* v. *Crawford*, 4 A. R. 371, sufficiently establish this proposition, but they do not help the purchaser where he has gone behind the decree and acquired notice of a defect going to the very foundation of the action. That, as it seems to me, is this defendant's position. It is clear beyond a question that his solicitor in examining the title saw and read O'Sullivan's answer, and therefore had actual notice, not only of the nature of the latter's interest, which alone might not be so material, but also of the fact that the equity of redemption had before action been reconveyed to his *cestui que trust*. The notice thus acquired by the solicitor in the course of the transaction is imputed to the defendant—*Bradley* v. *Riches*, 9 Ch. D. 189, 195; *Rolland* v. *Hart*, L. R. 6 Ch. 678, 682—who cannot, as I think, be protected by a decree, on its face a consent decree, obtained under the circumstances I have adverted to. As the late Chief Justice of this Court

* Now reported 5 O. R. 404.

observed, in *Shaw* v. *Crawford*, 4 A. R. at p. 385, the line
of decisions referred to only extends to protect purchasers
who had no knowledge of the alleged defect.

The appeal therefore fails, unless the conveyance from
the company to the defendant Damer can be treated as an
execution of the power of sale in their mortgage. If it
can, there is nothing in the circumstances which entitles
the plaintiff to be relieved against it. It does not appear
that the sale was in fact a disadvantageous one. There is no
reason to doubt that it was made in good faith, and without collusion with the purchaser, for the purpose of
realizing the company's claim, and, if within the power, it
does not contravene any of its requirements : *Warner* v.
Jacob, 20 Ch. D. 220 ; *Latch* v. *Furlong*, 12 Gr. 303.

I therefore come to the remaining question, which is of
a two-fold character :

1. Whether the power authorized a sale of the renewal
term, and

2. If it did, whether the conveyance to Damer may be
treated as an execution of it.

On the first point, I am of opinion, with some doubt
arising from the extremely informal language of the whole
instrument, that the sale of the renewal term was within
the power. Except the *habendum*, the terms of the mortgage are appropriate to a mortgage by way of assignment
of the term. The *habendum* explains that it was intended
to be by demise merely. Whether by assignment or
demise a renewal of the lease by the mortgagor is considered as a graft upon the old lease, and subject in equity
to the same mortgage as affected it: *Coote* on Mortgages,
4th ed. 244 ; *Smith* v. *Chichester*, 2 Dr. & War. 393 ; 1 Con.
& Law. 486 ; *Fector* v. *Philpott*, 12 Price 197 ; *James* v.
Dean, 11 Ves. 383 ; 15 Ves. 236 ; *Moody* v. *Matthews*, 7 Ves.
174 ; *Collett* v. *Hooper*, 13 Ves. 255.

The power of sale (not following the usual form, which
when the mortgage is by demise is confined to the interest
of the mortgagee, while the mortgage itself contains an
express declaration of trust by the mortgagor, of the

nominal reversion for the purchaser) extends to the whole interest of which the mortgagor had power to dispose, namely the whole term, including the nominal reversion, though the mortgage itself is limited to a lesser interest. If the renewal term is subject to the trusts and provisions of the mortgage, it must be subject *inter alia* to the power of sale conferred by it, which cannot, I think, be limited to the term in existence at its date.

The other point is one of some nicety. It is to be observed in the first place that it is in favour of a purchaser that the deed is relied upon as an execution of the power, and secondly, that if the decree and final order were invalid the equity of redemption had not been cut off at the date of the sale to Damer; the company were nothing more than mortgagees, and the power was not extinguished.

They erroneously supposed that they had acquired the absolute title to the whole term under the decree, and that they could pass it by virtue of their ownership. "But the mere circumstance that the party intended to pass the property in another manner is not always decisive of the effect of an instrument. The rule *cum quod ayo non vulet ut ago, valeat quantum valere potest,* interferes with the mode, and directs its force to the effect. Therefore, whatever may be the words, the instrument will operate according to the effect the parties intended to give it:" *Touch-stone,* 514; *Roe* v. *Tranmarr,* 2 Sm. L. C. 6th ed. vol. ii. p. 468; *Sugden* on Powers, 66, 104 (7).

The cases on the subject of the execution of powers where the donee has an interest in the estate are apposite, and may be referred to. The general rule is, "that where a man has both a power and an interest, and does an act generally as owner of the land, without reference to his power, the land shall pass by virtue of his ownership. He has an estate grantable in him and also a power to limit a use; and when he grants the land itself, without any reference to his authority, it implies his intent to grant an estate as owner of the land, and not to limit a use in pursuance of his power:" *Sugden* on Powers, 8th ed., 343.

But to this rule˜there are exceptions. In Sir *Edward Clere's Case*, 6 Co. 17, it was held that where a disposition would be absolutely void if it did not enure as an execution of the power, effect would be given to it by treating it as such.

And on this principle it is, says Sir E. Sugden, p. 347, "that where a man has both a power and an interest, and he creates an estate which will not have an effectual continuance in point of time, if it be fed out of his interest, it shall take effect by force of the power. As, where a tenant for life, with power of leasing, grants a lease for a term absolute, without referring to or mentioning his power, the lease, if it be supplied out of his interest, would expire with his life, and it shall, therefore, operate as an execution of the power." And on p. 344, he quotes from L. C. J. Parker's judgment in *Thomlinson* v. *Dighton*, 10 Mod. 36 : " That the point decided in Sir *Edward Clere's Case*, has since been carried much farther, as that, where the disposition would have some effect, but not all intended by the parties, there, to the end that the main design of the parties may be observed, the estate shall pass in another way than the parties intended." The illustration being in effect the same as given above, a lease for a term absolute, by a tenant for life with power of leasing.

The author of the " Original view of Executory Interests," states the proposition thus : " Where a man has both a power and an interest, and he creates an estate which would not or might not endure for the period assigned to it by the term of its creation, if it were fed out of his interest, it shall take effect by force of the power :" Real and Personal Property, 5th ed. 796.

In *Carver* v. *Richards*, 27 Beav. 488, affirmed on appeal *1b.* 499, the Master of the Rolls says (p. 495) : " It is, as I consider, the rule of this Court, that if the intention to pass the property subject to the power be clearly established, even though the intention to dispose of it under or by virtue of the power is not shewn, still that equity will give effect to the disposition and hold that the property passes under the power. This proposition seems to have been expressly decided in *Wade* v. *Paget*, 1 Bro. C. C.

364, although the report of that case seems, in many respects, to be imperfect."

This decision is referred to with approval in the last edition of *Sugden* on Powers, pp. 348, 349. The author comments upon *Denn* v. *Roake*, 4 Bligh. N. S. 1; 2 Bing. 497; 5 B. & C. 720, where, in the Court below, the contrary doctrine was advanced, *i. e.*, that there must be not only an intention to dispose of the property, but to dispose of it under the power, and says that it was strongly observed upon in argument at the Bar of the House of Lords, where he, as counsel for the respondent, had felt unable to support it. "If," he continues, "the intention to pass the property can be collected, it will pass under the power, although the donee supposed that it would work by force of his interest. There is no conflict; he intends the property to pass, and thinks he has all the interest in it, whereas he really has only a power. The intention governs, and the power will support the disposition." The judgment of the Chancellor (Lyndhurst) in the last case seems to state the rule, if I may say so, with accuracy. The instrument in that case was a will. He says (4 Bligh. N. S. at p. 21): "If the will, which is insisted upon as an execution of the power, does not refer to the power, and if the dispositions of the will can be satisfied without their being considered to be an execution of the power, unless there are other circumstances to shew that it was the intention of the devisor to execute the power of appointment by the will, under such circumstances the Courts have uniformly decided that the will is not to be considered an execution of the power."

On the question of intention, I may refer to *Maundrell* v. *Maundrell*, 7 Ves. 566; 10 Ves. 246, 258. In that case, a man had interests in two different estates, and powers over them. He executed an instrument reciting the power over one of them and his interest in it, and as to it expressly executed his power and conveyed his interest by lease and release. As to the other, he recited, not that he had power to appoint, but that he was seized in fee, and conveyed his interest in it by lease and release. It was held that the latter estate passed out of his interest only

and not by force of the power, from the *apparent intention*
not to execute the power.   Lord Eldon says (10 Ves. 257):
" The authority of *Sir Edward Clere's Case*, as well as all
general doctrine, seem to furnish this ; that it is not necessary to recite, that (the donee) means to execute the power;
if the act is one, that he can do only by that authority.
Though the form may not at first suggest, that he proposes
to exercise it, the purpose of the act makes it necessary to
hold, that he did intend it.   On the other hand, it is in
general clear, that where a party has both an authority and
an interest, and does an act, purporting to mean to pass the
interest, he shall be held to intend that, and not to exercise
his authority."   See also *Blake* v. *Marnell*, 2 Ball. & B.
35, 38, 39 ; *Re Morgan*, 7 Ir. Ch. R. at pp. 50, 51, 56 ;
Minchin v. *Minchin*, 5 Ir. R. Eq. series 258, 265, 273 ;
Deedes v. *Graham*, 16 Gr. 167 ; *Blagge* v. *Miles*, 1 Story,
C. C. 426.

To apply these authorities to the case before us: The
mortgagees could have sold and assigned the existing term
to Damer under the power.   Or they could have assigned
to him the lesser interest embraced in their mortgage, in
other words, could have assigned the mortgage. We
find that they have executed an instrument, using apt
words of conveyance, which shews that they intended to
sell and assign the term absolutely, and not merely to
transfer their mortgage interest.

The former they could not do except by means of the
power.   Their interest as mortgagees by demise would not
enable them to do it.   The tenor of the instrument forbids
the supposition that they intended to pass their mortgage
interest merely. and as the estate created by the conveyance would not be effectual for the period assigned to it,
that is to say, as a conveyance of the term, if it be treated
as an assignment of the mortgagees' interest, that being all
which they could convey apart from the power, I see no
reason why it may not be supported as an exercise of the
power, even though the grantors supposed they were conveying by virtue of their own title as owners of the term,
the act being one they could only do by virtue of the
power.

Seeing that the intention was to dispose of the property subject to the power, I do not think we can infer that it was not meant to exercise the power as well as to sell under any title the mortgagees believed to be vested in them by the foreclosure, as either or both modes might have been resorted to to ensure a good title to the purchaser. If the title under the foreclosure fails, I think the title under the power, the language of the instrument being sufficient, may stand good : *Re Alison, Johnson v. Mounsey*, 11 Ch. D. 284.

PATTERSON, J. A., concurred.

SPRAGGE, C. J. O., died before judgment was delivered.

Judgment reversed. Action dismissed.

[This case has been since argued in the Supreme Court.]

LANGTRY v. DUMOULIN.

*Appeal—Strangers to record—Trustee—Cestuis que trustent—Rector—
Churchwardens.*

Upon an application by the Churchwardens of St. James's Church for
leave to appeal from the judgment of the Chancery Divisional Court
(5 O. R. 644) in their own names, or in the name of the rector, the
defendant (who declined to carry the case further) as their trustee.

Held, that the rector was not a trustee for the applicants, but would
himself, if the contention should prevail, be beneficially entitled to the
fruits of the litigation ; and that the applicants had not such an interest as entitled them to be made parties to the action ; and the
application was therefore refused.

The event rendered it unnecessary to consider whether or not the application was properly made to this Court.

THE judgment of Ferguson, J., at the trial of the action
(5 O. R. 499) and the judgment of the Chancery Divisional
Court on re-hearing (5 O. R. 644) were in favour of the
plaintiffs.

The defendant Dumoulin, the Rector of St. James's
Church, did not desire to appeal from the judgment of the
Divisional Court, and intimated, before the case was taken
there, that he would be satisfied with the decision of that
Court, and, if it was against him, would not carry the case
further.

On the 26th January, 1885,* *Howland* and *Arnoldi,* for
the Churchwardens and Vestry of St. James's Church
moved to substitute the Churchwardens for the Rector as
defendants, and for leave to appeal to this Court in the
name of the Churchwardens, or in the name of the
Rector as their trustee.

The motion was made without notice to the plaintiffs or
the other defendants, but upon notice to the defendant
Dumoulin.

S. H. Blake, Q.C., for the defendant Dumoulin, stated
the position which his client took, and made no opposition
to the motion.

Present.—BURTON, PATTERSON, OSLER, JJ.A., and ROSE, J.

The facts in question in the case are fully stated in the two reports in the Court below, and in the judgment of Patterson, J.A., in this Court.

Howland. The contention of the defendant in the Court below was, that the lands granted previously to the patent of 1836 were not given as an endowment of, or as appurtenant to, the Rectory, but as appurtenant to the Church of St. James, for the benefit of its parishioners. This contention, whether well founded or not, shews the interest the churchwardens and vestry have in defending the suit and appealing. The defence has all along been sustained at the risk and expense of the vestry by the consent of the rector. Churchwardens have also an interest as remaindermen representing the interest of the vestry. In this particular case the congregation are very much interested in preventing the diversion of the fund to other churches, for the reason that if they succeed, the fund will be applied in lightening their burdens, such as the payment of assistant ministers, interest on the church debt, &c. The applicants' interests are affected by the judgment of the Court below, and they should, therefore, be allowed to appeal. The application is properly made to the Court of Appeal, and *ex parte*.

The following authorities were referred to: Secs. 13-15, 32-39, and Rules 95, 102, 103 (a), O. J. A.; Chy. G. O. 61; *McPherson* v. *McKay*, 4 A. R. 501; *Steer's* Parish Law, 136, 137; *Osborne* v. *Usher*, 6 Brown Parl. Cas. 20, 26; *Attorney-General* v. *Fowler*, 15 Ves. 85; *Lyster* v. *Kirkpatrick*, 26 U. C. R. 217; *Fletcher* v. *Fletcher*, 4 Ha. 67, 71, 78; *Crossley* v. *Crowther*, 9 Ha. 384; *Turquand* v. *Fearon*, 4 Q. B. D. 280; *Auster* v. *Holland*, 3 D. & L. 740; *Laws* v. *Bott*, 16 M. & W. 300; *Whitehead* v. *Hughes*, 2 Dowl. 258; *Mills* v. *Jennings*, 13 Ch. D. 639; *Re Anglo-Californian Gold Mining Co.*, 1 Dr. & Sm. 628; *Watson* v. *Cave*, 17 Ch. D. 19; *Bruff* v. *Cobbold*, L. R. 7 Ch. 217; *Wood* v. *Madras*, 23 Ch. D. 248; *Crawcour* v. *Salter*, 30 W. R. 329; *In re St. Nazaire Co.*, 12 Ch. D. 88; *Re Tucker*, 12 Ch. D. 308; *Re Markham*, 16 Ch. D. 1; *Parmiter* v. *Parmiter*, 2 D. F. & J. 526.

January 28th, 1885. PATTERSON, J. A.—The plaintiffs
conclude their statement of claim by asking to have it
declared that the ¦lands embraced in letters patent of
4th September, 1820, and indenture of 4th July, 1825,
which are set out in the statement, and the revenues
thereof, are subject to the operation of the various Acts of
Parliament mentioned in the statement, or are, at any
rate, subject to be dealt with as in the twenty-fifth paragraph of the statement set forth; and that the defendant
Dumoulin is a trustee of the said lands and the revenues
thereof, and holds the same upon and for the intent and purposes in the statement set forth ; and for consequent relief.

The patent of 4th September, 1820, granted four acres
of land in York to trustees in trust to hold the same for
the sole use and benefit of the resident clergyman of the
town of York, and his successors, appointed or to be
appointed rectors of the Episcopal Church therein, to
which the said land was appurtenant: provided, nevertheless, that whenever the Lieut.-Governor of the Province
should erect a parsonage or rectory in the said town of
York, and present to such parsonage or rectory an incumbent or minister of the Church of England, who should
have been duly ordained according to the rites of the said
Church, then and whenever the same should happen,
the said trustees were to convey to such incumbent or
minister being so appointed as aforesaid, and his successors forever, as a sole corporation, to and for the same uses
and upon the same trusts.

The indenture of 4th July, 1825, was a deed by which
trustees in whom certain lots in York were vested by
patent of 20th April, 1819, conveyed the lands to other
trustees upon trust to hold the same for the sole use and
benefit of the resident clergyman of the town of York, and
his successors, appointed or to be appointed incumbent of
the parsonage or rectory of the Episcopal Church, according
to the rites and ceremonies of the Church of England
therein, to which the land was appurtenant, with a proviso similar to that of the patent of 1820.

After setting out these deeds the plaintiffs go on to
shew the incorporation of York as the city of Toronto:
the erection of a parsonage or rectory, and the conveyance
of the lands to the Honorable and Reverend John Strachan,
the rector of St. James's, and his successors, as a sole corporation, to and for the same uses and upon the same
trusts mentioned and expressed in the letters patent and
indenture; the presentation in 1847 of the Rev. Henry
James Grasett, M.A., to be incumbent in the place of Dr.
Strachan, and his possession of the lands, and the receipt
of the rents, issues, and profits thereof to his own use
until the time of his death.

Then they set out the Act of 29 and 30 Vict. ch. 16,
passed in 1866, which gave power to the incorporated
Synod or the Church Society, with the consent of the
Synod, to sell and absolutely dispose of any lands granted
by the Crown in the diocese as a glebe of, or appurtenant
to, or appropriated for, any rectory, by whatever name the
same might be called, or in whomsoever the title thereto
might be vested, and other statutory enactments concerning the incorporated Synod, &c., and *inter alia* the provision of 41 Vict. ch. 69 (O.) for the distribution of the proceeds of the lands amongst the incumbents of other
churches of the Church of England, after appropriating
$5,000 a year to the incumbent of St. James's.

Then the death of the Rev. Mr. Grasett on the 20th
March, 1882, is stated, and the presentation of the defendant Dumoulin on the 19th August of the same year.

Paragraphs 14 to 24 are occupied with matters not
important to be now mentioned, and paragraph 25, which
is referred to in the prayer, submits that, even if the lands
be not subject to the Acts of Parliament, the Court should
declare the excess of the revenues to be applicable to the
support and maintenance of the clergy of the parish, other
than St. James's, which now form part of Toronto.

The defendant in his answer admits all the allegations
relating to the deeds and the incumbency of the rectory.
In his 7th paragraph he submits that the several Acts

referred to in the statement of claim do not affect his
right to the lands; and that, notwithstanding anything in
the Acts contained, his rights as the incumbent of the
Church, parsonage, and rectory are the same as if those
Acts had not been passed.

The action was tried before Mr. Justice Ferguson, who
gave judgment for the plaintiffs, and that judgment was
affirmed on rehearing before the Divisional Court of the
Chancery Division.

The defendant does not desire to appeal from that
decision, and has declined to permit an appeal to be prosecuted in his name; but the churchwardens of St. James's,
instructed, as they say, by the vestry of the parish, apply
for leave to appeal on the ground that the rector, in whose
name the defence has hitherto been conducted, was acting
on their behalf and as their trustee; and that they are
beneficially interested in the subject matter of the litigation.

Mr. Howland, for the applicants, has presented the case
to us with clearness and ability; but we are not able to
accede to his proposition that the relationship of trustee and
cestuis que trustent appears, or that his clients have such
an interest as entitles them to be made parties to the
action.

It is clearly enough shewn that the defence has been so
far conducted at the instance, and at the expense of the
churchwardens. Indeed, in one proceeding in the action it
became necessary to decide whether they were not chargeable with maintenance for the part they took, and the
opinion of the Divisional Court was not unanimous in their
favour. But while the rector so far yielded to their wishes,
he very distinctly intimated that his consent was not to
extend beyond the rehearing. This intimation was given,
as we gather from the papers before us, quite long enough
before the rehearing to enable the present applicants to
have themselves made parties to the record, if they had
been so disposed. and if they were really the *cestuis que
trustent* of the defendant. But they were nevertheless, as
for all present purposes may be assumed, entitled to wait

until the nominal defendant had definitely refused to proceed further, and then take such action as they should deem best. The ordinary right of a *cestui que trust* is to compel his trustee, on a proper indemnity, to lend his name. If the defendant is trustee for the applicants, and has so far, in that character, represented them in the action, there ought not to have arisen the necessity for an application like the present. The fact is, however, that the defendant does not admit that he occupies the position, or is liable to the duties of trustee, and the applicants have not attempted to enforce against him their contention that he occupies that position. He has been served with notice of this application, and has attended, not for the purpose of opposing or consenting to the motion, but merely to disclaim further connection with the proceedings.

The applicants nevertheless urge that they have an interest in the subject matter of the action such as entitles them to obtain leave from this Court to appeal.

The application is, I believe, the first of the kind which has been made to this Court. In England it was held, before the Judicature Act, that a party interested, though not a party to the cause, might obtain leave to appeal. *Parmiter* v. *Parmiter*, 2 D. F. & J. 526, which was cited by Mr. Howland, was an instance of that, and is also an authority for moving *ex parte*. If we adopt the practice, we must do so without any express direction, for neither in our Judicature Act, nor in the English Judicature Act, is there any provision on the subject. Applications of the kind seem, in England, to be not uncommon. We have been referred to some cases in which they were made, *e. g.*, *Re Markham*, 16 Ch. D. 1, and two or three others which I find also in a note at p. 55 of Mr. Langton's edition of *Maclennan's* Jud. Act. *Crawcour* v. *Salter*, 30 W. R. 329, and one or two other cases are there cited as authority for the proposition that one who is not a party can obtain leave only when his interest is such that he might have been made a party by service. This again calls attention to the anomalous nature of this application by parties who, if their contention as to their interest is correct, are already represented on the record by their trustee. But if he is warranted in disclaiming that character, then what is their interest ?

The tenure under the titles from the Crown, and the deed which vested the lands in Dr. Strachan, was for the use of the incumbent and his successors. That is, the use declared by the patent of 1820 and by the deed of 1825, and the later conveyance to the rector as a corporation sole.

The tenure is precisely that which was the subject of discussion in *Lyster* v. *Kirkpatrick*, 26 U. C. R. 217.

The fee is vested in the rector for his own use and that of his successors, without any trust for the members of his congregation, or for the church wardens of his Church.

The interest asserted by the applicants is not that of owners either at law or in equity.

If they could successfully attack the judgment against which they desire to appeal, the result would be, that the whole property, in place of an income of $5,000, would belong, not to the congregation, but to the incumbent. The congregation might no doubt reasonably hope that in that case they would derive benefit by having less occasion to contribute to the maintenance of their church. But the burden which might thus be lightened is the creature of later times and different circumstances from those in which the tenure originated on which these lands were granted. It does not create an interest in the lands themselves which a Court could recognize by making them parties to a contest respecting the title.

In *McPherson* v. *McKay*, 4 A. R. 501, it was held that land granted in trust for the incumbent for the time being of a particular Church, and which was enjoyed by the incumbent only in the character of incumbent of the Church, might without violence to the language of the statute there in question be held to be " in trust for or to the use of the congregation." But that was for the purpose of a statute which, upon a union of several religious bodies, provided that, in certain cases, property held in trust for or to the use of a particular congregation should belong to the united Church, and in certain other cases should not be interfered with; and the question arose in consequence of the incumbent having joined the united Church while his congregation refused to enter the union. The legal estate was in the trustees who remained with the congregation, and it was held that the incumbent, by ceasing to belong to the Church in connection with which the congregation was, ceased to be the *cestui que trust*. There was really no such question as that now in discussion, nor does anything in the case suggest that the congregation could, otherwise than through the trustees, have become party to such an action as the present. The question for decision was not as to the title, but was whether the property came within the description of property with which the statute dealt.

It cannot be seriously contended that the churchwardens or any representative of the congregation or parish of St. James could have brought an action in respect of these lands, as *e.g.* trespass, or a proceeding to restrain waste.

The incumbent is by English law bound to repair, and restore buildings in his benefice, and to leave them in repair for his successor. The law is stated in a learned judgment by Bayley, J., in *Wise* v. *Metcalfe*, 10 B. & C. 299, 312. That case, and also *Huntley* v. *Russell*, 13 Q. B. 572, and *Ross* v. *Adcock*, L. R. 3 C. P. 655, are examples of actions by the incoming incumbent against the executors of his predecessor for dilapidations.

Suits in equity by the owner of the advowson, or of the next presentation, or the patron of the living, to restrain waste are easily found in the reports, but none, so far as I am aware, which recognize a right in the people who may happen to belong to the particular parish: *Duke of St. Albans* v. *Skipwith*, 8 Beav. 354; *Strachy* v. *Francis*, 2 Atk. 217; *Duke of Marlborough* v. *St. John*, 5 DeG. & Sm. 174; *Sowerby* v. *Fryer*, L. R. 8 Eq. 417; *Holden* v. *Weekes*, 1 J. & H. 278.

On these grounds it seems to us very clear that the applicants could not be made parties to this action, and therefore would have no right now to intervene in order to appeal from the judgment, even if it were conceded that the English practice is applicable to this Court to the extent of allowing us to hear a person who may be interested, but is not a party to the record.

Under the circumstances we are not required to decide whether or not that practice should be followed here.

We refuse the application.

The defendant Dumoulin, who appears upon it, should be paid his costs by the applicants.

BURTON, J. A.—I agree with the judgment just pronounced that the applicants have not made out a case for being added or substituted as parties to the record, and that their motion for leave to appeal consequently fails.

The application is founded upon an entire misapprehension of the rights of the incumbent under the patents from the Crown which have been referred to, granted at a time when the rights of the laity to interfere with the management of the Church property were not recognized by law or by the Church of England as they are at present.

There can be no question that under the patents which have been referred to, the lands embraced in them were either vested in, or were held to the use of, the incumbent as a corporation sole, who in that character was entitled to all the rights, profits, and emoluments derivable from them.

It is not necessary now to inquire who would be the parties to be benefited under the first grant for the use of the parishioners and inhabitants of the town of York, or whether the trusts were not too vague and indefinite to be given effect to in a court of justice, although it is clear that the congregation of St. James's were not the beneficiaries intended.

It is sufficient for the present purpose to say that that grant was surrendered, and all we have now to deal with are, the grants and the trusts which were created under them which were valid and subsisting in 1866, at which time the Incumbent and his successors were alone entitled to the lands for their own use.

If, therefore, the Act of 1866 did not apply, the incumbent is still entitled absolutely for life to the rents and profits of these lands. He would hold them for his own uses without reference to the wishes of his congregation.

Such an application as the present would not have been entertained for a moment at the time when the lands were conveyed to the first incumbent.

These lands were granted by the State for the support of the incumbent with a view and to the intent that he should not be left to depend upon the voluntary contributions of the parishioners. But for the recent legislation no one but the incumbent could have any interest in them or their proceeds, and if the contention of the applicants be well founded, and the Acts do not apply, he is still entitled to them absolutely. Being of opinion therefore that the churchwardens have no *locus standi*, I have not thought it necessary to consider the question of whether the application to add them as parties should have been made in this Court or in the Court below. It should, I think, be dismissed, with costs.

OSLER, J. A.—I agree in the result. I think we ought not to do anything to facilitate an appeal in this case.

1. The applicants have not clearly made out that they really occupy the position of *cestuis que trustent*. 2. They had distinct notice so long ago as September last, and before the rehearing, that the defendant denied that they had any right as such, or that he represented them in any way. Nothing can be clearer than the position he then took with regard to them and their right to interfere with or control the action. They might and ought then to have applied to the Divisional Court to be added as parties defendants, if they meant to carry the case further in the event of the defendant declining to do so. After two

decisions upon the merits I think we should not aid the present applicants to delay the further prosecution of the suit by enabling them to appeal, a course which might have been taken in the first instance, and while the defendant was willing to defer to their wishes in regard to the conduct of the suit, instead of taking the chances of a favourable decision from the Divisional Court

ROSE, J., concurred.

Application refused, with costs.

LEE v. MacMAHON.

Sale of land—Contract—False representations—Election—Delay—Judge· at trial—Divisional Court.

The defendant, in January, 1882, bought land in Manitoba from the plaintiff for speculative purposes, paying $500 in cash, and giving a mortgage for the balance of the purchase money. Before the conveyances were executed the defendant in answer to inquiries made by him to persons on the spot received unfavourable accounts of the property, which were, however, explained away by the agent of the plaintiff. The defendant resisted payment of the mortgage, on which this action was brought, and counter claimed for a return of the $500, upon the ground of false representations by the plaintiff's agent. On the 27th July, 1882, the defendant visited the land and found it worthless, and in the end of August or the beginning of September gave notice of his intention to repudiate the contract. Armour, J., who tried the action, without a jury, found that the defendant was induced to purchase by false representations, but that he had by his delay elected to affirm the contract. The Queen's Bench Divisional Court affirmed the first finding, but set aside the second and gave judgment in the defendant's favour, Armour, J., concurring in that judgment.

Held, that the question of false representations was peculiarly one for the Judge at the trial, and that his finding should not be disturbed, especially as it was concurred in by the Divisional Court.

Held, also, (BURTON, J.A., dissenting) that the defendant had not by lapse of time, acquiescence, or delay, lost his right to rescind.

Per BURTON, J.A.—There was evidence to justify the finding of Armour, J., that the defendant had made his election, and no sufficient grounds were shewn for disturbing it; but as Armour, J., concurred in the judgment of the Divisional Court, and as the merits of the case did not call for interference, the judgment of the Divisional Court should be affirmed.

THIS was an appeal by the plaintiff from the judgment of the Queen's Bench Division, reported 2 O. R. 654.

The facts are fully stated, and the authorities cited are referred to in the report of the case in the Court below and in the judgments delivered in this Court.

The appeal was heard on the 20th day of November, 1884.[*]

Osler, Q. C., *Clute*, and *Hilton*, for the appellant.
Britton, Q. C., for the respondent.

January 26, 1885. BURTON, J. A.—The defendant, for mere speculative purposes, purchased from one Baker, an agent of the plaintiff, and his associates, certain land in Port-

[*]*Present*—BURTON, PATTERSON, MORRISON, and OSLER, JJ.A.

age la Prairie; the purchase was made on the 11th January, 1882, but the deed and mortgage to secure the balance of the purchase money, were not executed till a few days subsequently.

The purchase was made through their agent at Kingston, but as sales were being made at other places, it so happened that the particular block 47, which the defendant desired to purchase, had been sold to some one else. The agent offered to give him in lieu of it block 48, but the defendant insisted on his right to have this particular block, and the other sale was eventually cancelled and the sale to the defendant carried out. The agent does not appear to have pressed the purchase. The defendant made several offers for the land which were refused, the vendors naming $1,500 as their price, and refusing to take less, and the defendant then offered to take it at the price asked, and wrote out a memorandum of the purchase which was signed.

After signing this memorandum, and before signing the mortgage, defendant wrote to a person of the name of Georgen, who was examined under a commission, in reference to the property, and he got an answer, he says, in the ordinary course of mail; he has not kept the answer, but he says it gave an unfavourable account of the property, and he says he handed the letter to Baker, who told him that Georgen was prejudiced against the property. He then wrote to Dr. Hagarty, but is unable to give the precise date; shortly after the other letter, however, and the answer to this letter also has unfortunately not been preserved; but we may form some idea of its contents from the views expressed by Dr. Hagarty on his examination, in which he states "that the map was a fraud, and that the parties who perpetrated it should be chastised according to law for obtaining money under false pretences," and he also gives an unfavourable account of the property.

The cash payment of $500 was made, and the mortgage executed on the 18th January.

This suit is upon the covenant in the mortgage, to recover the instalment which matured on the 18th July, 1882, and was commenced on the 21st September of that year.

The payment is resisted on the ground that the plaintiff and his associates through their agent, made certain misrepresentations to the defendant to induce him to purchase, and that he did purchase on the faith of those representations. These representations are thus set forth in the statement of defence:

4. While offering said blocks and lots for sale as aforesaid the said William F. Baker, for the purpose of inducing the said John Arthur McMahon to purchase in said tract, stated to him, that he had been all over the said land, and that it was all high and dry, that the Saskatchewan Avenue ran through the south of the said estate, and that the Assiniboine River ran along the south side of the town as shewn on a plan he then produced, and that the built up and business part of the town extended over on the Lee estate as shewn on said plan.

5. The said John Arthur McMahon was induced by the said representations to purchase one of the blocks in said tract then offered for sale by the said William F. Baker, to wit: Block 47 as laid out on a plan of said Lee estate, for the price or sum of $1,500.

And the defendant counter claimed on the same ground to be repaid the sum of $500.

The case was tried before Mr. Justice Armour, without a jury, who found that the defendant was induced to purchase by the false representations of Baker, but that he had disentitled himself to be relieved of the purchase by his delay in repudiating it, and he found in favour of the plaintiff.

The Divisional Court reversed that decision, and in giving judgment the learned Chief Justice says: " But for the extraordinary map of the town, professing to shew the position of the Lee and Baker estate, we should have unanimously decided that the defence failed as to the soil and general character of the land."

As I entirely agree with that view of the evidence upon the other points, I propose to deal with that one represen-

tation only, and with the action of the Divisional Court
in reversing the decision of the learned Judge below on
the point of election.

The map marked red which was produced with the
commission is not the map which was produced at the
time of sale, nor was any coloured map then produced; a
map was produced similar to it in other respects, and it is
alleged on the one side but denied on the other, that there
was a pencil tracing on the map produced, corresponding
with the limits so marked in red on the plan annexed to
the commission, which it is said was subsequently coloured,
and issued by Lee and his associates.

If the pencil tracing was not there, there is an end of
the case, as the business part of the town is on the locality
over which those words are printed; if however they were
there, the question would remain, whether the representation was of a material fact, and of such a nature as was
calculated to induce the defendant to enter into the contract, and whether the defendant was thereby induced to
enter into it.

I should be inclined to agree with the Court below that
the map in this case was calculated to mislead, and that
being so, I should have thought that in a case of an ordinary purchase, the inference would be that he acted on
the inducement so held out, and that the onus would be
on the other side to shew that he did not, but if I had
been trying this case, I confess that I should have been
incredulous enough to doubt whether any such effect was
produced on the defendant's mind. He was avowedly
purchasing with the view to take advantage of the existing mania for speculation in that description of property.
The statement that the business portion of the town
extended to the pencil limit was accompanied by the statement that the population was only about 3,500, and he
seems to have placed much more reliance on representations
that that speculation was still continuing, or as he himself
expresses it, "that the property was all right," and that, as
he says, he was informed by letter from a brother of

Baker's, "things were booming," when he got to Portage
la Prairie.

It is, however, no part of our duty to reverse the
Divisional Court upon a question of fact unless it is shewn,
not that there is room for a difference of opinion, but that
they are manifestly wrong; but then, assuming the representation to be false, the effect is to render the contract
voidable not void, the party defrauded having the right on
discovering the fraud, to elect whether he will continue to
treat the contract as binding, or will disaffirm it.

In such cases the question is, has the person on whom
the fraud was practised, having notice of the fraud, elected
not to avoid the contract ? or has he elected to avoid it ? or
has he made no election? See *Clough* v. *The London and
North Western R. W. Co.*, L. R. 7 Ex. 26.

It seems to have been left open in a recent case whether
this election must be made within a reasonable time : *Morrison* v. *The Universal Marine Ins. Co.*, L. R. 8 Ex. 197.

The better opinion seems to be that so long as he has
made no election he retains the right to determine it either
way, subject to this, that if in the interval while he is
deliberating an innocent third party has acquired an interest in the property, or if in consequence of his delay the
position even of the wrongdoer is affected, it will preclude
him from exercising his right to rescind.

Lapse of time, however, without rescinding, will furnish
evidence that the party has determined to affirm the contract, and, as remarked by Mr. Justice Mellor, in giving
the judgment of the Exchequer Chamber in the case I have
above referred to (L. R. 7 Ex. at p. 35), "when the lapse of
time is great, it probably would in practice be treated as
conclusive evidence to shew that he has so determined."

So also it must be a material element in coming to a
conclusion upon such a point to consider the nature of the
property which is the subject of the contract. I cannot for
a moment doubt, that if the subject matter of this contract
had been a mine, or timber limits, or a colliery, it would
have been incumbent on the defendant to have acted

promptly on the discovery of the fraud; should not the same rule be applied in the circumstances of this case, where it is manifest that all parties were dealing with the land, not for ordinary purposes, but in reference to the prevailing fever for making purchases in that land of promise? The lands had been in fact sold to another purchaser when the defendant insisted on his own purchase being completed, and they might readily have been sold at an advance before the defendant gave notice of his intention to rescind. The plaintiff cannot of course complain that he will be in a worse position if the contract be set aside by reason of any deterioration between the time the delusion was practised upon the defendant and the time it was discovered, but if, after that discovery is made, the defendant, instead of promptly giving notice of his intention to rescind, continues to hold the property until its market value decreases, the tribunal dealing with the facts may fairly and reasonably draw the inference that he had elected to affirm the contract and take his chances. A man is not at liberty to play fast and loose as to a misrepresentation of which he complains, he is not to be permitted to inflict a greater loss upon the other party than he would have suffered had he come forward at the earliest moment after he discovered the misrepresentation.

The evidence then discloses that the defendant was informed very shortly after the sale that the land was utterly worthless. He went up himself to Portage la Prairie, arriving there on the 27th July, and saw it; he gave notice to the plaintiff of his intention to repudiate the contract about the latter part of August or beginning of September, and he states his reason thus:

" Because the property was so bad it was utterly worthless for building purposes, and therefore I tendered back the property, *if the property had been perfectly dry I would not have had any occasion.*"

Q. "That is it? A. It was not anything like it was represented."

Q. "The whole point is, that it was not dry? A. Of course that increases it. And as I have explained, the town could not grow on account of that big slough."

So that his repudiation is not put upon the ground that he was deceived by the representation as to the location of the business part of the town, but on grounds as to which the Court has found there was in fact no representation on which he relied, and as to which he received information within a few days from the making of the contract.

Is not this notice in effect an admission by the defendant that he gave up all reliance upon the representation as to the location of the business part of the town, if he ever relied on it, and would be willing to take to the property if the representations as to its being high and dry had proved true, and was there not evidence upon which the Judge of first instance might well have found, that there was so much delay as to satisfy him that there was an adoption and an affirmance of the contract?

It appears to me that there was evidence upon which the learned Judge was justified in finding that the defendant had made his election, and no sufficient grounds have been shewn for interfering with that finding. It may be said that the judgment we are now dealing with is that of the Divisional Court, and not that of the learned Judge of first instance. I freely admit that we ought not to interfere with that judgment unless satisfied that it is incorrect, but that is merely to formulate a statement of our duty in any case that comes before us. We are surely called upon to say, whether the Court has exercised a proper discretion in interfering with the decision of the Judge of first instance, who having seen the witnesses has come to a conclusion upon the facts.

The House of Lords in a recent case reversed the judgment of the Court of Appeal, in which that Court had reversed the decision of the Admiralty Judge upon a question of fact. The learned Lord who delivered the judgment remarked : " The question was one of credit, and on such a point the opinion of the learned Judge and the assessors who saw and heard the witnesses, ought to have very great weight, unless it was fairly overbalanced by legitimate inferences from undisputed facts, or by con-

clusions to be drawn from a comparison of the oral
evidence with other statements previously made by or
on behalf of the same parties."

In the present case it is true there was not any great
.conflict of evidence, but very much might depend upon
the manner in which the defendant gave his evidence in
deciding whether he had not in fact delayed in the expectation of a rise in the market; bearing in mind the natuie
of the property and the fluctuations in its value from day
to day, is there anything upon the evidence from which a
Court could properly say that the learned Judge's inferences and conclusions were not well founded ?

I entirely agree with the Court below that the defendant is not entitled to any special consideration.   I do
not think any of the parties before the Court required
its protection; they were each and every one of them
apparently well able to take care of themselves, and under
the circumstances, I am not sure that it would be going
too far to say that the maxim of *caveat emptor* might
fairly be applied to the defendant.

But when the learned Chief Justice adds : " If the case
had been heard by a jury they might well have found
against the defendant upon the whole case, and we should
not have felt inclined to interfere;" I do not understand
why that should not hold good when the case has been
tried by a Judge who, presumably as competent as a jury
to deal with such a question, has found for the plaintiff.

If there was no evidence to support such a finding, or
the inferences drawn by the Judge are manifestly erroneous, then it was the duty of the Court to interfere ; but
unless that is so, the reversal would seem to be unwarranted, and it is as much our duty now to deal with that
question as it was open to the Divisional Court to do so.

I cannot avoid thinking that more weight was attached
to the making of this so-called fraudulent plan by the
Court below, rather than in ascertaining from the evidence
how far the plan had operated upon the defendant's mind
in inducing him to purchase.   In dealing with this part of

the question, the Chief Justice states as a reason for not
reversing the verdict on the point of misrepresentation,
" that they could not do so without sanctioning the use of
an instrument so calculated to deceive."

The evidence that was relied upon was of the most
meagre description, and for myself I believe it never was
relied on, a conviction which is strengthened from the circumstance that it was not referred to as a ground for repudiating the purchase. With great deference to the learned
Chief Justice, I think that the case of *Hurd* v. *Lindsay
Petroleum Co.*, L. R. 5 P. C. 221, has not much application.
The parties there occupied a fiduciary position, and there
was no evidence to shew that the fraud was not discovered
until shortly before the filing of the bill. No such relationship existed here, and there is distinct evidence that very
shortly after the sale, the defendant was advised that the
property was worthless, and if he did originally rely upon
the statement as to the business part of the town, he
did not make that the ground of his repudiation, and
allowed considerable time to pass even after he had become
fully aware of the actual facts by personal inspection. I
say considerable time, because the delay must, I think, be
considered in reference to the subject matter. Here the
subject matter was a gambling in property; the value of
which fluctuated from day to day.

These were all facts which could not have been with-
held from a jury, in order to enable them to form an
opinion as to whether the defendant had or had not elected
to affirm the contract, and were considered by the Judge,
who has arrived at the conclusion that he had. If such
had been the conclusion of the jury, I gather from the
remarks of the Chief Justice the Court would not have
interfered; and if that be a sound view, why should a
different rule be adopted when the Judge has so decided?
But then Mr. Justice Armour appears to have concurred
in the judgment of the Divisional Court, reversing his
finding upon the question of adoption; but for this circumstance, I should have been of opinion that his finding

should not have been interfered with, but that the parties to the litigation should have been left as he left them. For similar reasons I think that we ought not now to interfere with the decision of the Divisional Court, notwithstanding the very strong opinion I entertain upon both the points of defence. I should myself have arrived at a different conclusion, but as they have found in favour of the defendant, and Mr. Justice Armour has apparently re-considered his decision, I do not think that the merits of the case call upon us to interfere.

I concur, therefore, with my learned Brothers in dismissing the appeal.

OSLER, J. A.—I do not see my way to reverse the judgment of the Court below.

The learned Judge who tried the case, without a jury, found that the plaintiff had been induced to purchase the land in question by the representations of Baker, and that such representations were false.

The reasons for his judgment at the trial have not been reported, but as he took part in the judgment of the Divisional Court, which is now before us, we have the advantage of knowing that the particular false representation relied upon and proved to the satisfaction of both tribunals, as one which influenced the defendant to purchase, was that which related to the position of the business portion of the town.

The questions whether this representation was material, whether it was false, and whether the defendant was influenced by it, were peculiarly questions for the learned Judge who tried the cause to decide. He had the advantage of seeing and hearing the principal parties in the witness box, and on all these points the case would turn very much on his opinion of their credibility. If there was evidence in support of his finding, I think we could not interfere, especially as it has been concurred in by the Divisional Court. But, after a careful consideration of the evidence, I must say that I am entirely of opinion with

the Court below that the map was designedly prepared for
the purpose of deception, and was itself directly calculated
to mislead intending purchasers as to the position of the
business portion of the town, apart from any actual verbal
assertion on the subject. That Baker did make the representation as to this, I consider abundantly proved. Whether
it influenced the defendant, I should have had more doubt,
looking at the then prevailing mania for speculation in
North-West lands. But on that point I conceive, there
being evidence in support of it, we are specially bound to
respect the finding of the Judge of first instance. The
argument, that the defendant, was not or ought not to have
been influenced or misled by the false map and false statement, does not come very persuasively from those who put
them forward, nor should a Court of justice be astute to
support a claim, which arises out of what I cannot help
characterizing as a manifest fraud. When a mania for
speculation exists, the least that is to be demanded of those
who seek to take advantage of it is, that they shall use no
unfair means in doing so.

The next question is, whether the defendant has lost his
right to be relieved from the contract by reason of acquiescence or lapse of time or delay in repudiating it after
discovery of the fraud ?

The learned Judge at the trial at first thought he had,
but he afterwards concurred with the other members of
the Divisional Court in holding that he had not. There
is no reason therefore to suppose, that the finding at the
trial on this point proceeded upon any estimate the learned
Judge formed of the veracity of the witnesses, from their
demeanour, &c.

The facts are undisputed upon which this question must
depend. It was quite competent for the Divisional Court
to take a different view from the Judge of the first instance of the inference proper to be drawn from them, and
even if we may think it would have been more satisfactory
not to have interfered with his decision, we cannot for that
reason re-establish it, and reverse the judgment of the

Divisional Court. We can only do that if we are quite
satisfied that they were wrong; *Hale* v. *Kennedy*, 8 A.
R. 157, and *Symington* v. *Symington*, L. R. 2 Sc. App. 415.

I think the result of the evidence is fairly stated on
this point in the Court below.

The defendant bought the land in January, 1882. Before
the deed was made, he wrote to a friend at Portage La
Prairie making some general inquiries with regard to the
character of the property. He received an unfavorable
reply, which he shewed to Baker, who told him, as Baker
himself admits, that his friend was prejudiced against the
property; that his statements were not true, and that his
reason for making them was, that he thought he was
interested in property in other parts of the town. Subsequently he wrote to a Dr. Hagarty, a real estate agent,
who also gave an unsatisfactory answer. Baker advised
him to pay no attention to this letter either, and for the
same reason. After this the defendant had an offer for the
property at an advance upon the price he had given for it,
which was withdrawn, the intending purchaser saying he
had heard the property was bad, though in what respect
is not stated. As late as the month of March the defendant was holding it as high as $5,000.

After one month the "boom" was over, and it could not
be sold at all. In the end of July the defendant visited
Portage la Prairie, and then for the first time became
aware of the actual condition and position of the property.
He returned to Kingston about the 10th or 12th of August
and in the end of that month, or the beginning of September, requested the plaintiff to take it back, and executed a
re-conveyance of it.

There is no evidence that the property had fallen in
value between the time the defendant was in Portage la
Prairie and the date of the re-conveyance.

Now the question here is, whether the vendee has lost
his right by reason of acquiescence, lapse of time, or delay,
to elect to avoid this contract, which was at some time
certainly voidable on the ground of the vendor's fraud.

In *Clough* v. *The London and North Western R. W. Co.*, L. R. 7 Ex. 26, we find the law thus laid down, p. 35: "In such cases the question is, has the person on whom the fraud is practised, *having notice of the fraud*, elected not to avoid the contract? or has he elected to avoid it? or has he made no election? We think that so long as he has made no election he retains the right to determine it either way, subject to this, that if in the interval whilst he is deliberating, an innocent third party has acquired an interest in the property, or if in consequence of his delay the position even of the wrongdoer is affected, it will preclude him from exercising his right to rescind. And lapse of time without rescinding will furnish evidence that he has determined to affirm the contract; and when the lapse of time is great, it probably would in practice be treated as conclusive evidence to shew that he has so determined."

In *The Lindsay Petroleum Co.* v. *Hurd*, L. R. 5 P. C. 221, 239, it is said: "The doctrine of laches in Courts of Equity is not an arbitrary or a technical doctrine. Where it would be practically unjust to give a remedy, either because the party has, by his misconduct, done that which might fairly be regarded as equivalent to a waiver of it, or where by his conduct and neglect he has, though perhaps not waiving that remedy, yet put the other party in a situation in which it would not be reasonable to place him if the remedy were afterwards to be asserted, in either of these cases, lapse of time and delay are most material. * * Two circumstances, always important in such cases, are, the length of the delay and the nature of the acts done during the interval, which might affect either party and cause a balance of justice or injustice in taking the one course or the other, so far as relates to the remedy."

In *Erlanger* v. *The New Sombrero Phosphate Co.*, 3 App. Cas. 1218, 1230, the statement in the first part of the foregoing extract was approved of as containing the nearest approach to a definition of the equitable doctrine upon this head, a doctrine which, though I think it was argued to the contrary, is not confined to cases where a fiduciary position exists between the parties, but is that which is applied whenever, as between vendor and purchaser, either party seeks to avoid the contract on the ground of fraud: See per Lord

Hatherley in *Erlanger's Case*, at p. 1243; *Clough* v. *London and North Western R. W. Co.*, *supra*; *Pollock* on Contracts, 495, 506, 516, note.

To apply the principles laid down in these cases to the one before us. If the defendant, after receiving Georgen's letter, had concluded the purchase, or if, after receiving Dr. Hagarty's letter, he had continued to deal with the property without in either case making further inquiry, I should have had no difficulty in inferring acquiescence and an election on his part to affirm the contract, and this although we have not been informed in what respects either of these persons told him the property was unsatisfactory. He was clearly put upon inquiry, and if he made none, the inference would be irresistible that he was satisfied to take the property in the one case, or to retain it in the other, whether the representations which had been made to him were true or false. But he shewed the letters to Baker, and cannot I think, by Baker and his principals, especially considering the business connection between them, be accused of having acted imprudently in resting satisfied with the representations made by him as to the interested motives of the writers, at all events for the comparatively short period during which fictitious and inflated values prevailed. When the general fall in values occurred, the necessity of a prompt inquiry into the condition of these particular lands would not be apparent, and therefore I think no improper delay is imputable to the defendant before he went to Portage la Prairie in the end of July, 1882. He then had notice of the actual condition of affairs, and it is his conduct after that time that is to be looked at. It does not appear that he attempted to sell the property, or did any other act with relation to it subsequently, and there is no evidence that there was any further depreciation in its value, or that the plaintiff has been placed by the delay of five or six weeks in a worse position than if the defendant had elected to avoid the deed while at Portage la Prairie, and had then given notice of his intention to do so. I am therefore of opinion that the defendant had not by lapse of time, acquiescence, or delay, lost his right to rescind, and that the appeal should be dismissed.

PATTERSON and MORRISON, JJ.A., concurred.

Appeal dismissed, with costs.

HUGHES V. MOORE ET AL.

Sale of goods—Agreement—Written instrument—Admissibility of parol evidence to explain terms as to price.

The plaintiff bought the office and plant of a newspaper, gave a chattel mortgage thereon to W., and placed P. in charge. The defendants made advances to P. for the purpose of carrying on the business. W. sold the property by auction for the amount of the mortgage debt to the defendants, who, supposing that P. was the owner, wished to secure themselves for the advances made to him. The defendants then agreed to sell the property to the plaintiff; but a dispute arose as to the price, and this action was brought to obtain specific performance of the agreement. There was written evidence of the agreement in a document signed by the defendant Moore, part of which was as follows : " Price of this office to be what it has cost Mr. Horton (the other defendant) and myself." Specific performance was decreed by consent, and it was referred to the Master at London to take the accounts, and to report what was the true agreement between the parties.

Held, [reversing the decision of the Master and of Ferguson, J.,] that the defendants had the right to shew before the Master what they meant by the reference to the cost of the office as fixing the price ; and that, upon the evidence, the true agreement between the parties was, that the price was to be the amount paid to W., *plus* the advances to P.

THIS was an appeal by the defendants from the judgment of Ferguson, J., dismissing an appeal from the report of the Master at London.

The action was brought to enforce specific performance of an agreement to sell the office and plant of a newspaper called the *Elgin Gazette.* It appeared that the plaintiff bought the property in question in 1879 or 1880, and gave a chattel mortgage thereon to one White for $500, payable with interest at eight per cent. in February, 1881.   One Pankhurst was associated with him in the purchase, and though he failed to advance his share of the purchase money, there appeared to have been an understanding that he or his wife might in some event become the owner.

At all events the property was taken to Aylmer, and Pankhurst became the editor of the paper, and the ostensible manager and proprietor of the business.

After it had been published for some time at Aylmer, the defendants, who for business purposes of their own desired that a paper of that kind should be published in St. Thomas, suggested to Pankhurst that it would be better to publish it there, which he agreed to do.   They accordingly made advances to him to meet the expenses incurred in the removal, and afterwards in carrying on and publishing the paper.   In the latter end of March, or the beginning of April, 1881, the mortgagee offered the property for sale by auction, and the defendants became the purchasers for the amount of the mortgage debt.   They supposed that Pankhurst was the owner and mortgagor, and their object was to make themselves secure for the advances they had made to him.

The present action arose out of what took place between the defendants and the plaintiff's agent, one R. W. Rule, at and soon after the sale.   The defendants admitted that there was an offer or agreement on their part to sell the property to the plaintiff, and were willing and asked that the agreement, as they understood it, might be specifically performed.   The dispute between the parties was as to the price; the plaintiff contending that he was to have the property on payment of what the defendants paid the mortgagee for it at the sale, while the defendants alleged that they were to be paid, not only that sum, but also the advances they had made to Pankhurst.   Both parties demanding specific performance of "the only and true agreement" between them, the case came before Proudfoot, J., on motion for judgment on the pleadings on the 31st January, 1883, and by consent of counsel a decree was made declaring "that the agreement for the sale of the office and plant of the *Elgin Gazette*, in the pleadings mentioned, ought to be specifically performed," &c., and referring it to the Master at London to take accounts and make inquiries, and *inter alia* "to ascertain and state what is the true agreement between the plaintiff and defendants in respect of such sale."

On the 21st January, 1884, the Master reported as follows:

"1. That the true agreement between the plaintiff and defendants in respect of the sale in the said judgment mentioned is: That the plaintiff purchased from the defendants the office and plant in the proceedings and pleadings mentioned, at the price which the same had previously cost the defendants, when they purchased under the chattel mortgage sale from one White, the mortgagee, and as set out in the plaintiff's statement of claim.

"2. That the price which the same had cost the defendants was $530 paid to the said White in full of his claim, and a claim for rent of the buildings in which the said office and plant stood, due to one Welding, the amount of which properly chargeable against the office and plant in question was $26.25, which the defendants had paid to the said Welding, making the total price paid by the defendants for the said office and plant $556.25."

An appeal from these findings was dismissed by Ferguson, J., who was of opinion that no sufficient reasons existed for varying or reversing any of the conclusions of the Master.

The material parts of the evidence taken before the Master are set out in the judgments herein.

The appeal was heard on the 9th day of December, 1884.*

H. Becher, for the appellants. The true agreement upon the evidence was, that the plaintiff purchased from the defendants the office and plant in question at the price referred to in the letter from Moore to Rule of the 13th

---

* *Present.*—HAGARTY, C.J.O., BURTON, PATTERSON, and OSLER, JJ.A.

April, 1881. The Master should have found that the defendants, in addition to the sum allowed them by him, were also entitled to be paid $325, the amount lent to John C. Pankhurst, $26.25, additional for rent, and $20 for insurance premiums.

Bayly, Q. C., for the respondents. The Master was warranted upon the evidence in finding as he did: *Lawrence* v. *Ketchum*, 4 A. R. 92.

January 26, 1885. HAGARTY, C. J. O.—It is not easy to understand why the defendants should have purchased at the sale, if it was merely for the purpose of paying off the chattel mortgage, and then handing the property over to the plaintiff.

Mr. Rule says, p. 9: "Before the sale I made arrangements with Moore that I was to settle as to the chattel mortgage with White, and to arrang: with Moore and Horton the amount they should be out, with interest. * * I had made an arrangement with these defendants before the sale that they were to satisfy White's claim, and I was to pay the defendants and get the plant back."

Then at the sale Rule bid $20 over what the defendants bid; the auctioneer did not accept his bid, not thinking him good for it. I hardly see why he bid if he had made a previous arrangement with the defendants, and he says he considered there was a conspiracy to prevent his getting it. He says he was bidding at the sale for the plaintiff: that the instructions he had from the plaintiff were to sell if a good price was got, if not, to settle the mortgage; the object he had in bidding was, to bring the price up and try and sell the property. Immediately after the sale Rule heard the defendants talking of an amount they had been out to Pankhurst; it was Horton, Moore. and White who spoke of what they had paid to Pankhurst, and who said he had deceived them.

The plaintiff states that he had bought the office and plant for $500 cash, bill of sale $500, he to have half interest, Pankhurst the other half; that was not carried out because Pankhurst could not raise $500: that he had instructed

Rule, and that, if the sale was enough to pay the mortgage and himself, to let it go, if not, to arrange about the mortgage. When he heard that it had been knocked down to Moore, and he had given possession to Pankhurst, he made up his mind that he had lost the office. He was told that if he could raise $150 he could purchase.

Rule was prevented before the, Master from shewing that before the sale he knew from Pankhurst as to the expenses incurred by the defendants respecting the paper after the removal to St. Thomas. I think the question should have been allowed to shew Rule's knowledge of the true position of affairs, as the plaintiff had left him the conduct of the matter, and relies chiefly on his evidence. Mr. Rule was thus enabled to say, "I was not at all aware myself that they had been at expense."

Moore's evidence is directly opposed to Rule as to any understanding or agreement, and he swears most positively that he informed him that they would, if they bought it do so to secure their claim for advances: that after he bought he told Rule if he wanted it he could have it, he could have it for what it cost them, and might thus get back the money which he said Pankhurst owed him. He fully explains his understanding of the terms of the receipt or contract which he signed. Rule does not deny nor was he asked as to telling Moore that Pankhurst owed him.

Horton's evidence is important. He says Rule had told him that Pankhurst owed him money: that up to the sale Horton thought the chattel mortgage was from Pankhurst; that if he had known it was the plaintiff's property, he would have known the purchase would not have done them any good: they did not want to make anything out of it: that a few moments after the sale Moore asked him, in Rule's presence, if in case they could get their money out of the sale they might let Rule have the property, as Pankhurst owed him a good deal. Horton answered in presence of Rule, that all he wanted was, to get what we had advanced Pankhurst. Rule asked how much that was, and Moore answered about $1,000. It was assented to that he might get anything beyond what was coming to them. They then went to Horton's office, and they gave Rule an order to get possession, after that he came and asked them to advance $400 to run the office, which they declined. Rule gave up the property, and they put Pankhurst in possession again.

I think the evidence heavily preponderates in favour of holding that Mr. Rule fully understood the defendants' object in purchasing was to protect themselves for their advances.

The plaintiff's claim must rest on the document of April 12, 1881. The $150 is received on purchase of office and plant of the Elgin *Gazette*, formerly owned by Pankhurst, and bought by Moore. "Price to be what it has cost Mr. Horton and myself."

Next day Moore writes that he heard Rule understood the matter differently, and states his understanding, and adds: "If you understood it different, you had better cancel the bargain and get your money back, as that is the condition I sold on."

Pankhurst strongly corroborates Moore's evidence as to his understanding. He was present when money was paid. He says: "After Rule paid it I said to him my impression was, that they required the amount advanced to me in addition to the amount of the chattel mortgage."

As soon as the alleged misunderstanding was known to the plaintiff or Mr. Rule—which was the next day—they could have either received back the $150, or at once abandoned the matter, or have with reasonable promptness insisted on their supposed rights. Nearly twenty months after, this action was brought.

Mr. Rule accounts for the long delay by saying: "We were all working together to get the material sold to some one else to make a good sale, so that the plaintiff and defendant could get their money." In the fall of 1882, he says, Moore told him he had sold to a man for $1,500, and wished the matter to stand as it was, as nothing would be paid until Spring.

In November, 1882, in answer to a demand from the plaintiff, Moore gave the account of their claim, shewing a balance after crediting the $150 paid. I would gather from Moore's evidence that when he rendered this account he did not understand that the plaintiff seriously insisted on the claim now urged.

It would have been far more convenient if it had been ascertained and found at the trial whether any concluded agreement had really been made or not. If they differed immediately after the signing of the receipt as to the sense in which they understand some words of doubtful import, I think the Court would not have decreed specific performance.

Then it is, apparently by consent, referred to the Master to find the true agreement between the parties.

My view on the general merits would be, that there was no concluded agreement made at the time ; no *consensus animorum*; but that the conduct of the parties in the long interval between the alleged bargain and the commencement of this suit shews that the only real agreement, if there be any, must be as the defendants construe and understand it.

I think the burden was on the plaintiff to have either accepted defendants' view, or promptly have insisted on their rights as they understood them. With full notice of defendants' understanding, they do not either take back the $150, or say they will hold them to their version. If I have to find that there was an agreement concluded, my decision must be in favour of defendants' version of it. It is more consonant with reason—it seems the only explanation of their purchase—and I think their evidence reads with much greater force than that offered by plaintiff.

BURTON, J. A.—I agree with the rest of the Court that parol evidence was clearly admissible to shew what the defendant Moore intended by the reference in the memorandum of the 12th April, as to the price being what the office had cost Mr. Horton and himself.

I think it perfectly clear that, upon the defendants intimating to the plaintiff that there was a misunderstanding, it was open to the plaintiff to consider the proposal at an end, and to call for a return of the money. But we have to deal with the matter as we now find it, after the long delay by the plaintiff to avail himself of the opportunity to recede from the proposal, his filing a bill to have this agreement specifically performed, and the submission by the defendants to have the agreement carried out, but pointing out that the terms were different from those alleged by the plaintiff, the subsequent consent of all parties to a decree for specific performance of the agreement for the sale.

It appears to me, that, under this decree, all that was open to the parties was the construction to be placed upon the words to which I have referred. Whether, in other words, the contention of the plaintiff that they were restricted to the amount of the White mortgage and a small sum to which the property was liable for rent, or that of the defendants that the true agreement was that the plaintiff purchased the office at the price referred to in the letter of the 13th April, or in the classic language of that letter, "all they were out on it," or about $1,000.

This letter conveyed a clear intimation to the plaintiff of what the defendants meant by the language in the receipt of the previous day.

There was no other agreement between the parties. It was open to the plaintiff, upon receiving that intimation, to say, I never so understood the matter, the result being that no agreement would have been arrived at, and he would have been entitled to a return of his money.

Instead of taking that course, he leaves the matter in abeyance for months, and eventually files a bill to have the agreement for the sale specifically performed. He had been told that the defendants did not recognize his construction of the document, and therefore he could not have contemplated the specific performance of that agreement as he understood it, and the only possible result at the hearing must have been, but for the submission in the

defendants' answer, a dismissal of his bill on the ground
that there was no concluded agreement.

But at the hearing both parties, agreeing that there had
been a sale, but differing as to the terms, consented to a
decree recognizing an agreement for sale. And the reference to the Master practically was, to ascertain what
" the defendants were out on account of the office." The
plaintiff knew that that was the only agreement the defendants recognised, and that, therefore, was the agreement, or
there was none. The inquiry before the Master was, whether
the payments claimed to have been made to Pankhurst
were in fact made. If these payments are now admitted,
no further reference will be necessary. Those payments
are $225 ; $26.50 for rent and $20 for insurance.

Making the total sum.................$530	00
	225 00
	26 50
	20 00
	$801 50
Less the payment made $150 00	
And the allowance for rent.... 350 00	
$500	00
	$301 50

with interest from the times they were advanced.

If these amounts are now agreed to, a reference back may
be dispensed with.

The appeal should be allowed, with costs, with a declaration to this effect. If the plaintiff desires a reference, it
should be at his risk as to costs, in the event of his failing
to reduce the amount claimed.

OSLER, J. A.—We have not the advantage of knowing
the grounds on which the Master proceeded further than
they may be inferred from the report of the proceedings
before him.

It, therefore, becomes necessary to examine the evidence.

The form of the decree causes some embarrassment. It first declares that the agreement in the pleadings mentioned (each party setting up a different one) ought to be specifically performed, and then directs the Master to find out what the true agreement is. On such a reference the evidence might be of a character which would absolutely preclude the Master from finding the existence of any agreement whatever, a not improbable contingency in the present case, looking at the wide divergence between the parties on the question of price.

I may say, in the first place, that the evidence wholly fails to support the allegation in the statement of claim, that the defendants made an agreement, which they afterwards repudiated, with Rule, the plaintiff's agent, to bid for the property at the sale under the chattel mortgage, and in the event of their becoming the purchasers, to transfer it to the plaintiff on repayment of what they should advance for it. No plausible reason is suggested why they should have made such an agreement, the defendants deny it, and Rule's conduct in bidding against them at the sale is totally inconsistent with it.

The plaintiff does not indeed rely upon any such agreement, and the allegation seems to have been made rather with the view of giving colour to his version of the actual agreement, the written evidence of which, as both parties admit, is contained in the following document, which was given to Rule by the defendant Moore on its date:

"St. Thomas, Ont., April 12th, 1881.

"Received from R. W. Rule the sum of $150, on purchase of office and plant of *Elgin Gazette*, formerly owned by J. C. Pankhurst, and bought by me. I am to have a chattel mortgage for balance of purchase, payable in one year at farthest ; chattel mortgage to be made by Alfred H. Hughes, who is the purchaser, provided, if Hughes cannot give a legal chattel mortgage, this purchase and receipt to be null and void, and money to be returned. Price of this office to be what it has cost Mr. Horton and myself.

"Elijah Moore."

The case turns entirely upon the expression "price of this office to be what it has cost Mr. Horton and myself;" the plaintiff insisting that it necessarily limits the price

to the amount the defendants had paid to White, and a
further small sum which had been paid for the rent of the
office, and that the defendants were not at liberty to shew
that they meant by it to include also what they had
advanced to Pankhurst. The Master adopted the defendants' contention as appears from the following note of
his ruling:

"Objection by PLAINTIFF.—That evidence cannot be given
to vary the written contract. This is conceded by defendants, who offer this evidence to shew advances by defendants to Pankhurst in connection with the office and plant
in question, and to shew what it has cost the defendants.

" Mr. BAYLY objects to evidence of any advances made
by the defendants to Pankhurst, as such cannot be under
any circumstances part of what the office and plant cost
them (the defendants), the office never belonging to Pankhurst at any time.

" NOTE.—From the words of the agreement, which leaves
the specific price of the office and plant an open question
and the subject of inquiry, I think I am bound to accept
any evidence from the defendants, which does not go to
the extent of setting up a verbal agreement as to Pankhurst's debt, to alter, vary, or add to the written agreement.
As to the cost or price of the office and plant, if the evidence
on being taken goes so far as that, then, I think, it will be
inadmissible, and may be so argued on closing the hearing
under the reference."

I am unable to concur in this view, as I think it clear
that the defendants had the right to shew what they
meant by the reference to the cost of the office as fixing
the price. The expression is an ambiguous one, not in
terms inconsistent with the contention of either party. It
is capable of meaning, according to circumstances and to
the real intention and agreement of the parties, either the
whole of the defendants' outlay in connection with the
office, or merely what they had paid to the mortgagee
Parol evidence was therefore admissible to shew what
the parties meant, just as it would have been to identify
the subject matter of the contract, and if, either as to subject matter or price there was no *consensus ad idem*, if

both did not mean the same thing, the only result would be
that there was no contract at all between the parties: See
Phillips v. *Bistolli*, 2 B. & C. 511; *Greene* v. *Bateman*, 2
Woodbury & Minot 359; *Malins* v. *Freeman*, 2 Keen
25; *Cochrane* v. *Willis*, L. R. 1 Ch. 58; *Riley* v.
Spotswood, 23 C. P. 318; *Smith* v. *Hughes*, L. R. 6 Q. B.
597.

What the defendants meant is evident; they had all
along been dealing with Pankhurst as the owner of the
concern, and the moneys they had advanced to him were in
connection with it. Moore says, and Rule does not deny
it, that Rule told him on the day of the sale that the office
and plant belonged to Pankhurst, and the receipt of the
12th April, which Rule says was read to him when he paid
the $150, is on its face expressed to be for the office and
plant of the *Gazette*, formerly owned by J. C. Pankhurst.

If it was antecedently improbable that the defendants
would advance money to buy in the property for the plaintiff's benefit, it is still more unlikely that, when they had
become the absolute owners of it, they would sell it to him
on a year's credit for just what they had paid for it. Then
the defendant Horton swears, "a few minutes after the sale
Moore asked me in Rule's presence if in case we could get
our money out of the sale, we might let Rule have the
property, as Pankhurst owed him a good deal; I answered
in the presence of Rule, that all that I wanted was to get
what we had advanced Pankhurst; Rule asked how much
that was, and Moore said about $1,000; it was assented to
that he might get anything beyond what was coming to us."
And Moore said: "I saw Mr. Rule before the mortgage sale,
and told him that Mr. Horton and I had a claim on the
office and plant, and that I was going to buy it under the
chattel mortgage to secure our claim and make it sure; he
said Pankhurst was also indebted to him to a considerable
amount, and he'd like to secure his too, if he could; I told
him if I bought the office that day, that after Mr. Horton
and I had found out what it had cost us I would let him
have it for what it did cost us; of course, he understood
that I meant what money it had cost us; I told him so;
both what we had already advanced and what we had to
pay that day; I say of course he understood it, because he

wanted me to buy it in for him, and I would not do it. I had some conversation with Mr. Rule after the sale, I think at Mr. Horton's office, and then we told him that if he wanted the office and plant, and would pay us just what it cost us, he could have it, and get his money owed him by Pankhurst back."

And on the 13th April, the day after the receipt was given, Moore, who appears to have heard, probably from Pankhurst, that there was some misapprehension on Rule's part, wrote to him as follows :

"In the matter of sale of printing office, I am told you understand different from me. What the office cost Mr. Horton and myself is all we are out on it, or about $1,000, and the chattel mortgage must draw interest at 8 per cent. If you understood it different, you had better cancel the bargain and get your money back, as that is the conditions I sold it on."

Rule received this letter on the same day, and it was at once communicated to his principal. Before considering the subsequent dealings of the parties we may refer to Rule's evidence as to the bargain, which is not inconsistent with what the defendants say was their understanding of it. He said he knew the defendants were having the paper removed to St. Thomas, and were taking an interest in it, and had heard from Pankhurst that they had incurred expense about the paper after its removal. He also heard a conversation between the defendants themselves immediately after the sale under the chattel mortgage as to an amount they said they had been "out" to Pankhurst. As to the arrangement with Moore he said :

"Before the sale, I made arrangements with Moore that he was to settle as to the chattel mortgage with Mr. White, and to arrange with Moore & Horton the amount they should be out, with interest. We considered it a conclusive bargain, and after the sale they delivered it over to my possession, and I considered it to bind the bargain. They delivered it by a writing to Mr. Pankhurst to deliver it to me ; I got possession then. I retained possession for about an hour, when Mr. Pankhurst returned with a second order, under which I gave up the goods again. I had no more conversation with them any more after that, for about a

week, when Mr. Pankhurst told me that if I would pay
$150 within a certain time they would continue the bar-
gain. I got the $150 from Mr. Hughes, and paid it. * *
Mr. Pankhurst told me that if I would pay $150 within a
specified time, I should have the property as agreed. Mr.
Pankhurst was a sort of medium between the plaintiff
and defendants. The price he said I should have it at
was what it had cost the defendants, and the landlord's
dues. He did not mention the amounts, but only the $150
to be paid on account; my understanding was $530 and
half the rent. In conversing with Mr. Moore, I did not go
into the items of what it had cost them, and he did not
mention any sums at the time, and I mentioned none; very
few words passed. I counted out the $150, and he read
and copied the receipt 'B.'"

Taking Rule's evidence most strongly in his own favour,
he nowhere expressly says that his agreement with the
defendants was, that he was only to pay them the amount
they might pay or had paid to White. He says, that was
his understanding, and though it is not quite easy to see
how he could have so understood the matter, he is to
some extent corroborated by Pankhurst, who was called
by the defendants, and says: "After Rule paid it (the
$150) I said to him that my impression was, that they re-
quired the amount advanced to me in addition to the
amount of the chattel mortgage and the rent then paid,
and he said I was mistaken, and that all he had to pay
was what it had cost them at the sale."

The defendant Moore's evidence is also rather suggestive
that the price had only been mentioned in general terms,
and that Rule might have misunderstood the language
employed, and both parties agree that no amount or items
were mentioned when the receipt was given.

The inclination of my opinion would be, that while the
proof of the contract alleged by the plaintiff entirely fails,
the evidence up to this stage did not sufficiently establish
that relied upon by the defendants. And I should not
have thought that a contract binding on the plaintiff had
resulted from the subsequent dealings between the parties.
The plaintiff says (p. 13) that after he had seen the letter
of the 13th April, he saw Moore and Pankhurst, and told

them he would pay no borrowed money: that Moore did not assent to this, and the matter went on in that way for nearly a year: that Moore wanted the thing to remain as it was, to try to sell the property for enough to pay all parties, "and it remained at that. I was not consenting to pay any money only the price they had agreed on. I was not willing to pay any more. Rule had no authority beyond that price."

Rule's evidence (p. 12) is to the same effect. The defendant Moore says that about a week after he sent the letter he saw Rule, who said he would see the plaintiff and they would come up and get the items and make out the chattel mortgage: that they never came.

" The last understanding was, that he and the plaintiff were to come up and give the chattel mortgage, and they never came ; nothing was said as to what was to become of the office and plant then, but it was understood when I saw Mr. Hughes some time after between Mr. Hughes, and first with Mr. Rule, that we would try and sell the office and get all we could for it, and after we were paid I understood that the balance was to go to Mr. Hughes, or Mr. Rule ; I thought to Mr. Rule."

I think that while this shews that the defendants were willing that the plaintiff should have the benefit of any sale they might make after recouping their own outlay, it would fall short of proving an actual contract on the part of the plaintiff to buy it.

Still we have to deal with the fact that the parties have by the decree consented that there was a contract between them, and with the further fact that neither of them has made any application to vacate it. Considering these facts, and that the plaintiff consented to the decree with the knowledge he has all along had of the defendants' contention as to price, I think that he must be taken to have consented, not only that there was a contract, but that it was as the defendants have alleged it to be, if on the reference the contention of the latter as to what they meant by the expression " price of office and plant," should be proved, as I think it is proved beyond a doubt.

I am, therefore, of opinion that the appeal should be allowed, and that it should be referred back to the Master to report that the true agreement between the parties is that alleged by defendants in their statement of defence, and to take the accounts between them on the footing mentioned in the reasons of appeal.

If the parties can agree upon the figures, the reference back to the Master may be dispensed with. I do not think that a personal order for payment of the purchase money should be made on any ground.

PATTERSON, J. A., concurred.

Appeal allowed, with costs.

LUMSDEN ET AL. V. DAVIES.

Sale and re-sale of goods—Conditional contract as to re-sale—Delivery—Statute of Frauds.

Defendant sold the plaintiffs some tea, and verbally agreed that he would take back, at an advance of ten cents a pound, such part thereof as the plaintiffs should have in stock unsold at a certain date :

Held, [affirming the decision of the Queen's Bench Division] that there was but one entire conditional contract, not one contract to sell the tea to the plaintiffs, and another to buy it back ; and therefore the delivery of the tea by the defendant satisfied the Statute of Frauds, and the plaintiffs were entitled to recover for the defendant's refusal to take back the unsold tea.

Williams v. *Burgess*, 10 A. & E. 499, considered and followed.

THIS was an appeal by the defendant from the judgment of the Queen's Bench Division, discharging an order *nisi* to set aside the judgment of Morrison, J. A., at the trial, in favour of the plaintiffs.

The action was first tried in 1881 before Galt, J., who non-suited the plaintiffs.

In Hilary Term, 1881, the Court of Queen's Bench set aside the nonsuit and ordered a new trial. (See 46 U. C. R. 1.)

The facts appear in the former report of the case and in the present judgments, where the authorities are also referred to.

The appeal was heard on the 27th day of January, 1885.*

Laidlaw, for the appeal.
McCarthy, Q.C., contra.

March 3, 1885. BURTON, J.A.—I was at first inclined to think that this case was distinguishable from *Burgess* v. *Williams*, 10 A. & E. 499, where the contract might be regarded as a 'conditional sale, and that this was in truth an independent contract of re-sale, and was within the operation of the Statute of Frauds.

Further reflection has, however, led me to the conclusion that the defendant's promise is not an independent original

---

* *Present.*—BURTON, PATTERSON, OSLER, JJ.A., and ROSE, J.

contract, but rather a part of the same contract by which
the plaintiffs agreed to become the purchasers of the tea, and
by which the plaintiffs' purchase became a qualified and
not an absolute purchase. According to the plaintiffs'
evidence and the finding of the learned Judge the plaintiffs
would not have made this purchase. The promise and
undertaking of the defendant formed thus part of the
original contract, and that contract it appears to me was
taken out of the operation of the Statute of Frauds by the
delivery of the tea on the one side and the payment of the
money on the other. That being so it seems to fall within
the principle of such cases as *Burgess* v. *Williams*, and the
judgment below would appear therefore to be correct.

The appeal should, I think, be dismissed, with costs.

PATTERSON, J.A.—The finding of fact by the learned
Judge who tried this action, is thus expressed in his judgment: " In this case I find that the defendant offered and
sold to the plaintiffs the teas in question, viz: 10,852
pounds for $5,250.36 ; and as an inducement to plaintiffs
to purchase, promised them that, if they would take the
teas, he, the defendant, would pay them an advance of
ten cents a pound for all of such teas as they would have
on hand in stock unsold in February, 1880. On these terms
plaintiffs purchased the teas."

Mr. Laidlaw's contention for the defendant is, that if the
agreement to receive back the unsold teas, and pay for
them at the original selling price, plus ten cents per lb. if
made out, it is as an agreement distinct from the sale of
the teas to the plaintiffs, and that, under the 17th section
of the Statute of Frauds, that agreement cannot be allowed
to be good.

It certainly is not left beyond doubt, by the learned
Judge's memorandum of his finding, whether he understood
the whole agreement as one, or regarded it as divisible
into two.

In the Divisional Court it was considered, as expressed
in the judgment of the Court, which was delivered, I

believe, by the Chief Justice, that there was no room for disturbing the finding of the learned Judge, who gave weight and credit to the plaintiff's evidence. In that I entirely agree, but in 'which of the two ways the finding was understood, is still left to inference.

The Court had already given a judgment in the action, in setting aside a nonsuit, (46 U. C. R. 1) and the judgment now in appeal refers to the former one as deciding that the contract was valid under the Statute of Frauds. That former decision was chiefly supported, by the learned Judge who delivered it, by the authority of *Burgess* v. *Williams*, 10 A. & E. 499.

Taking all these things together, we shall, I think, be correct in understanding the view of the Court below to have been that there was but one entire contract, not that there was one contract to sell the teas to the plaintiffs and another to buy them back.

I believe that is the way we all understand the finding at the trial; and that if we adopt the opinion of the learned Judge, who gave credit to the plaintiffs' evidence as against the contradictory evidence of the defendant, we should ourselves conclude from the evidence that the whole was one agreement for the purchase by the plaintiffs of the teas, on the terms that they were to pay the agreed prices, and to have the right in February to return such of the teas as remained unsold, and receive back the price they paid with ten cents per lb. added.

Understanding the contract in this way, the Statute of Frauds creates less difficulty.

The 17th section enacts that no contract for the sale of any goods, wares, or merchandize, for the price of £10 sterling or upwards, shall be allowed to be good, except the buyer shall *first* accept part of the goods so sold and actually receive the same: or *secondly*, shall give something in earnest to bind the bargain, or in part payment: or *thirdly*, unless some memorandum or note in writing of the said bargain be made and signed by the parties to be charged with such contract, or their agents thereto' lawfully authorized.

Here the plaintiffs, who were the buyers, fulfilled the first and second articles. They accepted and actually received the goods, and they paid for them. The contract for the sale was therefore good, and was of course good as to all its terms. That is the doctrine of *Burgess* v. *Williams*, whether the terms relating to the return of the goods be called a condition, or simply a part of the contract.

I do not think this case is distinguishable in principle from *Burgess* v. *Williams*. The distinction suggested by Mr. Laidlaw, from the circumstance that the person charged in that case was the vendee, who had actually received the chattel which he afterwards refused to return, while here the vendee is charging the vendor upon his promise to receive back or repurchase the goods, does not appear to receive support from the terms of the statute. By the statute the effect of acceptance and receipt or payment by the buyer, is that *the contract* is allowed to be good; and the contract includes all that is to be done by both parties.

Gardner v. *Grout*, 2 C. B. N. S. 340, for a reference to which I am indebted to my Brother Rose, is an instance in which the seller was charged upon a contract which was taken out of the statute by the buyer's acceptance and actual receipt of a portion of the goods.

I agree that the appeal must be dismissed, with costs.

OSLER, J.A.—A second argument of this appeal has not changed my opinion. The principal question is, whether the agreement is within the 17th section of the Statute of Frauds.

The agreement declared on and proved was, that the defendant, being desirous of selling to the plaintiffs a quantity of tea, as an inducement to the plaintiffs to buy, promised them that if they would take the teas he would pay them an advance of ten cents per pound for all of such teas as they should have in stock unsold in February, 1880, and would take back the same, and that the plain-

tiffs purchased the tea on these terms. The plaintiffs paid
the defendant for the teas and in February, 1880, had in
stock unsold a large quantity, which the defendant refused
to take back at the price plaintiffs paid for them, or to pay
the advance of ten cents per pound.

On the first trial the plaintiffs were nonsuited on the
ground that the agreement for the re-sale or return was
within the Statute of Frauds, and that there was no
memorandum in writing to satisfy the statute. The nonsuit was set aside, the Court holding that the agreement
was entire, consisting of one conditional contract of sale,
and that the delivery of the goods thereunder to the
plaintiffs satisfied the statute.

On the second trial before Morrison, J.A., without a
jury, the plaintiffs had judgment, which the Divisional
Court refused to disturb otherwise than by reducing the
damages ; and the present appeal is from that decision.

On the question of fact there is no reason to interfere
with the finding, which is supported by evidence amply
sufficient, if believed by the learned Judge, to prove the
somewhat unusual contract these parties entered into.

We have next to determine whether a writing was necessary within the Statute of Frauds. That depends upon
whether the contract was an entire contract for the sale of
the teas by Davies to Lumsden, subject to the condition and
agreement upon which the latter now rely, or two separate
contracts, one, the sale by Davies to Lumsden, and another
for a resale by Lumsden to Davies, at an advance of so
much of the stock as should remain unsold in February.
If the contract was entire the original delivery and acceptance took the whole out of the statute.

I am of opinion that the contract was one entire and
conditional contract as declared on, and as proved, and I
think that Mr. Laidlaw has not succeeded in shewing that
the case of *Burgess* v. *Williams*, 10 A. & E. 499, upon
which the Divisional Court relied, is inapplicable, or that
its authority has been shaken in any way.

In that case the plaintiff sold a mare to the defendant for £20, subject to the condition that if it proved to be in foal the defendant should return it on receiving £12. Here the defendant sells tea to the plaintiffs, subject to a condition that the former shall take back all of it that remains unsold at a certain date, and pay the plaintiffs ten cents per pound advance on the invoice price.

The only difference between the two cases is, that in the former the condition is enforced by and for the advantage of the vendor, and in the latter by and for the advantage of the vendee of the goods—a difference which does not affect the principle of the decision.

The case is thus referred to in the 8th Am. ed., from the 8th London ed., of *Addison* on Contracts, 1883, p. 926: "The acceptance takes the whole contract out of the statute. * * If, therefore, the contract is made defeasible on certain conditions, the conditions will stand good as part of the contract." It is also cited, without observation, for the same proposition in *Chitty* on Contracts, 11th ed. p. 380 ; in *Benjamin* on the Contract of Sale, 3rd Eng. ed. p. 148 ; *Ib.* 3rd Am. ed., p. 169 ; and in *Story* on Sales, 4th ed., 1874, p. 292.

In *Browne* on the Statute of Frauds, 4th ed. p. 355, 356, citing this case, it is said : "A stipulation that the subject of the sale may be returned in a certain event, is not to be regarded as a contract for a re-sale so as to be affected by the statute. * * But it may be necessary to distinguish between such a case as this, where the stipulation to return is annexed to the original sale by way of condition, and the case of a stipulation to re-sell at a future time for the same or a different price, though made contemporaneously with the original sale. It must depend, it seems, upon whether the latter is a complete transaction of itself, and, in some degree, upon the language used by the parties."

In a note the writer comments on *Burgess* v. *Williams*: "It must be observed that the stipulation was to return, not to receive back, and was made in favor of the vendor, not of the vendee."

As I have said I think that makes no difference in principle, if the contract is single. If it was, and there was a delivery to the *plaintiffs* in the character of vendees of the goods, the defendant might have shewn what the true terms of the bargain were, had *he* been the party suing and the plaintiffs resisting the action. The position of the parties is reversed in this action, but I think their rights are the same in either case, viz., to shew all the terms of the contract.

Some of the American cases cited, illustrate the distinction pointed out in the text of *Browne* on Frauds; *Fay v. Wheeler*, 44 Vt. 292; *Wooster v. Sage*, 6 Hun. (N. Y.) 285; 67 N. Y. App. 67; *Hagar v. King*, 38 Barb. 200; *Blanchard v. Trim*, 38 N. Y. App. 225.

The case of *Tomkinson v. Staight*, 17 C. B. 697, is also in the plaintiffs' favour on the application of the general principle. Williams, J., says, p. 707: "The Legislature has thought, that, where there is a fact so consistent with the existence of a contract of sale as the actual acceptance of part of the goods sold, the necessity of written evidence of the contract might safely be dispensed with. But it is clear that it was not meant to go to all the terms of the contract; and that acceptance * * only establishes the broad fact of the relation of vendor and vendee."

See also *Fry* on Specific Performance, sec. 559.

I think the appeal fails, and should be dismissed, with costs.

ROSE, J.—Having been favoured with a perusal of the judgment of my Brother Osler, I desire to concur without adding more than a reference to two or three authorities shewing that the Courts have always treated an acceptance by the vendee as taking the case out of the statute, so as to enable the vendee to enforce performance as against the vendor. The reason for this conclusion seems plain when we look at the wording of the 17th section of the statute. The contract is not to be allowed to be good except, (1) the buyer shall accept part of the goods so sold, or actually receive the same; (2) or give something in earnest to bind the bargain or in part payment; (3) or that some note or memorandum in writing of the said

bargain be made and signed by the parties to be charged
by such contract, or their agents thereunto lawfully
authorized.

It will be observed that exceptions one and two are acts
in which both vendor and vendee concur. (1) The vendor
delivers; the vendee accepts and receives. (2) The vendee gives, and the vendor receives. In neither of these is
anything said about the party to be charged. This language is used in the third exception, for the manifest
reason that it would be absurd for the pursuing party or
plaintiff to furnish evidence of the contract by producing
a memorandum signed by himself alone.

In *Gardner* v. *Grout*, 2 C. B. N. S. 340, after the sale
agreed on, the buyer went to the vendor's warehouse and
got samples of the goods sold, which he promised to pay for
when he took away the bulk ; and the samples so taken
were weighed and entered against him in the vendor's
book. The vendor then refused to complete the sale, but
held that there had been a part acceptance *making the
bargain complete.*

Smith v. *Hudson*, 6 B. & S. 431, was an action by the
assignees of the vendee, an adjudicated bankrupt, against
the vendor for non-delivery of certain corn. Held, that
the vendor was not bound because the vendee had not
accepted the goods. Blackburn, J., said p. 448 : " In order
to satisfy it (the 17th section) there must have been an
acceptance and receipt of the goods to bind both the purchaser and vendor."

Nicholson v. *Bower*, 1 E. & E. 172 was a case similar to
Smith v. *Hudson*. In *Nicholson* v. *Bower*, the vendee,
believing it to be dishonest to receive the goods after
becoming insolvent, and, determining to stop payment,
purposely abstained from accepting them. A verdict in
favour of his assignees against the vendor was set aside on
the ground that there had been no acceptance in fact by
the vendee.

An interesting case recognizing the same principle may
be found in the United States Courts, viz., *Washington
Ice Co.* v. *Webster*, 62 Me. 341.

The above cases, and probably others, may be found in *Benjamin's* work on Sales of Personal Property, 3rd Eng., 4th Am. ed.

It follows, therefore, that the case of *Burgess* v. *Williams* cannot be disting uished on the ground that there the action was by the vendor, and being of the opinion that the contract is one, entire and indivisible; the condition forming part of the original agreement, I am unable to distinguish it on any other ground.

In my opinion it governs this case, and the appeal fails.

Appeal dismissed, with costs.

O'CALLAGHAN V. BERGIN.

Solicitor and client—Negligence—Investing money for client.

A solicitor entrusted with moneys to invest, did so on property of insufficient value, and his client, shortly after the loan, desired him to realize
the amount advanced, which the solicitor endeavored to do by getting
the owner to effect another loan from a Building Society.   He desired
his client to release his mortgage for that purpose, undertaking
to obtain security on chattel property for any deficiency before
acting on the release.   The society refused to advance more than $800,
which it was stipulated should be paid to the client, thus leaving a
balance due him of about $150.   The solicitor procured from the mort-
gagor a chattel mortgage on cattle, &c., variously valued at from $100
to $130 : such security being made out in the name of the client, and
only requiring his affidavit of *bona fides* to have it registered.   This the
client refused to accept, and instituted proceedings against his solicitor
for the surplus of his claim ; and the Judge of the County Court gave a
verdict and judgment for $177 against the latter.
On appeal, this Court [BURTON, J. A., dissenting,] being of opinion that
the plaintiff had of his own wrong lost the benefit of the chattel mortgage, reduced the judgment by $117, thus limiting the verdict to $60,
with Division Court costs, but refused to either party costs of the appeal.

APPEAL from the judgment of the Judge of the County
Court of the United Counties of Stormont, Dundas, and
Glengarry.

The action was against a solicitor who was charged
with negligently and unskilfully advancing to one Hilderbroom, upon insufficient security, the sum of $855.50,
intrusted to the defendant by the plaintiff for investment,
and with subsequently inducing the plaintiff to release the
security upon the defendant's assurance that the plaintiff
would not suffer any pecuniary loss thereby.   The plaintiff
claimed from the defendant for the loss and damage that
he had sustained in the premises, the sum of $185.

It appeared from the evidence that the plaintiff had
been re-paid $800 of the moneys advanced, and had been
offered a chattel mortgage as security for the balance, but
that he had refused to accept it, and had then brought
this action.

The learned Judge of the County Court gave judgment for the plaintiff for $177.70, and the defendant
appealed.

The facts are fully set out in the judgments on the present appeal, which was heard on the 2nd and 3rd days of February, 1885.[*]

S. H. Blake, Q.C., for the appellant.
Moss, Q C., for the respondent.

March 3, 1885. HAGARTY, C. J. O.—I fully agree with the judgment of my brother Osler, that the case fails as to the attempt to charge defendant for negligence causing damage to plaintiff in the investment of the money advanced by plaintiff on mortgage. Even admitting the retainer, the evidence of which I think is very unsatisfactory, I see no actionable negligence. The property was valued by the agent of the building society as worth several hundred dollars beyond plaintiff's advance.

The company, acting on their rules as to requiring a certain margin, would only advance $800.

Plaintiff did not attempt to realize his security, and allowed interest to accumulate without taking any step.

I think plaintiff's claim must depend entirely on the latter branch of the case.

The learned Judge does not tell us whether he finds his verdict on a personal promise of defendant absolutely to be responsible to plaintiff for the balance coming to him over and above the $800 if he would discharge his mortgage, or whether he holds him guilty of actionable negligence in obtaining sufficient security from Landry by chattel mortgage for such balance.

I think the finding on the evidence could only have properly been on the latter ground; that all that could be found was his undertaking that before he gave up the discharge he would get sufficient security in chattel property. He obtains a chattel mortgage on horses and cows from Landry to plaintiff, as far as we can see properly executed, and only requiring plaintiff's affidavit to be duly registered. Plaintiff refuses to accept it, saying the security was not

[*] Present.—HAGARTY, C.J.O., BURTON and OSLER, JJ.A.

sufficient. I cannot see that even then he gave defendant to understand that he would hold him responsible.

I am strongly of opinion that his only remedy was for negligence resulting in damage to plaintiff in taking security which turned out to be insufficient; plaintiff's damage being the difference between the value of the security and the claim to be secured.

I cannot in this view understand plaintiff's right wholly to repudiate or refuse acceptance of the direct mortgage made to him and useless to any one else, and thus emphatically damaging himself by his own wrong.

The chattel property was variously valued by his witnesses, one of them valuing it as high as $130. In such a case we might certainly have looked for some evidence to shew that plaintiff in refusing to accept this security gave defendant to understand that he held him personally responsible.

The whole of the value, whatever it was, was as I think, wrongfully and wantonly lost by plaintiff's own conduct, and the utmost extent of defendant's liability should be the deficiency, which would only be from $50 to (at the outside) $60.

I rest my judgment not on any questions of contradictory evidence, but on the evidence of the plaintiff and his witnesses.

BURTON, J. A.—This is an appeal from the Judge of the County Court, of the United Counties of Stormont, Dundas and Glengarry, who gave judgment in favour of the plaintiff for $177.70, in an action against a solicitor for having taken, as he alleges, an insufficient security for a loan of money, and in inducing him to release that security upon payment of a portion of the amount secured by it on receiving the defendant's assurance that he would save him harmless and procure sufficient security for the balance due.

That in pursuance of the engagement, the defendant did shortly afterwards procure a chattel mortgage, but on examining the property covered by it, the plaintiff found it to be insufficient and refused to accept it, and claiming from the defendant the loss consequent upon the premises.

The defendant denies the retainer, and alleges that he acted in the transaction as the solicitor of one Hilderbroom, and that the plaintiff applied to him to see if he had any application for loans, that he informed him of this one, mentioned the security, and made no representation as to the sufficiency, but on the contrary it was understood that the plaintiff should make all necessary inquiries for himself.

That the land was ample and sufficient security for the amount advanced.

That the plaintiff some time after became dissatisfied with the security, and requested the defendant to procure a loan from a loan company, in order to enable the plaintiff to obtain his money without the expense of legal proceedings. That he agreed to take whatever could be obtained from the loan company, and the balance, if any, the plaintiff agreed with the then owner of the mortgaged premises to have secured by chattel mortgage on certain of his chattel property.

He denies that the plaintiff released his mortgage at the request of the defendant, or that he agreed to hold him harmless or free from loss by reason of his doing so.

That a mortgage was prepared and executed on certain chattel property, but that plaintiff refused to accept it, and that it was sufficient to cover the balance of the claim.

These were the issues presented for trial, and the learned Judge has found that the defendant was acting as solicitor for the plaintiff as well as for Hilderbroom, and that he undertook the duty of investing his money upon proper and sufficient security.

Had he been acting merely as the solicitor of Hilderbroom, as he alleges, there would, of course, have been no liability to this plaintiff, but it is perfectly manifest upon the evidence that, although the expenses of the mortgage security were to be paid by the borrower, the defenant undertook to act as the adviser of the plaintiff, and investigated the title for him. Had that title proved

defective there could be no doubt of his liability, if it were
a defect for which a solicitor might be held liable. But
it would not follow that he undertook any thing more
than to see that the title was correct and the mortgage
properly executed with the usual provisions.

But the evidence goes further, and shews that the
defendant was entrusted with moneys by the plaintiff for
investment, and that the defendant in this instance acted
as a scrivener, and that he frequently acted as a valuator.
The plaintiff also swears that he knew nothing of the
property himself, but he told the defendant to accept it if
he thought it good security, and that he lent the money
on the defendant's assurance that it was a good security.

The defendant himself admits that he went out to
examine the property and entered a valuation in his docket,
and the Judge draws from this the conclusion, which I
think almost every one else would draw, that he did so
in order to ascertain and advise the plaintiff, whether it
was a security upon which he could safely advance his
money.

In addition to which he made a charge to the plaintiff
for his commission on the investment, although, for reasons
satisfactory to himself, he afterwards abandoned the claim.

This being then, as found by the learned Judge, the
position of the defendant, what duties did it impose upon
him ?

I do not think it can admit of any doubt that, when a
solicitor undertakes a business of that nature, he must be
bound to exercise a reasonable amount of care and attention
in making investments for his client.

I do not wish to be understood that he might not have
sufficiently discharged his duty if he had in good faith
acted upon the opinion of competent surveyors.

But here the evidence of the plaintiff is that he advanced
the money upon the distinct understanding that the defendant would satisfy himself of the sufficiency of the security,
and he admits himself that he went out and personally
examined it.

The learned Judge has also found upon evidence, quite sufficient to warrant the conclusion, that the property was not worth more than $800. It is true that a witness, George McDonald, a valuator for a loan company, who did not go out to examine the property, saw the valuation the applicant had placed upon it and recommended his company to advance $1000 on it, but the company declined to advance more than $800, for which sum they eventually sold it to a purchaser, who admits he would not have purchased even at that price, if it had not adjoined his own farm.

Upon this evidence the learned Judge came to the conclusion that the defendant had not fulfilled his duty to the plaintiff in investing his money upon a sufficient security.

Having come to that conclusion, there was a sufficient motive for the defendant entering into the engagement the learned Judge finds he did enter into, in order to induce the plaintiff to sign the release.

If it be true that the defendant did enter into an engagement of that nature to see that he got sufficient security by chattel mortgage, I take it to be quite clear that the plaintiff was not bound, when he found the property covered by it to be insufficient in value, to accept it at all, and that it cannot be said that to the extent of the value of the articles contained in it he cannot recover damages. I venture very confidently to assert that there is no such rule in law, and properly so. He had a right to stand upon his agreement, and he might very seriously have compromised his position had he accepted such a security after he had had an opportunity of examining it.

Unexplained it would have been conclusive evidence against him that the defendant's contract had been carried out.

Assuming the learned Judge's finding to be correct, I think that no one in the plaintiff's position was under any obligation to receive any thing short of satisfactory security, and was not called upon to expose himself to the risk of being unable subsequently to shew that it had only been received on account.

a promise made by the defendant that he should be
secured for the balance due to him, a promise which he
finds that the defendant failed to perform. Judgment
appears to have been given on this ground for the plaintiff for $177.70.

On the argument of the appeal it was contended that
the evidence shewed the existence of actionable negligence
on the solicitor's part in investing the plaintiff's money on
bad and insufficient security.

The leaning of the learned Judge's opinion is undoubtedly in that direction, although, as I have said, there
is no actual finding on the point.

I think, however, with great respect, that the evidence
does not support this view, bearing in mind that the *onus*
of proof of negligence and of damage resulting therefrom
rests on the plaintiff.

Assuming that there was a retainer, the facts are, that
the loan was made in August, 1881, the solicitor having
first satisfied himself, from an examination of the property
and from the fact (which was proved), that Hilderbroom,
the proposed borrower, had paid $1,200 or $1,300 for it,
that it was a sufficient security. The term of the loan
was three years, but the plaintiff became dissatisfied with
the security a few months after it was taken, and told the
defendant it was better to get back the money on it if he
could. In the judgment of the learned Judge it is observed
that the defendant himself said a few minutes [months?]
after the loan was made by him that the property was not
a sufficient security for the money. I do not, however,
find this statement in the report of the evidence. It is
possibly one of the numerous errors in the appeal book, of
which we have had reason to complain.

In February, 1882, Hilderbroom sold the property to
one Landry, for whom the defendant appears to have acted.
The price is not directly stated, but it cannot have been
for less, and was probably for $100 more than the amount
secured by the plaintiff's mortgage. As a part of that
transaction (the sale to Landry) it was expected that a

sufficient sum would be borrowed by Landry to pay off the plaintiff, but the Canada Permanent Loan Company, to whom the application was made, refused to advance more than $800, although their valuator had recommended, and at the trial swore, that he thought the property a good security for a loan of $1,000.

The plaintiff instead of requiring the property to be sold under his mortgage, which was at this time in default, some delay having occurred in carrying out the loan, consented— it is not just now material to consider on what terms he did so—to discharge his mortgage on receipt of the proceeds of the loan. If the property had been brought to the hammer under the plaintiff's mortgage, and had then failed to produce enough to pay him off, it might have been difficult to hold that a finding, that there had been negligence on the part of the solicitor, was wrong, although that is not the conclusion I should myself have arrived at, looking at the evidence alone. But as the plaintiff chose to discharge his mortgage in reliance, as he says, upon the solicitor's undertaking to obtain security for the balance, I think he cannot now say that his damage necessarily resulted from the latter's negligence in the original valuation.

The case must rest, as I understand the learned Judge to put it, upon the defendant's undertaking.

I think the weight of evidence is, that there was an undertaking of some kind, on the faith of which the plaintiff signed the discharge of his mortgage ; and there seems no sufficient reason for saying that it was not such an undertaking as the learned Judge has found. That finding, however, must be read with reference to what passed between the parties at the time, and from what the plaintiff says it is clear that, though the defendant's undertaking was absolute, the nature of the security spoken of and that which he undertook to procure was a chattel mortgage from Landry. If the promise was absolute, the fact that the goods included in the chattel mortgage were not sufficient in value would not discharge him from his liability to make good any deficiency, and the plaintiff would not,

by accepting the mortgage, have lost his recourse against
him for it. The defendant had no means of compelling
Landry to give him a chattel mortgage. It was, as we
may infer, to have been given, as between Landry and
Hilderbroom, on account of the purchase money of the
property; and it seems to me manifest that the plaintiff
should have taken it for whatever it was worth, and cannot
hold the defendant liable for more than the difference
between that and the balance due to him on the Hilderbroom mortgage.

This is one of the points taken in the reasons for appeal,
and to this extent I think the appeal should be allowed.

The value of the chattels, according to the plaintiff's
estimate, was about $125. On the whole, I think $117 a
not unreasonable value, and that the judgment should be
reduced to $60; the plaintiff recovering Division Court
costs, and neither party having any costs of this appeal.

CORPORATION OF THE VILLAGE OF BRUSSELS V. JOHN D. RONALD.

Municipal bonus—Mortgage—Bond—Conditions—Performance—Damages.

The plaintiffs under a by-law granted the defendant a bonus of $20,000 to aid him in the manufacture of steam fire engines and agricultural implements, subject to a condition in the by-law that he should give a mortgage on the factory premises for $10,000, and a bond for $10,000, to be conditioned, (1) for the carrying on of such manufactures for 20 years; (2) during that period to keep $30,000 invested in the factory; and (3) to insure the building and plant in plaintiffs' favour for $10,000. The defendant gave the bond and mortgage, the latter containing a covenant for insurance, and he invested the $30,000, as stipulated for. He also made a further mortgage on the premises to the plaintiffs for $3,000, not mentioned in the by-law. The factory was one in which 18 to 25 men might have been employed, and which could have turned out 100 mowers in a year. In the course of two years only 20 mowers were constructed, and the number of persons employed dwindled down from 18 or 20 to two or three.

Held, that the performance contemplated by the parties of the contract to carry on manufactures, was one reasonably commensurate with the capabilities of the factory; and that, upon the evidence, the defendant had failed in the performance.

Held, also, that the $10,000 mortgage was given as a security for any damages the plaintiffs might sustain by the defendant's default, to an extent not greater than $10,000, and not as a charge for that specific sum.

Held, also, that, as the $3,000 mortgage was not authorized by the by-law, as to it the plaintiffs were not entitled to any relief.

Remarks upon elements to be considered by the Master in assessing the damages.

THIS was an appeal by the plaintiffs from the judgment of Proudfoot, J., pronounced on the 18th day of May, 1882, reported 4 O. R. 1.

There was also a cross-appeal by the defendant as mentioned in the judgment of the Court.

The appeal and cross-appeal were heard on the 27th day of January, 1885.*

The facts are stated and the authorities cited referred to in the report of the case in the Court below and in the present judgment.

Robinson, Q. C., and *Bain*, Q. C., for the plaintiffs.
Alexander Bruce, for the defendant.

Present.—HAGARTY, C.J.O., BURTON, PATTERSON, and OSLER, JJ.A.

March 3, 1885.   OSLER, J. A.—This is an appeal from
the judgment of Mr. Justice Proudfoot, and the questions raised are in some respects of a novel and difficult
nature.

Under the powers conferred by the Municipal Act, R. S.
O. ch. 174 sec. 454, subsec. 5, the corporation of the village
of Brussels, who are the plaintiffs and appellants, in order
to promote manufactures within their limits, granted to
the respondent a bonus of $20,000, in debentures of the
village, to aid him in the manufacture of steam fire engines
and agricultural implements.   The by-law under which
the bonus was authorized took effect on the 1st September,
1878, and recites that the debentures are to be handed
over subject to the terms, conditions, and restrictions mentioned in the 5th clause, which is as follows:

"Before any of the said debentures are handed over to the said John D.
Ronald, he shall satisfy the reeve of the said municipality that he has
purchased the site or premises for the carrying on of the said manufactory,
and that he has erected and completed the necessary buildings thereon,
and he shall then be entitled to receive the one-half of the said debentures, and he shall be entitled to receive the balance thereof immediately
after he shall have commenced to carry on the manufactures heretofore
mentioned therein.   But before receiving any part of such debentures, he
shall execute and deliver to the reeve, on behalf of the said municipality,
a first mortgage upon the said premises, for the sum of $10,000, and also
bond of himself, personally, for the further sum of $10,000, which said
mortgage and bond shall be conditioned for the carrying on of said manufactures for the term of twenty years next ensuing the date thereof, without interruption for a longer period than three months at any one time,
unless in case of loss by fire, as shall render such interruption unavoidable, but in no case for a longer period than twelve months, and shall be
further conditioned that he shall at all times during the continuance of
the said term of twenty years, have and keep invested in the said manufactory in the premises and plant therefor, at least the sum of $30,000,
and that he shall immediately upon the execution thereof, insure the said
building and plant against fire in some company to be approved by the
said municipality, in favour of said municipality, for the sum of $10,000,
and keep the same so insured during the said term, the loss if any to be
made payable to the said municipality."

On the 27th January, 1879, the defendant executed a
bond in the penal sum of $10,000, reciting the by-law con-
ditioned, (1) for the carrying on at all times during the

period of twenty years next after the date of the bond
the manufactures in question, without interruption for a
longer period than three months at any one time, "unless
in case of loss by fire as shall render such interruption
unavoidable" (*sic*); but in no case for a longer period than
twelve months; (2) and at all times during said twenty
years to have and keep invested in said manufactures on
the premises and plant thereof at least the sum of $30,000;
(3) and for payment of taxes and performance of statute
labor.

He also executed a mortgage which recites the by-law,
and is expressed to be in consideration of the delivery of
the debentures for $20,000.

The proviso is, that the mortgage shall be void on performance of the same conditions as those mentioned in the
bond.   There is a covenant by the mortgagee to observe
the proviso, and also a covenant to insure the buildings on
the lands, to the amount of not less than $10,000.   The
bond does not refer to the insurance, nor is the mortgage
expressed to be given as security for $10,000 or any speci-
fic sum.

The defendant acquired the site, erected the necessary
buildings, and had the factory in partial operation by the
end of December, 1878.   He was permitted to use one-
half of the debentures when the land was purchased and
the building completed, and the rest were finally handed
over to him on the execution of the securities.

He was allowed to apply part of the proceeds in purchasing a site for and erecting a private residence for himself, &c., in payment of a mortgage on his property in
Chatham, and of some old debts incurred before he came
to Brussels.

In November or December, 1880, (the date is not given
in the appeal book,) the plaintiffs brought this action to
foreclose the mortgage and to enforce payment of the
penalty of the bond.

The fifth paragraph of the bill of complaint thus sets
forth the grounds of the action and the nature of the relief
sought.

"The plaintiffs charge that the defendant, John D. Ronald, has not at any time since the execution thereof complied with the conditions of the said bond and mortgage by engaging in or carrying on the manufacture of agricultural implements in the premises aforesaid, or elsewhere in the said village of Brussels, in the manner contemplated or intended by said indenture, and further that the defendant, John D. Ronald, has not now, nor has he had for a time long since past the sum of $30,000 invested in the said manufactory in the plant and premises thereof, but only a very much smaller sum, to wit, the sum of $20,000 or thereabouts, and although all conditions have been performed, all things happened, and all times elapsed necessary to entitle the plaintiffs to a performance of the conditions of the said mortgage and bond on the part of the defendant, John D. Ronald, yet the defendant, John D. Ronald, has therein wholly failed and made default, whereby the plaintiffs submit that they are entitled to have the equity of redemption in the said lands foreclosed, and also to recover the amount of the penalty provided by the said bond, namely, the sum of $10,000, and to have judgment and execution against the defendant, John D. Ronald, therefor."

These allegations are denied by the answer.

The bill was also filed to foreclose a further mortgage on the premises, made by the defendant to the plaintiffs for $3,000.

The case came on for hearing at Goderich before the late Chief Justice of this Court, when Chancellor, on the 20th April, 1881.

He found as a fact that the defendant had invested $30,000 in the premises and plant of the manufactory as required by the by-law, but upon the other question, viz., whether he had carried on the manufactures, the learned Chancellor held that, according to his view of the construction of the agreement, "the bargain had not been performed within any reasonable meaning that the parties could have had in their minds in entering into the agreement."

He expressed himself as being averse from ordering an immediate foreclosure, and directed the bill to be retained for six months in order to give the defendant an opportunity to perform his agreement, and to enable the parties to come to some arrangement.

In March, 1881, the case came before Mr. Justice Proudfoot on motion for judgment. It was alleged that the defendant had not succeeded in performing his agreement, and no further contention appears to have been raised on this point.

On the questions of fact the learned Judge followed the Chancellor's findings, but held that the forfeitures which the defendant had incurred were such as the Court would relieve against, and that the mortgage and bond had been merely taken as security for any damages the plaintiffs might sustain from the nonperformance of the defendant's undertaking. He therefore directed a reference to ascertain what damages the plaintiffs had in any way sustained, by reason of the failure of the defendant to perform his agreement, to carry on for the period of twenty years from the date of the said mortgage and bond the manufacture of steam fire engines and agricultural implements as in the pleadings mentioned; reserving further directions and costs.

As to the $3,000 mortgage, the learned Judge held the plaintiffs not entitled to recover, as it had been taken without consideration, and was not authorized by the by-law.

The plaintiffs appeal from this judgment on the ground substantially, that the defendant having made default in performance of the conditions, his right to perform them had terminated and all his estate in the premises should have been ordered to be foreclosed, or that if the mortgage was not in accordance with the by-law it should be reformed and declared to be a security for payment of $10,000, and that the appellants were entitled to be paid that sum on default in performance of the conditions, and that the usual order for payment should have been made, and for foreclosure on default.

As to the bond, that it was a security for an ascertained damage of $10,000, being one half of the amount of the bonus, and not merely security for unascertained damages.

And that, if the plaintiffs' claim was for damages only, such damages had been, by the agreement and conduct of the parties fixed at $20,000, that being the sum agreed upon as the value to the appellants of the performance by the respondent of the conditions imposed upon him.

The plaintiffs also appealed from the judgment as to the $3,000 mortgage.

The defendant, with his reasons against appeal, gave notice by way of cross-appeal that he would contend that upon the evidence it should not have been found that he had failed to carry out the manufacture of steam fire engines and agricultural implements, &c.

The questions we are asked to determine (apart from that which arises in respect of the $3,000 mortgage) are:

(1) Assuming the mortgage to be reformed so as to make it a security for a specific sum of $10,000, as required by the by-law, whether the sums secured by mortgage and bond are to be regarded as liquidated damages, the plaintiffs being entitled, on the findings, to foreclosure of the former on non-payment of $10,000 and to an absolute judgment for a further sum of $10,000 upon the bond; or whether the instruments are, as the Court below held them to be, security merely for such damages as the plaintiffs may have sustained, and may in future from time to time sustain, by the non-performance of the agreement.

(2) If they stand as security merely, then on what principle or by what rule the damages are to be ascertained.

(3) On the cross-appeal whether upon the evidence and the proper construction of the agreement the defendant can be held to have failed to carry on the manufactures mentioned in the by-law.

It will be convenient first to dispose of the cross-appeal. Upon the best consideration I have been able to give to the evidence, I think we ought not to interfere with the late Chancellor's finding.

The question was one of some difficulty, as the parties had not defined the extent to which the defendant was to carry on the manufactures, either by reference to the number of workmen to be employed, or the minimum of machines to be turned out yearly. The argument for the defendant is, that he is not obliged to manufacture on a more extensive scale than is warranted by his sales, and that if his factory is not absolutely closed and some work is being done there, though no more than two or three hands may be employed, or ten machines or so constructed in a year, the agreement is literally performed, as it cannot be said that manufactures are not being carried on.

I am of opinion, however, that what the plaintiffs are entitled to is a substantial performance of the agreement, and that the defendant's ability to carry on the manufactures at a profit is not the test or measure of his liability. What is a substantial performance under all the circumstances of the case is a question which admits of a wide solution, and in attempting to answer it one would desire to use terms of some elasticity.

I should be inclined to say that the performance contemplated or intended by the parties was one reasonably commensurate with the capabilities of the factory, having regard to its size, the quantity and value of the machinery and plant, and the number of hands which could be employed in it.

Taking this as a guide, and allowing the defendant a wide discretion in its application, I think it must be held that he has failed to carry on the business within the meaning of his agreement.

The manufactory was one in which at a moderate estimate from eighteen to twenty-five men might have been employed, and which could have turned out one hundred mowers, the only agricultural implement manufactured by defendant, in a year. In the course of two years only twenty mowers were constructed, and the number of persons employed dwindled down from eighteen or twenty, to two or three, the establishment becoming, as the learned

Chancellor described it, a mere repairing shop. To reduce
the business to such dimensions is only one degree short of
not carrying it on at all, in other words, to carry it on in
a nominal and illusory manner.

I think, therefore, the cross-appeal must be dismissed.

Then as to the plaintiffs' appeal. In its origin and
nature a municipal bonus is a voluntary gift, and conditions may be imposed by the donors in default of obser-
vance of which the right to it may never be acquired, as
e. g., in the case of *Luther* v. *Wood*, 19 Gr. 348, or on non-
performance of which after it has been paid over the donee
may become liable to repay it, as in the *Corporation of
Haldimand* v. *The Hamilton and North-Western R.W. Co.*,
27 C. P. 228.

We have not to consider here the right of the intended
donee to enforce the gift (see *Grand Junction R. W. Co.*
v. *Peterborough*, 8 S. C. R. 76; *Re Stratford and Huron
R. W. Co. and The Corporation of Perth*, 38 U. C. R. 112),
but the rights of the municipality under the agreements
they have taken for the performance of the conditions they
annexed to it.

These rights are to be determined, not by anything peculiar to the position of a municipality granting a bonus
under the statute, but upon the proper construction of the
contracts the parties have entered into.

Both parties ask that the bond and mortgage may be
reformed so as to be in accordance with the by-law, and to
the extent of inserting therein anything which has been
omitted, I think they are entitled to that relief. The
mortgage will then stand as a security for the specific sum
of $10,000, and a further condition of each will be to
insure the buildings and plant in the sum of $10,000, as
the by-law requires.

The first question is one which depends upon the intention of the parties, to be gathered from the instruments.
" The principle is, that, although the parties may have used
the term 'liquidated damages,' yet if the Court can see,
upon the whole of the instrument taken together, that

there was no intention that the entire sum should be paid absolutely on non-performance of any of the stipulations of the deed, they will * * consider it as being in the nature of a penalty only :" *Green* v. *Price*, 13 M. & W. 695, 701, 16 M. & W. 346. Here the parties have neither designated the principal sums as liquidated damages, nor have they in terms expressed an intention that the bonus, *qua* bonus, shall be repaid wholly or in part in any given event.

I think the rules of construction applicable are those laid down in the cases of *Davies* v. *Penton*, 6 B. & C. 216, and *Reynolds* v. *Bridge*, 6 E. & B. 528. In the former Bayley, J., says, p. 223: "Where the sum which is to be a security for the performance of an agreement to do several acts, will, in case of breaches of the agreement, be in some instances too large and in others too small a compensation for the injury thereby occasioned, that sum is to be considered a penalty." And in *Reynolds* v. *Bridge*, Mr. Justice Coleridge, at p. 541, after referring to the case of an agreement to pay a particular sum which is much less than the sum named as payable upon the breach, says: " Then comes the case where there are several provisions, the breach of some of which will produce an ascertainable damage, but the breach of others an uncertain damage. In that case * * inasmuch as there is one provision in respect of which the sum cannot be taken as liquidated damages, it cannot be so taken for any provision; for, if it could, the contract would mean liquidated damages in one case and not in another."

The general question is very much discussed and the authorities, including the leading case of *Kemble* v. *Farren*, 6 Bing. 141, reviewed in the recent case of *Wallis* v. *Smith*, 21 Ch. D. 243, but nothing is laid down which absolutely conflicts with these propositions.

To apply them to the present case: we have two agreements, which the parties are entitled to have read together and in connection with the by-law, securing separate sums of $10,000, one in the shape of a bond with a penalty, and the other in the shape of a mortgage, each of which is for the performance of the same conditions, viz.: (1) to carry on the manufacture for twenty years, (2) to keep invested

$30,000 in the premises and plant of the manufactory, and (3) to insure the building and plant in favour of the municipality in the sum of $10,000.

The damage for the breach of the first of these stipulations is not ascertainable with any high degree of certainty. For the second it may depend upon the actual value of the premises, &c., from time to time, and may be large or trifling, according to circumstances. But as regards the third, if the action is brought before the occurrence of a loss, the damage is assessable with accuracy, and must necessarily be trifling, consisting merely of what it would cost the plaintiffs to procure the insurance: while, if brought after a loss, it depends upon the value of the premises destroyed, but can in no event exceed the amount which ought to have been insured: *Douglass* v. *Murphy*, 16 U. C. R. 113; *Mayne* on Damages, 3rd ed. p. 242. Yet if the sums secured by these instruments are liquidated damages, the plaintiffs would be entitled to recover the whole $20,000 upon breach of the condition to insure, though the actual damage might not exceed $100, and could never be more than $10,000. This consideration alone suffices to shew that the principal sums must be regarded as penalties, or, as Lord Westbury said, in *Thompson* v. *Hudson*, L. R. 4 H. L. at p. 30, "conventional sums put in by the parties plainly for the purpose of securing the performance of the agreement contained in the engagement between them."

There is another circumstance which points in the same direction, namely, that the mortgage contains a covenant to perform the conditions, shewing that what the plaintiffs really desired was a security for the continued performance of the work.

This conclusion practically disposes of the principal appeal, as it is not alleged in the reasons of appeal that the decree is defective in not giving directions to the Master as to the principle on which the damages are to be measured or ascertained.

On the argument we were urged to lay down some rule
on this point, but on consideration it seems to me that we
are not in a position to do so authoritatively. The question may admit of more than one view being taken of it,
and it may be difficult to say that either is wrong. I have,
however, no objection to state for myself how it strikes
me at present.

The object of the plaintiffs in granting the bonus was,
of course, to increase the general prosperity of the municipality. That object would, to some extent, be directly
attained by the increase in the wage-earning and tax-
paying population, who would, besides contributing to the
general burdens, also bear their share of the taxation
required to meet the debentures issued for the bonus under
the by-law.

Further, if the manufactures are not carried on, it may
be said that during the existence of that state of things so
much of the yearly assessment to meet the interest and
sinking fund for the debentures is absolutely lost.

There may be other elements of damage, but these occur
to me as being the most obvious and, at least as regards
the latter, the most readily ascertained.

As to the second mortgage for $3,000, of which the plain-
tiffs also seek foreclosure, I see no reason to change the
view which, I think, was expressed on the argument.

That mortgage was not authorized by the by-law, and
appears upon its face to have been taken without consideration. I think Mr. Justice Proudfoot properly held that
as to it the plaintiffs were not entitled to relief.

In one respect a formal correction should be made in the
decree.

It seems to have been erroneously assumed that the
principal mortgage contained no covenant for insurance
on the part of the mortgagor. No doubt, if this mistake
had been noticed in drawing up the decree, it would at
once have been corrected.

The decree may be varied by directing the Master to
ascertain what sums, if any, the plaintiffs have paid for

premiums of insurance on the mortgaged premises, and declaring that the same form a charge upon the land, &c.

With this variation, I think the decree is right, and the appeal should be dismissed.

HAGARTY, C. J. O., BURTON and PATTERSON, JJ. A., concurred.

Appeal dismissed, with costs.

.

NELSON v. THORNER.

Practice—Judgment under Rule 80, O. J. A.—Evidence for jury— Discretion of Judge.

A *primâ facie* case for judgment under Rule 80, O. J. A., was made by the plaintiff in an action upon two bills of exchange accepted by a married woman who, in her defence alleged, amongst other things, that she accepted the bills as agent of her husband, but there being evidence on which the jury might have been justified in finding that the business, in which such acceptances were given, was hers, the Court refused to interfere with the discretion of the County Court Judge in directing judgment to be entered for the plaintiff, the defendant having declined to comply with the condition of paying the amount of the claim into Court to abide the result of a trial.

THIS was an appeal by the defendant from an order made by the Judge of the County Court of the county of Wentworth, permitting the plaintiff to sign final judgment in the action under Rule 80 of the Ontario Judicature Act.

The action was upon two bills of exchange accepted by the defendant, a married woman.

An appearance was entered in the action and the plaintiff then moved for an order to sign final judgment. This was opposed on the ground that the defendant had accepted the bills sued on merely as agent for her husband, and that it was not shewn that she had any separate estate, or carried on the trade or business in connection with which the bills had been given, separately from her husband.

The defendant and her husband were cross-examined upon the affidavits made by them in opposition to the motion. An option to pay the amount claimed into Court, or to give security for the claim as a condition of being allowed to defend having been declined, leave was given to the plaintiff to sign final judgment.

The appeal was argued on the 2nd day of December, 1884.*

Mackelcan, Q.C., for the appeal.
Walker, contra.

December 18, 1884. The judgment of the Court was delivered by

OSLER, J.A.—I have with some hesitation arrived at the conclusion that the appeal fails. The question whether such an order should have been made was one, which in the circumstances, to some extent, rested in the discretion of the Judge, and therefore the Court ought not to interfere, unless, as Lord Selborne said in a similar case under the English Judicature Act, for strong and substantial reasons : *Wallingford* v. *Mutual Society*, 5 App. Cas. 685.

"It is a very valuable and important part of the new procedure introduced by the Judicature Act, that the means should exist of coming by a short road to final judgment, when there is no real *bond fide* defence to an action. But it is of at least equal importance, that parties should not in any such way, by a summary proceeding in Chambers, be shut out from their defence, when they ought to be admitted to defend." Ib. p. 693.

Now here the plaintiff made out a *primâ facie* case, and the defendant was offered, but refused to accept, leave to defend conditionally.

What we have to consider, therefore, is, whether the order offends against the principle on which the rule (80)

ought to be applied, which is, I think, very clearly stated in the judgment of Cotton, L. J., in *Ray* v. *Barker*, 4 Ex. D. 279, 284. " If the defendant's affidavit sets up a good defence, the Court has no discretion, and cannot order the money claimed to be paid into Court. But an alternative is allowed in which leave to defend may be given, namely, where the defendant discloses ' such facts as may be deemed sufficient to entitle him to defend ;' and it is this state of facts to which the discretionary power given by the sixth rule (Rule 85, O. J. A.) is directed. The affidavit may not make it clear that there is a defence, but the defendant may be able at the trial to establish a *bonâ fide* defence." See also per Lord Blackburn, 5 App. Cas. 704.

I think this is a case in which we cannot say that the Judge was wrong in imposing a condition, and in exercising his discretion in favour of the plaintiff. The defendant did not make out a clear defence on the merits. She undoubtedly accepted the bills sued on, and neither she nor her husband ventured to say that she accepted them as his agent, or because she was carrying on the business for him. The business was carried on in her name : the goods were bought on her account, she herself gave a chattel mortgage on the stock to some creditors, and she and her husband permitted others to sue and obtain judgments against her, for debts incurred in carrying it on. All these creditors dealt with her as the owner of the business, and not with her husband, and the latter swears he treated it as his wife's business, and was always willing the goods should be hers. There is evidence on which a jury would be justified in finding that the business was really the wife's, and not the husband's : See *Cooper* v. *Blacklock*, 5 A. R. 535. As against creditors whom both husband and wife had deliberately procured to deal with her as the owner of the business, it may be that neither of them could be heard to say to the contrary, or to allege that the property was not the wife's separate property, and liable to seizure on execution against her.

I do not agree that the right of the husband's creditors is the test in such circumstances.

It might very well be, looking at the shuffling, equivocating manner in which both of them gave their evidence, that in another proceeding a jury would have little difficulty in finding as against her, that her name was used only as a cloak and a fraud against her husband's creditors.

But when we see that neither of them will venture to swear that the goods were the husband's goods, we cannot be surprised that the learned Judge was not satisfied that there was a *bonâ fide* defence on the merits, and that he thought leave to defend conditionally was as much as the defendant could reasonably ask.

On the ground, therefore, that the order was made in the exercise of a discretion, which, in the circumstances, we think the learned Judge had, and that we cannot say he came to a wrong conclusion, the appeal should be dismissed.

Appeal dismissed, with costs.

COLLINS v. HICKOK.

Practice—Rule 80 O. J. A.—Immediate judgment—Defence on merits.

Where on moving for immediate judgment under marginal Rule 80 O.J. A. the plaintiff makes out a *primâ facie* case for granting an order therefor, it is not sufficient for the defendant, in opposing the application, to swear that he has a good defence on the merits ;—he must shew the nature of his defence, and give some reason for thinking that such defence exists in fact.

THIS was an appeal by the defendant from an order made by the County Judge of Wentworth, on the 24th of September, 1884, directing final judgment to be signed for the amount indorsed on the writ of summons with interest and costs ; and execution to be issued therefor pursuant to the marginal Rule 80 of the Ontario Judicature Act.

The appeal came on to be heard on the 16th March, 1885.*

Mackelcan, Q. C., for the appellant, contended that under the facts appearing in the case it was one that should have been directed to proceed to trial in the usual way, and ought not to have been decided in this summary manner ; that it never was intended that the rights of parties should be thus summarily disposed of where the defendant had pledged his oath to a good defence on the merits.

Kittson, for respondents.

Ray v. *Barker,* 4 Ex. D. 279; *Thorne* v. *Seel,* W. N. 1878, p. 215; Anon. W. N. 1876, p. 12, were referred to.

April 17, 1885. OSLER, J.A.—The affidavits filed on behalf of the plaintiffs make out a *primâ facie* case for granting an order under Rule 80, shewing the existence of a debt for goods sold &c., invoices of which had from time to time been delivered with the goods, to the defendant : and four persons deposed to the fact that the defendant admitted the account and promised to pay it.

Present.—HAGARTY, C.J.O., BURTON, PATTERSON, and OSLER, JJ.A.

In his affidavit in answer the defendant says : " The plaintiffs never delivered to me particulars of their alleged account of $153.15 sued for herein, and I deny that I owe them the said sum or any portion thereof * * I have a good defence to this action on the merits and I deny that I ever admitted that I owed the plaintiffs the said sum of $153.15 or any portion thereof."

The learned Judge not being satisfied that the defendant had a good defence to the action on the merits, or that he had disclosed facts sufficient to entitle him to defend, made the order complained of.

The power to direct judgment to be summarily signed is no doubt one that should be exercised with great caution, and the most scrupulous discretion. A defendant ought not, except upon strong and apparent grounds, to be deprived of the opportunity of making any, even plausible, defence in the usual way. The object of the rule however is that the creditor may not be delayed by a defence which is merely for time. When therefore, the plaintiff has made out a *primâ facie* case, the defendant is required *to satisfy the Judge* that he *has* a good defence to the action on the merits, or at least that the plaintiff's claim is so doubtful as to make it a fair case to try : *Spence* v. *Davis,* 1 C. P. D. 719, 721.

It is not sufficient for him merely to swear that he has a good defence on the merits. Experience has shewn that a general statement of that kind in an affidavit means little or nothing. He must shew the nature of his defence, and give some reason for thinking that it exists in point of fact. He must, as Lord Blackburn says, in *Wallingford* v. *The Mutual Benefit Society,* 5 App. Cas. 685, 704, " condescend upon particulars." If he cannot satisfy the Judge that he has a defence upon the merits, or a counter-claim, or set off, he may disclose such facts as the Judge may deem sufficient to entitle him to defend the action upon terms. But in either case the *facts* must be shewn upon which the Judge is asked to hold his hand. See *Runnacles* v. *Mesquita,* 1 Q. B. D. 416 ; *Girvin* v. *Grepe,* 13 Ch. D. 174 ; Ch. Forms, 12th ed. 114.

It is not enough merely to deny the existence of the debt
—to say as the defendant has here contented himself with
saying: " I deny that I owe the said sum, or any part thereof:" that is no more than, if so much as, saying that there
is a defence on the merits, and the value of such a statement
depends altogether upon what we are not informed of, viz.
the meaning the defendant in his own mind attached to it.

Lord Blackburn's judgment in the case already cited of
Wallingford v. *The Mutual Benefit Society*, really covers
the whole ground. He says : " If the Judge is satisfied upon the affidavits before him that there really is
a defence upon the merits, it is a matter of right that the
defendant should he able to raise it." And then, speaking
of what the defendant must shew in order to be allowed to
defend under the second part of the rule, that is when he
discloses such facts as may be deemed sufficient to entitle
him to defend, though a defence on the merits is not clearly
shewn, he says : " It is not enough to swear ' I say I owe
the man nothing.' Doubtless if it was true that you owed
the man nothing as you swear that would be a good
defence. But that is not enough, you must satisfy the
Judge that there is reasonable ground for saying so. So
again if you swear that there was fraud, that will not do.
It is difficult to define it, but you must give such an extent
of definite facts pointing to the fraud as to satisfy the
Judge that those are the facts which make it reasonable
that you should be allowed to raise that defence, and
so of illegality, and every other defence that might be
mentioned."

In that case there were disputed accounts and counter-
claims, and strong reasons existed as one of the Lords
pointed out, upon the face of the mortgage bonds on
which the action was brought, against summarily assuming
without going into an account between the parties that
the sum claimed was really due. The affidavit moreover
contested the whole debt, upon grounds specifically stated.
See also *Barber* v. *Russell*, 9 P. R. 433 cited by Mr.
MacKelcan, where an example will be found of a very
full and sufficient affidavit in answer to an application of
this kind.

In the case before us the defendant denies in general terms the admission he is alleged to have made, and if the case had turned upon the admissions it might perhaps have been better that no order for leave to sign judgment should have been made. But as to the other evidence of the debt, while the defendant impliedly admits that there were dealings between himself and the plaintiffs, he confines his affidavit to a mere denial of the delivery of the particulars of the account, &c., and of his owing them the sum claimed. I think it is not a satisfactory affidavit. It is drawn on a very fine line and should be judged accordingly. See *Ebrard* v. *Gassier*, 28 Ch. D. 232, 52 L. T. N. S. 63. The bald and limited expressions " I say, that I deny that I owe: " " I say, that I deny that I admitted," &c., used in answer to distinct and precise allegations of fact, are not calculated to convey the impression of candor and sincerity on the part of the deponent, nor have casuists failed to argue that they do not necessarily involve the denial of any assertion of fact.

I think the learned Judge was right in declining to be satisfied by it, either that there was a defence on the merits or that there was any reason for allowing the defendant to defend upon terms.

Therefore, in my opinion, we should dismiss the appeal.

HAGARTY, C. J. O., BURTON, and PATTERSON, JJ.A., .concurred.

Appeal dismissed, with costs.

COTTINGHAM ET AL. V. COTTINGHAM ET AL.

Sale of lands—Excess in quantity—Payment for excess—Sale by the acre or in bulk—Rectification—Rescission.

In proceeding to a sale of lands under a decree of the Court of Chancery in 1876, one parcel was advertised as containing 100 acres, and was bid off by one A. at $31 per acre, which in the agreement to purchase signed by A., as well as in the conveyance to him, was described as "100 acres more or less, composed of the east part of lot 9," &c.: he paying or securing according to the conditions of sale, the sum of $3,100. In reality the portion so sold contained $124\frac{68}{100}$ acres, a fact neither party to the transaction was aware of when sold. There was no provision in the conditions of sale for compensation. The purchaser became aware that there was an excess on the same day, immediately after the sale, but the vendors not until long afterwards, though before the execution of the conveyance. In the report on sale several of the sales were referred to as at so much per acre, while the one in question was mentioned as a sale at a bulk sum of $3,100.

After the conveyance to A. he had been obliged to take proceedings against G. T., the person who had conveyed the land in question to the father of the vendors, to obtain possession of the portion in dispute and which he succeeded in obtaining. The vendors, however, refused to interpose in such proceedings or assist A. in any way in such litigation.

Held—[reversing the judgment of FERGUSON, J., 5 O. R. 704,] that the sum of $3,100 was bid for the whole parcel; that the sale being a sale in bulk, and there being no provision in the conditions of sale for compensation, there could be no rectification after the execution of the conveyance, nor could there have been, under the circumstances of this case, a rescission of the contract, had such relief been asked for. There was no mistake as to what was intended to be sold, or in the price intended to be paid for it.

PATTERSON, J. A., dissenting.

THIS was an appeal from a judgment of Ferguson, J., pronounced on the 4th of March, 1884, in favour of the plaintiffs upon their petition against Thomas R. Adam.

The bill of complaint in the cause was filed for the sale or partition of the lands of William Cottingham, who died on the 19th May, 1874, intestate, the plaintiffs being his children and heirs-at-law, and the defendant Lucy A. Cottingham his widow.

Under the decree a large portion of the lands of the intestate were in April, 1876, sold, and among them the east part of lot nine in the fifth concession of Fenelon, was sold to Thomas R. Adam for $31.00 per acre, the advertisement of sale stating that the part so sold to Adam contained " 100 acres," só that the purchase money was computed as being $3,100, which sum Adam paid or secured.

The petition now in question was filed by the plaintiffs in May, 1881, who prayed under the circumstances to have it declared that the lot sold to Adam contained $124\frac{6}{100}$ acres, and to have an order against Adam for the payment of a sum for the excess of acreage or possession of the same; for an occupation rent (Adam having been in possession of the whole lot), and for a rectification of the deed to Adam, and the mortgage given by him to secure part of the purchase money.

Adam answered the petition, and the issues raised were tried before Ferguson, J., at Lindsay, on the 9th and 10th days of November, 1882.

In the course of the evidence it was proved that George Taylor, who had conveyed the premises in question to William Cottingham (the intestate), had gone into possession of a portion of the lands conveyed to Adam, claiming to hold the same as not having been embraced in the conveyance from him to Cottingham. That Adam had applied to the plaintiffs to have possession of this portion of the easterly part of lot No. 9 delivered to him, and threatened in case of their neglecting or refusing to give him such possession to apply to the Master for a warrant to proceed on the title. Adam subsequently instituted proceedings against Taylor to recover possession of this portion of the property; in which he recovered judgment and subsequently filed a bill seeking to restrain Taylor and his wife from trespassing on the premises or interfering with his, Adam's, possession thereof, and an injunction for that purpose was ordered in the cause. The Cottinghams refused to interpose in these proceedings, or assist Adam in any way to carry them on.

Judgment was delivered on the 4th of March, 1884, in favour of the petitioners, ordering Adam to pay the petitioners for the excess of acreage at $31 per acre, or to deliver up possession of the $24\frac{66}{100}$ acres, as he might elect, and ordering him to pay the costs. The decree was for the delivery up of possession. This judgment is reported in 5 O. R. 704, where the facts of the case are more fully set out.

Adam thereupon appealed to this Court, and the same came on to be heard on the 10th and 11th of February, 1885.*

Moss, Q. C., and *Hopkins*, for the appellant.

The laches and negligence of which the petitioners in this case have been guilty are sufficient to prevent their obtaining any relief in this matter.

The evidence in the matter shews that while the appellant was endeavouring to make out and enforce his purchase against another person in possession, the petitioners stood by without offering him the slightest assistance, and without themselves asserting any claim ; they are therefore not now entitled to take any benefit, or obtain any advantage from his exertions and expenditure.

It is clearly established that in the case of the appellant's purchase the premises were not sold by the acre ; but were simply put up in that manner at the sale ; a lump sum being mentioned in the written contract or agreement to purchase and signed by the appellant at the time of sale.

Here the sale was subject to the approval of the Master ; and the only sale approved of by him was a sale of the whole parcel, being No. 26 of the parcels enumerated in the advertisement, at the lump sum of $3,100. His report on sale finds a sale for $3,100 ; and the report having been duly confirmed, no relief can possibly be obtained until such report is rectified or set aside.

It is also shewn that the intention was to sell all the right and title of the petitioners in the lot in question, that is, " the east part," not 100 acres. The purchaser had a right to suppose he was bidding and purchasing the whole parcel ; and having effected the purchase in that view he

---

*Present. –HAGARTY, C. J. O., BURTON, PATTERSON, and OSLER, JJ. A.

cannot now be compelled to accept a part of what was so offered for sale, and in like manner bought by him.

But even if it can be contended that this lot was sold by the acre, the advertisement plainly stated what the acreage was, so that the price must be taken as fixed with reference to the quantity named; and a vendor cannot be permitted to advertise a lot as containing 100 acres, and then seek to compel the purchaser to pay for 125 acres at the same rate.

If the petitioners are entitled to any relief at this late day, rescission of the contract is the only one they can obtain; rectification is certainly out of the question. The effect of rectifying the contract in the manner sought by the petitioners is simply obliging the appellant to enter into a contract that he never intended to make, and which it is shewn he never would have willingly entered into : to obtain such relief they must shew a mutual mistake.

Under any circumstances, they cannot enforce specific performance with a parol variation.

Had the petitioners alleged and proved any fraud or fraudulent practices in obtaining the agreement in the terms in which it is expressed, they might have been entitled to the relief they now ask. Any fraud, however, is entirely out of the question, therefore, the conveyance having been executed in pursuance of the bargain entered into, the petitioners cannot have the relief they ask on the simple ground that the property proves to be of more value, comparatively, than the parties to the sale had contemplated. In the position of these parties, the statute of frauds is an insuperable bar to the relief sought.

In any view of the case, the relief, accorded to the petitioners, could not be afforded on petition; to obtain such, it was necessary to file a bill seeking such remedy. The evidence shews, and the evidence is confirmed by the circumstances attending the sale, that the petitioners waived any claim or right to have the premises surveyed in order to obtain the contents of the parcel purchased by the appellant.

S. H. Blake, Q. C., and *Hudspeth*, Q. C., for respondents.

At the trial in this case, the learned Judge determined, as a fact, that the parcel of land in question here was sold and purchased at $31 an acre. No doubt all parties, vendors as well as purchasers, thought and believed that the lot contained only 100 acres, but the price or purchase money to be paid, as also the biddings, were at so much per acre, and not so much for the whole property put up as "Parcel No. 26;" and in the view of the learned Judge, the attempt to prove that the parcel was bid for by the audience and knocked down to the appellant at $3,100 signally failed, and the conclusion arrived at by his Lordship should not, under the rule prevailing in the several Courts, be now disturbed.

The evidence here establishes clearly, that on the day of sale, and shortly after the sale had taken place, the appellant became aware of the fact that there was an excess of land, notwithstanding which he concealed the fact from the vendors and allowed them to proceed in completing the sale and conveyance to him as for "one hundred acres more or less," although he was well aware that the premises described in the conveyance embraced a quantity of land largely in excess of that specified in the deed, and it was not until upwards of three years after the transaction had been consummated, that the vendors or their solicitor had any intimation of or reason to believe that there existed, the unreasonable difference in quantity that an actual survey of the premises disclosed.

There is no question that the excess does exist, and his Lordship at the trial determined that the delay which had taken place did not under the circumstances shewn in the evidence establish the fact of laches on the part of the petitioners. A man cannot be guilty of neglect of, or indifference to his interests when he is kept in ignorance of those interests.

Hill v. *Buckley*, 17 Ves. 394, 401; *Allen* v. *Richardson*, 13 Ch. D. 524; *Besley* v. *Besley*, 9 Ch. D. 103; *Joliffe* v.

Baker, 11 Q. B. D. 255; *Follis* v. *Porter*, 11 Gr. 442; *Campbell* v. *Edwards*, 24 Gr. 152; *Superior Savings and Loan Soc.* v. *Lucas*, 44 U. C. R. 106; *Boyd* v. *Simpson*, 26 Gr. 278; *In re Turner and Skelton*, 13 Ch. D. 130; *Bos* v. *Helsham*, L. R. 2 Ex. 72; *Whittemore* v. *Whittemore*, L. R. & Eq. 603; *Dart's* V. & P. 5th ed. 645 *et seq.* and 742 *et seq.*, were referred to.

April 17, 1885. HAGARTY, C. J. O.—There are many cases in the books on the subject of compensation, but they all are as to compensation to a purchaser who claims that he has not or cannot get as much land or rent, &c., as he contracted or bid for, and in most of the cases there is a clause providing as in the last case of *Palmer* v. *Johnson*, 13 Q. B. D. 351. "If any error, misstatement, or omission in the particulars be discovered, the same shall not annul the sale, but compensation shall be allowed by the vendor or purchaser as the case may require."

Of this condition, Mr. Dart says (p. 134): "Such a condition must be taken to contemplate and provide for *only* such misdescription, mistake, or error, as, in the absence of the condition, would be a ground for avoiding the contract: *Leslie* v. *Tompson*, 9 Hare 273." The head note to *Palmer* v. *Johnson*, gives the effect of the decision. "The plaintiff purchased at a sale by auction certain property belonging to the defendant described in particulars of sale as producing a net annual rental of £39 (setting out the condition of sale as already given). After the conveyance (without any covenants) had been executed by defendant to plaintiff, it was discovered by plaintiff that the rental of £39 was a gross rental, the net rental being considerably less. Held, that, notwithstanding the error was not discovered till after the conveyance, the plaintiff was entitled to compensation under the conditions of sale."

This decision seems to put an end to the difficulty occasioned by the direct opposition to the judgments of Sir George Jessel, in *Re Turner* and *Skelton*, 13 Ch. D. 130, and of Malins, V.C., in *Allen* v. *Richardson*, in the same volume, p. 532, the latter decision being supported by the subsequent judgment of the Divisional Court in *Joliffe* v. *Baker*, 11 Q. B. D. 255.

We must now consider that where the compensation clause is found, the closing of the matter by conveyance does not necessarily preclude a claim on either vendor or vendee's part.

In the case before us there is no compensation clause in the conditions. It was suggested that the sale being under the order of the Court, it was within the right of the latter to do full justice between the parties, as I understood the counsel, with larger powers, and less adherence to strict construction of contracts, than in ordinary cases.

Cann v. *Cann*, 3 Sim. 447, is often cited. There was a sale by the Court with the usual compensation condition. After conveyance, and entry into possession, the purchaser discovered that the rental was less than stated. The purchase money had been paid into Court.

Before the cause was heard for further directions he presented a petition praying compensation, and that the amount thereof should be paid to him out of the money then standing to the credit of the cause.

It was shewn in answer that the mistake was merely from inadvertence, and not intentional, that the purchaser had paid no more than fair value, and that another person was willing to take his place, and it would be better for the infants to repay him the purchase money and interest, and to resell, &c.

The V. C. Shadwell, held that the question was, whether, "there having been a misrepresentation as to the value of the property, in respect of which the purchaser had a right of action, the circumstance of his having taken a conveyance, has destroyed that right * * as the Court would not have permitted him to bring an action for damages on account of the misrepresentation, I am of opinion that he is entitled to be recouped out of the purchase money."

In *Re Perriam*, 49 L. T. N. S. 710, before Pearson, J., compensation was given to a purchaser after conveyance for variation from particulars of sale. The Judge said: "Under the circumstances, I do not think that I can refuse what they ask (vendees, petitioners for compensation), the purchase money being still in Court." He considered that after the money had been distributed he could not make any order.

In *Daniell's* Chy. Pr. 5th ed., 1170, it is stated that either vendors or purchasers may apply, and a form of summons is given, Vol. of Forms No. 1419, calling on purchaser to shew cause why he should not, in addition to his purchase money, pay such sum as the Judge may direct as, *e. g.*, by reason of the premises being described in particulars of sale as containing by admeasurement ten acres instead of twelve acres.

The general subject is discussed in *Fry*, 540 *et seq.*; also at p. 344, sec. 744, he says: "Where there is a mistake of both parties, but not about the very subject of the contract, it will not be a ground for rectifying the contract. Therefore where both parties were under a mistake as to the duration of a leasehold interest, so that the price was considerably less than if the actual extent of the interest had been known, and the vendors filed a bill asking for a reassignment of the extra term which the purchasers took under the assignment, Knight Bruce, V.C., held that the lease was the substance sold and not a term of the supposed duration, and that the vendors ought to have known what was the condition of the property they proposed to sell, and dismissed the bill;" citing *Okill* v. *Whittaker*, 1 DeG. & Sm. 83, affirmed by Lord Cottenham, 2 Phil. 338.

The Vice-Chancellor's judgment is very full and clear, and my Brother Burton quotes Lord Cottenham's language, which seems to me very much in point in the case before us.

The thing sold here was the east part of the lot: the vendors and vendee equally so understood it.

In the absence of any clause for compensation, it is not easy to see what the vendors can ask except rescission of the contract. As the Vice-Chancellor says (1 DeG. & Sm. 88, 89) "The question is, what was the thing which the vendors intended to sell, and the purchaser to buy? Was it a term of eight or nine years, or was it a specific lease, erroneously supposed not to have more than eight or nine years to run? That is the material question * * it must be impossible, I think, to give the plaintiffs relief in this case upon any other footing than that of rescinding the contract wholly; * * and upon what ground is that sought in a case where, I repeat, there is a total absence of unfair dealing, and where the peculiar doctrines of specific performance are entirely beside the question ?"

The law is much discussed in *Nicol* v. *Chambers*, 11 C. B. 1007, where many cases are commented on.

The sale was on 22nd April, 1876. The deed bears date 12th December, 1876, but does not appear to have been actually executed till much later, as we find a letter from vendors' solicitors to defendant, dated 12th April, 1877, stating that the deeds had been ready a long time and asking him to close the matter. This is merely to be noted as shewing that there was no hurry at all events on defendant's part to close the matter by conveyance.

In a requisition as to title, dated 9th December, 1876, from defendant's solicitor Mr. Martin, we find the objection (amongst others) that "the land is not sufficiently described."

The land was sold as under lease to Bryson expiring in 1878. This lease described the land as composed of the east part of No. 9, 100 acres, be the same more or less. It expired October, 1878.

On the 14th November, 1878, Adam brings ejectment against Taylor and his wife for the east part of the lot, 100 acres, more or less. They defended for the whole. Judgment entered on 6th May, 1879. This suit was brought by order of the Court. Mr. Hudspeth's firm acting for plaintiff, the now defendant.

During the progress of the suit the Taylors offered to give up the 100 acres to Adam, the now defendant, they retaining the surplus of the lot, and to receive a deed therefor from the Cottinghams.

In 1879 the plaintiff had the exact quantity ascertained, and then Mr. Hudspeth wrote to the defendant demanding payment at $31 per acre for the extra 24 acres.

It seems there was a decree in Chancery at Adam's suit against Taylor, 20th October, 1879, as I understand, to quiet Adam's claim against him, and declaring that Adam was entitled to the whole 124 acres as against Taylor.

The petition here does not ask that the whole contract should be rescinded, but merely payment for the excess or restoration of the excess, or rectification of the conveyance. The petition was not filed till May 11th, 1881.

It is seldom, I think, that we find relief asked by the vendor of property under such extraordinary circumstances as are here disclosed.

The vendors held the land under deed from Geo. Taylor as far back as 1861, in which it is described as 120 acres, more or less.

It is found as a fact that the land was sold by vendors and bought by defendant under the common belief that it contained 100 acres.

I am unable to see any decisive force in the argument, that because it was put up or bid off at so much per acre therefore, we must hold that the bargain meant that it was a sale only of 100 acres of land at so much per acre, and that if it were really more or less in quantity, the payment was only to be for the ultimately ascertained quantity.

The sale seems to me to have been of a named estate, assumed by both to be of about a particular size, and that the bidding on the assumed acreage was merely a method of fixing the price for the whole.

We must remember it was not held or sold as a half-lot, but as the easterly part of a lot. This part was defined and ascertainable on the ground by fences, otherwise it might be difficult to avoid the charge of vagueness, especially as to any title in Cottingham over and above 100 acres.

The auction here was very unlike that described in *Winch* v. *Winchester*, before Sir W. Grant, 1 V. & B. 375, when the auctioneer was asked what quantity he sold the farm for, he replied, "forty-one acres. If the purchaser does not like to take it so, it shall be measured, and if it proves more, the excess must be paid for; if less, an abatement will be made."

The defendant, in a bill for specific performance, stated this, and that on measurement there was only thirty-six acres, and asked for compensation.

The estate had been sold as containing by estimation 41 acres, be the same more or less. Sir W. Grant held that the defendant could not be made to take the land without compensation, and as he was willing to take it, compensation was directed.

Immediately after the sale, the defendant here became aware that there was some surplus,

There was apparently some talk about the Taylors making some claim, and defendant spoke to Mr. Hudspeth, who told him that he had bought the whole property ; and adds, that his recollection of the conversation is, that defendant was aware there was more land in it, which induced him to buy. Mr. Hudspeth says his idea was that if there was perhaps an acre over defendant would get it. He also told defendant that Taylor had no claim.

I am wholly unable to understand the proceedings on behalf of the vendors in this ejectment of *Adam* v. *Taylor*, and the Chancery proceedings in the same name.

The ejectment suit as already noticed, brought out the fact of the overplus claimed by the Taylors, even if the facts were not known before ; and yet it is nearly three years after the sale, and sometime after the conveyance and payment of the purchase money by cash and mortgage that this demand for an increased price is made on defendant.

It appears to me that no relief could be given to the vendors, except by rescinding the whole contract. I think they could not force the bargain on the purchaser at a price increased nearly twenty-five per cent.

A man who thinks he is buying about 100 acres, costing some $3,000, must not, I think, be forced to pay some $3,800. The language of Tindal, C. J., is often quoted : " It is, at all events, a safe rule to adopt, that where the misdescription, although not proceeding from fraud, is in a material and substantial point, so far affecting the subject matter of the contract, that it may reasonably be supposed, that, but for such misdescription, the purchaser might never have entered into the contract at all, in such case the contract is avoided altogether, and the purchaser is not bound to resort to the clause of compensation :" *Flight* v. *Booth*, 1 Bing. N. C., at p. 377.

I think under the evidence before us, it would be eminently unfair to rescind the contract after a possession so long as that enjoyed by defendant.

The remarks of the Court already noticed in *Okill* v. *Whittaker*, are much against such a course.

Price v. *North*, 2 Y. & C. Ex. 620, may be referred to. The lapse of time and omission to apply earlier is discussed. The Court says, if the party applying be allowed to open the biddings four years after knowledge of the facts why not twenty years ? That was a sale by the Court, and a larger acreage was found to be in the land purchased than stated in the particulars. The case failed on other grounds, but the remarks made by the Court on the general law are valuable. " One reason (p. 627) is, that the purchaser upon the faith that he has obtained the benefit of his contract, may have laid out large sums of money on the premises, and to say that in four years afterwards the Court might alter his interest in the property, would be to say that the Court might do it after any indefinite time."

From almost the day of the auction sale the vendors knew there was some surplus, and with that knowledge after long delay, with the amplest opportunity of ascertaining the true extent of the land, they proceeded to answer requisitions to clear up the title, to confirm the sale and complete it all by conveyance—introducing the words, " more or less " into the description—then with the fullest knowledge of the claims of Taylor to over twenty acres, use the defendant's name to obtain full possession of the property. Finally, in October, 1879, demand payment from defendant, and after another seven months' delay file this petition.

I do not think that in thus proceeding the plaintiffs have any higher right against defendant from the fact of the sale having been made under the Court. If the defendant had been seeking relief on any ground of fraud or misrepresentation he would have to do so by petition, or application in the cause, as the Court would not permit

him in action to charge fraud in their sale, such is the
doctrine laid down in such cases as *Cann* v. *Cann, supra.*

Here they have closed the whole dealing with the defendant by conveyance, and if they desire to impeach the
whole proceeding and have the bargain rescinded, it would
seem that they should do so by an independent proceeding.

I think in a case of this, in my opinion, extraordinary
character we should lay much stress on the fact that the
only relief asked by the vendors is payment for the extra
quantity or delivery up of possession thereof, and that the
only relief allowable in such a case, viz., rescission of the
contract is not prayed for.

I think the appeal should be allowed.

BURTON, J. A.—In the view I take of the sale being for
a bulk sum of $3,100, the price per acre being only a
mode of arriving at the sum bid, it is not necessary for me
to consider some of the questions with which some of my
learned Brothers have dealt very fully.

In placing my opinion as to the sale in opposition to
that of the learned Judge who tried the case, I wish to
guard against its being supposed that I assume to overrule
him upon any question of fact, or to prefer the evidence of
one witness where he possibly may have preferred another;
in fact I do not consider that upon the evidence of what
actually occurred at the sale there is any very material
conflict, but assuming the state of facts most favourable
to the petitioners, I am unable to convince myself that
the inference drawn is the correct one.

Both parties were at the time of the sale ignorant that
there was the large overplus which the parcel sold was
some time subsequently found to contain. The vendors
stated that it contained 100 acres, and the strongest confirmation that they intended to sell the lot in the mass or
lump, or as a one hundred acre farm, is to be found in the
fact that the record of the sale, that which constituted the
effectual contract between the parties, did not treat it as a
sale and purchase at so much per acre, but as a sale of the
farm for $3,100.

A remark is made by the learned Judge who decided *Leslie* v. *Tompson*, 9 Ha. 268, which does not carry conviction to my mind when he says, (p. 274), "the actual designation of the number of acres contained in the lot negatives the presumption of any intention on the part of the vendors to sell in the lump."

I confess that a statement that a piece of land contained a fixed number of acres would, to my mind, lead rather to the presumption that the vendor had measured and ascertained the quantity, and that the acreage so agreed upon or ascertained would have fully as much to do with the ascertainment of the purchase money as the price per acre, and that the two multiplied together constituted the price; that would seem the natural inference, and that was what was actually done in this case. On the contrary, if there were any qualifying expressions such as "containing by estimation," or "more or less," or other similar phrases, the inference would be, that the actual price could only be ascertained after a measurement had been made.

In *Hill* v. *Buckley*, 17 Ves. 394, Sir William Grant, then Master of the Rolls, used expressions (p. 401) which tend strongly to shew that in a case like the present where the farm sold was represented as containing a certain fixed quantity, "the presumption is, that in fixing the price regard was had on both sides *to the quantity*, which both suppose the estate to consist of. The demand of the vendor and the offer of the purchaser are supposed to be influenced in an equal degree by the quantity, which both believe to be the subject of their bargain."

It appears to me the same principle must govern where the property is described as containing a fixed number of acres, whether the price be named in one bulk sum, or at so much per acre, it was that piece of land known as the farm in the occupation of James Bryson, which the one was selling and the other purchasing, and this seems to be the view taken of the matter by Mr. *Dart* in his book on Vendors and Purchasers, at p. 652.

I think that the circumstance also that in four cases out
of the twenty-six parcels sold they were referred to as
sales at so much per acre, and were so returned to the
Court, whereas this was returned as a sale at a bulk sum
is not without weight.

The course pursued by the petitioners has not always
been consistent. Their solicitor has at times treated the sale
as in point of fact of the easterly 100 acres, and I was
inclined during the argument to think that it would
probably have to be so treated, as the north-east part of a
lot containing 100 acres more or less would at first sight,
and without something more to define it, appear to be too
vague and indefinite a description to embrace anything,
but when we refer to the evidence I incline to think the
parcel sold was a well ascertained parcel of land divided
from the westerly 100 acres by a sufficiently defined
boundary; and that it was the farm then in the occupation
and possession of the tenant Bryson, which in the contemplation of both parties was put up at the auction for sale,
and sold.

During the investigation of the title some objection was
made which as to the easterly 100 acres was cured by a
tax deed, and the solicitors for the petitioners in reply,
said: "this is immaterial, as you only purchased the 100
acres."

This contention would have been intelligible enough,
and it is to be regretted that they had not taken their
stand upon that, and executed a deed which would have
embraced only the easterly 100 acres, had they taken that
stand, I think that the purchaser i en.'envouring to
enforce specific performance of the sale of the whole would
have failed in consequence of the mistake as to the acreage, and for this branch of the case, it would have been
immaterial whether the sale was in bulk or by the acre;
the purchaser on the land being ascertained to be so much
in excess could not have enforced specific performance
unless he were willing to adopt the alternative of making
compensation for the excess.

And I apprehend that the vendors would have experienced a similar difficulty if they had attempted to enforce specific performance ; they sold the whole farm and not a portion of it. The petitioners could not have specific performance of the contract with variations, although the difference was so large that they might perhaps have been entitled to vacate it, or have attained the same result by resisting a suit for specific performance.

The petitioners' solicitors did not, however, convey the 100 acres and no more, although the deed was delivered after a question had arisen as to the acreage, but before the actual survey. In that deed the facts of the sale by auction is recited, and it is there declared that Adam was declared the highest bidder for and became the purchaser of the lands thereinafter mentioned, at the price or sum of $3,100, not at $31 per acre of which the sum of $3,100 had been paid, and the balance of which yet remained unpaid, and then the lands are described as the east part of 9, containing 100 acres more or less. I have already pointed out that this must mean the whole property intended to be sold or it is void for uncertainty, and have stated why in my opinion the whole property passed.

If, then, I am right in saying that before conveyance the petitioners could have had no relief except a rescission, it would seem to be a much stronger case against any relief after they have with notice that there was a question of this kind raised, executed a conveyance to the purchaser.

I must confess that I see very great difficulty in drawing a distinction in principle between this case and *Okill* v. *Whittaker*, 1 De G. & Sm. 83, although, as pointed out by the Vice-Chancellor when the case was before him, the delay and other facts relied on were sufficient to prevent a rescission.

Lord Cottenham in that case uses language very appropriate to the present case. He says (2 Phil. at p. 340): " Suppose a party proposed to sell a farm, describing it as all my farm of 200 acres, and the price was fixed on that supposition, but it afterwards turned out to be 250 acres, could he afterwards come and ask for a reconveyance of the farm or payment, of the difference ? Clearly not ; the only equity being that the thing turns out more valuable than either of the parties supposed."

Cases are of course to be found where the Court has rectified a conveyance, on the ground that it included property never intended to be dealt with ; but I am unable to find any case where the vendor intended to sell the entire farm, but made a mistake as to the quantity comprised in it, in which after conveyance, relief has been granted. But in the present case there is no question as to the identity of the property sold, and I do not think that even a decree for rescission could at this late period be properly granted, although it is not necessary to say how that would be, that not being the form of relief sought. What the petition amounts to is a bill for specific performance with variations after conveyance executed, and the alternative prayer is for the delivery of possession, not for a conveyance which would seem to be the more appropriate prayer. The petitioners seem hardly to have decided even at the time of presenting their petition whether to treat the deed as a deed of the 100 acres or a deed of the whole ; if it was a deed of the 100 acres only, a decree for payment of the additional 24 acres, which has never been conveyed, would appear to be unwarranted, whilst a decree for possession only would seem scarcely an adequate measure of relief if the deed covers the whole.

I do not think that it makes any difference that the sale was made under the authority of the Court, or that infants are interested. The property offered for sale was described as containing 100 acres ; all parties knew what the property was. The solicitors conducting the sale thought it was being sold for $3,100, that being the sum at which the vendors were willing to dispose of the farm and the purchaser to take it.

All parties having acted in ignorance of the actual acreage at the time of the sale, and no fraud being shewn,

I think no case for relief has been made out and the petition should have been dismissed.

I am, therefore, of opinion that the appeal should be allowed.

OSLER, J. A.—It will be convenient first shortly to notice the material facts.

The property was sold pursuant to the decree in the present suit and was described in the advertisement of the sale as parcel 26, *east part* of lot No. 9, in the 5th concession of the township of Fenelon, 100 acres; leased to James Bryson until October 1st, 1878, at a rental of $150.

At the sale, which took place on the 22nd April, 1876, the appellant became the purchaser. The property was put up at so much per acre, and was knocked down to his bid of $31 per acre. He immediately afterwards signed a contract to purchase "parcel 26, mentioned in the within particulars for the sum of $3,100, and upon the terms mentioned in the above conditions of sale, and subject to a lease to Bryson," &c.

No doubt exists as to the identity of the property intended to be sold, or that the vendors intended to sell and the appellant to buy all their estate and interest in the lot in question as then in possession of Bryson, although at the time of the sale, as the learned Judge expressly finds, both parties supposed that the quantity was 100 acres as stated in the advertisement and contract. It must also be taken to appear from the evidence, though there is no finding on that point, that neither party intended that any survey or measurement should be made for the purpose of ascertaining the quantity.

The conditions of sale contain no clause for compensation either way.

After the sale, and if that be material, on the same day, the appellant was informed that the property exceeded or over-ran the 100 acres to some, though not to what, extent.

The report on the sale was filed on the 6th June, 1876, and reports that the appellant was declared the highest bidder for, and had become the purchaser of parcel 26 at the price or sum of $3,100.

Demand of abstract of title was served the 24th November, 1876, and on the 2nd December following, the abstract was delivered. Among the instruments abstracted are, (1) the deed from George Taylor, the previous owner of the lot to the father of the vendors, dated the 20th August, 1861, in which it is described as the east part of nine in the fifth concession of Fenelon, 120 acres, more or less; and (2) a deed from the warden, &c., of the county to him, dated 9th January, 1871, conveying the east *half* of lot 9 in the 5th concession, sold for taxes on the 7th December, 1869.

There is also a decree dated the 19th September, 1872, in a suit of *Taylor* v. *Cottingham*, which, though not set forth on the abstract, was presumably brought to the notice of the vendee, with the other documents of title, declaring that the deed of the 20th August, 1861, to the vendor's father was valid, and that Taylor had no estate or interest in the land conveyed by it except a right to a lease for a short term which has long since expired.

Requisitions upon the abstract and answers thereto, passed between the parties on the 9th December, 1876, and the 22nd January, 1877. So far as the evidence shews, it was upon the examination of the abstract that the purchaser first became aware that there might be anything like so large an excess as twenty acres. It does not seem to have been otherwise noticed by the vendors, and their attention was not called to it by the purchaser.

On the 12th of April, 1877, the vendors' solicitors wrote to the appellant stating that " the deeds in this matter" had been ready a long time, and asking him to close it at once. The deed bears date the 12th December, 1876.

There is no evidence as to when it was actually delivered and registered, but it seems to have been prepared by the vendors' solicitors and executed and delivered without the knowledge of or examination by the purchaser. The property is described therein as 100 acres, more or less, composed of the east *part* of lot 9, &c.

The next occurrence in order of date is a notice from
the purchaser to the vendors' solicitor on the 15th of
October, 1878, a fortnight after the expiration of Bryson's
lease, that he had executed a mortgage and paid into Court
the purchase money of the land, pursuant to the conditions of sale, and that one Taylor being in possession of
part of the property (the east part, &c.,) he required possession to be delivered as against him, and that in default
an application would be made to the Master at Lindsay
to consider the occupation of Taylor as an objection to the
title and to compel delivery of possession. As appears
from the answer to the petition and the evidence, a warrant to consider the title was accordingly obtained from
the Master, who directed the vendors to bring an action
to eject the Taylors. On the 14th of November, 1878, an
action was commenced in the name of the purchaser
against George and Elizabeth Taylor. The land was
described in the writ as in the deed to Adam. On the
19th December the solicitor for the Taylors wrote to the
vendors' solicitors proposing to settle by releasing all
claims to the east 100 acres, and that the Cottingham
estate should release their claim to the residue of the lot
which was said to comprise twenty acres.

This proposition was declined by letter of the 30th
December, 1878, in which the vendor's solicitor pointed out
that all matters in dispute between the Cottinghams and
Taylor relating to the land had been settled by the above-
mentioned decree of the 19th September, 1872 ; and as to
the acreage, that inquiry would be made and such steps
taken as might be necessary to protect the interests of the
estate.

The action of ejectment was subsequently brought to
trial in April, 1879, and judgment signed therein on the
6th May following.

In the meantime, in the month of March, 1879, the
vendors' solicitor had procured a survey and measurement
to be made of the land, from which it appeared that there
was an actual excess in it of $24\frac{68}{100}$ acres over 100 acres.

The Taylors were subsequently dispossessed under a writ of *hab. fac. poss.* issued in May, 1879, but the vendors' solicitor appears to have refused to direct the sheriff to give formal possession of more than 100 acres. The consequence of this was that the Taylors re-entered upon the westerly $24\frac{68}{100}$ acres of the east part, and Adam shortly afterwards forcibly ejected them therefrom, and successfully defended upon his title an action of trespass brought against him by the Taylors therefor. As, however, they continued to trespass on and attempt to take possession of the land, he brought an action against them to quiet the title, in which, on the 20th October, 1879, a decree was made declaring that he was entitled to the whole $124\frac{68}{100}$ acres under his deed.

Three days afterwards the vendors' solicitor wrote to him demanding payment for the $24\frac{68}{100}$ acres at $31 per acre and interest, " being the surplus land over the 100 acres settled for."

This was the first intimation that the vendors had given to the purchaser of the existence of such a claim, or of their intention to make such a demand ; nor was anything done to follow it up until the 30th April, 1881, more than a year and a half later, when the purchaser was served with notice of intention to present the petition on which the proceedings before us are founded,

The reason for the delay is thus set forth in the petition:

" 18. Your petitioners delayed making this application after they became aware that the said lands contained more than one hundred acres in order that the litigation between the said Taylor and the said Adam might be concluded; and the said Adam having been now declared entitled to hold the said $124\frac{68}{100}$ths acres as against the said Taylor under his conveyance from your petitioners, your petitioners desire to receive such relief from this honorable Court as they are entitled to in the premises."

The relief asked is in the alternative that the appellant may be ordered to pay for the excess of acreage at the same rate per acre as he paid " for the 100 acres offered for sale and purchased by him," or that he may be ordered to deliver up possession of the excess of acreage and to account for the rents and profits.

The petition proceeds upon the, as it seems to me, erroneous assumption, that, while the effect of the deed undoubtedly is to convey 124 acres, the actual sale was of 100 acres only.

The state of facts with which we have to deal is this. The sale was not a sale of 100 acres as alleged in the petition, but of a known tract of land, sufficiently described in the circumstances as the easterly part of lot No. 9, in the 5th concession of Fenelon; the number of acres being also, though erroneously, stated in the description.

2. The parties believed at the time, that the acreage was correctly stated as 100 acres, but it was not in fact intended that any survey or measurement should be made.

3. The sale was by auction, the price being ascertained by a bidding of so much per acre upon the assumed quantity.

4. The conditions of sale do not provide that any error, or omission in the description, &c., shall be made the subject of compensation.

5. The conveyance has been executed, but subsequently to the contract and before the completion thereof by conveyance, the purchaser had learned that there was a possible excess of at least twenty acres in the tract.

6. The sale was one under the direction of the Court.

The question then is, whether on this state of facts the vendor is entitled to any, and if so, to what relief.

We may first notice what the rights of the parties would have been if the mistake had been disclosed to the Court or to the vendors before the execution of the conveyance.

The sale was of a known and defined tract of land, but the price, though at so much per acre, was ascertained upon an assumed quantity of 100 acres. If the purchaser had insisted on completing the purchase, he would not have been permitted to do so, except upon the terms of paying for the excess at the same rate per acre as the rest of the property; or even if the sale had not been professedly by measurement, but the quantity had been so much understated in the contract, the vendors would have been entitled to compensation as a condition of carrying out the contract: *Sugden* on Vendors and Purchasers, 325, 326; *Dart* on Vendors and Purchasers, 550, 644-5, 651; *Leslie* v. *Tompson*, 9 Hare 268.

On the other hand, the vendors could not, the excess being so considerable, and involving so large an addition to the whole purchase money, have enforced the contract against the purchaser so as to compel him to pay for the larger acreage: *Price* v. *North*, 2 Y. & C. 620. In short, the contract was one which would have been rescinded if the purchaser declined to pay for the larger acreage.

So, again, if there had been such a deficiency in the acreage, instead of an excess, specific performance would have been decreed only at the instance of the purchaser, and with compensation: *Sugden*, p. 324; and see *Re Arnold*, 14 Ch. D. 270. And if the vendor, having discovered the deficiency, had omitted to communicate the fact to the purchaser the latter would be entitled to compensation even after the completion of the contract. This, however, would be on the ground of fraud or misrepresentation: *Sugden*, 324, 325; *Shovel* v. *Bogan*, 2 Eq. Cas. Ab. 688.

Then what effect has the execution of the conveyance upon the rights of parties here? It is unnecessary to do more than refer to cases like *Cann* v. *Cann*, 3 Sim. 447, in which the contract expressly provides for compensation. The most recent cases of that class are *Phelps* v. *White*, L. R. 5 Ir. 318, and *Palmer* v. *Johnston*, 13 Q. B. D. 351. In such cases it is settled that the execution of the conveyance does not preclude the parties from resorting to the contract.

In *Sugden* on Vendors and Purchasers, 14th ed. 324, it is said that after conveyance even a large excess or deficiency has not been considered a ground for relieving a vendor or purchaser.

A case sufficient as a defence to a suit for specific performance may be insufficient to enable the vendee to rescind a contract after conveyance.

In *Dart* on Vendors and Purchasers, 747, citing *Vigers* v. *Pike*, 8 Cl. & F. 645, 646; *Wilde* v. *Gibson*, 1 H. L. Cas. 605, 617; and at page 517 of the same work, citing *Okill* v. *Whittaker*, 2 Ph. 338, 11 Jurist, 141, 681, it is laid down that the vendor, after the execution of the contract, has no remedy if the property proves to be as respects either quantity or quality more valuable than was imagined.

In the last case the residue of a lease of which twenty years were in fact unexpired, was sold under the impression that only eight years were to run, and the price was fixed on that supposition. It was held that the vendors were bound by the conveyance. Lord Cottenham in affirming the decree of Knight-Bruce, V. C., dismissing the plaintiffs' bill said: "Suppose a party proposed to sell a farm describing it 'as all my farm of 200 acres,' and the price was fixed on that supposition, but it afterwards turned out to be 250 acres, could he afterwards come and ask for a reconveyance of the farm, or payment of the difference? Clearly not; the only equity being that the thing turns out more valuable than either of the parties supposed. And whether the additional value consists in a longer term or a larger acreage is immaterial. * * Here the plaintiffs did intend to sell all the remaining interest in the lease, but by their own mistake they misdescribed what that interest was."

In the report of the same case in 11 Jur. 681, we find the following language: "Here, in fact, the vendor comes and asks that the purchaser may pay more than he has contracted to pay, because the property turns out more valuable than he thought it to be. A purchaser may resist specific performance on the ground of mistake, but you cannot on this ground come to rescind or alter the original contract. The object of the present bill is to introduce a new term into the contract, either to make the purchaser pay more for the property, or to convert him into a trustee for the vendor."

I think it is extremely difficult to distinguish that case from the present and it appears to me to be an answer to the claim of the vendors in this proceeding. They cannot have a rectification of the conveyance, and thus compel the purchaser to pay a larger price than he agreed to give, nor a rescission of the contract, for there was no mistake as to what was intended to be sold or the price intended to be paid for it.

The case is different in principle from those in which relief has been granted, because more or less land has passed than has been contracted for, *e.g.*, where the sale was strictly a sale of 100 acres at so much an acre and in laying off the quantity by measurement the surveyor erroneously included 118 acres by the metes and bounds. *Gilmour* v. *Morgan*, 2 J. J. Marshall, or where part of the land contracted for by a particular has been omitted; *Leuty* v. *Hillas*, 2 DeG. & J. 110; or where the conveyance comprises more land than the vendor intended to deal with, as when the sale was of farm A. and by mistake part of the farm B. was included in the conveyance: *Taylor* v. *Beversham*, Rep. T. Finch 80; *Sugden*, 326; or where the mistake has been caused by even an innocent misrepresentation of the party, or an agent of the party, seeking to take advantage of it, and there has been no negligence on the part of the other party: *Carpmael* v. *Powis*, 11 Jur. N. S. 158, 10 Beav. 36. See also *Payne* v. *Upton*, 87 N. Y. 327; *Garrard* v. *Frankel*, 30 Beav. 445; *Harris* v. *Pepperell*, L. R. 5 Eq. 1; *Bloomer* v. *Spittle*, L. R. 13 Eq. 427; *Paget* v. *Marshall*, 28 Ch. D. 255; *Gun* v. *McCarthy*, 13 L. R. Ir. 304; *Jones* v. *Clifford*, 3 Ch. D. 779, 791, and *Besley* v. *Besley*, 9 Ch. D. 103, the decision in which is said in *Palmer* v. *Johnson*, 13 Q. B. D. 351, to be not law, and in which it would seem relief should have been granted on the equity administered in *Carpmael* v. *Powis*, *supra*, as the report does not indicate that there was any contract for compensation.

But even if it be thought that there is anything in these or other authorities which would have warranted the vendors in asking for the only relief they could by possibility have been entitled to, viz., a rescission on the ground of mistake, there are circumstances in this case, which, as it appears to me, make it inequitable to interfere.

The conduct of the vendors after the sale in delivering an abstract, in which they set forth the conveyance to Cottingham, describing the east part of the lot as containing 120 acres—their answer to the purchaser's requisition for a better description, in which, not referring to that deed, they content themselves with saying that the abstract shewed a good title to the east *half* of the lot, referring to the sheriff's sale for taxes, and concluding, "the sale was only for 100 acres," when they knew that, whether for 100 acres or more, it was of the whole parcel of land in question— Mr. Hudspeth's declaration to the purchaser that he had bought the whole of it, and the fact that it was not intended to verify the contents by a survey before completing the sale—all these circumstances coupled with the fact that the vendors' solicitors in preparing the deed, altered the description by adding thereto the words "more or less," might well lead the purchaser to believe, and the Court to conclude that the vendors knew there might be a surplus, and were willing that he should take whatever he could acquire in the lot by the description of the east part, although they would not assume the responsibility of *proving a title* to more than 100 acres. The course pursued by the vendors after the expiration of the lease to Bryson, adds force to this conclusion, as it shews that it was not until after the purchaser had at his own expense established his title to the whole property as against the squatter Taylor, that any claim was made upon him in respect of the excess.

Then there is the great and unexplained delay in taking proceedings. Apart from the knowledge which might be imputed to the vendors from the possession of the title deeds and the preparation of the abstract, their solicitor undoubtedly had express notice of the fact of the excess as early as the 19th November, 1878 (not the 23rd October, 1879, as is inadvertently stated in the judgment), during the pendency of the action of ejectment brought by him, under the direction of the Master, to meet the objection which had been made to the title in consequence of Taylor's possession. Yet that action was prosecuted to judgment after an actual survey had been made of the land, and possession delivered in it without any intimation to the purchaser that a claim would be made upon him; and he was, on Taylor again going into possession, left at his own expense to defend his title in an action of trespass, and after that to file a bill against the Taylors to quiet the title, with the same reticence on the part of the vendors. And though at last a demand was made on the 23rd October, 1879, the matter was allowed to sleep for another year and a-half, the purchaser in the meantime improving the property by building, draining, fencing, &c. There was thus a delay of two and a-half years from the date of the contract, the vendors having all the time in the office of their own solicitor the means of discovering the mistake, and a further delay of two and a-half years after express notice of it—in all a delay of five years. It was pre-eminently a case in which redress should have been promptly sought, and, if we say that the transaction can now be undone, we must hold that it can be undone at any indefinite time, so long as the purchaser has not parted with the property: *Price* v. *North*, 2 Y. & C. 620; *Harris* v. *Pepperell*, L. R. 5 Eq. 1, 5.

I have considered whether the fact that the sale was under the direction of the Court should in the circumstances make any difference in our decision. If the purchaser had made any misstatement to, or had in any way misled the Court or the vendors, I should have thought that the sale ought to be set aside. I do not find anything in his conduct to lead me to such a conclusion; and I have already pointed out why he might well have supposed that the vendors were cognizant of the actual condition of affairs.

On this point I may refer to the cases of *Else* v. *Else*, L. R. 13 Eq. 196; *Re Bunister*, 12 Ch. D. 131; *In re Arnold*, 14 Ch. D. 270; and *Boswell* v. *Coaks*, 27 Ch. D. 424, 456, 457.

I think, therefore, that the appeal should be allowed.

PATTERSON, J.A.—At a sale under an order of the Court of Chancery for the purpose of partition amongst the heirs of William Cottingham, Thomas R. Adam became the purchaser of a parcel of land which had been described in the advertisement of the sale as " Parcel No. 26. The east part of lot No. 9 in the fifth concession Fenelon ; 100 acres, leased to James Bryson until the first of October, 1878, at the rental of $150; frame house, &c." The sale was on 22nd April, 1876.

The lands had been offered for bids at so much an acre, and Adam's bid for parcel No. 26 was $31 an acre. He signed a memorandum which was prepared by the vendors' solicitor or his clerk in these words : " I agree to purchase parcel No. 26, mentioned in the within particulars, for the sum of $3,100, and upon the terms mentioned in the above conditions of sale, and subject to a lease to James Bryson which expires on the 1st October, 1878, at $150 per year." The conveyance to Adam bears date 12th December, 1876, but whether executed at that date or not, there is reason to infer that it was not accepted by Adam for some time after that, probably not till later than October, 1878, although the evidence does not afford us information as to the exact date, and it is perhaps not very important to know it.

A petition was presented to the Court on behalf of the heirs on the 11th of May, 1881, alleging that subsequently to the sale the petitioners discovered that the parcel contained upwards of 124 acres, and not 100 acres as was erroneously stated in the advertisement, and praying that Adam be ordered to pay for the excess over 100 acres at $31 an acre, or to restore the excess to the heirs and pay an occupation rent for the time he had it; that the conveyance to Adam, and a mortgage executed by him to secure four-fifths of the purchase money may, if necessary, be rectified ; and for further and other relief.

There are many other allegations in the petition which I do not at present notice.

An answer was filed by Adam, and the matter was heard, in the same way as an action in which issues of fact were joined, by Mr. Justice Ferguson at Lindsay, in November, 1882. At the close of the trial the learned Judge intimated his finding upon the disputed questions of fact, but did not dispose of the matter until 4th March, 1884, when he delivered a considered judgment.

In that judgment he thus stated his findings at the trial: " At the trial of the petition I found as facts that the lands were sold and purchased at $31 per acre, each party thinking that there were only 100 acres in the parcel, and that the biddings and the price or purchase money were so much per acre and not so much for the parcel of land, and that the evidence to shew that the lands were knocked down at $3,100 failed; that on the day of the sale, but after the sale had taken place, the purchaser learned and knew that there was an excess of land, but that the vendors did not, nor did the vendors' solicitor, then or for a long time afterwards know this, and that the first knowledge of it the vendors or their solicitor had was at or soon before the 23rd October, 1879; that the excess above referred to exists; and I decided that the delay was not, under the circumstances, too great."

In the conveyance to Adam the land was described as " that certain parcel or tract of land and premises situate, lying, and being in the township of Fenelon, in the county of Victoria, and province of Ontario, containing by admeasurement 100 acres more or less, and being composed of the east part of lot 9 in the 5th concession of the said township of Fenelon."

The learned Judge, in allusion to this description said: " Counsel for Adam, the purchaser, rested his argument mainly upon the fact that the words ' more or less' occurred in the description in the conveyance to his client, and that what was sold and purchased was the ' east part' of the lot. The peculiarity of this case is, that both parties were at the time of the sale ignorant of the existence of the excess in quantity of the land, but before taking his conveyance the purchaser was aware of it, and the vendor was not, nor was the vendor's solicitor, and in this conveyance the words ' more or less' occur for the first time. All the descriptions prior to this in the conveyance say ' the east part, 100 acres,' without any further expression in this respect." This last observation is not quite accurate if intended to apply to documents of earlier date than the advertisement for sale under which Adam bought.

Then the learned Judge, after referring to some authorities, continued thus: "The sale in the present case was by measurement. It was $31 per acre for the 100 acres mentioned in the advertisement. If the purchaser had been obliged to bring a suit for specific performance of his agreement, it seems to me clear that he could have got only the 100 acres. Then did the vendors waive any of their rights when the words 'more or less' were inserted in the conveyance under the circumstances that I have stated? Can they be held to have done an act of waiver, they or their solicitor not having at the time any knowledge of the material fact? I certainly think not, and I am of opinion that the petitioners are entitled to relief. I think there should be an order upon Adam, the purchaser, to pay the petitioners for the excess of acreage, viz., $24\frac{68}{100}$ acres, at the same rate per acre as he paid for the 100 acres, and interest; or that there should be an order for the delivery of possession of this $24\frac{68}{100}$ acres of land to the plaintiffs, or the plaintiffs and others, as the case may be, who were entitled to the estate before the sale and conveyance to Adam."

The order was for the last mentioned relief, Adam having elected to give up the excess rather than pay for it.

I have quoted the judgment in the learned Judge's own language, in preference to attempting to state the effect of it, partly because the repeated references to the facts connected with the sale and the conveyance shew the very clear opinion which he had formed from the testimony of the witnesses who were examined before him; and partly because upon one point, which may or may not turn out to be important, I am not sure that I can say what he thought, or whether he formed a decided opinion or not. That point is the legal operation of the deed to Adam as conveying the whole parcel of $124\frac{68}{100}$ acres, or only the east 100 acres of the lot.

Lot No. 9 is nominally a 200 acre lot, but, to use a common expression, it overruns; the excess being $24\frac{68}{100}$ acres.

The whole lot had once belonged to a man named Taylor, who conveyed the parcel now in question to William Cottingham, on 20th August, 1861, describing it as "containing by admeasurement 120 acres, more or less, and being composed of the east part of lot No. 9 in the 5th concession of Fenelon."

It is said, though I think not by any of the witnesses, that Taylor had at an earlier date conveyed the west 100 acres of the lot to one Wager.

William Cottingham made a lease to James Bryson for a term of five years from the 1st of October, 1873, in which the premises were described as "being composed of the east part of lot No. 9 in the 5th concession, 100 acres, be the same more or less;" which lease is the same mentioned in the advertisement, and in Adam's memorandum of agreement to purchase.

There is evidence of the existence of a fence of some kind between the Wager portion of the lot and the Cottingham portion. This evidence is not very distinct, but I have no doubt the limits or approximate limits of the two parts were known, and that the land intended to be sold at the auction and that which Adam intended to buy was the whole of the Cottingham part. On that particular there was no difference of understanding between vendor and vendee.

The error was in calling the quantity 100 acres and in computing the price as if that was the correct acreage.

I am inclined to think that the deed which was ultimately executed was sufficient to convey the whole tract. Without at this moment discussing that point, I shall assume that the deed had that effect.

Now when Adam, intending to buy the definite piece of land which in fact contained 124 acres, bid $31 an acre, and particularly since it has been conveyed to him, why should he not pay for it? If we leave out of view the difficulty created at common law by the receipt for purchase money which an ordinary conveyance usually contains, it is not easy to see how he could have resisted a common law action for land sold and conveyed, so long as the facts are taken to be as found by the learned Judge. A judgment in such an action would be equivalent to the first alternative proposed by the learned Judge for the decree. It would be simply enforcing the contract, and in that respect would present the condition which Lord Cottenham referred to as wanting in *Okill* v. *Whittaker*, 2 Phil. 338; 11 Jur. 681, when he said (I quote from the Jurist): "Here in fact, the vendor comes and asks that the purchaser may pay more than he has contracted to pay, because the property turns out more valuable than he thought it."

But Adam has a right to say that although he did offer $31 an acre, he did so supposing that he was buying only 100 acres, and that if he had known that the quantity was larger he would not have bought.

It would, I apprehend, be out of the question to attempt to enforce against the purchaser specific performance of a contract made under such a misapprehension, particularly when the misapprehension was induced by the vendor's misdescription of the property.

The heirs here really demand payment of a debt. "Where a lien is raised for purchase money under the usual equity in favor of a vendor, it is for a debt really due to him, and equity merely provides a security for it." *Sugden* on Vendors and Purchasers, 13th ed., p. 245. But at the same time the demand for payment of the debt for the price of the excess over 100 acres, is a demand for the specific performance of the purchaser's part of the contract, and equity would require that he should have the option to give up the bargain if he has done nothing to disentitle himself to that relief.

This brings us to consider the second alternative proposed by the learned Judge, being that which is embodied in the decree from which Adam appeals.

It will be noticed that the first, or rejected alternative, payment, assumes that the bargain was for the whole tract of 124 acres; while the second, or the restoration of the twenty-four acres, treats the actual purchase as confined to the easterly one hundred.

I have already alluded to the difficulty in taking the latter view of the purchase. My idea is, that it was resorted to, as it appears to have been in some negotiations between the parties, and was allowed to find its way into the decree, not because the parties were supposed to have intended to deal on that footing, but because it was thought that the contract may have been governed by the mistaken reference to the quantity, and may have come to have the unintended effect of a contract for the east 100 acres.

I do not think it can fairly be so treated.

I think we have to consider the demand for specific performance of the contract to pay $31 an acre for the whole tract, and the purchaser's claim for relief, on the understanding that the subject of the sale was the whole tract, and the price to be paid $31 for each acre it contained.

The right of Adam to be relieved from his bargain is not so clear as it would have been when he first discovered that there was a larger quantity of land than one hundred acres. He acquired that knowledge, according to the finding of the learned Judge, on the day of the sale, though not till after the sale. There is evidence to support a finding that he knew it before the sale, if Mr. Hudspeth's recollection is to be relied on when he tells us that Adam more than once spoke of his reason for buying being that he knew there was a surplus. But, confining ourselves to the facts as found, we have Adam taking the conveyance of the land long after he had acquired the knowledge that he was getting more than 100 acres, and whether or not he knew the full extent of the excess, with the knowledge that it was far beyond what the words " more or less " would cover. Taylor told him on the day of the sale that there was an overplus of sixteen or eighteen acres ; and his solicitors had before them the deed from Taylor to Cottingham where the tract was called 120 acres more or less.

Under these circumstances, one does not readily see why he should be relieved from the full payment of his purchase money.

COTTINGHAM V. COTTINGHAM.

This conclusion does not at all depend upon the correct construction of the conveyance itself, because, whether it ought to be construed as conveying the whole 124 acres, or only 100, Adam insists on the former, and in fact took the deed as being a conveyance of the larger quantity.

I accept the findings of fact at the trial, not only because I see no reason to dissent from them, but because I think I should myself have come to the same conclusions; and I think that upon those findings the proper decree would be for the payment of the unpaid purchase money.

The order actually made is, I think, more favourable to Adam, and less favourable to the heirs, than Adam had any right to look for; but inasmuch as it has been accepted on the part of the heirs, we ought not to disturb it merely because relief of another kind would seem more appropriate.

I shall presently notice the contention on the part of Adam founded on certain things that happened after the sale and after the conveyance. At present I am discussing the case without reference to those considerations.

The learned Judge's finding that the land was sold and bought at so much an acre, and not at so much for the parcel, has been impugned.

There can scarcely be said to be a conflict of evidence respecting what took place at the auction. Every one agrees that the biddings were for so much an acre; but a son of Adam deposes that the auctioneer, as a rule, announced not only the bid per acre, but also the total amount to which the bid brought up the price of the parcel. I do not know that that would make any difference in the character of the sale; but so far as young Adam's evidence may be considered in conflict with that of the auctioneer or other witnesses, we should of course accept the learned Judge's finding, even if we did not ourselves see the evidence in the same light. But while the evidence of the son failed to establish that the auctioneer sold in bulk, the fact that it was adduced for that purpose may be worth remembering when we are asked now to find as a fact that the sale was after all a sale in bulk, and not a sale by the acre.

The contention is, that the land was put up by the acre only as a way of arriving at the bulk sum for which the sale was to be made, and that this was true of all the twenty-six parcels sold except four. In support of this contention, the purchaser relies upon the circumstance that at the sale the gentleman who was acting as clerk, and who was either a clerk or partner of the vendors' solicitor, kept a list of the parcels sold, computed the price at the bid per acre upon the supposed acreage of the parcel, and filled up a memorandum for the purchaser to sign with the sum so arrived at; but, in the four exceptional cases, inserting the price per acre only. Reliance is also placed on the auctioneer's return to the Court, in which he reported all the parcels as having each been sold for a bulk sum, including parcel 26, $3,100, except the four which he reported as sold at so much an acre.

This return would, no doubt, be *primâ facie* evidence against the vendors, but it is merely the auctioneer's statement to his employers and not any part of the transaction with the purchaser. It is merely a report that contracts had been made, most of which were of the character of that which was signed by Adam, and it adds nothing to the effect of those contracts. Its use in evidence is principally as a matter to be considered, by way of a test, in connection with the affirmative evidence given by the auctioneer and by Mr. Hudspeth as to the sale being by the acre and not otherwise, and we have the learned Judge's conclusion upon the whole of that evidence.

I have not been able to see so much force in the contention which is based upon the form of the written contract as to give it weight against the finding of the Judge to whom it was addressed soon after the witnesses had been before him.

The entry of the four lots as being sold by the acre, while others are noted as if sold for bulk sums, does

not strike me as more than *primâ facie* evidence, if
no better evidence were forthcoming, of the two sets of
parcels having been sold on different principles; but when
we take with it the explanation given by Mr. Hudspeth,
and also look at the descriptions in the advertisement of
the sale, the entries seem to me consistent with the finding that there was no difference in the mode of selling the
several parcels.

The four exceptional parcels are 16, 23, 24, and 25.
Three of these, viz., 16, 24, and 25, are described as containing, respectively, 100, 100, and 75 acres. Parcel 23 is
merely called " North half, Lot 1, 9th] concession, Ops,
being all that part west of the creek ; " and it is the only
parcel in the whole twenty-six, the acreage of which is
not mentioned.

Mr. Hudspeth's explanation is found in an affidavit, to
which his attention was called at the trial by counsel for
Mr. Adam, where he said, " as there were a number of
parcels, the contents of which were unknown, lands cut
off by ponds, rivers, and streams, I instructed the auctioneer, Mr. William L. Russell, to put up all the lands by
the acre, and the lands were accordingly sold at so much
the acre."

It may be noted in passing, though it cannot be anything like authority, that in one reported case, *Leslie* v.
Tompson, 9 Hare 268, the mention of the number of acres
in the particulars was held to negative an intention to sell
by the lump.

Now when we find that three out of twenty-five lots,
each one of which was advertized as containing a definite
number of acres, are noted as sold at a price per acre, while
the other twenty-two lots are put down as sold for a sum
which is the price bid per acre multiplied by the stated
number of acres, and when the uncontradicted evidence is,
that the sales of all the parcels were conducted by the
auctioneer in precisely the same way, it is not an unreasonable inference that in every case the purchaser understood
that he was to pay for every acre in the parcel, while he

was not to pay for more than was there ; that in these three cases something was known which cast uncertainty upon the nominal acreage, and in the other cases the named amount was supposed to be correct,

When the measurements of the four exceptional parcels came to be made, the contracts for them would become essentially the same as those for the other parcels ; but if the surveyor who measured them happened to return the contents as more or less than the true amount, a thing which is possible, and of which we have a recorded instance in *Leslie* v. *Tompson*, 9 Hare 268, it could scarcely be maintained that either party would be bound by a computation made upon the erroneous measurement.

There is no ground for the suggestion which I think was made at the bar, that the preparation of the memorandum by Mr. Woodward, the clerk, and the signature of it by the purchaser, varied the contract made between the purchaser and the auctioneer. The object of that transaction was not to make a bargain, but to record one already made ; and I venture to think that the importance of proving that the contract now insisted on was made as soon as the bid was accepted and the lot "knocked down" was understood at the trial when the younger Adam persistently asserted that the parcel was sold by the auctioneer for the bulk sum.

No sufficient reason has, in my opinion, been shewn for taking a different view of the facts from that taken by the learned Judge.

If we should hold, contrary to the finding of the learned Judge, that parcel No. 26 was not sold by the acre, but simply for $3,100, which is what the appellant desires us to do, the vendors not knowing or supposing that it contained more than one hundred acres, and the purchaser either having no more correct information, or if he had, being under no obligation to communicate it, there might be greater difficulty in supporting the claim of the heirs for relief; and if they should be held entitled to relief it would be in a different form from that offered in either of the alternatives proposed by the learned Judge in the Court below.

The ground of the claim would be mistake.

The mistake as to the quantity of land would be a mutual mistake in one sense, but not in the sense which would afford a ground for reforming the deed. The hypothesis is, that this deed contained exactly what both parties intended it to contain, although the vendors would not have agreed to it had it not been for their mistaken idea of what they were selling. They meant to sell the whole parcel which they conveyed, and they meant to convey it, but they erroneously thought it contained only 100 acres.

The position would not resemble that in *Leuty* v. *Hillas*, 2 DeG. & J. 110, where the defendant had obtained a conveyance which described, along with the land he had contracted for, a piece of the premises which the same vendor had sold to the plaintiff; and where Lord Cranworth, L.C., held him to be a trustee of the piece of land for the plaintiff, and made a decree for its conveyance to the plaintiff.

In *Harris* v. *Pepperell*, L. R. 5 Eq. 1, also, in which a decree was made by Lord Romilly, M. R., for rectification of a conveyance, the error was in the parcels. In that case the error was not common to both parties, but the decree seems to have been the result of a choice given to the defendant between having the deed annulled or rectified.

Paget v. *Marshall*, 28 Ch. D. 255, before Bacon, V.C., was like *Harris* v. *Pepperell*, both in its facts and in the decree.

But although this deed could not be reformed, would the mistake of the vendors afford sufficient ground for rescinding the contract, assuming for the moment that the parties could be restored to their original position ?

The case of *Okill* v. *Whittaker*, 1 DeG. & S. 83; 2 Phil. 338; 11 Jur. 141, 681, is cited as bearing against the right to rescind. The sale there was of a lease which both parties assumed to have only eight years to run, but

which had in fact considerably more. The purchaser
lived six years after his purchase and the assignment to
him, and the bill was not filed till two or three years after
his death.   Knight Bruce, V. C., said it was impossible to
give the plaintiffs relief upon any other footing than that
of rescinding the contract wholly or from the outset, and
he pointed out why under the circumstances, that could
not be done, dwelling particularly on the absence of
explanation as to how the mistake occurred, and the failure of the plaintiffs to shew when the truth was discovered.   "In such a case as this," he concluded by saying,
(11 Jur. 144) "after all that has occurred, the Court is
asked to rescind the contract.   I am of opinion that such
a bill must be dismissed, with costs."   In this judgment I
understand the learned Vice-Chancellor to refuse to rescind
the contract, not because such relief was inappropriate or
such as a court of equity could not give, but because of
the unexplained laches of the plaintiffs and the change of
position of the parties.

   The decree was affirmed by Lord Cottenham, L.C., without calling on the defendant.   I understand him to have
taken the same view of the plaintiff's position as the Vice-
Chancellor.   He said, as reported in 2 Phillips at p. 340 :
" It is impossible on this bill to give any relief.   It goes far
beyond any of the cases that have been cited.   The plaintiffs do not ask to rescind the transaction altogether : nor
could they ; for after ten years' occupation and expectation
of the benefit of renewal, it would be impossible to restore
the purchaser to his original situation.   What they say is,
that the contract was improperly executed by the assignment, and they ask that what remains of the term after
the expiration of the eight years may be reassigned.   But
what is that, but to call upon this Court to decree specific
performance of a contract with a variation ?   For the thing
that both the vendor agreed to sell and the purchaser to
buy, was the residue of the term, and not a portion of the
residue."

   Then he made use of this illustration, which is relied
upon as authority that a mistake as to the acreage of a
parcel of land is not such a mistake as will entitle either

vendor or purchaser to ask the Court to rescind the contract :

"Suppose a party proposed to sell a farm, describing it as 'all my farm of 200 acres,' and the price was fixed on that supposition, but it afterwards turned out to be 250 acres, could he afterwards come and ask for a re-conveyance of the farm, or payment of the difference ? Clearly not ; the only equity being that the thing turns out more valuable than either of the parties supposed. And whether the additional value consists in a longer term or a larger acreage, is immaterial."

I do not understand this passage to be intended to lay down any such general proposition as that for which it is cited. The immediate object of the Lord Chancellor was to shew that the Court could not compel the purchaser to pay more than he had agreed to pay ; and he treated the bill as having for its object to introduce a new term into the contract either to make the purchaser pay more for the property or to convert him into a trustee for the vendor. He had already pointed out that rescission was out of the question, for the same reason given by the Vice-Chancellor, not that such relief was inappropriate or unwarranted by the principles of equity, but because of the change of the position of the purchaser.

The decision in *Okill* v. *Whittaker* is thus stated by Lord St. Leonards, in the chapter of *Vendors and Purchasers* where the subject of rescinding a contract is discussed : "Where a man sold and assigned a leasehold estate believing and representing that there was only eight years to run, and it afterwards appeared that a life was still in being, which did not drop for some years, so that the purchaser obtained a longer term than he bargained for, yet the seller's bill for relief was dismissed, with costs."

I do not find it laid down in that work that a mistake in value affords no ground for relief. The contrary is incidentally asserted in a paragraph preceding that which I have just quoted, where it is said : "A seller may have a title to relief on the ground of undervalue, improvidence and haste in the execution of the contract, or the like, and yet if he file his bill on the ground of fraud when none

exists, the bill may be dismissed; but if a proper case for
relief is made out, the mere superaddition of an allegation
of fraud, not proved, will not prevent the plaintiff from
succeeding:" *Sugden* on Vendors and Purchasers, 13th ed.,
p. 207. And, again, (p. 233): "A conveyance executed
will not, however, be easily set aside on account of the
inadequacy of the consideration. * * But a conveyance obtained for an inadequate consideration, from one
not conusant of his right, by a person who had notice of
such right, will be set aside, although no actual fraud or
imposition be proved."

There is a full discussion of the doctrine in *Story's*
Equity Jurisprudence. In section 141 I find it said : "So
if the mistake be in the *quantity* of the land sold, as four
acres instead of eight, this is sufficient to justify a Court
of Equity in rescinding the contract; it being proved that
the deficiency was material in the object of the purchase.
And this would be so although the land was described as
being eight acres ' more or less,'—those words being confined to a reasonable allowance for small errors in surveys,
and for variations in instruments."

This proposition must, of course, be read along with the
more general statement contained in section 151, where it
is said: "The general ground upon which all these distinctions proceed is that mistake or ignorance of facts in
parties, is a proper subject of relief only when it constitutes a material ingredient in the contract of the parties,
and disappoints their intention by a mutual error; or
where it is inconsistent with good faith, and proceeds from
a violation of the obligations which are imposed by law
upon the conscience of either party. But where each
party is equally innocent, and there is no concealment of
.acts which the other party has a right to know, and no
surprise or imposition exists, the mistake or ignorance,
whether mutual or unilateral, is treated as laying no
foundation for equitable interference. It is strictly
damnum absque injuriâ."

A number of cases were cited to us in which the right
to compensation by a purchaser for deficiency in the
quantity of land professed to be sold was in question. They
usually turned on some stipulation in the conditions of
sale, and have little direct bearing on the present question,

except when we find some Judge drawing the distinction between the rights of parties as restricted by the condition and the right when no condition existed. The judgment of Stuart, V. C., in *Cordingley* v. *Cheesebrough*, 8 Jur. N. S. 585, 587, is an instance of this.

I do not think any purpose would be served by discussing these cases.

The opinion which I derive from the authorities is, that a mistake in regard to the quantity of land may afford ground for equitable relief, even when the land is not sold by the acre, but that the circumstances of each case must be carefully considered before deciding that it is a case for rescission.

Adhering, as I do to the findings of fact by the Court below, and regarding as I do the real question as being the right of the heirs to enforce payment of that part of the purchase money which the purchaser has neither paid nor secured, which question is not altered by the purchaser having elected and the heirs having submitted to have the decree for the alternative relief which has been granted, I feel I can only pursue the discussion of the legal question of the right to rescind, in its application to this case, upon facts which to me are hypothetical and not the real facts of the case, a proceeding which would consume time without an adequate purpose. A number of things would necessarily enter into the discussion, which could not be satisfactorily dealt with except in relation to the ascertained facts connected with the sale itself. One thing would be the knowledge which Adam had of the existence of the surplus land at latest immediately after the sale, and certainly a long time before the conveyance. It may be that he was under no obligation to communicate his knowledge to the vendor, but that would be one thing to be considered.

Then we should have to determine whether the circumstance that this was a sale under an order of the Court, and that Adam was in a sense taking directly from the Court, particularly the interest of the infant heirs on whose behalf the deed was executed by an officer of the Court, did not create a duty which might not have existed in other circumstances. It may be that the principle on which in *Boswell* v. *Coaks*, 27 Ch. D. 424, the purchaser's neglect, when he was obtaining the Judge's sanction to the sale, to disclose a fact which affected the value of the property sold was held by the Court of Appeal to be a fraud, and for which, ten or twelve years after the sale, the transaction was set aside, would be found not clearly to apply when the purchaser had not to take so active a part in procuring approval of the sale and the execution of the deed; but that is another matter which would necessarily engage our attention.

We should, moreover, have to contend with the circumstance that some of the evidence which, on the assumption that the land was not sold by the acre, would bear materially on the right to a rescission, is the very evidence on which it has been found that the land was sold by the acre.

The discussion would possibly result in shewing that the equities are not unlike those dealt with by Sir G. J. Turner, V.C., in *Leslie* v. *Tompson*, 9 Hare. 268. In that case, there had been a sale of property in four lots. In the particulars of lot 1 there had been an understatement of about twenty acres in the quantity of the property which it comprised; and in lots 2, 3, and 4 there had been an overstatement by about ten acres. The question, upon a case stated, was, whether the purchaser was bound to pay compensation for the surplus in lot 1, and to receive compensation for the deficiency in the other lots. The Vice-Chancellor held that the conditions of sale did not apply, and then made some observations which might be found not inapposite to the facts we have before us. " I entertain some doubt," he said (p. 273), " whether, under the circumstances of this case, the vendors could have been relieved, if they had filed their bill to have the contract delivered up to be cancelled. I am rather disposed to think that, under the circumstances stated in the special case, they might have been relieved ; for it appears upon the special case; that the particulars of sale were prepared from some previous conditions and particulars of sale, and from the report of a surveyor prepared on a former occasion, and which particulars and report were erroneous. I am disposed to think, therefore, that as the vendors have in preparing the particulars in this case proceeded on former conditions of sale drawn up on the report of a surveyor, which is incorrect, and have therefore entered into the contract under a mistaken conception of the amount of property comprised in the particulars, they would be entitled to relief."

We have in t l.is] assage an explanation of how the mistake happened, which was one of the particulars the absence of which, in the judgment of Knight Bruce, V.C., stood in the way of a rescission of the contract in *Okill* v. *Whittaker;* and it is an explanation which does not appear to me of more force than that which in the present case is found in the fact that the sale was conducted by persons whose knowledge of the matters they were dealing with was derived entirely from the papers in their hands, one of which was the lease given by William Cottingham to Bryson, the latest document affecting the property in which the quantity was called 100 acres. To say that the means of correcting their mistake, or rather of avoiding it, existed in a deed from Taylor to Cottingham which they had or might have had, or ought to have had, in their custody, and which they might and perhaps, if attention had been called to it, would have read, is merely to say that there ought to have been no mistake. It does not touch the value of the explanation.

Then the Vice-Chancellor adds another remark, which fits this case wonderfully well. "One argument," he said, (p. 273), "put by Mr. Prendergast, appeared to me at first to be entitled to weight. It was that the vendors did not intend to sell the lot by admeasurement, but that they meant to sell the lot in the mass or lump. It was, upon that point that I felt some hesitation during the discussion before me. The conclusion, however, to which I have arrived is this, that the actual designation of the number of acres contained in the lot negatives the presumption of any intention on the part of the vendors to sell in the lump."

Without, therefore, attempting to exhaust the subject of the right to a rescission of this contract, I shall content myself with stating my strong impression that, even if the sale had been, in form and intention, a sale for a bulk sum, I should, in view of the other circumstances shewn by the evidence, hold that the heirs were entitled to equitable relief by way of rescission, unless disentitled by reason of something that occurred after the sale.

I shall refer to these subsequent events, although if I am right in considering that the claim of the heirs is for a debt for which the Court can give the remedies which a Court either of law or of equity could formerly have given, the subsequent events may not be of much importance. Whatever significance belongs to them will relate rather to the other branch of the case, for to quote again from Lord St. Leonards (p. 211): "A right to rescind a contract may, like most other rights, be lost by acquiescence or relinquished by confirmation."

The report on the sale bears date 22nd May, 1876.

The investigation of the title proceeded leisurely on till the end of January, 1877. The abstract furnished by the vendors' solicitor is dated 2nd December, 1876, and was delivered in pursuance of a requisition dated about a week earlier; then under date 9th December, 1876, there are objections from the purchaser's solicitor; and on 22nd January, 1877, a reply from the vendors.

It does not appear at what stage the deed, which bears date 12th December, 1876, was actually executed, but we have a letter from Messrs. Hudspeth and Woodward to Mr. Adam, dated 12th April, 1877, saying that the deed has been ready for a long time, and asking to have the matter closed at once.

We are not informed of any prompt response to this. In fact we hear of nothing further till after Bryson's lease fell in on 1st October, 1878. That event was followed on 15th October, 1878, by a formal notice from Mr. Adam to Mr. Hudspeth that he had executed a mortgage and paid money into Court pursuant to the conditions of sale: that one Mrs. Taylor being in possession of a portion of the land, Adam required delivery of possession as against Mrs. Taylor within one week; and that in default he would apply to the Master to consider Mrs. Taylor's occupation as an objection to the title, and make application to the Court to compel Mr. Hudspeth to deliver possession.

Thereupon an order was made for an action to be brought in the name of Adam to recover possession, and on 14th November, 1878, an action was commenced against George Taylor and his wife, the land being described in the writ, as it was in the deed to Adam, as the east part of lot No. 9, in the 5th concession of the township of Fenelon, containing one hundred acres, more or less. Taylor and his wife defended for the whole of the lands claimed, although we are told that what they really disputed was the right of Cottinghnm to more than the one hundred acres, and after a trial, judgment was recovered and entered up against them on the 6th of May, 1879.

On the execution of the writ of possession a dispute arose. One of Adam's causes of complaint is, that Mr. Hudspeth refused to give him possession or to direct the sheriff to give him possession of more than the east one hundred acres. This complaint is made in Adam's answer to the petition, where he also says that Mr. Hudspeth at the time of the action had the land surveyed. Unfortunately Mr. Adam's state of health prevented his examination at the trial, and Mr. Hudspeth was only able to speak of these matters from his recollection of having heard evidence given in another action concerning them, and not from any recollection of the occurrences themselves. But one thing which is made plain enough as against Adam is, that the right which he now sets up to hold the 124 acres, while he paid only for 100, was disputed on the part of the heirs on the first occasion that arose, and before he had been let into actual possession.

In disputing the right which Adam asserted, Mr. Hudspeth may not always have put the claim of the heirs on the precise ground on which I think them best entitled to maintain it; but whether he insisted that Adam should pay for the surplus land, or that he should not have it because he had not paid for it, is immaterial upon the charge of lying by. That charge is disproved by the assertion of the claim of the heirs in either shape.

Going back to the requisitions, we find Mr. Adam's solicitor objecting on 9th December, 1876, that the land was not sufficiently described, besides making some other objections, to all which the reply of 22nd January, 1877, was "The abstract shews a good title to the east half of said lot, 100 acres, under the tax deed thereof to William Cottingham, and the sale was only of 100 acres."

This strikes me as a very strong piece of evidence against the present appellant. The character of the sale, as we now understand it, was misapprehended by the person who answered the requisition in the name of Hudspeth and Woodward; but when we find the express assertion that 100 acres only had been bought, answering a requisition which contained a notice that if any answer was unsatisfactory a warrant to consider the abstract would be applied for; and then the acceptance of the conveyance without alteration of the description, or any further objection, or any application to the Master; we have a very plain act of acquiescence in the answer, and a clear justification of Mr. Hudspeth's action when he afterwards, as Adam complains, resisted his attempt to obtain actual possession of the surplus land, or declined to aid him in obtaining it.

So far then, whatever we may think of the merits of the dispute or of the conception of the rights of the heirs which their solicitor sometimes acted on, he is certainly free from any imputation of misleading the purchaser or of acquiescing in his demands.

Then we learn from Mr. Adam that he ejected Mrs. Taylor *vi et armis*, for which an action of trespass was brought against him, but his defence was successful; and afterwards, as the Taylors persisted in trespassing on the land and attempting to take possession of it, he filed a bill against them and others, and obtained an injunction

against them.   The costs of this action, we are informed,
were paid by some of the defendants, who, unlike the
Taylors, were solvent.

Mr. Hudspeth tells us in his evidence that he waited
for the termination of the litigation between Adam and
Taylor before further pressing the claim of the heirs,
although his recollection is that during that time he had
conversations with Adam in which he claimed that Adam
should pay for the 24 acres, while Adam denied his liability and insisted that he had bought it all.   There is not
a word in evidence to contradict this or to suggest that as
a matter of fact Adam ever supposed the claim to be re-
ceded from.   The decree in Adam's action against Taylor
was pronounced 20th October, 1879, the learned Vice-
Chancellor who tried the action expressing his opinion
that whatever was the position with regard to the Cottingham estate, Adam was entitled to success as against
Taylor, an opinion quite in accordance with what I believe
we all agree was the legal operation of the deed, and then
three days afterwards Mr. Hudspeth or his firm made a
formal written demand for payment for the 24 acres at
$31 an acre, which was followed by the petition now be-
fore us.

There is only one way in which any thing done or
omitted, in the proceedings to which I have now referred,
strikes me as capable of affecting the right to equitable
relief.   I assume that the heirs have been all through
fully represented by Mr. Hudspeth and bound by his acts
or omissions, although that may not be quite fair, as we
find him occasionally speaking of the difficulty of getting
instructions.

If the heirs were now asking to have the sale entirely
set aside, their claim might reasonably be resisted by pointing out that they had allowed their vendee to treat the
land as his, and to incur trouble and expense in prosecut-
ing his suit for the injunction, after they had full knowledge of the facts they now rely upon.   That objection
would, however, go only to the form of the relief.   They

recognized the effect of the conveyance and the interest of the grantee in the land, but always asserted a claim of the kind set out in their notice of the 23rd October, 1879, though not always so precisely expressed. They said all along to Adam, "you have only paid for 100 acres and you cannot keep the rest of the land without paying for it;" and then when the litigation with Taylor is over, and Adam is free from further disturbance from him, they say: "Now pay us for the odd 24 acres."

I know of no rule of equity which, in the circumstances, interferes with the assertion of that demand.

I do not discuss the effect of the execution of the conveyance, because I do not think it is seriously contended that that incident can affect either a vendor's lien for unpaid purchase money, or the equity to have the transaction rescinded where a proper case of mistake is made out, and where no counter equity intervenes.

The late case of *Palmer* v. *Johnson*, 12 Q. B. D. 32 ; 13 Q. B. D. 351, sets at rest some questions on the subject respecting which there were conflicting decisions, but those were questions of a different nature and depending on different principles.

A technical question was raised both by the answer and the reasons of appeal, touching the jurisdiction to dispose of this matter on petition in place of in a substantive action.

I see no reason for entertaining such a question. In view of the course the matter has taken, the objection becomes a matter of words only. The appellant might, if he had been so advised, have taken his stand upon the objection, but he has answered as fully as to a bill; his case has been fully tried ; he has had a resort on the merits to this Court ; and I apprehend that the Supreme Court Act of 1879, 42 Vict. ch. 86 (D.), leaves no doubt of the right to resort to that Court also.

I think we should dismiss the appeal, with costs.

Appeal allowed, with costs. [PATTERSON, J.A , dissenting]

SCHROEDER ET AL. V. ROONEY.

*Setting aside judgment—Execution—Assignment—Execut...s—Fraud—
Estoppel—Appeal.*

The plaintiffs by their agent, Patrick R., in April, 1877, procured a judgment to be signed against Peter R., the defendant, who, for purposes of his own, suffered the judgment to go by default. No execution was ever issued thereon. After the death of Peter, the plaintiffs assigned the judgment to the wife of Patrick, who paid them $50 therefor ; and, on her application, ARMOUR, J., made an order allowing execution to issue against the executors of Peter. The executors then applied to set aside the judgment, as having been fraudulently obtained, and to be allowed to defend the action, or for such other order as should seem just; and upon such application, WILSON, C. J., made an order setting aside the judgment and all proceedings in the action, and directing the plaintiffs to repay the $50. This order was affirmed on appeal by the Common Pleas Division.

Held, that an appeal lay from the order of the Common Pleas Division, as it was in effect a final disposition of the whole matter and a bar to the plaintiffs' further proceeding ; but, although the members of this Court were all of opinion for different reasons that the order below was wrong, they did not agree as to which it should be modified or reversed, and therefore the appeal was dismissed, without costs.

Per HAGARTY, C. J. O., and OSLER, J. A. :—The judgment should merely be set aside and the executors allowed in to defend.

Per BURTON, J. A. :—The executors cannot be heard to allege their testator's fraudulent purpose ; they are estopped from confining the operation of the judgment within the limit of his intended fraud ; and the judgment should be allowed to stand.

Per PATTERSON, J. A. :—The judgment should not be set aside, but the order of ARMOUR, J., should be rescinded, and it should be declared that Patrick's wife as assignee of the judgment, was not entitled to issue execution, because the judgment was procured by Patrick, her husband, and suffered by Peter, for a fraudulent purpose, of which she had notice when she took the assignment.

THIS was an appeal by the plaintiffs from the judgment of the Common Pleas Division affirming the order of Wilson, C. J., at Chambers, setting aside the judgment signed for default of appearance and all proceedings in the action.

The order of Wilson, C. J., and the facts and arguments are fully set out in the present judgments.

The appeal was heard on the 10th day of March, 1885.[*]

O'Donohoe, Q.C., for the appellants.

O'Sullivan, for the respondents.

[*]*Present.*—HAGARTY, C. J. O., BURTON, PATTERSON, and OSLER, JJ.A.

April 20, 1885. HAGARTY, C. J. O.—We first heard of this case on 22nd May last, on an application by the plaintiffs for leave to appeal against a judgment of the Court of Common Pleas.

The Court had set aside a judgment obtained for default of appearance.

An order had been obtained to revive the judgment and leave to issue execution against the executors of the defendant. The executors then moved to have the judgment set aside and to allow them to defend the action, and for an order for administration of the estate of the defendant or for such order as might be just.

The matter appears to have been referred by the Master to a Judge, and it was heard at length before Wilson, C.J., who made the following order, dated the 1st of December, 1883 :

" Upon the application of the plaintiffs for an order that execution do issue upon the judgment entered herein on the 20th of April, 1877, against the executors of the defendant Peter Rooney, and upon reading the order made therein by the Master in Chambers, and upon reading the order on appeal therefrom made herein, and upon reading the notice of application of the executors of the defendant that this said judgment be vacated, and that they be allowed in to defend as by leave given, and upon hearing read the affidavits filed and the exhibits referred to therein on the several applications herein the depositions taken in Montreal and New York under order made herein, and upon hearing the parties by their counsel, the said application having been referred to a Judge in Chambers by the said Master in Chambers :

1. It is ordered that the said judgment for the plaintiffs of the 20th of April, 1877, against Peter Rooney for the sum of $2,189.31, and all proceedings in that action, be set aside with costs of the whole of these applications, to be paid by Patrick Rooney and his wife, Thomasina Piscod Rooney, in the proceedings mentioned, to the representatives of Peter Rooney.

2. It is further ordered that the said representatives shall pay to Patrick Rooney and his wife the sum of $50.00, paid to William Schroeder & Co., of New York, for the

assignment of the said judgment, with interest from the time of payment of the same, and the costs attending the procuring of the said assignment.

3. And it is further ordered that the claim by the one party against the other as above be set off and the balance struck between them; and that the party in whose favor the balance is shall be paid that sum by the other party."

In his full reasons for judgment the learned Chief Justice concludes: "I shall therefore set aside the judgment with the costs of the whole of these applications to be paid by Patrick Rooney and wife to the representatives of Peter Rooney; and I do order that the said representatives shall pay to Patrick and wife the sum of $50, paid to Schroeder for the assignment of the judgment, with interest from payment, with costs attending the procuring the assignment, and that the claim by the one party against the other be set off and the balance struck between them; and that the party in whose favour the balance is, shall be paid that sum by the other party."

The plaintiffs appealed against this order to the Divisional Court, and after argument the appeal was dismissed with costs.

The learned Judge Galt, who reviewed all the facts, said that he "was satisfied that there never was any legal claim by the plaintiffs against Peter Rooney; but even if there had been, I think at the time when this judgment was obtained it had ceased to exist."

When the matter came first before us we were of opinion that it was not an appealable matter, so far as the setting aside of the judgment and letting in the executors to defend was concerned. It was represented then to us that the judgment below was in effect a final disposition of the whole matter and a bar to the plaintiffs further proceeding.

Our view on this was that, in that aspect of the case, the plaintiffs did not require any leave, but had the right to appeal.

In the reasons of appeal, all but the last, No. 7, go to the general merits as to interfering with the judgment.

No. 7 complains that the learned Chief Justice exceeded

his jurisdiction in making the order of 1st December, sweeping away the cause of action herein. Said order was not asked for by the defendant's notice of motion upon which it was had, and was a surprise no less to counsel supporting than to counsel opposing the motion.

The respondents, in No. 6 of reasons against appeal, allege that they offered to proceed by pleading a defence in the original suit and treating the judgment of the Chief Justice below as simply allowing them in to defend; but this offer was refused by appellants, who claimed they were entitled to have execution issued, and would submit to no other order being made in the matter.

The judgment in the Court below does not in terms bar any further proceeding in this matter. The refusal to allow execution to issue practically has that effect.

I think the Court had a right in its discretion to set aside this judgment, and to let the executors in to defend on such terms as appeared just to the Court; and I do not think that we are called on to question such right, or to review its exercise.

Were it necessary for me to express an opinion on the subject, I am not prepared to say that I differ from the propriety of the action taken.

But I find much difficulty in upholding the judgment, if its effect be to prevent the plaintiffs from having the validity of their original claim tried on the merits in the usual course; and a very full examination of all the facts before us in evidence leads me to the conclusion that the plaintiffs should still be allowed their ordinary right of trial.

I think it impossible to acquit the deceased defendant of all blame, or, (to use the mildest term,) heedlessness, in allowing this judgment to be recovered against him, and his executors would have been accorded a large indulgence in being allowed to come in and defend.

The learned Judges below have not discussed the question or stated their reasons for practically putting a final bar to further proceedings.

I must therefore content myself with expressing my opinion, with all respect, that such a bar ought not to have been created.

I think the judgment below should be varied so far as it prevents further proceedings for the trial of the plaintiffs' claim.

I do not think that there should be any costs of appeal, as the whole case was brought before the Court, and not merely the part on which I hold that there was any right to appeal.

BURTON, J.A.—I agree with the learned Chief Justice that the order appealed from ought not to be allowed to stand. I also agree with him that, if the order had been as we at first supposed it to be, when application was originally made for leave to appeal, an order setting aside the judgment and letting the executors in to defend the action, we should very properly have refused to grant such leave; but I am not prepared to say, that, although in setting aside the present order the statute enables us to give the judgment which the Court below should have given, there is any evidence before us which would warrant us after the lapse of some seven or eight years in letting these parties in to defend.

It is not a case in which a Court below, having exercised a discretion, we are called upon to interfere with that discretion, but it is a case in which we are exercising for the first time the equitable jurisdiction which all Courts possess over their own proceedings. Treating it then as an application to be let in to defend, I feel clear, upon a perusal of Chief Justice Wilson's judgment, that he had not the slightest intention of granting the smaller measure of relief. On the contrary, he was clearly of opinion that no such relief could have been granted if the judgment had still been in Schroeder's hands, and it was his intention to set aside, as he has done, the whole proceedings. It is not therefore a case in which we are called upon to interfere with a Judge's exercise of discretion, but are called upon now to say whether a case for relief of that kind has been made out. If such a motion had been made by Peter Rooney as soon as possible after the judgment was signed, he would have been bound to account satisfactorily by affidavit for his non-appearance, and to have disclosed a good defence upon the merits; and it would seem that the usual affidavit that he has a good defence upon the merits would not suffice, but that the affidavit should shew what the nature of the defence is, and that it is a good answer to the action.

The learned Judges below differed as to the grounds upon which relief should be granted; Mr. Justice Galt being of opinion that the goods were not ordered by Peter. It is not, I think, very material to the present inquiry; but the evidence of John Rooney himself convinces me that the goods were ordered by the old firm, although they did not arrive in this country until some time after the dissolution and transfer to the new firm, and that in strictness Peter and John were the plaintiffs' debtors. No doubt, by ranking with the new firm's consent on the estate of the new firm, they may, in the absence of contract, have discharged Peter; but I do not agree with the Chief Justice of the Queen's Bench, that the affidavit proving the claim against them in insolvency furnishes any evidence of their abandonment of their claim against Peter, in consequence of the omission to state that they held him as security, as it is only when the plaintiffs hold a security given by the insolvent firm that such a statement has to be made.

If, as John states, these goods were not taken into account in his dealings with the new firm and credited to him, and he thought himself liable to the plaintiffs, one can understand his desire to make that appear in his litigation with Rooney & Dolan; but even on the assumption that it was obtained with any fraudulent object, I do not very well understand how he can be heard to object to the judgment on that ground.

The onus was upon the executors to shew that this judgment, signed so many years ago, and acted upon by Peter Rooney for his own benefit in his litigation with Rooney & Dolan, was invalid, and ought to be set aside; and they have failed to satisfy that onus in my opinion.

It is said that the plaintiffs did not know of the judgment being obtained until after Patrick purchased it; but, so far as the Schroeders were concerned, that cannot be a matter of the slightest importance—they, I have no doubt in good faith, (for I am free to admit that I attach more weight to Mr. Carl Schroeder's letters written at the time than I do to his subsequent affidavits), instructed Patrick to take proceedings against Peter; and even though it were made perfectly clear that the judgment was obtained for some collateral purpose of Peter and Patrick, the Schroeders were legally entitled to enforce it, whenever it came to their knowledge. It is therefore abundantly clear that in the Schroeders' hands the attempt to impeach the judgment must have failed. Let us then see how the case stands in the present position of matters.

In April, 1883, Mr. Justice Armour made an order for leave to issue execution against the executors of Peter Rooney. No attempt apparently was made before him to impeach the judgment; and if it had been, it could not have succeeded. (See *Thomas* v. *Williams,* 3 Dowl. 655.)

The judgment itself could not be attacked on such an application, although I think the learned Judge might have imposed a condition that credit should be given for the dividends received from the other estate both prior to and subsequent to its recovery.

With great respect, I do not think it was competent to the Chief Justice, even with the consent of Mr. Justice Armour, to deal with that order upon this application.

The learned Chief Justice was himself under a misapprehension in reference to the nature of the application, when he refers to it as an application to set aside that order. It was simply for an order vacating the judgment and allowing the executors in to defend.

It becomes important, in my judgment, only in the view
that had it been an appeal from Mr. Justice Armour's
order, the Court below might have dealt with the application in the same manner as Mr. Justice Armour could ;
and if that had been made apparent, I might perhaps have
taken the same view as my brother Patterson in refusing
leave to issue execution. But there is nothing whatever
to shew that any application was ever made to rescind
that order ; on the contrary, it appears in the reasons, and
was admitted upon the argument, that no such application
ever was made ; but, upon its being mentioned to the Chief
Justice that that order stood in the way, he said he
would obtain the consent of Mr. Justice Armour to deal
with it ; and he proceeded to deal with it upon the pending application, and without the consent of the parties.

I think, therefore, we have at present nothing to do
with that order. It was granted, and has never been
appealed against ; and we are now dealing with the case
as if it were a judgment in which no application to the
Court was necessary in order to enforce it by execution.

When we come then to consider it in that way, we find
that what we are dealing with, and what the Court below
was alone competent to deal with, is a substantive application on the part of the executors of Peter to set aside
this judgment,

I have already dealt with the case, as it presents itself
to me, on the hypothesis that the Schroeders were still the
holders of the judgment, and that the sole ground was
that there was originally a good defence to the action on
the merits. I find it very difficult to find any intelligible
ground for granting relief, now that Patrick has acquired
it from the Schroeders. We are not now inquiring, and
cannot inquire in the absence of the Schroeders, whether
the assignment was obtained from them under circumstances which entitle Patrick to hold it against them, but
assuming, for the purpose of this application, that Patrick
or his wife is the rightful owner of it, and granting for
the purpose of the argument that the judgment was con-

-cocted fraudulently between Patrick and Peter for some purpose of their own, which we can only conjecture, it is clear that it was done for the benefit of Peter, and the inference is, that he did benefit by it. But upon what principle could any Court be asked now to assist either of these parties ? One of them is placed in a difficulty which is not infrequently the result of fraudulent conduct, and the transaction has the appearance of being very unjust ; but Courts are bound by rules of law, and one of these is, that where parties are in *pari'delicto* the law favours him who is actually in possession. As I have already said, we we are not called upon now to consider whether there was any concealment practised by Patrick upon Schroeder which would entitle him to come in and set aside the assignment as between the parties before us. The Schroeders were at liberty to give the judgment to any one they chose, and it does not lie in the mouths of the executors, any more than it would have done in Peter's, if he had been living, to impeach it on the ground of fraud to which he was a party.

If Patrick had obtained the judgment in his own name, and without any consideration, for the purpose of carrying out some fraudulent scheme in favour of Peter, it might be very inequitable in him to turn round upon Peter afterwards, and endeavour to enforce it by execution ; but I know of no rule of law or equity which would prevent his doing so. If it were necessary for him to seek the active interposition of the Courts to enforce his claim it might be different. Here he has the judgment and the right to enforce it, and the executors are the parties seeking to set it aside. I think they cannot be heard to allege their testator's own fraudulent purpose. They are estopped from confining the operation of the judgment within the limits of his intended fraud. If it had been shewn that Patrick was acting merely as the agent of Peter or his estate in obtaining an assignment of the judgment, I could well understand the Court restraining him from enforcing it. The difficulty is, that there is no evidence to sustain that position.

A great deal of the material used in the Court below was not evidence in any sense of the word. The affidavits of Carl Schroeder are inconsistent with each other, and in direct variance with the letters written at the time when there was no inducement to misrepresent; and taking into account the great lapse of time, the deaths of parties, and the difficulty of placing the claim for relief upon any sufficient legal or equitable ground, I feel that it would be establishing a most dangerous precedent to set aside this judgment. The parties have chosen to allow the judgment to be signed, either because they believed a debt to exist, or for some purpose of their own, and a very strong case indeed ought to be shewn to warrant our interference.

I think the appeal should be allowed, with costs.

PATTERSON, J.A.—The plaintiffs recovered judgment on 20th April, 1877, against Peter Rooney by default of appearance to a specially indorsed writ. No execution has ever been issued on that judgment.

Peter Rooney is dead, and Mrs. Rooney, the wife of Patrick Rooney, asserts that the judgment has been assigned to her by the plaintiffs.

Without closely scrutinizing Mrs. Rooney's title to the judgment, we may discuss the question whether she, as assignee, ought now to be permitted to enforce the judgment by execution against the personal estate of Peter in the hands of his executors.

Mr. Justice Armour made an order allowing the issue of writs of execution against the executors of Peter Rooney. This was I think in July, 1883. Then we find a notice given on the part of the executors on 17th July, 1883, of an application to stay proceedings till 3rd September following, which was the first Monday following the long vacation; and for an order vacating the judgment and allowing the executors in to defend the action, and for an order for the administration of the estate of Peter, or for such other order and upon such terms as should be deemed just.

The application was referred by the Master to a Judge, and was heard before Wilson, C.J., who, on the 1st of December, 1883, made an order to set aside the judgment and all proceedings in the action.

If the order had merely set aside the judgment and let the executors in to defend, it may be that it would have been considered to be an interlocutory order, from which, under section 35 of the Judicature Act, there would have been no appeal. But though in one alternative of the application relief was asked in that shape, the learned Chief Justice made such "other order as he deemed just," by setting aside all the proceedings.

From the views which he expressed, to the effect that the proceedings were of a fictitious character, concocted between Patrick and Peter, with no reference to the interests of the nominal plaintiffs, against whom he seems to have thought Peter could not have successfully defended himself, and from his considering that Patrick obtained the assignment on behalf of the estate of Peter, and that the executors ought to refund to Patrick the $50 which he says he paid to Carl Schroeder for the claim, I do not doubt that the order does not go farther than the Chief Justice intended, and that he had no idea of merely placing the executors in a position to defend the action, notwithstanding that in one branch of the judgment delivered he only speaks of setting aside the judgment.

The assignee appealed to the Divisional Court of the Common Pleas Division, where the judgment was affirmed by Galt, J., and Rose, J., but not for the same reasons given by Wilson, C. J.

Galt, J., acted upon his reading of the evidence, which convinced him that Peter never owed the Schroeder firm, but that the goods had been ordered by and sold to the firm of Rooney & Dolan, and not to P. & J. Rooney : and Rose, J., adopted that conclusion without giving us the assistance of his own examination of the evidence, which is to be regretted, because almost every witness on both sides is contradicted either by himself or by reasonable inference from plain facts.

I do not propose to follow the judgments in appeal, either in the course taken in discussing the facts, or in whatever I may have to say upon the questions of law or of practice; but I shall adopt what seems to me the more convenient method of stating from my own point of view my impressions of the history of the transaction, as well as of the rights of the parties; while at the same time I think more importance than it deserves has been attached to the nature of the dealing between the Schroeder firm, and P. & J. Rooney, or Rooney & Dolan.

The goods for the price of which the judgment was obtained were invoiced to " P. & G. Rooney," which is evidently a clerical error for P. & J. Rooney, in three separate invoices dated 3rd, 14th, and 25th July, 1874. It seems to be satisfactorily shewn that they represented but one order, the dates of the invoices being the dates of the shipping of the goods, which may have been manufactured after the order was given.

I am satisfied that the order was given by P. & J. Rooney, whether by Peter through Patrick in Montreal, which Patrick thinks was the case, or by John in London to the London house, which is John's version. I have no idea that when Carl Schroeder, on 18th August, 1875, wrote to Patrick Rooney that the plaintiffs held Peter for the part of the debt of Rooney & Dolan which was contracted when Peter was a partner of the old firm, and when, in April, 1877, Peter suffered judgment for the same debt, they were dealing on a fabricated state of facts. There is no reason why they should have done so.

The affidavits or depositions on the part of the executors do not in the least shake me in that opinion. When John Rooney in an affidavit, to the admissibility of which Mr. O'Donohoe objects, swears that the goods were bought by him in London in May or June, 1874, but most likely in June, long after Peter had retired from the firm, I believe he is either swearing recklessly or intending to mislead. Hugh Dolan, John Rooney's partner, says in his deposition that he only remembers one purchase from plaintiffs by

Rooney & Dolan.　He certainly says that his partner
bought *these* goods in London, and that it was shortly after
his entering the firm; but against that we nave the fact
that goods were bought in December, or rathei invoiced in
that month, from the plaintiffs, and that that may be the
one purchase which Hugh correctly remembers as the only
one, while the theory requires two.　Then John Rooney
does not suggest how it was possible that, if he bought for
Rooney & Dolan, the goods were invoiced and sent to
P. & J. Rooney.

The affidavit of Carl Schroeder, which is also ' bjected
to, in which he swears that he "never understood that any
other person could be or was liable to us except Rooney
& Dolan," when contrasted with his letter of 18th August,
1875, shews that, if he fully understood the affidavit he
was swearing to, his memory is not to be relied on; and
Mr. Roughan, the book-keeper of Rooney & Dolan, when
he swears, as he does in one of his affidavits, that "never
at any time did Carl Schroeder or his firm look to Peter
Rooney for payment of any purchase either first or last, or
anticipate any such payment at any time from Peter
Rooney," is so obviously swearing to a matter of which he
could know nothing, that, even if he had not been compelled in cross-examination to admit that he knew nothing
of it, it stamps his affidavit with the character of recklessness, which is confirmed when we find him in his other
affidavit representing the July goods, as appearing in the
invoice-book of Rooney & Dolan, as being all comprised in
one purchase of 25th July, and by his including in his
affidavit, in place of facts, the argumentative deposition
that "if the goods delivered in said month of July to
Rooney & Dolan were ordered by Peter Rooney in the
preceding month of April or May, there was ample opportunity for William Schroeder & Co. to stop the delivery of
the goods to the new firm."

The mistake in putting all the three July items in one,
placing the last of them first, and giving its date as the
date of them all, is found also in an affidavit in which the

solicitor, who is himself one of the executors, details the
inquiries he made into the affairs in question. This circumstance suggests that one of the deponents may have
adopted the figures of the other without making independent enquiries, and naturally casts doubt on the value of
the affidavits.

We can surmise how the mistake happened from reading
Hugh Dolan's deposition where, looking at the invoice
book, he reads from page 71 the invoice of the 3rd July;
from page 72 that of the 14th July; and from page 70 that of
the 25th July; shewing that the latest invoice of the three
had found its way into the book before the others, and
that whoever extracted the figures, whether Hugh Dolan
or the solicitor, noted them in this order without noting
the dates of the last two entries.   The two gentlemen
may of course have noted them independently, but it is
odd that, if that were so, they should have agreed in
omitting to note all but one of the dates, and in overlooking the fact that that date was the latest of the three.

The solicitor himself is not always careful to separate
his statements of fact from his arguments or inferences.
Thus, professing to give, in one of his four affidavits, the
substance of letters written by Patrick Rooney, and alluding to the judgment, he inserted this statement: " They
could do nothing to enforce it, he said, without his assistance, or language to that effect. The judgment was one
got by defendant, and got, as he said, to be used for purposes apparently fraudulent."   These last words express
only the inference of the deponent, not the language of
the letter, as we learn when the letters are produced.

Then to this affidavit evidence, unsatisfactory as it is,
and to the affidavit of John Rooney, there is opposed the
evidence of John Rooney himself given in June, 1877, in
Montreal in the suit of *Dolan* v. *Rooney*, in which suit
this judgment is said to have been made use of, where
he distinctly swore that the goods were ordered by the
firm of P. & J Rooney before the new firm was formed ;
and there is the cross-examination of Mr. Roughan, who,

when confronted with the invoice-book, where the name of
P. & G. Rooney appears attached to the invoices which he
spoke of as the first purchase of Rooney & Dolan, admits
that he cannot possibly account for that circumstance.

Upon the whole evidence, it is to my mind impossible to
come to the conclusion of fact upon which the judgments
in the Divisional Court proceeded. I have no doubt that
Peter and John Rooney were the original debtors to the
plaintiffs; whether a novation was afterwards effected so
as to discharge Peter, or whether it is of much consequence
whether he was discharged or not, are other matters.

If the issue had to be tried whether or not such a novation had taken place, there would be evidence in the facts
before us proper to consider in support of the affirmative.
One piece of evidence would be the ranking on the estate
of Rooney and Dolan for the debt, the proof of claim as
an unsecured debt being made for the plaintiffs by Patrick
Rooney as their attorney in August, 1875; and their dividends being received, the last being payable on 10th July,
1878. But the evidence would not be all one way. Even the
statement, probably in a printed form, that they held no
security would only go for what it was worth as a statement of Patrick Rooney. It could have no effect on the
insolvent estate, which was liable either to Schroeder &
Co., or to Peter. There was no security of which the
creditors could have availed themselves.

In a contest between the plaintiffs and Peter Rooney,
the judgment which Peter permitted the plaintiffs to recover
would probably have been conclusive against him. But
that point being granted, does it follow that the present
assignee can be permitted to enforce the judgment?

I am not convinced, that, in any view of the case which
is in my judgment sustainable upon the evidence, it would
be proper to set the judgment aside.

It is said that it was recovered for a fraudulent purpose;
that Peter Rooney having been paid some $11,500 by the
firm of Rooney & Dolan, partly in cash and partly in notes,
half of which were indorsed by Francis Dolan, the father

of Hugh, which notes had been negotiated by Peter, Francis Dolan brought an action against him to recover $1,111.81, being one half of an amount which he alleged was an over payment for Peter's interest in the assets. This action was compromised by Peter paying $600. The act of settlement bears date 25th August, 1877. During the proceedings, or on the negotiation for settlement, the judgment now in question was produced for the purpose, as it is argued from the evidence, though not directly proved, of swelling Peter's claim on Rooney & Dolan by shewing his liability for these goods; and it is further argued that the purpose in suffering the judgment was that it might be so used. This argument has much support from the general evidence, and particularly from the fact that John Rooney was examined as a witness in the action, on behalf of Peter, to prove that Peter or his firm ordered the goods, and that no account had been taken of them in the statement of Peter's interest in the assets transferred to the new firm.

The inference from what we have before us, including several things in the evidence given by Patrick Rooney, is, I think, reasonable, if not inevitable, that the judgment was recovered and used for the purpose alleged; and I see no reason to refuse to carry the inference to the length that Peter obtained the intended advantage from the judgment, in his settlement with Francis Dolan.

There was nothing necessarily fraudulent in the transaction as thus stated. It would have been no fraud, but probably only an act of honesty, for Peter to pay the debt. It had once been his debt, and may have always been so; but whether or not he could have resisted the charge, yet inasmuch as Rooney & Dolan had not paid for the goods but had speedily become bankrupt, possibly by reason of the large sum they had to pay Peter, the injustice of throwing the loss upon Schroeder & Co. might reasonably have been recognized by him, and this more particularly as he had the security of the notes with Francis Dolan's indorsements. Thus the suffering of the judgment as he did was not necessarily a fraud of Peter either on the plaintiffs or on Dolan. The fraud would be in his intention to cheat the Schroeders after inducing Dolan to allow for the claim.

But, whether fraudulent or not, I understand the judgment to be precisely what Peter as well as Patrick intended it should be. If I am correct in this, Peter could not have asked to have it set aside; and his executors merely stand in his place.

The question then comes to that which I stated at the start, should the assignee be allowed to have execution upon the judgment against the executors?

Mrs. Rooney cannot claim, as purchaser for value or in any other way, a stronger position than Patrick himself could claim if he had taken the assignment in his own name.

The introduction of her name, and the pretence of paying Carl Schroeder for the judgment are both shams, as I think may be fairly inferred from her own evidence and from that of her husband, as well as from the affidavit of Carl, though if the matter were doubtful I should not rely much on that affidavit.

Some reliance was placed, on the part of the executors, on letters from Patrick Rooney, and on some other negotiations, in which he professed to be willing to forego the judgment if certain money was sent to his sister in Ireland. I h .ve not been able to see in all this anything more than grounds for perhaps forming an unfavorable idea of Patrick's title to be considered straight-forward, and perhaps for giving rise to that kind of prejudice which, though it may not be unjust, is apt, unless guarded against, to lead to making bad law. He apparently always asserted the judgment as something that he could enforce if he pleased; and if, under those circumstances, any dealings were had with the estate in dependence on anything short of a binding agreement with him, they cannot be made the ground of a claim in a court of law.

I think the relief of the executors, if they are entitled
to any, cannot be put on the right to avoid the judgment,
or on any agreement or estoppel between them and Patrick,
but simply upon the necessity for the assignee satisfying
the Court, under rule 356 of the Judicature Act, that she
is entitled to issue execution.

That necessity may arise from the lapse of six years from
the judgment, or from the change of parties by the death
of Peter. Here both circumstances concur.

There is no reason which is valid in law, upon which
either Peter in his life time or his executors since his death
could, so far as I can perceive, have opposed the issue of
execution by the plaintiffs.

The nominal plaintiffs are, however, not the actors at
present, and there are rather strong reasons for holding
that this assignee does not succeed to their rights.

Patrick Rooney never intended the judgment to exist
for the benefit of the Schroeder firm. He did not proceed
against his brother when, as appears from evidence which
he cannot dispute, the plaintiffs desired him to do so ; but
he proceeded only when a purpose of Peter's was to be
served by the judgment, and he then did so without the
knowledge of the principals in whose name he acted. He
did not press the judgment during Peter's life, although he
knew that Peter had money, and although his power of
attorney from the plaintiffs remained effective ; and when
at last, after Peter's death, he saw a prospect of making
use of the judgment, he did not apprise his principals of
the facts. It is more than doubtful if he told them there
was a judgment. Carl Schroeder says he did not know of
it, and Patrick does not really contradict him. The assignment, which is dated 29th January, 1883, contains the word
" judgment," but not in such a way as to call attention to
that as being a word of any importance. The words are:
" All and every claim, demand, cause of action, and judgment." Nothing was paid or agreed to be paid for that
assignment ; but some weeks later Patrick, being advised
that the transaction would be safer if he paid money, went

again to Carl and paid him $50, and gave his wife's note for $50 more.   Carl calls these sums each $100, and swears that they were credited to Patrick in his account.

This would seem to have been on 20th February, 1883, as of which date we have a rather unusual sort of document, a kind of combined affidavit and deed of confirmation, purporting to be sworn before a notary in New York by Carl Schroeder, giving particulars of the judgment, and confirming the assignment of it.

In his affidavit made in the cause Carl says he signed a paper when the money transaction took place.   This February transaction is not alluded to by Patrick further than the payment of the money, of which he gives substantially the same account as Carl, only calling the amount $50 in place of $100, and not telling us that the payment was placed to his own credit.

I am of opinion that the present applicant is not entitled to leave to issue execution.

I think the whole history of the judgment and the dealings in respect of it, as detailed by Patrick himself, supports the view that it was obtained as a fraudulent scheme arranged between the two brothers Patrick and Peter to aid Peter in his suit with Francis Dolan, without giving the nominal plaintiffs any benefit from it.   I have already said that Peter could not ask the Court to assist him to avoid the judgment.   His purpose in suffering it succeeded; but even if it had failed, its fraudulent character would bind him to his act.   Many decisions on this principle are collected in *Kerr* on Frauds, under the title "Parties," such as *Cecil* v. *Butcher*, 2 J. & W. 572 ; *Doe* v. *Roberts*, 2 B. & Ald. 369, &c.

Had Patrick been able, without more than a formal proceeding, or the ministerial act of an officer of the Court, to issue a regular execution in the name of the plaintiffs, the defendant or his executors might not have been able to resist it.   But he has now to ask the active aid of the Court, not as attorney for the nominal plaintiffs, but on his own behalf, and to enable him to carry out for his own benefit the fraud on the plaintiffs which was originally planned in the scheme to help Peter against Dolan. Possibly the case might be different if the plaintiffs, knowing of the judgment, and intending to dispose of it, had assigned it to Patrick, as they might have assigned it, either gratis or for value, to a stranger; though I do not say that even in that case the terms on which Patrick and Peter dealt might not afford some answer against Patrick. But if the first dealing is properly regarded as tainted by a fraud, which would have stood in Peter's way, and disabled him from obtaining relief from the Court, it is also proper to refuse to aid Patrick in turning the fraud to his own benefit. *In pari delicto potior est conditio possidentis.* See *Holman* v. *Johnson*, Cowp. 341, 343, per Lord Mansfield.

Then there is another matter which I think we should not overlook. The plaintiffs are not before us, and I am not satisfied that a sufficient case is made for interfering with their judgment in their absence, even so far as to let the executors in to defend. I should so hold even if a strong case of merits were made ; but as it is, I am by no means led by the materials before us to the opinion that Peter may not always have been liable both in law and in justice to pay the debt.

To justify us in setting aside the judgment in the absence of the plaintiffs it ought to be very satisfactorily shewn that they have really parted with all their interest in it. We have no such satisfactory evidence. We have an instrument, or rather two instruments, those of 29th January, and 20th February, by which, in terms, Carl Schroeder says he assigns the judgment, but what was his authority? He is not one of the plaintiffs, and we have only his own declarations to show that he has any right to act for them. One of these declarations is contained in the affidavit which Mr. O'Donohoe objects to being used in evidence—an objection which has more in it than I was inclined to think during the argument—but, the affidavit being put in by the executors, Mr. O'Donohoe has at least the right to avail himself of anything he finds in it in his favour. Carl there states that he is the New York representative of the plaintiffs, and is himself a partner of the firm of William Schroeder & Co., the plaintiffs—all of which amounts to no more than that the plaintiffs, of whom Carl is not one, traded as William Schroeder & Co., and that the same style is retained, and that he is now a member of the firm. In his declaration of 20th February, 1883, he says that the judgment formed part of the assets of the firm in 1879, when he became a partner. I place very little reliance on anything in that document, even if it were regular evidence, as a statement of fact. But it is perfectly plain from Patrick's evidence that no member of the plaintiffs' firm had ever heard of the judgment in 1879, nor had Carl heard of it; and it is more than doubtful if any of them ever heard of it till after the assignment. Therefore Carl's statements are far from proving authority in him to deal with the judgment, certainly not to give it away; and there is besides plenty of room for hesitation before accepting the evidence as sufficient proof of an intention to assign it.

My opinion is, that we should reverse the judgment of the Divisional Court so far as it affirms the order to set aside the judgment and the order for the executors to pay money to Patrick Rooney; and that in place thereof we should follow Chief Justice Wilson's finding on the other branch of the application, and make the order, which I think ought to have been made, to discharge the order of Mr. Justice Armour, which gave leave to issue execution, with a further declaration, which I shall state after discussing some technical questions.

There are technical objections taken to the interference with Mr. Justice Armour's order.

It was appealable to the Divisional Court only. The motion heard by Chief Justice Wilson was first made before the Master, and was merely to set aside the judgment and let the executors in to defend.

An order to set aside the judgment would of course have rendered the order for execution effete; but the latter

order would become operative again, if the order to vacate
the judgment should be reversed.

But although the notice of motion only attacked the
judgment, and although there would no appeal lie from
Mr. Justice Armour's order to the Chief Justice, any more
than to the Master who referred this motion to him, the
Chief Justice states in his judgment that the executors of
Peter had moved to set aside that order, and that Mr.
Justice Armour had permitted him to deal with it as he
might have done himself if he had heard the whole merits
of the case.

He accordingly considered both motions and held that
the first order should be rescinded, and that the judgment
should be set aside.

The order as drawn up said nothing of the first branch,
perhaps because the more extensive relief, by setting aside
the judgment and all proceedings, made it seem unnecessary to do so.

If the technical grounds relied upon sustain the objection,
we shall be bound to give effect to it, and the result of that
in connection with my opinion on the other branch of the
case would be that the judgment in *Schroeder* v. *Rooney*
should stand, and that the order for execution, of which I
disapprove, should also stand unaffected by this appeal.

But I do not think the objection is, upon the whole,
entitled to prevail.

It would have been competent to Mr. Justice Armour to
review his own order, though perhaps not in the face of an
objection by either party. The right of the party dissatisfied with the order was to appeal to the Court; and
possibly if both parties had appeared before him consenting
to his reconsidering it, they would have been taken to
have substituted that proceeding for an appeal, and have
been precluded from any further appeal: *Thompson* v.
Becke, 4 Q. B. 759. Here the matter was reconsidered by
Chief Justice Wilson in place of Mr. Justice Armour by
consent of the latter, and I apprehend with the same effect
as if Mr. Justice Armour had himself reconsidered it in

view of the additional evidence which was adduced upon the second application.

From the learned Chief Justice's statement that the executors had moved to set aside the order I understand that the propriety of that order being allowed to stand was a subject of discussion, and there is no intimation in the judgment he delivered that his .right to entertain the question was disputed. *Consensus tollit errorem.*

Had such an objection been urged the executors might have taken advice whether or not they should formally appeal from the order to the Divisional Court, or apply to have it reconsidered.

In place of that an appeal from the judgment generally was had, and was dismissed.

The assignee in appealing to this Court has, in the fifth reason of appeal, again raised the question of the propriety of Mr. Justice Armour's order, contending that it was proper and ought not to have been disturbed.

I cannot say that, on the score of irregularity, I am pressed with any difficulty in considering the whole matter as before us, and I have no reason to doubt that everything has been advanced on both sides which could be urged in either form of the motion.

Then looking at Rule 356, which relates to the application for leave to issue execution, we find that the Court or Judge upon the application may order that any issue or question necessary to determine the rights of the parties shall be tried in any of the ways in which any question in an action may be tried.

By this means the rights of the parties may be determined in the one proceeding as effectually as formerly in an action of revivor or in an action upon the judgment.

That has practically been done in the present case, so far as the rights of Patrick Rooney or his wife, assuming one of them to be really the assignee of the judgment, are concerned.

I think our judgment should declare that Thomasina Piscod Rooney is not entitled to issue execution, because the judgment in question was procured by Patrick and was suffered by Peter Rooney for a fraudulent purpose, of which she, when she took the alleged assignment, had notice.

I think there should be no costs of the appeal to either side.

OSLER, J. A.—I think the objection we have to deal with relates more to the form of the order made by the learned Chief Justice, as affirmed by the Divisional Court, than to anything actually expressed in the judgment.

The motion made on behalf of the executors was for an order vacating the judgment, and "allowing the executors in to defend the action," and the conclusión arrived at by the Chief Justice, and by my Brother Galt, as expressed in their opinions, is, that the judgment should be set aside. There was no motion to set aside the order permitting execution to issue ; we have nothing to do with that. No question of the kind was argued before us, and it is clear that an independent motion for the purpose, by way of appeal to the Divisional Court from the order of Armour, J., would have been out of time. The order as drawn up goes a good deal further than merely setting aside the judgment. It sets aside all the proceedings in the action.

We ought not to entertain an appeal from a decision setting aside a judgment by default on a specially indorsed writ, on the merits, which leaves the parties at liberty to prosecute the action. Such a decision is merely interlocutory, and does not finally dispose of the action. It is largely a matter of discretion with the Judge or Divisional Court whether in any particular case it is proper to set aside such a judgment, notwithstanding lapse of time, &c. or other reasons usually urged against the interference of the Court on such applications. In this case I am of opinion that very substantial reasons are to be found in the opinions referred to, for setting aside this judgment at the instance of the executors, whose duty it is to see that the estate of Peter Rooney is properly administered. These reasons are that in the circumstances (1) it is extremely doubtful whether any debt existed for which the Schroeders could have recovered judgment against Peter in a contested action: *Scarf* v. *Jardine*, 7 App. Cas. 345. And (2) it is also doubtful whether it was ever intended that there should be any *real* judgment recovered between the parties at all.

I think that in administering the estate in bankruptcy, or in an administration action, the trustee or executors or other creditors could go behind the judgment and prove these facts; and in that event neither the plaintiffs nor Patrick Rooney, who stands in their shoes, not merely as their assignee, but also as the active agent in recovering the judgment, could prove upon it in competition with the honest creditors of the estate. See *Ex parte Banner, Re Blythe*, 17 Ch. D. 480. *Ex parte Revell, In re Tollemache* (No. 1), 13 Q. B. D. 720.

Therefore the order is right in my opinion as regards setting aside the judgment. No one has suggested or argued that Mrs. Rooney is not the assignee of it, or that the Schroeders have any interest in it. But in setting aside all the proceedings in the action it goes, I think, too far, and certainly further than the Court was asked or perhaps intended to go. The judgment was a judgment by default, and if set aside the parties have a right to try the question in the usual way.

The decision of the Court below should, therefore, be modified to this extent.

With regard to the result of the appeal. In *Regina* v. *Browne*, 6 A. R. 386, 401, this Court, as then constituted, rather pointedly observed, in reviewing the judgment of the Court of Common Pleas : " The difference of opinion in this case is somewhat remarkable; because, while the majority of the Court below agreed in remanding the prisoner for extradition, the learned Judges who composed the majority differed in the grounds on which their judgment proceeded; and we affirm the judgment of the Court for reasons which none of the learned Judges deemed sufficient."

Following that precedent it may not be without interest to notice that the difference of opinion in the present case is even more remarkable, for although there was no expressed difference of opinion in the Court below, and the members of this Court agree, though for at least three different reasons, that the judgment is wrong, they nevertheless cannot agree that it shall to any extent whatever be modified or reversed.

I would concur with the Chief Justice in the following order: That the judgment of the Court below be varied as follows, viz.: That the judgment for the plaintiffs of the 30th April, 1877, against Peter Rooney in the proceedings mentioned, be and the same is hereby set aside without [or upon] payment of costs, and that the plaintiffs, or the said Thomasina Piscod Rooney, as their assignee, be at liberty to revive this action in the name of the said Thomasina Piscod Rooney as plaintiff, against Charles McManus and Dennis Ambrose O'Sullivan, executors of the last will and testament, &c., of the said Peter Rooney, deceased, as defendants; the said Charles McManus and Dennis Ambrose O'Sullivan undertaking to appear in the said action, and not to set up any defence founded upon the Statute of Limitations.

And no costs of appeal to either party.

Appeal dismissed, with costs.

[This case has been since carried to the Supreme Court.]

VanKoughnet v. Denison.

Sale of land—Restrictive covenant—Ambiguous description—Parol evidence —Maps not referred to in deed, admissibility of—Changing names of streets.

D. sold to the predecessor in title of the plaintiff certain lands, and the deed contained the following (which was held to amount to a covenant, the benefit of which passed to the plaintiff):—"Bellevue square is private property, but it is always to remain unbuilt upon except one residence with the necessary outbuildings including porter's lodge." The land having been sold under mortgage, a portion came again to the hands of D., who proceeded to convey parts of it for building purposes.
Held, that parol evidence was admissible to shew what was meant by "Bellevue square," no plan or description being incorporated in the deed.
Held, also, that D.'s liability under the restrictive agreement not to build on Bellevue square, revived on his again acquiring the property.
Certain maps of the city of Toronto, made by city surveyors in 1857 and 1858, shewing thereon a square marked "Bellevue square," were offered in evidence to shew the boundaries of the square. It was shewn that the defendant knew of these maps, but they were not prepared under his instructions.
Held, that the maps could not be received in evidence to shew the boundaries of the square.
Per HAGARTY, C.J.O., and OSLER, J.A.—The maps were admissible to shew that there was such a square known as Bellevue square, but not as evidence of title or boundary.
Per BURTON, J.A., and PATTERSON, J.A.—The maps were not admissible in evidence without its being shewn that they had been prepared under the instructions of the defendant or on information given by him.
The parol evidence shewing that but a portion of the land claimed by the plaintiff to be the square was undoubtedly within the limits of the square, the appeal was allowed as to all but that portion.
Remarks on the serious consequences likely to arise from the constant changes in the names of streets in the city of Toronto.

THIS was an appeal by the defendants from the judgment of Boyd, C., reported 1 O. R. 349, where, and in the present judgments, the facts and authorities are stated, and came to be heard before this Court on the 28th and 29th of October, 1884.*

S. H. Blake, Q. C., and *Black,* for the appellants.
J. Maclennan, Q. C., for the respondents.

January 15th, 1885.   HAGARTY, C. J. O.—I do not see any difficulty on the point raised as to the covenant in the deed from defendant to Bovell not running with the land.

Present—HAGARTY, C.J.O., BURTON, PATTERSON, and OSLER, JJ.A.

Such an objection would only arise in an action based on
the covenant asking for damages at plaintiff's suit as
purchaser from Bovell.

The remedy here sought is not of that description, but
an application to the Court's power to hold the defendant, as the original vendor, to the due performance of the
agreement which formed part of the consideration for
the purchase, viz., that " Bellevue Square was always to
remain unbuilt upon, except one residence with the necessary outbuildings, including porter's lodge."

This deed was in 1860.

It contained the further agreement on vendee's part, his
heirs, assigns, &c., not to permit any business of a public
nature such as a tavern, &c., to be carried on on the
property conveyed.

A burden is thus imposed on the property sold, and on
this adjacent property of the vendor. Any purchaser of
either property with notice, would be held bound by these
respective provisions.

The law is very clearly stated by Lord Cottenham in
the well-known Leicester Square Case : *Tulk* v. *Moxhay*, 2
Ph. 774, (1848.) He says : " It is said that, the covenant
being one which does not run with the land, this Court
cannot enforce it; but the question is, not whether the
covenant runs with the land, but whether a party shall be
permitted to use the land in a manner inconsistent with the
contract entered into by his vendor, and with notice of
which he purchased."

In *London and South Western R. W. Co.* v. *Gomm*, in
appeal, 20 Ch. D. 562, Sir Geo. Jessel held that the doctrine should not be extended beyond negative or restrictive
covenants, and that where there was a covenant, express or
implied, as, for instance, not to build so as to obstruct a
view, or not to use a piece of land otherwise than as a
garden, the Court would interfere. " This," he said, (p. 583,)
" is an equitable doctrine, establishing an exception to the
rules of common law which did not treat such a covenant
as running with the land, and it does not matter whether

it proceeds on analogy to a covenant running with the land, or on analogy to an easement."

We may also refer to *McLean* v. *McKay*, L. R. 5 P. C. 327, an appeal from New Brunswick.

I do not see that the plaintiff has disabled himself from claiming this right by any unnecessary delay or laches on his part, or on the part of those from whom he claimed.

When Bovell bought from the defendant in 1860, the whole of the property was in mortgage to a building society. Bovell's lot was released therefrom. Down to 1869 the property was beyond his control, except by his paying off the mortgage. It was sold under power of sale in 1866 to Mr. Coate, and in 1869 was conveyed by Coate's vendee to the defendant. In 1869, and before reconveyance to defendant, a street, as a continuance of Denison avenue, was opened from south to north about through the centre of the block said to be Bellevue square, but we do not see at what date. The west half or part thus cut off from the rest was sold in lots and built on by various persons.

Until about 1872, no attempt seems to have been made to sell or use portions of the remaining eastern part, and then plaintiff gives the notice of March, 1872.

Nothing further seems to have been done till shortly before the filing of the bill in this case.

I do not see how plaintiff could have interfered at any earlier period, nor can I see how the alienation of the western portion can affect his rights. He has done nothing to bring himself within the principle so clearly set forth in *Duke of Bedford* v. *Trustees of the British Museum*, 2 My. & K. 552, and again discussed in *Sayers* v. *Collyer*, 24 Ch. D. 180, before Pearson, J., confirmed in appeal, Weekly Notes, Nov. 15, 1884, p. 202.

I do not think that defendant can be released from the legal consequences of his original agreement, by any of the facts shewn in evidence, arising from the sale and alienation of large portions of the property originally called Bellevue Square, by title paramount, created by himself prior to his·

agreement. I also agree that he fails in establishing any trusts created, or supposed to be created, on the portion of the land that has come back to his possession, which can affect plaintiff's right to enforce the original bargain.

I think the sole difficulty in the case arises from the apparent uncertainty of the northern boundary of the alleged square.

As to the maps produced from the city treasurer's office, of the date of 1858, and also proved to have been in other places in the city, I do not see how they could have been wholly rejected. They appear to have been prepared by very well known city surveyors, and defendant admits that he saw these maps, and he says he went to Mr. Unwin the surveyor to see how the square had happened to appear on them. He does not tell us what information (if any) he received on the subject.

I think this evidence was receivable, as we would receive evidence that a board was seen on or near land, calling it by a certain name, or a name placed as a designation of a newly opened street, or that a public directory years ago, before any difficulty had arisen on the subject, contained addresses of people as resident on a place called " Bellevue Square," or that plans laying out the Bellevue property for sale, shewing this square, were posted about the town, as often occurs in Toronto.

The mere fact that it was not proved that the owners of the property had authorized the so calling of the square, must not, I think, require the total rejection of the evidence as far as it goes. The question for discussion is, what was Bellevue Square? Defendant denies its existence. But the name has been impressed by him on premises mentioned by him in deeds of lands given by him to others as well as to the plaintiff's vendor.

We do not receive maps so produced as evidence of title, or as to boundary, but merely to help in the elucidation of the proposition denied by defendant, was there any place known or called " Bellevue Square," and what was it ?

Such cases as *Pipe* v. *Fulcher*, 1 El. & El. 111; *Van Every* v. *Drake*, 9 C. P. 478; *Wilberforce* v. *Hearfield*, 5 Ch. D. 709, shew us somewhat of the extent to which such evidence may or may not be admissible.

I think it should not have been wholly rejected, but my judgment does not turn on its admissibility for any purpose. I merely use it as shewing that prior to the sale to Bovell, maps were published by well known city surveyors shewing the square on plans of the city, and that defendant was aware of these publications.

I think that three sides of the remains of the space originally called Bellevue Square are defined with reasonable certainty, east, west, and south. The present western boundary is a street opened some years ago, dividing the portions sold under superior title, and the portion remaining in defendant's control.

The whole difficulty is as to the northern boundary. A street, now called Nassau street, is the first street running east and west north of the southern boundary called Bellevue Terrace. Along the whole line of this street are parcels of land with buildings, also sold by title superior.

If the defendant had been proved to have authorized the surveyors to mark these maps of 1857-8 with Bellevue Square, or that they were furnished by him with a plan or survey to enable them so to do, I think the plaintiff's case would have been proved with reasonable certainty, and the cross street there marked from east to west, and apparently bisecting the block of land between Cambridge street and the street called Bellevue Terrace, would have been held to be the northern boundary of the square. Or, if the plaintiffs had shewn that at the time of the contract to sell to Bovell, the defendant was cognizant of the fact that maps were in circulation in the city, so placing and describing "Bellevue Square," I think we might safely assume that vendor and vendee in that transaction understood the square to be as there shewn.

But for reasons we assume to have been satisfactory to plaintiff, no attempt has been made to prove any such facts.

It is not easy to believe that some more distinct evidence could not have been obtained, as some at least of the well known surveyors whose names appear on these maps are still alive, to bring home to defendant some direct knowledge of the reason for the square appearing on the maps. But we must apply the rule "*de non apparentibus et non existentibus eadem est ratio.*" Nor can we find any evidence as to when the defendant first knew of such maps being in existence, whether before or after the sale to Bovell.

We are thus deprived of the help which might otherwise have been given to define the northern boundary.

The plaintiffs have then practically to depend on the evidence given by defendant. As to his knowledge of the city maps, see p. 40 of the appeal case. At part of that page he is asked: "What did you suppose to be the 'Bellevue Square' mentioned in this deed to Dr. Bovell? A. Well, I do not know what. I did intend to build myself a house on a lot in front of the old homestead years ago.

Q. And that was what you meant by Bellevue Square? A. If I meant anything I meant that, but I certainly did not mean any portion of the old place."

Q. It says here (in the deed) the street running east and west alongside of Bellevue Square? A. Yes, which would have been the place I would have built upon if I had built."

Q. That would be near the present residence? A. In front of it, towards the south."

Again, p. 43:

Q. "So that there is still 188 feet in your name? A. Yes."

Q. "Is your homestead upon that 188 feet? A. No. No part of it, and never was."

The defendant, by his trust deed of 30th August, conveyed the homestead lot and all north of the 188 feet in trust for his daughter, retaining to himself the 188 feet.

It is under this trust deed apparently, that the interests in the other defendants in the suit arise, and they have no interest in this front 188 feet.

We cannot see any legal evidence on which we can venture to place the northern boundary of the square beyond the 188 feet, and we think the decree must not extend beyond it.

The result must be that the bill must be dismissed as to all the defendants except Mr. Denison, with costs, and the appeal of all the defendants except Mr. Denison be allowed, with costs.

As to the costs of appeal between the plaintiff and the principal defendant: If the latter had appealed solely on the ground of the Court below having included in its decree some of the land north of the 188 feet, and succeeded on that contention, he would be entitled to his costs of appeal. But as he has appealed on the whole case, denying any right whatever in the plaintiff, we think our proper course must be to give no costs of appeal to either party.

It is not unlike the case where a plaintiff obtains a verdict for possession of a lot of 100 acres. The whole title is disputed, but defendant shews title by Statute of Limitations to, say, twenty-five acres, and the Court below improperly decides against him, *then if he limit his application to the Court above* as to this twenty-five acres and succeed, we think he would get his costs. If he go into the title question again as to the whole property, we think the Court would give no costs to either party: none to plaintiff, as he had judgment for too much; none to defendant, because he asked for too much.

That there be no costs of appeal as between plaintiff and defendant Denison; and that as to him the decree below be varied by declaring the northern boundary of the space called Bellevue Square to be a line drawn parallel to the northern line of Bellevue Terrace, at a distance of 188 feet north from such northern line.

We cannot part from the consideration of this case, without calling attention to the very serious inconvenience, and extra labour and trouble, in the investigation of the titles, boundaries, and head-letters in this city, arising from the numerous and constant changes in the names of streets.

Much confusion and uncertainty is introduced into the examination of title deeds and maps, and some very serious mistakes are likely to be made—and possibly have been made—by these changes.

This constant shifting of names, must also materially increase the difficulty of obtaining reliable evidence from persons as to their recollection of the position and state of property, and the identity of premises in former years.

The reason for change ought to be very cogent and unanswerable, to warrant alterations likely to work much mischief when disputes arise as to the rights of property.

BURTON, J.A.—The Court, upon the argument, expressed an opinion adverse to the contention of the appellants upon all the points taken in the appeal with one exception, and we have none of us seen any reason upon further consideration to change our views as to them.

The exception I refer to relates to the location of the square referred to in the deed to Dr. Bovell, which alludes to it merely as Bellevue Square, not referring to any map or plan, and the onus was upon the plaintiff of shewing what the square was. It was not a public square that was intended. The allusion to it is simply in these terms: "Bellevue square is private property, but is always to remain unbuilt upon, except one residence, with the necessary out-buildings, including porter's lodge."

Has the plaintiff satisfied that onus? There can be no question that parol evidence was admissible in order to ascertain the subject to which the deed refers, and all circumstances necessary to place the Court in the position of the parties, so as to enable it to judge of the meaning of the instrument.

The plaintiffs rely in the first place upon the mortgages given by Col. Denison in 1862, but the description given in those mortgages does not carry the case any farther than the deed itself. The mortgage was of the whole property, (with the exception of the 400 feet south of Bellevue Place, on part of which the appellant's house stands), and in the description of the mortgaged premises by metes and bounds, one of the boundaries is thus described: "Thence south along the easterly limit of Lippincott street, and in a line with the easterly limit of Lippincott street, produced 1210 feet, more or less, to a point in the line of the southerly limit of the street in front of Bellevue square; thence along the line of the southerly limit of that street to the east side of Denison avenue."

The mortgage in fact covered all that portion of land now shewn as the extension of Bellevue place, lying to the west of Denison avenue, and the only information which this description affords is, that there was a square, but of what size, shape, or dimensions is not shewn, bounded on the south by a street which at that time only extended to the west side of Denison avenue, and had not at that time been opened out to the westward of Denison avenue.

The plaintiff endeavours to supplement this evidence by producing certain maps of the city of Toronto, in which a square (not identical in size in each map) is shewn, but with great deference, I think no proper foundation was laid for the reception of these maps as evidence. It is not shewn that the map was prepared by the instructions of Colonel Denison, or that he had any knowledge of the existence of such a map at the time he entered into the contract in question. As Mr. Justice Patteson remarked in the case of *Wakeman* v. *West*, 7 C. & P. 479, in reference to the danger of admitting such evidence:

"I might choose to make a map of my property, and might add all my neighbours, but my map would not bind them."

I do not think the map could, even if it were an ancient map, be receivable in a case of this nature as evidence of reputation.

In *Pipe* v. *Fulcher*, 1 El. & El. 111, Mr. Justice Wightman says (p. 116): "Hearsay evidence of reputation is admissible to prove a public right, and a public right only."

Mr. Justice Stephen thus refers to the admissibility of such evidence:

" Statements of facts in issue, made in published maps or
charts, generally offered for public sale, *as to matters of
public notoriety,* such as the relative positions of towns or
countries, are themselves relevant facts, but such statements are irrelevant *if they relate to matters of private
concern.*"

The learned Chancellor referred to a case of *White* v.
Lisle, 4 Madd. 224, as supporting his view as to the reception of this evidence, but without conceding its applic-
ability to a case similar to the present, and conceding that
it may be admissible in cases of private right where a class
or district of persons are concerned, as where a covenant
had been entered into generally with the purchasers of lots
bordering on a square; I may say that there is nothing
here to shew that any class of persons had any rights with
the exception of the plaintiff. It was simply a contract
between his predecessor in title and Col. Denison, and so
far as the rest of the public are concerned, Col. Denison
was at liberty to use the square as he chose.

I concede, that from the manner in which Col. Denison,
who had an opportunity of explaining what the square
he referred to was, gave his explanation, very slight evidence of his knowledge of the existence of the city maps
at the time he entered into the covenant in question, would
have sufficed to sustain the learned Judge's finding.

He does not say, when asked what he meant by Bellevue Square, " I meant a certain portion of the property,"
defining it, but his answer is, " *Well, I do not know what.*
I did intend to have built myself a house on a lot in front
of the old homestead years ago. If I meant anything, I
meant that, but I certainly did not mean any portion of
the old place." And he subsequently goes on to explain,
that what he meant was a block in front of the present
residence towards the south.

This, somewhat vague as it is, is, in my opinion, the only
legal evidence of the situation and extent of the square;
and as Col. Denison had the opportunity of explaining
the position more definitely if he could, I think we may

assume as against him that it extended to the full extent of the 188 feet, which is referred to by him as lying in front of the homestead.

We may have our suspicions, from the fact that a porter's lodge was referred to in connection with the residence, that a larger square was intended, but we cannot decide questions of this nature by conjecture, we must consider upon whom is the onus of proof, and to the extent that that party has not succeeded in satisfying that onus, it is our duty to decide in favour of his opponent.

I cannot agree with the learned Judge below that this is the case of a person, who, having executed an instrument, seeks to lessen its force or effect by his own unsupported parol testimony. The deed is silent as to the extent or limits of the square. If any knowledge by Col. Denison of the existence of these maps at the time he entered into the contract, had been traced home to him, I quite agree that he could not reasonably hope that any Court would listen to an attempt to cut down the limits of the square thus described, by parol evidence, and especially by evidence given in the way I have mentioned; but there is, in my opinion, no evidence of any square at all if we strike out Col. Denison's testimony; and I think we ought to assume, as the persons who prepared these plans are alive, and could have proved the fact, if they were authorized by Col. Denison to insert the square as there delineated, that they could not do so.

I think in the course we propose taking, we are giving to the plaintiff the extreme right to which he has shewn himself entitled upon the evidence, and that the decree as to Col. Denison should be varied by restricting it to the square running back 188 feet from the street, and that as to the other defendants the bill should be dismissed, with costs.

PATTERSON, J. A.—I concur in the judgment delivered by his Lordship the Chief Justice. Nothing turns, in that judgment, upon the maps of the city which were received

in evidence in the Court below. I merely desire to say
that I have serious doubts of the admissibility of those
maps as evidence without more being shewn than was
shewn at the trial to connect the defendants in some way
with them, or to shew them to have been recognized by
the defendants as correct delineations of the alleged square.
On this point I may refer, in addition to the authorities
cited by my Brother Burton, to the judgment of the
Privy Council, in *Clark* v. *Elphinstone*, 6 App. Cas. 164,
where, at p. 172, some remarks are made by Sir Montague
E. Smith, upon some evidence of this character.

OSLER, J. A.—I agree that the plaintiff, though not in
terms the assignee of it, can maintain an action to enforce
a restrictive or negative covenant of this kind made by the
defendant with his predecessor in title,— that the language
of the deed is sufficient to constitute a covenant,—and that
the defendant Denison having again acquired the lands
which, by his covenant, he had burdened with the equity the
plaintiff seeks to enforce, may now be compelled to observe
it.   These are propositions clearly borne out by numerous
authorities.   It is sufficient to refer to the well-known case
of *Tulk* v. *Moxhay*, 11 Beav. 571, 2 Ph. 774, and to *Hay-
wood* v. *The Brunswick Building Society*, 8 Q. B. D. 403;
London and South Western R. W. Co. v. *Gomm*, 20 Ch.
D. 562; *McLean* v. *McKay*, L. R. 5 P. C. 327; *Sayers* v.
Collyer, 24 Ch. D. 180; *Lewin* on Trusts, 6th ed., 702.
    The defendant is not in a position to invoke against the
plaintiff the rule laid down in the leading case of *The Duke
of Bedford* v. *Trustees of the British Museum*, 2 My. & K.
552, and cognate cases such as *Peek* v. *Mathews*, L. R. 3 Eq.
510, and *Sayers* v. *Collyer*, 24 Ch. D. 180, because the
acts upon which he relies as having changed the character
and circumstances of the square, and the surrounding
property, are acts to which the plaintiff was no party,
in which he has not acquiesced, and which he was powerless to prevent. There does not appear to be any less valid
reason, apart from the hardship of the case (which is not

a reason), why so much of the original square as remains, and can be ascertained, should not still be subject to the defendant's covenant, than there was for fastening it upon the whole square twenty years ago. *Fry* on Specific Performance, 2nd ed. sec. 402.

The real, and as it has always seemed to me, the substantial difficulty in the case is, the question of fact which arises upon the evidence, namely, the identification of the property. The southern, eastern, and western boundaries of a plot of ground called Bellevue Square, are, I consider, sufficiently proved. It is with regard to the evidence for the northern boundary that I have felt myself unable to agree with the learned Chancellor. I cannot think that a square of this kind is to be looked upon as other than what it is in fact in the deed to Dr. Bovell, described as being : viz., private property, and not at all as of a public or *quasi* public nature. There is no evidence of its dedication to the public in any sense.

Certain maps of the city prepared, for anything known to the contrary, as a matter of private enterprise by the surveyors, whose names appear thereon, were produced at the trial. Their reception was objected to, and so far as they were admitted and made use of to prove or define the limits of the square in question, I am clearly of opinion that they were improperly admitted and used, on the short ground that it was not shewn either that they had been authorized, or prepared from information given by the defendant, or that he had in anyway recognized them as authentic. I refer on this point without repeating them, to the cases cited in the opinions which have just been delivered, and to *Clark* v. *Elphinstone*, 6 App. Cas. 164.

As, therefore, the decree proceeds upon the map of 1857 in declaring the northern boundary, it cannot be sustained to its full extent. But there is evidence given by the principal defendant himself, upon which we can properly find that the northern boundary was at least as far as 188 feet north of the south boundary.

The plaintiff may be satisfied with that, and if so, the decree should be varied accordingly.

If, however, he does not desire to take it in this form, we have no alternative but to allow the appeal, and dismiss the action against all the defendants.

RE CORPORATION OF THE TOWNSHIP OF ROMNEY AND CORPORATION OF THE TOWNSHIP OF MERSEA.

Drainage by-law—R. S. O. ch. 174, sec. 529—Petitioners—Land owners—Description of land—Private grievance.

A by-law was passed by the township of Mersea, providing for the drainage of lands in Mersea and Romney, and assessing property owners in both townships.

Held, that the by-law was invalid because the petition therefor did not describe the property to be benefited, and the by-law itself, which did shew the property to be benefited, disclosed that the petitioners were not the majority of the owners of such property.

Per BURTON, J. A.—Upon the evidence the corporation intended by the by-law to remedy a private grievance, and upon that ground also the by-law was bad.

THIS was an appeal by the corporation of Romney from the judgment of Armour, J., discharging an order *nisi* obtained by the appellants to quash a by-law passed by the township of Mersea for the drainage of lands in Mersea and Romney, assessing property-owners, &c., in both townships therefor.

The rule was as follows :

Upon reading the affidavits and papers filed, it is ordered that the corporation of the township of Mersea, upon notice to be given to them, their solicitor or agent, do appear and shew cause why the by-law of the said township of Mersea finally passed on the 2nd December last, called " The Bell and Extension Drain By-law," and known as by-law No. 330, should not be quashed in so far as it affects the township of Romney or any of the ratepayers

thereof, or the lands, roads and ditches therein, or why the
same should not be altogether quashed and set aside on the
following amongst other grounds : That a majority number
of the owners, as shewn by the last revised assessment
roll on the property to be benefited by the proposed drainage works in the township of Mersea, did not petition the
council of the corporation of the township of Mersea to pass
the said by-law, or to have the said lands either in Romney
or Mersea, or any of them, in the by-law mentioned and in
the report of their engineer to the Council of Romney set
forth and charged, drained : That the lands mentioned in
the petition asking for a drain, and the stopping up of culverts running to the north drains across the tenth concession of Mersea, and on which petition the report of the
engineer and by-law purport to be founded, are not identical, and there was and is no petition whereby the by-law
can be supported or founded : That the only petition upon
which the said by-law is founded contains ten names of
parties alleged to be owners assessed, whose property would
be benefited, who thereby sought to have a drain from lot
18 in front of the ninth concession to the centre of lot 21,
thence north to the line in front of the tenth concession,
and along the tenth concession from lot 18 eastward into
Romney to a drain called the Two Creeks Drain, and the
closing of the culverts across the tenth concession in an
assessment apparently of not over thirty assessed owners,
the by-law not only extends over those lots and concessions,
but is extended down and along Two Creeks Drain and
Two Creeks for some miles in Romney, and incorporating
the complaint of John W. Malott of his lands being over-
flowed by another drain, enacts the making of such extension of said proposed works, and charges the lands of over
fifty-three separately assessed lots and parts of lots and
the roads in Romney, and over or about thirty-four separately assessed lots or parts of lots in Mersea and its
roads along several concessions, none of which were con-
plated by said petition, so that they are entirely dissimilar,
and the by-law is bad : That the said council were not
authorized to remedy a complaint of an individual by
incorporating a supposed remedy therefor in said by-law,
and levying a tax therefor, that said by-law is bad in that
respect also ; and the council having no power to assess
lands as they have done on such a complaint, the by-law
would be bad on that ground also alone : That under the
circumstances disclosed by the affidavits and papers filed,

the said by-law is bad so far as it may, under the drainage laws, affect the township of Romney or bind that corporation to pass a by-law to raise the moneys imposed by it on lands and roads in Romney : That the said by-law, on grounds set forth in the affidavits and papers filed, unlawfully imposes a duty on the corporation of the township of Romney, and unlawfully imposes a tax for said drainage works on the roads and lands of individuals in Romney, and on these and other grounds set forth in the affidavits and papers filed, ought to be quashed, with costs.

On motion of Mr. J. K. Kerr, Q. C., of counsel for the said corporation of the township of Romney.

By the Court.

JOHN WINCHESTER,

Registrar, Q. B. D.

After argument the learned Judge gave this judgment :

ARMOUR, J.—It is impossible for me sitting alone to hold, even were I so disposed, in the face of *Re Montgomery and Raleigh,* 21 C. P. 381, and *Re White and Sandwich East,* 1 O. R. 530, that the by-law in question is invalid by reason of the objection taken that a majority of all the owners benefited by the proposed drainage had not signed the petition on which the by-law was founded, but that only a majority of the owners within the boundaries of a particular area benefited by it had signed the petition, or that this objection is such an one as suffices to render the by-law invalid.

Nor do I think the by-law open to the objection that it was passed with the twofold purpose of draining the particular area and of removing Malott's cause of complaint, for I think the facts shew that it was passed for the single purpose of draining the particular area, and though the effect of such drainage would be to remove Malott's cause of complaint.

I think, therefore, the order *nisi* must be discharged, with costs.

The appeal from this judgment was heard on the 9th day of December, 1884.*

C. R. *Atkinson,* for the appellants.

Robinson, Q. C., for the respondents.

**Present :—*HAGARTY, C. J. O., BURTON, PATTERSON, and OSLER, JJ. A.

January 26, 1885. HAGARTY, C. J. O.—It is only on the first branch of the short judgment of my brother Armour that anything turns.

There is nothing, we think, in the second branch as to Malott's cause of complaint.

The main, we may say the only question necessary for discussion, arises thus : The statute seems to require as a condition precedent to the action of the municipality as follows : in sec. 529 of the Municipal Act, R. S. O. ch. 174, (substantially the same as sec. 570 of Municipal Act, 1883.) In case the majority in number of the persons as shewn by the last revised assessment roll, to be the owners (whether resident or non-resident), *of the property to be benefited* in any part of any township, &c., petitions the council for the deepening of any stream * * or *for draining of the property (describing it)*, the council may procure an examination to be made by an engineer of the streams * * proposed to be deepened, or of the locality proposed to be drained, and may procure plans and estimates to be made of the work by such engineer, and an assessment, to be made by such engineer, of the real property to be benefited by such deepening or drainage, stating as nearly as may be * * the proportion of benefit to be derived by such deepening or drainage, by any road or lot or portion of lot. And if the council be of opinion that the deepening, * * or the drainage *of the locality described*, or a portion thereof, would be desirable, the council may pass by-laws for the deepening * * or the draining of the locality, &c.

On 17th April, 1882, the following petition was presented to the Mersea Council :

To the Reeve and Deputy Reeve of the Township of Mersea :

GENTLEMEN,—Your petitioners on the 8th and 9th concessions desire that the water crossing the 10th concession on lot 21 be conveyed along the south side of 10th concession into the Two Creeks Drain in the township of Romney, and also extend west on south side of 10th concession road, say to side road ; also from 10th to 9th concession in the centre of lot 21; thence west on south side of 9th concession road, say to the Creighton side road, and that the culvert fronting lot 19 on 9th concession, also culvert on 10th concession fronting lot 21, be closed, and said drain be made sufficient, and a rate levied on said lots and parts of lots and roads benefited, and that money be borrowed to complete the work, and that the time for paying the principal and interest do not extend five years, and your petitioners will ever pray.

    (Signed)   GEORGE BELL,
                           CHRISTOPHER COULTER,
                           ALEXANDER WHUTTAL,
                           FRANCIS WHUTTAL,
                           WILLIAM EVERS,
                           JAMES ARMSTRONG,
                           MARY WILLANS,
                           JOSEPH DALES,
                           WILLIAM DALES,
                           ISAAC DALES, JR.

On 15th May following, according to the affidavit of Lamarshe, the reeve, "the prayer of George Bell's petition was granted, and the township engineer Alex. Baird, was instructed to make the necessary survey, plans, and estimates of cost."

On July 17th Baird presented his report, plans, and estimates of the Bell drain and its outlet, and the report was adopted.

On 25th August the by-law was read a first time and published.

On 29th September the Court of Revision met and adjourned to October 13th, and again to October 24th and November 4th, at which meetings eleven appeals made against the assessments in Mersea were heard and determined.

On 2nd December the by-law was read a third time and passed.

On 11th December the township of Romney, the appellants, served notice on the Mersea Council of application to be made to quash the by-law.

It is sworn that no opposition was made to the passing of the by-law on behalf of Romney, and no notice of appeal or for arbitration given.

This is the by-law No. 330:

"A by-law to provide for draining parts of the township of Mersea by the construction of the Bell Drain, and for borrowing on the credit of the municipality the sum of $4, 390 for completing the same.

"Provisionally adopted the 24th day of August, A.D. 1882.

"Whereas, a majority in number of the owners as shewn by the last revised assessment roll to be resident on the property hereinafter set forth, to be benefited by the construction of the Bell drain, have petitioned the Council of the said township of Mersea, praying that the waters crossing the 10th concession on lot 21 be conveyed along the south side of 10th concession into the Two Creeks Drain in the township of Romney, and extended west on the south side of the 10th concession road, &c., and whereas notice was served on the council by John W. Malott, complaining that the waters in the Dales and Extension Drain are overflowing his lands.

"And whereas, thereupon, the said council procured an examination to be made by Alexander Baird, P. L. S., being a person competent for such purpose, of the said locality proposed to be drained by the construction of said drain, and has also procured plans and estimates of the work to be made by the said Alexander Baird, and an assessment to be made by him of the real property to be benefited by the construction of said drain, stating, as nearly as he can, the proportion of benefit which in his opinion will be derived in consequence of such construction by every road and lot or portion of lot; the said assessment so made, and the report of the said Alexander Baird in respect thereof, and the said drain being as follows:

"'In compliance with your instructions, I have made a survey of the drain petitioned for by George Bell and others, and beg to report thereon as follows: The drain commences on the south side of the road between concessions 8 and 9, at the west side of lot No. 19; thence runs easterly along the south side of said road to the centre of lot 21; thence north across said road and through the centre of said lot 21 in the 9th concession to the south side of the road between concessions 9 and 10; thence east along the south side of the last mentioned road to Two Creeks Drain, in the township of Romney; thence

down this last mentioned drain in the township of Romney
and the creek of the same name, to the dead water in said
creek, 34 rods south of Talbot street on lot number 5 in
the 1st concession of the said township of Romney.

"'Connecting with the main drain on the road between
concessions 9 and 10 aforesaid, at the centre of lot 21, is
a branch drain which runs west along the south side of
the concession road last mentioned, to the east side of the
18 and 19 side road, Mersea.

"'I would recommend that the culvert on the 9th concession road, opposite the west part of lot 19, and the one
on the 10th concession road, opposite the centre of lot 21,
be removed and the excavation over which they stand be
filled in. My estimate of the cost of the work is $4,390.
This sum I assess against the lands and roads benefited as
per schedule, the drain to be kept in repair at the joint
expense of the lands and roads assessed for its construction, each paying in the same relative proportion as for
construction.'

"And whereas the said council are of opinion that the
drainage of the locality described is desirable :

"Be it therefore enacted by the said municipal council
of the township of Mersea, pursuant to the provisions of
ch. 174, of the Revised Statutes of Ontario :

"That the said report, plans, and estimates be adopted,
and the said drain and the works connected therewith be
made and constructed in accordance therewith."

Schedules are annexed to the by-law shewing an assessment on lots and roads as benefited.

Total cost, $4,390.
    Assessed against some 75 lots in Mersea.. $1980
    Roads in Mersea......................   970
    Against lands and roads in Romney 1440
                                         _____
                                          $4390

Seventy-eight properties are assessed in Romney.

These assessments on about 150 properties in the two
townships are the result of the ten freeholders' petition.

The question is, is there a sufficient legal foundation for
the action of the council ?

Can we hold that the statute has been complied with—
that the majority of the owners of the property to be

benefited in any part of the township have petitioned the
council for the *draining of any described property ?* or
is there in the petition anything from which it can be
inferred that petitioners are such majority, or where their
property is, beyond that they call themselves "your petitioners on the 8th and 9th concessions?" They ask that
the water crossing the 10th concession on lot 21 be conveyed along the south side of the 10th concession into the
Two Creeks Drain in Romney, and also extend west on
south side of 10th concession road, say to side road ; also
from 10th to 9th concessions in the centre of lot 21 ; then
west on south side of 9th concession road to the Creigh-
tons side road; then as to closing two named culverts,
and they ask that a rate be levied on said lots and parts
of lots and road benefited.

We are wholly unable to find any area or specified
locality or of any particular property described or shewn
in this petition.

In affidavits it is attempted to be shewn that some seven
lots formed the locality "immediately to be benefited."

Mr. Baird in one of his plans colors this alleged locality
" green." Outside of the green portions several lots
appear between them and Romney town line, and the
petition proposes to drain into the Two Creeks Drain or
watercourse in Romney.

Then the by-law asserts that a majority of the owners
resident on the property thereinafter set forth, to be benefited by the proposed drain, have petitioned, &c.

And that the engineer has examined the locality proposed to be drained by said drain, and has made assessments of the real property to be benefited by its
construction, and the proportion of benefit derivable by
every road and lot. It then proceeds to declare the
amounts to be assessed and levied, as already stated, on
some 150 properties and on a number of roads in said
township.

It seems very difficult to hold that the statute has been
complied with, so as to enable the council to pass this
by-law.

In one of the cases relied on by Mr. Justice Armour—
Re Montgomery and Corporation of Raleigh, 21 C. P. 381,
a very carefully considered judgment of the Court of Common Pleas was delivered by Mr. Justice Gwynne.

We shall have occasion to notice it more hereafter, especially in his reference to the petition on which the by-law there was grounded.

We have sent for the original papers, and find that the petition represented that it "would greatly benefit the township and the lands hereinafter mentioned," if certain drainage was carried out, and it prays therefor, and that the costs be "assessed and collected from the mentioned property as well as any property to be benefited in the adjoining municipalities," &c.

Then it subjoins a list of the lots and the signatures of each petitioner, shewing his lot.

The by-law in that case recited that a majority of the resident landowners of the lots, setting out the lots by name, had petitioned and that the council thought it would greatly benefit that portion of the township, and they instruct their surveyor to report, &c.

It recites appeals by two adjoining municipalities, and arbitrations had, and the amount awarded to be paid by each, and it merely assesses the Raleigh lots and roads enumerated at and for the amount to be paid by Raleigh. These lots appears to be the same referred to in the petition.

The report of the surveyor charged a number of lots in adjoining township.

We do not see how this case can aid this by-law under circumstances so very different.

It seemed conceded on the argument of this appeal, that, if the petitioners referred to a specified locality as the property requiring drainage, it might be sufficient to warrant the passing of a by-law, based on the report of the engineer, shewing other lands outside or beyond such locality to be benefited, and therefore assessable.

But even with this admission, assuming it for the argument to be proper, the case before us seems fatally defective — everything as to any particular locality being omitted, and no means therefore available to know if a majority had petitioned.

Gwynne, J., says, at p. 395: "In some future case it may be necessary to determine *what majority* is sufficient to procure the action of a council. Four concessions in a township may be interested, in different degrees, in a work which would drain *all the lands* in those concessions, but it might be of more importance to the owners of the lands *in one* of these concessions than to all the owners of lands in the other three to procure the construction of the work. As at present advised we do not see that a majority of the resident owners in the *one* concession would not comply with the terms of the Act, namely, ' In case a majority in number of the resident owners, as shewn by the last revised assessment roll, of the property to be benefited *in any part of any municipality*, do petition the council,' &c., but in the present case there appears to be no foundation for the objection."

In another place he says, p. 394 : " Treating the by-law, with the schedule thereto annexed, to be a finding by the council, impliedly, that these are the only lands in Raleigh benefited by the work, the petition appears to have been signed by a majority of the resident *owners* of the property assessed."

It seems clear that that case was not open to the objections pressed against the case before us.

In *Re White and Corporation of Sandwich*, 1 O. R. 530, before my Brother Cameron, the petition set out the lots to be drained; the applicant to quash the by-law was not a petitioner; nor was his land part of the land mentioned ; nor did he reside on any part of the land described.

The petitioners were a majority of the owners of the land mentioned. The applicant was assessed as a party benefited, and the by-law was held valid as against him. The learned Judge says: "As the tax for such drains is a local tax and the work can only be authorized on the principle of local taxation, in the first place, at the instance of the majority of those whose lands are to be improved

or benefited, it may be with much force contended that
only those petitioning and the minority coming within the
express terms of the petition can be made liable to pay
for the cost of the work."

He holds, however, that *Re Montgomery and Raleigh*, is
an authority binding on him to hold that others may be
bound, and he quotes largely from the judgment.

At all events *Re White and Corporation of Sandwich*,
is an authority as to the requirements of a proper petition.

In re Corporation of Essex and Rochester, 42 U. C. R.
523, the law is much discussed, but the points affecting
our case do not arise.

Re Corporations of Dover and Chatham, 5 O. R. 325,
does not touch the question.

As far as we possibly can, we desire to uphold the evident desire of the Legislature that all disputes and difficulties arising in these municipal matters should be settled
by the means provided in the statutes.   But whatever
appears plainly to be made a condition precedent to the
right of the municipality to initiate legislation, we are
bound to see that it exists.

We think we are bound to hold that there was nothing
before the council to warrant their adoption or passing of
this by-law, and that we must allow this appeal and quash
the by-law.

We do not desire to discuss any wider question than
that which we find necessary for the decision of the case.

BURTON, J.A.—I think the objection in the reasons of
appeal that the petition does not describe the property to
be benefited, and that the by-law based upon it, and which
does profess to shew the property benefited, and discloses
that the petitioners were not in point of fact the majority
in number of the owners of the property to be benefited,
is well taken, and is fatal to the validity of the by-law,
which the court below was asked to quash.

It is impossible to ascertain from the petition itself what
lands the council were asked to levy the rate upon, as the

lots or parts of lots benefited, if the petitioners intended to convey the meaning to the council that the lands, of which they were the respective owners in the 8th and 9th concessions, were the lands in respect of which the drainage was sought, and that they were willing to be assessed therefor. A by-law founded upon it might properly enough be upheld, but this petition read in connection with the by-law amounts to this, that ten persons, residing upon a particular concession in the township of Mersea, propose to tax between sixty and seventy owners of lands in other portions of the township, and some seventy-five in the township of Romney, on the alleged ground that their properties will be benefited. If that be the fact, then it must be manifest that a majority such as the statute contemplates, before the council can proceed to act, has not been obtained.

I do not think that either of the cases cited by the learned Judge support such a by-law as this, and I feel quite clear that a by-law based upon such a petition cannot be sustained.

This is sufficient to dispose of the case, but I cannot help feeling, notwithstanding the learned Judge's finding in reference to Malott's complaint, that the corporation did intend to remedy the grievance of which he complained at the expense of the ratepayers affected by this special rate. I merely refer to it in order that these municipal bodies may not entertain the impression that such a proceeding would be legal, or that a by-law tainted by such a proceeding, clearly made out, could be allowed to stand.

I think the appeal must be allowed, and the by-law quashed, with costs.

PATTERSON AND OSLER, JJ.A., concurred.

Appeal allowed, with costs.

STILLWELL v. RENNIE ET AL.

Jury separating—Consent of counsel—New trial.

At the trial it appeared that the counsel for P. had left the Court before the Judge's charge, having authorized F., counsel for two other defendants, to take on his behalf any objections he might think proper to the charge. The jury, after hearing the Judge's charge, were allowed to separate and be at large from Saturday till Monday, before giving their verdict, which was against the defendants P. and R.

Held, [reversing the decision of the Queen's Bench Division, 7 O. R. 355,] that such a proceeding could not be upheld except upon clear affirmative evidence of consent expressly and knowingly given ; and, therefore, where counsel for the defendant P. had left the Court before the Judge's charge, and it did not appear that he had authorized any one to represent him or his client, or that any one had consented or assumed to consent on behalf of P. to the jury separating, a new trial as to P. was directed.

Per OSLER, J. A.—Had F. assumed to represent the counsel for P. in assenting to the separation of the jury, P. would have been bound to the same extent as if his own counsel had taken a similar course, contrary to instructions.

AN appeal by the defendant Pattullo from the judgment of the Queen's Bench Division, (7 O. R. 355,) discharging an order *nisi* for a new trial, which he sought upon the ground that the jury had, after hearing the Judge's charge, been allowed to separate and be at large from Saturday to Monday before giving their verdict; and also upon the ground that while the jury were so at large, a public newspaper had published some comments upon the case calculated to prejudice the said defendant.

The facts and authorities cited appear in the report of the case in the Court below, and in the present judgments. The appeal was heard on the 15th May, 1885.*

McCarthy, Q. C., and *Wallace Nesbitt,* for the appellant. *Delamere,* for the respondent.

May 26, 1885. HAGARTY, C. J. O.—No statement of defence was fyled by either Knight or Rennie.

Defendant Pattullo defended the claim, Mr. Ball acting as his counsel.

**Present.—*HAGARTY, C. J. O., BURTON, PATTERSON, and OSLER, JJ.A.

Mr. Falconbridge acted as counsel for Knight and Rennie.

Under the old practice the appearance of counsel at a trial where no defence was pleaded, would have been merely in mitigation of damages.

Mr. Ball left the Court before the Judge had charged the jury, having requested Mr. Falconbridge, the counsel for the other defendants, to take any objections which he might think proper to the charge on behalf of Pattullo.

After the jury had been given in charge, and had retired to consider their verdict, they returned to Court declaring their inability to agree, except as to Knight. The jury were most anxious to get away by the train, it being Saturday afternoon, and they were allowed by the learned Judge to separate and to meet again on Monday morning and consider their verdict.

Mr. Delamere for the plaintiff consented to this, and so did Mr. Falconbridge on behalf of Rennie and Knight. But we see no statement of his offering any consent as to Pattullo.

In his affidavit he states that beyond Mr. Ball's request to take any exceptions to the charge, and telegraph the result to him, he " was in no sense left in charge of the case for the defendant Pattullo nor representing him."

On the Monday morning, Mr. Ball objected for Pattullo to the jury having been allowed to separate and to meet again, and asserted that he had never consented to them separating, or that they should meet again to consider their verdict.

They, however, were allowed to meet and did deliver their verdict, acquitting Knight, and $500 damages against Pattullo and Rennie.

Except on the clear consent of counsel in a civil suit, we do not see how it is possible to support a verdict rendered as this was. After the Judge's charge, and the jury being given in charge in the usual manner to consider their verdict, we have never heard of any separation and re-assembling having been allowed. Indeed, we may venture to say that we have never met in practice with any instance of such a thing having occurred even by consent.

We are unable to see anything in the statement of the case, or of the trial, to make us believe that Mr. Falconbridge professed to consent for Pattullo.

Mr. Ball in leaving the Court had no reason whatever for anticipating such an unusual event as the separation and subsequent assembling of the jury after being once given in charge. A verdict rendered as this has been, would without question have been held invalid, in the total absence of a defendant or his counsel. Nothing but an express consent could, in our opinion, have rendered such a proceeding effective.

If we rightly understand the view of the Court below, it was that they were not satisfied that Mr. Falconbridge did not consent.

With much respect, we may state our view to be that the proceeding could not be upheld except on clear affirmative evidence of consent—consent beyond reasonable doubt expressly and knowingly given.

As we understand the facts, there was no such evidence. If Mr. Falconbridge did expressly consent for Pattullo, another question, viz., as to his authority, would have been raised. But as already remarked, we cannot see that he gave the Court to understand that he was acting for Pattullo, or consenting on his behalf.

We think the proper course is, to allow the appeal, with costs as to defendant Pattullo, and make the rule absolute below for a new trial as to him, without costs.

BURTON, J. A.—I agree, and I only wish to add a word in reference to the extraordinary course taken at the trial; if the report before us be accurate, the result, I fear, of the recent changes in pleading.

I gather from the book that there was no defence by two of the defendants; a case in which formerly, whatever may be the present practice, an entry of judgment by default would have been made upon the record, and damages assessed against them, there being no issue to try. Instead of this a verdict appears to have been rendered in favour of one of these defendants, and a motion for a non-suit very strenuously urged in favour of the other, though unsuccessfully.

As to the third defendant, the one who had pleaded, no motion for a nonsuit appears to have been made, but Mr. McCarthy now makes an application for a nonsuit, based, however, upon the ground that although the evidence given on the part of the plaintiff might, unexplained, have been sufficient to go to the jury, when explained by the evidence of the defendant it was clear that no case was made out. I do not think that position tenable. If there was any evidence fit to be submitted to the jury at the end of the plaintiff's case, any explanation of that evidence on the part of the defendant was necessarily for the jury, and not for the Judge.

If the point had been taken at the close of the plaintiff's case, that there was no evidence fit to be submitted to the jury, it might have been renewed in the Divisional Court and before us with much force, for I think I never saw a case in which a large verdict for libel was sought to be sustained against a person, not the author of the libel or privy to its publication, upon more meagre evidence—some of it, in fact, not evidence at all, but a mere statement of the witness's impressions. I think if I had been asked, as presiding Judge at the trial to decide, as it would have been my duty to decide, whether there was any evidence that the defendant was the proprietor of the paper, so as to make him in law responsible for the acts of the publisher,—the onus of proving which was upon the plaintiff—I should have held that there was none, adopting the well-known aphorism of Mr. Justice Maule, in *Jewell* v. *Parr*, 13 C. B. 909, 916 : " When we say that there is no evidence to go to a jury, we do not mean that there is literally none, but that there is none which ought reasonably to satisfy a jury that the fact sought to be proved is established." A remark founded on sound sense, which was fully approved of and adopted in the House of Lords in *Jackson* v. *The Metropolitan R. W. Co.*, 3 App. Cas. 193, 207, and which has never been questioned in any subsequent decision.

That objection ought, however, to have been taken at a time when the plaintiff might possibly have supplied the omission, and cannot be urged now, and was not in fact urged except upon the ground I have mentioned, which is not, as I have said, in my opinion tenable.

OSLER, J. A.—It is not arguable, and Mr. Delamere did not attempt to argue, that without consent the jury could have been allowed to separate, after having been given in charge, and afterwards to reassemble and consider and deliver their verdict.

The only question therefore is, whether Mr. Falconbridge consented, or must be taken to have consented on behalf of Mr. Ball, the counsel for Pattullo, as he undoubtedly did on behalf of his own clients, to the separation of the jury. The note of the official reporter as to what occurred is as follows : " On application of the jury, and by consent of Mr. Falconbridge and Mr. Delamere, Mr. Ball having left for home immediately after his address to the jury, the jury were allowed to separate till Monday, when they were to assemble at 11 o'clock and consider as to their verdict."

The affidavits of Mr. Falconbridge and Mr. Ball, in effect, agree in stating that just before the jury left the Court, the latter asked the former to take such objections to the Judge's charge as he might think proper, of which Mr Ball's client might have the benefit, if it became necessary to move.

It does not appear that the plaintiff's counsel knew that Mr. Falconbridge had received any instructions to act for Mr. Ball. Nor is there any affidavit either that the plaintiff was misled into assenting to the course which was taken, by the belief that Mr. Falconbridge was acting for all the defendants, or that in fact he did act, or profess to act for Mr. Ball, or for any one but his own clients. Nor is anything of the kind asserted in the reasons against the appeal, which on this point merely urge that the counsel for Pattullo by absenting himself from the trial of the cause before the same was concluded, must be taken to have consented to the separation of the jury. I need hardly say that Mr. Delamere cited no authority for that proposition.

On such a state of facts, as I have mentioned, I am, with great deference, of opinion that there is nothing from which we can or ought to say that any consent was given, or must be taken to have been given, on behalf of the defendant Pattullo to the separation of the jury. If the plaintiff's counsel did not know or believe, and in the absence of an affidavit on this point we cannot assume that he did know or believe, that Mr. Falconbridge was to any extent instructed to represent Mr. Ball, then he was not misled by the consent actually given, and, therefore, there is no reason why a more extensive authority should be imputed than that which was actually conferred.

On this ground, and on this ground only, I agree that the appeal must be allowed.

If Mr. Falconbridge had assumed to represent Mr. Ball, and had assented to the separation of the jury, an entirely different question would have arisen. I should in that case be of opinion that, notwithstanding the limited nature of his instructions, the defendant would be bound by what he did, just as he would have been bound if Mr. Ball himself had taken a similar course contrary to instructions. The opposite party would have had the right to rely on the assumption, that counsel appearing in the cause was authorized to take, at least in a matter relating to the mere conduct of the cause, such course as commended itself to his judgment and discretion, even though of so unusual a character as occurred in the present case.

As to the motion for nonsuit I am clearly of opinion that there was evidence fit to be submitted, and which the learned Judge could not, with propriety, have ¦with_ drawn from the jury. On the general question I refer to the cases of *Murray* v. *The Canada Central R. W. Co.*, 7 A. R. 646, 8 App. Cas. 574; *McLaren* v. *The Canada Central R. W. Co.*, 8 A. R. 564, and in the Privy Council, 21 C. L. J. p. 114.

The appeal is on behalf of the defendant Pattullo only. As regards the two other defendants Rennie and Knight the case took rather an unusual course at the trial.

As appears from the statement on page nine of the appeal book, these defendants did not deliver any statement of defence. It is not stated that interlocutory judgment had been signed against them under Rule 206, (*Maclennan*, p. 344) and they would seem to have been allowed to defend at the trial as if they had pleaded in denial of their liability, and even to move for a nonsuit, instead of being confined to mitigation of damages.

In this way a verdict was found against the defendants Pattullo and Knight, as being the proprietors of the paper at the time of the publication of the article, with damages assessed at $500, and the defendant Knight, who as well as Rennie had not pleaded, had nevertheless a verdict found in his favour. On this appeal Rennie has not appeared, nor has any question been raised as to the disposition of the case as against him and Knight. As to those two defendants, therefore, who are not in a position to complain of what was done at the trial, we see no reason why the verdict and judgment should not stand. As to Pattullo the rule in the Court below should be made absolute for a new trial, without costs.

PATTERSON, J. A., concurred.

Appeal allowed, with costs.

FERGUSON V. McMARTIN.

County Court—Trial without a jury—Setting aside verdict and judgment—
Constitution of Court—Motion—Appeal—R. 510, O. J. A.

An action in the County Court of Carleton was tried without a jury by
the Junior Judge of that County, who, after consideration, entered a
verdict for the defendant.

A Court composed of the senior and junior Judges of Carleton, and the
Judge of the County Court of Prescott and Russell subsequently
assumed to set aside the verdict, and to enter judgment for the plaintiff,
dissentiente the junior Judge of Carleton.

Held, that the judgment of a Court so constituted was invalid, and that
the verdict at the trial was not affected thereby.

Per PATTERSON, J. A.—The verdict at the trial was a final judgment of
the Court, and could not be attacked except by an appeal to this Court.
Rule 510, O. J. A., gives a party no right to move in the County Court.

Per OSLER, J. A.—The party dissatisfied with the judgment at the trial
may, under Rule 510, O. J. A., move against it before the Judge himself; and an appeal to this Court may, under 45 Vict. ch. 6, sec. 4, as
properly be brought from the decision on such motion as from the judgment at the trial.

THIS was an appeal by the defendants from a judgment
of the County Court of Carleton, assuming to set aside the
verdict and judgment for the defendant enteied by the
Junior Judge of that county, who tried the case without
a jury.

The material facts are set out in the judgment of Patterson, J. A.

The appeal was heard on the 15th and 16th days of
February, 1885.*

J. Maclennan, Q. C., for the appeal.

Moss, Q. C., contra.

March 3, 1885.   PATTERSON, J. A.—This is an action in
the County Court of the county of Carleton to recover
damages for taking timber.   It was tried on the 14th and
15th December, 1883, before the Junior Judge of the
county, without a jury. His Honour took time to consider,
and on 12th January, 1884, he gave judgment for the
defendant.   He indorsed his finding on the copy of
pleadings.

Present.—HAGARTY, C.J.O., BURTON, PATTERSON, and OSLER, JJ.A.

" Verdict for defendant without costs, and I order judgment to be entered accordingly."

Judgment was entered upon that order, on 17th January. On 29th January an order was made in Chambers, on the application of the plaintiff, setting aside that judgment, and on the same day an order *nisi* was issued calling on the defendant to shew cause why the verdict found by his Honour Judge Lyon on 12th January, and the judgment entered thereon on 17th January should not be set aside, and a verdict and judgment entered for the plaintiff.

After argument this order was made absolute on 21st February, 1884.

Elaborate written judgments were delivered by the Senior and Junior Judges. The latter adhered to his previous decision and the former took a different view of the merits. We are informed, though the fact does not appear directly from the papers certified to this Court, that a third Judge, the Judge of the County Court of an adjoining county, sat with the two Judges of the county of Carleton, on the argument, and concurred with the judgment of the Senior Judge.

The defendant appeals from that judgment, stating the following as his first ground of appeal :

" Because the judgment at the trial was a judgment of the Court, and final judgment was entered thereon before any application to set the same aside, and the Judge or Court had no jurisdiction or authority to review the same or set it aside."

A reference to some provisions of the Judicature Act and the rules under it will shew the objection to be fatal.

The County Courts are governed by that Act in all matters in question on this appeal.

Rule 486 abolishes County Court terms, and enacts that there shall be sittings of the Court at and for the same periods as the terms. The abolished January term began, in 1884, on 7th January and ended on the 12th. The order now complained of was not made during any term, or period substituted therefor. It is headed: "Special January Sittings." I am not sure that I understand what that means. If it has reference to rule 488, which gives power to the Judges of County Courts to sit and act at any time for the transaction of any part of the business of such Courts, or for the discharge of any duty which, by any statute or otherwise, is required to be discharged out of or during term, it plainly recognizes the Judicature Act as applicable to the proceeding now questioned.

It may not be necessary at present to inquire whether the right to move against a verdict in the County Court can now be exercised at any time except during the periods corresponding with the term in which the motion could have been formerly made. It is clear that if the motion now in question had to rest upon the former law as found in the County Courts Act, R. S. O. ch. 43, secs. 29, 30; and in the C. L. P. Act, R. S. O. ch. 50, secs. 284, 285, 286, 287, 292, 293, the judgment could not be sustained, even if no objection were insisted on except the want of jurisdiction to make the order out of term.

The principal objection under the Judicature Act is to the jurisdiction itself, without special regard to the time at which, in this case, it was exercised.

Under the sections of the C. L. P. Act to which I have just adverted, the practice and procedure of the County Courts corresponded with those of the Superior Courts of law in the matter of moving against the findings of either jury or Judge. Therefore, under rule 490 of the Judicature Act, the practice and procedure for the time being of the High Court of Justice apply and extend to County Courts.

By sec. 28, subsec. 2, O. J. A., a Judge, sitting elsewhere than in a Divisional Court, is to decide all questions coming properly before him, and is not to reserve any case for the consideration of a Divisional Court.

This was the course pursued by Judge Lyon at the trial of this action.

Rules 307 to 314 provide for applications for new trials in jury cases, by orders *nisi*.

I believe those are the only motions in which such an order is expressly authorized by the Rules. Rule 405 forbids the granting of any such order, except in the cases where it is expressly authorized.

When a Judge has given judgment, either upon the findings of a jury, or when he tries an action without a jury, the rule which in cases in the High Court of Justice provides for reviewing his judgment is No. 510.

Under that rule the application may be either to a Divisional Court, or to the Court of Appeal.

No time was limited by the rules 316 and 317, for which rule 510 was substituted, nor is any time limited by rule 510 itself, for such an application. Now, by rule 523, an application to the Divisional Court of the Chancery Division to change or reverse any judgment is to be made at the time there fixed; and by rule 527, the time for applications in the Queen's Bench and Common Pleas Divisions under rule 510 is provided for, that time not being quite the same as prescribed for the Chancery Division. In this particular, therefore, there is not a uniform practice in the High Court.

When rule 510 authorizes an application to this Court against the judgment of a Judge who tries an action, there is no difficulty in understanding it, when read along with rule 490, and with the statute 45 Vict. ch. 6, sec. 4, which allows an appeal from every decision or order disposing of any right or claim, provided the decision or order is in its nature final, and not merely interlocutory, as applying to County Courts as well as to the High Court of Justice. But when it gives a choice between coming at once to the Court of Appeal and applying to a Divisional Court, can that be held to establish a practice and procedure which, under rule 490. shall apply and extend to County Courts?

There is, I apprehend, no doubt that a County Court, sitting at the times which represent the abolished terms, is intended to exercise the same functions which by rules

307, *et seq.*, are expressly given to Divisional Courts only, in hearing motions for new trials in jury cases.

It might not be easy to give a satisfactory reason, if we had to look merely at the language of rule 510, for holding that the power there given to Divisional Courts to review the judgment of a Judge, should not in like manner extend to a County Court.

But we have to bear in mind the subject matter of the different rules. In one case it is the verdict of a jury which is to be reviewed, not by the persons who pronounced it, but by the Court. If not reviewable under these rules, 307, &c., the verdict would always have to stand unchallenged. Besides, what the Court has to do is not to reverse or vary the verdict, but to consider whether the case should not be submitted to another jury.

In the other case the Judge has, under section 28, given his considered judgment, and the motion would be to himself to reconsider it.

In some counties, it is true, there may be a second Judge, so that the motion may not of necessity be to the same Judge, but may happen to be in the scarcely more satisfactory shape of an application to one Judge to reverse the judgment of another. That chance where it exists is an accident. The normal position is an appeal to the Judge to-day to reconsider and reverse what he did yesterday.

There is no analogy between such a proceeding and a motion to a Divisional Court which, under the express terms of section 29, must comprise at least two Judges, whose judgment is not in question.

It seems to me impossible, in the face of section 29, to treat the Divisional Court referred to in Rule 510, as having any counterpart in County Court procedure; and if it were possible, there would be no necessity for so treating it. To do so would be to encourage and justify proceedings in those Courts, which would involve delay and expense, while they could seldom serve any useful purpose when the Judges, in obedience to section 28, consider the judgments they give after a trial.

A case can be as fully argued and as carefully considered on a motion for judgment, as upon a motion to reverse a judgment given without consideration.

In the present case the learned Judge took time to consider before he pronounced judgment after the trial.

The anomaly of rehearing the case before the junior Judge, or before the two Judges, was perceived; and an attempt was made to avoid it by constituting a Court of three Judges.

There is no warrant that we are aware of for that proceeding. There is certainly none to be found in the statutes to which we were referred, viz., the Local Courts Act and the County Courts Act, R. S. O. chs. 42 and 43.

The judgment in question was that of a majority of the Court so constituted, the two Judges of the county of Carleton differing in their views. That cannot be recognized as a valid judgment of the County Court of the county of Carleton.

This objection to the judgment, which however is not distinctly taken as a ground of appeal, might suffice to cause the allowance of the appeal. But the ground of which notice is distinctly given is fatal to the judgment. I have shewn why I hold that Rule 510 cannot be construed so as to give a right to move in the County Court itself, or to attack the judgment anywhere but in this Court; and if the right is not given by that rule it nowhere exists. But I do not say that the right to appeal depends on Rule 510, or that that rule must have any necessary application to the procedure of the County Courts The judgment being in its nature final, an appeal is given by the direct effect of 45 Vict. ch. 6, sec. 4, (O.) without the aid of the Judicature Act.

We cannot help the respondent by treating this as an appeal from the judgment at the trial, as I thought we were justified in doing in *Williams* v. *Crow*, 10 A.R. 301, because the appellant is supporting that judgment and attacking the proceeding which assumed to reverse it. We must allow the appeal, and the appellant should have his costs of the appeal, but only such costs as would have been incurred if he had appealed only on the ground of the jurisdiction on which he has succeeded. We have not reached the merits of the contest, having been stopped *in limine*, and a good deal of the expense, particularly of printing, must have been connected with that part of the contest which we have not reached. We fix this item of costs to be taxed as the cost of an appeal book of ten pages.

The order in the Court below is, of course, to be vacated, but there should no costs of the motion there for two reasons: because there was no jurisdiction there to entertain it; and because the question of jurisdiction on which the appellant now succeeds was not raised there.

OSLER, J. A.—We have been referred to nothing in the Local Courts Act, or the County Courts Act, R. S. O. chs. 42, 43, which confers authority upon the Judges of the County Courts of two or three, or any number of counties, to sit together and constitute a Court for any purpose.

So far as the proceedings complained of depend upon the action of a tribunal so constituted, they were merely *coram non judice* and void. That is the case in *Davison v. McCuaig*,[*] where the Judges of the County of Carleton have assumed to overrule the judgment at the trial of the Judge of the united counties of Prescott and Russell, *dissentiente* the latter, whose judgment, therefore, simply stands.

In the present case the Judge of Prescott and Russell and the senior Judge of Carleton have assumed to overrule the judgment at the trial of the junior Judge of Carleton, *dissentiente* the latter. But even if it be said that the Judges of Carleton were lawfully sitting together under section 12 of the Local Courts Acts, treating Judge Daniel as not present, still, as they differed in opinion the judgment at the trial was not affected. The appeal in each case must, therefore, be allowed.

[*]This case was heard at the same time, and no more formal disposition made of it.—A. G.

The question whether a County Court Judge, who has tried a case without a jury, or has directed judgment upon findings of a jury on the facts, can rehear, or reconsider the judgment pronounced by him at or after the trial, or otherwise set aside such judgment, and grant a new trial, is one not entirely free from difficulty, and not really necessary to be determined upon the present appeals. But as the other members of the Court have expressed their views, I may briefly state my own, so far as I have been able to consider the question, although it is one which, having regard to its importance and its bearing in other respects upon the practice of the County Court, I should like to have heard fully argued.

I do not think we are at all embarrassed by sections 28 and 29 of the Judicature Act, the provisions of which, in their essence and by their very terms, are applicable only to the High Court and Divisional Courts thereof. They have no more application or relation to County Courts than has, e. g., section 23, which provides for the distribution of business in the High Court, and many other sections of the Act. I cannot, therefore, see their bearing upon the construction of Rule 510.

Rule 490 provides that, subject to the provisions of the Act and to rules of Court, the *pleadings, practice,* and *procedure* for the time being of the High Court shall apply and extend to County Courts, wherever the present pleadings, practice, and procedure of the latter correspond with those of the Superior Courts of law.

That rule therefore applies the new rules of practice relating to the trial of an action, whether by a jury, or a Judge alone without a jury, and the subsequent proceedings, to the County Courts, the practice and procedure in those Courts in all these particulars having corresponded, generally speaking, with that of the Superior Courts of law, at the time of the passing of the Judicature Act: C. L. P. Act, R. S. O. ch. 50, secs. 256, 287 (2), 284, 292; A. J. Act, R. S. O. ch. 49, sec. 49; C. C. Act, R. S. O. ch. 43, sec. 29.

To illustrate the way in which the machinery of the High Court is thus applied to the County Court, I may take rule 307, which provides that where there has been a trial by a jury, any application for a new trial shall be to a Divisional Court.

There being no Divisional Courts in the County Court, the practice of the High Court can here only be applied by holding that as to the former the application must be made to the Judge, sitting as a Court in the County Court Sittings, corresponding to the periods formerly known as Terms, or at any other period, under Rule 488.

If this construction is admissible, and I hardly see how it can be controverted without denying the existence of the right to move for a new trial in jury cases, it appears to me to follow that Order XXXVI., relating to motion for judgment, is also part of the practice and procedure in the County Court, except as to any rules of that order which relate to procedure in a particular division of the High Court. I do not think that the difficulty in applying Rule 510 of that order is greater than it is in the case of many other rules. That rule gives the right to move against the judgment of the Judge ; that is the main thing. In the County Court the motion cannot be made to a Divisional Court for the reason I have already mentioned, and it cannot, I think, be made in the alternative to the Court of Appeal, as I apprehend it was not intended by rules, which deal with practice and procedure, to give a new right of appeal in County Court actions: *Attorney-General* v. *Sillem*, 2 H. & C. 581, 10 H. L. Cas. 704. The only forum, therefore, in which such a motion could be made under that rule, is the County Court itself, before the Judge of that Court in the County Court " sittings." There is, no doubt, an anomaly in rehearing the decision before the Judge who pronounced it, but substantially the same thing occurred when the Judge heard an application for a new trial in a case tried by him without a jury prior to the Judicature Act, and does still occur on motion for new trial in jury cases, when he has to reconsider an objection to his own ruling at the trial. Moreover, there is a practical convenience in this exposition of the rule, for, while the party who complains merely of the judgment is not likely to incur the expense of rehearing the case before the Judge, but will go direct to the Court of Appeal under 45 Vict. ch. 6, sec. 4 (the only Act by which an appeal is given from the judgment of a Judge,) there may be cases in which it is sought to invoke the application of Rule 321, or where the findings of the jury on the facts are objected to as well as the judgment of the Judge thereon, and where, therefore, it is desirable that the whole case should be reheard before the Judge, instead of partly before him and partly before the Court of Appeal, with a possible result of the decision of the latter Court being useless in consequence of the granting of a new trial by the Judge upon the facts. So again, in a case tried before a Judge, the party may be dissatisfied or not with the judgment, but the circumstances may be such that the proper relief is the granting of a new trial under the discretionary jurisdiction of the Court, a jurisdiction which, I think, exists by analogy to the practice of the High Court, in that respect, in cases which would not be embraced by Rule 510.

Upon the whole, the inclination of my opinion is, that while the right of appeal from the judgment of the Judge in a case tried without a jury, or upon findings of fact by a jury, depends upon the recent Act, and is not given by Rule 510, or the County Court Act, R. S. O. ch. 43, sec. 35, the party dissatisfied with the judgment, may, if he desires to do so, move against it before the Judge himself; and that the appeal to the Court of Appeal may as properly be brought from the decision on such motion as from the judgment at the trial.

I refer to sections 77, 80, of O. J. Act, Rules 264, 471, 490; C. L. P. Act, ch. 50, secs. 256, 287 (2), 284, 287, 292, 293: *Pryor* v. *City Offices Co.*, 10 Q. B. D. 504; *Re King* v. *Hawkesworth*, 4 Q. B. D. 371.

HAGARTY, C. J. O., and BURTON, J. A., concurred.

Appeal allowed.

HOBBS ET AL. V. GUARDIAN INSURANCE COMPANY.

HOBBS ET AL. V. NORTHERN INSURANCE COMPANY.

Fire insurance—11th statutory condition—Gunpowder explosion—Subsequent Fire.

Where the damage complained of in actions upon fire policies, which were subject to the statutory conditions, was caused by an explosion of gunpowder accidentally set fire to, and by the fire subsequently result-ing from the explosion :

Held, [affirming the decision of the C. P. Div. 7 O. R. 634, and of the Q. B. Div. 8 O. R. 342] that, upon the construction of the 11th statu-tory condition, the defendants were not liable except for the damages caused by the after fire.

THESE actions were brought to recover amounts due under policies of fire insurance. The plaintiffs' loss was occasioned by some gunpowder stored in the insured pre-mises being accidentally set fire to, the admitted damage being $2,778. The loss by the explosion of gunpowder was admitted to have been $2,088.50, and the loss by the after fire, $694.50. The defendants denied their liability for the loss occasioned by the explosion save to the extent of the fire which ensued. The parties agreed to submit the facts of the cases to Chief Justice Wilson, at the London Fall Assizes, 1884, without argument, and a formal verdict was entered by him for the plaintiffs in each case.

The defendants moved in the *Guardian Case* before the Common Pleas Division, and in the *Northern Case*, before the Queen's Bench Division, to set aside the verdicts and to enter judgment for the defendants, which motions were argued during the Michaelmas Sittings, 1884, and were granted, the plaintiffs' verdicts being set aside and judg-ment ordered for the defendants in each case ; (7 O. R. 634, 8 O. R. 342.)

The plaintiffs appealed from these judgments, and the appeals were heard together on the 29th day of April, 1884.*

**Present.—*HAGARTY, C.J.O., BURTON, PATTERSON, and OSLER, JJ.A.

Gibbons, for the appellants. There being a positive insurance against fire, there could be no limitation by implication. A gunpowder explosion is a "fire." The insurance was against "fire," and the implication sought would not be an interpretation of a doubtful phrase, but a contradiction of the terms of the covenant to insure. No implication could make a gunpowder explosion other, in fact and law, than a "fire"—there is no exception of that class of fire, known as gunpowder explosion in this policy, or the statutory conditions. Fire applied to the gunpowder was in any case the cause of the loss. The intention of the Legislature in framing the condition 11 was evidently to prevent the company, by any condition of their own, from exempting themselves from liability from two classes of "fire" therein described; it was not the intention thereby to limit the liability of the company to these two classes. By condition 10, the insured are allowed to keep not more than twenty-five pounds of gunpowder. Here they had less than that amount. If the case is to be governed by implications at all, it would be implied that the company assumed the risk of that gunpowder being ignited. It has been the practice of insurance companies to pay such losses even where specially exempted by proper conditions, and it should be clearly shewn that the intention of both parties was to exempt this class of loss, if the company desire to be exempted.

A. H. Marsh, for the respondents. The rights of the parties must be ascertained by construction of the contract between them, and there is no clause in that contract which can be construed into an undertaking on the part of the respondents to make good a loss caused by the explosion of gunpowder. The true construction of the 11th statutory condition is arrived at by reading it in the light of the maxim *expressio unius exclusio est alterius*. So read it means that the company will not make good any *loss caused by explosion* except a loss caused by the explosion of coal gas in a building not forming part of gas works, and as to any other explosion, and as to lightning they will

be liable only for the *loss by fire caused by such explosion*
or lightning. Upon the question of the application of
this maxim to the construction of written instruments.
I refer to : *Hare* v. *Horton*, 5 B. & Ad. 715 ; *Blackburn* v.
Flavelle, 6 App. Cas. 628, 634 ; *Adams* v. *Bancroft*, 3
Sumner (Circ. Ct.) per Story, J. at p. 387 ; *Briggs* v.
French, 2 Sumner (Circ. Ct.) per Story, J. at p. 257 ; *Baker*
v. *Ludlow*, 2 Johns. Cases 289 ; *Voorhees* v. *Presbyterian*
Church, 5 How. Pr. 58, 71, 72 ; *Curtiss* v. *Leavitt*, 15 N.
Y. at p. 259 ; *Sill* v. *Village of Corning*, 15 N. Y. at
p. 568 ; *Van Steenburg* v. *Kortz*, 10 Johns. Rep. at p. 170 ;
The Chautauque County Bank v. *White*, 6 Barb. 589, 599 ;
Allen v. *Dykers*, 3 Hill N. Y. 593, 597.

May 12, 1885. HAGARTY, C. J. O.—The same question
arises in each of these cases.

In neither of the policies have the company followed the
requirements of our Insurance Act. There are no statutory
conditions, or declared variations, or additional conditions.
Each assurance is " against loss or damage by fire."

In the *Guardian Case* the condition No. 9 declares that
loss from fires caused by lightning will be made good * *
neither will the company be responsible for loss or damage
by explosion, except for such loss or damage, as arises from
explosion by common gas, nor " for any loss or damage
occurring on premises where more than twenty-five pounds
of gun or blasting powder, or more than five gallons of
coal, or other mineral oil, are kept in stock," unless specially
permitted, &c.

Section 10. " Nor for any damage done by fire occasioned
by earthquake, hurricane, or volcanic eruptions."

Under our statute law the statutory conditions must be
considered as embodied in every policy, and if the company
desire to vary the statutory conditions, or omit any of them,
or add new conditions, it must be done in a specified manner, and subject to the judgment of the Court as to their
being reasonable.

This has not been done here, and practically we seem to
be governed solely by the statutory conditions.

We have then to read the contract to be answerable for loss or damage by fire as qualified or explained by the statutory conditions.

Section 11. " The company will make good loss caused by the explosion of coal gas in a building not forming part of gas works, and loss by fire caused by any other explosion, or by lightning."

I suppose we must take the words of this condition as professing to make more clear and intelligible the general contract to insure against losses by fire in the event of explosion.

If the liability, unexplained or modified, left the company responsible for all losses caused by explosion, where fire was the exploding agent, then the words of the statutory condition would be idle and useless, unless they modified or qualified the general liability.

To prevent misunderstanding, it is provided that, except in gas works, the insurers must make good loss caused by explosion of coal gas.

I presume it will not be disputed that, under such words, we would have to hold that they were not liable for such an explosion in gas works or buildings forming part thereof.

Then it is added they must pay for loss by fire, caused by any other explosion or by lightning.

It seems to me as if the Legislature said in effect, now to prevent questions arising as to explosions, we define the liability to be as follows, &c., &c. " *All* loss caused by explosion of coal gas," that will cover the rending of the building besides the consequent fire loss. But then they add and " loss *by fire* caused by any other explosion."

Can this be held to cover the loss to the building shattered and blown into the air and completely destroyed by the mere explosive force of a barrel of gunpowder ?

It seems to me that in the latter case it is only the loss by fire that is provided against.

I do not see how we can give the latter words any meaning except as restrictive of the preceding words.

Coal gas explosion involves all damage from wreck of the building, as well as fire, all other explosions are confined to loss by fire.

If it do not mean that, I cannot guess what it means.

In the policy of the Northern Company we may refer to the conditions to shew that such a construction is in the contemplation of insurers, although we cannot allow the conditions to vary or limit those provided by our statute.

No. 6. Declares (i) that they will not pay " loss or damage by explosion *except loss or damage to a building or to property contained therein caused by explosion of coal gas in such building.*"

From this we gather that, although it was reasonable to pay for damage to the building, caused by wreckage by a coal gas explosion, it was not so considered as to other explosions.

I think the appeal must be dismissed.

Burton, J. A.—This case and one against the Northern Insurance Company were argued together, the point in each case being the same, viz.: whether under the terms of the contract the companies were liable for a loss which was occasioned by a concussion or disturbance of the atmosphere, by an explosion of gunpowder upon the premises of the assured.

The conditions in the case of each policy were not the statutory conditions, but the companies' own conditions, not stated to be variations of the statutory conditions. It is clear therefore according to the construction of the statute laid down by the Privy Council in *Parsons* v. *The Citizens*, 7 App. Cas. 96, that the statutory conditions alone are to be looked at as governing the liability of these defendants. It is manifest that the companies would not be liable if their own conditions could be read into the contract. The whole difficulty arises from the way in which the 11th statutory condition is framed, not stating that the company will not be liable for certain losses, but stating that they will be liable for explosions caused in a particular way, and for fires caused by other explosions.

We have to decide what is the meaning of the parties to these contracts, to be gathered from the whole instrument.

In the case of the Guardian the contract is to make good all such loss or damage as shall happen by fire to the property insured, according to the tenor of the terms and conditions of the policy.

That of the Northern is that, subject to the terms and conditions, if the property described shall be destroyed or damaged by fire, the company will make good the loss.

Condition ten qualifies the general words by providing, that, even though a loss by fire be sustained, the company will not be liable under certain circumstances, and great stress was laid by the plaintiff's counsel on the sub-section F, which provides that the companies shall not be liable for a loss or damage occurring while petroleum and other enumerated articles are stored or kept in the building insured, or containing the property insured, without permission, as shewing that for any other losses not included in this exception the company would be liable. But as I read that sub-section, it is merely intended to provide that, although the loss comes within the risk insured against as a loss by fire, the company will not hold themselves responsible if it occurs whilst those prohibited articles are upon the premises.

I do not propose to enter into the disquisition in which some American Judges, to whose decisions we were referred, have indulged as to the philosophical or scientific meaning of the term explosion, further than to say that, assuming it to be beyond doubt that explosion may be described "as rapid combustion and hence a fire," which would be a good reason for the companies being made responsible for the lost gunpowder, if covered by the insurance, it appears to me that according to the plain and ordinary understanding of men of business, the words of this policy would not extend to such loss or damage as is here admitted to have been sustained.

The risk referred to in the body of the policy is against loss or damage by fire, that is by actual ignition. Assuming, though not conceding, that without the words of the 11th condition, a loss caused by the rending or destruction of the building caused by explosion only, would come within the words of the policy, it seems to me that all ambiguity is removed by the terms of that condition, as shewing that the contracting parties did not intend to include explosion within the terms "loss by fire."

I do not read it as an exception, but as explanatory of what they mean by a loss or damage by fire; in other words, they say in the 11th condition, in addition to the losses insured against in the body of this policy, we will hold ourselves responsible for loss caused by the explosion of coal gas, and for loss by fire caused by any other explosion.

The use of this language leads me irresistibly to the conclusion that the parties never intended to include a risk of this kind.

It was perhaps rather a stretch of authority on the part of the Legislature, or those who framed these conditions, to extend the liability of the assurers beyond the express words of the policy, but, I suppose, they must have ascertained that in practice the insurance companies had extended their risks to cover losses by explosion in the one particular case mentioned, and so may have felt that, in adopting a general form of policy, they were not extending the liability usually intended to be covered, but the companies might, if not satisfied with it, have excluded even this one risk by a variation in the condition; in the view which I take of the case, this was not necessary.

The policy in the body of it covered loss or damage caused by the direct action of fire. The condition imposed by the Legislature, and in effect adopted by the defendants in consequence of their non-compliance with the directions of the statute, extended this liability in one particular case to loss by explosion, and impliedly relieved them from all others, by confining their responsibility in other cases of explosion to loss by fire caused by the explosion.

The operation of a condition so worded, and coupled as we find it with a loss by fire caused by lightning, would seem to limit the liability to this one particular cause of explosion, according to the rule " *Expressum facit cessare tacitum.*"

For a mere injury by lightning, although the electric spark is of the nature of fire, if the premises insured were not set on fire, the companies would not be liable under these policies with the statutory conditions, and so also for a mere injury by explosion not causing fire.

In order to bring the case within the words of the policy (reading it without the condition) it must be shewn that the damage resulted from actual ignition.

And this is rendered more clear by the words of the condition, and reading the two together as we are bound to read them, I think we are driven to the conclusion that the damage here was not within the risks insured against, but was caused by a concussion or disturbance of the atmosphere, and that the mere circumstance that the explosion was upon the premises, and not just outside their limits, can make no difference.

I do not think the argument sound which places a liability upon these defendants, on the ground that the explosion was the result of fire.

The proximate cause of the loss was the explosion, the *causa causans ;* the fact that that explosion was brought about by fire is immaterial ; fire, no doubt, was the remote cause of the damage, the *causa sine qua non ;* as remarked by Mr. Justice Byles in one of the cases quoted, a shot from a cannon falling amongst crockery-ware, might, in one sense, be said to occasion a loss by fire, but it would not fall within the words of the contract, which must be understood in their plain and ordinary sense.

I am of opinion, therefore, that the appeals should be dismissed, with costs, and judgment entered for the defendants, with costs.

PATTERSON, J. A., concurred.

OSLER, J.A.—I concur in dismissing the appeal in these cases, for the reasons stated in the opinion of my Lord, and of my Brother Rose, in the Guardian case.

Appeal dismissed, with costs.

JOSEPH HALL MANUFACTURING CO. V. HAZLITT ET AL.

Sale of goods on credit—Property in goods passing—Trade.

The plaintiffs sold to U. & Co. certain wheels, &c., to be used in their manufactory under a written agreement, whereby it was stipulated that the right and property to the goods should not pass to them until the whole price thereof was paid : the right of possession merely passing : such right to be forfeited and the plaintiffs to be at liberty to resume possession in case of default in the payments being made, or in case of seizure for rent, &c., or upon any attempt by U. & Co. to sell or dispose thereof without the consent of the plaintiffs, it being expressly declared that the sale was conditional only, and punctual payment of the instalments being essential to its existence. U. & Co. placed the machinery in the flume belonging to their factory, which was held by them under a lease from H. & Co., and subsequently the sheriff having seized other chattels belonging to U. & Co., they surrendered the possession of the premises and delivered the key thereof to H. & Co. Default having been made by U. & Co., the plaintiffs demanded the wheels of H. & Co., which demand H. & Co. refused to comply with, assigning as a reason that they had not possession thereof, and in the following month the wheels were sold under proceedings to enforce payment of the liens of certain mechanics.

Held, [affirming the judgment of the Common Pleas Division, 8 O. R. 465,] that the plaintiffs were entitled to recover the value of the goods.

THIS was an appeal by the defendants from the judgment of the Common Pleas Division (8 O. R. 465.)

The facts and arguments appear in the former report, and in the present judgments.

The appeal was heard on the 2nd day of June, 1885.*

McCarthy, Q.C., and *Poussette*, for the appellants.
C. H. Ritchie for the respondent.

Present—HAGARTY, C.J.O., BURTON, PATTERSON, and OSLER, JJ.A.

June 30, 1885. BURTON, J. A.—The property in the wheels in question in this case never passed out of the plaintiffs. By the express terms of the contract between them and the purchasers, no property was to pass until payment of the price; but it is said that such a stipulation can be of no avail where, from the nature of the property, the vendor must have known that in order to be made use of it must necessarily be built into, and become part of, the building, and would then fall within the rule "*quicquid plantatur solo solo cedit.*"

The owner of the property would not cease to be owner, but there might be a difficulty in asserting his rights; if, for instance, a man should convert a quantity of bricks and erect them into a house they would have lost their legal identity as chattels so as to be incapable of recaption by the original owner; but if the purchasers in this case had placed these wheels on their own property could they have successfully resisted a claim by their vendor on the ground that they had converted them into freehold, although the vendor must be held to have known that it was intended so to use the property that it would be annexed to the freehold? He would be entitled to rely on the agreement between him and his vendee that, as between them, it should under all circumstances be regarded as personal property.

It is not a necessary inference from the simple fact of annexation, where the chattel is severable without material injury to itself or to the freehold, that the chattel becomes the property of the freeholder; but it is always open to inquiry under what circumstances it was annexed, and whether an agreement did or did not exist under which the owner would be at liberty to take it away again, as in *Lancaster* v. *Eve*, 5 C. B. N. S. 717, where a pile had been driven into the bed of the river, and where Williams, J., observed that to apply the maxim I have quoted there must be such a fixing to the soil as reasonably to lead to the inference that it was intended to be incorporated with the soil.

I do not at all question the decisions referred to by Mr. McCarthy, that what are commonly known as trade or tenant's fixtures form part of the land and pass by a conveyance, whether that conveyance be absolute or by way of mortgage ; so that although a person occupying the position of tenant might remove them they would nevertheless, as between grantor and grantee or mortgagor and mortgagee, pass as part of the land so as not to require a bill of sale of them as fixtures, but as pointed out in *Holland* v. *Hodgson*, L. R. 7 C. P. 328, if a tenant, having only a limited interest in land and an absolute interest in the fixtures, were to convey not only his limited interest in the land and his right to enjoy the fixtures during the term so long as they continued part of the land, but also his power to sever those fixtures and dispose of them absolutely a different question might arise.

This, however, is not a case between mortgagor and mortgagee, but the simple question is, whether, it being clear that as between the plaintiffs and the purchaser the property in question remained a chattel and the property of the plaintiffs, it ceased to be so because the purchaser, who had subsequently leased a property from Hazlitt, put up a mill upon it, and placed these wheels in it in such a manner as to become fixtures, had incurred a forfeiture of the lease or surrendered it to his landlord.

It is rather a startling proposition, it is true that even at this late date the " divine right " of landlords still exists to make the debt due to them by their tenants out of the goods of strangers, and that they are still at liberty to appropriate without compensation fixtures which, perhaps by inadvertence, a tenant may have neglected to remove during his term, but a Court would scarcely hold, unless compelled to do so by authority, that the owner of a chattel left in the possession of a tenant should lose his property in it through the default of that tenant.

It is not like the case of a purchaser advancing his money in the *bond fide* belief that the fixtures which he saw were really the property of the freeholder, but one in which a landlord claims that a forfeiture of the lease or a surrender of the term passes, not only the buildings and fixtures owned by the tenant, but those which he did not own, which he had no power to dispose of, and which had not become part of the freehold with the consent of the owner.

As to the forfeiture the evidence entirely fails, there may or may not have been a default which would have warranted the landlord in exercising his right of forfeiture, but he did not exercise it and the defendant is driven to rely upon the voluntary surrender of the term.

Here the tenant had no property in the wheels and could not convey what he did not have. If the property had passed and the vendor had taken a chattel mortgage and registered it, it is clear that a mere annexation would not have enabled a subsequent mortgagee of the freehold to claim them. Here, however, he had no title, and no presumption under the circumstances can arise (as would generally arise from the simple fact of annexation unexplained) that he intended to give them to another. There can be no presumption that a man intends to commit a fraud, which this defendant would have committed if he had, by annexing these chattels to the freehold, intended to defraud the true owner of them and give them to a stranger.

It is, one would suppose, too simple a proposition to require authority, that a person who has only the use of a chattel belonging to another cannot by annexing it to the soil make it part of the realty, but *D'Eyncourt* v. *Gregory*, L. R. 3 Eq. 382, is clear authority if any is required, and *Central Branch R. W. Co.* v. *Fritz*, 27 Am. Rep. 175, may also be referred to.

I think, therefore, that the finding at the trial as to the plaintiffs' right to the property was correct, and the demand and refusal were sufficient to entitle them to maintain this action, which should be considered as an action for preventing the plaintiffs from exercising their right to sever and remove the fixtures. And I am pleased to think that we are not compelled by any technical rule of law to deprive these plaintiffs of their just rights, and to hold the defendants entitled to property for which they never paid and to which they have no moral or equitable right.

The appeal, in my judgment, should be dismissed, with costs.

OSLER, J.A.—This case appears to me to have been well decided, for the reasons given in the opinion of the learned Chief Justice of the Common Pleas.

The wheels were unquestionably trade or tenant's fix-
                                                              nant Usborne
                                                              remove them

                                                              in the latter
                                                              the case just
                                                              rtgaged them

                                                              n which they
                                                              r five years.
                                                              time during
                                                              a surrender
                                                              ie had made
                                                              :hus become
                                                              ssion of the
                                                              eir removal.
                                                              iere was no
                                                              e plaintiffs'
                                                              and West-
minster *Loan and Discount Co. v. —*. , B. N. S. 798,
and other cases referred to in the judgment below. As between Usborne, the plaintiffs, and the defendants, the wheels still remained fixtures or chattels removable in the terms of the agreement, and never became, as contended, part of the freehold.

The *crux* propounded in the sixth reason of appeal, viz., " 6. The plaintiffs' proposition of law may be stated baldly as follows :—A, a contractor, steals nails from B, and uses

Subscribers will please change the word " mortgagee," in line 3 of page 757, to 'mortgagor.'

them in building C's house.   B demands from C the right
to remove the nails.   On refusal has B a right of action
against C for the value of the nails," is not applicable
where the question is one of the removability of fixtures
not intended in any event to become part of the realty:
Wake v. *Hall*, 8 App. Cas. 195, 203 ; *1homas* v. *Inglis*, 7
O. R. 588.

The case of *Mason* v. *Bickle*, 2 A. R. 291, seems to be
a decisive answer to the objection taken in the argument
that the plaintiffs had discounted the notes taken by them
for the price of the wheels.

I think the appeal should be dismissed.

HAGARTY, C.J.O., and PATTERSON, J.A., concurred.

Appeal dismissed, with costs,

SMITH V. FAIR.

Chattel mortgage—Curing defect—Subsequent conveyance—Intent to prefer— Evidence—Jury.

A formal defect in a chattel mortgage may be cured by a conveyance at any time before an execution reaches the sheriff's hands; but such conveyance, whether effected by a deed or by delivery only, has no retroactive operation and if void for intent to prefer under R. S. O. ch. 118, would not suffice to cure the defects. The intent to prefer is a question of fact for the jury; and therefore where the jury found that there was such intent, and where there was evidence to support the finding, the judgment of the County Judge setting aside the jury's verdict in favor of the execution creditor was reversed, but a new trial was directed in order that evidence might be given to shew that the bill of sale was made in order to carry out honestly the original mortgage contract. OSLER, J.A., dissenting.

AN appeal by the defendant from the judgment of the County Court of the county of Peel in an interpleader issue.

The issue was as to the ownership of certain goods seized by the sheriff of Peel on the 4th October, 1884, under an execution issued on a judgment recovered by the defendant against one Sanford, and claimed by the plaintiff under a bill of sale from Sanford, dated 23rd August, 1884.

The issue was tried by a jury in December, 1884.

It appeared from the evidence that on the 10th June, 1884, Sanford had made a chattel mortgage on the goods in question to the plaintiff, and that the hotel, in which the goods were, having subsequently been destroyed by fire, a part of the goods was taken to the plaintiff's house, and while the property was there the bill of sale in question was given.

The money was actually advanced on the chattel mortgage, and at the time it was given Sanford was quite solvent, so far as was shewn, but at the time of the execution of the bill of sale, Sanford was not in a position to pay his debts in full.

The chattel mortgage was defective for want of an affidavit of execution.

The jury gave a verdict in favour of the defendant, but the Judge of the County Court set it aside and gave judgment for the plaintiff, from which judgment the defendant appealed.

The appeal was heard on the 19th day of May, 1885.*

Lash, Q.C., and *W. L. Walsh*, for the appellant.

Moss, Q.C., and *H. P. Milligan*, for the respondent.

June 30, 1885. BURTON, J.A.—Whilst adhering to the views which I expressed in *Parke* v. *St. George*, 10 A. R. 496, that a mortgagee may, without any additional act on the part of the mortgagor, cure a formal defect in his mortgage by taking possession before the goods are bound by an execution, a point upon which I am, at the same time, quite free to admit that there is ample room for a difference of opinion, I agree with my Brother Patterson, that this appeal ought to be allowed, because there is no evidence that there was any taking of possession by the mortgagee at the time the bill of sale was given, and no finding of the jury at all upon the question, and the learned Judge states it as his opinion that the attempt to shew that the property was taken into possession under the mortgage was not made out.

This bill of sale does not profess to be made for the purpose of curing a defect in the mortgage, and, if the evidence is to be believed, could not have been made with any such object, but purports to be an independent sale of certain chattels embraced in the mortgage, the purchase money for which is to be credited on the mortgage. Such a sale, if the mortgagor was then insolvent was liable to question under chapter 118 of the R. S. O., and I agree with the other members of the Court that there was evidence for the jury on which they might reasonably come to the conclusion that it was made with intent to give a preference. If, therefore, that sale could not stand we are driven back on the mortgage, which was bad, unless

it is established that possession was taken under it either
with or without some active step on the part of the mortgagee. I do not think any sufficient ground has been
shewn for interfering with the finding of the jury upon
the evidence given at the trial, but if the plaintiff desires
it, I think he should be entitled to a new trial upon payment of costs, which perhaps under the circumstances
mentioned upon the argument and which the defendant
desired to show upon affidavits which we do not consider
ourselves justified in looking at, would best meet the
justice of the case.

In the absence of such a request, and payment within
thirty days of all costs, on the part of the plaintiff, the
appeal should be allowed, with costs.

PATTERSON, J.A.—I have not been able to satisfy myself
that the learned Judge of the County Court was right in
giving judgment for the plaintiff. I do not say that he
ought to have given judgment for the defendant, though I
believe that a judgment for the defendant would have
been proper, having regard to the finding of the jury and
the undisputed fact of Sanford's insolvency when he made
the bill of sale, which the jury found was made with intent
to prefer the plaintiff to other creditors; but I think that
the view of the learned Judge being against the sufficiency
of those facts to establish the liability of the goods to be
taken under the defendant's execution, his proper course
would have been to order a new trial for the purpose of
more fully elucidating the facts.

The plaintiff claimed, as he stated in his evidence, under
a chattel mortgage, and also under the bill of sale.

The latter, by itself, could not stand in the face of the
facts found and conceded to which I have just referred.

The plaintiff is forced to resort to the chattel mortgage,
using in aid such facts connected with the bill of sale
transaction as may serve his purpose.

The mortgage was, when first made, free from objection
under R. S. O. ch. 118, so far as appears from the evidence.

It is not shewn that at that time Sanford was not able to pay his debts in full. His evidence is to the contrary.

But the mortgage was defective as against creditors under ch. 119.

That was a defect which, as I pointed out in *Parkes* v. *St. George*, 10 A. R. at p. 535, could readily be cured by remedying what was wrong in connection with the deed itself, or by some act of the mortgagor, such as the execution of a new deed, or a delivery of the goods operating as a conveyance, at any time before a creditor had acquired a right to seize the goods, and so long as no subsequent purchaser or mortgagee had intervened.

I also expressed or intimated my opinion that the remedial effect of delivery of possession depended on the act of the mortgagor ; and that a mortgagee taking possession by virtue of his mortgage, without any act amounting to a delivery or new transfer by the mortgagor, would still hold merely under the defective conveyance which had not been accompanied by an immediate delivery and followed by an actual and continued change of possession.

Further consideration has not led me to change those views.

The difference between the English Bills of Sales Acts of 1854 and 1878, in which the state of possession at the time of the bankruptcy, or assignment for the benefit of creditors, or seizure in execution, is what is made material, while our Act requires the change of possession to be immediate, actual, and continued, is illustrated by the recent case of *Swire* v. *Cookson*, 9 App. Cas. 653.'

I have no doubt that the plaintiff's defective mortgage might have been replaced by a conveyance to which no objection could be taken under chapter 119, at any time before the defendant's execution reached the hands of the sheriff.

But such new conveyance, whether effected by a deed or by delivery only, would, if my views are correct, have no retroactive operation. From this it follows that, while perfectly unimpeachable under chapter 119, it would have to stand the test of chapter 118, and might run the risk of being held void against creditors by reason of intent to prefer &c.

That intent would have to be deduced, as in other cases, from whatever evidence existed, and it would not, of necessity, be inferred from the effect of the deed which might postpone creditors against whom the former defective conveyance would not have stood, nor from the fact that it was executed in order that it might have that effect.

I am of course now speaking without any reference to the recent Act, 48 Vict. ch. 26 sec. 2, O., by which force is given to the effect of a transfer without necessary regard to the intent. I have had occasion, in several cases which have come before us in this Court, to express the opinion that the existence of the intent which, under chapter 118, avoids an assignment is a question of fact to be decided, like any other question of fact, upon the whole evidence; and in *Brayley* v. *Ellis*, 9 A. R. at p. 592, I alluded to the effect of a promise to give a security in saving the security when given from the imputation of the forbidden intent, provided it would have been good if given at the time the promise was made.

My opinion on that point was not at variance with the opinions of other members of the Court, though we differed about the doctrine of pressure on which the judgment turned.

A promise to give property in security could not be evidenced more convincingly than by the making of a mortgage upon it; and I have a very strong opinion that, granted the absence of the forbidden intent, when a mortgage was given which happened not to operate as against creditors by reason of the omission of some formality required by chapter 119, no tribunal would hold that a subsequent transfer, either by deed or by delivery, made for the purpose of curing the defect, was made with intent to prefer &c., within the meaning of chapter 118, even though the immediate motive was to make the mortgagee secure against an expected execution. The intent would be held to be to perform the promise previously made in good faith and without any indirect purpose.

I am inclined to believe that these views are essentially the same as those acted upon by the learned Judge in the Court below, though I have enunciated them at greater length than he thought it necessary to do. But I cannot satisfy myself that we are in possession of the requisite facts to support a judgment for the plaintiff.

We of course start with the assumption, nothing being shewn to the contrary, of the good faith in every respect of the mortgage.

The learned Judge thought, and I agree with him, that the taking of possession under the mortgage was not made out ; and no question as to it was left to the jury.

The remedial conveyance then must be the bill of sale· If possession was given and taken at the time it was made or afterwards, that possession would be under the bill of sale rather than under the mortgage.

We have no finding that possession was taken, and very meagre grounds for inferring it, if indeed there is any ground except the execution of the bill of sale itself, and it appears to have been registered as required when possession is not changed.

The jury's finding is not attacked except by the contention that there was no evidence for the jury. I think there was evidence ; but I also think that evidence that the bill of sale was made in order to carry out honestly the transaction agreed on when the mortgage was made, would have been proper to submit as disproving the other intent.

The deed itself does not furnish internal evidence of the kind required, for it professes to be a new transaction for the taking of some of the mortgaged goods at a valuation in payment of so much of the alleged mortgage debt ; and, as a reason for the transaction, it recites matters which the plaintiff himself disproves.

The intent is a matter of fact, not of law. The fact as found is fatal to the plaintiff if I am right in considering that his title must rest on the deed, at least in the absence of a finding, founded upon evidence, of a delivery of possession apart from the transaction of the bill of sale.

For these reasons, I am of opinion that we should allow the appeal, with costs; and either direct judgment to be entered on the interpleader for the defendant, or order a new trial on payment of costs by the plaintiff within a limited time, in default of which payment the defendant should have judgment.

OSLER, J. A.—I shall consider the case as it is presented upon the evidence as reported to us, entirely discarding the affidavits which it has been sought to introduce. There is nothing in them on which at this stage of the case we could safely act.

The defendant's judgment was signed in September or the early part of October, 1884.

The chattel mortgage of June, 1884, though possibly made in good faith and as a security for money actually advanced at the time, was invalid against execution creditors, as it failed to comply with certain requirements of the Chattel Mortgage Act. It was given for the expressed consideration of $425, payable at the expiration of six months, with interest at 8 per cent., and the property in question, with other property included in it, was at the time at the hotel and premises occupied by the mortgagor.

The hotel was destroyed by fire a few days afterwards, and the goods were during the first week in July moved to the plaintiff's premises. The plaintiff said he did so at the mortgagor's request and for his own protection : that the latter told him he had no more use for them; and that he had better take the goods until they could have a settlement. The mortgagor's evidence was, that he had no other place to put the things when the hotel was burnt, and so he took them to Smith's. He thought it was not done at Smith's suggestion more than at his own. He went to live at Smith's and generally made it his home after the fire, but was not paying board.

As to the bill of sale. The plaintiff said that after discussing the question of a sale, it was proposed that he should take the goods at a valuation, and he agreed to do so and to give credit on the mortgage. He and Sanford made the valuation. The bill of sale untruly recites that the mortgage had become due in consequence of the sale, without the consent of the plaintiff, of a horse included therein, and that the plaintiff had thereupon, pursuant to the power therein contained, taken possession of the goods. The evidence of both parties was, that the horse had been sold with the consent of the mortgagee.

The learned Judge's note of the charge is very brief. He left to the jury the question, " Was the bill of sale made with a view of giving Smith a preference over other creditors of Sanford ? " This, he observed, did not affect the legal question of payment on the mortgage by delivering the goods.

There is a note that the verdict was to be entered according to the finding, subject to be otherwise entered according to judgment on legal points raised. What these " legal points " were, is not very clearly shewn. One, probably, was that the mortgagee having taken possession of the goods before the execution was issued, the defendant was not in a position to avoid it, or to take the goods out of his possession under the execution, because of the non-registration of the chattel mortgage.

The jury found that the bill of sale was made with the view of giving the plaintiff a preference over the other creditors of Sanford, and a verdict was entered for the defendant at the trial. This verdict the learned Judge afterwards set aside, and directed judgment for the plaintiff, on the ground that there was nothing to leave to the jury, and that they should have been directed to find for the plaintiff.

I have no doubt that under Rule 321, O. J. A., there is power to take this course in a proper case, and to direct judgment for one party or the other, notwithstanding the finding of the jury.

It is nevertheless, as Wilson, C. J., remarked in *Stewart v. Rounds*, 7 App. R. 515-518, a power which must be sparingly and cautiously exercised.

If the plaintiff is confined to his title under this bill of sale, I am not satisfied that there is not some evidence from which a jury might have said that it was made with intent (not, as the question was left to them, " with a view,") of giving the plaintiff a preference over the other creditors of the debtor. There is the untrue recital of the reason for the mortgagee having taken possession—the fact that the mortgage money was not then due—that the parties did not know of the irregularity in the chattel mortgage, so that the bill of sale could not be said to have been given with intent to correct it; the terms on which the mortgagor was living with the mortgagee, and that the former was undoubtedly insolvent, though not to the knowledge of the latter. These circumstances taken together were, I think, proper to be considered by the jury in determining whether the bill of sale was made by the grantor in fraud of the Act with the prohibited intent: R. S. O. ch. 118, sec. 2.

I have not noticed anything in the evidence as reported which shews that it was made in consequence of a request or pressure on the part of the mortgagee.

The case of *Brown v. Sweet*, 7 App. R. 725, cited by Mr. Moss, does not assist the plaintiff, as it arose upon the statute of Elizabeth (13 Eliz. ch. 5), and not upon the Fraudulent Preference Act: R. S. O. ch. 118, sec. 2.

The plaintiff is, however, in my opinion entitled to succeed on the ground that he had, as I understand the evidence, actually taken possession of the goods before Sanford's creditors had acquired any rights against them, and, indeed, before the commencement of any action against him. Whether he took such possession under the chattel mortgage or under the bill of sale can, I think, be of no importance. He had possession—a possession he had a right to acquire, though not to sell the goods, the mortgage not being in default, and I see no reason why it should not be attributed to the mortgage if the bill of sale is invalid. I say he had the right to take possession because the mortgage contains no clause giving the mortgagor the right to possession until default. If the mortgage was invalid merely because it did not comply with the formalities required by the Chattel Mortgage Act, R. S. O. ch. 125, I think we have already decided in *Parkes* v. *St. George*, 10 App. R. 406, that if the mortgagee takes possession of the goods before a creditor is in a position to seize them, his title cannot be impeached.

If the bill of sale is void, the execution creditor is still at liberty to sell the equity of redemption, his right to do that not being now in question.

I do not discuss any of the other questions which have been argued.

I think the appeal should be dismissed.

Appeal allowed, with costs.   [OSLER, J.A., dissenting.]

THE CORPORATION OF THE COUNTY OF YORK V. THE TORONTO GRAVEL ROAD AND CONCRETE CO.

Agreement, construction of—Implied qualification—Traction engine—Tramway—Right to use steam power on.

The defendant company, who were empowered by statute to run a traction engine over certain highways in the county of York, and who by their charter were allowed to construct a tramway in the county to be worked by horse or steam power, upon such terms as might be agreed on with the municipalities through which the road might pass, entered into an agreement with the county, whereby it was agreed that the company should be at liberty to lay down a tramway along a certain road: that the tolls to be collected should not exceed certain specified rates on one and two horse vehicles: that the company, if required, should run two passenger cars daily each way, or in lieu thereof an omnibus or sleigh: that in case horses, carriages, teams, or other vehicles or animals met the horses, waggons, carriages, or other vehicles of the company, the latter should have the right of way, and that "so soon as this agreement shall have been ratified by the said corporation, the said company shall forthwith withdraw their said traction engine from the public highways of the said county, and shall discontinue the use of the said traction engine, and of any other traction engine upon or along such public highways."

The company insisted that they were at liberty, under the agreement, to run a steam motor upon the said tramway. Thereupon an action was instituted by the corporation to restrain the use of steam power on the tramway, which relief the Court below, (PROUDFOOT, J.,) on the hearing of the cause, granted: upon appeal, this Court being equally divided, the appeal was dismissed with costs.

Per HAGARTY, C. J., and PATTERSON, J. A., [agreeing with PROUDFOOT, J.]—On the true construction of the agreement there was, if not an express, at least an implied qualification excluding the use of steam as a motive power.

Per BURTON, J. A., and ROSE, J.—What the company had agreed to abandon was only the right theretofore exercised by them;—under the general law, 31 Vict. ch. 34, R. S. O. ch. 186,—of using traction engines on the public highway, and that they were not restricted by the agreement from using steam motors on the tramway.

THIS was an appeal by the defendants from the judgment of Proudfoot, J., reported 3 O. R. 584, where and in the present judgments the facts giving rise to the action, the points relied on by counsel and authorities cited are clearly stated.

The appeal came on for hearing on the 8th of September, 1884.[*]

Robinson, Q. C., and *Osler*, Q. C., for the appellants.

[*] *Present.*—HAGARTY, C.J.O., BURTON, PATTERSON, JJ.A. and ROSE, J.

J. K. Kerr, Q. C., and *W. Cassels*, Q. C., for the respondents.

January 13, 1885. HAGARTY, C. J. O.—By 31 Vict. ch.
34, passed in 1868 R. S. O. ch. 186, traction engines were
allowed to be used on public highways, weight not to
exceed 20 tons, width of driving wheels to be at least 12
inches, and truck wheels four inches for first two tons, and
one-quarter of an inch for each further ton.

Certain restrictions are prescribed as to speed, &c., and
provision is made for settling the amount of toll to be levied
on them by arbitration, &c.   37 Vict. ch. 90, (O.) (March,
1874) amended defendants' charter, and allowed them to
make a double or single tramway of wood or iron, or of
wood and iron, and other material, from their gravel pits
in Scarborough to a point within the city. "And the
said road may be worked by horse or other power; but if
by steam, the rate of travelling shall not be greater than
10 miles per hour."

Sec. 3.—"Municipalities may permit them to construct
their road in, along, over and upon the highways, upon
such terms and conditions as may be agreed on between
them."

It seems clear that on granting the defendants the right
to lay their tramway on the highroad, the plaintiffs had
the right to impose such terms as they pleased, and that,
except on terms satisfactory to the county, the privilege
could not be obtained.

We must look to the state of things which led to the
agreement of August, 1874.

The defendants, under the Act of 1868, were running a
traction engine on the highway. It was represented in the
interest of persons using the highway to be "an intolerable
nuisance," and with much apparent reason.

The council was pressed to take action in the matter, and
they negotiated with the defendants, the result being this
agreement. I fully concur in the opinion of the learned
Judge below: "Their intention was to effect the removal

of steam from the highway, as it had been found so inconvenient and dangerous to farmers and others travelling
the road. I do not think it necessary (he says) to refer
further to the evidence on this subject, nor to enquire
whether, upon that evidence, I ought to conclude that the
defendants understood that they were only getting a qualified permission, for I think the agreement itself contains
stipulations that are only consistent with the view taken
by the Municipal Council, that if there is no express, there
is, at any rate, an implied qualification excluding the use of
steam, as a motive power."

He then points out the provision as to tolls, and the use
of an omnibus or sleigh, and the provision for teams meeting, as all clearly pointing to the use of horse power as the
motive power.

The petition to the Council from a very large number of
ratepayers, after setting forth the injury caused by the
running of the traction engine, sets out that the defendants
were willing to withdraw it from the road, if the plaintiffs
would give them leave to lay a tramway or street railway
on the road, and they requested the Council to grant that
privilege, on the defendants agreeing not to use "said engine
or any other engine of a similar character."

I have no doubt but that the plaintiffs in entering into
the agreement, fully thought they were bargaining for the
non user of steam on the public road, and the learned
Judge says: "I understood Mr. Robinson to concede that at
the time of the agreement both parties only thought of
horse-power, but that steam not being expressly excluded,
the statutory right was not interfered with."

I think the language of the deed points to a user of
horse-power alone. If any use of steam other than in a
traction engine had been contemplated, we should naturally
have looked for some agreement as to tolls, as provided
in the Traction Engine Act of 1868. A locomotive, or
"motor" as the phrase is, would hardly be left to the provision in the contract as to the tolls on a one-horse or two-
horse vehicle.

It is hardly within the bounds of belief that a corporation
anxious to abate the nuisance caused by a steam engine

on the high-road, would knowingly grant the privilege of
running other kinds of locomotives along a portion of the
road forever ; or that in providing against the continued
user of the traction engine then on their road, they would
knowingly leave it to the other party to run an ordinary
railway locomotive or steam motor in its stead.

A great deal of evidence was given as to the meaning to
be attached to " traction engine." It seems reasonably
clear, that if a man were buying or selling or contracting
for a " traction engine," it would be understood to be that
species of engine used to run on common roads.

But it may be urged that it has a wider significance,
and, as some of the witnesses considered, that it is a locomotive or movable steam engine used for the traction or
drawing of carriages on a railway or on common roads.

Every locomotive or steam motor is a traction engine,
but in its special technical and commercial sense, every
traction engine is not a locomotive or steam motor used
for rails.

In construing the agreement, we are to place ourselves
in the position of the parties, having before us all the surrounding circumstances, understanding the subject matter
about which they were dealing, and in short considering
all matters calculated to make us understand their understanding of the force and meaning of the words they were
using. We cannot go against the clear and obvious meaning of such words, but we may, I think, fairly inquire into
their meaning, if any other than one meaning can be fairly
gathered from them. 2 Taylor's Evidence, 985, sec. 1034.

The terms of every document must, in the absence of all
parol testimony, be construed in their primary sense, unless
the context evidently points out that in the particular
instance, and in order to effectuate the immediate intention
of the parties, they must be understood in some other and
peculiar sense. It may be stated generally, that if the
language be technical or scientific, and be used in a matter
relating to the art of science to which it belongs, its
technical or scientific must be considered its primary mean-

ing ; but if, on the other hand, the expressions have reference to the common transactions of life, they will be interpreted in their plain, ordinary, and popular meaning.

Lord Ellenborough, in *Robertson v. French*, 4 East 134, says the words are to be understood in ordinary plain popular sense, "unless the context evidently points out that they must, in the particular instance, and in order to effectuate the immediate intention of the parties to the contract, be understood in some other special and peculiar sense."

Erle, C. J., in *Carr v. Montefiore*, 5 B. & S., at p. 427, speaks of the contract being construed according to the same rules as all other written contracts, namely, the intention of the parties, which is to be gathered from the words of the instrument interpreted together with the surrounding circumstances. If the words of the instrument are clear in themselves, the instrument must be construed accordingly, but if they are susceptible of more meanings than one, then the Judge must inform himself by the aid of the Jury and the surrounding circumstances which bear on the contract.

The subject is very fully discussed in Leake 224 et seq. Mr. Leake quotes Lord Westbury's language in *Great Western R. W. Co. v. Rous*, L. R. 4 H. L. 650 : " The safer and wiser course for a court of justice is to follow the plain, literal meaning and interpretation of the words used, unless it can clearly find in some other part of the instrument, a rule for their construction that over-rules the obligation of abiding by the literal meaning, and enables you to give a more or less extended interpretation of the words."

In *Ford v. Beech*, 11 Q. B. 866 Parke B. says : " The common and universal principle ought to be applied, the agreement ought to receive that construction which the language will admit, and which will best effectuate the intention of the parties to be collected from the whole of the agreement, and that greater regard is to be had to the clear intent of the parties, than to any particular words which they may have used in the expression of their intent."

The rule is, *Ex antecedentibus et consequentibus optima fit interpretatio.*

The subject is also treated in Broom's Maxims, 542: " The Judge will not cavil about the propriety of words when the intent of the parties appears, but will rather apply the words to fulfil the intent, than destroy the intent by reason of the insufficiency of the words."

In *Fowell* v. *Frautee*, 3 H. & C. 461, Bramwell, B., says: " Words are to be construed according to their natural meaning, unless such a construction would either render them senseless, or would be opposed to the general scope and intent of the instrument, or unless there be some very cogent reason of convenience in favour of a different interpretation."

In the case before us, the corporation was not buying, or selling, or contracting for the manufacture of a traction engine, or any other kind of engine. They were endeavoring to get rid of a steam engine found to be a nuisance to the travelling public, and they agree, in consideration of defendants agreeing not to use such an engine on their road, to allow them to use part of their highway for a tramroad, with provisions evidently showing that both parties only contemplated the use of horse-power thereon. May it not be considered as if they said : " We allow you the tramway for horse-power, on condition of you withdrawing the engine you now have for drawing on the highway, and agree not to use any other engine for drawing on the highway."

When the defendants urge their right under their charter to use steam on their tramway, it must always be borne in mind, that the track allowed to them by this agreement, is a part of the highroad to be used by them in common with all other subjects, and not a track or roadway of their own property. In bargaining with the Municipality, they can only acquire the right to use the highway on the terms expressly agreed on. If the defendants' view be right, the only effect of the agreement would be, that instead of running a steam engine on the common road, it would be run on rails laid on such common road, to be used in common with every one else.

The argument as to the kind of rails for horse tramways and railroads is also to be considered.

As to any reformation of the contract, the defendants do not admit there was any mistake common to both parties. The general rule is in such a case against reformation.

In *Harris* v. *Pepperill*, L. R. 5 Eq. 1 : Lord Romilly referring to his own decision, in *Lord Bradford* v. *Lord Romney*, 30 Beav. 431, says (p. 4): that where there was a settlement on marriage, the marriage solemnized and children born, where the Court is called to rectify a mistake made on one side, the Court must require proof of the exact contract which both parties intended to enter into, as it is impossible to undo the marriage, or to remit the parties to the same position they were in before.

But the same rule does not apply in cases arising between vendors and purchasers, using these words in their widest sense. In such a case, if the deed be not actually executed, the Court will refuse specific performance, and at p. 5 he says :

" In the present case it is clear that the Court can put the parties in the same position as before the conveyance was executed, for if I hold that there has been a mistake and that the deed ought to be rectified, then I can give the defendant the option of having the whole contract annulled, or else of taking it in the form which the plaintiff intended. It is, therefore, a case where the Court can grant relief, and I am of opinion that the mistake was clearly proved."

The plaintiff had included too much land in the conveyance to the defendant, alleging his own mistake. The defendant insisted there was no mistake.

Bloomer v. *Spittle*, L. R. 13 Eq. 431, before the same Judge is to same effect. After the lapse of some years a deed was directed to be rectified, unless the party who denied the alleged mistake preferred having the whole transaction set aside, the purchase money and interest to be repaid, the other party charged with an occupation rent, and an inquiry as to repairs and lasting improvements.

Mr. Kerr in his work (Ed. 1883 p. 499), says in reference to *Harris* v. *Pepperell*, that it was undoubtedly well decided; but that Lord Romilly's distinction that there was

an exception to the general rule requiring the mistake to
be common to both parties, in the case of vendors and
purchasers, is not supported by the authorities.

He refers to *Garrard* v. *Frankel*, 30 Beav. 445, another
decision of the same Judge. He also states it to be sound,
but that, as I understand his views "the Court merely
abstained from setting the agreement aside, on the consent
of the defendant to submit to the variation claimed by the
plaintiff."

Mr Fry (340, Sec. 759)—Says that a mistake of one
party can never be a ground for compulsory rectification.
It may be a reason for setting the whole thing aside, but
never for imposing on one party the erroneous conception
of the other. He then (Sec. 760) states the decisions of
Lord Romilly already cited, but does not comment on them.

There is another aspect in which this case may be
viewed. I find on the evidence that the plaintiffs believed
and understood that they were getting rid of the use of
steam on their roads, and were in consideration thereof,
granting the privilege to the defendants to have a horse
tramway.

I also find, as a fact, that the defendants knew and
understood that the plaintiffs so understood the bargain
and they, the defendants, either accepted the privilege on
the same understanding, or (an alternative I do not care to
adopt) intentionally concealed the idea of reserving the
right to use steam.

The well-known case of *Smith* v. *Hughes*, L. R., 6 Q. B.
597. may be referred to. Lord Blackburn says at p. 607'
"If whatever a man's real intention may be, he so conducts
himself that a reasonable man would believe he was assenting to the terms proposed by the other party, and that
other party upon that belief enters into the contract with
him, the man thus conducting himself, would be equally
bound as if he had intended to agree to the other party's
terms."

The judgment of Hannen, J., in this case is quoted by Mr.
Kerr, (p. 488): "'The promiser is not bound to fulfil a promise in a sense in which the promisee knew at the time

the promiser did not intend it,' and in considering the question in what sense a promisee is entitled to enforce the promise, it matters not in what way the knowledge of the meaning in which the promiser made it is brought to the mind of the promisee, whether by express words, or by conduct, or by previous dealings, or by other circumstances. If, by any means he knew there was no real agreement between him and the promiser, he is not entitled to insist that the promise shall be fulfilled in a sense to which the mind of the promiser did not assent."

This last sentence seems to meet this case very fairly, if the present contention of the defendants as to their version of this contract be correct.

I think we must hold the defendants to the full knowledge that the plaintiffs were only dealing with them for a horse tramway. Their user of the road for many years shews their interpretation of the bargain.

The learned Judge below, while holding that the contract did not require rectification, says : "If horse power alone was in the contemplation of the parties, then the Company has not shewn that they got permission to use steam, or if that were not incumbent on them, to show where they got the right to make a tramway, it establishes, however, that the Municipality only gave a permission for a tramway worked by horse-power."

As I agree in the conclusion arrived at by the learned Judge, I do not think it necessary to rest my conclusion on the question whether a Court of Equity would not, if they could not rectify the contract in the absence of evidence of common mistake, avoid the contract altogether, unless the defendants would consent to accept it in the sense contended for by the plaintiffs.

BURTON, J. A.—The whole question turns upon the construction of the agreement of the 10th of August, 1874, and I think the learned Judge below was correct, when he came to the conclusion that he must hold the traction engines referred to in the agreement, were traction engines such as were then in use, and the use of which had been authorised by the Act of 1868.

No doubt in order to arrive at the real intention of the parties, and to make a correct application of the words and language of the contract to the subject matter of it, all the surrounding facts and circumstances are to be taken into consideration.

We find then, that some years before the date of the agreement, an Act of Parliament had been passed authorizing the use of traction engines, that is to say an engine designed to run upon the ordinary highways of the Province, and that under the authority of that Act, a traction engine had been and was in use by the defendants on the road in question.

The agreement in question refers to such traction engine, and the fact that it was used by the defendants under the authority of that Act of Parliament.

The use of it was objected to by the plaintiffs, but they were powerless to prohibit it, but on the 10th July, 1874, Mr. Lamond Smith, the Managing Director of the defendants' Company, wrote to the plaintiffs proposing to them to withdraw it, and not to place it or any other traction engine on the road again, if the County would grant them permission to make a tramway or Street Railway, under the provisions of their charter.

No one can possibly doubt the meaning of this proposal, that it had reference to the then traction engine, and any other engine of a like nature which the Company were authorized to use under the Act.

The charter to which they refer had been passed on the 24th of the previous month of March, under which they were authorised to construct a double or single tramway, from their gravel pits in the Township of Scarborough to the City of Toronto, which might be worked by horse or other power, but if by steam, the rate of travelling was not to be greater than ten miles per hour.

The Councils of the Municipalities through or in which the road might be constructed, might, by by-law, or otherwise, permit the company to construct the same in or along the highways, upon such terms and conditions as might be agreed upon between them.

This being the position of matters, the Company having the unquestionable right to use their traction engine, and having the power to build their railway and to use horse power or steam upon it, but only to build it on the public highway upon obtaining the consent of the Council, the proposal I have referred to was made, and resulted in the agreement in question. That instrument, which refers to the power of the company to build their railway along the public highways, with the consent of the municipal corporation, proceeds to define the terms and conditions on which it is granted. In the enumeration of these terms and conditions, not one word is said about the use of steam power, and I think we may fairly assume that the matter did not suggest itself to either of the contracting parties, but this at all events is clear, that there is no prohibition against its use : whether if it had been suggested the company would have accepted the license with such a condition annexed, or the county would have granted the permission, if the company would only accept it on the condition that they should abandon so much of their chartered rights, it is not possible now to say, all that we are permitted to know now is, what this agreement contains, and this accords the license upon certain conditions, of which the prohibition to use steam is not one.

Then comes the *quid pro quo*, that on the agreement, that is the agreement already set forth in detail, being ratified by the corporation, the company will do what? Will do what they proposed they would do if the corporation gave them the license, that is, they would withdraw their said traction engine from the public highways, and would discontinue the use and employment of the said traction engine, and of any other traction engine, upon or along such highways, in other words they would bind themselves to abandon their rights under the Act of 1868.

I think the expert evidence (unsatisfactory as that evidence is, as usual,) entirely beside the point, and in my opinion was not in the circumstances of this case admissible.

The parties have defined their meaning, by shewing that what they referred to was an engine which the company were authorised to use upon the public highway, that, they agreed to withdraw and not to use any other upon the highway. The true construction of that agreement was for the Court, and the only construction that can, I think, be placed upon it is, that if you, the county, grant us the license upon the terms you have dictated, we will agree to waive our rights under the general law.

What A. B. or C. may understand to be a traction engine is a matter with which we at present are not concerned. What these parties meant by traction engines is I think perfectly clear, there is no room for ambiguity, they were dealing with traction engines, which, but for the Act of Parliament it would have been illegal to use upon the highway, it was a valuable privilege which the company possessed, and it was the waiver of this privilege to which they consented, on the county granting a license to lay their tramway.

I do not think it necessary to impute bad faith to either side. My conviction is, on a perusal of the evidence, that it did not occur to either party to provide for this contingency, but it is not the province of a Court of Justice to make contracts for people, but to construe or enforce those which they have made, if, as suggested by the learned Chief Justice, the contract could be avoided altogether, the company would be remitted to their original right to use their traction engine on the highway itself, a result that the county would not, I apprehend, desire.

It appears to me clearly to be a case in which the parties have omitted to stipulate for something, which they would have stipulated for if they had thought of it, and which might have resulted in no agreement being arrived at, but we have merely to construe the contract they have made, and that contract leaves the defendants free to use steam power on their tramway.

I am of opinion therefore that the appeal should be allowed, with costs; but as the Legislature has interfered to prevent the exercise of this right by the company, there must be a reference back to the learned Judge to assess the compensation to which the defendants are entitled.

PATTERSON, J. A.—The plaintiffs seek to restrain the defendants from using steam as the motive power on their tramway.

The defendants were empowered by the Statute 37 Vict. cap. 90, (O.) passed 24th March, 1874, to construct a tramway of wood or iron, or wood and iron, and other materials; and it was enacted that the road might be worked by horse or other power, but if by steam the rate of travelling was not to be greater than ten miles an hour. There was also express power given to construct a wire tramway, and to operate or work it by a stationary steam-engine.

The statutory right to use steam is thus clear.

The same statute made applicable to the defendants certain clauses of the act respecting joint stock companies for the construction of roads and other works in Upper Canada,—C. S. U. C. cap. 49, including the clauses giving power to expropriate lands required for the undertaking; and it provided, by section 3, that the councils of the municipalities through or in which the tramways or roads might be laid out, constructed or pass, might, by by-law or otherwise, permit the company to construct the same in, along, over, and upon the highways and streets, upon such terms and conditions as might be agreed upon between them.

The defendants did not exercise their expropriation powers, but constructed their tramway along a highway by permission given by the county council by a document embodying the agreement with the defendants, dated 10th August, 1874.

The defendants' case is, that by that instrument they received permission to construct their tramway along the highway, without any restriction, imposed by the plaintiffs or agreed to by the defendants, of their statutory powers touching the working of the road.

The plaintiffs, on the other hand, assert that the permission was restricted to constructing a tramway to be worked by horse-power only. They go further and contend that the defendants expressly covenanted not to work it by steam.

The learned Judge in the Court below found against this latter contention. I agree with his finding; but, as it has been impugned before us, I shall notice the point a little more at length.

The defendant company had been incorporated in 1873 by 36 Vict. cap. 114, (O.,) principally for the purpose of working gravel pits, and hauling and disposing of the gravel. For the purposes of their business they used on the common highway a traction engine, under the authority of the general Act 31 Vict. cap. 4, (O.,) now R. S. O. cap. 186.

The use of this engine proved very annoying to travellers driving along the highway, in consequence of which a petition was signed by a number of persons and presented to the county council, in which the petitioners represented that they had arranged with the owners of the engine, who would withdraw it, and would not put any other traction engine on any roads belonging to the county of York, on condition that the council would give the company leave to lay a tramway or street railway on the side of the Kingston Road, in such a manner as not to impede the traffic; and they prayed the council to grant the company the privilege of constructing such tramway on the Kingston Road, upon their entering into a covenant with the county not to use the said engine, or any other engine of a similar character, upon the roads of the county.

Thereupon negotiations ensued, which resulted in the agreement of 10th August, 1874.

That document begins with the following recitals:—

Whereas the company are owners of a certain traction engine which, under the authority of an Act of the Parliament of Ontario, has been employed by the said company for the conveyance of freight, etc., over the public highways of the said county: and

Whereas by a certain other Act of Parliament of Ontario the said company were, amongst other things, authorised upon certain terms and conditions, to construct tramways for the conveyance of freight and passengers upon or along the public highways of the said county of York: and

Whereas one of such terms and conditions was, that before constructing said tramway upon or along such public highways, the consent of the said corporation should be first had and obtained: and

Whereas the said Company have applied to the said corporation for leave to lay down and construct a tramway upon or along the Kingston Road, being one of the publi highways of the said county, from their gravel beds or pits in the township of Scarboro through the township of York to the city of Toronto: and

Whereas the said corporation have agreed upon the terms and conditions hereinafter mentioned to give their consent to such application:

Now it is hereby agreed as follows:

Then follows the permission given which I shall have to discuss on the other branch of the controversy; and the instrument concludes with the agreement I am now dealing with in these words:

" 9. So soon as this agreement shall have been ratified by the said corporation the said company shall forthwith withdraw their said traction engine from the public highways of the said county, and shall discontinue the use and employment of the said traction engine, and of any other traction engine, upon or along such public highways."

This is what is relied on as a covenant not to work the tramway by steam.

It seems palpable on reading the recitals and this 9th clause, and on knowing the facts which I have mentioned, that the parties to this document had in their minds nothing but the engine that caused the grievance, and which engine they arranged to have discontinued; and that they meant simply to say that they did not stipulate only with respect to this particular engine, the removal of which would not cure the evil if another like it was put in its place or on any of the other roads of the county. This kind of machine

well known by the name of traction engine, and so described in the statute they recited, was evidently all that
was in contemplation.

The argument by which this clause is attempted to be
made to exclude a steam motor from the tramway has, I
confess, gone farther to dispose me against the whole case
of the plaintiffs than anything that has been advanced on
the part of the defendants. So far has it been from convincing me that either party intended to use, or believed
the other to understand the term as conveying anything
more than its popular meaning, that I am at a loss to
reconcile the conception on which this part of the case has
been conducted with the well understood rule which requires us to give effect to contracts in the sense in which
the parties to them understood the language they used.

We are gravely asked to construe the term by holding it,
in this clause of the contract, to cover whatever can be
brought within the etymological meaning of the word
"traction;" and expert after expert in mechanical engineering has been examined to tell us what he finds in a
dictionary. An illustration of the unreliable character of
testimony of this kind is unconsciously furnished by most
of these experts who, striving to shew that any engine that
draws may be called a traction engine because " traction "
is derived from " traho," yet refuse to go the length that
their etymological theory would require, and to admit that
stationary engines may come within the category. No
one of them pretends to know as part of his professional
knowledge, or to find in any scientific or other book, that
the term " traction engine," as a name for a specific kind of
machine, is ever applied to any locomotive except one for
use on a common highway, while every definition of the
term that has been quoted gives precisely the popular
meaning. One was read from a work of Brand & Cox. I
turn up another authority, which I happen to have at hand
as I write, Smith's Glossary of Terms and Phrases, and
read: "A traction engine is a locomotive for drawing
waggons along a highway."

One gentleman who gave his evidence was one of the most eminent civil engineers of the day, and his explanation makes it perfectly clear that while, in engineering, the word "traction" as applied to an engine relates to its power as a locomotive to draw a load from place to place, the term "traction engine" is not ordinarily if it is ever used to describe any locomotive except one which runs on ordinary roads.

This attempt on the plaintiffs' part to induce the Court to find that in making the agreement the members of the county council of York were using the term, not as descriptive of the engine they knew and wanted to get rid of, and other engines of that kind, but as descriptive of whatever engine could be designated by a derivative from "traho," suggests to me that little confidence has been felt in the real merits of their case. The same impression arises with even greater force from the circumstance that the plaintiffs thought it, for their safety, necessary to procure from the Legislature in 1881, pending this litigation, the statute 44 Vict. ch. 57, (O.,) declaring that thereafter the defendants should not have power to use locomotives propelled by steam, or steam motors, or other steam engines upon the tramway in question, unless permitted by by-law or resolution of the county council; but as that Act declares that nothing contained in it shall prejudice or affect the rights or contention of either party in this action, I pass on to consider whether under the proper construction of the document of 10th August, permission was granted without any limitation to use whatever motive power the defendants pleased.

We have a mass of evidence from the members of the council on the one hand, and members of the defendant company on the other, with that of some other persons, to shew what was talked of or understood at or before the execution of the deed. I should prefer to find the key to the construction of the document in its own terms. It is questionable whether we can properly give attention to the oral testimony, beyond gathering from it the state of facts with reference to which the agreement was made. If we had to weigh the evidence on the one side against that given on the other, I am afraid I should feel that the plaintiffs by their attempt in the conduct of the case to which I have adverted, to maintain what so strongly strikes me as unreal in fact and disingenuous, have thrown some weight into the scale of their opponents.

We must find, if possible, the meaning of the parties from the writing itself, seeking to ascertain from its provisions as a whole what was really intended, and not applying against the plaintiffs the rule of critical interpretation on which they invited us to find a meaning for "traction engine," which the contracting parties never thought of.

The first provision is that

" The said company shall be at liberty forthwith to lay down and construct a tramway in accordance with the last mentioned Act of Parliament of Ontario, for the carriage of freight and passengers upon and along the Kingston Road, from the gravel bed or pits of the said company in the townships of York and Scarboro to the city of Toronto."

This in its terms refers to the construction and not to the working of the road. It contains no restriction, but is not inconsistent with any restriction elsewhere to be found.

The part of the highway to be occupied is then defined, and the event of the company discontinuing the use of the tramway is provided for.

Then come the clauses on which most of the argument turns :

4. Tolls to be collected shall not exceed the same as for ordinary conveyances, viz., not more than 7 cents for cars drawn by one horse, and 10 cents for cars drawn by two horses.

5. The said company shall, if required, run not less than two passenger cars daily each way (or in lieu thereof an omnibus or sleigh), from the Don bridge to Norway, at such hours as may be found most convenient for the company and the public, so long as the said tramway is in use.

In case of horses, carriages, teams, or other vehicles or animals meeting or being overtaken by the horses, waggons, carriages or other vehicles of the said company, travelling upon the said tramway, the said company shall have the first and immediate right of way over and upon said tramway.

It cannot in view of these clauses be said that the permission to construct the tramway upon the highway given by the first clause of the agreement was unconditional. These clauses 4, 5, and 6 are conditions annexed to or restrictions of the right which the defendants would have enjoyed if governed only by their statutes. The question then is, to what extent should it be held, on a fair construction of the instrument, the statutory right was restricted; or the question may perhaps more properly take another shape:—Permission was required from the municipal council before the powers could be exercised: Did the council grant permission to exercise all or only some of the statutory powers?

It is clearly implied that the permission was only accorded on the terms that tolls should be paid, notwithstanding that clause 4 is framed as limiting the amount for the protection of the defendants. The regulation of the tolls by reference to the number of horses, and in no other way, is, as it strikes me, a very satisfactory indication that the agreed user was only to be by cars drawn by horses. The two following clauses have less direct significance, but they indicate that only vehicles drawn by horses were in contemplation.

The onus is on the defendants to shew unrestricted permission. They have nothing to shew but the first clause, which, taking the whole document together, must be read as merely conceding the right to construct, subject to restrictions as to user. The statute expressly mentions horse power and steam power. We find the restrictive clauses dealing with one of those motors and not the other, and at the same time bearing evidence, emphasized by clause 4 being drawn in the interest of the defendants, of the agreement involving payment in the form of tolls. It seems impossible to say that the learned Judge was wrong in holding that no right to use steam was conceded.

The principle of construction laid down by Lord Cotten-ham, in *Lloyd* v. *Lloyd*, 2 My. & C. at p. 202, seems very apposite. The passage reads thus :

"If the provisions are clearly expressed, and there is nothing to enable the Court to put upon them a construc-tion different from that which the words import, no doubt the words must prevail; but if the provisions and expres-sions be contradictory, and f there be grounds appearing upon the face of the instrument affording proof of the real intention of the parties, then that intention will prevail against the obvious and ordinary meaning of the words. If the parties have themselves furnished a key to the meaning of the words used, it is not material by what ex-pression they convey their intention."

Here we have the first clause which by itself would give all the powers contended for. It is shewn by the subse-quent provisions that that was not the intention of the parties. The instrument does, I think, afford proof of the extent to which it was intended and understood that the permission should go.

I may add that a careful perusal of the evidence has not tended to cause me to doubt that this construction does justice to the real understanding of those concerned. Statements to the effect that the defendants or those acting for them never intended to forego any of their rights, and would not have made the agreement if they had supposed they were doing so, do not influence my view. It was not a question of foregoing any right. The question was the use of this highway, and how much of the statutory right did the county agree should be exercised over the highway.

I do not doubt the correctness of the suggestion that neither party thought, at the time of the making of the agreement, of the tramway being run by steam. One member of the defendant company was asked would they have agreed in 1874 to a stipulation as to their right to use steam, and his answer was: "It was never mentioned at our board, and we would not have agreed to it had it been."

Evidence like this certainly does not prove the contemplation of using steam at the date in question.

Witnesses on both sides agree that the subject of tolls was treated as an important one.

Mr. Morton, a leading member of the defendant company, is very emphatic in his evidence on the point. At one meeting of the council, where he was one of the audience, he says the main thing discussed was, getting as much as possible out of the company for tolls; at another part of his evidence we have this dialogue :—

"Q. You there discussed the terms upon which you would withdraw the traction engine? A. Yes.

Q. And the subject also was discussed as to tolls which you should pay? A. Yes; that is what took me there.

Q. You objected to pay tolls? A. Altogether.

Q. They insisted you should pay tolls? A. Yes.

Q. The result was they decided you should pay tolls? A. When we came to a general understanding, I agreed to submit it to the directors; the question of tolls had arisen before that.

Q. At a previous meeting? A. I had a previous meeting in my office. Mr. Leslie first brought a memo. without tolls, and they insisted upon tolls, and I said I would never think of such a thing, and would abandon the whole thing, and was making arrangements to run on another roadway, and then Mr. Wheeler and these gentlemen came up and talked about the question of tolls, and invited me to that meeting in the County Chamber."

We can easily understand from this evidence why the clause 4 in the agreement took the shape of limiting the amount of tolls to be charged; but it also confirms the opinion that the privilege granted was only co-extensive with the tolls to be paid.

This is not answered by Mr. Osler's suggestion that the reason why horses only were mentioned was, that the Road Acts gave no power to collect tolls upon steam vehicles. We are dealing with an agreement, and not with the statutory power to collect tolls from persons who have a common law right to use the highway.

I think we should dismiss the appeal, with costs.

Rose J.—I agree with the learned Judge below in the construction of the term "traction engine." I would also agree in the conclusion he arrived at that the defendants

had no right to use steam, were I able to form the opinion
that it was necessary to obtain permission to use steam.   I
however think that when the defendants obtained the
right to make a tramway, such right, carried with it the
right to exercise all the powers and privileges conferred
upon them by the Amending Act of 1874, unless by the
express terms of the agreement such rights and privileges
were taken away.

The onus of shewing that the plaintiffs had prohibited
the defendants from using steam or any other motive
power rested upon the plaintiffs.   Any doubt in the matter
prevents their succeeding in this action.

This should be so, for rights and franchises should not
be taken away by implication.

The judgment below rests upon the finding that a permission was granted to use horses only as a motive or
traction power.   If so, it is clear that the defendants could
not use any other of the motive or traction powers permitted by the Act of Parliament.

The learned Judge in his judgment says : " I understood
Mr. Robinson to concede that at the time of the agreement
both parties only thought of horse power."   It seems to me
this is the fact.   If so, then it did not occur to the plaintiffs that the defendants some day might use steam, and
consequently the plaintiffs could not have intended to prohibit the use of steam.   The Amending Act is recited in
the agreement.   I suppose the reference to it is as sufficient a statement of its terms as if they had been set out in
full, even if its being an Act of Parliament did not place
the plaintiffs in the position of having full notice of its
provisions.

In this view the agreement may fairly be read thus :

Recite that the company are owners of a traction engine.

That by Act of Parliament the company are authorized
to construct a tramway and to transport thereon cars, &c ,
drawn or propelled by horse or other power including steam.

That before constructing the tramway the consent of the
municipality must be obtained.

That the company have applied to the municipality for permission to construct a tramway upon which to transport cars, etc., drawn or propelled by horse or other power, including steam.

That the municipality have agreed to give their consent to construct such tramway upon which to transport cars, &c., drawn or propelled by horse or other power, including steam.

Agreement according to recitals followed by provisions having reference to the use of horse power, and an undertaking by the company, to withdraw the traction engine then in use, and discontinue the use of that engine or any other traction engine upon or along such public highways.

Here we would expect to find an agreement by the company or a prohibition by the municipal corporation as to the use of any power other than horse power, and no doubt we would have found it had it been thought of, and had an agreement been come to by the parties.

Because it was not thought of, I cannot conclude that the defendants were prohibited from using power other than horse power.

The defendants say if such a condition had been insisted upon they would not have entered into the agreement. It is of course difficult for them now to know what they would then have done, but it is sufficient for their purpose that they did not agree.

For these reasons I agree with my Brother Burton in thinking the appeal should be allowed, and also that there should be a reference back to assess the compensation.

The Court being equally divided, the appeal was dismissed, and the judgment appealed from stood affirmed.

[This case was affirmed in the Supreme Court on the 16th Nov., 1885.]

PLUMB v. STEINHOFF.

Survey—Description—Evidence.

In an action of ejectment the question was as to the position of lot 5 in the 18th concession, the plaintiff's lot, which was granted in 1807, and lot 24 in the 17th concession, the defendant's lot, the patent for which was issued at a later date. No traces remained of the surveyor's work on the ground. In the former patent the concession line was given as the southerly boundary of the lot, with a distance of 84 chains more or less from thence to the river:

Held, [in this reversing the judgment of FERGUSON, J., reported 1 O. R. 614,] that notwithstanding there was no evidence of the actual position of the line as run upon the ground, and that all the land in both concessions at the date of the patent belonged to the Crown, the distance of 84 chains thus given could not be treated as fixing the position of the concession line as at an absolute distance of 84 chains at least from the river.

THIS was an appeal by the defendant from the judgment of Ferguson, J., (reported 2 O. R. 614), and came on to be heard before this Court on the 8th and 11th days of February, 1884.*

Atkinson, for the appellant.
Moss, Q. C., and *Nesbitt,* for the respondent.

The facts of the case and the points relied on sufficiently appear in the former report, and in the present judgment.

September 5, 1884. PATTERSON, J. A.—The plaintiff owns lot No. 5 in the 18th concession of Dover East, and the defendant owns lot No. 24 in the 17th concession. These lots both adjoin the township line between Dover East and Chatham, the 18th concession lying north of the 17th. The matter in dispute is the position of the concession line which runs between these two lots.

The action is an action to recover land of which the defendant has possession, which he claims as part of lot 24, and which the plaintiff claims as part of lot 5.

The land is marsh land, unfit for cultivation, or even for use as meadow land without draining, and was unoccupied

Present.—SPRAGGE, C.J.O., BURTON, PATTERSON, and OSLER, JJ.A.

until the defendant, six or seven years ago, took actual
possession of the piece now in dispute, and by means of
ditches, dykes, and pumping apparatus, drained it and
made it cultivable.

He bought lot 24 in 1876, and shortly after his purchase
procured Mr. Fraser, a surveyor, to ascertain the northern
line of the lot, and he took possession and made his improvements in accordance with the line so found.   The plaintiff
now alleges that Mr. Fraser's line is considerably too far
north, and that the defendant has consequently encroached
seven or eight chains, or even more, upon his lot No. 5.

The burden of proving this allegation is, of course, upon
the plaintiff.

It is not pretended that the plaintiff, or any one through
whom he claims, ever actually occupied the land, wherefore
the plaintiff is driven to show a paper title, or rather, his
title to lot 5 not being disputed, he has to shew that the
tract in dispute is really part of lot No. 5.

That lot was patented with other lands in 1807 to Lord
Selkirk.

The case has been argued before us, and was apparently
treated in the Court below, as if the plaintiff claimed under
the patentee, and I discuss it in the first place on that footing.   I believe, however, that the fact is that the plaintiff
claims title only under a sale for taxes, and therefore not
in privity with the earlier paper title.   The grant contained
in the patent is of a tract thus described :

" All that parcel or tract of land, situate in the township
of Dover, &c., containing by admeasurement 920 acres, be
the same more or less, being lots Nos. 19, 1, 2, 3, 4, and 5,
in the 18th concession of the said township of Dover,
together with, &c., which said 920 acres of land are butted
and bounded, or may be otherwise known as follows, that
is to say : commencing in front of the said concession at
the easterly angle of the said lot No. 5 on the easterly
limit of the said township of Dover ; thence north forty-
five degrees west eighty-four chains, more or less, to Great
Bear Creek ; thence south-westerly following the several
courses of the said creek and Chenal Ecartè to the allow-

ance for road in front of lot No. 19 between the 17th and 18th concessions; thence north forty-five degrees east eighteen chains, more or less, to the allowance for road between lots Nos. 19 and 1; then south forty-five degrees east thirty-five chains, more or less, to the allowance for road in front of lot No. 1 between the 17th and 18th concessions; thence north forty-five degrees east one hundred and fifty chains, more or less, to the place of beginning."

A survey of that part of the township of Dover had been made in 1804 by a surveyor named Hambly, who carried out instructions issued from the surveyor general's office on the 15th December, 1803, to Abraham Iredell.

Two parallel lines running north-west from the river Thames, which will have to be frequently mentioned, are the township line, or base line, between Dover and Chatham, and a line between the western and eastern divisions of the township, called the division line, or Little Bear line.

The concession lines are at right angles to those running north-east from the western boundary on lake St. Clair and the Chenal Ecarté, or south-west from the base line.

The concessions on each side of the division line are numbered from 1 to 18, but those on opposite sides of the line do not correspond in width. The concession lines of the two systems are not in any concession continuous lines, but each line in the eastern division is considerably to the south of the line of the same number in the western division.

The lots are numbered from the western extremity on lake St. Clair, the lot next to the division line on the west being No. 19.

There were originally five lots in each concession between the division line and the base line, which Hambly appears to have numbered 1, 2, 3, 4, and 5, but which seem to have been also known in all the concessions south of the 18th, as Nos. 20, 21, 22, 23, and 24. This explains how lot 24 in the 17th concession happened to be immediately in rear of lot 5 in the 18th. There was also adjoining the base line a 19th concession, or rather there was a line marked on the base line as 19th concession line, which ran only across or partly across the width of one lot when it struck the Large Bear Creek, which with the Chenal Ecartè into which it falls at lot No. 2. bounds the 18th concession, making the lots in that concession of unequal depths.

Hambly shews by his diary and field notes, and by his plan, that he laid out the concessions along the base line from 3 to 18 inclusive (Nos. 1 and 2 having been laid out by Iredell) of the uniform depth of sixty-eight chains, or including the allowance for road in front of each concession, sixty-nine chains; and he gives the distance in the 19th concession as fifty-six and a half chains until the line intersects a line called the purchase line, which was the extreme north-western limit of the base line. At some point in this space of fifty-six and a half chains he places the river.

His field note of lot 19 is: "Open meadow to 10.50 chains; then poplar thickets, thorns, plumb bushes, grape vines, &c., to 16 chains; at 18 chains X Large Bear Creek trending south-westerly; then fine open meadow to 34 chains; then maple, elm, ash, chiefly oak, to 56½ chains, and intersected the purchase line run by Abraham Iredell, Esquire."

The uncertainty is the reading of the symbolic cross. If the meaning is that at 18 chains he begins to "cross the river" he must make the distance from the 18th concession line to the river 69 + 18 or 87 chains. If he means that at 18 chains he is "across the river" he allows certainly not more than two chains for the width of the river, because he gives at least 16 chains of dry land before reaching it. According to the evidence the river must have been from three to four chains wide, and therefore two chains was an underestimate.

The description in the patent must have been intended to follow Hambly's report.

It shews that in the Surveyor General's office there was no idea that there was a distance of 18 chains from the front of the 19th concession to the river, yet the 84 chains mentioned in the description will not even allow Hambly's 16, as 69 + 16 would be 85.

I may have to notice by-and-by the effect of these and
other details. My present object is chiefly to point out
that Hambly, according to his report, actually laid out all
these concessions. In his diary he notes that he planted
stakes at some concession lines, usually mentioning only
those where he happened to encamp for the night, thus:
"Sunday, July 1st, 1804. Continued the said line, planted
6th concession stake, and encamped." He mentions on
other days planting the 9th, 12th, 14th, and 16th concession
stakes, the last of these was on the 6th July.

Then on 7th, "Town line continued to 20 chains and
left off on account of deep and wet marsh; then went and
opened the 16th concession line, and encamped late."

On Sunday, 8th July, he continued to open that line till
he reached Little Bear River which crosses it. He did
further work on that line on 21st July. On 9th August,
he "went to the 18th concession post and continued a line
through the meadows." On 10th August, "went to the
17th concession post, ran a line, and then continued the
line between Chatham and Dover, beginning at the 17th
concession post." And on 11th August, "went to Large
Bear Creek, and continued the line as per field book."

After this the diary shews his work at the division line
where, on the 14th August, he planted the 18th, 17th, and
16th concession posts. These I understand to be for the
western concessions which he continued down to the 13th,
when the hardships attendant on the survey, and the
sickness of himself and his men brought his work there
to an end.

In Hambly's field notes he gives the boundary of each
concession on the base line, that of the 3rd concession
being a beech tree and all the others "pickets" of iron-
wood or black ash.

There are notes also of his survey of concessions 13 to
18 on the division line; of concession lines 15, 16, 17, and
18, running from the division line to the base line, and of
concessions 13, 14, 15, 16, 17, and 18, on the west side of
the division line.

Hambly notes other work in traversing the rivers, &c., which it is not necessary now to refer to. I should, however, notice his letter of 11th July, 1804, to the Surveyor-General. I have mentioned that on the 7th July he had run the 16th concession line as far as Little Bear River, and that on the 21st he resumed the running of that line. He had in the meantime, as his diary shews, gone up the river to pay a visit to Lord Selkirk, and had been otherwise occupied. On the 11th, the date of the letter, he " travelled down the township line, and arrived at Mr. Iredell's late." In the letter he reports the running of the division line of Chatham and Dover, and says (amongst other things): "I have ran the 16th concession of the eastern division of Dover, the lot No. 1 of which crosses the river De Luce on a large marsh." The river De Luce seems to be the same as Little Bear Creek.

Thus we have the fact that, before the issue of the patent, there had been an actual survey made by order of the Government, and duly returned to the Surveyor-General's office.

It is evident the patent was framed with reference to this survey. It ignores, it is true, the 19th concession, and treats the land all the way to the river as being the 18th concession; but, as all that part of the township beyond the river was already, as I infer it was, the property of Lord Selkirk, and as there was really nothing of the 19th concession but a few acres in the triangle formed by the river, the base line, and the north line of 18, there was little object in describing it as in concession 19; we are not, however, much concerned with the effect of the description on the title to the triangle, as the land in question is at a distance from it.

The plaintiff has to establish that the line over which he charges the defendant with encroaching, is the front of the 18th concession, or the allowance for road between the 17th and 18th concessions. This he must do whether he relies on the general description of " lot 5, in the 18th concession," or on the description by metes and bounds.

It is proved and is conceded that no trace of Hambly's work upon the ground at this concession line remains. The concession line, if ever marked by blazed trees, which is not probable, as there is evidence that the place was a marsh without trees, has long been obliterated ; and no post, whether planted by Hambly, or by any one to mark the place of Hambly's post, exists.

If the place of the line can be established, it must be by evidence of a different sort.

The plaintiff relies on the mention in the patent of eighty-four chains, more or less, as the distance from the concession line to the river, which, although a chain less than the distance given by Hambly in his field notes and · plan, may have been made so by adding together Hambly's figures of sixty-eight chains for the 18th, and sixteen for the 19th concessions, overlooking his allowance for road between the two concessions, and the contention is, that no direct evidence being available of the actual position of the line as run upon the ground, the plaintiff has the right to take an absolute distance of eighty-four chains from the river, as the position of the concession line. It may have been, and I think it was also urged that the whole region being vested in the Crown in 1807, the grant ought to be construed as giving eighty-four chains from the river, whether or not the terminus of that distance agreed with the concession line as surveyed.

The argument in this shape is clearly untenable in the face of the description in the patent, which gave the concession line as the boundary, whether more or less than the named distance from the river, and the question must be, as it was treated throughout the judgment of the learned Judge, what is the true position of the original line ?

I believe I am right in saying that what I have mentioned is the entire case made by the plaintiff.

Two surveyors, who had made measurements for him, shewed that taking 84 chains from the river as the place to which the plaintiff's title extended, the defendant had encroached, the extent being computed at 8 chains 16 links by one surveyor, and 7 chains 72 links by the other, the difference between them arising from one measuring from the water as he found it, and the other allowing nearly half a chain because he was told that the drainage had swollen the volume of water in the river.

These surveyors also stated, that if the concessions were divided equally, with the surplus apportioned proportionately among them, the encroachment would appear to be somewhat greater. They speak of the proportionate division being "under the statute," and I notice that the learned Judge inadvertently adopts that expression, but the statute affords no authority for resorting to such a process in order to replace a lost concession line.

There are in the statute (R. S. O., cap. 146). minute directions concerning side lines of lots, including the useful rule contained in section 65, under which a line of a somewhat arbitrary kind may be established by apportioning the space between two undisputed posts or limits, when no intermediate limit can be ascertained, but there is no such rule applicable to concession lines.

The provisions of sections 38 and 39 of that statute, and those of section 462 of the Municipal Act, R. S. O., cap. 174, under which steps may be taken by County Councils, or in some cases by the Councils of other municipalities, for procuring an authoritative survey and marking of concession lines, even though, as in this case, the line has become obliterated, are, I believe, the only enactments specially dealing with the retracing of lost concession lines, and they do not support the assumed right to apportion the distance between any two points farther apart than the depth of two concessions. This subject was discussed in *Boley* v. *McLean*, 41 U. C. R. 260, and in cases there cited.

Even if the rule in section 65 could be applied to concession lines, its application would fail in a case like this for want of undisputed limits between which to divide.

I understand the surveyors to take as one undisputed point, the third concession line, where Iredell's work stopped,

and as the other the Large Bear Creek; but the latter, though
a fixed natural object, is not the limit of any concession.
It is simply a natural feature which occurs a certain distance beyond the 18th concession, and somewhere in the
19th concession.

The plaintiff does not and cannot contend that it should
be held, as a conclusion of law, that the concession line is
either eighty-four or eighty-five chains from the river.
We have to deal simply with the question of fact,
where was the line placed in the original survey. The
inquiry is not, as was apparently assumed by one of the
surveyors who gave evidence for the plaintiff, affected by
the circumstance that in 1807, when this patent issued,
there was no express statutory provision such as that first
contained in section 32 of 12th Victoria ch. 35, and now
forming section 46 of R. S. O., ch. 146, which declares that
all boundary lines of townships, cities, towns, and villages,
all concession lines, governing points, and all boundary
lines of concessions, sections, blocks, gores, and commons,
and all side lines and limits of lots surveyed, and all posts
or monuments marked, placed, or planted at the front
angles of any lots or parcels of land, under government
authority, shall be the true and unalterable boundaries of
all and every such townships, cities, towns, villages, concessions, sections, blocks, gores, commons, and lots or parcels
of land respectively, whether the same upon admeasurement be found to contain the exact width, or more or less
than the exact width mentioned or expressed in any letters
patent, grant, or other instrument in respect of such township, city, town, village, concession, section, block, gore,
common, lot or parcel of land.

The facts that the land had, before the issue of the
patent, been surveyed into concessions and lots, and that
the land was granted by a description which had reference
to that survey, the starting point in the abuttals being the
front of the concession at the easterly angle of lot No. 5,
would have made the inquiry precisely the same before

the passing of the Statute of 1848, as in the case of a grant made after that date.

The description before us being intended, as I take it clearly to be intended, to refer to a definite spot as the easterly angle of lot 5, namely, the spot where Hambly planted, as he reported to the department, a black ash picket or post, from which spot the distance to the river is described as eighty-four chains, more or less; and the grant being in express terms confined to the 18th concession; I am not prepared to hold without doubt that the measurement back from the river of eighty-four chains is proper evidence, if nothing else were shewn, of the original *situs* of the line, particularly when the question does not arise between the grantee and the Crown, his grantor, but between him and a grantee of land bounded by the allowance for road upon the same concession line.

At most, the description and the field notes and plan would be only evidence for a jury to take for what it is worth. If we assume that it is to that extent proper evidence, we have to see how far it carries the proof. I am still speaking only of the evidence adduced on the part of the plaintiff, and before referring to that given for the defendant, I shall notice one or two other points.

The plaintiff's two surveyors measured from the front of the 3rd concession where Hambly's work began, to the Great Bear Creek; and they both tell us that allowing sixty-nine chains for each of the fifteen concessions, No. 3 to No. 17, and eighty-five chains more for 18 and 19, there is still a surplus of land. One of them, Mr. McDonell, says it is three chains thirty-four links; and dividing it proportionately he allots twenty-seven links to concessions 18 and 19 in respect of the eighty-five chains, and the rest, or three chains and seven links, to the other fifteen concessions, which, as I compute it, gives each of those concessions a fraction over twenty links. I do not say that twenty-seven links to eighty-five chains, and twenty links to sixty-nine chains are in the same ratio. I merely refer to the evidence given.

The other surveyor, Mr. Passmore, does not tell us what his measurement was, but he says the result of it was, that he had thirty-six links to give as proportionate distance for eighty-four chains, thirty-six links more to the distance given in the patent. That would, I think, allow about twenty-nine links to each of the fifteen other concessions, and would shew Mr. Passmore's whole measurement to be four chains and thirty-five links, apparently agreeing with Mr. McDonell's three chains and thirty-four links, with one chain added from the eighty-five chains, as Mr. Passmore takes the distance of eighty-four as representing the 18th and 19th concessions.

This apportionment is, as I have said, unwarranted by law. I now quote the figures to shew that the plaintiff's own evidence shews affirmatively what every one at all acquainted with the subject would assume without proof, that Hambly's work, as represented by him upon paper, cannot possibly coincide with the work he did upon the ground.

The result shewn is that there is a variance of nearly four and a-half chains between the distance actually measured now, and that laid down by him. At what part or parts of his survey the irregularities occurred, of which this is merely the gross result, it is, of course, impossible, so far as this part of the evidence goes, even to conjecture.

Mr. Atkinson called our attention to one discrepancy in the figures given as the measurements in connection with this very 18th concession, which make the length of the river that represents the hypothenuse of a right angled triangle, less than that of the base of the triangle.

Common experience prepares us to find irregularities in every part of the work, and the touching accounts which Mr. Hambly's diary and letters contain of the hardships and difficulties he had to contend with, do not lead us to look for such exceptional accuracy in the survey, as must be assumed if we treat these measurements back from the river as sufficient proof of the place of the concession line.

Having regard to these considerations, and to the fact that, since the statute provides a proceeding by which obliterated concession lines may be authoritatively retraced and marked, it is not necessary to resort to so uncertain a method as that now relied on; my opinion is, that the evidence ought not to be held sufficient.

But if we assume, for the purpose of the present discussion, that it is evidence on which a verdict could be sustained, we must see what effect ought to be given to the evidence offered for the defendant.

We must not forget that the onus of proof is upon the plaintiff, who has to establish that the defendant is occupying some land of his.

The defendant does not necessarily undertake to shew where the true line is, but being in actual possession, his evidence fulfils its purpose if it makes it clear that, upon the whole testimony, it would be unsafe to hold that the plaintiff's case is made out. An important part of the defendant's case was the evidence from the records of the Crown Lands department relating to a survey made by a Mr. Smith, in 1810, three years after the patent to Lord Selkirk, and two years before the date of the order in Council under which the patent for the defendant's lot was issued.

There is, of course, no pretence that the survey of 1810 can in any way control the operation of the deed of 1807. The value of the evidence touching that survey consists in the light it may throw upon the earlier survey, or the assistance it may afford us in deciding upon the propriety of adopting the conclusion which the plaintiff asks us to draw from the fact that the defendant occupies land within eighty-four chains of the river.

It will be remembered that Iredell was instructed in 1803, to lay out the parts of Dover and Chatham then unsurveyed, and that Hambly's work was a continuation of what Iredell had begun. Then on 23rd August, 1809, instructions were sent to Smith " for the survey of the remaining parts of Dover and Chatham." He was to do this according to rough plans, called in the instructions *bruillon* plans, which were sent for his guidance, but which are not forthcoming.

It must have been by these plans that the instruction was conveyed to make an alteration in one part of Hambly's survey. I have mentioned that the concessions Nos. 3 to 18, laid out by Hambly between the division line and the base line, contained each five 200 acre lots, which Hambly numbered 1, 2, 3, 4, 5. Smith made a new division of lots 2, 3, and 4, in all the concessions from 3 to 17, running down the centre of lot 3 a road called Baldoon street, and laying out on each side of the road lots of 100 acres each, thus making in each concession six 100 acre lots out of the three 200 acre lots. I gather from the correspondence in evidence that this was done, at the instance and in part at the expense of Lord Selkirk, for purposes relating to the settlement of immigrants upon the lands.

Smith was not required to interfere with lots 1 or 5 (otherwise 20 and 24), but the survey of the Baldoon street lots seems to have necessitated his tracing the division line and the base line as well as all the concession lines. His diary and field notes shew with much detail what was done by him, or the men who worked under him and under his assistant in two parties, in order to meet Lord Selkirk's desires to have the survey pushed rapidly forward, one party apparently working on the east side of Baldoon street and the other on the west side.

Smith mentions posts at the ends of nearly every concession line; but it would not be easy to decide from what he says, whether they were posts planted by Hambly or by himself.

The references to them are found in three documents, viz. : his diary, his field notes of the base line, and his field notes of the several concession lines. An extract or two from each of these will shew the general character of these references. Thus in the diary we find an entry 27th April, 1810, " from post 12 and 13 on Baldoon street to post con-

cession 7 on base of Dover and Chatham; then along
Chatham line sixty-nine chains to post concession 8; then
S. 45° W. to post 15 and 16 on Baldoon street;" and on
2nd May, "from 39 and 40 N. 45° W. sixty-nine chains to
post 42 and 43; then N. 45° E. 75.65 to the base of Dover
and Chatham, concession 17; then N. 45° W. sixty-nine
chains along the base of Chatham to concession post 18;
then N. 45° W. sixty-nine chains to concession post 19, on
the base of Dover and Chatham; then N. 45° W. five
chains to the border of Big Bear Creek."

It will be noticed that when in these extracts and other
similar entries he simply mentions a post, he does so in
the same way, whether the post is one of those on Baldoon
street, all of which were of his own planting, or one on the
base line. This language, therefore, merely shews that
when the work was being done, on the days here referred
to, the posts were already there. But in an earlier part of
the diary we have an account of his planting the Baldoon
street posts, and he has left no such record of work on the
base line.

It will be further noticed, that no post is here mentioned
at concession 17. In the field notes of the base line many
posts are noted as *marked*, including one in front of the
2nd concession, which was surveyed by Iredell. One post,
namely at concession 17, he says he *planted*, and a number
of concessions are noted in the field notes without anything
being said as to the posts, although the posts of nearly all
of them are mentioned in the diary. I read the notes
referring to the concessions 17, 18, and 19:

"69—16th concession—black ash swamp to ten chains,
then meadow wet; at 65 a small inlet on the left; 69
planted post 17th concession."

"69—17th concession—water grass meadow—at 30 a
point of wood R. H. distant eight chains running parallel
with the line ten chains. Forty chains across wood on the
left, distant thirty-five chains; sixty the same woods end
in a point; at sixty-nine marked post, concession 18th."

"69—18th concession—water grass meadow; at sixty-
nine marked post, concession 19."

" 5.0—19th concession—at 5.0 the border of Big Bear Creek."

" 3.59—Over Big Bear Creek."

" 38.00—Through a wood to the intersection of the Indian boundary running east from the Forks of the Chenal Ecartè, where a cedar post is planted, being the west angle of Chatham."

The field notes of the concession lines refer to posts at five points on each line, viz.:—those at the extremities on the base line and division line; the posts in the centre on Baldoon street; the posts dividing the Baldoon street survey from the two outside lots 1 and 5 or 20 and 24. The last two are as a rule, though not invariably, noted as *planted*. The centre post in one concession is noted as *planted*, in all the others the entry is " 75.65 a post in the centre of Baldoon street."

Then as to those at the ends of the concessions, the notes run in each alternate concession from the Little Bear line and from the base line. The post at the starting point is never noted, but the last entry always is " 75.65, post on the base of Dover," or " 75.65 post on Little Bear line "—except in regard to concession lines 6 and 7. In these we find " 75.65 planted a post on the base line of Dover " and " 75.65 planted a post on Little Bear line."

Here again we have the same classes of entries respecting the posts which may or may not have been Hambly's, and those which certainly were Smith's.

It happened that the 17th concession line was run *from* the base line and therefore we find here nothing said about its post on the base line.

A good deal was said in the discussion, of the evidence respecting this 17th concession post. The facts as to it are, that Hambly in his diary speaks of it as " the 17th concession post "; in his field notes he says it was an ash picket. Smith in his field notes says he planted a post at the 17th concession, and in his diary when he mentions having reached the base line at concession 17, he says nothing of any post. Smith notes that he planted a post

at another point on the base line, where Hambly reported
one, viz:—at concession 6 ; and also at one or two places
on the division line.

I shall defer what I have to say on the question, whether
this evidence indicates that Smith merely retraced Hambly's
work, until I note some other matters of fact.

There are letters in evidence written by Smith to the
surveyor general ; one is dated 14th August, 1810. He
mentions that he had postponed the survey of Chatham
till the summer should be over ; and, speaking of the completion of the survey of Dover, he says, "I found no
surveys in Dover. that is, visible lines, except two, the
base of Dover and Chatham and a third concession line,
(run so incorrect as made a departure of one chain east in
75), yet these were lines sufficient to give me a deal
of trouble, loss of time and augmentation of expense, for
to preserve the settlements of the Thames and Big Bear
Creek, and to prevent the clashing of surveys, I had first
to ascertain the variation of the old lines and calculate
latitude and longitude before I could proportion the concessions, all which created more loss of time and far more
trouble and labour than if no survey had ever been performed, and no patent issued. To guide the eye to the
place of reference, I was obliged to give temporary names
to the principal lines. Mr. McDonell, on the part of Lord
Selkirk, was very particular, and I have the satisfaction
to think he is satisfied with the survey, a plan of which
and notes I had to deliver to him on account of the settlers
that were in waiting, as well as for the guidance of the
person who traced the lines, and there is nothing now
remaining but your approbation."

In a letter dated 10th April, 1810, he said: "Hitherto I
have seen no interior surveys in the townships but the 3rd
concession line on the Thames ;" and on the 7th December,
1810, he said, "I saw no surveys in Dover but the 3rd
concession line and the base of Chatham, and which were
no saving of work, for I had to run them over, and the
base especially and unavoidably when turning the heads
of the northern sections. The survey of the Baldoon tract
was done when the swamps were breaking up and the
party lying idle ; in fact I spared no pains to render the
work satisfactory."

"There would have been less trouble if no old surveys had appeared at all, for they occasioned some delay in ascertaining the difference of variation, and fixing the *Nonius* to the same before any parallel or angular lines could be extended. * * Chatham is now under survey by my assistant and my son, and I expect to join them in a few days." In the margin of this letter is this note by the writer: "This difference not to be ascertained but by running along the old blazes a considerable distance."

From this correspondence I understand Smith to report that the 3rd concession line and the base line were blazed lines, and that he found no other blazed lines. He says nothing about posts, but defines his meaning by the term "interior surveys," evidently denoting concession lines.

Then other facts are proved by oral testimony. It is shewn by Mr. McDonell, one of the surveyors, and I believe the correctness of his evidence is not questioned, that the concession lines as actually opened or recognised as far as the 17th concession line, correspond with the concession lines in Chatham, which run from the same base line.

This correspondence was to be secured according to the instructions originally given to Iredell in 1803. He is there told, "the division line between Dover and Chatham you will consider as your grand line of communication, from whence in Chatham you will run your concession lines to the north-east, and in Dover to the south-west." In this method of surveying, the lines being run in each direction from the same starting point, it is clear there could be no "jog" such as occurs where the starting place of one line is the terminus of the other.

At the end of Smith's instructions is the following: "Note—In Chatham continue the concessions by the dotted line in order to prevent the jog, break, or off-set in the said concession lines."

We have not the *bruillon* plan on which the dotted lines appeared; but I see no reason to doubt that those lines were intended to secure the carrying out of the scheme laid down for Iredell to follow, and that they were extensions into Chatham of the Dover lines. This view was not accepted by the learned Judge in the Court below ; but I think his attention cannot have been directed to Iredell's instructions on the point ; and I think also it is supported by our finding upon Smith's plan of his survey of Dover, which was returned to the Department before he made the survey of Chatham, dotted extensions into Chatham of several of the Dover concession lines.

There is no trace upon the ground of Smith's survey, or of the post of which he speaks at the 18th concession of Dover ; but there is on the Chatham side a line traceable by blazes. It was by producing this line into the township of Dover that the defendant's surveyor fixed the line up to which the defendant occupies. These blazes are not shewn to be as old as Smith's survey, and from the evidence I take it that they are of much more recent date. The line on which they occur is, however, shewn by Mr. McDonell to be reputed to be Smith's line. Very old blazes are found on some other lines, some which cut from trees on the 17th concession line in Dover were produced, and the computation made of the annual growths would carry their dates fully as far back as Hambly's survey, and perhaps even farther back. Without, however, placing great stress on these computations which are liable to be fallacious, it is sufficient for my purpose to note, that according to Mr. McDonell who speaks from long knowledge of the place, and who is the principal witness for the plaintiff, it is not doubted that the lines on which the roads are opened are Smith's lines.

Mr. McDonell further measured the depth of the concessions Nos. 3 to 17, as so fixed by what he considers Smith's survey, together with Nos. 1 and 2, which it is not contended that Smith disturbed, although he includes them in his field notes with the others. In the field notes and on his plan Smith gives each of the concessions 1 and 2 a depth of sixty-seven chains fifty links. McDonell finds them to be respectively 64.09 and 69.53. Then while Smith marks each of the other concessions sixty-nine chains, McDonell finds their depths as actually laid out varying from 69.07 to 71.34, the gross overplus in the fifteen concessions being twelve chains seventy-two links.

The 17th concession is in this computation reckoned up to the line to which the defendant holds, and as being 69.71 in depth ; the 16th concession, bounded by the 17th concession line where the old blazes were found, is 69.41. Smith allows sixty-nine chains for concession 18, and five chains for concession 19, making seventy-four chains in place of Hambly's eighty-five, or the eighty-four of the Selkirk patent. By McDonell's measurement the defendant's fence is seventy-six chains and eighty-four links from the river. Therefore, if Smith's work correctly indicates the line of concession 18, whether we take his work as noted by himself, or as evidenced by the line in Chatham, the defendant is on his own ground.

I have now, I think, alluded to all the facts that have a very direct bearing on what we have to decide, but there are some other things shewn, which it may not be amiss to notice. One thing is, that a comparison of the position of some streams which cross the base line and are understood by the surveyor McDonell to be the same mentioned in the field notes of both Hambly and Smith, with the lines now found on the ground, and with the position assigned them in the field notes, tends to support the contention that the lines on the ground are not where Hambly reported them to be.

Then there is the result of the different surveys or theories, as tested with reference to the quantity of land.

Lord Selkirk's patent calls it 920 acres more or less.

On Smith's plan there are quantities marked on each of the lots 1 to 5 which amount in all to 808.20 acres. Add to this 10.70 acres for lot 19 and you have 818.90 acres, or 101.10 acres less than the nominal 920 acres.

Mr. McDonell computed the actual contents of the five lots, as defined by what he calls Smith's survey, and made 857.59 acres. Add as before 10.70 for lot 19, and the actual area appears to be 868.29, or only 51.71 short of 920.

Now, as the plaintiff claims to advance 8.16 chains, or 7.72, according to one or the other of his surveyors, beyond the line to which Mr. McDonell computed the quantity, let us see how much, if he succeeds, the patent would cover.

Take the concession to be 151 chains in width, which is a little less than Smith makes it. A strip 151 chains by 8.16 will contain upwards of 123 acres. One of 151 chains by 7.72 will contain over 116 acres. Add these results to the computed area of 868.29 and we have either 991 or 984 acres as against the 920 of the patent, an excess of 71 or 64 acres.

Now what is the effect of all this evidence?

If I had to decide where was the 18th concession line as run or marked by Hambly, I should have difficulty in holding it affirmatively proved that Smith's line was identical with Hambly's. I might think it unlikely that in the six years following Hambly's survey all trace of his posts had disappeared, and much more probable that Smith found those posts, or found the place of any one that had disappeared and planted one in its place; but I could not lay my hand on direct evidence of that.

There is much force in the argument that Smith, by giving the uniform depth of 69 chains to each concession from the 3rd to the 18th, conveys the idea that the posts he speaks of were just where his own chaining of 69 chains happened to come to, while if he chained merely from one of Hambly's posts to another, the probability would be so strong as to amount almost to a certainty, that he would have found the distances somewhat irregular; still we have grounds for caution in drawing this inference from the fact that Smith's field notes give the depth of concessions 1 and 2 as each 67.50 chains, giving the details as to timber, &c., just as if he had surveyed that part of the base line and marked the limits of those concessions; while we know from his own letters as well as from other evidence, that he found the rear lines of number 2 fixed and marked by the blazed line which was the only interior survey he found. Hambly notes that that line was marked on the base line by a beech tree, and Smith himself began one stage of his Baldoon street survey on 24th April, 1810, by planting a post at the opposite end of it on the Little Bear line. We also learn from Mr. McDonell's measurements, that in place of 67.50 being the correct depth of each of those two concessions as laid out, the figures are 64.09 and 69.53.

Furthermore, there is the important fact that Smith's diary contains no note of his chaining along the base line, except only those parts of the line chained in "turning the head of the northern sections," as he expresses it, and this work seems to have been confined to eight of the fifteen concessions affected by the Baldoon street survey, there being no note of his chaining the line along concessions 3, 5, 8, 10, 12, 14, or 16.

It was Smith's duty, so far as we can judge, to adhere to Hambly's landmarks. His instructions inform him that the lines already run were shewn in yellow upon the *bruillon* plans, and as those plans were doubtless prepared with reference to Iredell's and Hambly's returns, all these concession lines would be thus indicated. Hambly's survey was comparatively recent when Smith's was made, and no reason has been given for supposing that while the base line as he ran it, with all the inaccuracies which gave Smith so much trouble, was traceable, the posts planted along it were all gone. An inference to the contrary may well be drawn from Smith's express mention of planting one or two posts in that line.

Upon the whole I cannot say that the evidence preponderates against the conclusion that Smith did his duty, and merely retraced along the base line the work done by Hambly.

As I have already remarked, I might find it difficult to say that he is proved to have done so if an issue of that sort were presented for decision.

But we have another consideration of some significance in Smith's statement that Lord Selkirk's agent, who had been very particular in the matter of this survey, was satisfied with it. I take the fact to be made out, as satisfactorily as could be hoped for under the circumstances, that the line to which the defendant holds is the line described by Smith, or is at all events no nearer the river than that line.

All the evidence, the Chatham line with which it agrees, the depth of the concession from the front of 17 which seems fixed as Smith's line, and the distance from the river which nearly agrees with that laid down on Smith's field notes and plan, point in that direction. If this is so we have the line which Lord Selkirk's agent understood to be that which bounded the Baldoon street survey, and ran between it and the 18th concession, and with which he was satisfied.

This is a fact the significance of which, having regard to the then recent date of Hambly's survey, in accordance with which the patent had only three years before been issued, cannot be overestimated.

The effect of what the plaintiff asks will be to assign to the operation of the patent 60 or 70 acres more than the area named in it, and (assuming the 17th concession line on the ground to be unchangeable) to reduce the defendant's lot to one of 61 or 62 chains, in place of its present size of 69.71.

The case on which he asks the Court to do this, weak as it was as launched by him, when it depended entirely on the backward measurement from the river, is in my judgment much further weakened by the evidence concerning Smith's survey.

Balancing probabilities merely, I am of opinion that there would be better reason for holding that Smith's survey adopted the same lines which Hambly had marked, than for saying that Hambly's line can now properly be ascertained in the mode relied on by the plaintiff. But taking the whole case together, I think the decision that the plaintiff has sustained his claim ought not to be supported.

We have not been given on this appeal the particulars of the title of either of the litigant parties, because it was admitted at the trial, after some evidence of the plaintiff's claim of title had been given, that the plaintiff was the owner of lot 18. I observe from the note we have of the evidence, that the plaintiff is grantee under a person who bought the lot at sheriff's sale for taxes, and there is nothing noted to shew that he derives title under any conveyance from the patentee.

It has not been urged that that interferes with his right to set up any question touching the original survey which he has set up; but it may be an additional reason why he must be held to proof of the land he claims being strictly part of lot number five in the 18th concession, without being treated as in privity with the patentee, or entitled to any aid, if any could be derived from the description in the patent.

The case has evidently not been looked at in this aspect. The judgment now in appeal proceeds, and the expert evidence by at least one of the plaintiff's surveyors, and in fact the surveys by both of them have proceeded on the assumption that the line was to be put 84 chains from the river.

There is no pretence of authority for that except by the reading of the patent, for Hambly put it 85 chains away.

This view seems to me to add force to what at the beginning I intimated as my opinion, that the patent is not proper evidence, or any evidence, of the position of the concession line.

The other purpose for which it has been argued it was receivable, namely, to shew that, without necessary reference to the survey, a grant had been made of a tract running 84 chains from the river, I have already answered. But an additional and conclusive answer would be found in the fact that the plaintiff does not take under the patent.

The evidence is thus shewn to consist only of Hambly's notes and plan. If by them the plaintiff's case can be sustained he ought to recover for a chain more than has been awarded to him, but for the reasons I have given we are of opinion that he has failed to prove what was incumbent upon him, and that we should allow the appeal, with costs, and dismiss the action, with costs.

SPRAGGE, C. J. O., died before judgment was given.

BURTON and OSLER, JJ. A., concurred.

Appeal allowed, with costs.

[This case has since been appealed to the Supreme Court, and stands for judgment there.]

A DIGEST

OF

ALL THE REPORTED CASES

DECIDED IN

THE COURT OF APPEAL,

CONTAINED IN THIS VOLUME.

ACTION FOR DECEIT.

See DECEIT, &c.

AGENT TO PURCHASE LANDS.

See PRINCIPAL AND AGENT.

AGREEMENT.

See CONSTRUCTION OF, &c.,—SALE OF GOODS, 1.

——— FOR PARTNERSHIP.

In June, 1874, the plaintiff and defendant by writing entered into an agreement for supplying together the iron for the Grand Junction Railway, and providing for the division of the surplus or profits. No division of the profits was made and the defendant went on investing the receipts from that enterprise in other contracts, and the plaintiff claimed a like interest in them also, which the defendant denied his right to.

Held, that the onus of negativing such right of the plaintiff rested on the defendant, and having failed to negative his right to such share, the Court declared him entitled thereto, and directed a reference to take the accounts between the parties. *Cameron v. Bickford.* 52.

———FOR SALE OF LANDS.

By a contract for the sale and purchase of land the vendee agreed to pay $4,000, part of the purchase money, on the execution of the agreement (which was paid accordingly) and an additional portion of the purchase money was to be paid within sixty days thereafter, the balance remaining out on mortgage. After the expiration of the sixty days the vendor instituted proceedings to recover the amount agreed to be then paid, and at the trial, CAMERON, J., directed judgment to be entered for the defendants with liberty to the plaintiff to bring a fresh action which by an order of the Divisional Court, was set aside, (3 O. R. 573.)

On appeal, this Court (HAGARTY, C. J. O., dissenting) discharged that order, with costs.

Per BURTON and PATTERSON, JJ. A. The agreement to convey the lands, and that to pay the money at the expiration of sixty days, were not mutual but dependent, so that the vendor before being entitled to recover the purchase money must shew that he was ready, willing, and able to convey ; and that the purchaser, until he did so, could not be called on to pay his money and rely on the ability of the vendor to convey the estate, or in the event of his being unable to do so, look to him for repayment.

Per ROSE, J. Without determining that point expressly, the neglect and delay of the vendor to take the necessary steps to shew his title to the lands, part of which the vendor admitted was vested in one Y., were such as disentitled him to call for payment, and therefore that the finding of the Judge at the trial was correct. *McDonald* v. *Murray et al,* 101.

[This case has been carried to the Supreme Court.]

ALIMONY.

In an action for alimony the defendant relied upon a divorce granted on his own petition by the Circuit Court of St. Louis County, Missouri, where he then resided : the wife (the present plaintiff) having made no defence thereto though notified of the proceedings. It appeared that the domicile of the husband at the time of the marriage and of the divorce was Canadian, though the marriage was celebrated at Detroit, and the wife was an American citizen. It was proved that the evidence of

desertion by the wife as alleged by the husband, and on which the decree for divorce was founded, was untrue.

Held, that the decree having been obtained on an untrue statement of facts, and for a cause not recognized by our law, could not be set up as a bar to the wife's claim for alimony.

Held, also, that the non-feasance of the wife in failing to appear or defend the action for divorce did not amount to collusion on her part so as to estop her from impeaching the validity of the decree made in that action.

Held, also, [affirming the decision of the Court appealed from, and following *Harvey* v. *Farnie,* 5 Pro. D. 153 ; 6 Pro. D. 35 ; 8 App. Cas. 43], that the jurisdiction to divorce depends upon the domicile of the parties, *i. e.,* of the husband, and that this being Canadian, the Missouri Court had no jurisdiction.

Per HAGARTY, C. J. O.—There is no safe ground for distinction between domicile for succession, and for matrimonial purposes, or a domicile by residence. *Magurn* v. *Magurn,* 178.

AMBIGUOUS DESCRIPTION.

See SALE OF LANDS, 3.

APPEAL.

Upon an application by the Churchwardens of St. James's Church for leave to appeal from the judgment of the Chancery Division Court (5 O. R. 644) in their own names, or in the name of the rector, the defendant (who declined to carry the case further) as their trustee.

Held, that the rector was not a trustee for the applicants, but would himself, if the contention should prevail, be beneficially entitled to the fruits of the litigation ; and that the applicants had not such an interest as entitled them to be made parties to the action ; and the application was therefore refused.

The event rendered it unnecessary to consider whether or not the application was properly made to this Court. *Langtry* v. *Dumoulin*, 544.

[Leave given to appeal by Supreme Court, 16th November, 1885.]

See also COUNTY COURT—MUNICIPAL ACT—SETTING ASIDE JUDGMENT.

APPEAL FOR COSTS.

J., one of the defendants, had bid for and had become purchaser of a lot of land sold under the provisions of the R. S. O. ch. 216, by certain parties claiming to be trustees of the Colored Wesleyan Methodist Church, whose proceedings in respect of such attempted sale were impeached in the action to which J. was made a party defendant, although he avowed his willingness to withdraw from the purchase, and by his answer disclaimed all interest in the result of the suit, and alleged that no effort had been made by him to have the sale carried out, as he was aware that the same would have to be first confirmed by the members of the said church. At the trial judgment was pronounced setting aside the sale, and ordering the defendants generally to pay costs.

Held, [varying the judgment of the Court below], that under the circumstances a formal disclaimer was not required and J. was ordered to be paid his costs of the appeal but the action in the Court below was dismissed as against him without costs.

Per OSLER, J. A.—The rule as to an appeal on the question of costs appears to be this, that if in making the order complained of there has been any violation of principle, or the court has proceeded on a wrong general rule, or if the discretion of the court has been exercised upon any misapprehension of fact a Court of Appeal will interfere but not otherwise. *Wansley* v. *Smallwood*, 439.

ARBITRATION.

See MUNICIPAL ACT.

ASSIGNEE, ELECTION BY.

See INSOLVENCY ACT, 1875, 1, 2, 3.

ASSIGNMENT.

On the dissolution of partnership between L. and W., the latter transferred all his interest in the partnership to L., who subsequently became insolvent and assigned all his estate, including that part of it which had formerly been assets of the partnership, to the defendants, in trust to pay " the claims of his creditors ratably and proportionately, and without preference or priority, recognizing such liens, claims, charges, and priorities as the law directs."

Held, [reversing the judgment of the Court below, 5 O R. 104] that under the terms of the deed there was no priority between the separate creditors of L and the joint creditors of L., and W., all being creditors of L, and that both classes of creditors were entitled to be paid *pari passu*. *Moorehouse* v. *Bostwick*, 76.

ASSIGNMENT BY PAROL.

See PAROL ASSIGNMENT.

BAIL, FIXING.

See FIXING BAIL.

BENEFICIARY, EVIDENCE OF.

See WILL, &c.

BOND.

See MUNICIPAL BONUS.

CA. SA. TO FIX BAIL.

See FIXING BAIL.

CHANGING NAMES OF STREETS.

See SALE OF LANDS, 3.

CHATTEL MORTGAGE.

A formal defect in a chattel mortgage may be cured by a conveyance at any time before an execution reaches the sheriff's hands ; but such conveyance, whether effected by a deed or by delivery only, has no retroactive operation, and if void for intent to prefer under R. S. O. ch. 118, would not suffice to cure the defects. The intent to prefer is a question of fact for the jury ; and therefore where the jury found that there was such intent, and where there was evidence to support the finding, the judgment of the County Judge setting aside the jury's verdict in favor of the execution creditor was reversed, but a new trial was directed in order that evidence might be given to shew that the bill of sale was made in order to carry out honestly the original mortgage contract.

OSLER, J.A., dissenting. *Smith* v. *Fair*, 755.

CHURCHWARDENS.

See APPEAL.

CONFLICTING EVIDENCE.

The learned Judge who tried the case, in which the evidence was conflicting and irreconcilable, rested his conclusion in favor of the defendant on the documentary evidence and the probabilities arising in the case. This Court, while not differing from the Judge as to the credibility of the parties or their witnesses, having come to a different conclusion on the whole evidence, allowed the appeal and reversed the decision of the Court below. *Cameron* v. *Bickford*, 52.

CONSENT OF COUNSEL.

See JURY SEPARATING.

CONSTITUTION OF COURT.

See COUNTY COURT.

CONSTRUCTION OF AGREEMENT.

The defendant company, who were empowered by statute to run a traction engine over certain highways in the county of York, and who by their charter were allowed to construct a tramway in the county to be worked by horse or steam power, upon such terms as might be agreed on with the municipalities through which the road might pass, entered into an agreement with the county, whereby it was agreed that the company should be at liberty to lay down a tramway along a certain road : that the tolls to be collected should not exceed certain specified rates on one and two horse vehicles ; that the company, if required, should run two passenger cars daily each way, or in lieu thereof an omnibus or sleigh ; that in case horses, carriages, teams, or other vehicles or animals met the horses, waggons, carriages. or other vehicles of the company, the latter should have the right of way, and that "so soon as this agreement shall have been ratified by the said corporation, the said company shall forthwith withdraw their said traction engine from the public highways of the said county, and shall discontinue the use of the said traction engine, and of any other traction engine upon or along such public highways."

The company insisted that they were at liberty, under the agreement, to run a steam motor upon the said tramway. Thereupon an action was instituted by the corporation to restrain the use of steam power on the tramway, which relief the Court below (PROUDFOOT, J.,) on the hearing of the cause, granted : upon appeal, this Court being equally divided, the appeal was dismissed, with costs.

Per HAGARTY, C. J., and PATTERSON, J. A., [agreeing with PROUDFOOT, J.]—On the true construction of the agreement there was, if not an express, at least an implied qualification excluding the use of steam as a motive power.

Per BURTON, J. A., and ROSE, J.—What the company had agreed to abandon was only the right theretofore exercised by them ; under the general law, 31 Vict. ch. 34, R. S. O. ch. 186,—of using traction engines on the public highway, and that they were not restricted by the agreement from using steam motors on the tramway. *The Corporation of the County of York* v. *The Toronto Gravel Road and Concrete Co.,* 765.

[Affirmed by Supreme Court, 16th November, 1885]

CONTRACT.

See SALE OF LANDS.

COSTS.

See PRACTICE, 1—APPEAL FOR.

COUNTY COURT.

An action in the County Court of Carleton was tried without a jury by the junior Judge of that county, who, after consideration, entered a verdict for the defendant.

A Court composed of the senior and junior Judges of Carleton, and the Judge of the County Court of Prescott and Russell subsequently assumed to set aside the verdict, and to enter judgment for the plaintiff, *dissentiente* the junior Judge of Carleton.

Held, that a judgment of a Court so constituted was invalid, and that the verdict at the trial was not affected thereby.

Per PATTERSON, J. A.—The verdict at the trial was a final judgment of the Court, and could not be attacked except by an appeal to this Court. Rule 510, O. J. A., gives a party no right to move in the County Court.

Per OSLER, J. A.—The party dissatisfied with the judgment at the trial may, under Rule 510, O. J. A., move against it before the Judge himself ; and an appeal to this Court may under 45 Vict. ch. 6, sec. 4 as properly be brought from the decision on such motion as from the judgment at the trial. *Ferguson* v. *McMartin*, 731.

COUNTY COURT, PARTITION BY.

See PARTITION &c.

COVENANTS, DEPENDENT OR MUTUAL.

See AGREEMENT FOR SALE OF LANDS.

CREDIT, SALE OF GOODS ON.

See SALE OF GOODS, 3.

CREDITOR VALUING SECURITY.

See INSOLVENCY ACT, 1875, 1, 2, 3.

CROSS ACTION.

See SALE BY SAMPLE.

CURING DEFECT.

[IN CHATTEL MORTGAGE.]

See CHATTEL MORTGAGE.

DAMAGES.

See MUNICIPAL BONUS.

DEATH OF MARRIED WOMAN BY ACCIDENT.

See RAILWAY ACCIDENT.

DEATH OF ONE PARTNER, EFFECT OF—ON SURETY.

See GUARANTEE TO A FIRM.

DECEIT, ACTION FOR.

The defendants other than the company being directors of the defendant company, made certain representations concerning the affairs of the company, which they believed to be true, but which were not in fact correct, and procured the plaintiff and others to take stock in the company.

Held, affirming the judgment of the Court below, 2 O. R. 218, in an action to recover back the amount of the subscriptions paid by the plaintiffs, and to remove their names from the list of stockholders, that the defendants were not liable. PATTERSON, J. A., *dubitante. Petrie* v. *Guelph Lumber Co. et al.; Stewart* v. *Guelph Lumber Co. et al.; Inglis* v. *Guelph Lumber Co. et al.*, 336.

2. The plaintiff upon the assurance of the defendant that a land

warrant issued to one of the North-West Mounted Police Force would entitle the holder to 160 acres of Dominion lands, and which warrant on its face expressly stated that the party was entitled to 160 acres, purchased such warrant from the defendant for $312. In consequence of various Acts of the Legislature and orders in Council, lands in the North-West territory, which at the time this warrant was issued, were held for sale at $1, were increased to $2 per acre, so that on the presentation of the warrant to the proper officer, the plaintiff would only be credited with $160 on the purchase of land at the established price. The defendant was not aware of this change. In an action brought by the plaintiff the Queen's Bench Division held that he was not entitled to recover back his purchase money as having been obtained by misrepresentation.

On appeal this Court being equally divided, the appeal was dismissed. *McKenzie* v. *Dwight*, 381.

DEFECT, CURING.
See CHATTEL MORTGAGE.

DEFECTS IN FENCES.
See RAILWAY COMPANY.

—— IN QUALITY.
See SALE BY SAMPLE.

DELAY.
See SALE OF LANDS, 1.

DELIVERY.
See SALE OF GOODS, 2.

DELIVERY, PLACE OF.
See SALE BY SAMPLE.

DEPENDENT COVENANTS.
See AGREEMENT FOR SALE OF LANDS.

DESCRIPTION OF LAND.
See DRAINAGE BY-LAW — EJECTMENT.

DIRECTORS.
See DECEIT, ACTION FOR.

DISCLAIMER.
See APPEAL FOR COSTS.

DISCRETION OF JUDGE.
See PRACTICE, 2.

DOMICILE.
See ALIMONY.

DOMINION ELECTION LAW.

The jurisdiction of the Provincial Legislature over " property and civil rights" does not preclude the Parliament of Canada from giving to an informer the right to recover, by a civil action, a penalty imposed as a punishment for bribery at an election.

The Dominion Election Act 1874, by sec. 109, provides that all penalties and forfeitures (other than fines in cases of misdemeanour) imposed by the Act shall be recoverable, with full costs of suit, by any person who will sue for the same, by action of debt or information, in any of Her Majesty's Courts in the Province in which the cause of action arose, having competent jurisdiction.

Held, that this enactment was valid. *Doyle* v. *Bell,* 326.

DOMINION LAND ACTS.

See DECEIT, &c., 2.

DRAINAGE BY-LAW.

A by-law was passed by the township of Mersea, providing for the drainage of lands in Mersea and Romney, and assessing property owners in both townships.

Held, that the by-law was invalid because the petition therefor did not describe the property to be benefited, and the by-law itself, which did shew the property to be benefited, disclosed that the petitioners were not the majority of the owners of such property.

Per BURTON, J.A.—Upon the evidence the corporation intended by the by-law to remedy a private grievance, and upon that ground also the by-law was bad. *Re Corporation of the Township of Romney and Corpo ration of the Township of Mersea,* 712.

· *See* ALSO MUNICIPAL ACT.

EJECTMENT.

In an action of ejectment the question was as to the position of lot 5 in the 18th concession, the plaintiff's lot, which was granted in 1807, and lot 24 in the 17th concession, the defendant's lot, the patent for which was issued at a later date. No traces remained of the surveyor's work on the ground. In the former patent the concession line was given as the southerly boundary of the lot, with a distance of 84 chains more or less from thence to the river :

Held, [reversing the judgment of FERGUSON, J., reported 1 O. R. 614,] that notwithstanding there was no evidence of the actual position of the line as run upon the ground, and that all the land in both concessions at the date of the patent belonged to the Crown, the distance of 84 chains thus given could not be treated as fixing the position of the concession line as at an absolute distance of 84 chains at least from the river. *Plumb* v. *Steinhoff,* 788.

ELECTION.

See SALE OF LANDS, 1.

—— BY ASSIGNEE.

See INSOLVENCY ACT 1875, 1, 2, 3.

ESTOPPEL.

See PATENT—SETTING ASIDE JUDGMENT.

EVIDENCE FOR JURY.

See EJECTMENT—PRACTICE, 2.

EXCESS OF LANDS SOLD.

See SALE OF LANDS, 2.

EXECUTION.
See SETTING ASIDE JUDGMENT.

EXECUTION OF POWER.
See MORTGAGE OF LEASE.

EXECUTORS.
See SETTING ASIDE JUDGMENT.

FALSE REPRESENTATIONS.
See SALE OF LANDS, 1.

FINDING OF JURY.
See NEGLIGENCE.

FIRE INSURANCE.
Where the damage complained of in actions upon fire policies, which were subject to the statutory conditions, was caused by an explosion of gunpowder accidentally set fire to, and by the fire subsequently resulting from the explosion :

Held, [affirming the decision of the C. P. Div. 7 O. R 634, and of the Q. B. Div. 8 O. R. 342] that, upon the construction of the 11th statutory condition, the defendants were not liable except for the damages caused by the after fire. *Hobbs et al.* v. *Guardian Ins. Co., Hobbs et al.* v. *Northern Ins. Co.,* 741.

[Since argued in Supreme Court, and stands for judgment.]

FIXING BAIL.
Held, reversing the judgment of the Court below, that proceedings to

104—VOL. XI A.R.

fix bail cannot be maintained on a writ of *ca. sa.* which is made returnable immediately after the execution thereof : for such purpose it is necessary that the writ should be returnable on a day certain. [HAGARTY, C. J. O. dissenting.] *Proctor* v. *Mackenzie et al,* 486,

---

FORECLOSURE, IRREGULARITY IN.
See MORTGAGE OF LEASE.

FOREIGN DIVORCE.
See ALIMONY.

FRAUD.
See ALIMONY — SETTING ASIDE JUDGMENT.

GOODS, PROPERTY IN—PASSING.
See SALE OF GOODS, 3.

—— SALE OF, ON CREDIT.
See SALE OF GOODS, 3.

GUARANTEE, NOTICE TO DETERMINE.
[EFFECT OF ON SURETY.]
See GUARANTEE TO A FIRM.

GUARANTEE TO A FIRM.

By a written agreement made in April, 1879, the defendant guaranteed to C. & Sons, or the members for the time being forming such firm, the price of any goods supplied by C. & Sons to one Q. to the amount of $5,000, and which he agreed should be a continuing guarantee. C. died in September, 1881, after which the sons who were named as executors in his will, carried on the same business under the like firm name until December, 1882, when the assets of the partnership were transferred to the plaintiffs, a joint stock company. Q. continued to obtain goods from the sons, and the plaintiffs since the formation of the joint stock company, until the spring of 1883.

Meanwhile, and on the 5th of April, 1882, the defendant being dissatisfied with the manner in which Q. was conducting his business, wrote to the firm forbidding them to supply any more goods to Q. under such guarantee :

Held, (1) [BURTON, J. A., dissenting], affirming the judgment of Rose, J., reported 5 O. R. 189, that such notice put an end to defendant's liability for any goods subsequently supplied to Q. ; but, *Held*, (2) reversing the judgment of ROSE, J., that the death of C. had not that effect. *The Cosgrave Brewing and Malting Co. of Toronto* v. *Starrs*, 156.

GUNPOWDER EXPLOSION.

See FIRE INSURANCE.

IMMEDIATE JUDGMENT.

[UNDER RULE 80 O. J. A.]

See PRACTICE, 2. 3.

IMPEACHING JUDGMENT,

See PARTITION BY COUNTY COURT.

IMPLIED QUALIFICATION.

See CONSTRUCTION OF AGREEMENT.

INCORPORATED COMPANY.

J. H. B., one of the defendants, a director of the defendant company, personally owned a vessel "The United Empire," valued by him at $150,000 ; and was possessed of the majority of the shares of the company, some of which he had assigned to others of the defendants in such numbers as qualified them for the position of directors of the company, the duties of which they discharged. Upon a proposed sale and purchase by the company of the vessel "The United Empire" the board of directors (including J. H. B.), at their board meeting adopted a resolution approving of the purchase by the company of such vessel ; and subsequently at a general meeting of the shareholders, including J. H. B. and those to whom he had transferred portions of the stock, a like resolution was passed, the plaintiff alone dissenting.

Held, (reversing the judgment of the Court below, 6 O. R. 300), that although the purchase on the resolution of the directors alone might have been avoided, the resolution of the shareholders validated the transaction, and that there is not any principle of equity to prevent J. H. B. in such a case from exercising his rights as a shareholder as fully as other members of the company.

Per BURTON, J. A.—In dealings of this nature the relative positions of the shareholders and directors are those of principals and agents, not those of *cestuis que trustent* and trustees. *Beatty* v. *North-Western Transportation Company et al.*, 205.

[Since argued in the Supreme Court, and stands for judgment.]

INDEPENDENT COVENANTS.

See AGREEMENT FOR SALE OF LANDS.

INJUNCTION.

See TRADE NAME.

INSOLVENCY ACT, 1875.

1. When an assignee in insolvency elects, under sec. 84 of the Insolvent Act, 1875, to allow a creditor to retain, at a valuation, the property which he holds as security for his debt, the creditor becomes a purchaser at that valuation, freed from any right or equity to redeem on the part of the insolvent or his estate. *Bell* v. *Ross et al.*, 45$_8$.

2. Where the secured creditor has valued his security for the purpose of proof, the policy and express language of the Insolvent Act, 1875, require that the decision of the assignee shall be promptly made. *Ib.*

3. A formal resolution of the assignee allowing the creditor to retain the property is not necessary. There-

fore where the assignee had ample means of knowing the value of the assets before the creditor proved his claim and valued his security in January, 1879, and where no meeting of creditors was held after that date till the 30th of July, following, and the estate was sold without any reference to the security; and where nothing further was done by the assignee until the 13th October, following, when he wrote to the creditor: "Your claim as filed shews a balance over security of $3,091.13, but Mr. Leitch (the purchaser of the estate) disputes your claim to any dividend, on the ground," &c., it was

Held, that the assignee had signified his election to allow the creditor to retain the security, and his abandonment of any right to redeem it for the estate. *Ib.*

INSPECTION.

See SALE BY SAMPLE.

INTENT TO PREFER.

See CHATTEL MORTGAGE.

INVESTING MONEY FOR CLIENT.

See SOLICITOR AND CLIENT.

JUDGMENT, IMPEACHING.

See PARTITION BY COUNTY COURT.

JUDGMENT.

[UNDER RULE 80 O. J. A.]

See PRACTICE, 2, 3.

JURY SEPARATING.

At the trial it appeared that the counsel for P. had left the Court before the Judge's charge, having authorised F., counsel for two other defendants, to take on his behalf any objections he might think proper to the charge. The jury, after hearing the Judge's charge, were allowed to separate and be at large from Saturday till Monday, before giving their verdict, which was against the defendants P. and R.

Held, [reversing the decision of the Queen's Bench Division, 7 O. R. 355,] that such a proceeding could not be upheld except upon clear affirmative evidence of consent expressly and knowingly given ; and, therefore, where counsel for the defendant P. had left the Court before the Judge's charge, and it did not appear he had authorised any one to represent him or his client, or that any one had consented or assumed to consent on behalf of P. to the jury separating, a new trial as to P. was directed.

Per OSLER, J. A.—Had F. assumed to represent the counsel for P. in assenting to the separation of the jury, P. would have been bound to the same extent as if his own counsel had taken a similar course, contrary to instructions. *Stillwell* v. *Rennie et al.*, 724.

LAND OWNERS.

See DRAINAGE BY-LAW.

——WARRANTS.

See DECEIT &c.

LIABILITY OF RAILWAYS FOR KILLING ON.

See RAILWAY ACCIDENT.

——[OF REGISTRAR] FOR EXCESS OF FEES.

See REGISTRAR OF DEEDS.

MAPS NOT REFERRED TO IN DEED.

[ADMISSIBILITY OF,]

See SALE OF LANDS, 3.

MERITS, DEFENCE ON.

See PRACTICE, 3.

MISREPRESENTATION.

See DECEIT, ACTION FOR.

MORTGAGE OF LEASE.

In a mortgage of leasehold premises, the *habendum* was as follows : " To hold to the said mortgagees, their successors and assigns, for the residue now unexpired of the term, and every renewal term, save and except one day thereof." The mortgage contained a power of sale to be exercised in default of payment, without notice. The mortgagor, K., assigned his equity of redemption to O'S., in trust to pay off the mortgage, but O'S., after renewing the lease for a term of twenty-one years in his own name, reconveyed to K. without paying off the mortgage. The mortgagees, with knowledge that the beneficial interest was in K., filed a bill for foreclosure against O'S. alone, and O'S. filed an answer and disclaimer, stating his position as above, but ultimately withdrew his disclaimer and consented to a decree for foreclosure. After decree and final order of foreclosure, the mortgagees sold to D., reciting in their conveyance the foreclosure proceedings, and making no mention of the power of sale. D.'s solicitors accepted the title after searching the foreclosure proceedings.

Held, that the decree so obtained was invalid, and that D. had notice of and was affected by the irregularity, and could not be protected as an innocent purchaser for value without notice.

But, *held*, that the power in the mortgage authorised a sale of the renewal term, and that the conveyance to D., though not purporting to be made in exercise of the power, was nevertheless a valid exercise of it, and as the sale was made in good faith and was not a disadvantageous one, the decree for redemption pronounced by PROUDFOOT, J., was reversed. *Kelly* v. *Imperial Loan and Investment Company et al.* 526.

[Affirmed in Supreme Court 16th November, 1885.]

MORTGAGE, MORTGAGEE, MORTGAGOR.

See MUNICIPAL BONUS.

MOTION.

See COUNTY COURT.

MOUNTED POLICE FORCE.

See DECEIT, &c.

MUNICIPAL ACT.

Under the drainage clauses of the Municipal Act a by-law was passed by the township of Chatham, founded on the report, plans, and specifications of a surveyor to authorise the drainage of certain lands in that township. In order to obtain a sufficient fall it was necessary to continue the drain into the adjoining township of Dover. The surveyor assessed certain lots and roads in Dover, and also the town line between Dover and Chatham for part of the cost of the works in proportion to the benefit in his judgment derived by them therefrom. Dover appealed from the report on several grounds, and three arbitrators were appointed pursuant to the Act. At their last meeting they all agreed that the lands and roads in Dover were benefited by the work, but R. F., one of the arbitrators, thought $500 should be taken off the town line. W. D., another of the arbitrators, was of opinion that while the bulk sum assessed was not too great, the assessment on lands and roads should be varied but that this was for the Court of Revision to do. A memorandum to this effect was signed by W. D. and A E., the third arbitrator; at the foot of which R. F. also signed a memorandum that he dissented and declined to be present at the adjourned meeting to sign the award "*if in accordance with the above memoranda.*" Later, on the same day, the two arbitrators, W. D. and A. E., met and signed an award determining that the assessment on the lands and roads in Dover and the town line should be sustained and confirmed, and also that on the town line between Dover and Chatham.

Held, (1) *per* HAGARTY, C. J. O., and OSLER, J. A., [affirming the judgment of CAMERON, J.,) that the award was bad (*a*) as formally sanctioning and confirming the particular assessme on lands and roads and the town line, instead of the aggregate amount assessed, the latter being the only award contemplated at the last meeting, at which all three arbitrators were presnt : (*b*) because one of the arbitrators had recorded his dissent from the adjustment or scheme of assessment, and yet by the award purported to sanction or affirm it.

Per BURTON and PATTERSON, JJ.A., *contra*, that the duty of the arbitrators was confined to ascertaining the correctness of the proportions payable by each township : that all other objections as to the amounts of the assessment were for the Court of Revision, and that the award did not substantially differ from the memorandum signed at the last meeting of the arbitrators. *Essex* v. *Rochester*, 42 U. C. R. 523, and *Thurlow* v. *Sidney* 1 O. R. 249, commented on.

Held, (2) that the report of the surveyor, incorporated in the by-law, sufficiently shewed the termini of the proposed work, and that under the circumstances it was not open to the objections that it did not expressly state that the work was to be constructed at the expense of both townships and in what proportions, and that it determined, in apparent disregard of section 554, that the work was to be kept in repair by Chatham at the joint expense of Chatham and Dover. OSLER, J. A., dissenting.

Held, (3) upon the true construction of the drainage sections of the Municipal Act, that when drainage works are extended and continued into an adjoining township beyond the limits of the township in which they are commenced, the roads in the former township and the town line are liable to be assessed in proportion to the benefits derived by them therefrom. OSLER, J. A., dissenting. *Corporation of Dover* v. *Corporation of Chatham*, 248.

[Since argued in the Supreme Court, and stands for judgment.]

MUNICIPAL BONUS.

The plaintiffs under a by-law granted the defendant a bonus of $20,000 to aid him in the manufacture of steam fire engines and agricultural implements, subject to a condition in the by-law that he should give a mortgage on the factory premises for $10,000, and a bond for $10,000, to be conditioned, (1) for the carrying on of such manufactures for 20 years ; (2) during that period to keep $30,000 invested in the factory ; and (3) to insure the building and plant in plaintiffs' favor for $10,000. The defendant gave the bond and mortgage, the latter containing a covenant for insurance, and he invested the $30,000 as stipulated for. He also made a further mortgage on the premises to the plaintiffs for $3,000 not mentioned in the by-law. The factory was one in which 18 to 25 men might have been employed, and which could have turned out 100 mowers in a year. In the course of two years only 20 mowers were constructed, and the number of persons employed dwindled down from 18 or 20 to two or three.

Held, that the performance contemplated by the parties of the contract to carry on manufactures, was one reasonably commensurate with the capabilities of the factory; and that, upon the evidence, the defendant had failed in the performance.

Held, also, that the $10,000 mortgage was given as a security for any damages the plaintiffs might sustain by the defendant's default, to an extent not greater than $10,000, and not as a charge for that specific sum.

Held, also, that, as the $3,000 mortgage was not authorized by the by-law, as to it the plaintiffs were not entitled to any relief.

Remarks upon elements to be considered by the Master in assessing plaintiffs' damages. *Corporation of the Village of Brussels* v. *John D. Ronald*, 605.

MUTUAL COVENANTS.

See AGREEMENT FOR SALE OF LANDS.

NEGLIGENCE.

Where, after calling out the name of the next station, a railway train was slowed up on approaching and passing it, but was not brought to a full stop, and the plaintiff, who had purchased a ticket for that station, received injuries on alighting there:

Held, that there was evidence of an invitation to alight, and that it was for the jury to say whether she had acted in a reasonably prudent and careful manner in availing herself of it. *Edgar and Wife* v. *The Northern R.W. Co.*, 452.

See also SOLICITOR AND CLIENT.

NEW TRIAL.

See JURY SEPARATING.

NONSUIT.

See PRACTICE, 1.

NOTICE OF ACTION.

See REGISTRAR OF DEEDS.

NOVELTY, WANT OF,

[IN PATENT.]

See PATENT.

ONUS OF PROOF.

See AGREEMENT FOR PARTNERSHIP.

PAROL ASSIGNMENT.

On the occasion of the defendant effecting a purchase of land from one H., against whom the plaintiff had a claim for money advanced to effect the original purchase jointly by H. and himself, and in the conveyance of a portion of which he refused to join until assured by his solicitor, with defendant's assent, that part of the purchase money would be paid to the solicitor, out of which the solicitor agreed to pay the amount due the plaintiff, whereupon the plaintiff joined in the conveyance to the defendant which was duly registered. The defendant and H., however, made other arrangements for discharging all the purchase money, no portion of which was paid to the solicitor or the plaintiff.

Held, (affirming the judgment of Proudfoot, J.,) that under the circumstances an equitable assignment had been made of so much of the purchase money as the plaintiff's demand amounted to, and for which purchase money H. had a vendor's lien ; and that the defendant was bound to pay the same to the plaintiff.

Burton, J.A., dissenting. *Armstrong* v. *Farr,* 186.

PAROL EVIDENCE.

See Sale of Lands, 3.

—— TO EXPLAIN TERMS AS TO PRICE.

[Admissibility of.]

See Sale of Goods, 1.

PARTITION BY COUNTY COURT.

When proceedings for a partition in a County Court have terminated by an order confirming such partition and nothing remains to be done by way of enforcing the judgment, such judgment cannot afterwards be impeached on the ground of fraud or deception on the Court otherwise than in resisting an action in which it is relied on, or by bringing an action for the express purpose of setting it aside. *Jenking* v. *Jenking et al.,* 92.

PARTNERSHIP.

The fact that the plaintiff who had for some years acted as the legal ad-

viser of the defendant, was appointed one of the directors of the railway company, at ·the same time that he claimed to be interested with the defendant in the construction of a railroad, formed no ground for the defendant refusing to account to the plaintiff for his share of the profits of the enterprise. *Cameron* v. *Bickford,* 52.

See also Agreement for Partnership—Trade Name.

PARTNERSHIP CREDITORS.

See Assignment.

PATENT.

In 1882, one C., obtained a patent for what he called "The Paragon Counter Check book," which, in his application, he stated to be : "In a black leaf check book of double leaves, one half of which are bound together, while the other half fold in as fly leaves, both being perforated across so that they can be readily torn out, the combination of the black leaf bound into the book next the cover and provided with (a) tape across its ends ; the said black leaf having the transferring composition on one of its sides only."

In anticipation of procuring such patent, C. had, in January, 1882, sold one-half thereof to the defendant with whom he entered into partnership ; and on the 31st of July following, formally assigned such half interest to him, which. on a dissolution of such partnership, four months afterwards. he re-assigned to C., who the same day assigned the whole interest to the plaintiffs.

Prior to such dissolution the defendant applied for and obtained a patent of what he called "Butterfield's Improved Paragon Check Book," which embodied several things claimed to be improvements on previous books, and defendant avowedly thereunder proceeded with the manufacture of books. The plaintiffs thereupon instituted proceedings to restrain such manufacture by the defendant, claiming the same to be an infringement of their patent, and at the trial of that action, Boyd, C., granted the relief prayed.

On appeal, this Court, while holding that the acts of the defendant amounted to an infringement of the patent granted to C., reversed the judgment of the Chancellor on the ground that such patent was void for want of novelty; and that the defendant was not estopped by his conduct from shewing that the patent was void. *The Grip Printing and Publishing Company of Toronto* v. *Butterfield*, 145.

[Reversed in Supreme Court, 16th November, 1885.]

PAYMENT OF PURCHASE MONEY.

See AGREEMENT FOR SALE OF LAND.

PECUNIARY LOSS.

See RAILWAY ACCIDENT.

PENALTIES.

See DOMINION ELECTION LAW.

105—VOL. XI A.R.

PETITIONERS.

See DRAINAGE BY-LAW.

PLACE OF DELIVERY.

See SALE BY SAMPLE.

PLAN, SALE OF LOTS BY.

See SALE OF LOTS, &c.

POSSESSION CONTRARY TO DEED.

See VOID DEED BY MARRIED WOMAN.

POWER OF SALE.

See MORTGAGE OF LEASE.

PRACTICE.

I. At the trial of a case with a jury, the Judge of the County Court at the conclusion of the plaintiff's evidence and without hearing any evidence on the part of the defendants, nonsuited the plaintiff. In the following term the Judge set the nonsuit aside and entered judgment for the plaintiff, claiming a right under the circumstances to do so. On appeal this Court, while satisfied with the ruling of the Judge on the legal liability of the defendants, set the nonsuit aside and ordered a new trial upon the facts, so as to afford the defendants an opportunity of adducing evidence : but under the circumstances, refused the costs of the appeal.

Rules 311, 312, 319, and 321 of O. J. Act discussed. *Baker* v. *The Grand Trunk Railway Company of Canada*, 68,

2. A *primâ facie* case for judgment under Rule 80, O. J. A., was made by the plaintiff in an action upon two bills of exchange accepted by a married woman who, in her defence alleged, amongst other things, that she accepted the bills as agent of her husband, but there being evidence on which the jury might have been justified in finding that the business, in which such acceptances were given, was hers, the Court refused to interfere with the discretion of the County Court Judge in directing judgment to be entered for the plaintiff, the defendant having declined to comply with the condition of paying the amount of the claim into Court to abide the result of a trial. *Nelson* v. *Thorner*, 616.

3. Where on moving for immediate judgment under marginal Rule 80, O. J. A. the plaintiff makes out a *primâ facie* case for granting an order therefor, it is not sufficient for the defendant, in opposing the application, to swear that he has a good defence on the merits;—he must shew the nature of the defence, and give some reason for thinking that such defence exists in fact. *Collins* v. *Hickok*, 620.

See ALSO APPEAL FOR COSTS— FIXING BAIL—PARTITION BY COUNTY COURT.

PREFERENCE.

See CHATTEL MORTGAGE.

PRINCIPAL AND AGENT.

An agent employed to purchase lands is not authorised to purchase lands which are subject to mortgage. Where, however, the principal was made aware of the incumbrance and still agreed to accept two lots out of ten lots alleged by the agent to have been bought for himself and his principal, this was deemed a waiver of the objection to the act of the agent and to the right of the principal to demand a return of the money placed in his agent's hands. But the principal having ascertained that the two lots offered to him fell short in quantity, of which fact the agent was aware when offering them :

Held, under these circumstances, that the principal's right of action revived and that he was entitled to enforce payment from the agent of the principal money and interest. *Butterworth* v. *Shannon*, 86.

PRIORITIES.

See ASSIGNMENT.

PRIVATE GRIEVANCE.

See DRAINAGE BY-LAW.

PROPERTY IN GOODS PASSING.

See SALE OF GOODS, 3.

PROPERTY AND CIVIL RIGHTS.

See DOMINION ELECTION LAW.

PROSPECTUS,

See ACTION FOR DECEIT.

PURCHASE FROM DIRECTOR OF INCORPORATED COMPANY.

See INCORPORATED COMPANY.

PURCHASE MONEY, PAYMENT OF.

See AGREEMENT FOR SALE OF LANDS.

PURCHASER WITH NOTICE.

See MORTGAGE OF LEASE.

QUALITY, DEFECTS IN.

See SALE BY SAMPLE.

RAILWAY ACCIDENT.

Held, [reversing the judgment of the Q. B. D. (1 O. R. 545) BURTON, J. A., dissenting] that under the provisions of Lord Campbell's Act, Imp. Stat. 9-10 Vict. ch. 93, R. S. O. ch. 128, the husband of a woman killed by accident, suing as her administrator is entitled to recover damages for himself and her children, although there may be no evidence shewing that she was entitled for life to rents or other income.

Per BURTON, J.A.—The injury contemplated by the statute means injury resulting in the loss of money present or prospective but proximate or direct. *Lett* v. *St Lawrence and Ottawa Railway Company,* 1.

[Affirmed in Supreme Court 16th November, 1885.]

See also NEGLIGENCE.

RAILWAY COMPANY.

Sheep belonging to the plaintiff escaped from his premises on to the highway, and from thence owing to defects in the fences of the defendants into lands of theirs, whence they strayed on to the railway track where they were killed by a passing train.

Held, (reversing the judgment of the County Judge), that the defendants were not answerable in damages for the loss, the sheep not being lawfully on the highway. *Daniels* v. *Grand Trunk R. W. Co.,* 471.

See also NEGLIGENCE.

RAILWAY CROSSING.

When the defendants, the Canada Southern Railway Company, were locating their road, an agent was employed by them for the purpose of obtaining the right of way from the several land owners along their line of road, and amongst others the agent purchased such right of way across the plaintiff's farm for a sum which the plaintiff swore was much less than he would have accepted therefor, in consequence of the agent agreeing that a certain crossing underneath the railway, where trestle work was to be constructed, should be continued permanently.

Several years afterwards the company, desiring to make an alteration in the construction of the road by substituting a solid earth embankment for the trestle-work, proceeded to effect such alteration, when the plaintiff instituted proceedings to restrain the company from destroying or interfering with the crossing.

Held, (varying the judgment of Proudfoot, J., 4 O. R. 28,) that the plaintiff was not entitled to such crossing in perpetuity, but that under the circumstances there should be a new valuation of the lands conveyed to the company, and if the parties could not agree on the amount or the mode of ascertaining it, a reference for the purpose should be made to the Master. *Clouse* v. *The Canada Southern R. W. Co.*, 287.

[Since argued in Supreme Court and stands for judgment.]

2. The agent of a railway company while engaged in obtaining the right of way agreed with one S., through whom the plaintiff claimed, for the right of crossing his property, and S. executed an agreement to convey to the company $4\frac{17}{100}$ acres of his farm for that purpose in consideration of $1,650; such agreement before being executed having had indorsed thereon a memorandum that S. should " have liberty to remove for his own use all buildings on the said right of way ; and it is also further agreed that in the event of there being constructed on the same lot a trestle bridge of sufficient height to allow of the passage of cattle, the said company will so construct their fence to each side thereof as not to impede the passage thereunder."

The company did construct a trestle bridge which the plaintiff, as well as S. whilst owner of the lot, continued to use for the purpose of passing under the railway from one portion of the farm to another for upwards of ten years, when the company determined to convert the trestle bridge into a solid embankment :

Held, that the company were at liberty so to change the bridge, but that the plaintiff was, as in *Clouse* v. *Canada Southern R. W. Co.,* (ante

p. 287), entitled to a re-valuation of the land conveyed.

BURTON, J. A., dissenting, who thought the plaintiff had under the circumstances failed to establish any claim for relief. *Erwin* v. *Canada. Southern R. W. Co.*, 306.

[Since argued in Supreme Court and stands for judgment.]

RATIFICATION BY SHAREHOLDERS.

See INCORPORATED COMPANIES.

RECTIFICATION.

See SALE OF LANDS, 2.

RECTOR.

See APPEAL.

REGISTRAR OF DEEDS.

Where a registrar of deeds is dismissed before the expiration of the year, having received in fees an amount in excess of that specified in the statute (R. S. O. ch. 111, sec. 104), he is bound to return and pay over to the municipality a proportionate amount of such excess, although not in office at the time prescribed by the statute for making his return of fees ; but,

Semble, that the treasurer could not maintain an action for such fees before the 15th of January, the day named in the Act for sending in his return.

Held, also, that the defendant was not entitled to notice of action. *The Corporation of the County of Bruce* v. *McLay*, 477.

RENTS OR OTHER INCOME.

See RAILWAY ACCIDENT.

———

REPRESENTATION OF OPINION.

See DECEIT, &c., 2.

———

RESALE OF GOODS.

See SALE OF GOODS, 2.

———

RESCISSION.

See DECEIT, 2—SALE OF LANDS, 2.

———

RESTRICTIVE COVENANT.

See SALE OF LANDS, 3.

———

REVALUATION OF LAND.

See RAILWAY CROSSING, 1, 2.

———

REVERSING FINDING OF JUDGE.

See CONFLICTING EVIDENCE.

———

SALE BY ACRE OR IN BULK.

See SALE OF LANDS, 2.

———

SALE BY SAMPLE.

The defendants agreed with one W., who stated incorrectly that he was acting as broker for the plaintiff, for the purchase by sample of a quantity of cotton waste at 1¼ cents per lb., to be delivered at St. Catharines. In reality W. was selling for his own benefit, as he arranged to purchase the waste at one cent a pound. Instead of inspecting the goods at St. Catharines, the defendants requested W. to consign them to their house in Cincinnati, U. S., which the plaintiff did by direction of W. The plaintiff, at the request of W., made out a bill of lading in the name of the defendants and drew on them for the price at 1¼ cents per lb., which draft was accepted by the defendants, the plaintiff paying W. his profit in cash. On the goods reaching Cincinnati, an inspection took place when they were found greatly inferior to the sample. The defendants rejected the goods but refused to return them to the plaintiff at St. Catharines, although he was willing to accept them there. In an action on the bill of exchange.

Held, affirming the judgment of SENKLER, Co. J., that the defect in quality formed no ground of defence, that the plaintiff's contract was to deliver the goods at St. Catharines, where the inspection ought *primâ facie* to have taken place, and that the only redress of the defendants was by cross-action. *Towers* v. *Dominion Iron and Metal Company,* 315.

———

SALE OF GOODS.

1. The plaintiff bought the office and plant of a newspaper, gave a chattel mortgage thereon to W., and placed P. in charge. The defendants made advances to P. for the purpose of carrying on the business. W. sold the property by auction for the

amount of the mortgage debts to the defendants, who, supposing that P. was the owner, wished to secure themselves for the advances made to him. The defendants then agreed to sell the property to the plaintiff; but a dispute arose as to the price, and this action was brought to obtain specific performance of the agreement. There was written evidence of the agreement in a document signed by the defendant Moore, part of which was as follows: " Price of this office to be what it has cost Mr. Horton (the other defendant) and myself." Specific performance was decreed by consent, and it was referred to the Master at London to take the accounts, and to report what was the true agreement between the parties.

Held, (reversing the decision of the Master and of Ferguson, J.,) that the defendants had the right to shew before the Master what they meant by the reference to the cost of of the office as fixing the price; and that, upon the evidence, the true agreement between the parties was, that the price was to be the amount paid to W., *plus* the advances to P. *Hughes* v. *Moore et al.*, 569.

2. Defendant sold the plaintiffs some tea, and verbally agreed that he would take back, at an advance of ten cents a pound, such part thereof as the plaintiffs should have in stock unsold at a certain date:

Held, (affirming the decision of the Queen's Bench Division) that there was but one entire conditional contract, not one contract to sell the tea to the plaintiffs, and another to buy it back; and therefore the delivery of the tea by the defendant satisfied the Statute of Frauds, and the plaintiffs were entitled to recover for the defendant's refusal to take back the unsold tea.

Williams v. *Burgess*, 10 A. & E. 499, considered followed. *Lumsden et al.* v. *Davies*, 585.

3. The plaintiffs sold to U. & Co. certain wheels, &c., to be used in their manufactory under a written agreement, whereby it was stipulated that the right and property to the goods should not pass to them until the whole price thereof was paid: the right of possession merely passing: such right to be forfeited and the plaintiffs to be at liberty to resume possession in case of default in the payments being made, or in case of seizure for rent, &c., or upon any attempt by U. & Co. to sell or dispose thereof without the consent of the plaintiffs, it being expressly declared that the sale was conditional only, and punctual payment of the instalments being essential to its existence. U. & Co. placed the machinery in the flume belonging to their factory, which was held by them under a lease from H. & Co., and subsequently the sheriff having seized other chattels belonging to U. & Co., they surrendered the possession of the premises and delivered the key thereof to H. & Co. Default having been made by U. & Co. in payment of the moneys due the plaintiffs, they demanded of H. & Co. a delivery up of the wheels, which demand H. & Co. refused to comply with, assigning as a reason that they had not possession thereof, and in the following month the wheels were sold under proceedings to enforce payment of the liens of certain mechanics.

Held, affirming the judgment of the Common Pleas Division, 8 O. R. 465, that the plaintiffs were entitled to recover the value of the goods. *Joseph Hall Manufacturing Co.* v. *Hazlitt et al.*, 749.

SALE OF LANDS.

The defendant, in January, 1882, bought land in Manitoba from the plaintiff for speculative purposes, paying $500 in cash, and giving a mortgage for the balance of the purchase money. Before the conveyances were executed the defendant in answer to inquiries made by him to persons on the spot received unfavourable accounts of the property, which were, however, explained away by the agent of the plaintiff. The defendant resisted payment of the mortgage, on which this action was brought, and counter-claimed for a return of the $500, upon the ground of false representations by the plaintiff's agent. On the 27th July, 1882, the defendant visited the land and found it worthless, and in the end of August or the beginning of September gave notice of his intention to repudiate the contract. Armour, J., who tried the action, without a jury, found that the defendant was induced to purchase by false representations, but that he had by his delay elected to affirm the contract. The Queen's Bench Divisional Court affirmed the first finding, but set aside the second, and gave judgment in the defendant's favour, Armour, J., concurring in that judgment.

Held, that the question of false representations was peculiarly one for the Judge at the trial, and that his finding should not be disturbed, especially as it was concurred in by the Divisional Court.

Held, also, (BURTON, J. A., dissenting,) that the defendant had not by lapse of time, acquiescence, or delay, lost his right to rescind.

Per BURTON, J. A.—There was evidence to justify the finding of Armour, J., that the defendant had made his election, and no sufficient

grounds were shewn for disturbing it; but as Armour, J., concurred in the judgment of the Divisional Court, and as the merits of the case did not call for interference, the judgment of the Divisional Court should be affirmed. *Lee* v. *MacMahon*, 555.

2. In proceeding to a sale of lands under a decree of the Court of Chancery in 1876, one parcel was advertised as containing 100 acres, and was bid off by one A. at $31 per acre, which in the agreement to purchase signed by A., as also in the conveyance to him, was described as "100 acres more or less, composed of the east part of lot 9," &c.: he paying or securing according to the conditions of sale, the sum of $3,100. In reality the portion so sold contained $124\frac{68}{100}$ acres, a fact neither party to the transaction was aware of when sold. There was no provision in the conditions of sale for compensation. The purchaser became aware that there was an excess on the same day, immediately after the sale, but the vendors not until long afterwards, although before the execution of the conveyance. In the report on sale several of the sales were referred to as at so much per acre, while the one in question was mentioned as a sale at a bulk sum of $3,100.

After the conveyance to A. he had been obliged to take proceedings against G. T., the person who had conveyed the land in question to the father of the vendors, to obtain possession of the portion in dispute and which he succeeded in obtaining. The vendors, however, refused to interpose in such proceedings or assist A. in any way in such litigation.

Held—[reversing the judgment of FERGUSON, J., 5 O. R. 704,] that the sum of $3,100 was bid for the whole parcel; that the sale being a sale in bulk, and there being no provision in the conditions of sale for compensation, there could be no rectification after the execution of the conveyance, nor could there have been, under the circumstances of this case, a rescission of the contract, had such relief been asked for. There was no mistake as to what was intended to be sold, or in the price intended to be paid for it.

PATTERSON, J. A., dissenting. *Cottingham et al.* v. *Cottingham et al.*, 624.

3. D. sold to the predecessor in title of the plaintiff certain lands, and the deed contained the following (which was held to amount to a covenant, the benefit of which passed to the plaintiff) :—" Bellevue square is private property, but it is always to remain unbuilt upon except one residence with the necessary outbuildings including porter's lodge." The land having been sold under a mortgage, a portion came again to the hands of D., who proceeded to convey parts of it for building purposes.

Held, that parol evidence was admissible to shew what was meant by " Bellevue square," no plan or description being incorporated in the deed.

Held, also, that D's liability under the restrictive agreement not to build on Bellevue square, revived on his again acquiring the property.

Certain maps of the city of Toronto, made by city surveyors in 1857 and 1858, shewing thereon a square marked " Bellevue square," were offered in evidence to shew the boundaries of the square. It was shewn that the defendant knew of these maps, but they were not prepared under his instructions.

Held, that the maps could not be received in evidence to shew the boundaries of the square.

Per HAGARTY, C.J.O., and OSLER, J.A.—The maps were admissible to shew that there was such a square known as Bellevue square, but not as evidence of title or boundary.

Per BURTON, J.A. and PATTERSON, J.A.—The maps were not admissible in evidence without its being shewn that they had been prepared under the instructions of the defendant or on information given by him.

The parol evidence shewing that but a portion of the land claimed by the plaintiff to be the square was undoubtedly within the limits of the square, the appeal was allowed as to all but that portion.

Remarks on the serious consequences likely to arise from the constant changes in the names of streets in the city of Toronto. *Vankoughnet* v. *Denison*, 699.

SAMPLE, SALE BY.

See SALE BY SAMPLE.

SALE OF LOTS BY PLAN.

The mere fact of the owner of lands selling them in lots according to a plan shewing streets and lanes adjoining the several lots does not bind him to continue such streets and lanes, unless a purchaser is materially inconvenienced by the closing of any of them.

The defendants, the City of Toronto, announced a sale by auction of city lots, the advertisement stating that " lanes run in rear of the several lots." A plan of the land shewing the streets and lanes was exhibited at the sale, and was incorporated in the contracts of purchase. At such sale the plaintiff purchased a lot situate on the north side of Baldwin street, which lot abutted on a lane running from east to west; a lane also ran in rear of other lots situate on Huron street, all of which were bought by the defendant M., such lane joining at right angles the lane in rear of the plaintiff's lot. The land in rear of the lots on Huron street was subsequently closed.

Held, (reversing the judgment of FERGUSON, J., 7 O. R. 194), that, as the plaintiff had ready access to the streets by the lane on which his lot abutted, he could not prevent the city from closing up other lanes on the property. *Carey* v. *City of Toronto*, 416.

[Since argued in Supreme Court and stands for judgment.]

SEPARATE CREDITORS.

See ASSIGNMENT.

SETTING ASIDE JUDGMENT.

The plaintiffs by their agent, Patrick R., in April, 1877, procured a judgment to be signed against Peter R., the defendant, who, for purposes of his own, suffered the judgment to go by default. No execution was ever issued thereon. After the death of Peter, the plaintiffs assigned the judgment to the wife of Patrick, who paid them $50 therefor; and, on her application, ARMOUR, J., made an order allowing execution to issue against the executors of Peter. The executors then applied to set aside

the judgment as having been fraudulently obtained, and to be allowed to defend the action, or for such other order as should seem just; and upon such application, WILSON, C.J., made an order setting aside the judgment and all proceedings in the action, and directing the plaintiffs to repay the $50. This order was affirmed on appeal by the Common Pleas Division.

Held, that an appeal lay from the order of the Common Pleas Division, as it was in effect a final disposition of the whole matter and a bar to the plaintiffs' further proceeding; but, although the members of this Court were all of opinion for different reasons that the order below was wrong, they did not agree as to the extent to which it should be modified or reversed, and therefore the appeal was dismissed, without costs.

Per HAGARTY, C.J.O., and OSLER, J.A.—The judgment should merely be set aside and the executors allowed in to defend.

Per BURTON, J. A.—The executors cannot be heard to allege their testator's fraudulent purpose; they are estopped from confining the operation of the judgment within the limit of his intended fraud; and the judgment should be allowed to stand.

Per PATTERSON, J.A.—The judgment should not be set aside, but the order of ARMOUR, J., should be rescinded, and it should be declared that Patrick's wife as assignee of the judgment, was not entitled to issue execution, because the judgment was procured by Patrick, her husband, and suffered by Peter, for a fraudulent purpose, of which she had notice when she took the assignment. *Schroeder et al.* v. *Rooney*, 673.

See also COUNTY COURT.

SHAREHOLDERS, RATIFICATION BY.

See INCORPORATED COMPANY.

SHARE OF PROFITS.

See INCORPORATED COMPANY.

SOLICITOR AND CLIENT.

A solicitor entrusted with moneys to invest, did so on property of insufficient value, and his client, shortly after the loan, desired him to realize the amount advanced, which the solicitor endeavored to do by getting the owner to effect another loan from a building society, and desired his client to join in releasing his mortgage for that purpose, he undertaking to obtain security on chattel property for any deficiency before acting on the release. The society refused to advance more than $800, which was stipulated should be paid to the client, thus leaving a balance due him of about $150. The solicitor procured from the mortgagor a chattel mortgage on cattle, &c., variously valued at from $100 to $130 : such security being made out in the name of the client, and only requiring his affidavit of *bona fides* to have it registered. This the client refused to accept, and instituted proceedings against his solicitor for the surplus of his claim ; and the Judge of the County Court gave a verdict and judgment for $177 against the latter.

On appeal, this Court (BURTON, J.A., dissenting,) being of opinion that the plaintiff had of his own wrong lost the benefit of the chattel mortgage, reduced the judgment by $117, thus limiting the verdict to $60, with

Division Court costs, but refused to either party costs of the appeal. *O'Callaghan* v. *Bergin*, 594.

STRANGERS TO THE RECORD.

See APPEAL.

STATUTE OF FRAUDS.

See SALE OF GOODS, 2.

STATUTORY CONDITION (11TH.)

See FIRE INSURANCE.

STEAM POWER, RIGHT USE ON TRAMWAY.

See CONSTRUCTION OF AGREEMENT.

STREETS AND LANES SHEWN ON PLAN.

See SALE OF LOTS BY PLAN.

———— CHANGING NAMES OF

See SALE OF LANDS, 3.

SUBSEQUENT FIRE.

See FIRE INSURANCE.

SURVEY.

See EJECTMENT.

TRACTION ENGINE.

See CONSTRUCTION OF AGREEMENT.

TRADE NAME.

The plaintiff and defendant Beatty, carried on business as partners from 1st May, 1877, to 28th August, 1879, during which time Beatty prepared a series of headline copy books, published as " Beatty's System of Practical Penmanship," but spoken of as " Beatty's Headline Copy Books" and "Beatty's Copies," from the sales of which large profits were realized by the firm. At the date last mentioned Beatty having sold his interest to the plaintiff for $20,000, retired from the firm, the most valuable asset thereof being the series of copy books. Subsequently, and in the year 1882, Beatty, at the instance of his co-defendants, the publishing company, in consideration of a royalty to be paid to him, and with the express purpose of enabling the company to publish a copy book to be called "Beatty's" prepared another series of headline copy books differing only to a colorable extent from the former series. The title of the new series was " Beatty's New and Improved Headline Copy Books," the name "Beatty" being printed conspicuously on the cover ; and the books were in such a form and cover as to lead the public to believe that they were the books published by the plaintiff, and it was shewn that the plaintiff's business was injured by the sale of the new series.

Held, (affirming the judgment of FERGUSON, J.) that the conduct of the defendants in publishing the new series was illegal, inasmuch as by simulating the plaintiff's books, they deprived him of the profits he would otherwise have made ; and that he was entitled to a perpetual injunction, restraining defendants from issuing, advertising, publishing, or selling, or offering for sale the books called " Beatty's New and Improved Headline Copy Books" in and with its present cover, or in any other form of cover calculated to lead persons to believe that it was the plaintiff's book. *Gage v. Canada Publishing Company*, 402.

[Affirmed in Supreme Court 16th November, 1885.]

TRAMWAY, RIGHT TO USE STEAM POWER ON.

See CONSTRUCTION OF AGREEMENT.

TRIAL BY JURY.

See PRACTICE, 1.

TRIAL WITHOUT A JURY.

See COUNTY COURT.

TRUSTEE &c.

See APPEAL—INCORPORATED COMPANY.

UNCORROBORATED EVIDENCE OF BENEFICARY.

See WILL, &c.

UNDER CROSSING, VERBAL AGREEMENT FOR.

See RAILWAY CROSSING, 1.

UNDER CROSSING, WRITTEN AGREEMENT FOR.

See RAILWAY CROSSING, 2.

VENDOR AND PURCHASER.

See AGREEMENT FOR SALE OF LANDS.

VENDOR'S LIEN.

See PAROL EVIDENCE.

VERDICT, SETTING ASIDE.

See COUNTY COURT

VOID DEED BY MARRIED WOMAN.

In 1834 C. A., a married woman, conveyed to a *bonâ fide* purchaser, in fee, the east half of a lot of land granted to her by the Crown, but the conveyance was invalid by reason of the want of the usual certificate by justices of the peace on the deed, and her grantee never did enter into possession. In or about the year 1866, the two sons of C. A. went and resided on the west half of the land upon the understanding and agreement with their mother that they were to have the whole lot, but no conveyance was executed to them until 1875. During the interval, however, the sons paid the taxes on the whole property, and cut timber at times on the east half.

Held (reversing the judgment of the Q. B. D., reported 2 O. R. 352) that this was a sufficient " actual possession or enjoyment " of the east half of the lot to prevent the operation of section 13 of R. S. O. ch.

127 (36 Vict. ch. 18, s. 12), by means of which such void deed would be rendered valid. OSLER, J. A. dissenting. *Elliott* v. *Brown et al.*, 228.

WANT OF NOVELTY,

[IN PATENT.]

See PATENT.

WILL, VALIDITY OF.

The testator, by his will made in June, 1880, gave the bulk of his property to the plaintiff his sister, with whom, in the Autumn before his death, he had quarrelled, and it did not appear that she saw him again before he died. The defendant, another sister, claimed under a second will made an hour or two before the testator's death. The evidence shewed that the testator was a very determined man, and not easily influenced ; that he was suffering from excessive indulgence in drink ; that he latterly spoke in very bitter and offensive terms of the defendant, and had frequently said that she should have nothing ; that he had frequently, and as late as a few days before his death, stated that if he died everything was arranged, and that the plaintiff would get his property. Shortly before his death the defendant had him brought to her house. On the night of his death the physician in attendance told defendant that if anything was to be settled it should be done at once. A solicitor was sent for to draw a will. The defendant instructed him before he saw the testator, and upon her instructions the will was drawn, which gave the bulk of the property to the defendant, and a bequest of

$1,000 to the plaintiff. This the solicitor read over to the testator, and asked him if he approved of it. He made a sign of dissent. The defendant urged the testator to give the plaintiff the $1,000, but (as the defendant stated) he said $10 was enough for the plaintiff. The solicitor thereupon went away leaving the will with the defendant, and during his absence it was signed.

The evidence of various witnesses for the defence was conflicting as to the incidents which happened during this time and until the testator's decease; and while they all spoke of the testator's unwillingness to give the plaintiff more than $10, there was no evidence, other than that of the defendant, of his desire to give her the bulk of his property or to make any disposition of it.

Held, reversing the judgment of Proudfoot, J., that the second will could not be established on the uncorroborated evidence of the defendant, and the prior will was declared to be the testator's last will. *Hogg v. Maguire*, 507.

WRITTEN INSTRUMENT.

See SALE OF GOODS, 1.

Lightning Source UK Ltd.
Milton Keynes UK
UKHW012140180219
337529UK00012B/1329/P